Treasures of the Catholic Church

2,000 years of the Writings of Saints and Martyrs in 5 Minutes a Day.

(condensed from The Office of Readings)

Fr. James Altman

ISBN: 978-1-80623-869-9

Printed in the United States of America

Acknowledgements

I never would dare to pretend that this project came to fruition all on my own efforts. Oh no – that would be arrogance beyond measure. Every holy person who has inspired my life of Faith deserves credit. These are just a few, with apologies to the many not here named – always remember, God knows and any Grace that flows here from flows also to you:

My great-grandparents, James and Maude, who helped raise my mom in Faith.

My great-aunt Frances, who, after Vatican II, said "I don't care what they say, they're not taking away my Rosary!"

My mom and dad, who to this day have provided me with guidance and support.

My brother and sisters and their witness of Faith in overcoming challenges.

Mother Mathias and Mother Michaela, Ursaline nuns, in 3rd and 4th grade.

Nick and Mary Ann Lambros, and James, John and Alexis, friends for over 45 years, who work overtime to keep me humble.

Eileen Bradford, a holy spiritual woman in my mid-teens.

Fr. Dan Zaloga, a brilliant spiritual director before seminary.

Raymond Leo Cardinal Burke, my first Bishop and a Lion of the Church.

Jan Eggers, and her "Jan-isms" of praying the Holy Rosary multiple times a day, and who personally is responsible for inspiring me to Adoration of The Holy Eucharist.

Fr. William Lynn, SJ, a holy Catholic Jesuit, and my first spiritual director.

Fr. Richard Tomasek, SJ, another holy Catholic Jesuit, and second spiritual director.

Fr. John Horn, SJ, another great holy Catholic Jesuit, who rescued my vocation.

Fr. John Murphy, SJ, another holy Jesuit, a magnificent formation advisor.

Joan Bond, Paul and Peg Klinkhammer, Jan Minarcin, and all the Assumption staff.

Msgr. Hundt, Diocese of La Crosse, who spent my first three years of seminary teaching me the meaning of sacrificial priesthood.

Msgr. Kachel, Diocese of La Crosse, who spent the second three years of my seminary teaching me the meaning of sacrificial priesthood.

Msgr. Diermeier, Diocese of La Crosse, who spent years after ordination teaching me the meaning of sacrificial priesthood.

Fr. Jim Weigner and Fr. Greg Michaud, La Crosse, holy priests and loyal friends.

Mr. Chris Carstens, La Crosse Director of Sacred Liturgy, who inspired me to bring all things sacred and holy into my parishes.

Barb Swieciak, the best housekeeper with which any priest could be blessed.

Jeff and Sandy Reinhart, the first family I came to love in this Diocese.

John and Dana Wogerman, from Sts. Peter and Paul. I wanted 13 of my own children and lo, our Father who knows the longing of our hearts, brought this family of 13 children, to my first parish.

Dee Garabaldi, whose joyful voice I would recognize if I were in a coma.

Julie Pisula, whose Faith in all adversity continues to humble me.

The Hansen Clan, John, Donna and Thomas, Paul and Karla, Mary and Tim, Amy and Tom, who exude Faith in all things.

Jeff, Sandy and Gabe Ashbeck, whose life of prayer humbles me.

Chris and Andrea Bires and their 10 children, whose reverence at Holy Mass inspires me.

Roberto and Maria - profoundly holy and profoundly behind the scenes - they took care of my parents and me at St. James.

Donna Walz, Ken and Mary Ann Schelfhout and Sue Schaller, whose unwavering support at St. James made so much possible.

Georgia and Tim Stockman, and Georgia's rescue of Sacred Music at St. James, hallelujah

Joe and Mary Lehn, and their very, very holy and calming effect on my vigorous approach to things.

Providence Academy, especially Dr. Scott and Jill Marshall and their whole family.

Zach Liebert and Fr. Aaron Liebert, the Coppernalls, the Olsons, the Heilmans, the Pronschinskes, the Van Hoofs, and the entire Latin Mass Community at St. James. They are the ones who red-pilled me. I did not see it coming, but I remember the exact moment it happened. And as is the case, once you have been red-pilled, there is no going back.

The Wolf Pack (Todd & Melanie, Natalie, Abbie, Preston, Chandler, Ethan) who I miss very much.

Doug and Kristen Strauss and their beautiful family.

Mike Peeters, a stalwart Sacristan who learned his way around the Missale Romanum.

Dr. Louise Smyth and Dr. Kim Couri, profoundly faithful Catholics who have intervened and saved my life for over 10 years, essentially at no cost. They literally saved my life.

Greg and Toni Whittaker and their entire Clan of 12 children, 9 in-laws, and something like 60+ grandchildren, from White Post Virginia. I have never met a total family of such prayer.

Marco Lopez, whose capacity to overcome challenges I hardly can imagine has inspired me to work harder in the Lord's Vineyard, and to do this work without complaining.

The person in the State of Washington who sent me a 1st class relic of St. Thomas More, but whose address I lost and do not know how to thank personally.

Hermit David, who bravely disputes any errors in my thinking, and keeps my mind focused on the Truths revealed in The Apocalypse.

There are so many others, friends, prayer warriors, supporters, and in my rush to get this done, I know I have not named all of you. Please forgive me. I'll make up for it in the next book!

My soul magnifies the Lord

And my spirit rejoices in God my Savior;

Because He has regarded the lowliness of His handmaid;

For behold, henceforth all generations shall call me blessed;

Because He who is mighty has done great things for me,

and holy is His name;

And His mercy is from generation to generation

on those who fear Him.

He has shown might with His arm,

He has scattered the proud in the conceit of their heart.

He has put down the mighty from their thrones,

and has exalted the lowly.

He has filled the hungry with good things,

and the rich He has sent away empty.

He has given help to Israel, his servant, mindful of His mercy

Even as he spoke to our fathers,

to Abraham and to his posterity forever.

Gospel of St Luke 1:46-55

Sunday of the 1st Week in Advent

From a catechetical instruction by St. Cyril of Jerusalem, Bishop & Doctor

On the twofold coming of Christ

We do not preach only one coming of Christ, but a second as well, much more glorious than the first. The first coming was marked by patience; the second will bring the crown of a divine kingdom.

In general, whatever relates to our Lord Jesus Christ has two aspects. There is a birth from God before the ages, and a birth from a virgin at the fullness of time. There is a hidden coming, like that of rain on fleece, and a coming before all eyes, still in the future.

At the first coming he was wrapped in swaddling clothes in a manger. At his second coming he will be clothed in light as in a garment. In the first coming he endured the cross, despising the shame; in the second coming he will be in glory, escorted by an army of angels.

We look then beyond the first coming and await the second. At the first coming we said: *Blessed is he who comes in the name of the Lord.* [Ps 118:26] At the second we shall say it again; we shall go out with the angels to meet the Lord and cry out in adoration: *Blessed is he who comes in the name of the Lord.* [Ps 118:26]

The Savior will not come to be judged again, but to judge those by whom he was judged. At his own judgment he was silent; then he will address those who committed the outrages against him when they crucified him and will remind them: *You did these things, and I was silent.* [Ps 50:21]

His first coming was to fulfill his plan of love, to teach men by gentle persuasion. This time, whether men like it or not, they will be subjects of his kingdom by necessity. The prophet Malachi speaks of the two comings. *And the Lord whom you seek will come suddenly to his temple* [Mal 3:1]: that is one coming.

Again, he says of another coming: *Look, the Lord almighty will come, and who will endure the day of his entry, or who will stand in his sight? Because he comes like a refiner's fire, a fuller's herb, and he will sit refining and cleansing.* [Mal 3:2]

These two comings are also referred to by Paul in writing to Titus: *The grace of God the Savior has appeared to all men, instructing us to put aside impiety and worldly desires and live temperately, uprightly, and religiously in this present age, waiting for the joyful hope, the appearance of the glory of our great God and Savior, Jesus Christ.* [Ti 2:11] Notice how he speaks of a first coming for which he gives thanks, and a second, the one we still await.

That is why the faith we profess has been handed on to you in these words: *He ascended into heaven, and is seated at the right hand of the Father, and he will come again in glory to judge the living and the dead, and his kingdom will have no end.*

Our Lord Jesus Christ will therefore come from heaven. He will come at the end of the world, in glory, at the last day. For there will be an end to this world, and the created world will be made new.

Monday of the 1st Week in Advent

From a pastoral letter by St. Charles Borromeo, Bishop

The Season of Advent

Beloved, now is the acceptable time spoken of by the Spirit, the day of salvation, peace and reconciliation: the great season of Advent. This is the time eagerly awaited by the patriarchs and prophets, the time that holy Simeon rejoiced at last to see. This is the season that the Church has always celebrated with special solemnity. We too should always observe it with faith and love, offering praise and thanksgiving to the Father for the mercy and love he has shown us in this mystery. In his infinite love for us, though we were sinners, he sent his only Son to free us from the tyranny of Satan, to summon us to heaven, to welcome us into its innermost recesses, to show us truth itself, to train us in right conduct, to plant within us the seeds of virtue, to enrich us with the treasures of his grace, and to make us children of God and heirs of eternal life.

Each year, as the Church recalls this mystery, she urges us to renew the memory of the great love God has shown us. This holy season teaches us that Christ's coming was not only for the benefit of his contemporaries; his power has still to be communicated to us all. We shall share his power, if, through holy faith and the sacraments, we willingly accept the grace Christ earned for us, and live by that grace and in obedience to Christ.

The Church asks us to understand that Christ, who came once in the flesh, is prepared to come again. When we remove all obstacles to his presence he will come, at any hour and moment, to dwell spiritually in our hearts, bringing with him the riches of his grace.

In her concern for our salvation, our loving mother the Church uses this holy season to teach us through hymns, canticles and other forms of expression, of voice or ritual, used by the Holy Spirit. She shows us how grateful we should be for so great a blessing, and how to gain its benefit: our hearts should be as much prepared for the coming of Christ as if he were still to come into this world. The same lesson is given us for our imitation by the words and example of the holy men of the Old Testament.

Tuesday of the 1st Week in Advent

From a sermon by St. Gregory Nazianzen, Bishop & Doctor

The marvel of the Incarnation

The very Son of God, older than the ages, the invisible, the incomprehensible, the incorporeal, the beginning of beginning, the light of light, the fountain of life and immortality, the image of the archetype, the immovable seal, the perfect likeness, the definition and word of the Father: he it is who comes to his own image and takes our nature for the good of our nature, and unites himself to an intelligent soul for the good of my soul, to purify like by like. He takes to himself all that is human, except for sin. He was conceived by the Virgin Mary, who had been first prepared in soul and body by the Spirit; his coming to birth had to be treated with honor, virginity had to receive new honor. He comes forth as God, in the human nature he has taken, one being, made of two contrary elements, flesh and spirit. Spirit gave divinity, flesh received it.

He who makes rich is made poor; he takes on the poverty of my flesh, that I may gain the riches of his divinity. He who is full is made empty; he is emptied for a brief space of his glory, that I may share in his fullness. What is this wealth of goodness? What is this mystery that surrounds me? I received the likeness of God, but failed to keep it. He takes on my flesh, to bring salvation to the image, immortality to the flesh. He enters into a second union with us, a union far more wonderful than the first.

Holiness had to be brought to man by the humanity assumed by one who was God, so that God might overcome the tyrant by force and so deliver us and lead us back to himself through the mediation of his Son. The Son arranged this for the honor of the Father, to whom the Son is clearly obedient in all things.

The Good Shepherd, who lays down his life for the sheep, came in search of the straying sheep to the mountains and hills on which you used to offer sacrifice. When he found it, he took it on the shoulders that bore the wood of the cross, and led it back to the life of heaven.

Christ, the light of all lights, follows John, the lamp that goes before him. The Word of God follows the voice in the wilderness; the bridegroom follows the bridegroom's friend, who prepares a worthy people for the Lord by cleansing them by water in preparation for the Spirit.

We need God to take our flesh and die, that we might live. We have died with him, that we may be purified. We have risen again with him, because we have died with him. We have been glorified with him, because we have risen again with him.

Wednesday of the 1st Week in Advent

From a sermon by St. Bernard, Abbot & Doctor

God's Word will come to us

We know that there are three comings of the Lord. The third lies between the other two. It is invisible, while the other two are visible. In the first coming he was seen on earth, dwelling among men; he himself testifies that they saw him and hated him. In the final coming *all flesh will see the salvation of our God* [Lk 3:6], and *they will look on him whom they pierced.* [Jn 19:37] The intermediate coming is a hidden one; in it only the elect see the Lord within their own selves, and they are saved. In his first coming our Lord came in our flesh and in our weakness; in this middle coming he comes in spirit and in power; in the final coming he will be seen in glory and majesty.

Because this coming lies between the other two, it is like a road on which we travel from the first coming to the last. In the first, Christ was our redemption; in the last, he will appear as our life; in this middle coming, he is our rest and consolation.

In case someone should think that what we say about this middle coming is sheer invention, listen to what our Lord himself says: *If anyone loves me, he will keep my word, and my Father will love him, and we will come to him.* [Jn 14:23] There is another passage of Scripture which reads: *He who fears God will do good* [Eccl 7:18], but something further has been said about the one who loves, that is, that he will keep God's word. Where is God's word to be kept? Obviously in the heart, as the prophet says: *I have hidden your words in my heart, so that I may not sin against you.* [Ps 119:11]

Keep God's word in this way. Let it enter into your very being, let it take possession of your desires and your whole way of life. Feed on goodness, and your soul will delight in its richness. Remember to eat your bread, or your heart will wither away. Fill your soul with richness and strength.

If you keep the word of God in this way, it will also keep you. The Son with the Father will come to you. The great Prophet who will build the new Jerusalem will come, the one who makes all things new. This coming will fulfill what is written: *As we have borne the likeness of the earthly man, we shall also bear the likeness of the heavenly man.* [1 Cor 15:49] Just as Adam's sin spread through all mankind and took hold of all, so Christ, who created and redeemed all, will glorify all, once he takes possession of all.

Thursday of the 1st Week in Advent

From a commentary on the Diatessaron by St. Ephrem, Deacon & Doctor

Keep watch; he is to come again

To prevent his disciples from asking the time of his coming, Christ said: *About that hour no one knows, neither the angels nor the Son. It is not for you to know times or moments.* [Mt 24:36] He has kept those things hidden so that we may keep watch, each of us thinking that he will come in our own day. If he had revealed the time of his coming, his coming would have lost its savor: it would no longer be an object of yearning for the nations and the age in which it will be revealed. He promised that he would come but did not say when he would come, and so all generations and ages await him eagerly.

Though the Lord has established the signs of his coming, the time of their fulfillment has not been plainly revealed. These signs have come and gone with a multiplicity of change; more than that, they are still present. His final coming is like his first. As holy men and prophets waited for him, thinking that he would reveal himself in their own day, so today each of the faithful longs to welcome him in his own day, because Christ has not made plain the day of his coming.

He has not made it plain for this reason especially, that no one may think that he whose power and dominion rule all numbers and times is ruled by fate and time. He described the signs of his coming; how could what he has himself decided be hidden from him? Therefore, he used these words to increase respect for the signs of his coming, so that from that day forward all generations and ages might think that he would come again in their own day.

Keep watch; when the body is asleep nature takes control of us, and what is done is not done by our will but by force, by the impulse of nature. When deep listlessness takes possession of the soul, for example, faint-heartedness or melancholy, the enemy overpowers it and makes it do what it does not will. The force of nature, the enemy of the soul, is in control.

When the Lord commanded us to be vigilant, he meant vigilance in both parts of man: in the body, against the tendency to sleep; in the soul, against lethargy and timidity. As Scripture says: *Wake up, you just* [Eph 5:14], and *I have risen, and am still with you* [Mt 28]; and again, *Do not lose heart. Therefore, having this ministry, we do not lose heart.* [2 Cor 4:1]

Friday of the 1st Week in Advent

From the Proslogion by Saint Anselm, Bishop & Doctor

Desire for the vision of God

Insignificant man, escape from your everyday business for a short while, hide for a moment from your restless thoughts. Break off from your cares and troubles and be less concerned about your tasks and labors. Make a little time for God and rest a while in him.

Enter into your mind's inner chamber. Shut out everything but God and whatever helps you to seek him; and when you have shut the door, look for him. Speak now to God and say with your whole heart: *I seek your face; your face, Lord, I desire.* [Ps 27:8]

Lord, my God, teach my heart where and how to seek you, where and how to find you. Lord, if you are not here where shall I look for you in your absence? Yet if you are everywhere, why do I not see you when you are present? But surely you dwell in "light inaccessible." And where is light inaccessible? How shall I approach light inaccessible? Or who will lead me and bring me into it that I may see you there? And then, by what signs and under what forms shall I seek you? I have never seen you, Lord my God; I do not know your face.

Lord most high, what shall this exile do, so far from you? What shall your servant do, tormented by love of you and cast so far from your face? He yearns to see you, and your face is too far from him. He desires to approach you, and your dwelling is unapproachable. He longs to find you, and does not know your dwelling place. He strives to look for you, and does not know your face.

Lord, you are my God and you are my Lord, and I have never seen you. You have made me and remade me, and you have given me all the good things I possess, and still I do not know you. I was made in order to see you, and I have not yet done that for which I was made.

Lord, how long will it be? How long, Lord, will you forget us? How long will you turn your face away from us? When will you look upon us and hear us? When will you enlighten our eyes and show us your face? When will you give yourself back to us?

Look upon us, Lord, hear us and enlighten us, show us your very self. Restore yourself to us that it may go well with us whose life is so evil without you. Take pity on our efforts and our striving toward you, for we have no strength apart from you.

Teach me to seek you, and when I seek you show yourself to me, for I cannot seek you unless you teach me, nor can I find you unless you show yourself to me. Let me seek you in desiring you and desire you in seeking you, find you in loving you and love you in finding you.

Saturday of the 1st Week in Advent

From a treatise On the Value of Patience, by Saint Cyprian, Bishop and Martyr

We hope for what we do not see

Patience is a precept for salvation given us by our Lord, our teacher: *Whoever endures to the end will be saved.* [Mt 24:13] And again: *If you persevere in my word, you will truly be my disciples; you will know the truth, and the truth will set you free.* [Jn 8:31-32]

Dear brethren, we must endure and persevere if we are to attain the truth and freedom we have been allowed to hope for; faith and hope are the very meaning of our being Christians, but if faith and hope are to bear their fruit, patience is necessary.

We do not seek glory now, in the present, but we look for future glory, as Saint Paul instructs us when he says: *By hope we were saved. Now hope which is seen is not hope; how can a man hope for what he sees? But if we hope for what we do not see, we wait for it in patience.* [Ro 8:24-25] Patient waiting is necessary if we are to be perfected in what we have begun to be, and if we are to receive from God what we hope for and believe.

In another place the same Apostle instructs and teaches the just, and those active in good works, and those who store up for themselves treasures in heaven through the reward God gives them. They are to be patient also, for he says: *Therefore while we have time, let us do good to all, but especially to those who are of the household of the faith. But let us not grow weary in doing good, for we shall reap our reward in due season.* [Gal 6:9-10]

Paul warns us not to grow weary in good works through impatience, not to be distracted or overcome by temptations and so give up in the midst of our pilgrimage of praise and glory, and allow our past good deeds to count for nothing because what was begun falls short of completion.

Finally the Apostle, speaking of charity, unites it with endurance and patience. *Charity,* he says, *is always patient and kind; it is not jealous, is not boastful, is not given to anger, does not think evil, loves all things, believes all things, hopes all things, endures all things.* [1 Cor 13:4-7] He shows that charity can be steadfast and persevering because it has learned how to endure all things.

And in another place he says: *Bear with one another lovingly, striving to keep the unity of the Spirit in the bond of peace.* [Eph 4:3] He shows that neither unity nor peace can be maintained unless the brethren cherish each other with mutual forbearance and preserve the bond of harmony by means of patience.

Sunday of the 2nd Week in Advent

From a commentary on Isaiah by Eusebius of Caesarea, Bishop

The voice in the wilderness

The voice of one crying in the wilderness: Prepare the way of the Lord, make straight the paths of our God. [Is 40:3] The prophecy makes clear that it is to be fulfilled, not in Jerusalem but in the wilderness: it is there that the glory of the Lord is to appear, and God's salvation is to be made known to all mankind.

It was in the wilderness that God's saving presence was proclaimed by John the Baptist, and there that God's salvation was seen. The words of this prophecy were fulfilled when Christ and his glory were made manifest to all: after his baptism the heavens opened, and the Holy Spirit in the form of a dove rested on him, and the Father's voice was heard, bearing witness to the Son: *This is my beloved Son, listen to him.* [Mt 17:5]

The prophecy meant that God was to come to a deserted place, inaccessible from the beginning. None of the pagans had any knowledge of God, since his holy servants and prophets were kept from approaching them. The voice commands that a way be prepared for the Word of God: the rough and trackless ground is to be made level, so that our God may find a highway when he comes. *Prepare the way of the Lord* [Is 40:3]: the way is the preaching of the Gospel, the new message of consolation, ready to bring to all mankind the knowledge of God's saving power.

Climb on a high mountain, bearer of good news to Zion. Lift up your voice in strength, bearer of good news to Jerusalem. [Is 40:9] These words harmonize very well with the meaning of what has gone before. They refer opportunely to the evangelists and proclaim the coming of God to men, after speaking of the voice crying in the wilderness. Mention of the evangelists suitably follows the prophecy on John the Baptist.

What does Zion mean if not the city previously called Jerusalem? This is the mountain referred to in that passage from Scripture: *Here is mount Zion, where you dwelt.* [Ps 74:2] The Apostle says: *You have come to mount Zion.* [Heb 12:22] Does not this refer to the company of the apostles, chosen from the former people of the circumcision?

This is the Zion, the Jerusalem, that received God's salvation. It stands aloft on the mountain of God, that is, it is raised high on the only-begotten Word of God. It is commanded to climb the high mountain and announce the word of salvation. Who is the bearer of the good news but the company of the evangelists? What does it mean to bear the good news but to preach to all nations, but first of all to the cities of Judah, the coming of Christ on earth?

Monday of the 2nd Week in Advent

From a treatise on The Ascent of Mount Carmel by Saint John of the Cross, Priest & Doctor

In Christ God has spoken to us

Under the ancient law prophets and priests sought from God revelations and visions which indeed they needed, for faith had as yet no firm foundation and the gospel law had not yet been established. Their seeking and God's responses were necessary. He spoke to them at one time through words and visions and revelations, at another in signs and symbols. But however he responded and what he said and revealed were mysteries of our holy faith, either partial glimpses of the whole or sure movements toward it.

But now that faith is rooted in Christ, and the law of the gospel has been proclaimed in this time of grace, there is no need to seek him in the former manner, nor for him so to respond. By giving us, as he did, his Son, his only Word, he has in that one Word said everything. There is no need for any further revelation.

This is the true meaning of Paul's words to the Hebrews when he urged them to abandon their earlier ways of conversing with God, as laid down in the law of Moses, and to set their eyes on Christ alone: *In the past God spoke to our fathers through the prophets in various ways and manners; but now in our times, the last days, he has spoken to us in his Son.* [Heb 1:1-2] In effect, Paul is saying that God has spoken so completely through his own Word that he chooses to add nothing. Although he had spoken but partially through the prophets he has now said everything in Christ. He has given us everything, his own Son.

Therefore, anyone who wished to question God or to seek some new vision or revelation from him would commit an offense, for instead of focusing his eyes entirely on Christ he would be desiring something other than Christ, or beyond him.

God could then answer: *This is my beloved Son in whom I am well pleased; hear him.* [Mt 3:17] In my Word I have already said everything. Fix your eyes on him alone for in him I have revealed all and in him you will find more than you could ever ask for or desire.

I, with my Holy Spirit, came down upon him on Mount Tabor and declared: *This is my beloved Son in whom I am well pleased; hear him.* [Mt 3:17] You do not need new teachings or ways of learning from me, for when I spoke before it was of Christ who was to come, and when they sought anything of me they were but seeking and hoping for the Christ in whom is every good, as the whole teaching of the evangelists and apostles clearly testifies.

Tuesday of the 2nd Week in Advent

From the dogmatic constitution on the Church of the Second Vatican Council *Lumen Gentium*

The eschatological character of the pilgrim Church

The Church, to which we are all called in Christ Jesus and in which we acquire holiness through the grace of God, will reach its perfection only in the glory of heaven, when the time comes for the renewal of all things, and the whole world, which is intimately bound up with man and reaches its perfection through him, will, along with the human race, be perfectly restored in Christ.

Lifted above the earth, Christ drew all things to himself. Rising from the dead, he sent his life-giving Spirit upon his disciples, and through the Spirit established his Body, which is the Church, as the universal sacrament of salvation. Seated at the right hand of the Father, he works unceasingly in the world, to draw men into the Church and through it to join them more closely to himself, nourishing them with his own body and blood, and so making them share in his life of glory.

The promised renewal that we look for has already begun in Christ. It is continued in the mission of the Holy Spirit. Through the Spirit it goes on developing in the Church: there we are taught by faith about the meaning also of our life on earth as we bring to fulfillment – with hope in the blessings that are to come – the work that has been entrusted to us in the world by the Father, and so work out our salvation.

The end of the ages is already with us. The renewal of the world has been established, and cannot be revoked. In our era it is in a true sense anticipated: the Church on earth is already sealed by genuine, if imperfect, holiness. Yet, until a new heaven and a new earth are built as the dwelling place of justice, the pilgrim Church, in its sacraments and institutions belonging to this world of time, bears the likeness of this passing world. It lives in the midst of a creation still groaning and in travail as it waits for the sons of God to be revealed in glory.

Wednesday of the 2nd Week in Advent

From a discourse on the Psalms by Saint Augustine, Bishop & Doctor

God's promises are held out to us by his Son

God established a time for his promises and a time for their fulfillment. The time for promises was in the time of the prophets, until John the Baptist; from John until the end is the time of fulfillment.

God, who is faithful, put himself in our debt, not by receiving anything but by promising so much. A promise was not sufficient for him; he chose to commit himself in writing as well, as it were making a contract of his promises. He wanted us to be able to see the way in which his promises were redeemed when he began to discharge them. And so the time of the prophets was, as we have often said, the foretelling of the promises.

He promised eternal salvation, everlasting happiness with the angels, an immortal inheritance, endless glory, the joyful vision of his face, his holy dwelling in heaven, and after resurrection from the dead no further fear of dying. This is as it were his final promise, the goal of all our striving. When we reach it, we shall ask for nothing more. But as to the way in which we are to arrive at our final goal, he has revealed this also, by promise and prophecy.

He has promised men divinity, mortals immortality, sinners justification, the poor a rising to glory. But, brethren, because God's promises seemed impossible to men - equality with the angels in exchange for mortality, corruption, poverty, weakness, dust and ashes - God not only made a written contract with men, to win their belief but also established a mediator of his good faith, not a prince or angel or archangel, but his only Son. He wanted, through his Son, to show us and give us the way he would lead us to the goal he has promised.

It was not enough for God to make his Son our guide to the way; he made him the way itself, that you might travel with him as leader, and by him as the way.

Therefore, the only Son of God was to come among men, to take the nature of men, and in this nature to be born as a man. He was to die, to rise again, to ascend into heaven, to sit at the right hand of the Father, and to fulfill his promises among the nations, and after that to come again, to exact now what he had asked for before, to separate those deserving his anger from those deserving his mercy, to execute his threats against the wicked, and to reward the just as he had promised.

All this had therefore to be prophesied, foretold, and impressed on us as an event in the future, in order that we might wait for it in faith, not find it a sudden and dreadful reality.

Thursday of the 2nd Week in Advent

From a sermon by Saint Peter Chrysologus, Bishop

Love desires to see God

When God saw the world falling to ruin because of fear, he immediately acted to call it back to himself with love. He invited it by his grace, preserved it by his love, and embraced it with compassion. When the earth had become hardened in evil, God sent the flood both to punish and to release it. He called Noah to be the father of a new era, urged him with kind words, and showed that he trusted him; he gave him fatherly instruction about the present calamity, and through his grace consoled him with hope for the future. But God did not merely issue commands; rather with Noah sharing the work, he filled the ark with the future seed of the whole world. The sense of loving fellowship thus engendered removed servile fear, and a mutual love could continue to preserve what shared labor had effected.

God called Abraham out of the heathen world, symbolically lengthened his name, and made him the father of all believers. God walked with him on his journeys, protected him in foreign lands, enriched him with earthly possessions, and honored him with victories. He made a covenant with him, saved him from harm, accepted his hospitality, and astonished him by giving him the offspring he had despaired of. Favored with so many graces and drawn by such great sweetness of divine love, Abraham was to learn to love God rather than fear him, and love rather than fear was to inspire his worship.

God comforted Jacob by a dream during his flight, roused him to combat upon his return, and encircled him with a wrestler's embrace to teach him not to be afraid of the author of the conflict, but to love him. God called Moses as a father would, and with fatherly affection invited him to become the liberator of his people.

In all the events we have recalled, the flame of divine love enkindled human hearts and its intoxication overflowed into men's senses. Wounded by love, they longed to look upon God with their bodily eyes. Yet how could our narrow human vision apprehend God, whom the whole world cannot contain? But the law of love is not concerned with what will be, what ought to be, what can be. Love does not reflect; it is unreasonable and knows no moderation. Love refuses to be consoled when its goal proves impossible, despises all hindrances to the attainment of its object. Love destroys the lover if he cannot obtain what he loves; love follows its own promptings, and does not think of right and wrong. Love inflames desire which impels it toward things that are forbidden. But why continue?

It is intolerable for love not to see the object of its longing. That is why whatever reward they merited was nothing to the saints if they could not see the Lord. A love that desires to see God may not have reasonableness on its side, but it is the evidence of filial love. It gave Moses the temerity to say: *If I have found favor in your eyes, show me your face.* [Ex 33:13] It inspired the psalmist to make the same prayer: *Show me your face.* [Ex 33:13] Even the pagans made their images for this purpose: they wanted actually to see what they mistakenly revered.

Friday of the 2nd Week in Advent

From a treatise Against Heresies by Saint Irenaeus, Bishop, Doctor & Martyr

Eve and Mary

The Lord, coming into his own creation in visible form, was sustained by his own creation which he himself sustains in being. His obedience on the tree of the cross reversed the disobedience at the tree in Eden; the good news of the truth announced by an angel to Mary, a virgin subject to a husband, undid the evil lie that seduced Eve, a virgin espoused to a husband.

As Eve was seduced by the word of an angel and so fled from God after disobeying his word, Mary in her turn was given the good news by the word of an angel, and bore God in obedience to his word. As Eve was seduced into disobedience to God, so Mary was persuaded into obedience to God; thus the Virgin Mary became the advocate of the virgin Eve.

Christ gathered all things into one, by gathering them into himself. He declared war against our enemy, crushed him who at the beginning had taken us captive in Adam, and trampled on his head, in accordance with God's words to the serpent in Genesis: *I will put enmity between you and the woman, and between your seed and her seed; he shall lie in wait for your head, and you shall lie in wait for his heel.* [Gen 3:15]

The one lying in wait for the serpent's head is the one who was born in the likeness of Adam from the woman, the Virgin. This is the seed spoken of by Paul in the letter to the Galatians: *The law of works was in force until the seed should come to whom the promise was made.* [Gal 3:19] He shows this even more clearly in the same letter when he says: *When the fullness of time had come, God sent his Son, born of a woman.* [Gal 4:4] The enemy would not have been defeated fairly if his vanquisher had not been born of a woman, because it was through a woman that he had gained mastery over man in the beginning, and set himself up as man's adversary.

That is why the Lord proclaims himself the Son of Man, the one who renews in himself that first man from whom the race born of woman was formed; as by a man's defeat our race fell into the bondage of death, so by a man's victory we were to rise again to life.

Saturday of the 2nd Week in Advent

From a sermon by Blessed Isaac of Stella, Abbot

Mary and the Church

The Son of God is the first born of many brothers. Although by nature he is the only-begotten, by grace he has joined many to himself and made them one with him. For to those who receive him *he has given the power to become the sons of God.* [Jn 1:12]

He became the Son of man and made many men sons of God, uniting them to himself by his love and power, so that they became as one. In themselves they are many by reason of their human descent, but in him they are one by divine rebirth.

The whole Christ and the unique Christ – the body and the head – are one: one because born of the same God in heaven, and of the same mother on earth. They are many sons, yet one son. Head and members are one son, yet many sons; in the same way, Mary and the Church are one mother, yet more than one mother; one virgin, yet more than one virgin.

Both are mothers, both are virgins. Each conceives of the same Spirit, without concupiscence. Each gives birth to a child of God the Father, without sin. Without any sin, Mary gave birth to Christ the head for the sake of his body. By the forgiveness of every sin, the Church gave birth to the body, for the sake of its head. Each is Christ's mother, but neither gives birth to the whole Christ without the cooperation of the other.

In the inspired Scriptures, what is said in a universal sense of the virgin mother, the Church, is understood in an individual sense of the Virgin Mary, and what is said in a particular sense of the virgin mother Mary is rightly understood in a general sense of the virgin mother, the Church. When either is spoken of, the meaning can be understood of both, almost without qualification.

In a way, every Christian is also believed to be a bride of God's Word, a mother of Christ, his daughter and sister, at once virginal and fruitful. These words are used in a universal sense of the Church, in a special sense of Mary, in a particular sense of the individual Christian. They are used by God's Wisdom in person, the Word of the Father.

This is why Scripture says: *I will dwell in the inheritance of the Lord.* [Ps 27:29] The Lord's inheritance is, in a general sense, the Church; in a special sense, Mary; in an individual sense, the Christian. Christ dwelt for nine months in the tabernacle of Mary's womb. He dwells until the end of the ages in the tabernacle of the Church's faith. He will dwell forever in the knowledge and love of each faithful soul.

Sunday of the 3rd Week in Advent

From a sermon by Saint Augustine, Bishop & Doctor

The voice is John, the Word is Christ

John is the voice, but the Lord *is the Word who was in the beginning.* [Jn 1:1] John is the voice that lasts for a time; from the beginning Christ is the Word who lives for ever.

Take away the word, the meaning, and what is the voice? Where there is no understanding, there is only a meaningless sound. The voice without the word strikes the ear but does not build up the heart.

However, let us observe what happens when we first seek to build up our hearts. When I think about what I am going to say, the word or message is already in my heart. When I want to speak to you, I look for a way to share with your heart what is already in mine.

In my search for a way to let this message reach you, so that the word already in my heart may find a place also in yours, I use my voice to speak to you. The sound of my voice brings the meaning of the word to you and then passes away. The word which the sound has brought to you is now in your heart, and yet it is still also in mine.

When the word has been conveyed to you, does not the sound seem to say: *The word ought to grow, and I should diminish?* [Jn 3:30] The sound of the voice has made itself heard in the service of the word, and has gone away, as though it were saying: *My joy is complete.* [Jn 15:11] Let us hold on to the word; we must not lose the word conceived inwardly in our hearts.

Do you need proof that the voice passes away but the divine Word remains? Where is John's baptism today? It served its purpose, and it went away. Now it is Christ's baptism that we celebrate. It is in Christ that we all believe; we hope for salvation in him. This is the message the voice cried out.

Because it is hard to distinguish word from voice, even John himself was thought to be the Christ. The voice was thought to be the word. But the voice acknowledged what is was, anxious not to give offense to the word. *I am not the Christ, he said, nor Elijah, nor the prophet. And the question came: Who are you, then? He replied: I am the voice of one crying in the wilderness: Prepare the way for the Lord.* [Jn 1:20-23]

The voice of one crying in the wilderness is the voice of one breaking the silence. *Prepare the way for the Lord*, he says, as though he were saying: "I speak out in order to lead him into your hearts, but he does not choose to come where I lead him unless you prepare the way for him."

To prepare the way means to pray well; it means thinking humbly of oneself. We should take our lesson from John the Baptist. He is thought to be the Christ; he declares he is not what they think. He does not take advantage of their mistake to further his own glory.

If he had said, "I am the Christ," you can imagine how readily he would have been believed, since they believed he was the Christ even before he spoke. But he did not say it; he acknowledged what he was. He pointed out clearly who he was; he humbled himself.

He saw where his salvation lay. He understood that he was a lamp, and his fear was that it might be blown out by the wind of pride.

Monday of the 3rd Week in Advent

From a discourse On the Contemplation of God by William of Saint-Thierry, Abbot

He loved us first

Truly you alone are the Lord. Your dominion is our salvation, for to serve you is nothing else but to be saved by you! O Lord, salvation is your gift and your blessing is upon your people; what else is your salvation but receiving from you the gift of loving you or being loved by you? That, Lord, is why you willed that the Son at your right hand, the man whom you made strong for yourself, should be called Jesus, that is to say, Savior, *for he will save his people from their sins,* [Mt 1:21] *and there is no other in whom there is salvation.* [Acts 4:12] He taught us to love him by first loving us, *even to death on the cross.* [Phil 2:5-10] By loving us and holding us so dear, he stirred us to love him who had first loved us to the end.

And this is clearly the reason: you first loved us so that we might love you--not because you needed our love, but because we could not be what you created us to be, except by loving you.

In many ways and on various occasions you spoke to our fathers through the prophets. Now in these last days you have spoken to us in the Son, your Word; by him the heavens were established and all their powers came to be by the breath of his mouth.

For you to speak thus in your Son was to bring out in the light of day how much and in what way you loved us, for you did not spare your own Son but delivered him up for us all. He also *loved us and gave himself up for us.* [Eph 5:1-2]

This, Lord, is your Word to us, this is your all-powerful message: while all things were in midnight silence (that is, were in the depths of error), he came from his royal throne, the stern conqueror of error and the gentle apostle of love.

Everything he did and everything he said on earth, even enduring the insults, the spitting, the buffeting--the cross and the grave--all of this was actually you speaking to us in your Son, appealing to us by your love and stirring up our love for you.

You know that this disposition could not be forced on men's hearts, my God, since you created them; it must rather be elicited. And this, for the further reason that there is no freedom where there is compulsion, and where freedom is lacking, so too is righteousness.

You wanted us to love you, then, we who could not with justice have been saved had we not loved you, nor could we have loved you except by your gift. So, Lord, as the apostle of your love tells us, and as we have already said, *you first loved us:* you are first to love all those who love you.

Thus we hold you dear by the affection you have implanted in us. You are the one supremely good and ultimate goodness. Your love is your goodness, the Holy Spirit proceeding from the Father and the Son! From the beginning of creation it was he who hovered over the waters--that is, over the wavering minds of men, offering himself to all, drawing all things to himself. By his inspiration and holy breath, by keeping us from harm and providing for our needs, he unites God to us and us to God.

Tuesday of the 3rd Week in Advent

From The Imitation of Christ ~ Thomas a Kempis

On humility and peace

Do not care much who is with you and who is against you; but make it your greatest care that God is with you in everything you do.

Have a good conscience, and God will defend you securely; no one can hurt you if God wishes to help you.

If you know how to suffer in silence, you will surely receive God's help. Since he knows best the time and the way to set you free, resign yourself to him, for God helps you and frees you from all confusion.

It is often good for us, and helps us to remain humble, if others know our weaknesses and confront us with them.

When a man humbles himself for his faults, he more easily pleases others and mollifies those he has angered.

God protects and frees a humble man; he loves and consoles a humble man; he favors a humble man; he showers him with graces; then, after his suffering, God raises him up to glory.

He reveals his secrets to a humble man and in his kindness invitingly draws that man to himself. When a humble man is brought to confusion, he experiences peace, because he stands firm in God and not in this world. Do not think that you have made any progress unless you feel that you are the lowest of all men.

Above all things, keep peace within yourself, then you will be able to create peace among others. It is better to be peaceful than learned.

The passionate man often thinks evil of a good man and easily believes the worst; a good and peaceful man turns all things to good.

A man who lives at peace suspects no one. But a man who is tense and agitated by evil is troubled with all kinds of suspicions; he is never at peace with himself, nor does he permit others to be at peace.

He often speaks when he should be silent, and he fails to say what would be truly useful. He is well aware of the obligations of others but neglects his own.

So be zealous first of all with yourself, and then you will be more justified in expressing zeal for your neighbor.

You are good at excusing and justifying your own deeds, and yet you will not listen to the excuses of others. It would be more just to accuse yourself and excuse your brother.

If you wish others to put up with you, first put up with them.

Wednesday of the 3rd Week in Advent

From a treatise Against Heresies by Saint Irenaeus, Bishop, Doctor & Martyr

When Christ comes, God will be seen by men

There is one God, who by his word and wisdom created all things and set them in order. His Word is our Lord Jesus Christ, who in this last age became man among men to unite end and beginning, that is, man and God.

The prophets, receiving the gift of prophecy from this same Word, foretold his coming in the flesh, which brought about the union and communion between God and man ordained by the Father. From the beginning the word of God prophesied that God would be seen by men and would live among them on earth; he would speak with his own creation and be present to it, bringing it salvation and being visible to it. He would *free us from the hands of all who hate us,* Canticle of Zechariah [Lk 1:67-80] that is, from the universal spirit of sin, and enable us *to serve him in holiness and justice all our days.* Man was to receive the Spirit of God and so attain to the glory of the Father.

The prophets, then, foretold that God would be seen by men. As the Lord himself says: *Blessed are the clean of heart, for they shall see God.* [Mt 5:8] In his greatness and inexpressible glory *no one can see God and live* [Ex 33:20], for the Father is beyond our comprehension. But in his love and generosity and omnipotence he allows even this to those who love him, that is, even to see God, as the prophets foretold. *For what is impossible to men is possible to God.* [Mt 19:26]

By his own powers man cannot see God, yet God will be seen by men because he wills it. He will be seen by those he chooses, at the time he chooses, and in the way he chooses, for God can do all things. He was seen of old through the Spirit in prophecy; he is seen through the Son by our adoption as his children, and he will be seen in the kingdom of heaven in his own being as the Father. The Spirit prepares man to receive the Son of God, the Son leads him to the Father, and the Father, freeing him from change and decay, bestows the eternal life that comes to everyone from seeing God.

As those who see light are in the light sharing its brilliance, so those who see God are in God sharing his glory, and that glory gives them life. To see God is to share in life.

Thursday of the 3rd Week in Advent

From the dogmatic constitution on Divine Revelation of the Second Vatican Council *Dei Verbum*

Christ brings all revelation to perfection

God, who through the Word creates all things and keeps them in being, provides men with unfailing testimony to himself in creation. With the intention of opening up the way of salvation from above, he also revealed himself to our first parents from the very beginning.

After their fall, he lifted them up to hope for salvation by the promise of redemption, and watched over mankind with unceasing care, in order that he might give eternal life to all who in persevering in good works seek out salvation.

In his own good time God called Abraham, to make of him a mighty nation. After the patriarchs, he taught this nation through Moses and the prophets to acknowledge himself alone as the living and true God, a provident father and just judge, and to look forward to the promised Savior. So, through the ages, he prepared a way for the Gospel. After speaking *at various times and in different ways through the prophets, God has finally spoken to us in these days through the Son.* [Heb 1:1-2]

He sent his Son, the eternal Word who enlightens all men, to dwell among men and make known to them the innermost things of God. Jesus Christ, the Word made flesh, sent as *a man to men, speaks the words of God* 1 Thess 2:13, and brings to perfection the saving work that the Father gave him to do.

To see him is to see the Father also. By his whole presence and self-revelation, by words and actions, by signs and miracles, especially by his death and glorious resurrection from the dead, and finally by sending the Spirit of truth, he completes revelation and brings it to perfection, sealing by divine testimony its message that God is with us to free us from the darkness of sin and death, and to raise us up to eternal life.

The Christian dispensation, because it is the new and definitive covenant, will never pass away, and no new public revelation is any longer to be looked for before the manifestation in glory of our Lord Jesus Christ.

Friday of the 3rd Week in Advent

From a discourse on the psalms by Saint Augustine, Bishop & Doctor

The desire of your heart constitutes your prayer

In the anguish of my heart I groaned aloud. [Ps 38:9] There is a hidden anguish which is inaudible to men. Yet when a man's heart is so taken up with some particular concern that the hurt inside finds vocal expression, one looks for the reason. And one will say to oneself: perhaps this is what causes his anguish, or perhaps such and such has happened to him. But who can be certain of the cause except God, who hears and sees his anguish? Therefore the psalmist says: *In the anguish of my heart I groaned aloud.* For if men hear at all, they usually hear only bodily groaning and know nothing of the anguish of the heart from which it issues.

Who then knows the cause of man's groaning? *All my desire is before you.* [Ps 38:10] No, it is not open before other men, for they cannot understand the heart; *but before you is all my desire.* If your desire lies open to him who is your Father and who sees in secret, he will answer you.

For the desire of your heart is itself your prayer. And if the desire is constant, so is your prayer. The Apostle Paul had a purpose in saying: *Pray without ceasing.* [1 Thess 5:17] Are we then ceaselessly to bend our knees, to lie prostrate, or to lift up our hands? Is this what is meant in saying: *Pray without ceasing?* Even if we admit that we pray in this fashion, I do not believe that we can do so all the time.

Yet there is another, interior kind of prayer without ceasing, namely, the desire of the heart. Whatever else you may be doing, if you but fix your desire on God's Sabbath rest, your prayer will be ceaseless. Therefore, if you wish to pray without ceasing, do not cease to desire.

The constancy of your desire will itself be the ceaseless voice of your prayer. And that voice of your prayer will be silent only when your love ceases. For who are silent? Those of whom it is said: *Because evil has abounded, the love of many will grow cold.* [Mt 24:12]

The chilling of love means that the heart is silent; while burning love is the outcry of the heart. If your love is without ceasing, you are crying out always; if you always cry out, you are always desiring; and if you desire, you are calling to mind your eternal rest in the Lord.

And all my desire is before you. What if the desire of our heart is before him, but not our groaning? But how is that possible, since the groaning is the voice of our desire? And therefore it is said: *My groaning is not concealed from you.* It may be concealed from men, but it is not concealed from you. Sometimes God's servant seems to be saying in his humility: *My anguish is not concealed from you.* At other times he seems to be laughing. Does that mean that the desire of his heart has died within him? If the desire is there, then the groaning is there as well. Even if men fail to hear it, it never ceases to sound in the hearing of God.

Sunday of the 4th Week in Advent
are taken from the office of the day (see December 17th-24th)

December 17th

From a letter by Saint Leo the Great, Pope & Doctor

The mystery of our reconciliation with God

To speak of our Lord, the son of the Blessed Virgin Mary, as true and perfect man is of no value to us if we do not believe that he is descended from the line of ancestors set out in the Gospel. Matthew's gospel begins by setting out *the genealogy of Jesus Christ, son of David, son of Abraham* [Mt 1:1], and then traces his human descent by bringing his ancestral line down to his mother's husband, Joseph. On the other hand, Luke traces his parentage backward step by step to the actual father of mankind, to show that both the first and the last Adam share the same nature.

No doubt the Son of God in his omnipotence could have taught and sanctified men by appearing to them in a semblance of human form as he did to the patriarchs and prophets, when for instance he engaged in a wrestling contest or entered into conversation with them, or when he accepted their hospitality and even ate the food they set before him. But these appearances were only types, signs that mysteriously foretold the coming of one who would take a true human nature from the stock of the patriarchs who had gone before him. No mere figure, then, fulfilled the mystery of our reconciliation with God, ordained from all eternity. The Holy Spirit had not yet come upon the Virgin nor had the power of the Most High overshadowed her, so that within her spotless womb Wisdom might build itself a house and the Word become flesh. The divine nature and the nature of a servant were to be united in one person so that the Creator of time might be born in time, and he through whom all things were made might be brought forth in their midst.

For unless the new man, by being made *in the likeness of sinful humanity* [Phil 2:7], had taken on himself the nature of our first parents, unless he had stooped to be one in substance with his mother while sharing the Father's substance and, being alone free from sin, united our nature to his, the whole human race would still be held captive under the dominion of Satan. The Conqueror's victory would have profited us nothing if the battle had been fought outside our human condition. But through this wonderful blending the mystery of new birth shone upon us, so that through the same Spirit by whom Christ was conceived and brought forth we too might be born again in a spiritual birth; and in consequence the evangelist declares the faithful to *have been born not of blood, nor of the desire of the flesh, nor of the will of man, but of God.* [Jn 1:13]

December 18th

From a letter to Diognetus

God has revealed his love through the Son

No man has ever seen God or known him, but God has revealed himself to us through faith, by which alone it is possible to see him. God, the Lord and maker of all things, who created the world and set it in order, not only loved man but was also patient with him. So he has always been, and is, and will be: kind, good, free from anger, truthful; indeed, he and he alone is good.

He devised a plan, a great and wonderful plan, and shared it only with his Son. As long as he preserved this secrecy and kept his own wise counsel he seemed to be neglecting us, to have no concern for us. But when through his beloved Son he revealed and made public what he had prepared from the very beginning, he gave us all at once gifts such as we could never have dreamt of, even sight and knowledge of himself.

When God had made all his plans in consultation with his Son, he waited until a later time, allowing us to follow our own whim, to be swept along by unruly passions, to be led astray by pleasure and desire. Not that he was pleased by our sins: he only tolerated them. Not that he approved of that time of sin: he was planning this era of holiness. When we had been shown to be undeserving of life, his goodness was to make us worthy of it. When we had made it clear that we could not enter God's kingdom by our own power, we were to be enabled to do so by the power of God.

When our wickedness had reached its culmination, it became clear that retribution was at hand in the shape of suffering and death. The time came then for God to make known his kindness and power (how immeasurable is God's generosity and love!). He did not show hatred for us or reject us or take vengeance; instead, he was patient with us, bore with us, and in compassion took our sins upon himself; he gave his own Son as the price of our redemption, the holy one to redeem the wicked, the sinless one to redeem sinners, the just one to redeem the unjust, the incorruptible one to redeem the corruptible, the immortal one to redeem mortals. For what else could have covered our sins but his sinlessness? Where else could we-wicked and sinful as we were-have found the means of holiness except in the Son of God alone?

How wonderful a transformation, how mysterious a design, how inconceivable a blessing! The wickedness of the many is covered up in the holy One, and the holiness of One sanctifies many sinners.

December 19th

From a treatise Against Heresies by St Irenaeus, Bishop, Doctor & Martyr

The plan of redemption through the Incarnation

God is man's glory. Man is the vessel which receives God's action and all his wisdom and power.

Just as a doctor is judged in his care for the sick, so God is revealed in his conduct with men. That is Paul's reason for saying: *God has made the whole world prisoner of unbelief that he may have mercy on all.* [Rom 11:30-32] He was speaking of man, who was disobedient to God, and cast off from immortality, and then found mercy, receiving through the Son of God the adoption he brings.

If man, without being puffed up or boastful, has a right belief regarding created things and their divine Creator, who, having given them being, holds them all in his power, and if man perseveres in God's love, and in obedience and gratitude to him, he will receive greater glory from him. It will be a glory which will grow ever brighter until he takes on the likeness of the one who died for him.

He it was who took on the likeness of sinful flesh, to condemn sin and rid the flesh of sin, as now condemned. He wanted to invite man to take on his likeness, appointing man an imitator of God, establishing man in a way of life in obedience to the Father that would lead to the vision of God, and endowing man with power to receive the Father. He is the Word of God who dwelt with man and became the Son of Man to open the way for man to receive God, for God to dwell with man, according to the will of the Father.

For this reason *the Lord himself gave* as the sign of our salvation, the one who was born of *the Virgin, Emmanuel.* [Is 7:14] It was *the Lord himself who saved them,* [Mt 1:18-23] for of themselves they had no power to be saved. For this reason Paul speaks of the weakness of man, and says: *I know that no good dwells in my flesh* [Rom 7:18]; he means that the blessing of our salvation comes not from us but from God. Again, he says: *I am a wretched man; who will free me from this body doomed to die?* [Rom 7:24] Then he speaks of a liberator, thanks to Jesus Christ our Lord.

Isaiah says the same: *Hands that are feeble, grow strong! Knees that are weak, take courage! Hearts that are faint, grow strong! Fear not-see, our God is judgement and he will repay. He himself will come and save us.* [Is 35:3-4] He means that we could not be saved of ourselves but only with God's help.

December 20th

From a homily In Praise of the Virgin Mother by Saint Bernard of Clairvaux, Abbot & Doctor

The whole world awaits Mary's reply

You have heard, O Virgin, that you will conceive and bear a son; you have heard that it will not be by man but by the Holy Spirit. The angel awaits an answer; it is time for him to return to God who sent him. We too are waiting, O Lady, for your word of compassion; the sentence of condemnation weighs heavily upon us.

The price of our salvation is offered to you. We shall be set free at once if you consent. In the eternal Word of God we all came to be, and behold, we die. In your brief response we are to be remade in order to be recalled to life.

Tearful Adam with his sorrowing family begs this of you, O loving Virgin, in their exile from Paradise. Abraham begs it, David begs it. All the other holy patriarchs, your ancestors, ask it of you, as they dwell in the country of the shadow of death. This is what the whole earth waits for, prostrate at your feet. It is right in doing so, for on your word depends comfort for the wretched, ransom for the captive, freedom for the condemned, indeed, salvation for all the sons of Adam, the whole of your race.

Answer quickly, O Virgin. Reply in haste to the angel, or rather through the angel to the Lord. Answer with a word, receive the Word of God. Speak your own word, conceive the divine Word. Breathe a passing word, embrace the eternal Word.

Why do you delay, why are you afraid? Believe, give praise, and receive. Let humility be bold, let modesty be confident. This is no time for virginal simplicity to forget prudence. In this matter alone, O prudent Virgin, do not fear to be presumptuous. Though modest silence is pleasing, dutiful speech is now more necessary. Open your heart to faith, O blessed Virgin, your lips to praise, your womb to the Creator. See, the desired of all nations is at your door, knocking to enter. If he should pass by because of your delay, in sorrow you would begin to seek him afresh, the One whom your soul loves. Arise, hasten, open. Arise in faith, hasten in devotion, open in praise and thanksgiving. *Behold, the handmaid of the Lord,* she says, *be it done to me according to your word.* [Lk 1:38]

December 21st

From a commentary of Luke by Saint Ambrose, Bishop & Doctor

Mary Visits Elizabeth

When the angel revealed his message to the Virgin Mary he gave her a sign to win her trust. He told her of the motherhood of an old and barren woman to show that God is able to do all that he wills.

When she hears this Mary sets out for the hill country. She does not disbelieve God's word; she feels no uncertainty over the message or doubt about the sign. She goes eager in purpose, dutiful in conscience, hastening for joy.

Filled with God, where would she hasten but to the heights? The Holy Spirit does not proceed by slow, laborious efforts. Quickly, too, the blessings of her coming and the Lord's presence are made clear: as soon as *Elizabeth heard Mary's greeting the child leapt in her womb, and she was filled with the Holy Spirit.* [Lk 1:41]

Notice the contrast and the choice of words. Elizabeth is the first to hear Mary's voice, but John is the first to be aware of grace. She hears with the ears of the body, but he leaps for joy at the meaning of the mystery. She is aware of Mary's presence, but he is aware of the Lord's: a woman aware of a woman's presence, the forerunner aware of the pledge of our salvation. The women speak of the grace they have received while the children are active in secret, unfolding the mystery of love with the help of their mothers, who prophesy by the spirit of their sons.

The child leaps in the womb; the mother is filled with the Holy Spirit, but not before her son. Once the son has been filled with the Holy Spirit, he fills his mother with the same Spirit. John leaps for joy, and the spirit of Mary rejoices in her turn. When John leaps for joy Elizabeth is filled with the Holy Spirit, but we know that though Mary's spirit rejoices she does not need to be filled with the Holy Spirit. Her son, who is beyond our understanding, is active in his mother in a way beyond our understanding. Elizabeth is filled with the Holy Spirit after conceiving John, while Mary is filled with the Holy Spirit before conceiving the Lord. Elizabeth says: *Blessed are you because you have believed.* [Lk 1:45]

You also are blessed because you have heard and believed. A soul that believes both conceives and brings forth the Word of God and acknowledges his works.

Let Mary's soul be in each of you to proclaim the greatness of the Lord. Let her spirit be in each to rejoice in the Lord. Christ has only one mother in the flesh, but we all bring forth Christ in faith. Every soul receives the Word of God if only it keeps chaste, remaining pure and free from sin, its modesty undefiled. The soul that succeeds in this proclaims the greatness of the Lord, just as Mary's soul magnified the Lord and her spirit rejoiced in God her Savior. In another place we read: *Magnify the Lord with me.* [Ps 34:3-4] The Lord is magnified, not because the human voice can add anything to God but because he is magnified within us. Christ is the image of God, and if the soul does what is right and holy, it magnifies that image of God, in whose likeness it was created and, in magnifying the image of God, the soul has a share in its greatness and is exalted.

December 22nd

From a commentary on Luke by Venerable Bede, Priest & Doctor

The Magnificat

Mary said: My soul proclaims the greatness of the Lord, my spirit rejoices in God my Savior. [Lk 1:46-47]

The Lord has exalted me by a gift so great, so unheard of, that language is useless to describe it, and the depths of love in my heart can scarcely grasp it. I offer then all the powers of my soul in praise and thanksgiving. As I contemplate his greatness, which knows no limits, I joyfully surrender my whole life, my senses, my judgment, for my spirit rejoices in the eternal Godhead of that Jesus, that Savior, whom I have conceived in this world of time.

The Almighty has done great things for me, and holy is his name. [Lk 1:49]

Mary looks back to the beginning of her song, where she said: *My soul proclaims the greatness of the Lord.* Only that soul for whom the Lord in his love does great things can proclaim his greatness with fitting praise and encourage those who share her desire and purpose, saying: *Join with me in proclaiming the greatness of the Lord; let us extol his name together.* [Ps 34:3]

Those who know the Lord, yet refuse to proclaim his greatness and sanctify his name to the limit of their power, *will be called least in the kingdom of heaven.* [Mt 5:19] His name is called holy because in the sublimity of his unique power he surpasses every creature and is far removed from all that he has made.

He has come to the help of his servant Israel for he has remembered his promise of mercy. [Lk 1:54]

In a beautiful phrase Mary calls Israel the servant of the Lord. The Lord came to his aid to save him. Israel is an obedient and humble servant, in the words of Hosea: *Israel was a servant, and I loved him.* [Hos 11:1]

Those who refuse to be humble cannot be saved. They cannot say with the prophet: *See, God comes to my aid; the Lord is the helper of my soul.* [Ps 54:4] But *anyone who makes himself humble like a little child is greater in the kingdom of heaven.* [Mt 18:4]

The promise he made to our fathers, to Abraham and his children for ever. [Lk 1:55]

This does not refer to the physical descendants of Abraham, but to his spiritual children. These are his descendants, sprung not from the flesh only, but who, whether circumcised or not, have followed him in faith. Circumcised as he was, Abraham believed, and this was credited to him as an act of righteousness.

The coming of the Savior was promised to Abraham and to his descendants for ever. These are the children of promise, to whom it is said: *If you belong to Christ, then you are descendants of Abraham, heirs in accordance with the promise.* [Gal 3:29]

December 23rd

From a treatise against the heresy of Noetus by Saint Hippolytus, Priest

The manifestation of the hidden mystery

There is only one God, brethren, and we learn about him only from sacred Scripture. It is therefore our duty to become acquainted with what Scripture proclaims and to investigate its teachings thoroughly. We should believe them in the sense that the Father wills, thinking of the Son in the way the Father wills, and accepting the teaching he wills to give us with regard to the Holy Spirit. Sacred Scripture is God's gift to us and it should be understood in the way that he intends: we should not do violence to it by interpreting it according to our own preconceived ideas.

God was all alone and nothing existed but himself when he determined to create the world. He thought of it, willed it, spoke the word and so made it. It came into being instantaneously, exactly as he had willed. It is enough then for us to be aware of a single fact: nothing is coeternal with God. Apart from God there was simply nothing else. Yet although he was alone, he was manifold because he lacked neither reason, wisdom, power nor counsel. All things were in him and he himself was all. At a moment of his own choosing and in a manner determined by himself, God manifested his Word, and through him he made the whole universe.

When the Word was hidden within God himself he was invisible to the created world, but God made him visible. First God gave utterance to his voice, engendering light from light, and then he sent his own mind into the world as its Lord. Visible before to God alone and not to the world, God made him visible so that the world could be saved by seeing him. This mind that entered our world was made known as the Son of God. All things came into being through him; but he alone is begotten by the Father.

The Son gave us the law and the prophets, and he filled the prophets with the Holy Spirit to compel them to speak out. Inspired by the Father's power, they were to proclaim the Father's purpose and his will.

So the Word was made manifest, as Saint John declares when, summing up all the sayings of the prophets, he announces that this is the Word through whom the whole universe was made. He says: *In the beginning was the Word, and the Word was with God, and the Word was God. Through him all things came into being; not one thing was created without him.* [Jn 1:1-3] And further on he adds: *The world was made through him, and yet the world did not know him. He entered his own creation, and his own did not receive him.* [Jn 1:10-11]

December 24th

From a sermon by Saint Augustine, Bishop & Doctor

Truth has arisen from the earth, and justice looked down from heaven

Awake, mankind! For your sake God has become man. *Awake, you who sleep, rise up from the dead, and Christ will enlighten you.* Eph 5:14 I tell you again: for your sake, God became man.

You would have suffered eternal death, had he not been born in time. Never would you have been freed from sinful flesh, had he not taken on himself the likeness of sinful flesh. You would have suffered everlasting unhappiness, had it not been for this mercy. You would never have returned to life, had he not shared your death. You would have been lost if he had not hastened to your aid. You would have perished, had he not come.

Let us then joyfully celebrate the coming of our salvation and redemption. Let us celebrate the festive day on which he who is the great and eternal day came from the great and endless day of eternity into our own short day of time.

He *has become our justice, our sanctification, our redemption, so that, as it is written: Let him who glories glory in the Lord.* 1 Cor 1:30

Truth, then, has arisen from the earth: Christ who said, *I am the Truth,* Jn 14:16 was born of the Virgin. *And justice looked down from heaven* Ps 85:11*:* because believing in this new-born child, man is justified not by himself but by God.

Truth has arisen from the earth: because *the Word was made flesh.* Jn 1:14 *And justice looked down from heaven:* because *every good gift and every perfect gift is from above.* James 1:17

Truth has arisen from the earth: flesh from Mary. *And justice looked down from heaven:* for *man can receive nothing unless it has been given him from heaven.* Jn 3:27

Justified by faith, let us be at peace with God Rom 5:1*:* for *justice and peace have embraced one another.* Ps 85:10 *Through our Lord Jesus Christ:* for *Truth has arisen from the earth. Through whom we have access to that grace in which we stand, and our boast is in our hope of God's glory.* Rom 5:2 He does not say: "of our glory," but *of God's glory:* for *justice* has not proceeded from us but *has looked down from heaven.* Therefore *he who glories, let him glory,* not in himself, but *in the Lord.*

For this reason, when our Lord was born of the Virgin, the message of the angelic voices was: *Glory to God in the highest, and peace to his people on earth.* Lk 2:14

For how could there be peace on earth unless *Truth has arisen from the earth,* that is, unless Christ were born of our flesh? And *he is our peace who made the two into one:* Eph 2:14 that we might be men of good will, sweetly linked by the bond of unity.

Let us then rejoice in this grace, so that our glorying may bear witness to our good conscience by which we glory, not in ourselves, but in the Lord. That is why Scripture says: *He is my glory, the one who lifts up my head.* Ps 3:3 For what greater grace could God have made to dawn on us than to make his only Son become the son of man, so that a son of man might in his turn become son of God?

Ask if this were merited; ask for its reason, for its justification, and see whether you will find any other answer but sheer grace.

December 25th

Christmas Day

From a sermon by Saint Leo the Great, Pope & Doctor

Christian, remember your dignity

Dearly beloved, today our Savior is born; let us rejoice. Sadness should have no place on the birthday of life. The fear of death has been swallowed up; life brings us joy with the promise of eternal happiness.

No one is shut out from this joy; all share the same reason for rejoicing. Our Lord, victor over sin and death, finding no man free from sin, came to free us all. Let the saint rejoice as he sees the palm of victory at hand. Let the sinner be glad as he receives the offer of forgiveness. Let the pagan take courage as he is summoned to life.

In the fullness of time, chosen in the unfathomable depths of God's wisdom, the Son of God took for himself our common humanity in order to reconcile it with its creator. He came to overthrow the devil, the origin of death, in that very nature by which he had overthrown mankind.

And so at the birth of our Lord the angels sing in joy: *Glory to God in the highest,* Lk 2:14 and they proclaim *peace to his people on earth* as they see the heavenly Jerusalem being built from all the nations of the world. When the angels on high are so exultant at this marvelous work of God's goodness, what joy should it not bring to the lowly hearts of men?

Beloved, let us give thanks to God the Father, through his Son, in the Holy Spirit, because in his great love for us he took pity on us, and *when we were dead in our sins he brought us to life with Christ* [Eph 2:5], so that in him we might be a new creation. Let us throw off our old nature and all its ways and, as we have come to birth in Christ, let us renounce the works of the flesh.

Christian, remember your dignity, and now that you share in God's own nature, do not return by sin to your former base condition. Bear in mind who is your head and of whose body you are a member. Do not forget that you have been rescued from the power of darkness and brought into the light of God's kingdom.

Through the sacrament of baptism you have become a temple of the Holy Spirit. Do not drive away so great a guest by evil conduct and become again a slave to the devil, for your liberty was bought by the blood of Christ.

December 29th
Fifth day within the Octave of Christmas

From a sermon by Saint Bernard of Clairvaux, Abbot & Doctor

In the fullness of time the fullness of divinity appeared

The goodness and humanity of God our Savior have appeared in our midst. [Tit 3:4] We thank God for the many consolations he has given us during this sad exile of our pilgrimage here on earth. Before the Son of God became man his goodness was hidden, for God's mercy is eternal, but how could such goodness be recognized? It was promised, but it was not experienced, and as a result few believed in it. *Often and in many ways the Lord used to speak through the prophets.* [Heb 1:1] Among other things, God said: *I think thoughts of peace and not affliction.* [Jer 29:11] But what did men respond, thinking thoughts of affliction and knowing nothing of peace? They said: *Peace, peace, there is no peace.*[Jer 6:14; Jer 8:11] This response made the *angels of peace weep bitterly* [Isa 33:7], saying: *Lord, who has believed our message?*[Isa 53:1] But now men believe because they see with their own eyes, and because *God's testimony has now become even more credible.* He has gone so far as to *pitch his tent* [Jn 1:14] in the sun so even the dimmest eyes can see him.

Notice that peace is not promised but sent to us; it is no longer deferred, it is given; peace is not prophesied but achieved. It is as if God the Father sent upon the earth a purse full of his mercy. This purse was burst open during the Lord's passion to pour forth its hidden contents-the price of our redemption. It was only a small purse, but it was very full. As the Scriptures tell us: *A little child has been given to us* [Lk 2:11]*, but in him dwells all the fullness of the divine nature.*[Col 2:9] The fullness of time brought with it the fullness of divinity. God's Son came in the flesh so that mortal men could see and recognize God's kindness. When God reveals his humanity, his goodness cannot possibly remain hidden. To show his kindness what more could he do beyond taking my human form? My humanity, I say, not Adam's-that is, not such as he had before his fall.

How could he have shown his mercy more clearly than by taking on himself our condition? For our sake the Word of God became as grass. What better proof could he have given of his love? Scripture says: *Lord, what is man that you are mindful of him;*[Ps 8:5] *why does your heart go out to him?*[Song 5:6] The incarnation teaches us how much God cares for us and what he thinks and feels about us. We should stop thinking of our own suffering and remember what he has suffered. Let us think of all the Lord has done for us, and then we shall realize how his goodness appears through his humanity. The lesser he became through his human nature the greater was his goodness; the more he lowered himself for me, the dearer he is to me. *The goodness and humanity of God our Savior have appeared,*[Titus 3:4] says the Apostle.

Truly great and manifest are the goodness and humanity of God. He has given us a most wonderful proof of his goodness by adding humanity to his own divine nature.

December 30th
Sixth day within the Octave of Christmas

From a treatise On the Refutation of All Heresies by Saint Hippolytus, Priest

The Word made flesh makes man divine

Our faith is not founded upon empty words; nor are we carried away by mere caprice or beguiled by specious arguments. On the contrary, we put our faith in words spoken by the power of God, spoken by the Word himself at God's command. God wished to win men back from disobedience, not by using force to reduce him to slavery but by addressing to his free will a call to liberty.

The Word spoke first of all through the prophets, but because the message was couched in such obscure language that it could be only dimly apprehended, in the last days the Father sent the Word in person, commanding him to show himself openly so that the world could see him and be saved.

We know that by taking a body from the Virgin he refashioned our fallen nature. We know that his manhood was of the same clay as our own; if this were not so, he would hardly have been a teacher who could expect to be imitated. If he were of a different substance from me, he would surely not have ordered me to do as he did, when by my very nature I am so weak. Such a demand could not be reconciled with his goodness and justice.

No. He wanted us to consider him as no different from ourselves, and so he worked, he was hungry and thirsty, he slept. Without protest he endured his passion, he submitted to death and revealed his resurrection. In all these ways he offered his own manhood as the first-fruits of our race to keep us from losing heart when suffering comes our way, and to make us look forward to receiving the same reward as he did, since we know that we possess the same humanity.

When we have come to know the true God, both our bodies and our souls will be immortal and incorruptible. We shall enter the kingdom of heaven, because while we lived on earth we acknowledged heaven's King. Friends of God and coheirs with Christ, we shall be subject to no evil desires or inclinations, or to any affliction of body or soul, for we shall have become divine.

It was because of our human condition that God allowed us to endure these things, but when we have been deified and made immortal, God has promised us a share in his own attributes.

The saying "Know yourself" means therefore that we should recognize and acknowledge in ourselves the God who made us in his own image, for if we do this, we in turn will be recognized and acknowledged by our Maker. So let us not be at enmity with ourselves, but change our way of life without delay. *For Christ who is God, exalted above all creation*[Phil 2:9], has taken away man's sin and has refashioned our fallen nature. In the beginning God made man in his image and so gave proof of his love for us. If we obey his holy commands and learn to imitate his goodness, we shall be like him and he will honor us. God is not beggarly, and for the sake of his own glory he has given us a share in his divinity.

December 31st
Seventh day within the Octave of Christmas

From a sermon of Saint Leo the Great, Pope & Doctor

The birthday of the Lord is the birthday of peace

Although the state of infancy, which the majesty of the Son of God did not disdain to assume, developed with the passage of time into the maturity of manhood, and although after the triumph of the passion and the resurrection all his lowly acts undertaken on our behalf belong to the past, nevertheless today's feast of Christmas renews for us the sacred beginning of Jesus' life, his birth from the Virgin Mary. In the very act in which we are reverencing the birth of our Savior, we are also celebrating our own new birth. For the birth of Christ is the origin of the Christian people; and the birthday of the head is also the birthday of the body.

Though each and every individual occupies a definite place in this body to which he has been called, and though all the progeny of the church is differentiated and marked with the passage of time, nevertheless as the whole community of the faithful, once begotten in the baptismal font, was crucified with Christ in the passion, raised up with him in the resurrection and at the ascension placed at the right hand of the Father, so too it is born with him in this Nativity, which we are celebrating today.

For every believer regenerated in Christ, no matter in what part of the whole world he may be, breaks with that ancient way of life that derives from original sin, and by rebirth is transformed into a new man. Henceforth he is reckoned to be of the stock, not of his earthly father, but of Christ, who became Son of Man precisely that men could become sons of God; for unless in humility he had come down to us, none of us by our own merits could ever go up to him.

Therefore the greatness of the gift which he has bestowed on us demands an appreciation proportioned to its excellence; for blessed Paul the Apostle truly teaches: *We have received not the spirit of this world, but the Spirit which is from God, that we might understand the gifts bestowed on us by God.*[1 Cor 2:12] The only way that he can be worthily honored by us is by the presentation to him of that which he has already given to us.

But what can we find in the treasure of the Lord's bounty more in keeping with the glory of this feast than that peace which was first announced by the angelic choir on the day of his birth? For that peace, from which the sons of God spring, sustains love and mothers unity; it refreshes the blessed and shelters eternity; its characteristic function and special blessing is to join to God those whom it separates from this world.

Therefore, may those *who were born, not of blood nor of the will of the flesh nor of the will of man, but of God,*[Jn 1:13] offer to the Father their harmony as sons united in peace; and may all those whom he has adopted as his members meet in the firstborn of the new creation who came not to do his own will but the will of the one who sent him; for the grace of the Father has adopted as heirs neither the contentious nor the dissident, but those who are one in thought and love. The hearts and minds of those who have been reformed according to one and the same image should be in harmony with one another.

The birthday of the Lord is the birthday of peace, as Paul the Apostle says: *For he is our peace, who has made us both one;*[Eph 2:14] for whether we be Jew or Gentile, *through him we have access in one Spirit to the Father.*[Eph 2:18]

Sunday after Christmas

The Holy Family

From an address by Pope Paul VI

Nazareth, a model

Nazareth is a kind of school where we may begin to discover what Christ's life was like and even to understand his Gospel. Here we can observe and ponder the simple appeal of the way God's Son came to be known, profound yet full of hidden meaning. And gradually we may even learn to imitate him.

Here we can learn to realize who Christ really is. And here we can sense and take account of the conditions and circumstances that surrounded and affected his life on earth: the places, the tenor of the times, the culture, the language, religious customs, in brief everything which Jesus used to make himself known to the world. Here everything speaks to us, everything has meaning. Here we can learn the importance of spiritual discipline for all who wish to follow Christ and to live by the teachings of his Gospel.

How I would like to return to my childhood and attend the simple yet profound school that is Nazareth! How wonderful to be close to Mary, learning again the lesson of the true meaning of life, learning again God's truths. But here we are only on pilgrimage. Time presses and I must set aside my desire to stay and carry on my education in the Gospel, for that education is never finished. But I cannot leave without recalling, briefly and in passing some thoughts I take with me from Nazareth.

First, we learn from its silence. If only we could once again appreciate its great value. We need this wonderful state of mind, beset as we are by the cacophony of strident protests and conflicting claims so characteristic of these turbulent times. The silence of Nazareth should teach us how to meditate in peace and quiet, to reflect on the deeply spiritual, and to be open to the voice of God's inner wisdom and the counsel of his true teachers. Nazareth can teach us the value of study and preparation, of meditation, of a well-ordered personal spiritual life, and of silent prayer that is known only to God.

Second, we learn about family life. May Nazareth serve as a model of what the family should be. May it show us the family's holy and enduring character and exemplifying its basic function in society: a community of love and sharing, beautiful for the problems it poses and the rewards it brings; in sum, the perfect setting for rearing children – and for this there is no substitute.

Finally, in Nazareth, the home of a craftsman's son, we learn about work and the discipline it entails. I would especially like to recognize its value – demanding yet redeeming – and to give it proper respect. I would remind everyone that work has its own dignity. On the other hand, it is not an end in itself. Its value and free character, however, derive not only from its place in the economic system, as they say, but rather from the purpose it serves.

In closing, may I express my deep regard for people everywhere who work for a living. To them I would point out their great model, Christ their brother, our Lord and God, who is their prophet in every cause that promotes their well being.

January 1st

Mary, Mother of God

From a letter by Saint Athanasius, Bishop & Doctor

The Word took our nature from Mary

The Apostle tells us: *The Word took to himself the sons of Abraham, and so had to be like his brothers in all things*[Heb 2:16-17]. He had then to take a body like ours. This explains the fact of Mary's presence: she is to provide him with a body of his own, to be offered for our sake. Scripture records her giving birth, and says: *She wrapped him in swaddling clothes*[Lk 2:7]. Her breasts, which fed him, were called blessed. Sacrifice was offered because the child was her firstborn. Gabriel used careful and prudent language when he announced his birth. He did not speak of "what will be born *in you"* to avoid the impression that a body would be introduced into her womb from outside; he spoke of "what will be born *from you"*[Lk 1:31] so that we might know by faith that her child originated within her and from her.

By taking our nature and offering it in sacrifice, the Word was to destroy it completely and then invest it with his own nature, and so prompt the Apostle to say: *This corruptible body must put on incorruption; this mortal body must put on immortality*[1 Cor 15:53-54].

This was not done in outward show only, as some have imagined. This is not so. Our Savior truly became man, and from this has followed the salvation of man as a whole. Our salvation is in no way fictitious, nor does it apply only to the body. The salvation of the whole man, that is, of soul and body, has really been achieved in the Word himself.

What was born of Mary was therefore human by nature, in accordance with the inspired Scriptures, and the body of the Lord was a true body: It was a true body because it was the same as ours. Mary, you see, is our sister, for we are all born from Adam.

The words of Saint John: *The Word was made flesh*[Jn 1:14], bear the same meaning, as we may see from a similar turn of phrase in Saint Paul: *Christ was made a curse for our sake*[Gal 3:13]. Man's body has acquired something great through its communion and union with the Word. From being mortal it has been made immortal; though it was a living body it has become a spiritual one; though it was made from the earth it has passed through the gates of heaven.

Even when the Word takes a body from Mary, the Trinity remains a Trinity, with neither increase nor decrease. It is for ever perfect. In the Trinity we acknowledge one Godhead, and thus one God, the Father of the Word, is proclaimed in the Church.

Second Sunday after Christmas

Readings are from the day (January 2nd-5th)

Monday from January 2 to Epiphany

From the book On the Holy Spirit by Saint Basil the Great, Bishop & Doctor

The Lord gives life to his body in the spirit

A spiritual man is one who no longer lives by the flesh but is led by the Spirit of God, one called a son of God, remade in the likeness of God's Son. As the power of sight is active in a healthy eye, so the Holy Spirit is active in a purified soul.

We may form a word either as a thought in the heart or as a sound on the lips. So the Holy Spirit, bearing witness to our spirit, cries out in our hearts, saying: *Abba, Father*, or speaks in our place, as Scripture says: *It is not you who speak; it is the Spirit of the Father who speaks in you.*[Mt 10:20]

In the gifts that he distributes we can see the Spirit as a whole in relation to its parts. We are all members of one another, but with different gifts according to the grace God gives us. So *the eye cannot say to the hand, I do not need you, nor can the head say to the feet, I have no need of you*[1 Cor 12:21]. All the members together make up the body of Christ in the unity of the Spirit, and render each other a necessary service through their gifts. God has arranged the various parts of the body according to his own will, but there exists among them all a spiritual fellowship which makes it natural for them to share one another's feelings and to be concerned for one another. If one member suffers, all suffer with it; if one member is honored, all rejoice together. Moreover, as parts are present in a single whole, so each of us is in the Spirit since all who make up the one body have been baptized into the one Spirit.

As the Father is seen in the Son, so the Son is seen in the Spirit. To worship in the Spirit, then, is to have our minds open to the light, as we may learn from our Lord's words to the Samaritan woman. Misled by the tradition of her country, she imagined that it was necessary to worship in a certain place, but our Lord gave her a different teaching. He told her that one must worship in Spirit and in truth, and clearly by the truth he meant himself.

As we speak of worship in the Son because the Son is the image of God the Father, so we speak of worship in the Spirit because the Spirit is the manifestation of the divinity of the Lord. Through the light of the Spirit we behold the Son, the splendor of God's glory, and through the Son, the very stamp of the Father, we are led to him who is the source both of his stamp, who is the Son, and of its seal, who is the Holy Spirit.

Tuesday from January 2 to Epiphany

From a treatise on John by Saint Augustine, Bishop & Doctor

The double commandment of love

The Lord, the teacher of love, full of love, came in person *with summary judgment on the world*[Jn 9:39], as had been foretold of him, and showed that the law and the prophets are summed up in two commandments of love.

Call to mind, brethren, what these two commandments are. They ought to be very familiar to you; they should not only spring to mind when I mention them, but ought never to be absent from your hearts. Keep always in mind that we must love God and our neighbor: *Love God with your whole heart, your whole soul, and your whole mind, and your neighbor as yourself.*[Mk 12:28-31]

These two commandments must be always in your thoughts and in your hearts, treasured, acted on, fulfilled. Love of God is the first to be commanded, but love of neighbor is the first to be put into practice. In giving two commandments of love Christ would not commend to you first your neighbor and then God but first God and then your neighbor.

Since you do not yet see God, you merit the vision of God by loving your neighbor. By loving your neighbor you prepare your eye to see God. Saint John says clearly: *If you do not love your brother whom you see, how will you love God whom you do not see!*[1 Jn 4:20]

Consider what is said to you: Love God. If you say to me: Show me whom I am to love, what shall I say if not what Saint John says: *No one has ever seen God!*[Jn 1:18] But in case you should think that you are completely cut off from the sight of God, he says: *God is love, and he who remains in love remains in God*[1 Jn 4:16]. Love your neighbor, then, and see within yourself the power by which you love your neighbor; there you will see God, as far as you are able.

Begin, then, to love your neighbor. *Break your bread to feed the hungry, and bring into your home the homeless poor; if you see someone naked, clothe him, and do not look down on your own flesh and blood*[Isa 58:7].

What will you gain by doing this? *Your light will then burst forth like the dawn*[Isa 58:8]. Your light is your God; he is your *dawn*, for he will come to you when the night of time is over. He does not rise or set but remains for ever.

In loving your neighbor and caring for him you are on a journey. Where are you traveling if not to the Lord God, to him whom we should love with our whole heart, our whole soul, our whole mind? We have not yet reached his presence, but we have our neighbor at our side. Support, then, this companion of your pilgrimage if you want to come into the presence of the one with whom you desire to remain for ever.

Wednesday from January 2 to Epiphany

From The Five Hundred Chapters by Saint Maximus the Confessor, Abbot

A mystery ever new

The Word of God, born once in the flesh (such is his kindness and his goodness), is always willing to be born spiritually in those who desire him. In them he is born as an infant as he fashions himself in them by means of their virtues. He reveals himself to the extent that he knows someone is capable of receiving him. He diminishes the revelation of his glory not out of selfishness but because he recognizes the capacity and resources of those who desire to see him. Yet, in the transcendence of mystery, he always remains invisible to all.

For this reason the apostle Paul, reflecting on the power of the mystery, said: *Jesus Christ, yesterday and today: he remains the same for ever*[Heb 13:8]. For he understood the mystery as ever new, never growing old through our understanding of it.

Christ is God, for he had given all things their being out of nothing. Yet he is born as man by taking to himself our nature, flesh endowed with intelligent spirit. A star glitters by day in the East and leads the wise men to the place where the incarnate Word lies, to show that the Word, contained in the Law and the Prophets, surpasses in a mystical way knowledge derived from the senses, and to lead the Gentiles to the full light of knowledge.

For surely the word of the Law and the Prophets when it is understood with faith is like a star which leads those who are called by the power of grace in accordance with his decree to recognize the Word incarnate.

Here is the reason why God became a perfect man, changing nothing of human nature, except to take away sin (which was never natural anyway). His flesh was set before that voracious, gaping dragon as bait to provoke him: flesh that would be deadly for the dragon, for it would utterly destroy him by the power of the Godhead hidden within it. For human nature, however, his flesh was to be a remedy since the power of the Godhead in it would restore human nature to its original grace.

Just as the devil had poisoned the tree of knowledge and spoiled our nature by its taste, so too, in presuming to devour the Lord's flesh he himself is corrupted and is completely destroyed by the power of the Godhead hidden in it.

The great mystery of the divine incarnation remains a mystery for ever. How can the Word made flesh be essentially the same person that is wholly with the Father? How can he who is by nature God become by nature wholly man without lacking either nature, neither the divine by which he is God nor the human by which he became man?

Faith alone grasps these mysteries. Faith alone is truly the substance and foundation of all that exceeds knowledge and understanding.

Thursday from January 2 to Epiphany

From a sermon by Saint Augustine, Bishop & Doctor

The vision of the Word will fulfill all our desires

What man knows all the treasures of wisdom and knowledge hidden in Christ, concealed in the poverty of his flesh? *Scripture says: Although he was rich he became poor for our sake to enrich us by his poverty*[2 Cor 8:9]. He showed himself poor when he assumed our mortal nature and destroyed death, yet he promised us riches, for he had not been robbed of his wealth but was keeping it in reserve.

How great are the blessings of his goodness which he reserves for those who fear him and shows to those who hope in him! Until he gives them to us in their plentitude, we can have only the faintest conception of them; but to enable us to receive these blessings, he who in his divine nature is the equal of the Father assumed the condition of a slave and became like us, and so restored to us our likeness to God. The only Son of God became a son of man to make many men sons of God. He instructed slaves by showing himself in the form of a slave, and now he enables free men to see him in the form of God.

For *we are the sons of God, and although what we shall be has not yet been revealed, we know that when he appears we shall be like him for we shall see him as he is*[1 Jn 3:2]. For what are those treasures of wisdom and knowledge, what those divine riches, if not the one thing that can fulfill our longing? What are the great blessings of his goodness, if not the one thing that will content us? Therefore: *Show us the Father, and all our desires will be satisfied*[Jn 14:8].

Christ speaks both in us and for us when, in one of the psalms, he says to the Father: *I shall be satisfied when your glory is revealed*[Ps 16:15]. For he and the Father are one, and whoever sees him sees the Father also. *The Lord of hosts, is himself the king of Glory*[Ps 24:10]. He will transform us and show us his face, and we shall be saved; all our longing will be fulfilled, all our desires will be satisfied.

But this has not yet been accomplished; he has not yet given us the vision that will satisfy every desire; we have not yet drunk our fill of the fountain of life. So while all this remains in the future and we still walk by faith, absent from the Lord, while we still hunger and thirst for justice and, with inexpressible longing yearn for God's beauty, let us reverently celebrate the day he was born into our own servile condition.

Since we can as yet form no conception of his generation by the Father before the daystar, let us keep the festival of his birth of a virgin in the hours of the night. Since it is still beyond our understanding that *his name endures for ever and existed before the sun*[Ps 72:17], let us at least recognize his dwelling that he has placed beneath the sun. We cannot as yet behold him as the only Son, abiding for ever in his Father, so let us recall *his coming forth like a bridegroom from his chamber*[Ps 19:6]. We are not yet ready for the banquet of our Father, so let us contemplate the manger of Jesus Christ our Lord.

Friday from January 2 to Epiphany

From a Sermon by Saint Gregory of Nazianzus, Bishop & Doctor

The baptism of Christ

Christ is bathed in light; let us also be bathed in light. Christ is baptized; let us also go down with him, and rise with him.

John is baptizing when Jesus draws near. Perhaps he comes to sanctify his baptizer; certainly he comes to bury sinful humanity in the waters. He comes to sanctify the Jordan for our sake and in readiness for us; he who is spirit and flesh comes to begin a new creation through the Spirit and water.

The Baptist protests; Jesus insists. Then John says: *I ought to be baptized by you*[Mt 3:14]. He is the lamp in the presence of the sun, the voice in the presence of the Word, the friend in the presence of the Bridegroom, the greatest of all born of woman in the presence of the firstborn of all creation, the one who leapt in his mother's womb in the presence of him who was adored in the womb, the forerunner and future forerunner in the presence of him who has already come and is to come again. *I ought to be baptized by you:* we should also add: *and for you*, for John is to be baptized in blood, washed clean like Peter, not only by the washing of his feet.

Jesus rises from the waters; the world rises with him. The heavens like Paradise with its flaming sword, closed by Adam for himself and his descendants, are rent open. The Spirit comes to him as to an equal, bearing witness to his Godhead. A voice bears witness to him from heaven, his place of origin. The Spirit descends in bodily form like the dove that so long ago announced the ending of the flood and so gives honor to the body that is one with God.

Today let us do honor to Christ's baptism and celebrate this feast in holiness. Be cleansed entirely and continue to be cleansed. Nothing gives such pleasure to God as the conversion and salvation of men, for whom his every word and every revelation exist. He wants you to become a living force for all mankind, lights shining in the world. You are to be radiant lights as you stand beside Christ, the great light, bathed in the glory of him who is the light of heaven. You are to enjoy more and more the pure and dazzling light of the Trinity, as now you have received – though not in its fullness – a ray of its splendor, proceeding from the one God, in Christ Jesus our Lord, to whom be glory and power for ever and ever. Amen.

Saturday from January 2 to Epiphany

From a sermon by Saint Augustine, Bishop & Doctor

God became man so that man might become God

Beloved, our Lord Jesus Christ, the eternal creator of all things, today became our Savior by being born of a mother. Of his own will he was born for us today, in time, so that he could lead us to his Father's eternity. God became man so that man might become God. The Lord of the angels became man today so that man could eat the bread of angels.

Today, the prophecy is fulfilled that said: *Pour down, heavens, from above, and let the clouds rain the just one: let the earth be opened and bring forth a savior*[Isa 45:8]. The Lord who had created all things is himself now created, so that he who was lost would be found. Thus man, in the words of the psalmist, confesses: *Before I was humbled, I sinned*[Ps 118:67]. Man sinned and became guilty; God is born a man to free man from his guilt. Man fell, but God descended; man fell miserably, but God descended mercifully; man fell through pride, God descended with his grace.

My brethren, what miracles! What prodigies! The laws of nature are changed in the case of man. God is born. A virgin becomes pregnant with man. The Word of God marries the woman who knows no man. She is now at the same time both mother and virgin. She becomes a mother, yet she remains a virgin. The virgin bears a son, yet she does not know man; she remains untouched, yet she is not barren. He alone was born without sin, for she bore him without the embrace of a man, not by the concupiscence of the flesh but by the obedience of the mind.

Epiphany

(Solemnity, January 6th or Sunday between January 2nd and January 8th)

From a sermon by Saint Leo the Great, Pope & Doctor

The Lord has made his salvation known to the whole world

The loving providence of God determined that in the last days he would aid the world, set on its course to destruction. He decreed that all nations should be saved in Christ.

A promise had been made to the holy patriarch Abraham in regard to these nations. He was to have a countless progeny, born not from his body but from the seed of faith. His descendants are therefore compared with the array of the stars. The father of all nations was to hope not in an earthly progeny but in a progeny from above.

Let the full number of the nations now take their place in the family of the patriarchs. Let the children of the promise now receive the blessing in the seed of Abraham, the blessing renounced by the children of his flesh. In the persons of the Magi let all people adore the Creator of the universe; let God be known, not in Judea only, but in the whole world, so that *his name may be great in all Israel*[Ps 75:2].

Dear friends, now that we have received instruction in this revelation of God's grace, let us celebrate with spiritual joy the day of our first harvesting, of the first calling of the Gentiles. Let us give thanks to the merciful God, *who has made us worthy,* in the words of the Apostle, *to share the position of the saints in light, who has rescued us from the power of darkness, and brought us into the kingdom of his beloved Son*[Col 1:12-13]. As Isaiah prophesied: *the people of the Gentiles, who sat in darkness, have seen a great light, and for those who dwelt in the region of the shadow of death a light has dawned*[Isa 9:2]. He spoke of them to the Lord: *The Gentiles, who do not know you, will invoke you, and the peoples, who knew you not, will take refuge in you*[Isa 55:5].

This is *the day that Abraham saw, and rejoiced to see*[Jn 8:56], when he knew that the sons born of his faith would be blessed in his seed, that is, in Christ. Believing that he would be the father of the nations, he looked into the future, *giving glory to God, in full awareness that God is able to do what he has promised*[Rom 4:21].

This is the day that David prophesied in the psalms, when he said: *All the nations that you have brought into being will come and fall down in adoration in your presence, Lord, and glorify your name*[Ps 85:9]. Again, *the Lord has made known his salvation; in the sight of the nations he has revealed his justice*[Ps 97:2].

This came to be fulfilled, as we know, from the time when the star beckoned the three wise men out of their distant country and led them to recognize and adore the King of heaven and earth. The obedience of the star calls us to imitate its humble service: to be servants, as best we can, of the grace that invites all men to find Christ.

Dear friends, you must have the same zeal to be of help to one another; then, in the kingdom of God, to which faith and good works are the way, you will shine as children of the light: through our Lord Jesus Christ, who lives and reigns with God the Father and the Holy Spirit for ever and ever. Amen.

Monday after Epiphany to the Baptism of the Lord

From a sermon by St Peter Chrysologus, Bishop

In choosing to be born for us, God chose to be known by us

In the mystery of our Lord's incarnation there were clear indications of his eternal Godhead. Yet the great events we celebrate today disclose and reveal in different ways the fact that God himself took a human body. Mortal man, enshrouded always in darkness, must not be left in ignorance, and so be deprived of what he can understand and retain only by grace.

In choosing to be born for us, God chose to be known by us. He therefore reveals himself in this way, in order that this great sacrament of his love may not be an occasion for us of great misunderstanding.

Today the Magi find, crying in a manger, the one they have followed as he shone in the sky. Today the Magi see clearly, in swaddling clothes, the one they have long awaited as he lay hidden among the stars.

Today the Magi gaze in deep wonder at what they see: heaven on earth, earth in heaven, man in God, God in man, one whom the whole universe cannot contain now enclosed in a tiny body. As they look, they believe and do not question, as their symbolic gifts bear witness: incense for God, gold for a king, myrrh for one who is to die.

So the Gentiles, who were the last, become the first: the faith of the Magi is the first fruits of the belief of the Gentiles.

Today Christ enters the Jordan to wash away the sin of the world. John himself testifies that this is why he has come: *Behold the Lamb of God, behold him who takes away the sins of the world*[Jn 1:29]. Today a servant lays his hand on the Lord, a man lays his hand on God, John lays his hand on Christ, not to forgive but to receive forgiveness.

Today, as the psalmist prophesied: *The voice of the Lord is heard above the waters*[Ps 28:3]. What does the voice say? *This is my beloved son, in whom I am well pleased*[Mt 3:17; Mt 17:5; Mk 1:11; Mk 9:6; Lk 3:22; Lk 9:35; 2 Pet 1:17].

Today the Holy Spirit hovers over the waters in the likeness of a dove. A dove announced to Noah that the flood had disappeared from the earth; so now a dove is to reveal that the world's shipwreck is at an end for ever. The sign is no longer an olive-shoot of the old stock: instead, the Spirit pours out on Christ's head the full richness of a new anointing by the Father, to fulfil what the psalmist had prophesied: *Therefore God, your God, has anointed you with the oil of gladness above your fellows*[Heb 1:9].

Today Christ works the first of his signs from heaven by turning water into wine. But water [mixed with wine] has still to be changed into the sacrament of his blood, so that Christ may offer spiritual drink from the chalice of his body, to fulfill the psalmist's prophecy: *How excellent is my chalice, warming my spirit*[Ps 23:5].

Tuesday after Epiphany to the Baptism of the Lord

From a sermon on the Epiphany attributed to Saint Hippolytus, Priest

Water and the Spirit

That Jesus should come and be baptized by John is surely cause for amazement. To think of the infinite river that gladdens the city of God being bathed in a poor little stream of the eternal; the unfathomable fountainhead that gives life to all men being immersed in the shallow waters of this transient world! He who fills all creation, leaving no place devoid of his presence, he who is incomprehensible to the angels and hidden from the sight of man, came to be baptized because it was his will. And *behold, the heavens opened and a voice said: "This is my beloved Son in whom I am well pleased."* Mt 3:17; Mt 17:5; Mk 1:11; Mk 9:6; Lk 3:22; Lk 9:35; 2 Pet 1:17

The beloved Father begets love, and spiritual light generates light inaccessible. In his divine nature he is my only Son, though he was known as the son of Joseph. *This is my beloved Son*. Though hungry himself, he feeds thousands; though weary, he refreshes those who labor. He has no place to lay his head yet holds all creation in his hand. By his passion [inflicted on him by others], he frees us from the passions [unleashed by our disobedience]; by receiving a blow on the cheek he gives the world its liberty; by being pierced in the side he heals the wound of Adam.

I ask you now to pay close attention, for I want to return to that fountain of life and contemplate its healing waters at their source.

The Father of immortality sent his immortal Son and Word into the world; he came to us men to cleanse us with water and the Spirit. To give us a new birth that would make our bodies and souls immortal, he breathed into us the spirit of life and armed us with incorruptibility. Now if we become immortal, we shall also be divine; and if we become divine after rebirth in baptism through water and the Holy Spirit, we shall also be coheirs with Christ after the resurrection of the dead.

Therefore, in a herald's voice I cry: Let peoples of every nation come and receive the immortality that flows from baptism. This is the water that is linked to the Spirit, the water that irrigates Paradise, makes the earth fertile, gives growth to plants, and brings forth living creatures. In short, this is the water by which a man receives new birth and life, the water in which even Christ was baptized, the water into which the Holy Spirit descended in the form of a dove.

Whoever goes down into these waters of rebirth with faith renounces the devil and pledges himself to Christ. He repudiates the enemy and confesses that Christ is God, throws off his servitude, and is raised to filial status. He comes up from baptism resplendent as the sun, radiant in his purity, but above all, he comes as a son of God and a coheir with Christ. To him and to his most holy and life-giving Spirit be glory and power now and for ever. Amen.

Wednesday after Epiphany to the Baptism of the Lord

From a sermon by St Proclus of Constantinople, Bishop

The waters are made holy

Christ appeared in the world, and, bringing beauty out of disarray, gave it luster and joy. He bore the world's sin and crushed the world's enemy. He sanctified the fountains of waters and enlightened the minds of men. Into the fabric of miracles he interwove ever greater miracles.

For on this day land and sea share between them the grace of the Savior, and the whole world is filled with joy. Today's feast of the Epiphany manifests even more wonders than the feast of Christmas.

On the feast of the Savior's birth, the earth rejoiced because it bore the Lord in a manger; but on today's feast of the Epiphany it is the sea that is glad and leaps for joy; the sea is glad because it receives the blessing of holiness in the river Jordan.

At Christmas we saw a weak baby, giving proof of our weakness. In today's feast, we see a perfect man, hinting at the perfect Son who proceeds from the all-perfect Father. At Christmas the King puts on the royal robe of his body; at Epiphany the very source enfolds and, as it were, clothes the river.

Come then and see new and astounding miracles: the Sun of righteousness washing in the Jordan, fire immersed in water, God sanctified by the ministry of man.

Today every creature shouts in resounding song: *Blessed is he who comes in the name of the Lord*[Ps 118:26; Lk 13:35]. Blessed is he who comes in every age, for this is not his first coming.

And who is he? Tell us more clearly, I beg you, blessed David: *The Lord is God and has shone upon us*[Ps 118:27]. David is not alone in prophesying this; the apostle Paul adds his own witness, saying: *The grace of God has appeared bringing salvation for all men, and instructing us*[Tit 2:11-12]. Not for some men, but *for all*. To Jews and Greeks alike God bestows salvation through baptism, offering baptism as a common grace for all.

Come, consider this new and wonderful deluge, greater and more important than the flood of Noah's day. Then the water of the flood destroyed the human race, but now the water of baptism has recalled the dead to life by the power of the one who was baptized. In the days of the flood the dove with an olive branch in its beak foreshadowed the fragrance of the good odor of Christ the Lord; now the Holy Spirit, coming in the likeness of a dove, reveals the Lord of mercy.

Thursday after Epiphany to the Baptism of the Lord

From a commentary on the Gospel of John by Saint Cyril of Alexandria, Bishop & Doctor

The gift of the Holy Spirit to all mankind

In a plan of surpassing beauty the Creator of the universe decreed the renewal of all things in Christ. In his design for restoring human nature to its original condition, he gave a promise that he would pour out on it the Holy Spirit along with his other gifts, for otherwise our nature could not enter once more into the peaceful and secure possession of those gifts.

He therefore appointed a time for the Holy Spirit to come upon us: this was the time of Christ's coming. He gave this promise when he said: *In those days,* that is, the days of the Savior, *I will pour out a share of my Spirit on all mankind*[Joel 2:28; Acts 2:17].

When the time came for this great act of unforced generosity, which revealed in our midst the only-begotten Son, clothed with flesh on this earth, a man born of woman, in accordance with Holy Scripture, God the Father gave the Spirit once again. Christ, as the first-fruits of our restored nature, was the first to receive the Spirit. John the Baptist bore witness to this when he said: *I saw the Spirit coming down from heaven, and it rested on him*[Jn 1:32].

Christ "received the Spirit" in so far as he was man, and in so far as man could receive the Spirit. He did so in such a way that, though he is the Son of God the Father, begotten of his substance, even before the incarnation, indeed before all ages, yet he was not offended at hearing the Father say to him after he had become man: *You are my son; today I have begotten you*[Ps 2:7; Heb 5:5].

The Father says of Christ, who was God, begotten of him before the ages, that he has been "begotten today," for the Father is to accept us in Christ as his adopted children. The whole of our nature is present in Christ, in so far as he is man. So the Father can be said to give the Spirit again to the Son, though the Son possesses the Spirit as his own, in order that we may receive the Spirit in Christ. The Son therefore took to himself the seed of Abraham, as Scripture says, and became like his brothers in all things.

The only-begotten Son receives the Spirit, but not for his own advantage, for the Spirit is his, and is given in him and through him, as we have already said. He receives it to renew our nature in its entirety and to make it whole again, for in becoming man he took our entire nature to himself. If we reason correctly, and use also the testimony of Scripture, we can see that Christ did not receive the Spirit for himself, but rather for us in him; for it is also through Christ that all gifts come down to us.

Friday after Epiphany to the Baptism of the Lord

From a sermon by Saint Maximus of Turin, Bishop

The mystery of the Lord's baptism

The Gospel tells us that the Lord went to the Jordan River to be baptized and that he wished to consecrate himself in the river by signs from heaven.

Reason demands that this feast of the Lord's baptism, which I think could be called the feast of his birthday, should follow soon after the Lord's birthday, during the same season, even though many years intervened between the two events.

At Christmas he was born a man; today he is reborn sacramentally. Then he was born from the Virgin; today he is born in mystery. When he was born a man, his mother Mary held him close to her heart; when he is born in mystery, God the Father embraces him with his voice when he says: *This is my beloved Son in whom I am well pleased: listen to him* [Mt 3:17; Mt 17:5; Mk 1:11; Mk 9:6; Lk 3:22; Lk 9:35; 2 Pet 1:17]. The mother caresses the tender baby on her lap; the Father serves his Son by his loving testimony. The mother holds the child for the Magi to adore; the Father reveals that his Son is to be worshipped by all the nations.

That is why the Lord Jesus went to the river for baptism, that is why he wanted his holy body to be washed with Jordan's water.

Someone might ask, "Why would a holy man desire baptism?" Listen to the answer: Christ is baptized, not to be made holy by the water, but to make the water holy, and by his cleansing to purify the waters which he touched. For the consecration of Christ involves a more significant consecration of the water.

For when the Savior is washed all water for our baptism is made clean, purified at its source for the dispensing of baptismal grace to the people of future ages. Christ is the first to be baptized, then, so that Christians will follow after him with confidence.

I understand the mystery as this. The column of fire went before the sons of Israel through the Red Sea so they could follow on their brave journey; the column went first through the waters to prepare a path for those who followed. As the apostle Paul said, what was accomplished then was the mystery of baptism. Clearly it was baptism in a certain sense when the cloud was covering the people and bringing them through the water.

But Christ the Lord does all these things: in the column of fire he went through the sea before the sons of Israel; so now, in the column of his body, he goes through baptism before the Christian people. At the time of the Exodus the column provided light for the people who followed; now it gives light to the hearts of believers. Then it made a firm pathway through the waters; now it strengthens the footsteps of faith in the bath of baptism.

Saturday after Epiphany to the Baptism of the Lord

From a sermon by Faustus of Riez, Bishop

The marriage of Christ and the Church

On the third day there was a wedding[Jn 2:1-11]. What wedding can this be but the joyful marriage of man's salvation, a marriage celebrated by confessing the Trinity or by faith in the resurrection. That is why the marriage took place "on the third day," a reference to the sacred mysteries which this number symbolizes.

Hence, too, we read elsewhere in the Gospel that the return of the younger son, that is, the conversion of the pagans, is marked by song, and music and wedding garments.

Like a bridegroom coming from his marriage chamber[Ps 18:6] our God descended to earth in his incarnation, in order to be united to his Church which was to be formed of the pagan nations. To her he gave a pledge and a dowry: a pledge when God was united to man; a dowry when he was sacrificed for man's salvation. The pledge is our present redemption; the dowry, eternal life.

To those who see only with the outward eye, all these events at Cana are strange and wonderful; to those who understand, they are also signs. For, if we look closely, the very water tells us of our rebirth in baptism. One thing is turned into another from within, and in a hidden way a lesser creature is changed into a greater. All this points to the hidden reality of our second birth. There water was suddenly changed; later it will cause a change in man.

By Christ's action in Galilee, then, wine is made, that is, the law withdraws and grace takes its place; the shadows fade and truth becomes present; fleshly realities are coupled with spiritual, and the old covenant with its outward discipline is transformed into the new. For, as the Apostle says: *The old order has passed away; now all is new!*[2 Cor 5:17] The water in the jars is not less than it was before, but now begins to be what it had not been; so too the law is not destroyed by Christ's coming, but is made better than it was.

When the wine fails, new wine is served: the wine of the old covenant was good, but the wine of the new is better. The old covenant, which Jews follow, is exhausted by its letter; the new covenant, which belongs to us, has the savor of life and is filled with grace.

The good wine[Jn 2:10], that is, good precepts, refers to the law; thus we read: *You shall love your neighbor but hate your enemy*[Mt 5:43]. But the Gospel is a better and a stronger wine: *My command to you is: love your enemies, pray for your persecutors*[Mt 5:44].

The Baptism of the Lord

A sermon by St Gregory Nazianzen, Bishop & Doctor

The baptism of Christ

Christ is bathed in light; let us also be bathed in light. Christ is baptized; let us also go down with him, and rise with him.

John is baptizing when Jesus draws near. Perhaps he comes to sanctify his baptizer; certainly he comes to bury sinful humanity in the waters. He comes to sanctify the Jordan for our sake and in readiness for us; he who is spirit and flesh comes to begin a new creation through the Spirit and water.

The Baptist protests; Jesus insists. Then John says: *I ought to be baptized by you*[Mt 3:14]. He is the lamp in the presence of the sun, the voice in the presence of the Word, the friend in the presence of the Bridegroom, the greatest of all born of woman in the presence of the firstborn of all creation, the one who leapt in his mother's womb in the presence of him who was adored in the womb, the forerunner and future forerunner in the presence of him who has already come and is to come again. *I ought to be baptized by you:* we should also add, *and for you*, for John is to be baptized in blood, washed clean like Peter, not only by the washing of his feet.

Jesus rises from the waters; the world rises with him. The heavens like Paradise with its flaming sword, closed by Adam for himself and his descendants, are rent open. The Spirit comes to him as to an equal, bearing witness to his Godhead. A voice bears witness to him from heaven, his place of origin. The Spirit descends in bodily form like the dove that so long ago announced the ending of the flood and so gives honor to the body that is one with God.

Today let us do honor to Christ's baptism and celebrate this feast in holiness. Be cleansed entirely and continue to be cleansed. Nothing gives such pleasure to God as the conversion and salvation of men, for whom his every word and every revelation exist. He wants you to become a living force for all mankind, lights shining in the world. You are to be radiant lights as you stand beside Christ, the great light, bathed in the glory of him who is the light of heaven. You are to enjoy more and more the pure and dazzling light of the Trinity, as now you have received – though not in its fullness – a ray of its splendor, proceeding from the one God, in Christ Jesus our Lord, to whom be glory and power for ever and ever. Amen.

Ash Wednesday

From a letter to the Corinthians by Saint Clement, Pope

Repent

Let us fix our attention on the blood of Christ and recognize how precious it is to God his Father, since it was shed for our salvation and brought the grace of repentance to all the world.

If we review the various ages of history, we will see that in every generation the Lord has *offered the opportunity of repentance*[Pope St. Clement] to any who were willing to turn to him. When Noah preached God's message of repentance, all who listened to him were saved. Jonah told the Ninevites they were going to be destroyed, but when they repented, their prayers gained God's forgiveness for their sins, and they were saved, even though they were not of God's people.

Under the inspiration of the Holy Spirit, the ministers of God's grace have spoken of repentance; indeed, the Master of the whole universe himself spoke of repentance with an oath: *As I live, says the Lord, I do not wish the death of the sinner but his repentance*[Ezek 18:23]. He added this evidence of his goodness: *House of Israel, repent of your wickedness. Tell the sons of my people: If their sins should reach from earth to heaven, if they are brighter than scarlet and blacker than sackcloth, you need only turn to me with your whole heart and say, "Father," and I will listen to you as to a holy people*[Isa 1:18].

In other words, God wanted all his beloved ones to have the opportunity to repent and he confirmed this desire by his own almighty will. That is why we should obey his sovereign and glorious will and prayerfully entreat his mercy and kindness. We should be suppliant before him and turn to his compassion, rejecting empty works and quarreling and jealousy which only lead to death.

Brothers, we should be humble in mind, putting aside all arrogance, pride and foolish anger. Rather, we should act in accordance with the Scriptures, as the Holy Spirit says: *The wise man must not glory in his wisdom nor the strong man in his strength nor the rich man in his riches. Rather, let him who glories glory in the Lord by seeking him and doing what is right and just*[Jer 9:23]. Recall especially what the Lord Jesus said when he taught gentleness and forbearance. *Be merciful,* he said, *so that you may have mercy shown to you. Forgive, so that you may be forgiven. As you treat others, so you will be treated. As you give, so you will receive. As you judge, so you will be judged. As you are kind to others, so you will be treated kindly. The measure of your giving will be the measure of your receiving*[Pope St. Clement].

Let these commandments and precepts strengthen us to live in humble obedience to his sacred words. As Scripture asks: *Whom shall I look upon with favor except the humble, peaceful man who trembles at my words*[Isa 66:2]*?*

Sharing then in the heritage of so many vast and glorious achievements, let us hasten toward the goal of peace, set before us from the beginning. Let us keep our eyes firmly fixed on the Father and Creator of the whole universe, and hold fast to his splendid and transcendent gifts of peace and all his blessings.

Thursday after Ash Wednesday

From a sermon by Saint Leo the Great, Pope & Doctor

Purification of spirit through fasting and almsgiving

Dear friends, at every moment *the earth is full of the mercy of God*[Ps 118:64], and nature itself is a lesson for all the faithful in the worship of God. The heavens, the sea and all that is in them bear witness to the goodness and omnipotence of their Creator, and the marvelous beauty of the elements as they obey him demands from the intelligent creation a fitting expression of its gratitude.

But with the return of that season marked out in a special way by the mystery of our redemption, and of the days that lead up to the paschal feast, we are summoned more urgently to prepare ourselves by a purification of spirit.

The special note of the paschal feast is this: the whole Church rejoices in the forgiveness of sins. It rejoices in the forgiveness not only of those who are then reborn in holy baptism but also of those who are already numbered among God's adopted children.

Initially, men are made new by the rebirth of baptism. Yet there is still required a daily renewal to repair the shortcomings of our mortal nature, and whatever degree of progress has been made there is no one who should not be more advanced. All must therefore strive to ensure that on the day of redemption no one may be found in the sins of his former life.

Dear friends, what the Christian should be doing at all times should be done now with greater care and devotion, so that the Lenten fast enjoined by the apostles may be fulfilled, not simply by abstinence from food but above all by the renunciation of sin.

There is no more profitable practice as a companion to holy and spiritual fasting than that of almsgiving. This embraces under the single name of mercy many excellent works of devotion, so that the good intentions of all the faithful may be of equal value, even where their means are not. The love that we owe both God and man is always free from any obstacle that would prevent us from having a good intention. The angels sang: *Glory to God in the highest, and peace to his people on earth*[Lk 2:14]. The person who shows love and compassion to those in any kind of affliction is blessed, not only with the virtue of good will but also with the gift of peace.

The works of mercy are innumerable. Their very variety brings this advantage to those who are true Christians, that in the matter of almsgiving not only the rich and affluent but also those of average means and the poor are able to play their part. Those who are unequal in their capacity to give can be equal in the love within their hearts.

Friday after Ash Wednesday

From a homily by Saint John Chrysostom, Bishop

Prayer is the light of the spirit

Prayer and converse with God is a supreme good: it is a partnership and union with God. As the eyes of the body are enlightened when they see light, so our spirit, when it is intent on God, is illumined by his infinite light. I do not mean the prayer of outward observance but prayer from the heart, not confined to fixed times or periods but continuous throughout the day and night.

Our spirit should be quick to reach out toward God, not only when it is engaged in meditation; at other times also, when it is carrying out its duties, caring for the needy, performing works of charity, giving generously in the service of others, our spirit should long for God and call him to mind, so that these works may be seasoned with the salt of God's love, and so make a palatable offering to the Lord of the universe. Throughout the whole of our lives we may enjoy the benefit that comes from prayer if we devote a great deal of time to it.

Prayer is the light of the spirit, true knowledge of God, mediating between God and man. The spirit, raised up to heaven by prayer, clings to God with the utmost tenderness; like a child crying tearfully for its mother, it craves the milk that God provides. It seeks the satisfaction of its own desires, and receives gifts outweighing the whole world of nature.

Prayer stands before God as an honored ambassador. It gives joy to the spirit, peace to the heart. I speak of prayer, not words. It is the longing for God, love too deep for words, a gift not given by man but by God's grace. The apostle Paul says: *"We do not know how we are to pray but the Spirit himself pleads for us with inexpressible longings*[Rom 8:26]*."*

When the Lord gives this kind of prayer to a man; he gives him riches that cannot be taken away, heavenly food that satisfies the spirit. One who tastes this food is set on fire with an eternal longing for the Lord: his spirit burns as in a fire of the utmost intensity.

Practice prayer from the beginning. Paint your house with the colors of modesty and humility. Make it radiant with the light of justice. Decorate it with the finest gold leaf of good deeds. Adorn it with the walls and stones of faith and generosity. Crown it with the pinnacle of prayer. In this way you will make it a perfect dwelling place for the Lord. You will be able to receive him as in a splendid palace, and through his grace you will already possess him, his image enthroned in the temple of your spirit.

Saturday after Ash Wednesday

From the treatise Against Heresies by Saint Irenaeus, Bishop, Doctor & Martyr

The friendship of God

Our Lord, the Word of God, first drew men to God as servants, but later he freed those made subject to him. He himself testified to this: *I do not call you servants any longer, for a servant does not know what his master is doing. Instead I call you friends, since I have made known to you everything that I have learned from my Father*[Jn 15:15]. Friendship with God brings the gift of immortality to those who accept it.

In the beginning God created Adam, not because he needed man, but because he wanted to have someone on whom to bestow his blessings. Not only before Adam but also before all creation, the Word was glorifying the Father in whom he dwelt, and was himself being glorified by the Father. The Word himself said: *Father, glorify me with that glory that I had with you before the world was*[Jn 17:5].

Nor did the Lord need our service. He commanded us to follow him, but his was the gift of salvation. To follow the Savior is to share in salvation; to follow the light is to enjoy the light. Those who are in the light do not illuminate the light but are themselves illuminated and enlightened by the light. They add nothing to the light; rather, they are beneficiaries, for they are enlightened by the light.

The same is true of service to God: it adds nothing to God, nor does God need the service of man. Rather, he gives life and immortality and eternal glory to those who follow and serve him. He confers a benefit on his servants in return for their service and on his followers in return for their loyalty, but he receives no benefit from them. He is rich, perfect and in need of nothing.

The reason why God requires service from man is this: because he is good and merciful he desires to confer benefits on those who persevere in his service. In proportion to God's need of nothing is man's need for communion with God.

This is the glory of man: to persevere and remain in the service of God. For this reason the Lord told his disciples: *You did not choose me but I chose you*[Jn 15:6]. He meant that his disciples did not glorify him by following him, but in following the Son of God they were glorified by him. As he said: *I wish that where I am they also may be, that they may see my glory*[Jn 17:24].

First Sunday of Lent

From a commentary on the psalms by Saint Augustine, Bishop & Doctor

In Christ we suffered temptation, and in him we overcame the devil

Hear, O God, my petition, listen to my prayer[Ps 54:2; Ps 60:2]. Who is speaking? An individual, it seems. See if it is an individual: *I cried to you from the ends of the earth while my heart was in anguish*[PS 60:3]. Now it is no longer one person; rather, it is one in the sense that Christ is one, and we are all his members. What single individual can cry from the ends of the earth? The one who cries from the ends of the earth is none other than the Son's inheritance. It was said to him: *Ask of me, and I shall give you the nations as your inheritance, and the ends of the earth as your possession*[Ps 2:8]. This possession of Christ, this inheritance of Christ, this body of Christ, this one Church of Christ, this unity that we are, cries from the ends of the earth. What does it cry? What I said before: *Hear, O God, my petition, listen to my prayer; I cried out to you from the ends of the earth*. That is, I made this cry to you *from the ends of the earth;* that is, on all sides.

Why did I make this cry? *While my heart was in anguish*. The speaker shows that he is present among all the nations of the earth in a condition, not of exalted glory but of severe trial.

Our pilgrimage on earth cannot be exempt from trial. We progress by means of trial. No one knows himself except through trial, or receives a crown except after victory, or strives except against an enemy or temptations.

The one who cries from the ends of the earth is in anguish, but is not left on his own. Christ chose to foreshadow us, who are his body, by means of his body, in which he has died, risen and ascended into heaven, so that the members of his body may hope to follow where their head has gone before.

He made us one with him when he chose to be tempted by Satan. We have heard in the gospel how the Lord Jesus Christ was tempted by the devil in the wilderness. Certainly Christ was tempted by the devil. In Christ you were tempted, for Christ received his flesh from your nature, but by his own power gained salvation for you; he suffered death in your nature, but by his own power gained life for you; he suffered insults in your nature, but by his own power gained glory for you; therefore, he suffered temptation in your nature, but by his own power gained victory for you.

If in Christ we have been tempted, in him we overcome the devil. Do you think only of Christ's temptations and fail to think of his victory? See yourself as tempted in him, and see yourself as victorious in him. He could have kept the devil from himself; but if he were not tempted he could not teach you how to triumph over temptation.

Monday of the First Week of Lent

From a Sermon by Saint Gregory Nazianzen, Bishop & Doctor

Let us show each other God's generosity

Recognize to whom you owe the fact that you exist, that you breathe, that you understand, that you are wise, and, above all, that you know God and hope for the kingdom of heaven and the vision of glory, now darkly and as in a mirror but then with greater fullness and purity. You have been made a son of God, coheir with Christ. Where did you get all this, and from whom?

Let me turn to what is of less importance: the visible world around us. What benefactor has enabled you to look out upon the beauty of the sky, the sun in its course, the circle of the moon, the countless number of stars, with the harmony and order that are theirs, like the music of a harp? Who has blessed you with rain, with the art of husbandry, with different kinds of food, with the arts, with houses, with laws, with states, with a life of humanity and culture, with friendship and the easy familiarity of kinship?

Who has given you dominion over animals, those that are tame and those that provide you with food? Who has made you lord and master of everything on earth? In short, who has endowed you with all that makes man superior to all other living creatures?

Is it not God who asks you now in your turn to show yourself generous above all other creatures and for the sake of all other creatures? Because we have received from him so many wonderful gifts, will we not be ashamed to refuse him this one thing only, our generosity? Though he is God and Lord he is not afraid to be known as our Father. Shall we for our part repudiate those who are our kith and kin?

Brethren and friends, let us never allow ourselves to misuse what has been given us by God's gift. If we do, we shall hear Saint Peter say: Be ashamed of yourselves for holding on to what belongs to someone else. Resolve to imitate God's justice, and no one will be poor. Let us not labor to heap up and hoard riches while others remain in need. If we do, the prophet Amos will speak out against us with sharp and threatening words: *Come now, you that say: When will the new moon be over, so that we may start selling? When will the sabbath be over, so that we may start opening our treasures*[Amos 8:5]?

Let us put into practice the supreme and primary law of God. He sends down rain on just and sinful alike, and causes the sun to rise on all without distinction. To all earth's creatures he has given the broad earth, the springs, the rivers and the forests. He has given the air to the birds, and the waters to those who live in water. He has given abundantly to all the basic needs of life, not as a private possession, not restricted by law, not divided by boundaries, but as common to all, amply and in rich measure. His gifts are not deficient in any way, because he wanted to give equality of blessing to equality of worth, and to show the abundance of his generosity.

Tuesday of the First Week of Lent

From a treatise on the Lord's Prayer by Saint Cyprian, Bishop & Martyr

He has given us life; he has also taught us how to pray

Dear brothers, the commands of the Gospel are nothing else than God's lessons, the foundations on which to build up hope, the supports for strengthening faith, the food that nourishes the heart. They are the rudder for keeping us on the right course, the protection that keeps our salvation secure. As they instruct the receptive minds of believers on earth, they lead safely to the kingdom of heaven.

God willed that many things should be said by the prophets, his servants, and listened to by his people. How much greater are the things spoken by the Son. These are now witnessed to by the very Word of God who spoke through the prophets. The Word of God does not now command us to prepare the way for his coming: he comes in person and opens up the way for us and directs us toward it. Before, we wandered in the darkness of death, aimlessly and blindly. Now we are enlightened by the light of grace, and are to keep to the highway of life, with the Lord to precede and direct us.

The Lord has given us many counsels and commandments to help us toward salvation. He has even given us a pattern of prayer, instructing us on how we are to pray. He has given us life, and with his accustomed generosity, he has also taught us how to pray. He has made it easy for us to be heard as we pray to the Father in the words taught us by the Son.

He had already foretold that the hour was coming when true worshipers would worship the Father in spirit and in truth. He fulfilled what he had promised before, so that we who have received the spirit and the truth through the holiness he has given us may worship in truth and in the spirit through the prayer he has taught.

What prayer could be more a prayer in the spirit than the one given us by Christ, by whom the Holy Spirit was sent upon us? What prayer could be more a prayer in the truth than the one spoken by the lips of the Son, who is truth himself? It follows that to pray in any other way than the Son has taught us is not only the result of ignorance but of sin. He himself has commanded it, and has said: *You reject the command of God, to set up your own tradition*[Mk 7:9].

So, my brothers, let us pray as God our master has taught us. To ask the Father in words his Son has given us, to let him hear the prayer of Christ ringing in his ears, is to make our prayer one of friendship, a family prayer. Let the Father recognize the words of his Son. Let the Son who lives in our hearts be also on our lips. We have him as an advocate for sinners before the Father; when we ask forgiveness for our sins, let us use the words given by our advocate. He tells us: *Whatever you ask the Father in my name, he will give you*[Jn 16:23]. What more effective prayer could we then make in the name of Christ than in the words of his own prayer?

Wednesday of the First Week of Lent

From a demonstration by Aphraates, Bishop

Circumcision of the heart

Law and covenant have been entirely changed. God changed the first pact with Adam, and gave a new one to Noah. He gave another to Abraham, and changed this to give a new one to Moses. When the covenant with Moses was no longer observed, he gave another pact in this last age, a pact never again to be changed.

He established a law for Adam, that he could not eat of the tree of life. He gave to Noah the sign of the rainbow in the clouds. He then gave Abraham, chosen for his faith, the mark and seal of circumcision for his descendants. Moses was given the Passover lamb, the propitiation for the people.

All these covenants were different from each other. Moreover, the circumcision that is approved by the giver of those covenants is the kind of spoken of by Jeremiah: *Circumcise your hearts*[Jer 4:4]. If God's pact with Abraham was firm, so also is this covenant firm and trustworthy, nor can any other law be laid down, whether it originates outside the law or among those subject to the law.

God gave Moses a law together with his prescriptions and precepts, and when it was no longer kept, he made the law and its precepts of no avail. He promised a new covenant, different from the first, though the giver of both is one and the same. This is the covenant that he promised: *All know me from the least to the greatest*[Heb 8:11]. In this covenant there is no longer any circumcision of the flesh, any seal upon the people.

We know, dearly beloved, that God established different laws in different generations which were in force as long as it pleased him. Afterward they were made obsolete. In the words of the apostle: *In former times the kingdom of God existed in each generation under different signs*[Dei Verbum §4].

Moreover, our God is truthful and his commandments are most trustworthy. Every covenant was proved firm and trustworthy in its own time, and those who have been circumcised in heart are brought to life and receive a second circumcision beside the true Jordan, the waters of baptism that bring forgiveness of sins.

Jesus, son of Nun, renewed the people's circumcision with a knife of stone when he had crossed the Jordan with the Israelites. Jesus, our Savior, renews the circumcision of the heart for the nations who have believed in him and are washed by baptism: circumcision by *the sword of his word, sharper than a two-edged sword*[Heb 4:12].

Jesus, son of Nun, led the people across the Jordan into the promised land. Jesus, our Savior, has promised the land of the living to all who have crossed the true Jordan, and have believed and are circumcised in heart.

Blessed, then, are those who are circumcised in heart, and have been reborn in water through the second circumcision. They will receive their inheritance with Abraham, the faithful leader and father of all nations, for his faith was credited to him for righteousness.

Thursday of the First Week of Lent

From a homily by Saint Asterius of Amasea, Bishop

Be shepherds like the Lord

You were made in the image of God. If then you wish to resemble him, follow his example. Since the very name you bear as Christians is a profession of love for men, imitate the love of Christ.

Reflect for a moment on the wealth of his kindness. Before he came as a man to be among men, he sent John the Baptist to preach repentance and lead men to practice it. John himself was preceded by the prophets, who were to teach the people to repent, to return to God and to amend their lives. Then Christ came himself, and with his own lips cried out: *Come to me, all you who labor and are overburdened, and I will give you rest*[Mt 11:28]. How did he receive those who listened to his call? He readily forgave them their sins; he freed them instantly from all that troubled them. The Word made them holy; the Spirit set his seal on them. The old Adam was buried in the waters of baptism; the new man was reborn to the vigor of grace.

What was the result? Those who had been God's enemies became his friends, those estranged from him became his sons, those who did not know him came to worship and love him.

Let us then be shepherds like the Lord. We must meditate on the Gospel, and as we see in this mirror the example of zeal and loving kindness, we should become thoroughly schooled in these virtues.

For there, obscurely, in the form of a parable, we see a shepherd who had a hundred sheep. When one of them was separated from the flock and lost its way, that shepherd did not remain with the sheep who kept together at pasture. No, he went off to look for the stray. He crossed many valleys and thickets, he climbed great and towering mountains, he spent much time and labor in wandering through solitary places until at last he found his sheep.

When he found it, he did not chastise it; he did not use rough blows to drive it back, but gently placed it on his own shoulders and carried it back to the flock. He took greater joy in this one sheep, lost and found, than in all the others.

Let us look more closely at the hidden meaning of this parable. The sheep is more than a sheep, the shepherd more than a shepherd. They are examples enshrining holy truths. They teach us that we should not look on men as lost or beyond hope; we should not abandon them when they are in danger or be slow to come to their help. When they turn away from the right path and wander, we must lead them back, and rejoice at their return, welcoming them back into the company of those who lead good and holy lives.

Friday of the First Week of Lent

From the Mirror of Love by Saint Aelred, Abbot

Christ, the model of brotherly love

The perfection of brotherly love lies in the love of one's enemies. We can find no greater inspiration for this than grateful remembrance of the wonderful patience of Christ. He who is *more fair than all the sons of men* offered his fair face to be spat upon by sinful men; he allowed those eyes that rule the universe to be blindfolded by wicked men; he bared his back to the scourges; he submitted that head which strikes terror in principalities and powers to the sharpness of the thorns; he gave himself up to be mocked and reviled, and at the end endured the cross, the nails, the lance, the gall, the vinegar, remaining always gentle, meek and full of peace.

In short, *he was led like a sheep to the slaughter, and like a lamb before the shearers he kept silent, and did not open his mouth*[Isa 53:7].

Who could listen to that wonderful prayer, so full of warmth, of love, of unshakable serenity – *Father, forgive them* [Lk 23:34] – and hesitate to embrace his enemies with overflowing love? *Father,* he says, *forgive them.* Is any gentleness, any love, lacking in this prayer?

Yet he put into it something more. It was not enough to pray for them: he wanted also to make excuses for them. *Father, forgive them, for they do not know what they are doing*[Lk 23:34]. They are great sinners, yes, but they have little judgment; therefore, *Father, forgive them* [Lk 23:34]. They are nailing me to the cross, but they do not know who it is that they are nailing to the cross: *if they had known, they would never have crucified the Lord of glory*[1 Cor 2:8]; therefore, *Father, forgive them* [Lk 23:34]. They think it is a lawbreaker, an impostor claiming to be God, a seducer of the people. I have hidden my face from them, and they do not recognize my glory; therefore, *Father, forgive them, for they do not know what they are doing* [Lk 23:34].

If someone wishes to love himself he must not allow himself to be corrupted by indulging his sinful nature. If he wishes to resist the promptings of his sinful nature he must enlarge the whole horizon of his love to contemplate the loving gentleness of the humanity of the Lord. Further, if he wishes to savor the joy of brotherly love with greater perfection and delight, he must extend even to his enemies the embrace of true love.

But if he wishes to prevent this fire of divine love from growing cold because of injuries received, let him keep the eyes of his soul always fixed on the serene patience of his beloved Lord and Savior.

Saturday of the First Week of Lent

From the Pastoral Constitution on the Church in the Modern World of the Second Vatican Council
Gaudium et spes

Man's deeper questionings

The world of today reveals itself as at once powerful and weak, capable of achieving the best or the worst. There lies open before it the way to freedom or slavery, progress or regression, brotherhood or hatred. In addition, man is becoming aware that it is for himself to give the right direction to forces that he has himself awakened, forces that can be his master or his servant. He therefore puts questions to himself.

The tensions disturbing the world of today are in fact related to a more fundamental tension rooted in the human heart. In man himself many elements are in conflict with each other. On one side, he has experience of his many limitations as a creature. On the other, he knows that there is no limit to his aspirations, and that he is called to a higher kind of life.

Many things compete for his attention, but he is always compelled to make a choice among them, and to renounce some. What is more, in his weakness and sinfulness he often does what he does not want to do, and fails to do what he would like to do. In consequence, he suffers from a conflict within himself, and this in turn gives rise to so many great tensions in society.

Very many people, infected as they are with a materialistic way of life, cannot see this dramatic state of affairs in all its clarity, or at least are prevented from giving thought to it because of the unhappiness that they themselves experience.

Many think that they can find peace in the different philosophies that are proposed.

Some look for complete and genuine liberation for man from man's efforts alone. They are convinced that the coming kingdom of man on earth will satisfy all the desires of his heart.

There are those who despair of finding any meaning in life: they commend the boldness of those who deny all significance to human existence in itself, and seek to impose a total meaning on it only from within themselves.

But in the face of the way the world is developing today there is an ever increasing number of people who are asking the most fundamental questions or are seeing them with a keener awareness: What is man? What is the meaning of pain, of evil, of death, which still persist in spite of such great progress? What is the use of those successes, achieved at such a cost? What can man contribute to society, what can he expect from society? What will come after this life on earth?

The Church believes that Christ died and rose for all, and can give man light and strength through his Spirit to fulfill his highest calling; his is the only name under heaven in which men can be saved.

So too the Church believes that the center and goal of all human history is found in her Lord and Master.

The Church also affirms that underlying all changes there are many things that do not change; they have their ultimate foundation in Christ, who is the same yesterday, today and for ever.

Sunday of the Second Week of Lent

From a sermon by Saint Leo the Great, Pope & Doctor

The law was given through Moses, grace and truth came through Jesus Christ

The Lord reveals his glory in the presence of chosen witnesses. His body is like that of the rest of mankind, but he makes it shine with such splendor that his face becomes like the sun in glory, and his garments as white as snow.

The great reason for this transfiguration was to remove the scandal of the cross from the hearts of his disciples, and to prevent the humiliation of his voluntary suffering from disturbing the faith of those who had witnessed the surpassing glory that lay concealed.

With no less forethought he was also providing a firm foundation for the hope of holy Church. The whole body of Christ was to understand the kind of transformation that it would receive as his gift. The members of that body were to look forward to a share in that glory which first blazed out in Christ their head.

The Lord had himself spoken of this when he foretold the splendor of his coming: *Then the just will shine like the sun in the kingdom of their Father*[Mt 13:43]. Saint Paul the apostle bore witness to this same truth when he said: *I consider that the sufferings of the present time are not to be compared with the future glory that is to be revealed in us*[Rom 8:18]. In another place he says: *You are dead, and your life is hidden with Christ in God. When Christ, your life, is revealed, then you also will be revealed with him in glory*[Col 3:3-4].

This marvel of the transfiguration contains another lesson for the apostles, to strengthen them and lead them into the fullness of knowledge. Moses and Elijah, the law and the prophets, appeared with the Lord in conversation with him. This was in order to fulfill exactly, through the presence of these five men, the text which says: *Before two or three witnesses every word is ratified*[Deut 19:15; Mt 18:16; 2 Cor 13:1]. What word could be more firmly established, more securely based, than the word which is proclaimed by the trumpets of both old and new testaments, sounding in harmony, and by the utterances of ancient prophecy and the teaching of the Gospel, in full agreement with each other?

The writings of the two testaments support each other. The radiance of the transfiguration reveals clearly and unmistakably the one who had been promised by signs foretelling him under the veils of mystery. As Saint John says: *The law was given through Moses, grace and truth came through Jesus Christ*[Jn 1:17]. In him the promise made through the shadows of prophecy stands revealed, along with the full meaning of the precepts of the law. He is the one who teaches the truth of prophecy through his presence, and makes obedience to the commandments possible through grace.

In the preaching of the holy Gospel all should receive a strengthening of their faith. No one should be ashamed of the cross of Christ, through which the world has been redeemed.

No one should fear to suffer for the sake of justice; no one should lose confidence in the reward that has been promised. The way to rest is through toil, the way to life is through death. Christ has taken on himself the whole weakness of our lowly human nature. If then we are steadfast in our faith in him and in our love for him, we win the victory that he has won, we receive what he has promised.

When it comes to obeying the commandments or enduring adversity, the words uttered by the Father should always echo in our ears: *This is my Son, the beloved, in whom I am well pleased; listen to him*[Mt 3:17; Mt 17:5; Mk 1:11; Mk 9:6; Lk 3:22; Lk 9:35; 2 Pet 1:17].

Monday of the Second Week of Lent

From the Catecheses by Saint John Chrysostom, Bishop

Christ and Moses

The Israelites witnessed marvels; you also will witness marvels, greater and more splendid than those which accompanied them on their departure from Egypt. You did not see Pharaoh drowned with his armies, but you have seen the devil with his weapons overcome by the waters of baptism. The Israelites passed through the sea; you have passed from death to life. They were delivered from the Egyptians; you have been delivered from the powers of darkness. The Israelites were freed from slavery to a pagan people; you have been freed from the much greater slavery to sin.

Do you need another argument to show that the gifts you have received are greater than theirs? The Israelites could not look on the face of Moses in glory, though he was their fellow servant and kinsman. But you have seen the face of Christ in his glory. Paul cried out: *We see the glory of the Lord with faces unveiled*[2 Cor 3:18].

In those days Christ was present to the Israelites as he followed them, but he is present to us in a much deeper sense. The Lord was with them because of the favor he showed to Moses; now he is with us not simply because of Moses but also because of your obedience. After Egypt they dwelt in desert places; after your departure you will dwell in heaven. Their great leader and commander was Moses; we have a new Moses, God himself, as our leader and commander.

What distinguished the first Moses? *Moses,* Scripture tells us, *was more gentle than all who dwelt upon the earth*[Num 12:3]. We can rightly say the same of the new Moses, for there was with him the very Spirit of gentleness, united to him in his inmost being. In those days Moses raised his hands to heaven and brought down manna, the bread of angels; the new Moses raises his hands to heaven and gives us the food of eternal life. Moses struck the rock and brought forth streams of water; Christ touches his table, strikes the spiritual rock of the new covenant and draws forth the living water of the Spirit. This rock is like a fountain in the midst of Christ's table, so that on all sides the flocks may draw near to this living spring and refresh themselves in the waters of salvation.

Since this fountain, this source of life, this table surrounds us with untold blessings and fills us with the gifts of the Spirit, let us approach it with sincerity of heart and purity of conscience to receive grace and mercy in our time of need. Grace and mercy be yours from the only-begotten Son, our Lord and Savior Jesus Christ; through him and with him be glory, honor and power to the Father and the life-giving Spirit, now and always and for ever. Amen.

Tuesday of the Second Week of Lent

From a commentary on the psalms by Saint Augustine, Bishop & Doctor

The passion of the whole body of Christ

Lord, I have cried to you, hear me[Ps 140:1]. This is a prayer we can all say. This is not my prayer, but that of the whole Christ. Rather, it is said in the name of his body. When Christ was on earth he prayed in his human nature, and prayed to the Father in the name of his body, and when he prayed drops of blood flowed from his whole body. So it is written in the Gospel: *Jesus prayed with earnest prayer, and sweated blood*[Lk 22:44]. What is this blood streaming from his whole body but the martyrdom of the whole Church?

Lord, I have cried to you, hear me; listen to the sound of my prayer, when I call upon you. Did you imagine that crying was over when you said: *I have cried to you?* You have cried out, but do not as yet feel free from care. If anguish is at an end, crying is at an end; but if the Church, the body of Christ, must suffer anguish until the end of time, it must not say only: *I have cried to you, hear me;* it must also say: *Listen to the sound of my prayer, when I call upon you* [Ps 140:1].

Let my prayer rise like incense in your sight; let the raising of my hands be an evening sacrificePs [140:2].

This is generally understood of Christ, the head, as every Christian acknowledges. When day was fading into evening, the Lord laid down his life on the cross, to take it up again; he did not lose his life against his will. Here, too, we are symbolized. What part of him hung on the cross if not the part he had received from us? How could God the Father ever cast off and abandon his only Son, who is indeed one God with him? Yet Christ, nailing our weakness to the cross (where, as the Apostle says: *Our old nature was nailed to the cross with him*[Rom 6:6]), cried out with the very voice of our humanity: *My God, my God, why have you forsaken me*[Ps 21:2; Mt 27:46; Mk 15:34]?

The evening sacrifice is then the passion of the Lord, the cross of the Lord, the oblation of the victim that brings salvation, the holocaust acceptable to God. In his resurrection he made this evening sacrifice a morning sacrifice. Prayer offered in holiness from a faithful heart rises like incense from a holy altar. Nothing is more fragrant than the fragrance of the Lord. May all who believe share in this fragrance.

Therefore, *our old nature,* in the words of the Apostle, *was nailed to the cross with him, in order,* as he says, *to destroy our sinful body, so that we may be slaves to sin no longer*[Rom 6:6].

Wednesday of the Second Week of Lent

From the treatise Against Heresies by Saint Irenaeus, Bishop, Doctor & Martyr

Through foreshadowing of the future,
Israel was learning reverence for God and perseverance in his service

From the beginning God created man out of his own generosity. He chose the patriarchs to give them salvation. He took his people in hand, teaching them, unteachable as they were, to follow him. He gave them prophets, accustoming man to bear his Spirit and to have communion with God on earth. He who stands in need of no one gave communion with himself to those who need him. Like an architect he outlined the plan of salvation to those who sought to please him. By his own hand he gave food in Egypt to those who did not see him. To those who were restless in the desert he gave a law perfectly suited to them. To those who entered the land of prosperity he gave a worthy inheritance. He killed the fatted calf for those who turned to him as Father, and clothed them with the finest garment. In so many ways he was training the human race to take part in the harmonious song of salvation.

For this reason John in the book of Revelation says: *His voice was as the voice of many waters*[Ezek 43:2; Rev 1:15; Rev 19:6]. The Spirit of God is indeed a multitude of waters, for the Father is rich and great. As the Word passed among all these people he provided help in generous measure for those who were obedient to him, by drawing up a law that was suitable and fitting for every circumstance.

He established a law for the people governing the construction of the tabernacle and the building of the temple, the choice of Levites, the sacrifices, the offerings, the rites of purification and the rest of what belonged to worship. He himself needs none of these things. He is always filled with all that is good. Even before Moses existed he had within himself every fragrance of all that is pleasing. Yet he sought to teach his people, always ready though they were to return to their idols. Through many acts of indulgence he tried to prepare them for perseverance in his service. He kept calling them to what was primary by means of what was secondary, that is, through foreshadowings to the reality, through things of time to the things of eternity, through things of the flesh to the things of the spirit, through earthly things to the heavenly things. As he said to Moses: *You will fashion all things according to the pattern that you saw on the mountain*[Ex 25:40].

For forty days Moses was engaged in remembering the words of God, the heavenly patterns, the spiritual images, the foreshadowings of what was to come. Saint Paul says: *They drank from the rock that followed them, and the rock was Christ*[1 Cor 10:4]. After speaking of the things that are in the law he continues: *All these things happened to them as symbols: they were written to instruct us, on whom the end of the ages has come*[1 Cor 10:11].

Through foreshadowings of the future they were learning reverence for God and perseverance in his service. The law was therefore a school of instruction for them, and a prophecy of what was to come.

Thursday of the Second Week of Lent

From a treatise on the psalms by Saint Hilary of Poitiers, Bishop & Doctor

The meaning of "the fear of the Lord"

Blessed are those who fear the Lord, who walk in his ways[Ps 127:1]. Notice that when Scripture speaks of the fear of the Lord it does not leave the phrase in isolation, as if it were a complete summary of faith. No, many things are added to it, or are presupposed by it. From these we may learn its meaning and excellence. In the book of Proverbs Solomon tells us: *If you cry out for wisdom and raise your voice for understanding, if you look for it as for silver and search for it as for treasure, then you will understand the fear of the Lord*[Prov 2:3-5]. We see here the difficult journey we must undertake before we can arrive at the fear of the Lord.

We must begin by crying out for wisdom. We must hand over to our intellect the duty of making every decision. We must look for wisdom and search for it. Then we must understand the fear of the Lord.

"Fear" is not to be taken in the sense that common usage gives it. Fear in this ordinary sense is the trepidation our weak humanity feels when it is afraid of suffering something it does not want to happen. We are afraid, or made afraid, because of a guilty conscience, the rights of someone more powerful, an attack from one who is stronger, sickness, encountering a wild beast, suffering evil in any form. This kind of fear is not taught: it happens because we are weak. We do not have to learn what we should fear: objects of fear bring their own terror with them.

But of the fear of the Lord this is what is written: *Come, my children, listen to me, I shall teach you the fear of the Lord*[Ps 33:12]. The fear of the Lord has then to be learned because it can be taught. It does not lie in terror, but in something that can be taught. It does not arise from the fearfulness of our nature; it has to be acquired by obedience to the commandments, by holiness of life and by knowledge of the truth.

For us the fear of God consists wholly in love, and perfect love of God brings our fear of him to its perfection. Our love for God is entrusted with its own responsibility: to observe his counsels, to obey his laws, to trust his promises. Let us hear what Scripture says: *And now, Israel, what does the Lord your God ask of you except to fear the Lord your God and walk in his ways and love him and keep his commandments with your whole heart and your whole soul, so that it may be well for you*[Deut 10:12-13]?

The ways of the Lord are many, though he is himself the way. When he speaks of himself he calls himself the way and shows us the reason why he called himself the way: *No one can come to the Father except through me*[Jn 14:6].

We must ask for these many ways, we must travel along these many ways, to find the one that is good. That is, we shall find the one way of eternal life through the guidance of many teachers. These ways are found in the law, in the prophets, in the gospels, in the writings of the apostles, in the different good works by which we fulfill the commandments. Blessed are those who walk these ways in the fear of the Lord.

Friday of the Second Week of Lent

From the treatise Against Heresies by Saint Irenaeus, Bishop, Doctor & Martyr

The covenant of the Lord

In the book of Deuteronomy Moses says to the people: *The Lord your God made a covenant on Horeb; he made this covenant, not with your fathers but with you*[Deut 5:2-3]. Why did God not make this covenant with their fathers? Because *the law is not aimed at the righteous*[1 Tim 1:9]. Their fathers were righteous: they had the power of the Decalogue implanted in their hearts and in their souls. That is, they loved the God who made them and did nothing unjust against their neighbor. For this reason they did not need to be admonished by written rebukes: they had the righteousness of the law in their hearts.

When this righteousness and love for God had passed into oblivion and had been extinguished in Egypt, God had necessarily to reveal himself through his own voice, out of his great love for men. He led the people out of Egypt in power, so that man might once again become God's disciple and follower. He made them afraid as they listened, to warn them not to hold their Creator in contempt.

He fed them with manna, that they might receive spiritual food. In the book of Deuteronomy Moses says: *He fed you with manna, which your fathers did not know, that you might understand that man will not live by bread alone but will live by every word of God coming from the mouth of God*[Deut 8:3; Mt 4:4; Lk 4:4].

He commanded them to love himself and trained them to practice righteousness toward their neighbor, so that man might not be unrighteous or unworthy of God. Through the Decalogue he prepared man for friendship with himself and for harmony with his neighbor. This was to man's advantage, though God needed nothing from man.

This raised man to glory, for it gave him what he did not have, friendship with God. But it brought no advantage to God, for God did not need man's love. Man did not possess the glory of God, nor could he attain it by any other means than through obedience to God. This is why Moses said to the people: *Choose life, that you may live and your descendants too; love the Lord your God, hear his voice and hold fast to him, for this is life for you and length of days*[Deut 30:19-20].

This was the life that the Lord was preparing man to receive when he spoke in person and gave the words of the Decalogue for all alike to hear. These words remain with us as well; they were extended and amplified through his coming in the flesh, but not annulled.

God gave to the people separately through Moses the commandments that enslave: these were precepts suited to their instruction or their condemnation. As Moses said: *The Lord commanded me at that time to teach you precepts of righteousness and of judgment*[Deut 4:5]. The precepts that were given them to enslave and to serve as a warning have been cancelled by the new covenant of freedom. The precepts that belong to man's nature and to freedom and to all alike have been enlarged and broadened. Through the adoption of sons God had enabled man so generously and bountifully to know him as Father, to love him with his whole heart, and to follow his Word unfailingly.

Saturday of the Second Week of Lent

From the treatise on Flight from the World by Saint Ambrose, Bishop & Doctor

Hold fast to God, the one true good

Where a man's heart is, there is his treasure also. God is not accustomed to refusing a good gift to those who ask for one. Since he is good, and especially to those who are faithful to him, let us hold fast to him with all our soul, our heart, our strength, and so enjoy his light and see his glory and possess the grace of supernatural joy. Let us reach out with our hearts to possess that good, let us exist in it and live in it, let us hold fast to it, that good which is beyond all we can know or see and is marked by perpetual peace and tranquility, a peace which is beyond all we can know or understand.

This is the good that permeates creation. In it we all live, on it we all depend. It has nothing above it; it is divine. No one is good but God alone. What is good is therefore divine, what is divine is therefore good. Scripture says: *When you open your hand all things will be filled with goodness*[Ps 144:16]. It is through God's goodness that all that is truly good is given us, and in it there is no admixture of evil.

These good things are promised by Scripture to those who are faithful: *The good things of the land will be your food*[Isa 1:19].

We have died with Christ. We carry about in our bodies the sign of his death, so that the living Christ may also be revealed in us. The life we live is not now our ordinary life but the life of Christ: a life of sinlessness, of chastity, of simplicity and every other virtue. We have risen with Christ. Let us live in Christ, let us ascend in Christ, so that the serpent may not have the power here below to wound us in the heel.

Let us take refuge from this world. You can do this in spirit, even if you are kept here in the body. You can at the same time be here and present to the Lord. Your soul must hold fast to him, you must follow after him in your thoughts, you must tread his ways by faith, not in outward show. You must take refuge in him. He is your refuge and your strength. David addresses him in these words: *I fled to you for refuge, and I was not disappointed*[Ps 21:6].

Since God is our refuge, God who is in heaven and above the heavens, we must take refuge from this world in that place where there is peace, where there is rest from toil, where we can celebrate the great sabbath, as Moses said: *The sabbaths of the land will provide you with food*[Lev 25:6]. To rest in the Lord and to see his joy is like a banquet, and full of gladness and tranquility.

Let us take refuge like deer beside the fountain of waters. Let our soul thirst, as David thirsted, for the fountain. What is that fountain? Listen to David: *With you is the fountain of life*[Ps 35:10]. Let my soul say to this fountain: *When shall I come and see you face to face*[Ps 41:3]? For the fountain is God himself.

Sunday of the Third Week of Lent

From a treatise on John by Saint Augustine, Bishop & Doctor

A Samaritan woman came to draw water

A woman came[Jn 4:7]. She is a symbol of the Church not yet made righteous but about to be made righteous. Righteousness follows from the conversation. She came in ignorance, she found Christ, and he enters into conversation with her. Let us see what it is about, let us see why *a Samaritan woman came to draw water*[Jn 4:7]. The Samaritans did not form part of the Jewish people: they were foreigners. The fact that she came from a foreign people is part of the symbolic meaning, for she is a symbol of the Church. The Church was to come from the Gentiles, of a different race from the Jews.

We must then recognize ourselves in her words and in her person, and with her give our own thanks to God. She was a symbol, not the reality; she foreshadowed the reality, and the reality camc to be. She found faith in Christ, who was using her as a symbol to teach us what was to come. *She came* then *to draw water*. She had simply come to draw water, in the normal way of man or woman.

Jesus says to her: Give me water to drink. For his disciples had gone to the city to buy food. The Samaritan woman therefore says to him: How is it that you, though a Jew, ask me for water to drink, though I am a Samaritan woman? For Jews have nothing to do with Samaritans[Jn 4:7-9].

The Samaritans were foreigners; Jews never used their utensils. The woman was carrying a pail for drawing water. She was astonished that a Jew should ask her for a drink of water, a thing that Jews would not do. But the one who was asking for a drink of water was thirsting for her faith.

Listen now and learn who it is that asks for a drink. *Jesus answered her and said: If you knew the gift of God, and who it is that is saying to you, "Give me a drink," perhaps you might have asked him and he would have given you living water.*

He asks for a drink, and he promises a drink. He is in need, as one hoping to receive, yet he is rich, as one about to satisfy the thirst of others. He says: *If you knew the gift of God*[Jn 4:10]. The gift of God is the Holy Spirit. But he is still using veiled language as he speaks to the woman and gradually enters into her heart. Or is he already teaching her? What could be more gentle and kind than the encouragement he gives? *If you knew the gift of God, and who it is that is saying to you, "Give me a drink," perhaps you might ask and he would give you living water*[Jn 4:10].

What is this water that he will give if not the water spoken of in Scripture: *With you is the fountain of life*[Ps 35:10]? How can those feel thirst who *will drink deeply from the abundance in your house*[Ps 35:9]?

He was promising the Holy Spirit in satisfying abundance. She did not yet understand. In her failure to grasp his meaning, what was her reply? *The woman says to him: Master, give me this drink, so that I may feel no thirst or come here to draw water*[Jn 4:15]. Her need forced her to this labor, her weakness shrank from it. If only she could hear those words: *Come to me, all who labor and are burdened, and I will refresh you*[Mt 11:28.] Jesus was saying this to her, so that her labors might be at an end; but she was not yet able to understand.

Monday of the Third Week of Lent

From a homily by Saint Basil the Great, Bishop & Doctor

Boast only of the Lord

The wise man must not boast of his wisdom, nor the strong man of his strength, nor the rich man of his riches[Jer 9:23]. What then is the right kind of boasting? What is the source of man's greatness? Scripture says: *The man who boasts must boast of this, that he knows and understands that I am the Lord*[Jer 9:24]. Here is man's greatness, here is man's glory and majesty: to know in truth what is great, to hold fast to it, and to seek glory from the Lord of glory. The Apostle tells us: *The man who boasts must boast of the Lord*[1 Cor 1:31]. He has just said: *Christ was appointed by God to be our wisdom, our righteousness, our sanctification, our redemption, so that, as it is written, a man who boasts must boast of the Lord.*

Boasting of God is perfect and complete when we take no pride in our own righteousness but acknowledge that we are utterly lacking in true righteousness and have been made righteous only by faith in Christ.

Paul boasts of the fact that he holds his own righteousness in contempt and seeks the righteousness in faith that comes through Christ and is from God. He wants only to know Christ and the power of his resurrection and to have fellowship with his sufferings by taking on the likeness of his death, in the hope that somehow he may arrive at the resurrection of the dead.

Here we see all overweening pride laid low. Humanity, there is nothing left for you to boast of, for your boasting and hope lie in putting to death all that is your own and seeking the future life that is in Christ. Since we have its first-fruits we are already in its midst, living entirely in the grace and gift of God.

It is God who is active within us, giving us both the will and the achievement, in accordance with his good purpose[Phil 2:13]. Through his Spirit, God also reveals his wisdom in the plan he has preordained for our glory.

God gives power and strength in our labors. *I have toiled harder than all the others,* Paul says, *but it is not I but the grace of God, which is with me*[1 Cor 15:10].

God rescues us from dangers beyond all human expectation. *We felt within ourselves that we had received the sentence of death, so that we might not trust in ourselves but in God, who raises the dead; from so great a danger did he deliver us, and does deliver us; we hope in him, for he will deliver us again*[2 Cor 1:9-10].

Tuesday of the Third Week of Lent

From a sermon by Saint Peter Chrysologus, Bishop

Prayer knocks, fasting obtains, mercy receives

There are three things, my brethren, by which faith stands firm, devotion remains constant, and virtue endures. They are prayer, fasting and mercy. Prayer knocks at the door, fasting obtains, mercy receives. Prayer, mercy and fasting: these three are one, and they give life to each other.

Fasting is the soul of prayer, mercy is the lifeblood of fasting. Let no one try to separate them; they cannot be separated. If you have only one of them or not all together, you have nothing. So if you pray, fast; if you fast, show mercy; if you want your petition to be heard, hear the petition of others. If you do not close your ear to others you open God's ear to yourself.

When you fast, see the fasting of others. If you want God to know that you are hungry, know that another is hungry. If you hope for mercy, show mercy. If you look for kindness, show kindness. If you want to receive, give. If you ask for yourself what you deny to others, your asking is a mockery.

Let this be the pattern for all men when they practice mercy: show mercy to others in the same way, with the same generosity, with the same promptness, as you want others to show mercy to you.

Therefore, let prayer, mercy and fasting be one single plea to God on our behalf, one speech in our defense, a threefold united prayer in our favor.

Let us use fasting to make up for what we have lost by despising others. Let us offer our souls in sacrifice by means of fasting. There is nothing more pleasing that we can offer to God, as the psalmist said in prophecy: *A sacrifice to God is a broken spirit; God does not despise a bruised and humbled heart*[Ps 50:19].

Offer your soul to God, make him an oblation of your fasting, so that your soul may be a pure offering, a holy sacrifice, a living victim, remaining your own and at the same time made over to God. Whoever fails to give this to God will not be excused, for if you are to give him yourself you are never without the means of giving.

To make these acceptable, mercy must be added. Fasting bears no fruit unless it is watered by mercy. Fasting dries up when mercy dries up. Mercy is to fasting as rain is to the earth. However much you may cultivate your heart, clear the soil of your nature, root out vices, sow virtues, if you do not release the springs of mercy, your fasting will bear no fruit.

When you fast, if your mercy is thin your harvest will be thin; when you fast, what you pour out in mercy overflows into your barn. Therefore, do not lose by saving, but gather in by scattering. Give to the poor, and you give to yourself. You will not be allowed to keep what you have refused to give to others.

Wednesday of the Third Week of Lent

From the book addressed to Autolycus by Saint Theophilus of Antioch, Bishop

Blessed are the clean of heart, for they will see God

If you say, "Show me your God," I will say to you, "Show me what kind of person you are, and I will show you my God." Show me then whether the eyes of your mind can see, and the ears of your heart hear.

It is like this. Those who can see with the eyes of their bodies are aware of what is happening in this life on earth. They get to know things that are different from each other. They distinguish light and darkness, black and white, ugliness and beauty, elegance and inelegance, proportion and lack of proportion, excess and defect. The same is true of the sounds we hear: high or low or pleasant. So it is with the ears of our heart and the eyes of our mind in their capacity to hear or see God.

God is seen by those who have the capacity to see him, provided that they keep the eyes of their mind open. All have eyes, but some have eyes that are shrouded in darkness, unable to see the light of the sun. Because the blind cannot see it, it does not follow that the sun does not shine. The blind must trace the cause back to themselves and their eyes. In the same way, you have eyes in your mind that are shrouded in darkness because of your sins and evil deeds.

A person's soul should be clean, like a mirror reflecting light. If there is rust on the mirror his face cannot be seen in it. In the same way, no one who has sin within him can see God.

But if you will you can be healed. Hand yourself over to the doctor, and he will open the eyes of your mind and heart. Who is to be the doctor? It is God, who heals and gives life through his Word and wisdom. Through his Word and wisdom he created the universe, for *by his Word the heavens were established, and by his Spirit all their array*[Ps 32:6]. His wisdom is supreme. God *by wisdom founded the earth, by understanding he arranged the heavens, by his knowledge the depths broke forth and the clouds poured out the dew*[Prov 3:19-20].

If you understand this, and live in purity and holiness and justice, you may see God. But, before all, faith and the fear of God must take the first place in your heart, and then you will understand all this. When you have laid aside mortality and been clothed in immortality, then you will see God according to your merits. God raises up your flesh to immortality along with your soul, and then, once made immortal, you will see the immortal One, if you believe in him now.

Thursday of the Third Week of Lent

From the treatise On Prayer by Tertullian, Priest

The spiritual offering of prayer

Prayer is the offering in spirit that has done away with the sacrifices of old. *What good do I receive from the multiplicity of your sacrifices*[Isa 1:11]*?* asks God. *I have had enough of burnt offerings of rams, and I do not want the fat of lambs and the blood of bulls and goats. Who has asked for these from your hands*[Isa 1:11]*?*

What God has asked for we learn from the Gospel. *The hour will come,* he says, *when true worshipers will worship the Father in spirit and in truth. God is a spirit*[Jn 4:23], and so he looks for worshipers who are like himself.

We are true worshipers and true priests. We pray in spirit, and so offer in spirit the sacrifice of prayer. Prayer is an offering that belongs to God and is acceptable to him: it is the offering he has asked for, the offering he planned as his own.

We must dedicate this offering with our whole heart, we must fatten it on faith, tend it by truth, keep it unblemished through innocence and clean through chastity, and crown it with love. We must escort it to the altar of God in a procession of good works to the sound of psalms and hymns. Then it will gain for us all that we ask of God.Since God asks for prayer offered in spirit and in truth, how can he deny anything to this kind of prayer? How great is the evidence of its power, as we read and hear and believe.

Of old, prayer was able to rescue from fire and beasts and hunger, even before it received its perfection from Christ. How much greater then is the power of Christian prayer. No longer does prayer bring an angel of comfort to the heart of a fiery furnace, or close up the mouths of lions, or transport to the hungry food from the fields. No longer does it remove all sense of pain by the grace it wins for others. But it gives the armor of patience to those who suffer, who feel pain, who are distressed. It strengthens the power of grace, so that faith may know what it is gaining from the Lord, and understand what it is suffering for the name of God.

In the past prayer was able to bring down punishment, rout armies, withhold the blessing of rain. Now, however, the prayer of the just turns aside the whole anger of God, keeps vigil for its enemies, pleads for persecutors. Is it any wonder that it can call down water from heaven when it could obtain fire from heaven as well? Prayer is the one thing that can conquer God. But Christ has willed that it should work no evil, and has given it all power over good.

Its only art is to call back the souls of the dead from the very journey into death, to give strength to the weak, to heal the sick, to exorcise the possessed, to open prison cells, to free the innocent from their chains. Prayer cleanses from sin, drives away temptations, stamps out persecutions, comforts the fainthearted, gives new strength to the courageous, brings travelers safely home, calms the waves, confounds robbers, feeds the poor, overrules the rich, lifts up the fallen, supports those who are falling, sustains those who stand firm.

All the angels pray. Every creature prays. Cattle and wild beasts pray and bend the knee. As they come from their barns and caves they look out to heaven and call out, lifting up their spirit in their own fashion. The birds too rise and lift themselves up to heaven: they open out their wings, instead of hands, in the form of a cross, and give voice to what seems to be a prayer.

What more need be said on the duty of prayer? Even the Lord himself prayed. To him be honor and power for ever and ever. Amen.

Friday of the Third Week of Lent

From the Moral Reflections on Job by Saint Gregory the Great, Pope & Doctor

The mystery of our new life in Christ

Holy Job is a type of the Church. At one time he speaks for the body, at another for the head. As he speaks of its members he is suddenly caught up to speak in the name of their head. So it is here, where he says: *I have suffered this without sin on my hands, for my prayer to God was pure*[Job 16:17].

Christ suffered without sin on his hands, for he committed no sin and deceit was not found on his lips. Yet he suffered the pain of the cross for our redemption. His prayer to God was pure, his alone out of all mankind, for in the midst of his suffering he prayed for his persecutors: *Father, forgive them, for they do not know what they are doing*[Lk 23:34].

Is it possible to offer, or even to imagine, a purer kind of prayer than that which shows mercy to one's torturers by making intercession for them? It was thanks to this kind of prayer that the frenzied persecutors who shed the blood of our Redeemer drank it afterward in faith and proclaimed him to be the Son of God.

The text goes on fittingly to speak of Christ's blood: *Earth, do not cover over my blood, do not let my cry find a hiding place in you*[Job 16:18]. When man sinned, God had said: *Earth you are, and to earth you will return*[Gen 3:19]. Earth does not cover over the blood of our Redeemer, for every sinner, as he drinks the blood that is the price of his redemption, offers praise and thanksgiving, and to the best of his power makes that blood known to all around him.

Earth has not hidden away his blood, for holy Church has preached in every corner of the world the mystery of its redemption.

Notice what follows: *Do not let my cry find a hiding place in you*[Job 16:18]. The blood that is drunk, the blood of redemption, is itself the cry of our Redeemer. Paul speaks of *the sprinkled blood that calls out more eloquently than Abel's*[Heb 12:24]. Of Abel's blood Scripture had written: *The voice of your brother's blood cries out to me from the earth*[Gen 4:10]. The blood of Jesus calls out more eloquently than Abel's, for the blood of Abel asked for the death of Cain, the fratricide, while the blood of the Lord has asked for, and obtained, life for his persecutors.

If the sacrament of the Lord's passion is to work its effect in us, we must imitate what we receive and proclaim to mankind what we revere. The cry of the Lord finds a hiding place in us if our lips fail to speak of this, though our hearts believe in it. So that his cry may not lie concealed in us it remains for us all, each in his own measure, to make known to those around us the mystery of our new life in Christ.

Saturday of the Third Week of Lent

From a sermon by Saint Gregory of Nazianzen, Bishop & Doctor

Serve Christ in the poor

Blessed are the merciful, because they shall obtain mercy[Mt 5:7; Jas 2:13], says the Scripture. Mercy is not the least of the beatitudes. Again: *Blessed is he who is considerate to the needy and the poor*[Ps 40:2]. Once more: *Generous is the man who is merciful and lends*[Ps 111:5]. In another place: *All day the just man is merciful and lends*[Ps 36:26]. Let us lay hold of this blessing, let us earn the name of being considerate, let us be generous.

Not even night should interrupt you in your duty of mercy. Do not say: *Come back and I will give you something tomorrow*[Prov 3:28]. There should be no delay between your intention and your good deed. Generosity is the one thing that cannot admit of delay.

Share your bread with the hungry, and bring the needy and the homeless into your house[Isa 58:7], with a joyful and eager heart. *He who does acts of mercy should do so with cheerfulness*[Rom 12:8]. The grace of a good deed is doubled when it is done with promptness and speed. What is given with a bad grace or against one's will is distasteful and far from praiseworthy.

When we perform an act of kindness we should rejoice and not be sad about it. *If you undo the shackles and the thongs*[Isa 58:6], says Isaiah, that is, if you do away with miserliness and counting the cost, with hesitation and grumbling, what will be the result? Something great and wonderful! What a marvelous reward there will be: *Your light will break forth like the dawn, and your healing will rise up quickly*[Isa 58:8]. Who would not aspire to light and healing.

If you think that I have something to say, servants of Christ, his brethren and coheirs, let us visit Christ whenever we may; let us care for him, feed him, clothe him, welcome him, honor him, not only at a meal, as some have done, or by anointing him, as Mary did, or only by lending him a tomb, like Joseph of Arimathaea, or by arranging for his burial, like Nicodemus, who loved Christ half-heartedly, or by giving him gold, frankincense and myrrh, like the Magi before all these others. The Lord of all asks for mercy, not sacrifice, and mercy is greater than myriads of fattened lambs. Let us then show him mercy in the persons of the poor and those who today are lying on the ground, so that when we come to leave this world they may receive us into everlasting dwelling places, in Christ our Lord himself, to whom be glory for ever and ever. Amen.

Sunday of the Fourth Week of Lent

From a treatise on John by Saint Augustine, Bishop & Doctor

Christ is the way to the light, the truth and the life

The Lord tells us: *I am the light of the world; he who follows me will not walk in darkness, but will have the light of life*. In these few words he gives a command and makes a promise. Let us do what he commands so that we may not blush to covet what he promises and to hear him say on the day of judgment: "I laid down certain conditions for obtaining my promises. Have you fulfilled them?" If you say: "What did you command, Lord our God?" he will tell you: "I commanded you to follow me. You asked for advice on how to enter into life. What life, if not the life about which it is written: *With you is the fountain of life?*"

Let us do now what he commands. Let us follow in the footsteps of the Lord. Let us throw off the chains that prevent us from following him. Who can throw off these shackles without the aid of the one addressed in these words: *You have broken my chains?* Another psalm says of him: *The Lord frees those in chains, the Lord raises up the downcast*.

Those who have been freed and raised up follow the light. The light they follow speaks to them: *I am the light of the world; he who follows me will not walk in darkness*. The Lord gives light to the blind. Brethren, that light shines on us now, for we have had our eyes anointed with the eye-salve of faith. His saliva was mixed with earth to anoint the man born blind. We are of Adam's stock, blind from our birth; we need him to give us light. He mixed saliva with earth, and so it was prophesied: *Truth has sprung up from the earth*. He himself has said: *I am the way, the truth and the life*.

We shall be in possession of the truth when we see face to face. This is his promise to us. Who would dare to hope for something that God in his goodness did not choose to promise or bestow?

We shall see face to face. The Apostle says: *Now I know in part, now obscurely through a mirror, but then face to face*. John the Apostle says in one of his letters: *Dearly beloved, we are now children of God, and it has not yet been revealed what we shall be. We know that when he is revealed we shall be like him, for we shall see him as he is*. This is a great promise.

If you love me, follow me. "I do love you," you protest, "but how do I follow you?" If the Lord your God said to you: "I am the truth and the life," in your desire for truth, in your love for life, you would certainly ask him to show you the way to reach them. You would say to yourself: "Truth is a great reality, life is a great reality; if only it were possible for my soul to find them!"

Monday of the Fourth Week of Lent

From a homily on Leviticus by Origen, Priest

Christ the high priest makes atonement for our sins

Once a year the high priest, leaving the people outside, entered that place where no one except the high priest might enter. In it was the mercy-seat, and above the mercy-seat the cherubim, as well as the ark of the covenant and the altar of incense.

Let me turn to my true high priest, the Lord Jesus Christ. In our human nature he spent the whole year in the company of the people, the year that he spoke of when he said: *He sent me to bring good news to the poor, to announce the acceptable year of the Lord, and the day of forgiveness*[Lk 4:18-19]. Notice how once in that year, on the day of atonement, he enters into the holy of holies. Having fulfilled God's plan, he passes through the heavens and enters into the presence of the Father to make him turn in mercy to the human race and to pray for all who believe in him.

John the apostle, knowing of the atonement that Christ makes to the Father for all men, says this: *Little children, I say these things so that you may not sin. But if we have sinned we have an advocate with the Father, Jesus Christ, the just one. He is the atonement for our sins*[1 Jn 2:1]. In the same way Paul refers to this atonement when he says of Christ: *God appointed him to be the atonement for our sins in his blood, through faith*[Rom 3:25]. We have then a day of atonement that remains until the world comes to an end.

God's word tells us: *The high priest shall put incense on the fire in the sight of the Lord. The smoke of the incense shall cover the mercy-seat above the tokens of the covenant, so that he may not die. He shall take some of the blood of the bull-calf and sprinkle it with his finger over the mercy-seat toward the east*[Lev 16:13].

God taught the people of the old covenant how to celebrate the ritual offered to him in atonement for the sins of men. But you have come to Christ, the true high priest. Through his blood he has made God turn to you in mercy and has reconciled you with the Father. You must not think simply of ordinary blood but you must learn to recognize instead the blood of the Word. Listen to him as he tells you: *This is my blood, which will be shed for you for the forgiveness of sins*[Mt 26:28].

There is a deeper meaning in the fact that the high priest sprinkles the blood toward the east. Atonement comes to you from the east. From the east comes the one whose name is Dayspring, he who is mediator between God and men. You are invited then to look always to the east: it is there that the sun of righteousness rises for you, it is there that the light is always being born for you. You are never to walk in darkness; the great and final day is not to enfold you in darkness. Do not let the night and mist of ignorance steal upon you. So that you may always enjoy the light of knowledge, keep always in the daylight of faith, hold fast always to the light of love and peace.

Tuesday of the Fourth Week of Lent

From a sermon by Saint Leo the Great, Pope & Doctor

The virtue of charity

In the gospel of John the Lord says: *In this will all men know that you are my disciples, if you have love for each other*[Jn 13:35]. In a letter of the same apostle we read: *Beloved, let us love one another, for love is from God, and everyone who loves is born of God and knows God; he who does not love does not know God, for God is love*[1 Jn 4:7].

The faithful should therefore enter into themselves and make a true judgment on their attitudes of mind and heart. If they find some store of love's fruit in their hearts, they must not doubt God's presence within them. If they would increase their capacity to receive so great a guest, they should practice greater generosity in doing good, with persevering charity.

If God is love, charity should know no limit, for God cannot be confined.

Any time is the right time for works of charity, but these days of Lent provide a special encouragement. Those who want to be present at the Lord's Passover in holiness of mind and body should seek above all to win this grace, for charity contains all other virtues and covers a multitude of sins.

As we prepare to celebrate that greatest of all mysteries, by which the blood of Jesus Christ did away with our sins, let us first of all make ready the sacrificial offerings of works of mercy. In this way we shall give to those who have sinned against us what God in his goodness has already given to us.

Let us now extend to the poor and those afflicted in different ways a more open-handed generosity, so that God may be thanked through many voices and the relief of the needy supported by our fasting. No act of devotion on the part of the faithful gives God more pleasure than that which is lavished on his poor. Where he finds charity with its loving concern, there he recognizes the reflection of his own fatherly care.

In these acts of giving do not fear a lack of means. A generous spirit is itself great wealth. There can be no shortage of material for generosity where it is Christ who feeds and Christ who is fed. In all this activity there is present the hand of him who multiplies the bread by breaking it, and increases it by giving it away.

The giver of alms should be free from anxiety and full of joy. His gain will be greatest when he keeps back least for himself. The holy apostle Paul tells us: *He who provides seed for the sower will also provide bread for eating; he will provide you with more seed, and will increase the harvest of your goodness*[2 Cor 9:10], in Christ Jesus our Lord, who lives and reigns with the Father and the Holy Spirit for ever and ever. Amen.

Wednesday of the Fourth Week of Lent

From a letter by Saint Maximus the Confessor, Abbot

The mercy of God to the penitent

God's will is to save us, and nothing pleases him more than our coming back to him with true repentance. The heralds of truth and the ministers of divine grace have told us this from the beginning, repeating it in every age. Indeed, God's desire for our salvation is the primary and preeminent sign of his infinite goodness. It was precisely in order to show that there is nothing closer to God's heart that, the divine Word of God the Father, with untold condescension, lived among us in the flesh, and did, suffered, and said all that was necessary to reconcile us to God the Father, when we were at enmity with him, and to restore us to the life of blessedness from which we had been exiled. He healed our physical infirmities by miracles; he freed us from our sins, many and grievous as they were, by suffering and dying, taking them upon himself as if he were answerable for them, sinless though he was. He also taught us in many different ways that we should wish to imitate him by our own kindness and genuine love for one another.

So it was that Christ proclaimed that he had come to call sinners to repentance, not the righteous, and that it was not the healthy who required a doctor, but the sick. He declared that he had come to look for the sheep that was lost, and that it was to the lost sheep of the house of Israel that he had been sent. Speaking more obscurely in the parable of the silver coin, he tells us that the purpose of his coming was to reclaim the royal image, which had become coated with the filth of sin. *You can be sure there is joy in heaven,* he said, *over one sinner who repents*[Lk 15:7; Ezek 18:23].

To give the same lesson he revived the man who, having fallen into the hands of brigands, had been left stripped and half-dead from his wounds; he poured wine and oil on the wounds, bandaged them, placed the man on his own mule and brought him to an inn, where he left sufficient money to have him cared for, and promised to repay any further expense on his return.

Again, he told of how that Father, who is goodness itself, was moved with pity for his profligate son who returned and made amends by repentance; how he embraced him, dressed him once more in the fine garments that befitted his own dignity, and did not reproach him for any of his sins.

So too, when he found wandering in the mountains and hills the one sheep that had strayed from God's flock of a hundred, he brought it back to the fold, but he did not exhaust it by driving it ahead of him. Instead, he placed it on his own shoulders and so, compassionately, he restored it safely to the flock.

So also he cried out: *Come to me, all you that toil and are heavy of heart. Accept my yoke*[Mt 11:28-30], he said, by which he meant his commands, or rather, the whole way of life that he taught us in the Gospel. He then speaks of a burden, but that is only because repentance seems difficult. In fact, however, *my yoke is easy,* he assures us, *and my burden is light*[Mt 11:28-30].

Then again he instructs us in divine justice and goodness, telling us to be like our heavenly Father, holy, perfect and merciful. *Forgive,* he says, *and you will be forgiven. Behave toward other people as you would wish them to behave toward you*[Mt 6:14-15].

Thursday of the Fourth Week of Lent

From a sermon by Saint Leo the Great, Pope & Doctor

Contemplating the Lord's passion

True reverence for the Lord's passion means fixing the eyes of our heart on Jesus crucified and recognizing in him our own humanity.

The earth – our earthly nature – should tremble at the suffering of its Redeemer. The rocks – the hearts of unbelievers – should burst asunder. The dead, imprisoned in the tombs of their mortality, should come forth, the massive stones now ripped apart. Foreshadowings of the future resurrection should appear in the holy city, the Church of God: what is to happen to our bodies should now take place in our hearts.

No one, however weak, is denied a share in the victory of the cross. No one is beyond the help of the prayer of Christ. His prayer brought benefit to the multitude that raged against him. How much more does it bring to those who turn to him in repentance.

Ignorance has been destroyed, obstinacy has been overcome. The sacred blood of Christ has quenched the flaming sword that barred access to the tree of life. The age-old night of sin has given place to the true light.

The Christian people are invited to share the riches of paradise. All who have been reborn have the way open before them to return to their native land, from which they had been exiled. Unless indeed they close off for themselves the path that could be opened before the faith of a thief.

The business of this life should not preoccupy us with its anxiety and pride, so that we no longer strive with all the love of our heart to be like our Redeemer, and to follow his example. Everything that he did or suffered was for our salvation: he wanted his body to share the goodness of its head.

First of all, in taking our human nature while remaining God, so that *the Word became man*[Jn 1:14], he left no member of the human race, the unbeliever excepted, without a share in his mercy. Who does not share a common nature with Christ if he has welcomed Christ, who took our nature, and is reborn in the Spirit through whom Christ was conceived?

Again, who cannot recognize in Christ his own infirmities? Who would not recognize that Christ's eating and sleeping, his sadness and his shedding of tears of love are marks of the nature of a slave?

It was this nature of a slave that had to be healed of its ancient wounds and cleansed of the defilement of sin. For that reason the only-begotten Son of God became also the son of man. He was to have both the reality of a human nature and the fullness of the godhead.

The body that lay lifeless in the tomb is ours. The body that rose again on the third day is ours. The body that ascended above all the heights of heaven to the right hand of the Father's glory is ours. If then we walk in the way of his commandments, and are not ashamed to acknowledge the price he paid for our salvation in a lowly body, we too are to rise to share his glory. The promise he made will be fulfilled in the sight of all: *Whoever acknowledges me before men, I too will acknowledge him before my Father who is in heaven*[Mt 10:32].

Friday of the Fourth Week of Lent

From an Easter letter by Saint Athanasius, Bishop & Doctor

The paschal sacrament brings together in unity of faith those physically separated from each other

Brethren, how fine a thing it is to move from festival to festival, from prayer to prayer, from holy day to holy day. The time is now at hand when we enter on a new beginning: the proclamation of the blessed Passover, in which the Lord was sacrificed. We feed as on the food of life, we constantly refresh our souls with his precious blood, as from a fountain. Yet we are always thirsting, burning to be satisfied. But he himself is present for those who thirst and in his goodness invites them to the feast day. Our Savior repeats his words: *If anyone thirsts, let him come to me and drink*[Jn 7:37].

He quenched the thirst not only of those who came to him then. Whenever anyone seeks him he is freely admitted to the presence of the Savior. The grace of the feast is not restricted to one occasion. Its rays of glory never set. It is always at hand to enlighten the mind of those who desire it. Its power is always there for those whose minds have been enlightened and who meditate day and night on the holy Scriptures, like the one who is called blessed in the holy psalm: *Blessed is the man who has not followed the counsel of the wicked, or stood where sinners stand, or sat in the seat of the scornful, but whose delight is in the law of the Lord, and who meditates on his law day and night*[Ps 1:1-2].

Moreover, my friends, the God who first established this feast for us allows us to celebrate it each year. He who gave up his Son to death for our salvation, from the same motive gives us this feast, which is commemorated every year. This feast guides us through the trials that meet us in this world. God now gives us the joy of salvation that shines out from this feast, as he brings us together to form one assembly, uniting us all in spirit in every place, allowing us to pray together and to offer common thanksgiving, as is our duty on the feast. Such is the wonder of his love: he gathers to this feast those who are far apart, and brings together in unity of faith those who may be physically separated from each other.

Saturday of the Fourth Week of Lent

From the pastoral constitution on the Church in the Modern World of the Second Vatican Council ~ *Gaudium et spes*

All human activity is to find its purification in the paschal mystery

Holy Scripture, with which the experience of the ages is in agreement, teaches the human family that human progress, though it is a great blessing for man, brings with it a great temptation. When the scale of values is disturbed and evil becomes mixed with good, individuals and groups consider only their own interests, not those of others.

The result is that the world is not yet a home of true brotherhood, while the increased power of mankind already threatens to destroy the human race itself.

If it is asked how this unhappy state of affairs can be set right, Christians state their belief that all human activity, in daily jeopardy through pride and inordinate self-love, is to find its purification and its perfection in the cross and resurrection of Christ.

Man, redeemed by Christ and made a new creation in the Holy Spirit, can and must love the very things created by God. For he receives them from God, and sees and reveres them as coming from the hand of God,

As he gives thanks for them to his Benefactor, and uses and enjoys them in a spirit of poverty and freedom, he enters into true possession of the world, as one having nothing and possessing all things. *For all things are yours, and you are Christ's, and Christ is God's*[1 Cor 3:21-23].

The Word of God, through whom all things were made, himself became man and lived in the world of men. As perfect man he has entered into the history of the world, taking it up into himself and bringing it into unity as its head. He reveals to us *that God is love*, and at the same time teaches us that the fundamental law of human perfection, and therefore of the transformation of the world, is the new commandment of love.

He assures those who have faith in God's love that the way of love is open to all men, and that the effort to restore universal brotherhood is not in vain. At the same time he warns us that this love is not to be sought after only in great things but also, and above all, in the ordinary circumstances of life.

He suffered death for us all, sinners as we are, and by his example he teaches us that we also have to carry that cross which the flesh and the world lay on the shoulders of those who strive for peace and justice.

Constituted as the Lord by his resurrection, Christ, to whom all power in heaven and on earth has been given, is still at work in the hearts of men through the power of his Spirit. Not only does he awaken in them a longing for the world to come, but by that very fact he also inspires, purifies and strengthens those generous desires by which the human family seeks to make its own life more human and to achieve the same goal for the whole world.

The gifts of the Spirit are manifold. He calls some to bear open witness to the longing for a dwelling place in heaven, and to keep this fresh in the minds of all mankind; he calls others to dedicate themselves to the service of men here on earth, preparing by this ministry the material for the kingdom of heaven.

Yet he makes all free, so that, by denying their love of self and taking up all earth's resources into the life of man, all may reach out to the future, when humanity itself will become an offering acceptable to God.

Sunday of the Fifth Week of Lent

From an Easter letter by Saint Athanasius, Bishop & Doctor

We keep the coming feast of the Lord through deeds, not words

The Word who became all things for us is close to us, our Lord Jesus Christ who promises to remain with us always. He cries out, saying: *See, I am with you all the days of this age*[Mt 28:20]. He is himself the shepherd, the high priest, the way and the door, and has become all things at once for us. In the same way, he has come among us as our feast and holy day as well. The blessed Apostle says of him who was awaited: *Christ has been sacrificed as our Passover*[1 Cor 5:7]. It was Christ who shed his light on the psalmist as he prayed: *You are my joy, deliver me from those surrounding me*[Ps 31:7]. True joy, genuine festival, means the casting out of wickedness. To achieve this one must live a life of perfect goodness and, in the serenity of the fear of God, practice contemplation in one's heart.

This was the way of the saints, who in their lifetime and at every stage of life rejoiced as at a feast. Blessed David, for example, not once but seven times rose at night to win God's favor through prayer. The great Moses was full of joy as he sang God's praises in hymns of victory for the defeat of Pharaoh and the oppressors of the Hebrew people. Others had hearts filled always with gladness as they performed their sacred duty of worship, like the great Samuel and the blessed Elijah. Because of their holy lives they gained freedom, and now keep festival in heaven. They rejoice after their pilgrimage in shadows, and now distinguish the reality from the promise.

When we celebrate the feast in our own day, what path are we to take? As we draw near to this feast, who is to be our guide? Beloved, it must be none other than the one whom you will address with me as our Lord Jesus Christ. He says: *I am the way*[Jn 14:6]. As blessed John tells us: it is Christ *who takes away the sin of the world*[Jn 1:29]. It is he who purifies our souls, as the prophet Jeremiah says: *Stand upon the ways; look and see which is the good path, and you will find in it the way of amendment for your souls*[Jer 6:16].

In former times the blood of goats and the ashes of a calf were sprinkled on those who were unclean, but they were able to purify only the body. Now through the grace of God's Word everyone is made abundantly clean. If we follow Christ closely we shall be allowed, even on this earth, to stand as it were on the threshold of the heavenly Jerusalem, and enjoy the contemplation of that everlasting feast, like the blessed apostles, who in following the Savior as their leader, showed, and still show, the way to obtain the same gift from God. They said: *See, we have left all things and followed you*[Mt 19:27]. We too follow the Lord, and we keep his feast by deeds rather than by words.

Monday of the Fifth Week of Lent

From the commentary on the psalms by Saint John Fisher, Bishop and Martyr

If anyone has sinned, we have an advocate with the Father

Our high priest is Christ Jesus, our sacrifice is his precious body which he immolated on the altar of the cross for the salvation of all men.

The blood that was poured out for our redemption was not that of goats or calves (as in the old law) but that of the most innocent lamb, Christ Jesus our Savior.

The temple in which our high priest offered sacrifice was not one made by hands but built by the power of God alone. For he shed his blood in the sight of the world, a temple fashioned by the hand of God alone.

This temple, however, has two parts. The first is the earth, which we now inhabit. The second is as yet unknown to us mortals.

Christ first offered sacrifice here on earth, when he underwent his most bitter death. Then, clothed in the new garment of immortality, with his own blood he entered into the holy of holies, that is, into heaven. There he also displayed before the throne of the heavenly Father that blood of immeasurable price which he had poured out seven times on behalf of all men subject to sin.

This sacrifice is so pleasing and acceptable to God that as soon as he has seen it he must immediately have pity on us and extend clemency to all who are truly repentant.

Moreover, it is eternal. It is offered not only each year (as with the Jews) but also each day for our consolation, and indeed at every hour and moment as well, so that we may have the strongest reason for comfort. That is why the Apostle adds: *He has secured an eternal redemption*[Heb 9:12].

All who have embarked on true contrition and penance for the sins they have committed, and are firmly resolved not to commit sins again for the future but to persevere constantly in that pursuit of virtues which they have now begun, all these become sharers in this holy and eternal sacrifice.

Saint John sets this before us in these words: *My little children, I am writing this to you so that you many not sin. But if anyone does sin we have an advocate with the Father, Jesus Christ the righteous one. And he is the propitiation for our sins, and not only for our sins but also for those of the whole world*[1 Jn 2:1-2].

Tuesday of the Fifth Week of Lent

From a sermon by Saint Leo the Great, Pope & Doctor

The cross of Christ is the source of all blessings, the cause of all graces

Our understanding, which is enlightened by the Spirit of truth, should receive with purity and freedom of heart the glory of the cross as it shines in heaven and on earth. It should see with inner vision the meaning of the Lord's words when he spoke of the imminence of his passion: *The hour has come for the Son of Man to be glorified*[Jn 12:23]. Afterward he said: *Now my soul is troubled, and what am I to say? Father, save me from this hour. But it was for this that I came to this hour. Father, glorify your Son*[Jn 12:27-28]. When the voice of the Father came from heaven, saying, *I have glorified him, and will glorify him again*[Jn 12:28], Jesus said in reply to those around him: *It was not for me that this voice spoke, but for you. Now is the judgment of the world, now will the prince of this world be cast out. And I, if I am lifted up from the earth, will draw all things to myself*[Jn 12:30-32].

How marvelous the power of the cross; how great beyond all telling the glory of the passion: here is the judgment-seat of the Lord, the condemnation of the world, the supremacy of Christ crucified.

Lord, you drew all things to yourself so that the devotion of all peoples everywhere might celebrate, in a sacrament made perfect and visible, what was carried out in the one temple of Judea under obscure foreshadowings.

Now there is a more distinguished order of Levites, a greater dignity for the rank of elders, a more sacred anointing for the priesthood, because your cross is the source of all blessings, the cause of all graces. Through the cross the faithful receive strength from weakness, glory from dishonor, life from death.

The different sacrifices of animals are no more: the one offering of your body and blood is the fulfillment of all the different sacrificial offerings, for you are the true *Lamb of God: you take away the sins of the world*[Jn 1:29]. In yourself you bring to perfection all mysteries, so that, as there is one sacrifice in place of all other sacrificial offerings, there is also one kingdom gathered from all peoples.

Dearly beloved, let us then acknowledge what Saint Paul, the teacher of the nations, acknowledged so exultantly: *This is a saying worthy of trust, worthy of complete acceptance: Christ Jesus came into this world to save sinners*[1 Tim 1:15].

God's compassion for us is all the more wonderful because Christ died, not for the righteous or the holy but for the wicked and the sinful, and, though the divine nature could not be touched by the sting of death, he took to himself, through his birth as one of us, something he could offer on our behalf.

The power of his death once confronted our death. In the words of Hosea the prophet: *Death, I shall be your death; grave, I shall swallow you up*[Hos 13:14, cf 1 Cor 15:54]. By dying he submitted to the laws of the underworld; by rising again he destroyed them. He did away with the everlasting character of death so as to make death a thing of time, not of eternity. *As all die in Adam, so all will be brought to life in Christ*[1 Cor 15:22].

Wednesday of the Fifth Week of Lent

From a commentary on the psalms by Saint Augustine, Bishop & Doctor

Jesus Christ prays for us and in us and is the object of our prayers

God could give no greater gift to men than to make his Word, through whom he created all things, their head and to join them to him as his members, so that the Word might be both Son of God and son of man, one God with the Father, and one man with all men. The result is that when we speak with God in prayer we do not separate the Son from him, and when the body of the Son prays it does not separate its head from itself: it is the one Savior of his body, our Lord Jesus Christ, the Son of God, who prays for us and in us and is himself the object of our prayers.

He prays for us as our priest, he prays in us as our head, he is the object of our prayers as our God.

Let us then recognize both our voice in his, and his voice in ours. When something is said, especially in prophecy, about the Lord Jesus Christ that seems to belong to a condition of lowliness unworthy of God, we must not hesitate to ascribe this condition to one who did not hesitate to unite himself with us. Every creature is his servant, for it was through him that every creature came to be.

We contemplate his glory and divinity when we listen to these words: *In the beginning was the Word, and the Word was with God, and the Word was God. He was in the beginning with God. All things were made through him, and without him nothing was made*. Here we gaze on the divinity of the Son of God, something supremely great and surpassing all the greatness of his creatures. Yet in other parts of Scripture we hear him as one sighing, praying, giving praise and thanks.

We hesitate to attribute these words to him because our minds are slow to come down to his humble level when we have just been contemplating him in his divinity. It is as though we were doing him an injustice in acknowledging in a man the words of one with whom we spoke when we prayed to God; we are usually at a loss and try to change the meaning. Yet our minds find nothing in Scripture that does not go back to him, nothing that will allow us to stray from him.

Our thoughts must then be awakened to keep their vigil of faith. We must realize that the one whom we were contemplating a short time before in his nature as God took to himself the nature of a servant; he was made in the likeness of men and found to be a man like others; he humbled himself by being obedient even to accepting death; as he hung on the cross he made the psalmist's words his own: *My God, my God, why have you forsaken me*[Mt 27:46; Ps 21:2]*?*

We pray to him as God, he prays for us as a servant. In the first case he is the Creator, in the second a creature. Himself unchanged, he took to himself our created nature in order to change it, and made us one man with himself, head and body. We pray then to him, through him, in him, and we speak along with him he along with us.

Thursday of the Fifth Week of Lent

From the dogmatic constitution on the Church of the Second Vatican Council
Lumen Gentium

The Church as sacrament of unity and salvation

See, the days are coming, says the Lord, when I will make a new covenant with the house of Israel and the house of Judah... I will plant my law within them and inscribe it in their hearts. I will be their God and they shall be my people... All shall know me, from the least to the greatest, says the Lord[Jer 31:31-34].

It was Christ who established this new covenant, the new testament in his blood, calling into being, from Jews and Gentiles, a people that was to form a unity, not in human fashion but in the Spirit, as the new people of God. Those who believe in Christ, reborn not of corruptible but of incorruptible seed through the word of the living God, not from the flesh but from water and the Holy Spirit, are constituted in the fullness of time as *a chosen race, a royal priesthood, a holy nation, a people God has made his own..., once no people but now the people of God*[1 Pet 2:9-10].

This messianic people has Christ as its head: Christ *who was given up for our sins and rose again for our justification*[Rom 4:25]; bearing now the name that is above every name, he reigns in glory in heaven. His people enjoy the dignity and freedom of the children of God, in whose hearts the Holy Spirit dwells as in a temple. They have as their law the new commandment of loving as Christ himself has loved us. They have as their goal the kingdom of God, begun on earth by God himself and destined to grow until it is also brought to perfection by him at the end of time, when Christ, our life, will appear, and *creation itself will be freed from slavery to corruption and take on the freedom of the glory of God's children*[Rom 8:21].

This messianic people, then, though it does not in fact embrace all mankind and often seems to be a tiny flock, is yet the enduring source of unity, hope and salvation for the whole human race. It is established by Christ as a communion of life, of love and of truth; it is also used by him as an instrument for the redemption of all, and is sent out into the whole world as the light of the world and the salt of the earth.

The Israel of old was already called the Church of God while it was on pilgrimage through the desert. So the new Israel, as it makes its way in this present age, seeking a city that is to come, a city that will remain, is also known as the Church of Christ, for he acquired it by his own blood, filled it with his Spirit, and equipped it with appropriate means to be a visible and social unity. God has called together the assembly of those who in faith look on Jesus, the author of salvation and the principle of unity and peace, and so has established the Church to be for each and all the visible sacrament of this unity which brings with it salvation.

Friday of the Fifth Week of Lent

From a treatise on faith addressed to Peter by Saint Fulgentius of Ruspe, bishop

Christ offered himself for us

The sacrifices of animal victims which our forefathers were commanded to offer to God by the holy Trinity itself, the one God of the old and the new testaments, foreshadowed the most acceptable gift of all. This was the offering which in his compassion the only Son of God would make of himself in his human nature for our sake.

The Apostle teaches that Christ *offered himself for us to God as a fragrant offering and sacrifice*[Eph 5:2]. He is the true God and the true high priest who for our sake entered once for all into the holy of holies, taking with him not the blood of bulls and goats but his own blood. This was foreshadowed by the high priest of old when each year he took blood and entered the holy of holies.

Christ is therefore the one who in himself alone embodied all that he knew to be necessary to achieve our redemption. He is at once priest and sacrifice, God and temple. He is the priest through whom we have been reconciled, the sacrifice by which we have been reconciled, the temple in which we have been reconciled, the God with whom we have been reconciled. He alone is priest, sacrifice and temple because he is all these things as God in the form of a servant; but he is not alone as God, for he is this with the Father and the Holy Spirit in the form of God.

Hold fast to this and never doubt it: the only-begotten Son, God the Word, becoming man offered himself for us to God as a fragrant offering and sacrifice. In the time of the old testament, patriarchs, prophets and priests sacrificed animals in his honor, and in honor of the Father and the Holy Spirit as well. Now in the time of the new testament the holy catholic Church throughout the world never ceases to offer the sacrifice of bread and wine, in faith and love, to him and to the Father and the Holy Spirit, with whom he shares one godhead.

Those animal sacrifices foreshadowed the flesh of Christ which he would offer for our sins, though himself without sin, and the blood which he would pour out for the forgiveness of our sins. In this sacrifice there is thanksgiving for, and commemoration of, the flesh of Christ that he offered for us, and the blood that the same God poured out for us. On this Saint Paul says in the Acts of the Apostles: *Keep watch over yourselves and over the whole flock, in which the Holy Spirit has appointed you as bishops to rule the Church of God, which he won for himself by his blood*[Acts 20:28].

Those sacrifices of old pointed in sign to what was to be given to us. In this sacrifice we see plainly what has already been given to us. Those sacrifices foretold the death of the Son of God for sinners. In this sacrifice he is proclaimed as already slain for sinners, as the Apostle testifies: *Christ died for the wicked at a time when we were still powerless, and when we were enemies we were reconciled with God through the death of his Son*[Rom 5:6-10].

Saturday of the Fifth Week of Lent

From a homily by Saint Gregory Nazianzen, Bishop & Doctor

We are soon going to share in the Passover

We are soon going to share in the Passover, and although we still do so only in a symbolic way, the symbolism already has more clarity than it possessed in former times because, under the law, the Passover was, if I may dare to say so, only a symbol of a symbol. Before long, however, when the Word drinks the new wine with us in the kingdom of his Father, we shall be keeping the Passover in a yet more perfect way, and with deeper understanding. He will then reveal to us and make clear what he has so far only partially disclosed. For this wine, so familiar to us now, is eternally new.

It is for us to learn what this drinking is, and for him to teach us. He has to communicate this knowledge to his disciples, because teaching is food, even for the teacher.

So let us take our part in the Passover prescribed by the law, not in a literal way, but according to the teaching of the Gospel; not in an imperfect way, but perfectly; not only for a time, but eternally. Let us regard as our home the heavenly Jerusalem, not the earthly one; the city glorified by angels, not the one laid waste by armies. We are not required to sacrifice young bulls or rams, beasts with horns and hoofs that are more dead than alive and devoid of feeling; but instead, let us join the choirs of angels in offering God upon his heavenly altar a sacrifice of praise. We must now pass through the first veil and approach the second, turning our eyes toward the Holy of Holies. I will say more: we must sacrifice ourselves to God, each day and in everything we do, accepting all that happens to us for the sake of the Word, imitating his passion by our sufferings, and honoring his blood by shedding our own. We must be ready to be crucified.

If you are a Simon of Cyrene, take up your cross and follow Christ. If you are crucified beside him like one of the thieves, now, like the good thief, acknowledge your God. For your sake, and because of your sin, Christ himself was regarded as a sinner; for his sake, therefore, you must cease to sin. Worship him who was hung on the cross because of you, even if you are hanging there yourself. Derive some benefit from the very shame; purchase salvation with your death. Enter paradise with Jesus, and discover how far you have fallen. Contemplate the glories there, and leave the other scoffing thief to die outside in his blasphemy.

If you are a Joseph of Arimathea, go to the one who ordered his crucifixion, and ask for Christ's body. Make your own the expiation for the sins of the whole world. If you are a Nicodemus, like the man who worshiped God by night, bring spices and prepare Christ's body for burial. If you are one of the Marys, or Salome, or Joanna, weep in the early morning. Be the first to see the stone rolled back, and even the angels perhaps, and Jesus himself.

Palm Sunday of the Lord's Passion

From a sermon by Saint Andrew of Crete, Bishop

Blessed is he who comes in the name of the Lord. Blessed is the king of Israel.

Let us go together to meet Christ on the Mount of Olives. Today he returns from Bethany and proceeds of his own free will toward his holy and blessed passion, to consummate the mystery of our salvation. He who came down from heaven to raise us from the depths of sin, to raise us with himself, we are told in Scripture, *above every sovereignty, authority and power, and every other name that can be named*[Eph 1:21], now comes of his own free will to make his journey to Jerusalem. He comes without pomp or ostentation. As the psalmist says: *He will not dispute or raise his voice to make it heard in the streets*[Mt 12:19]. He will be meek and humble, and he will make his entry in simplicity.

Let us run to accompany him as he hastens toward his passion, and imitate those who met him then, not by covering his path with garments, olive branches or palms, but by doing all we can to prostrate ourselves before him by being humble and by trying to live as he would wish. Then we shall be able to receive the Word at his coming, and God, whom no limits can contain, will be within us.

In his humility Christ entered the dark regions of our fallen world and he is glad that he became so humble for our sake, glad that he came and lived among us and shared in our nature in order to raise us up again to himself. And even though we are told that he has now ascended above the highest heavens – the proof, surely, of his power and godhead – his love for man will never rest until he has raised our earthbound nature from glory to glory, and made it one with his own in heaven.

So let us spread before his feet, not garments or soulless olive branches, which delight the eye for a few hours and then wither, but ourselves, clothed in his grace, or rather, clothed completely in him. We who have been baptized into Christ must ourselves be the garments that we spread before him. Now that the crimson stains of our sins have been washed away in the saving waters of baptism and we have become white as pure wool, let us present the conqueror of death, not with mere branches of palms but with the real rewards of his victory. Let our souls take the place of the welcoming branches as we join today in the children's holy song: *Blessed is he who comes in the name of the Lord. Blessed is the king of Israel*[Lk 13:35].

Monday of Holy Week

From a sermon by Saint Augustine, Bishop & Doctor

Let us too glory in the cross of the Lord

The passion of our Lord and Savior Jesus Christ is the hope of glory and a lesson in patience.

What may not the hearts of believers promise themselves as the gift of God's grace, when for their sake God's only Son, co-eternal with the Father, was not content only to be born as man from human stock but even died at the hands of the men he had created?

It is a great thing that we are promised by the Lord; but far greater is what has already been done for us, and which we now commemorate. Where were the sinners, what were they, when Christ died for them? When Christ has already given us the gift of his death, who is to doubt that he will give the saints the gift of his own life? Why does our human frailty hesitate to believe that mankind will one day live with God?

Who is Christ if not the Word of God: *in the beginning was the Word, and the Word was with God, and the Word was God*[Jn 1:1]? This Word of God *was made flesh and dwelt among us.* He had no power of himself to die for us: he had to take from us our mortal flesh. This was the way in which, though immortal, he was able to die; the way in which he chose to give life to mortal men: he would first share with us, and then enable us to share with him. Of ourselves we had no power to live, nor did he of himself have the power to die.

Accordingly, he effected a wonderful exchange with us, through mutual sharing: we gave him the power to die, he will give us the power to live.

The death of the Lord our God should not be a cause of shame for us; rather, it should be our greatest hope, our greatest glory. In taking upon himself the death that he found in us, he has most faithfully promised to give us life in him, such as we cannot have of ourselves.

He loved us so much that, sinless himself, he suffered for us sinners the punishment we deserved for our sins. How then can he fail to give us the reward we deserve for our righteousness, for he is the source of righteousness? How can he, whose promises are true, fail to reward the saints when he bore the punishment of sinners, though without sin himself?

Brethren, let us then fearlessly acknowledge, and even openly proclaim, that Christ was crucified for us; let us confess it, not in fear but in joy, not in shame but in glory.

The apostle Paul saw Christ, and extolled his claim to glory. He had many great and inspired things to say about Christ, but he did not say that he boasted in Christ's wonderful works: in creating the world, since he was God with the Father, or in ruling the world, though he was also a man like us. Rather, he said: *Let me not boast except in the cross of our Lord Jesus Christ*[Gal 6:14].

Tuesday of Holy Week

From the book On the Holy Spirit by Saint Basil, Bishop & Doctor

By one death and resurrection the world was saved

When mankind was estranged from him by disobedience, God our Savior made a plan for raising us from our fall and restoring us to friendship with himself. According to this plan Christ came in the flesh, he showed us the gospel way of life, he suffered, died on the cross, was buried and rose from the dead. He did this so that we could be saved by imitation of him, and recover our original status as sons of God by adoption.

To attain holiness, then, we must not only pattern our lives on Christ's by being gentle, humble and patient, we must also imitate him in his death. Taking Christ for his model, Paul said that he wanted to become like him in his death in the hope that he too would be raised from death to life.

We imitate Christ's death by being buried with him in baptism. If we ask what this kind of burial means and what benefit we may hope to derive from it, it means first of all making a complete break with our former way of life, and our Lord himself said that this cannot be done unless a man is born again. In other words, we have to begin a new life, and we cannot do so until our previous life has been brought to an end. When runners reach the turning point on a racecourse, they have to pause briefly before they can go back in the opposite direction. So also when we wish to reverse the direction of our lives there must be a pause, or a death, to mark the end of one life and the beginning of another.

Our descent into hell takes place when we imitate the burial of Christ by our baptism. The bodies of the baptized are in a sense buried in the water as a symbol of their renunciation of the sins of their unregenerate nature. As the Apostle says: *The circumcision you have undergone is not an operation performed by human hands, but the complete stripping away of your unregenerate nature. This is the circumcision that Christ gave us, and it is accomplished by our burial with him in baptism*[Col 2:11]. Baptism cleanses the soul from the pollution of worldly thoughts and inclinations: *You will wash me*[Ps 50:9], says the psalmist, *and I shall be whiter than snow* [Ps 50:9]. We receive this saving baptism only once because there was only one death and one resurrection for the salvation of the world, and baptism is its symbol.

Wednesday of Holy Week

From a treatise on John by Saint Augustine, Bishop & Doctor

The perfection of love

Dear brethren, the Lord has marked out for us the fullness of love that we ought to have for each other. He tells us: *No one has greater love than the man who lays down his life for his friends*[Jn 15:13]. In these words, the Lord tells us what the perfect love we should have for one another involves. John, the evangelist who recorded them, draws the conclusion in one of his letters: *As Christ laid down his life for us, so we too ought to lay down our lives for our brothers*[1 Jn 3:16]. We should indeed love one another as he loved us, he who laid down his life for us.

This is surely what we read in the Proverbs of Solomon: *If you sit down to eat at the table of a ruler, observe carefully what is set before you; then stretch out your hand, knowing that you must provide the same kind of meal yourself*[Prov 23:1]. What is this ruler's table if not the one at which we receive the body and blood of him who laid down his life for us? What does it mean to sit at this table if not to approach it with humility? What does it mean to observe carefully what is set before you if not to meditate devoutly on so great a gift? What does it mean to stretch out one's hand, knowing that one must provide the same kind of meal oneself, if not what I have just said: as Christ laid down his life for us, so we in our turn ought to lay down our lives for our brothers? This is what the apostle Paul said: *Christ suffered for us, leaving us an example, that we might follow in his footsteps*[1 Pet 2:21].

This is what is meant by providing "the same kind of meal." This is what the blessed martyrs did with such burning love. If we are to give true meaning to our celebration of their memorials, to our approaching the Lord's table in the very banquet at which they were fed, we must, like them, provide "the same kind of meal."

At this table of the Lord we do not commemorate the martyrs in the same way as we commemorate others who rest in peace. We do not pray for the martyrs as we pray for those others, rather, they pray for us, that we may follow in their footsteps. They practiced the perfect love of which the Lord said there could be none greater. They provided "the same kind of meal" as they had themselves received at the Lord's table.

This must not be understood as saying that we can be the Lord's equals by bearing witness to him to the extent of shedding our blood. He had the power of laying down his life; we by contrast cannot choose the length of our lives, and we die even if it is against our will. He, by dying, destroyed death in himself; we are freed from death only in his death. His body did not see corruption; our body will see corruption and only then be clothed through him in incorruption at the end of the world. He needed no help from us in saving us; without him we can do nothing. He gave himself to us as the vine to the branches; apart from him we cannot have life.

Finally, even if brothers die for brothers, yet no martyr by shedding his blood brings forgiveness for the sins of his brothers, as Christ brought forgiveness to us. In this he gave us, not an example to imitate but a reason for rejoicing. Inasmuch, then, as they shed their blood for their brothers, the martyrs provided "the same kind of meal" as they had received at the Lord's table.

Let us then love one another as Christ also loved us and gave himself up for us.

Holy Thursday

From an Easter homily by Saint Melito of Sardis, Bishop

The Lamb that was slain has delivered us from death and given us life

There was much proclaimed by the prophets about the mystery of the Passover: that mystery is Christ, and to him be glory for ever and ever. Amen.

For the sake of suffering humanity he came down from heaven to earth, clothed himself in that humanity in the Virgin's womb, and was born a man. Having then a body capable of suffering, he took the pain of fallen man upon himself; he triumphed over the diseases of soul and body that were its cause, and by his Spirit, which was incapable of dying, he dealt man's destroyer, death, a fatal blow.

He was led forth like a lamb; he was slaughtered like a sheep. He ransomed us from our servitude to the world, as he had ransomed Israel from the land of Egypt; he freed us from our slavery to the devil, as he had freed Israel from the hand of Pharaoh. He sealed our souls with his own Spirit, and the members of our body with his own blood.

He is the One who covered death with shame and cast the devil into mourning, as Moses cast Pharaoh into mourning. He is the One who smote sin and robbed iniquity of offspring, as Moses robbed the Egyptians of their offspring. He is the One who brought us out of slavery into freedom, out of darkness into light, out of death into life, out of tyranny into an eternal kingdom; who made us a new priesthood, a people chosen to be his own for ever. He is the Passover that is our salvation.

It is he who endured every kind of suffering in all those who foreshadowed him. In Abel he was slain, in Isaac bound, in Jacob exiled, in Joseph sold, in Moses exposed to die. He was sacrificed in the Passover lamb, persecuted in David, dishonored in the prophets.

It is he who was made man of the Virgin, he who was hung on the tree; it is he who was buried in the earth, raised from the dead, and taken up to the heights of heaven. He is the mute lamb, the slain lamb, the lamb born of Mary, the fair ewe. He was seized from the flock, dragged off to be slaughtered, sacrificed in the evening, and buried at night. On the tree no bone of his was broken; in the earth his body knew no decay. He is the One who rose from the dead, and who raised man from the depths of the tomb.

Good Friday of the Lord's Passion

From the Catecheses by Saint John Chrysostom, Bishop

The power of Christ's blood

If we wish to understand the power of Christ's blood, we should go back to the ancient account of its prefiguration in Egypt. Sacrifice a lamb without blemish, commanded Moses, and sprinkle its blood on your doors. If we were to ask him what he meant, and how the blood of an irrational beast could possibly save men endowed with reason, his answer would be that the saving power lies not in the blood itself, but in the fact that it is a sign of the Lord's blood. In those days, when the destroying angel saw the blood on the doors he did not dare to enter, so much less will the devil approach now when he sees, not that figurative blood on the doors, but the true blood on the lips of believers, the doors of the temple of Christ.

If you desire further proof of the power of this blood, remember where it came from, how it ran down from the cross, flowing from the Master's side. The gospel records that when Christ was dead, but still hung on the cross, a soldier came and pierced his side with a lance and immediately there poured out water and blood. Now the water was a symbol of baptism and the blood, of the holy eucharist. The soldier pierced the Lord's side, he breached the wall of the sacred temple, and I have found the treasure and made it my own. So also with the lamb: the Jews sacrificed the victim and I have been saved by it.

There flowed from his side water and blood. Beloved, do not pass over this mystery without thought; it has yet another hidden meaning, which I will explain to you. I said that water and blood symbolized baptism and the Holy Eucharist. From these two sacraments the Church is born: from baptism, the cleansing water that gives rebirth and renewal through the Holy Spirit, and from the Holy Eucharist. Since the symbols of Baptism and the Eucharist flowed from his side, it was from his side that Christ fashioned the Church, as he had fashioned Eve from the side of Adam. Moses gives a hint of this when he tells the story of the first man and makes him exclaim: Bone from my bones and flesh from my flesh! As God then took a rib from Adam's side to fashion a woman, so Christ has given us blood and water from his side to fashion the Church. God took the rib when Adam was in a deep sleep, and in the same way Christ gave us the blood and water after his own death.

Do you understand, then, how Christ has united his bride to himself and what food he gives us all to eat? By one and the same food we are both brought into being and nourished. As a woman nourishes her child with her own blood and milk, so does Christ unceasingly nourish with his own blood those to whom he himself has given life.

Holy Saturday

From an ancient homily for Holy Saturday

The Lord descends into hell

Something strange is happening – there is a great silence on earth today, a great silence and stillness. The whole earth keeps silence because the King is asleep. The earth trembled and is still because God has fallen asleep in the flesh and he has raised up all who have slept ever since the world began. God has died in the flesh and hell trembles with fear.

He has gone to search for our first parent, as for a lost sheep. Greatly desiring to visit those who live in darkness and in the shadow of death, he has gone to free from sorrow the captives Adam and Eve, he who is both God and the son of Eve. The Lord approached them bearing the cross, the weapon that had won him the victory. At the sight of him Adam, the first man he had created, struck his breast in terror and cried out to everyone: "My Lord be with you all." Christ answered him: "And with your spirit." He took him by the hand and raised him up, saying: "Awake, O sleeper, and rise from the dead, and Christ will give you light."

I am your God, who for your sake have become your son. Out of love for you and for your descendants I now by my own authority command all who are held in bondage to come forth, all who are in darkness to be enlightened, all who are sleeping to arise. I order you, O sleeper, to awake. I did not create you to be held a prisoner in hell. Rise from the dead, for I am the life of the dead. Rise up, work of my hands, you who were created in my image. Rise, let us leave this place, for you are in me and I am in you; together we form only one person and we cannot be separated.

For your sake I, your God, became your son; I, the Lord, took the form of a slave; I, whose home is above the heavens, descended to the earth and beneath the earth. For your sake, for the sake of man, I became like a man without help, free among the dead. For the sake of you, who left a garden, I was betrayed to the Jews in a garden, and I was crucified in a garden.

See on my face the spittle I received in order to restore to you the life I once breathed into you. See there the marks of the blows I received in order to refashion your warped nature in my image. On my back see the marks of the scourging I endured to remove the burden of sin that weighs upon your back. See my hands, nailed firmly to a tree, for you who once wickedly stretched out your hand to a tree.

I slept on the cross and a sword pierced my side for you who slept in paradise and brought forth Eve from your side. My side has healed the pain in yours. My sleep will rouse you from your sleep in hell. The sword that pierced me has sheathed the sword that was turned against you.

Rise, let us leave this place. The enemy led you out of the earthly paradise. I will not restore you to that paradise, but I will enthrone you in heaven. I forbade you the tree that was only a symbol of life, but see, I who am life itself am now one with you. I appointed cherubim to guard you as slaves are guarded, but now I make them worship you as God. The throne formed by cherubim awaits you, its bearers swift and eager. The bridal chamber is adorned, the banquet is ready, the eternal dwelling places are prepared, the treasure houses of all good things lie open. The kingdom of heaven has been prepared for you from all eternity.

Monday within the Octave of Easter

From an Easter homily by Melito of Sardis, Bishop

The Easter praise of Christ

We should understand, beloved, that the paschal mystery is at once old and new, transitory and eternal, corruptible and incorruptible, mortal and immortal. In terms of the Law it is old, in terms of the Word it is new. In its figure it is passing, in its grace it is eternal. It is corruptible in the sacrifice of the lamb, incorruptible in the eternal life of the Lord. It is mortal in his burial in the earth, immortal in his resurrection from the dead.

The Law indeed is old, but the Word is new. The type is transitory, but grace is eternal. The lamb was corruptible, but the Lord is incorruptible. He was slain as a lamb; he rose again as God. *He was led like a sheep to the slaughter*[Isa 53:7], yet he was not a sheep. He was silent as a lamb, yet he was not a lamb. The type has passed away; the reality has come. The lamb gives place to God, the sheep gives place to a man, and the man is Christ, who fills the whole of creation. The sacrifice of the lamb, the celebration of the Passover, and the prescriptions of the Law have been fulfilled in Jesus Christ. Under the old Law, and still more under the new dispensation, everything pointed toward him.

Both the Law and the Word came forth from Zion and Jerusalem, but now the Law has given place to the Word, the old to the new. The commandment has become grace, the type a reality. The lamb has become a Son, the sheep a man, and man, God.

The Lord, though he was God, became man. He suffered for the sake of those who suffer, he was bound for those in bonds, condemned for the guilty, buried for those who lie in the grave; but he rose from the dead, and cried aloud: *Who will contend with me? Let him confront me*[Isa 50:8]. I have freed the condemned, brought the dead back to life, raised men from their graves. Who has anything to say against me? I, he said, am the Christ; I have destroyed death, triumphed over the enemy, trampled hell underfoot, bound the strong one, and taken men up to the heights of heaven: I am the Christ.

Come, then, all you nations of men, receive forgiveness for the sins that defile you. I am your forgiveness. I am the Passover that brings salvation. I am the lamb who was immolated for you. I am your ransom, your life, your resurrection, your light, I am your salvation and your king. I will bring you to the heights of heaven. With my own right hand I will raise you up, and I will show you the eternal Father.

Tuesday within the Octave of Easter

From a discourse by Saint Anastasius of Antioch, Patriarch

It was necessary that Christ should suffer and so enter into his glory

Christ, who has shown by his words and actions that he was truly God and Lord of the universe, said to his disciples as he was about to go up to Jerusalem: *We are going up to Jerusalem now, and the Son of Man will be handed over to the Gentiles and the chief priests and scribes to be scourged and mocked and crucified*[Mk 10:33].

These words bore out the predictions of the prophets, who had foretold the death he was to die in Jerusalem. From the beginning holy Scripture had foretold Christ's death, the sufferings that would precede it, and what would happen to his body afterward. Scripture also affirmed that these things were going to happen to one who was immortal and incapable of suffering because he was God.

How could he have been God? Only by reflecting upon the meaning of the incarnation can we see how it is possible to say with perfect truth both that Christ suffered and that he was incapable of suffering, and why the Word of God, in himself incapable of suffering, came to suffer. In fact, man could have been saved in no other way, as Christ alone knew and those to whom he revealed it. For he knows all secrets of the Father. Even as the Spirit penetrates the depths of all mysteries.

It was necessary for Christ to suffer: his passion was absolutely unavoidable. He said so himself when he called his companions dull and slow to believe because they failed to recognize that he had to suffer and so enter into his glory. Leaving behind him the glory that had been his with the Father before the world was made, he had gone forth to save his people. This salvation, however, could be achieved only by the suffering of the author of our life, as Paul taught when he said that *the author of life himself was made perfect through suffering*[Heb 2:10]. Because of us he was deprived of his glory for a little while, the glory that was his as the Father's only-begotten Son, but through the cross this glory is seen to have been restored to him in a certain way in the body that he had assumed. Explaining what water the Savior referred to when he said: *He that has faith in me shall have rivers of living water flowing from within him*[Jn 7:38], John says in his gospel that *he was speaking of the Holy Spirit which those who believed in him were to receive, for the Spirit had not yet been given because Jesus had not yet been glorified*[Jn 7:39]. The glorification he meant was his death upon the cross for which the Lord prayed to the Father before undergoing his passion, asking his Father to give him the glory that he had in his presence before the world began.

Wednesday within the Octave of Easter

From an Easter homily by an ancient author

Christ the source of resurrection and life

Saint Paul rejoices in the knowledge that spiritual health has been restored to the human race. *Death entered the world through Adam,* he explains, *but life has been given back to the world through Christ*[Rom 5:12-21]. Again he says: *The first man, being from the earth, is earthly by nature; the second man is from heaven and is heavenly. As we have borne the image of the earthly man,* the image of human nature grown old in sin, *so let us bear the image of the heavenly man*[1 Cor 15:47-49]*:* human nature raised up, redeemed, restored and purified in Christ. We must hold fast to the salvation we have received. *Christ was the firstfruits,* says the Apostle; *he is the source of resurrection and life. Those who belong to Christ will follow him*[1 Cor 15:20]. Modeling their lives on his purity, they will be secure in the hope of his resurrection and of enjoying with him the glory promised in heaven. Our Lord himself said so in the gospel: *Whoever follows me will not perish, but will pass from death to life*[Jn 5:24].

Thus the passion of our Savior is the salvation of mankind. The reason why he desired to die for us was that he wanted us who believe in him to live for ever. In the fullness of time it was his will to become what we are, so that we might inherit the eternity he promised and live with him for ever.

Here, then, is the grace conferred by these heavenly mysteries, the gift which Easter brings, the most longed for feast of the year; here are the beginnings of creatures newly formed: children born from the life-giving font of holy Church, born anew with the simplicity of little ones, and crying out with the evidence of a clean conscience. Chaste fathers and inviolate mothers accompany this new family, countless in number, born to new life through faith. As they emerge from the grace-giving womb of the font, a blaze of candles burns brightly beneath the tree of faith. The Easter festival brings the grace of holiness from heaven to men. Through the repeated celebration of the sacred mysteries they receive the spiritual nourishment of the sacraments. Fostered at the very heart of holy Church, the fellowship of one community worships the one God, adoring the triple name of his essential holiness, and together with the prophet sings the psalm which belongs to this yearly festival: *This is the day the Lord has made; let us rejoice and be glad*[Ps 117:24]. And what is this day? It is the Lord Jesus Christ himself, the author of light, who brings the sunrise and the beginning of life, saying of himself: *I am the light of day; whoever walks in daylight does not stumble*[Jn 11:9]. That is to say, whoever follows Christ in all things will come by this path to the throne of eternal light.

Such was the prayer Christ made to the Father while he was still on earth: *Father, I desire that where I am they also may be, those who have come to believe in me; and that as you are in me and I in you, so they may abide in us*[Jn 17:24].

Thursday within the Octave of Easter

From the Jerusalem Catecheses

Baptism is a symbol of Christ's passion

You were led down to the font of holy baptism just as Christ was taken down from the cross and placed in the tomb which is before your eyes. Each of you was asked, "Do you believe in the name of the Father, and of the Son, and of the Holy Spirit?" You made the profession of faith that brings salvation, you were plunged into the water, and three times you rose again. This symbolized the three days Christ spent in the tomb.

As our Savior spent three days and three nights in the depths of the earth, so your first rising from the water represented the first day and your first immersion represented the first night. At night a man cannot see, but in the day he walks in the light. So when you were immersed in the water it was like night for you and you could not see, but when you rose again it was like coming into broad daylight. In the same instant you died and were born again; the saving water was both your tomb and your mother.

Solomon's phrase in another context is very apposite here. He spoke of *a time to give birth, and a time to die*[Eccl 3:]*2*. For you, however, it was the reverse: a time to die, and a time to be born, although in fact both events took place at the same time and your birth was simultaneous with your death.

This is something amazing and unheard of! It was not we who actually died, were buried and rose again. We only did these things symbolically, but we have been saved in actual fact. It is Christ who was crucified, who was buried and who rose again, and all this has been attributed to us. We share in his sufferings symbolically and gain salvation in reality. What boundless love for men! Christ's undefiled hands were pierced by the nails; he suffered the pain. I experience no pain, no anguish, yet by the share that I have in his sufferings he freely grants me salvation.

Let no one imagine that baptism consists only in the forgiveness of sins and in the grace of adoption. Our baptism is not like the baptism of John, which conferred only the forgiveness of sins. We know perfectly well that baptism, besides washing away our sins and bringing us the gift of the Holy Spirit, is a symbol of the sufferings of Christ. This is why Paul exclaims: *Do you not know that when we were baptized into Christ Jesus we were, by that very action, sharing in his death? By baptism we went with him into the tomb*[Rom 6:3-4].

Friday within the Octave of Easter

From the Jerusalem Catecheses

The anointing with the Holy Spirit

When we were baptized into Christ and clothed ourselves in him, we were transformed into the likeness of the Son of God. Having destined us to be his adopted sons, God gave us a likeness to Christ in his glory, and living as we do in communion with Christ, God's anointed, we ourselves are rightly called "the anointed ones." When he said: *Do not touch my anointed ones*[Ps 104:15], God was speaking of us.

We became "the anointed ones" when we received the sign of the Holy Spirit. Indeed, everything took place in us by means of images, because we ourselves are images of Christ. Christ bathed in the river Jordan, imparting to its waters the fragrance of his divinity, and when he came up from them the Holy Spirit descended upon him, like resting upon like. So we also, after coming up from the sacred waters of baptism, were anointed with chrism, which signifies the Holy Spirit, by whom Christ was anointed and of whom blessed Isaiah prophesied in the name of the Lord: *The Spirit of the Lord is upon me, because he has anointed me. He has sent me to preach good news to the poor*[Isa 61:1-2; Lk 4:18].

Christ's anointing was not by human hands, nor was it with ordinary oil. On the contrary, having destined him to be the Savior of the whole world, the Father himself anointed him with the Holy Spirit. The words of Peter bear witness to this: *Jesus of Nazareth, whom God anointed with the Holy Spirit*[Acts 10:38]. And David the prophet proclaimed: *Your throne, O God, shall endure for ever; your royal scepter is a scepter of justice. You have loved righteousness and hated iniquity; therefore God, your God, has anointed you with the oil of gladness above all your fellows*[Ps 44:7-8].

The oil of gladness with which Christ was anointed was a spiritual oil; it was in fact the Holy Spirit himself, who is called *the oil of gladness*[Heb 1:9] because he is the source of spiritual joy. But we too have been anointed with oil, and by this anointing we have entered into fellowship with Christ and have received a share in his life. Beware of thinking that this holy oil is simply ordinary oil and nothing else. After the invocation of the Spirit it is no longer ordinary oil but the gift of Christ, and by the presence of his divinity it becomes the instrument through which we receive the Holy Spirit. While symbolically, on our foreheads and senses, our bodies are anointed with this oil that we see, our souls are sanctified by the holy and life-giving Spirit.

Saturday within the Octave of Easter

From the Jerusalem Catecheses

The bread of heaven and the cup of salvation

On the night he was betrayed our Lord Jesus Christ took bread, and when he had given thanks, he broke it and gave it to his disciples and said: "Take, eat: this is my body." He took the cup, gave thanks and said: "Take, drink: this is my blood."[Mt 26:26-28; Mk 14:22-24; Lk 22:19-20; 1Cor 11:23-26]; Since Christ himself has declared the bread to be his body, who can have any further doubt? Since he himself has said quite categorically, *This is my blood*[Mt 26:26-28; Mk 14:22-24; Lk 22:19-20; 1Cor 11:23-26], who would dare to question it and say that it is not his blood?

Therefore, it is with complete assurance that we receive the bread and wine as the body and blood of Christ. His body is given to us under the symbol of bread, and his blood is given to us under the symbol of wine, in order to make us by receiving them one body and blood with him. Having his body and blood in our members, we become bearers of Christ and sharers, as Saint Peter says, in the divine nature.

Once, when speaking to the Jews, Christ said: *Unless you eat my flesh and drink my blood you shall have no life in you*[Jn 6:53]. This horrified them and they left him. Not understanding his words in a spiritual way, they thought the Savior wished them to practice cannibalism.

Under the old covenant there was showbread, but it came to an end with the old dispensation to which it belonged. Under the new covenant there is bread from heaven and the cup of salvation. These sanctify both soul and body, the bread being adapted to the sanctification of the body, the Word, to the sanctification of the soul.

Do not, then, regard the eucharistic elements as ordinary bread and wine: they are in fact the body and blood of the Lord, as he himself has declared. Whatever your senses may tell you, be strong in faith.

You have been taught and you are firmly convinced that what looks and tastes like bread and wine is not bread and wine but the body and the blood of Christ. You know also how David referred to this long ago when he sang: *Bread gives strength to man's heart and makes his face shine with the oil of gladness*[Ps 103:14-15]. Strengthen your heart, then, by receiving this bread as spiritual bread, and bring joy to the face of your soul.

May purity of conscience remove the veil from the face of your soul so that by contemplating the glory of the Lord, as in a mirror, you may be transformed from glory to glory in Christ Jesus our Lord. To him be glory for ever and ever. Amen

Second Sunday of Easter

Divine Mercy Sunday

From a sermon by Saint Augustine, Bishop & Doctor

A new creation in Christ

I speak to you who have just been reborn in baptism, my little children in Christ, you who are the new offspring of the Church, gift of the Father, proof of Mother Church's fruitfulness. All of you who stand fast in the Lord are a holy seed, a new colony of bees, the very flower of our ministry and fruit of our toil, my joy and my crown. It is the words of the Apostle that I address to you: *Put on the Lord Jesus Christ, and make no provision for the flesh and its desires*[Rom 13:14], so that you may be clothed with the life of him whom you have put on in this sacrament. *You have all been clothed with Christ by your baptism in him. There is neither Jew nor Greek; there is neither slave nor freeman; there is neither male nor female; you are all one in Christ Jesus*[Gal 3:27].

Such is the power of this sacrament: it is a sacrament of new life which begins here and now with the forgiveness of all past sins, and will be brought to completion in the resurrection of the dead. *You have been buried with Christ by baptism into death in order that, as Christ has risen from the dead, you also may walk in newness of life*[Rom 6:4].

You are walking now by faith, still on pilgrimage in a mortal body away from the Lord; but he to whom your steps are directed is himself the sure and certain way for you: Jesus Christ, who for our sake became man. For all who fear him he has stored up abundant happiness, which he will reveal to those who hope in him, bringing it to completion when we have attained the reality which even now we possess in hope.

This is the octave day of your new birth. Today is fulfilled in you the sign of faith that was prefigured in the Old Testament by the circumcision of the flesh on the eighth day after birth. When the Lord rose from the dead, he put off the mortality of the flesh; his risen body was still the same body, but it was no longer subject to death. By his resurrection he consecrated Sunday, or the Lord's day. Though the third after his passion, this day is the eighth after the Sabbath, and thus also the first day of the week.

And so your own hope of resurrection, though not yet realized, is sure and certain, because you have received the sacrament or sign of this reality, and have been given the pledge of the Spirit. *If, then, you have risen with Christ, seek the things that are above, where Christ is seated at the right hand of God. Set your hearts on heavenly things, not the things that are on earth. For you have died and your life is hidden with Christ in God. When Christ, your life, appears, then you too will appear with him in glory*[Col 3:1-4].

Monday of the Second Week of Easter

From an ancient Easter homily by Pseudo-Chrysostom

The spiritual Passover

The Passover we celebrate brings salvation to the whole human race beginning with the first man, who together with all others is saved and given life.

In an imperfect and transitory way, the types and images of the past prefigured the perfect and eternal reality which has now been revealed. The presence of what is represented makes the symbol obsolete: when the king appears in person no one pays reverence to his statue.

How far the symbol falls short of the reality is seen from the fact that the symbolic Passover celebrated the brief life of the firstborn of the Jews, whereas the real Passover celebrates the eternal life of all mankind. It is a small gain to escape death for a short time, only to die soon afterward; it is a very different thing to escape death altogether as we do through the sacrifice of Christ, our Passover.

Correctly understood, its very name shows why this is our greatest feast. It is called the Passover because, when he was striking down the firstborn, the destroying angel passed over the houses of the Hebrews, but it is even more true to say that he passes over us, for he does so once for all when we are raised up by Christ to eternal life.

If we think only of the true Passover and ask why it is that the time of the Passover and the salvation of the firstborn is taken to be the beginning of the year, the answer must surely be that the sacrifice of the true Passover is for us the beginning of eternal life. Because it revolves in cycles and never comes to an end, the year is a symbol of eternity.

Christ, the sacrifice that was offered for us, is the father of the world to come. He puts an end to our former life, and through the regenerating waters of baptism in which we imitate his death and resurrection, he gives us the beginning of a new life. The knowledge that Christ is the Passover lamb who was sacrificed for us should make us regard the moment of his immolation as the beginning of our own lives. As far as we are concerned, Christ's immolation on our behalf takes place when we become aware of this grace and understand the life conferred on us by this sacrifice. Having once understood it, we should enter upon this new life with all eagerness and never return to the old one, which is now at an end. As Scripture says: *We have died to sin – how then can we continue to live in it*[Rom 6:2]?

Tuesday of the Second Week of Easter

From a book addressed to Monimus by Saint Fulgentius of Ruspe, Bishop

The sacrament of unity and love

The spiritual building up of the body of Christ is achieved through love. As Saint Peter says: *Like living stones you are built into a spiritual house, to be a holy priesthood, offering spiritual sacrifices acceptable to God through Jesus Christ*[1 Pet 2:5]. And there can be no more effective way to pray for this spiritual growth than for the Church, itself Christ's body, to make the offering of his body and blood in the sacramental form of bread and wine. *For the cup we drink is a participation in the blood of Christ, and the bread we break is a participation in the body of Christ. Because there is one loaf, we who are many are one body, since we all share the same bread*[1 Cor 10:16-17]. And so we pray that, by the same grace which made the Church Christ's body, all its members may remain firm in the unity of that body through the enduring bond of love.

We are right to pray that this may be brought about in us through the gift of the one Spirit of the Father and the Son. The holy Trinity, the one true God, is of its nature unity, equality and love, and by one divine activity sanctifies its adopted sons. That is why Scripture says that *God's love has been poured into our hearts by the Holy Spirit he has given us*[Rom 5:5]. The Holy Spirit, who is the one Spirit of the Father and the Son, produces in those to whom he gives the grace of divine adoption the same effect as he produced among those whom the Acts of the Apostles describes as having received the Holy Spirit. We are told that *the company of those who believed were of one heart and soul*[Acts 4:32], because the one Spirit of the Father and the Son, who with the Father and the Son is one God, had created a single heart and soul in all those who believed.

This is why Saint Paul in his exhortation to the Ephesians says that this spiritual unity in the bond of peace must be carefully preserved. *I, therefore, a prisoner for the Lord,* he writes, *beg you to lead a life worthy of your calling, with all humility and meekness and with patience, bearing with one another in love, eager to maintain the unity of the Spirit in the bond of peace. There is one body and one Spirit*[Eph 4:1-4]. God makes the Church itself a sacrifice pleasing in his sight by preserving within it the love which his Holy Spirit has poured out. Thus the grace of that spiritual love is always available to us, enabling us continually to offer ourselves to God as a living sacrifice, holy and pleasing to him for ever.

Wednesday of the Second Week of Easter

From a sermon by Saint Leo the Great, Pope & Doctor

Christ lives in his Church

My dear brethren, there is no doubt that the Son of God took our human nature into so close a union with himself that one and the same Christ is present, not only in the firstborn of all creation, but in all his saints as well. The head cannot be separated from the members, nor the members from the head. Not in this life, it is true, but only in eternity will God be all in all, yet even now he dwells, whole and undivided, in his temple the Church. Such was his promise to us when he said: *See, I am with you always, even to the end of the world*[Mt 28:20].

And so all that the Son of God did and taught for the world's reconciliation is not for us simply a matter of past history. Here and now we experience his power at work among us. Born of a virgin mother by the action of the Holy Spirit, Christ keeps his Church spotless and makes her fruitful by the inspiration of the same Spirit. In baptismal regeneration she brings forth children for God beyond all numbering. These are the sons of whom it is written: *They are born not of blood, nor of the desire of the flesh, nor of the will of man, but of God*[Jn 1:13].

In Christ Abraham's posterity is blessed, because in him the whole world receives the adoption of sons, and in him the patriarch becomes the father of all nations through the birth, not from human stock but by faith, of the descendants that were promised to him. From every nation on earth, without exception, Christ forms a single flock of those he has sanctified, daily fulfilling the promise he once made: *I have other sheep, not of this fold, whom it is also ordained that I shall lead; and there shall be one flock and one shepherd*[Jn 10:16].

Although it was primarily to Peter that he said: *Feed my sheep,* yet the one Lord guides all pastors in the discharge of their office and leads to rich and fertile pastures all those who come to the rock. There is no counting the sheep who are nourished with his abundant love, and who are prepared to lay down their lives for the sake of the good shepherd who died for them.

But it is not only the martyrs who share in his passion by their glorious courage; the same is true, by faith, of all who are born again in baptism. That is why we are to celebrate the Lord's paschal sacrifice with the unleavened bread of sincerity and truth. The leaven of our former malice is thrown out, and a new creature is filled and inebriated with the Lord himself. For the effect of our sharing in the body and blood of Christ is to change us into what we receive. As we have died with him, and have been buried and raised to life with him, so we bear him within us, both in body and in spirit, in everything we do.

Thursday of the Second Week of Easter

From a sermon by Saint Gaudentius of Brescia, Bishop

The inheritance of the new Covenant

The heavenly sacrifice, instituted by Christ, is the most gracious legacy of his new covenant. On the night he was delivered up to be crucified he left us this gift as a pledge of his abiding presence.

This sacrifice is our sustenance on life's journey; by it we are nourished and supported along the road of life until we depart from this world and make our way to the Lord. For this reason he addressed these words to us: *Unless you eat my flesh and drink my blood, you will not have life in you*[Jn 6:53-58].

It was the Lord's will that his gifts should remain with us, and that we who have been redeemed by his precious blood should constantly be sanctified according to the pattern of his own passion. And so he commanded those faithful disciples of his whom he made the first priests of his Church to enact these mysteries of eternal life continuously. All priests throughout the churches of the world must celebrate these mysteries until Christ comes again from heaven. Therefore let us all, priests and people alike, be faithful to this everlasting memorial of our redemption. Daily it is before our eyes as a representation of the passion of Christ. We hold it in our hands, we receive it in our mouths, and we accept it in our hearts.

It is appropriate that we should receive the body of Christ in the form of bread, because, as there are many grains of wheat in the flour from which bread is made by mixing it with water and baking it with fire, so also we know that many members make up the one body of Christ which is brought to maturity by the fire of the Holy Spirit. Christ was born of the Holy Spirit, and since it was fitting that he should fulfill all justice, he entered into the waters of baptism to sanctify them. When he left the Jordan he was filled with the Holy Spirit who had descended upon him in the form of a dove. As the evangelist tells us: *Jesus, full of the Holy Spirit, returned from the Jordan*[Lk 4:1].

Similarly, the wine of Christ's blood, drawn from the many grapes of the vineyard that he had planted, is extracted in the winepress of the cross. When men receive it with believing hearts, like capacious wineskins, it ferments within them by its own power.

And so, now that you have escaped from the power of Egypt and of Pharaoh, who is the devil, join with us, all of you, in receiving this sacrifice of the saving passover with the eagerness of dedicated hearts. Then in our inmost being we shall be wholly sanctified by the very Lord Jesus Christ whom we believe to be present in his sacraments, and whose boundless power abides for ever.

Friday of the Second Week of Easter

From a sermon by Saint Theodore the Studite, Abbot

The precious and life-giving cross of Christ

How precious the gift of the cross, how splendid to contemplate! In the cross there is no mingling of good and evil, as in the tree of paradise: it is wholly beautiful to behold and good to taste. The fruit of this tree is not death but life, not darkness but light. This tree does not cast us out of paradise, but opens the way for our return.

This was the tree on which Christ, like a king on a chariot, destroyed the devil, the Lord of death, and freed the human race from his tyranny. This was the tree upon which the Lord, like a brave warrior wounded in his hands, feet and side, healed the wounds of sin that the evil serpent had inflicted on our nature. A tree once caused our death, but now a tree brings life. Once deceived by a tree, we have now repelled the cunning serpent by a tree. What an astonishing transformation! That death should become life, that decay should become immortality, that shame should become glory! Well might the holy Apostle exclaim: *Far be it from me to glory except in the cross of our Lord Jesus Christ, by which the world has been crucified to me, and I to the world*[Gal 6:14]*!* The supreme wisdom that flowered on the cross has shown the folly of worldly wisdom's pride. The knowledge of all good, which is the fruit of the cross, has cut away the shoots of wickedness.

The wonders accomplished through this tree were foreshadowed clearly even by the mere types and figures that existed in the past. Meditate on these, if you are eager to learn. Was it not the wood of a tree that enabled Noah, at God's command, to escape the destruction of the flood together with his sons, his wife, his sons' wives and every kind of animal? And surely the rod of Moses prefigured the cross when it changed water into blood, swallowed up the false serpents of Pharaoh's magicians, divided the sea at one stroke and then restored the waters to their normal course, drowning the enemy and saving God's own people? Aaron's rod, which blossomed in one day in proof of his true priesthood, was another figure of the cross, and did not Abraham foreshadow the cross when he bound his son Isaac and placed him on the pile of wood?

By the cross death was slain and Adam was restored to life. The cross is the glory of all the apostles, the crown of the martyrs, the sanctification of the saints. By the cross we put on Christ and cast aside our former self. By the cross we, the sheep of Christ, have been gathered into one flock, destined for the sheepfolds of heaven.

Saturday of the Second Week of Easter

From the constitution on the Sacred Liturgy of the Second Vatican Council *Sacrosanctum Concilium*

God's plan of salvation

In his desire that all men should be saved and come to the knowledge of the truth[1 Tim 2:3-4]*, God spoke in former times to our forefathers through the prophets, on many occasions and in different ways*[Heb 1:1-2]. Then, in the fullness of time he sent his Son, the Word made man, anointed by the Holy Spirit, to bring good news to the poor, to heal the broken-hearted as the physician of body and spirit and the mediator between God and men. In the unity of the person of the Word, his human nature was the instrument of our salvation. Thus in Christ there has come to be the perfect atonement that reconciles us with God, and we have been given the power to offer the fullness of divine worship.

This work of man's redemption and God's perfect glory was foreshadowed by God's mighty deeds among the people of the Old Covenant. It was brought to fulfillment by Christ the Lord, especially through the paschal mystery of his blessed passion, resurrection from the dead and ascension in glory: by dying he destroyed our death, and by rising again he restored our life. From his side, as he lay asleep on the cross, was born that wonderful sacrament which is the Church in its entirety.

As Christ was sent by the Father, so in his turn he sent the apostles, filled with the Holy Spirit. They were sent to preach the Gospel to every creature, proclaiming that we had been set free from the power of Satan and from death by the death and resurrection of God's Son, and brought into the kingdom of the Father. They were sent also to bring into effect this saving work that they proclaimed, by means of the sacrifice and sacraments that are the pivot of the whole life of the liturgy.

So, by baptism men are brought within the paschal mystery. Dead with Christ, buried with Christ, risen with Christ, they receive the Spirit that makes them God's adopted children, crying out: *Abba, Father;* and so they become the true adorers that the Father seeks.

In the same way, whenever they eat the supper of the Lord they proclaim his death until he comes. So, on the very day of Pentecost, on which the Church was manifested to the world, those *who received the word of Peter were baptized. They remained steadfast in the teaching of the apostles and in the communion of the breaking of bread, praising God and enjoying the favor of all the people*[Acts 2:41-42].

From that time onward the Church has never failed to come together to celebrate the paschal mystery, by *what was written about him in every part of Scripture*[Lk 24:44], by celebrating the eucharist in which the victory and triumph of his death are shown forth, and also by giving thanks *to God for the inexpressible gift*[2 Cor 9:15] he has given in Christ Jesus, *to the praise of God's glory.*

Sunday of the Third Week of Easter

From the first apology in defense of the Christians by Saint Justin, Martyr

The celebration of the eucharist

No one may share the eucharist with us unless he believes that what we teach is true, unless he is washed in the regenerating waters of baptism for the remission of his sins, and unless he lives in accordance with the principles given us by Christ.

We do not consume the eucharistic bread and wine as if it were ordinary food and drink, for we have been taught that as Jesus Christ our Savior became a man of flesh and blood by the power of the Word of God, so also the food that our flesh and blood assimilates for its nourishment becomes the flesh and blood of the incarnate Jesus by the power of his own words contained in the prayer of thanksgiving.

The apostles, in their recollections, which are called gospels, handed down to us what Jesus commanded them to do. They tell us that he took bread, gave thanks and said: *Do this in memory of me. This is my body*[Lk 22:19]. In the same way he took the cup, he gave thanks and said: *This is my blood.* The Lord gave this command to them alone. Ever since then we have constantly reminded one another of these things. The rich among us help the poor and we are always united. For all that we receive we praise the Creator of the universe through his Son Jesus Christ and through the Holy Spirit.

On Sunday we have a common assembly of all our members, whether they live in the city or the outlying districts. The recollections of the apostles or the writings of the prophets are read, as long as there is time. When the reader has finished, the president of the assembly speaks to us; he urges everyone to imitate the examples of virtue we have heard in the s. Then we all stand up together and pray.

On the conclusion of our prayer, bread and wine and water are brought forward. The president offers prayers and gives thanks to the best of his ability, and the people give their assent by saying, "Amen." The eucharist is distributed, everyone present communicates, and the deacons take it to those who are absent.

The wealthy, if they wish, may make a contribution, and they themselves decide the amount. The collection is placed in the custody of the president, who uses it to help the orphans and widows and all who for any reason are in distress, whether because they are sick, in prison, or away from home. In a word, he takes care of all who are in need.

We hold our common assembly on Sunday because it is the first day of the week, the day on which God put darkness and chaos to flight and created the world, and because on that same day our Savior Jesus Christ rose from the dead. For he was crucified on Friday and on Sunday he appeared to his apostles and disciples and taught them the things that we have passed on for your consideration.

Monday of the Third Week of Easter

From the commentary on the first letter of Peter by Saint Bede the Venerable, Priest & Doctor

A chosen race, a royal priesthood

You are a chosen race, a royal priesthood[1 Pet 2:9]. This praise was given long ago by Moses to the ancient people of God, and now the apostle Peter rightly gives it to the Gentiles, since they have come to believe in Christ who, as the cornerstone, has brought the nations together in the salvation that belonged to Israel.

Peter calls them *a chosen race* because of their faith, to distinguish them from those who by refusing to accept the living stone have themselves been rejected. They are *a royal priesthood* because they are united to the body of Christ, the supreme king and true priest. As sovereign he grants them his kingdom, and as high priest he washes away their sins by the offering of his blood. Peter says they are *a royal priesthood;* they must always remember to hope for an everlasting kingdom and to offer to God the sacrifice of a blameless life.

They are also called *a consecrated nation, a people claimed by God as his own*[1 Pet 2:9], in accordance with the apostle Paul's explanation of the prophet's teaching: *My righteous man lives by faith; but if he draws back, I will take no pleasure in him. But we,* he says, *are not the sort of people who draw back and are lost; we are those who remain faithful until we are saved*[Heb 10:38-39]. In the Acts of the Apostles we read: *The Holy Spirit has made you overseers, to care for the Church of God which he bought with his own blood*[Acts 20:28]. Thus, through the blood of our Redeemer, we have become *a people claimed by God as his own,* as in ancient times the people of Israel were ransomed from Egypt by the blood of a lamb.

In the next verse, Peter also makes a veiled allusion to the ancient story, and explains that this story is to be spiritually fulfilled by the new people of God, *so that,* he says, *they may declare his wonderful deeds*[Ps 95:3]. Those who were freed by Moses from slavery in Egypt sang a song of triumph to the Lord after they had crossed the Red Sea and Pharaoh's army had been overwhelmed; in the same way, now that our sins have been washed away in baptism, we too should express fitting gratitude for the gifts of heaven. The Egyptians who oppressed the people of God, and who can also stand for darkness or trials, are an apt symbol of the sins that once oppressed us but have now been destroyed in baptism.

The deliverance of the children of Israel and their journey to the long-promised land correspond with the mystery of our redemption. We are making our way toward the light of our heavenly home with the grace of Christ leading us and showing us the way. The light of his grace was also symbolized by the cloud and the pillar of fire, which protected the Israelites from darkness throughout their journey, and brought them by a wonderful path to their promised homeland.

Tuesday of the Third Week of Easter

From a sermon by Saint Augustine, Bishop & Doctor

Let us sing to the Lord a song of love

Sing to the Lord a new song; his praise is in the assembly of the saints[Ps 148:1-4]. We are urged to sing a new song to the Lord, as new men who have learned a new song. A song is a thing of joy; more profoundly, it is a thing of love. Anyone, therefore, who has learned to love the new life has learned to sing a new song, and the new song reminds us of our new life. The new man, the new song, the new covenant, all belong to the one kingdom of God, and so the new man will sing a new song and will belong to the new covenant.

There is not one who does not love something, but the question is, what to love. The psalms do not tell us not to love, but to choose the object of our love. But how can we choose unless we are first chosen? We cannot love unless someone has loved us first. Listen to the apostle John: *We love him, because he first loved us*[1 Jn 4:19]. The source of man's love for God can only be found in the fact that God loved him first. He has given us himself as the object of our love, and he has also given us its source. What this source is you may learn more clearly from the apostle Paul who tells us: *The love of God has been poured into our hearts*[Rom 5:5]. This love is not something we generate ourselves; it comes to us *through the Holy Spirit who has been given to us*[Rom 5:5].

Since we have such an assurance, then, let us love God with the love he has given us. As John tells us more fully: *God is love, and whoever dwells in love dwells in God, and God in him*[1 Jn 4:16]. It is not enough to say: *Love is from God*[1 Jn 4:7-8]. Which of us would dare to pronounce the words of Scripture: *God is love?* He alone could say it who knew what it was to have God dwelling within him. God offers us a short route to the possession of himself. He cries out: Love me and you will have me for you would be unable to love me if you did not possess me already.

My dear brothers and sons, fruit of the true faith and holy seed of heaven, all you who have been born again in Christ and whose life is from above, listen to me; or rather, listen to the Holy Spirit saying through me: *Sing to the Lord a new song*. Look, you tell me, I am singing. Yes indeed, you are singing; you are singing clearly, I can hear you. But make sure that your life does not contradict your words. Sing with your voices, your hearts, your lips and your lives: *Sing to the Lord a new song.*

Now it is your unquestioned desire to sing of him whom you love, but you ask me how to sing his praises. You have heard the words: *Sing to the Lord a new song,* and you wish to know what praises to sing. The answer is: *His praise is in the assembly of the saints;* it is in the singers themselves. If you desire to praise him, then live what you express. Live good lives, and you yourselves will be his praise.

From the first apology in defense of the Christians by Saint Justin, Martyr

Baptismal regeneration

Through Christ we received new life and we consecrated ourselves to God. I will explain the way in which we did this. Those who believe what we teach is true and who give assurance of their ability to live according to that teaching are taught to ask God's forgiveness for their sins by prayer and fasting and we pray and fast with them. We then lead them to a place where there is water and they are reborn in the same way as we were reborn; that is to say, they are washed in the water in the name of God, the Father and Lord of the whole universe, of our Savior Jesus Christ and of the Holy Spirit. This is done because Christ said: *Unless you are born again you will not enter the kingdom of heaven*[Jn 3:3], and it is obviously impossible for anyone, having once been born, to reenter his mother's womb.

An explanation of how repentant sinners are to be freed from their sins is given through the prophet Isaiah in the words: *Wash yourselves and be clean. Remove the evil from your souls; learn to do what is right. Be just to the orphan, vindicate the widow. Come, let us reason together, says the Lord. If your sins are like scarlet, I will make them white as wool; if they are like crimson, I will make them white as snow. But if you do not heed me, you shall be devoured by the sword. The mouth of the Lord has spoken*[Isa 1:16-20].

The apostles taught us the reason for this ceremony of ours. Our first birth took place without our knowledge or consent because our parents came together, and we grew up in the midst of wickedness. So if we were not to remain children of necessity and ignorance, we needed a new birth of which we ourselves would be conscious, and which would be the result of our own free choice. We needed, too, to have our sins forgiven. This is why the name of God, the Father and Lord of the whole universe, is pronounced in the water over anyone who chooses to be born again and who has repented of his sins. The person who leads the candidate for baptism to the font calls upon God by this name alone, for God so far surpasses our powers of description that no one can really give a name to him. Anyone who dares to say that he can must be hopelessly insane.

This baptism is called "illumination" because of the mental enlightenment that is experienced by those who learn these things. The person receiving this enlightenment is also baptized in the name of Jesus Christ, who was crucified under Pontius Pilate, and in the name of the Holy Spirit, who through the prophets foretold everything concerning Jesus.

Thursday of the Third Week of Easter

From the treatise Against Heresies by Saint Irenaeus, Bishop, Doctor & Martyr

The eucharist, pledge of our resurrection

If our flesh is not saved, then the Lord has not redeemed us with his blood, the eucharistic chalice does not make us sharers in his blood, and the bread we break does not make us sharers in his body. There can be no blood without veins, flesh and the rest of the human substance, and this the Word of God actually became: it was with his own blood that he redeemed us. As the Apostle says: *In him, through his blood, we have been redeemed, our sins have been forgiven*[Eph 1:7].

We are his members and we are nourished by creation, which is his gift to us, for it is he who causes the sun to rise and the rain to fall. He declared that the chalice, which comes from his creation, was his blood, and he makes it the nourishment of our blood. He affirmed that the bread, which comes from his creation, was his body, and he makes it the nourishment of our body. When the chalice we mix and the bread we bake receive the word of God, the eucharistic elements become the body and blood of Christ, by which our bodies live and grow. How then can it be said that flesh belonging to the Lord's own body and nourished by his body and blood is incapable of receiving God's gift of eternal life? Saint Paul says in his letter to the Ephesians that *we are members of his body*[Eph 5:30], of his flesh and bones. He is not speaking of some spiritual and incorporeal kind of man, *for spirits do not have flesh and bones*[Lk 24:39]. He is speaking of a real human body composed of flesh, sinews and bones, nourished by the chalice of Christ's blood and receiving growth from the bread which is his body.

The slip of a vine planted in the ground bears fruit at the proper time. The grain of wheat falls into the ground and decays only to be raised up again and multiplied by the Spirit of God who sustains all things. The Wisdom of God places these things at the service of man and when they receive God's word they become the eucharist, which is the body and blood of Christ. In the same way our bodies, which have been nourished by the eucharist, will be buried in the earth and will decay, but they will rise again at the appointed time, for the Word of God will raise them up to the glory of God the Father. Then the Father will clothe our mortal nature in immortality and freely endow our corruptible nature with incorruptibility, for God's power is shown most perfectly in weakness.

Friday of the Third Week of Easter

From a sermon by Saint Ephrem, Deacon & Doctor

The cross of Christ gives life to the human race

Death trampled our Lord underfoot, but he in his turn treated death as a highroad for his own feet. He submitted to it, enduring it willingly, because by this means he would be able to destroy death in spite of itself. Death had its own way when our Lord went out from Jerusalem carrying his cross; but when by a loud cry from that cross he summoned the dead from the underworld, death was powerless to prevent it.

Death slew him by means of the body which he had assumed, but that same body proved to be the weapon with which he conquered death. Concealed beneath the cloak of his manhood, his godhead engaged death in combat; but in slaying our Lord, death itself was slain. It was able to kill natural human life, but was itself killed by the life that is above the nature of man.

Death could not devour our Lord unless he possessed a body, neither could hell swallow him up unless he bore our flesh; and so he came in search of a chariot in which to ride to the underworld. This chariot was the body which he received from the Virgin; in it he invaded death's fortress, broke open its strongroom and scattered all its treasure.

At length he came upon Eve, the mother of all the living. She was that vineyard whose enclosure her own hands had enabled death to violate, so that she could taste its fruit; thus the mother of all the living became the source of death for every living creature. But in her stead Mary grew up, a new vine in place of the old. Christ, the new life, dwelt within her. When death, with its customary impudence, came foraging for her mortal fruit, it encountered its own destruction in the hidden life that fruit contained. All unsuspecting, it swallowed him up, and in so doing released life itself and set free a multitude of men.

He who was also the carpenter's glorious son set up his cross above death's all-consuming jaws, and led the human race into the dwelling place of life. Since a tree had brought about the downfall of mankind, it was upon a tree that mankind crossed over to the realm of life. Bitter was the branch that had once been grafted upon that ancient tree, but sweet the young shoot that has now been grafted in, the shoot in which we are meant to recognize the Lord whom no creature can resist.

We give glory to you, Lord, who raised up your cross to span the jaws of death like a bridge by which souls might pass from the region of the dead to the land of the living. We give glory to you who put on the body of a single mortal man and made it the source of life for every other mortal man. You are incontestably alive. Your murderers sowed your living body in the earth as farmers sow grain, but it sprang up and yielded an abundant harvest of men raised from the dead.

Come then, my brothers and sisters, let us offer our Lord the great and all-embracing sacrifice of our love, pouring out our treasury of hymns and prayers before him who offered his cross in sacrifice to God for the enrichment of us all.

Saturday of the Third Week of Easter

From a commentary on the gospel of John by Saint Cyril of Alexandria, Bishop & Doctor

Christ gave his own body for the life of all men

"I am dying for all men," says the Lord. "I am dying to give them life through myself and to redeem the whole human race through my humanity. In my death, death itself will die and man's fallen nature will rise again with me. I wanted to be like my brothers in every respect, so I became a man like you, a descendant of Abraham." Understanding this well Saint Paul says: *As the children of a family share the same flesh and blood, he too shared our human nature so that by his death he could destroy the power of the devil, the prince of death*[Heb 2:14]. Death itself and the prince of death could be destroyed only by Christ, who is above all, giving himself up as a ransom for all.

And so, speaking as a spotless victim offering himself for us to God the Father, Christ says in one of the psalms: *You desired no sacrifices or offerings, but you have prepared a body for me. You took no pleasure in holocausts or sin offerings. Then I said, "Behold, I am coming*[Ps 39:7-8]*."* He was crucified for all, desiring his one death for all to give all of us life in him. It was impossible for him to be conquered by death; nor could he who by his very nature is life be subject to corruption. Yet we know that Christ offered his flesh for the life of the world from his own prayer, *Holy Father, protect them*[Jn 17:15-21]*,* and from his words, *For their sake I consecrate myself*[Jn 17:19]. By saying that he consecrates himself he means that he offers himself to God as a spotless and sweet-smelling sacrifice. According to the law, anything offered upon the altar was consecrated and considered holy. So Christ gave his own body for the life of all, and makes it the channel through which life flows once more into us. How he does this I will explain to the best of my ability.

When the life-giving Word of God dwelt in human flesh, he changed it into that good thing which is distinctively his, namely, life; and by being wholly united to the flesh in a way beyond our comprehension, he gave it the life-giving power which he has by his very nature. Therefore, the body of Christ gives life to those who receive it. Its presence in mortal men expels death and drives away corruption because it contains within itself in his entirety the Word who totally abolishes corruption.

Sunday of the Fourth Week of Easter

From a homily on the Gospels by Saint Gregory the Great, Pope & Doctor

Christ the Good Shepherd

I am the good shepherd. I know my own – by which I mean, I love them – *and my own know me*[Jn 10:14]. In plain words: those who love me are willing to follow me, for anyone who does not love the truth has not yet come to know it.

My dear brethren, you have heard the test we pastors have to undergo. Turn now to consider how these words of our Lord imply a test for yourselves also. Ask yourselves whether you belong to his flock, whether you know him, whether the light of his truth shines in your minds. I assure you that it is not by faith that you will come to know him, but by love; not by mere conviction, but by action. John the evangelist is my authority for this statement. He tells us that *anyone who claims to know God without keeping his commandments is a liar*[1 Jn 2:4].

Consequently, the Lord immediately adds: *As the Father knows me and I know the Father; and I lay down my life for my sheep*[Jn 10:15]. Clearly he means that laying down his life for his sheep gives evidence of his knowledge of the Father and the Father's knowledge of him. In other words, by the love with which he dies for his sheep he shows how greatly he loves his Father.

Again he says: *My sheep hear my voice, and I know them; they follow me, and I give them eternal life*[Jn 10:27-28]. Shortly before this he had declared: *If anyone enters the sheepfold through me he shall be saved; he shall go freely in and out and shall find good pasture*[Jn 10:9]. He will enter into a life of faith; from faith he will go out to vision, from belief to contemplation, and will graze in the good pastures of everlasting life.

So our Lord's sheep will finally reach their grazing ground where all who follow him in simplicity of heart will feed on the green pastures of eternity. These pastures are the spiritual joys of heaven. There the elect look upon the face of God with unclouded vision and feast at the banquet of life for ever more.

Beloved brothers, let us set out for these pastures where we shall keep joyful festival with so many of our fellow citizens. May the thought of their happiness urge us on! Let us stir up our hearts, rekindle our faith, and long eagerly for what heaven has in store for us. To love thus is to be already on our way. No matter what obstacles we encounter, we must not allow them to turn us aside from the joy of that heavenly feast. Anyone who is determined to reach his destination is not deterred by the roughness of the road that leads to it. Nor must we allow the charm of success to seduce us, or we shall be like a foolish traveler who is so distracted by the pleasant meadows through which he is passing that he forgets where he is going.

Monday of the Fourth Week of Easter

From the book On the Holy Spirit by Saint Basil the Great, Bishop & Doctor

The Spirit gives life

Our Lord made a covenant with us through baptism in order to give us eternal life. There is in baptism an image both of death and of life, the water being the symbol of death, the Spirit giving the pledge of life. The association of water and the Spirit is explained by the twofold purpose for which baptism was instituted, namely, to destroy the sin in us so that it could never again give birth to death, and to enable us to live by the Spirit and so win the reward of holiness. The water into which the body enters as into a tomb symbolizes death; the Spirit instills into us his life-giving power, awakening our souls from the death of sin to the life that they had in the beginning. This then is what it means to be born again of water and the Spirit: we die in the water, and we come to life again through the Spirit.

To signify this death and to enlighten the baptized by transmitting to them knowledge of God, the great sacrament of baptism is administered by means of a triple immersion and the invocation of each of the three divine Persons. Whatever grace there is in the water comes not from its own nature but from the presence of the Spirit, since *baptism is not a cleansing of the body, but a pledge made to God from a clear conscience*[1 Pet 3:21].

As a preparation for our life after the resurrection, our Lord tells us in the gospel how we should live here and now. He teaches us to be peaceable, long-suffering, undefiled by desire for pleasure, and detached from worldly wealth. In this way we can achieve, by our own free choice, the kind of life that will be natural in the world to come.

Through the Holy Spirit we are restored to paradise, we ascend to the kingdom of heaven, and we are reinstated as adopted sons. Thanks to the Spirit we obtain the right to call God our Father, we become sharers in the grace of Christ, we are called children of light, and we share in everlasting glory. In a word, every blessing is showered upon us, both in this world and in the world to come. As we contemplate them even now, like a reflection in a mirror, it is as though we already possessed the good things our faith tells us that we shall one day enjoy. If this is the pledge, what will the perfection be? If these are the first-fruits, what will the full harvest be?

Tuesday of the Fourth Week of Easter

From a sermon by Saint Peter Chrysologus, Bishop & Doctor

Each one of us is called to be both a sacrifice to God and his priest

I appeal to you by the mercy of God[Rom 12:1]. This appeal is made by Paul, or rather, it is made by God through Paul, because of God's desire to be loved rather than feared, to be a father rather than a Lord. God appeals to us in his mercy to avoid having to punish us in his severity.

Listen to the Lord's appeal: In me, I want you to see your own body, your members, your heart, your bones, your blood. You may fear what is divine, but why not love what is human? You may run away from me as the Lord, but why not run to me as your father? Perhaps you are filled with shame for causing my bitter passion. Do not be afraid. This cross inflicts a mortal injury, not on me, but on death. These nails no longer pain me, but only deepen your love for me. I do not cry out because of these wounds, but through them I draw you into my heart. My body was stretched on the cross as a symbol, not of how much I suffered, but of my all-embracing love. I count it no loss to shed my blood: it is the price I have paid for your ransom. Come, then, return to me and learn to know me as your father, who repays good for evil, love for injury, and boundless charity for piercing wounds.

Listen now to what the Apostle urges us to do. *I appeal to you,* he says, *to present your bodies as a living sacrifice*[Rom 12:1]. By this exhortation of his, Paul has raised all men to priestly status.

How marvelous is the priesthood of the Christian, for he is both the victim that is offered on his own behalf, and the priest who makes the offering. He does not need to go beyond himself to seek what he is to immolate to God: with himself and in himself he brings the sacrifice he is to offer God for himself. The victim remains and the priest remains, always one and the same. Immolated, the victim still lives: the priest who immolates cannot kill. Truly it is an amazing sacrifice in which a body is offered without being slain and blood is offered without being shed.

The Apostle says: *I appeal to you by the mercy of God to present your bodies as a living sacrifice*. Brethren, this sacrifice follows the pattern of Christ's sacrifice by which he gave his body as a living immolation for the life of the world. He really made his body a living sacrifice, because, though slain, he continues to live. In such a victim death receives its ransom, but the victim remains alive. Death itself suffers the punishment. This is why death for the martyrs is actually a birth, and their end a beginning. Their execution is the door to life, and those who were thought to have been blotted out from the earth shine brilliantly in heaven.

Paul says: *I appeal to you by the mercy of God to present your bodies as a sacrifice, living and holy*[Rom 12:1]. The prophet said the same thing: *Sacrifice and offering you did not desire, but you have prepared a body for me*[Heb 10:5; Ps 39:7-8]. Each of us is called to be both a sacrifice to God and his priest. Do not forfeit what divine authority confers on you. Put on the garment of holiness, gird yourself with the belt of chastity. Let Christ be your helmet, let the cross on your forehead be your unfailing protection. Your breastplate should be the knowledge of God that he himself has given you. Keep burning continually the sweet-smelling incense of prayer. Take up the sword of the Spirit. Let your heart be an altar. Then, with full confidence in God, present your body for sacrifice. God desires not death, but faith; God thirsts not for blood, but for self-surrender; God is appeased not by slaughter, but by the offering of your free will.

Wednesday of the Fourth Week of Easter

From the treatise On the Trinity by Saint Hilary, Bishop & Doctor

The unity of the faithful in God through the incarnation of the Word and the sacrament of the Eucharist

We believe that the Word became flesh and that we receive his flesh in the Lord's Supper. How then can we fail to believe that he really dwells within us? When he became man, he actually clothed himself in our flesh, uniting it to himself for ever. In the sacrament of his body he actually gives us his own flesh, which he has united to his divinity. This is why we are all one, because the Father is in Christ, and Christ is in us. He is in us through his flesh and we are in him. With him we form a unity which is in God.

The manner of our indwelling in him through the sacrament of his body and blood is evident from the Lord's own words: *This world will see me no longer but you shall see me. Because I live you shall live also, for I am in my Father, you are in me, and I am in you*[Jn 14:19-20]. If it had been a question of mere unity of will, why should he have given us this explanation of the steps by which it is achieved? He is in the Father by reason of his divine nature, we are in him by reason of his human birth, and he is in us through the mystery of the sacraments. This, surely, is what he wished us to believe; this is how he wanted us to understand the perfect unity that is achieved through our Mediator, who lives in the Father while we live in him, and who, while living in the Father, lives also in us. This is how we attain to unity with the Father. Christ is in very truth in the Father by his eternal generation; we are in very truth in Christ, and he likewise is in us.

Christ himself bore witness to the reality of this unity when he said: *He who eats my flesh and drinks my blood lives in me and I in him*[Jn 6:56]. No one will be in Christ unless Christ himself has been in him; Christ will take to himself only the flesh of those who have received his flesh.

He had already explained the mystery of this perfect unity when he said: *As the living Father sent me and I draw life from the Father, so he who eats my flesh will draw life from me*[Jn 6:57]. We draw life from his flesh just as he draws life from the Father. Such comparisons aid our understanding, since we can grasp a point more easily when we have an analogy. And the point is that Christ is the wellspring of our life. Since we who are in the flesh have Christ dwelling in us through his flesh, we shall draw life from him in the same way as he draws life from the Father.

Thursday of the Fourth Week of Easter

From a treatise on John by Saint Augustine, Bishop & Doctor

The new commandment

A new commandment I give you, that you love one another[Jn 13:34-35]. This commandment that he is giving them is a new one, the Lord Jesus tells his disciples. Yet was it not contained in the Old Law, where it is written: *You shall love your neighbor as yourself*? Why does the Lord call it new when it is clearly so old? Or is the commandment new because it divests us of our former selves and clothes us with the new man? Love does indeed renew the man who hears, or rather obeys its command; but only that love which Jesus distinguished from a natural love by the qualification: *As I have loved you*[Jn 13:34-35].

This is the kind of love that renews us. When we love as he loved us we become new men, heirs of the new covenant and singers of the new song. My brothers, this was the love that even in bygone days renewed the holy men, the patriarchs and prophets of old. In later times it renewed the blessed apostles, and now it is the turn of the Gentiles. From the entire human race throughout the world this love gathers together into one body a new people, to be the bride of God's only Son. She is the bride of whom it is asked in the Song of Songs: *Who is this who comes clothed in white*[Song 8:5]? White indeed are her garments, for she has been made new; and the source of her renewal is none other than this new commandment.

And so all her members make each other's welfare their common care. When one member suffers, all the members suffer with him, and if one member is glorified all the rest rejoice. They hear and obey the Lord's words: *A new commandment I give you, that you love one another*[Jn 13:34-35]; not as men love one another for their own selfish ends, nor merely on account of their common humanity, but because they are all gods and sons of the Most High. They love one another as God loves them so that they may be brothers of his only Son. He will lead them to the goal that alone will satisfy them, where all their desires will be fulfilled. For when God is all in all, there will be nothing left to desire.

This love is the gift of the Lord who said: *As I have loved you, you also must love one another*[Jn 13:34-35]. His object in loving us, then, was to enable us to love each other. By loving us himself, our mighty head has linked us all together as members of his own body, bound to one another by the tender bond of love.

Friday of the Fourth Week of Easter

From a letter to the Corinthians by Saint Clement, Pope & Martyr

The preservation of unity

Beloved, Jesus Christ is our salvation, he is the high priest through whom we present our offerings and the helper who supports us in our weakness. Through him our gaze penetrates the heights of heaven and we see, as in a mirror, the most holy face of God. Through Christ the eyes of our hearts are opened, and our weak and clouded understanding reaches up toward the light. Through him the Lord God willed that we should taste eternal knowledge, *for Christ is the radiance of God's glory, and as much greater than the angels as the name God has given him is superior to theirs*[Heb 1:3-4].

So then, my brothers, let us do battle with all our might under his unerring command. Think of the men serving under our military commanders. How well disciplined they are! How readily and submissively they carry out orders! Not everyone can be a prefect, a tribune, a centurion, or a captain of fifty, but each man in his own rank executes the orders of the emperor and the officers in command. The great cannot exist without those of humble condition, nor can those of humble condition exist without the great. Always it is the harmonious working together of its various parts that insures the well-being of the whole. Take our own body as an example: the head is helpless without the feet; and the feet can do nothing without the head. Even our least important members are useful and necessary to the whole body, and all work together for its well-being in harmonious subordination.

Let us, then, preserve the unity of the body that we form in Christ Jesus, and let everyone give his neighbor the deference to which his particular gifts entitle him. Let the strong care for the weak and the weak respect the strong. Let the wealthy assist the poor and the poor man thank God for giving him someone to supply his needs. The wise man should show his wisdom not by his eloquence but by good works; the humble man should not proclaim his own humility, but leave others to do so; nor must the man who preserves his chastity ever boast of it, but recognize that the ability to control his desires has been given him by another.

Think, my brothers, of how we first came into being, of what we were at the first moment of our existence. Think of the dark tomb out of which our Creator brought us into his world where he had his gifts prepared for us even before we were born. All this we owe to him and for everything we must give him thanks. To him be glory for ever and ever. Amen.

From the commentary on the letter to the Romans by Saint Cyril of Alexandria, Bishop & Doctor

God's mercy has been extended to all; the whole world has been saved

Though many, we are one body, and members one of another, united by Christ in the bonds of love. *Christ has made Jews and Gentiles one by breaking down the barrier that divided us and abolishing the law with its precepts and decrees*[Eph 2:14-15]. This is why we should all be of one mind and if one member suffers some misfortune, all should suffer with him; if one member is honored, all should be glad.

Paul says: *Accept one another as Christ accepted you, for the glory of God*[Rom 15:7]. Now accepting one another means being willing to share one another's thoughts and feelings, bearing one another's burdens, and *preserving the unity of the Spirit in the bond of peace*[Eph 4:3]. This is how God accepted us in Christ, for John's testimony is true and he said that *God* the Father *loved the world so much that he gave his own Son for us*[Jn 3:16]. God's Son was given as a ransom for the lives of us all. He has delivered us from death, redeemed us from death and from sin.

Paul throws light on the purpose of God's plan when he says that Christ became the servant of the circumcised to show God's fidelity. God had promised the Jewish patriarchs that he would bless their offspring and make it as numerous as the stars of heaven. This is why the divine Word himself, who as God holds all creation in being and is the source of its well-being, appeared in the flesh and became man. He came into this world in human flesh not to be served, but, as he himself said, to serve and to give his life as a ransom for many.

Christ declared that his coming in visible form was to fulfill the promise made to Israel. *I was sent only to the lost sheep of the house of Israel*[Mt 15:24], he said. Paul was perfectly correct, then, in saying that Christ became a servant of the circumcised in order to fulfill the promise made to the patriarchs and that God the Father had charged him with this task, as also with the task of bringing salvation to the Gentiles, so that they too might praise their Savior and Redeemer as the Creator of the universe. In this way God's mercy has been extended to all men, including the Gentiles, and it can be seen that the mystery of the divine wisdom contained in Christ has not failed in its benevolent purpose. In the place of those who fell away the whole world has been saved.

Sunday of the Fifth Week of Easter

From a sermon by Saint Maximus of Turin, Bishop

Christ is the day

Christ is risen! He has burst open the gates of hell and let the dead go free; he has renewed the earth through the members of his Church now born again in baptism, and has made it blossom afresh with men brought back to life. His Holy Spirit has unlocked the doors of heaven, which stand wide open to receive those who rise up from the earth. Because of Christ's resurrection the thief ascends to paradise, the bodies of the blessed enter the holy city, and the dead are restored to the company of the living. There is an upward movement in the whole of creation, each element raising itself to something higher. We see hell restoring its victims to the upper regions, earth sending its buried dead to heaven, and heaven presenting the new arrivals to the Lord. In one and the same movement, our Savior's passion raises men from the depths, lifts them up from the earth, and sets them in the heights.

Christ is risen. His rising brings life to the dead, forgiveness to sinners, and glory to the saints. And so David the prophet summons all creation to join in celebrating the Easter festival: *Rejoice and be glad,* he cries, *on this day which the Lord has made*[Ps 117:24].

The light of Christ is an endless day that knows no night. Christ is this day, says the Apostle; such is the meaning of his words: *Night is almost over; day is at hand*[Rom 13:12]. He tells us that night is almost over, not that it is about to fall. By this we are meant to understand that the coming of Christ's light puts Satan's darkness to flight, leaving no place for any shadow of sin. His everlasting radiance dispels the dark clouds of the past and checks the hidden growth of vice. The Son is that day to whom the day, which is the Father, communicates the mystery of his divinity. He is the day who says through the mouth of Solomon: *I have caused an unfailing light to rise in heaven*[2 Chron 6:6-11]. And as in heaven no night can follow day, so no sin can overshadow the justice of Christ. The celestial day is perpetually bright and shining with brilliant light; clouds can never darken its skies. In the same way, the light of Christ is eternally glowing with luminous radiance and can never be extinguished by the darkness of sin. This is why John the evangelist says: *The light shines in the darkness, and the darkness has never been able to overpower it*[Jn 1:5].

And so, my brothers, each of us ought surely to rejoice on this holy day. Let no one, conscious of his sinfulness, withdraw from our common celebration, nor let anyone be kept away from our public prayer by the burden of his guilt. Sinner he may indeed be, but he must not despair of pardon on this day which is so highly privileged; for if a thief could receive the grace of paradise, how could a Christian be refused forgiveness?

Monday of the Fifth Week of Easter

From a sermon by Saint Gregory of Nyssa, Bishop

The firstborn of the new creation

The reign of life has begun, the tyranny of death is ended. A new birth has taken place, a new life has come, a new order of existence has appeared, our very nature has been transformed! This birth is not brought about *by human generation, by the will of man, or by the desire of the flesh, but by God*[Jn 1:13].

If you wonder how, I will explain in clear language. Faith is the womb that conceives this new life, baptism the rebirth by which it is brought forth into the light of day. The Church is its nurse; her teachings are its milk, the bread from heaven is its food. It is brought to maturity by the practice of virtue; it is wedded to wisdom; it gives birth to hope. Its home is the kingdom; its rich inheritance the joys of paradise; its end, not death, but the blessed and everlasting life prepared for those who are worthy.

This is the day the Lord has made[Ps 117:24] – a day far different from those made when the world was first created and which are measured by the passage of time. This is the beginning of a new creation. On this day, as the prophet says, God makes a new heaven and a new earth. What is this new heaven? you may ask. It is the firmament of our faith in Christ. What is the new earth? A good heart, a heart like the earth, which drinks up the rain that falls on it and yields a rich harvest.

In this new creation, purity of life is the sun, the virtues are the stars, transparent goodness is the air, and *the depths of the riches of wisdom and knowledge*[Rom 11:33], the sea. Sound doctrine, the divine teachings are the grass and plants that feed God's flock, the people whom he shepherds; the keeping of the commandments is the fruit borne by the trees.

On this day is created the true man, the man made in the image and likeness of God. For *this day the Lord has made* is the beginning of this new world. Of this day the prophet says that it is not like other days, nor is this night like other nights. But still we have not spoken of the greatest gift it has brought us. This day destroyed the pangs of death and brought to birth the firstborn of the dead.

I ascend to my Father and to your Father, to my God and to your God[Jn 20:17]. O what wonderful good news! He who for our sake became like us in order to make us his brothers, now presents to his true Father his own humanity in order to draw all his kindred up after him.

Tuesday of the Fifth Week of Easter

From a commentary on the gospel of John
by Saint Cyril of Alexandria, Bishop & Doctor

I am the vine, you are the branches

The Lord calls himself the vine and those united to him branches in order to teach us how much we shall benefit from our union with him, and how important it is for us to remain in his love. By receiving the Holy Spirit, who is the bond of union between us and Christ our Savior, those who are joined to him, as branches are to a vine, share in his own nature.

On the part of those who come to the vine, their union with him depends upon a deliberate act of the will; on his part, the union is effected by grace. Because we had good will, we made the act of faith that brought us to Christ, and received from him the dignity of adoptive sonship that made us his own kinsmen, according to the words of Saint Paul: *He who is joined to the Lord is one spirit with him*[1 Cor 6:17].

The prophet Isaiah calls Christ the foundation, because it is upon him that we as living and spiritual stones are built into a holy priesthood to be a dwelling place for God in the Spirit. Upon no other foundation than Christ can this temple be built. Here Christ is teaching the same truth by calling himself the vine, since the vine is the parent of its branches, and provides their nourishment.

From Christ and in Christ, we have been reborn through the Spirit in order to bear the fruit of life; not the fruit of our old, sinful life but the fruit of a new life founded upon our faith in him and our love for him. Like branches growing from a vine, we now draw our life from Christ, and we cling to his holy commandment in order to preserve this life. Eager to safeguard the blessing of our noble birth, we are careful not to grieve the Holy Spirit who dwells in us, and who makes us aware of God's presence in us.

Let the wisdom of John teach us how we live in Christ and Christ lives in us: *The proof that we are living in him and he is living in us is that he has given us a share in his Spirit*[1 Jn 4:13]. Just as the trunk of the vine gives its own natural properties to each of its branches, so, by bestowing on them the Holy Spirit, the Word of God, the only-begotten Son of the Father, gives Christians a certain kinship with himself and with God the Father because they have been united to him by faith and determination to do his will in all things. He helps them to grow in love and reverence for God, and teaches them to discern right from wrong and to act with integrity.

Wednesday of the Fifth Week of Easter

From a letter to Diognetus

The Christian in the world

Christians are indistinguishable from other men either by nationality, language or customs. They do not inhabit separate cities of their own, or speak a strange dialect, or follow some outlandish way of life. Their teaching is not based upon reveries inspired by the curiosity of men. Unlike some other people, they champion no purely human doctrine. With regard to dress, food and manner of life in general, they follow the customs of whatever city they happen to be living in, whether it is Greek or foreign.

And yet there is something extraordinary about their lives. They live in their own countries as though they were only passing through. They play their full role as citizens, but labor under all the disabilities of aliens. Any country can be their homeland, but for them their homeland, wherever it may be, is a foreign country. Like others, they marry and have children, but they do not expose them. They share their meals, but not their wives. They live in the flesh, but they are not governed by the desires of the flesh. They pass their days upon earth, but they are citizens of heaven. Obedient to the laws, they yet live on a level that transcends the law.

Christians love all men, but all men persecute them. Condemned because they are not understood, they are put to death, but raised to life again. They live in poverty, but enrich many; they are totally destitute, but possess an abundance of everything. They suffer dishonor, but that is their glory. They are defamed, but vindicated. A blessing is their answer to abuse, deference their response to insult. For the good they do they receive the punishment of malefactors, but even then they rejoice, as though receiving the gift of life. They are attacked by the Jews as aliens, they are persecuted by the Greeks, yet no one can explain the reason for this hatred.

To speak in general terms, we may say that the Christian is to the world what the soul is to the body. As the soul is present in every part of the body, while remaining distinct from it, so Christians are found in all the cities of the world, but cannot be identified with the world. As the visible body contains the invisible soul, so Christians are seen living in the world, but their religious life remains unseen. The body hates the soul and wars against it, not because of any injury the soul has done it, but because of the restriction the soul places on its pleasures. Similarly, the world hates the Christians, not because they have done it any wrong, but because they are opposed to its enjoyments.

Christians love those who hate them just as the soul loves the body and all its members despite the body's hatred. It is by the soul, enclosed within the body, that the body is held together, and similarly, it is by the Christians, detained in the world as in a prison, that the world is held together. The soul, though immortal, has a mortal dwelling place; and Christians also live for a time amidst perishable things, while awaiting the freedom from change and decay that will be theirs in heaven. As the soul benefits from the deprivation of food and drink, so Christians flourish under persecution. Such is the Christian's lofty and divinely appointed function, from which he is not permitted to excuse himself.

Thursday of the Fifth Week of Easter

From a treatise by Saint Gaudentius of Brescia, Bishop

The eucharist is the Lord's passover

One man has died for all, and now in every church in the mystery of bread and wine he heals those for whom he is offered in sacrifice, giving life to those who believe and holiness to those who consecrate the offering. This is the flesh of the Lamb; this is his blood. The bread that came down from heaven declared: *The bread that I will give is my flesh for the life of the world*[Jn 6:51]. It is significant, too, that his blood should be given to us in the form of wine, for his own words in the gospel, *I am the true vine*[Jn 15:1], imply clearly enough that whenever wine is offered as a representation of Christ's passion, it is his blood. This means that it was of Christ that the blessed patriarch Jacob prophesied when he said: *He will wash his tunic in wine and his cloak in the blood of the grape*[Gen 49:11]. The tunic was our flesh, which Christ was to put on like a garment and which he was to wash in his own blood.

Creator and Lord of all things, whatever their nature, he brought forth bread from the earth and changed it into his own body. Not only had he the power to do this, but he had promised it; and, as he had changed water into wine, he also changed wine into his own blood. *It is the Lord's passover*[Ex 12:11], Scripture tells us, that is, the Lord's passing. We are no longer to look upon the bread and wine as earthly substances. They have become heavenly, because Christ has passed into them and changed them into his body and blood. What you receive is the body of him who is the heavenly bread, and the blood of him who is the sacred vine; for when he offered his disciples the consecrated bread and wine, he said: *This is my body, this is my blood*[Mt 26:26-28]. We have put our trust in him. I urge you to have faith in him; truth can never deceive.

When Christ told the crowds that they must eat his flesh and drink his blood, they were horrified and began to murmur among themselves: *This teaching is too hard; who can be expected to listen to it*[Jn 6:60]? As I have already told you, thoughts such as these must be banished. The Lord himself used heavenly fire to drive them away by going on to declare: *It is the spirit that gives life; the flesh is of no avail. The words that I have spoken to you are spirit and life*[Jn 6:63].

Friday of the Fifth Week of Easter

From a sermon by Blessed Isaac of Stella, Abbot

Firstborn of many brothers

Just as the head and body of a man form one single man, so the Son of the Virgin and those he has chosen to be his members form a single man and the one Son of Man. *Christ is whole and entire, head and body*[Col 1:18; Eph 1:22-23], say the Scriptures, since all the members form one body, which with its head is one Son of Man, and he with the Son of God is one Son of God, who himself with God is one God. Therefore the whole body with its head is Son of Man, Son of God, and God. This is the explanation of the Lord's words: *Father, I desire that as you and I are one, so they may be one with us*[Jn 17:21-23].

And so, according to this well-known of Scripture, neither the body without the head, nor the head without the body, nor the head and body without God make the whole Christ. When all are united with God thcy become one God. The Son of God is one with God by nature; the Son of Man is one with him in his person; we, his body, are one with him sacramentally. Consequently those who by faith are spiritual members of Christ can truly say that they are what he is: the Son of God and God himself. But what Christ is by his nature we are as his partners; what he is of himself in all fullness, we are as participants. Finally, what the Son of God is by generation, his members are by adoption, according to the text: *As sons you have received the Spirit of adoption, enabling you to cry, Abba, Father*[Rom 8:15].

Through his Spirit, he gave men the power to become sons of God, so that all those he has chosen might be taught by the firstborn among many brothers to say: *Our Father, who are in heaven*[Mt 6:9-13]. Again he says elsewhere: *I ascend to my Father and to your Father*[Jn 20:17].

By the Spirit, from the womb of the Virgin, was born our head, the Son of Man; and by the same Spirit, in the waters of baptism, we are reborn as his body and as sons of God. And just as he was born without any sin, so we are reborn in the forgiveness of all our sins. As on the cross he bore the sum total of the whole body's sins in his own physical body, so he gave his members the grace of rebirth in order that no sin might be imputed to his mystical body. It is written: *Blessed is the man to whom the Lord imputes no sin*[Rom 4:8; Ps 31:2]. The blessed man of this text is undoubtedly Christ, who forgives sins insofar as God is his head. Insofar as this man is the head of the body, no sin is forgiven him. But insofar as the body that belongs to this head consists of many members, sin is not imputed to it.

Just in himself, it is he who justifies himself. He alone is both Savior and saved. In his own body on the cross he bore what he had washed from his body by the waters of baptism. Bringing salvation through wood and through water, he is the Lamb of God who takes away the sins of the world which he took upon himself. Himself a priest, he offers himself as sacrifice to God, and he himself is God. Thus, through his own self, the Son is reconciled to himself as God, as well as to the Father and to the Holy Spirit.

Saturday of the Fifth Week of Easter

From a discourse on the psalms by Saint Augustine, Bishop & Doctor

The Easter Alleluia

Our thoughts in this present life should turn on the praise of God, because it is in praising God that we shall rejoice for ever in the life to come; and no one can be ready for the next life unless he trains himself for it now. So we praise God during our earthly life, and at the same time we make our petitions to him. Our praise is expressed with joy, our petitions with yearning. We have been promised something we do not yet possess, and because the promise was made by one who keeps his word, we trust him and are glad; but insofar as possession is delayed, we can only long and yearn for it. It is good for us to persevere in longing until we receive what was promised, and yearning is over; then praise alone will remain.

Because there are these two periods of time – the one that now is, beset with the trials and troubles of this life, and the other yet to come, a life of everlasting serenity and joy – we are given two liturgical seasons, one before Easter and the other after. The season before Easter signifies the troubles in which we live here and now, while the time after Easter which we are celebrating at present signifies the happiness that will be ours in the future. What we commemorate before Easter is what we experience in this life; what we celebrate after Easter points to something we do not yet possess. This is why we keep the first season with fasting and prayer; but now the fast is over and we devote the present season to praise. Such is the meaning of the *Alleluia* we sing.

Both these periods are represented and demonstrated for us in Christ our head. The Lord's passion depicts for us our present life of trial – shows how we must suffer and be afflicted and finally die. The Lord's resurrection and glorification show us the life that will be given to us in the future.

Now therefore, brethren, we urge you to praise God. That is what we are all telling each other when we say *Alleluia.* You say to your neighbor, "Praise the Lord!" and he says the same to you. We are all urging one another to praise the Lord, and all thereby doing what each of us urges the other to do. But see that your praise comes from your whole being; in other words, see that you praise God not with your lips and voices alone, but with your minds, your lives and all your actions.

We are praising God now, assembled as we are here in church; but when we go our various ways again, it seems as if we cease to praise God. But provided we do not cease to live a good life, we shall always be praising God. You cease to praise God only when you swerve from justice and from what is pleasing to God. If you never turn aside from the good life, your tongue may be silent but your actions will cry aloud, and God will perceive your intentions; for as our ears hear each other's voices, so do God's ears hear our thoughts.

Sunday of the Sixth Week of Easter

From the commentary on the second letter to the Corinthians by Saint Cyril of Alexandria, Bishop & Doctor

God has reconciled us to himself through Christ and given us the ministry of reconciliation

Those who have a sure hope, guaranteed by the Spirit, that they will rise again lay hold of what lies in the future as though it were already present. They say: Outward appearances will no longer be our standard in judging other men. Our lives are all controlled by the Spirit now, and are not confined to this physical world that is subject to corruption. The light of the Only-begotten has shone on us, and we have been transformed into the Word, the source of all life. While sin was still our master, the bonds of death had a firm hold on us, but now that the righteousness of Christ has found a place in our hearts we have freed ourselves from our former condition of corruptibility.

This means that none of us lives in the flesh any more, at least not in so far as living in the flesh means being subject to the weaknesses of the flesh, which include corruptibility. *Once we thought of Christ as being in the flesh, but we do not do so any longer*[2 Cor 5:16], says Saint Paul. By this he meant that the Word became flesh and dwelt among us; he suffered death in the flesh in order to give all men life. It was in this flesh that we knew him before, but we do so no longer. Even though he remains in the flesh, since he came to life again on the third day and is now with his

Father in heaven, we know that he has passed beyond the life of the flesh; for *having died once, he will never die again, death has no power over him any more. His death was a death to sin, which he died once for all; his life is life with God*[Rom 6:8-10].

Since Christ has in this way become the source of life for us, we who follow in his footsteps must not think of ourselves as living in the flesh any longer, but as having passed beyond it. Saint Paul's saying is absolutely true that *when anyone is in Christ he becomes a completely different person: his old life is over and a new life has begun*[2 Cor 5:17]. We have been justified by our faith in Christ and the power of the curse has been broken. Christ's coming to life again for our sake has put an end to the sovereignty of death. We have come to know the true God and to worship him in spirit and in truth, through the Son, our mediator, who sends down upon the world the Father's blessings.

And so Saint Paul shows deep insight when he says: *This is all God's doing: it is he who has reconciled us to himself through Christ*[2 Cor 5:18]. For the mystery of the incarnation and the renewal it accomplished could not have taken place without the Father's will. Through Christ we have gained access to the Father, for as Christ himself says, no one comes to the Father except through him. *This is all God's doing,* then. *It is he who has reconciled us to himself through Christ, and who has given us the ministry of reconciliation*[2 Cor 5:18].

Monday of the Sixth Week of Easter

From the treatise On the Trinity by Didymus of Alexandria, Theologian

The Holy Spirit renews us in baptism

The Holy Spirit renews us in baptism through his godhead, which he shares with the Father and the Son. Finding us in a state of deformity, the Spirit restores our original beauty and fills us with his grace, leaving no room for anything unworthy of our love. The Spirit frees us from sin and death, and changes us from the earthly men we were, men of dust and ashes, into spiritual men, sharers in the divine glory, sons and heirs of God the Father who bear a likeness to the Son and are his co-heirs and brothers, destined to reign with him and to share his glory. In place of earth the Spirit reopens heaven to us and gladly admits us into paradise, giving us even now greater honor than the angels, and by the holy waters of baptism extinguishing the unquenchable fires of hell.

We men are conceived twice: to the human body we owe our first conception, to the divine Spirit, our second. John says: *To all who received him, who believed in his name, he gave power to become children of God. These were born not by human generation, not by the desire of the flesh, not by the will of man, but of God*[Jn 1:12-13]. All who believed in Christ, he says, received power to become children of God, that is, of the Holy Spirit, and to gain kinship with God. To show that their parent was God the Holy Spirit, he adds these words of Christ: *I give you this solemn warning, that without being born of water and the Spirit, no one can enter the kingdom of God*[Jn 3:5].

Visibly, through the ministry of priests, the font gives symbolic birth to our visible bodies. Invisibly, through the ministry of angels, the Spirit of God, whom even the mind's eye cannot see, baptizes into himself both our souls and bodies, giving them a new birth.

Speaking quite literally, and also in harmony with the words *of water and the Spirit,* John the Baptist says of Christ: *He will baptize you with the Holy Spirit and with fire*[Mt 3:11]. Since we are only vessels of clay, we must first be cleansed in water and then hardened by spiritual fire – for *God is a consuming fire*[Heb 12:29]. We need the Holy Spirit to perfect and renew us, for spiritual fire can cleanse us, and spiritual water can recast us as in a furnace and make us into new men.

Tuesday of the Sixth Week of Easter

From a commentary on the gospel of John by Saint Cyril of Alexandria, Bishop & Doctor

Christ is the bond of unity

All who receive the sacred flesh of Christ are united with him as members of his body. This is the teaching of Saint Paul when he speaks of the mystery of our religion *that was hidden from former generations, but has now been revealed to the holy apostles and prophets by the Spirit; namely, that the Gentiles are joint-heirs with the Jews, that they are members of the same body, and that they have a share in the promise made by God in Christ Jesus*[Eph 3:4-6].

If, in Christ, all of us, both ourselves and he who is within us by his own flesh, are members of the same body, is it not clear that we are one, both with one another and with Christ? He is the bond that unites us, because he is at once both God and man.

With regard to our unity in the Spirit, we may say, following the same line of thought, that all of us who have received one and the same Spirit, the Holy Spirit, are united intimately, both with one another and with God. Taken separately, we are many, and Christ sends the Spirit, who is both the Father's Spirit and his own, to dwell in each of us. Yet that Spirit, being one and indivisible, gathers together those who are distinct from each other as individuals, and causes them all to be seen as a unity in himself. Just as Christ's sacred flesh has power to make those in whom it is present into one body, so the one, indivisible Spirit of God, dwelling in all, causes all to become one in spirit.

Therefore, Saint Paul appeals to us to *bear with one another charitably, and to spare no effort in securing, by the bonds of peace, the unity that comes from the Spirit. There is but one body and one Spirit, just as there is but one hope held out to us by God's call. There is one Lord, one faith, one baptism, one God and Father of all, who is above all, and works through all, and is in all*[Eph 4:1-6]. If the one Spirit dwells in us, the one God and Father of all will be in us, and he, through his Son, will gather together into unity with one another and with himself all who share in the Spirit.

There is also another way of showing that we are made one by sharing in the Holy Spirit. If we have given up our worldly way of life and submitted once for all to the laws of the Spirit, it must surely be obvious to everyone that by repudiating, in a sense, our own life, and taking on the supernatural likeness of the Holy Spirit, who is united to us, our nature is transformed so that we are no longer merely men, but also sons of God, spiritual men, by reason of the share we have received in the divine nature. We are all one, therefore, in the Father and the Son and the Holy Spirit. We are one in mind and holiness, we are one through our communion in the sacred flesh of Christ, and through our sharing in the one Holy Spirit.

Wednesday of the Sixth Week of Easter

From a sermon of Saint Leo the Great, Pope & Doctor

The days between the resurrection and the ascension of Our Lord

Beloved, the days which passed between the Lord's resurrection and his ascension were by no means uneventful; during them great sacramental mysteries were confirmed, great truths revealed. In those days the fear of death with all its horrors was taken away, and the immortality of both body and soul affirmed. It was then that the Lord breathed on all his apostles and filled them with the Holy Spirit; and after giving the keys of the kingdom to blessed Peter, whom he had chosen and set above all the others, he entrusted him with the care of his flock.

During these days the Lord joined two of his disciples as their companion on the road, and by chiding them for their timidity and hesitant fears he swept away all the clouds of our uncertainty. Their lukewarm hearts were fired by the light of faith and began to burn within them as the Lord opened up the Scriptures. And as they shared their meal with him, their eyes were opened in the breaking of bread, opened far more happily to the sight of their own glorified humanity than were the eyes of our first parents to the shame of their sin.

Throughout the whole period between the resurrection and ascension, God's providence was at work to instill this one lesson into the hearts of the disciples, to set this one truth before their eyes, that our Lord Jesus Christ, who was truly born, truly suffered and truly died, should be recognized as truly risen from the dead. The blessed apostles together with all the others had been intimidated by the catastrophe of the cross, and their faith in the resurrection had been uncertain; but now they were so strengthened by the evident truth that when their Lord ascended into heaven, far from feeling any sadness, they were filled with great joy.

Indeed that blessed company had a great and inexpressible cause for joy when it saw man's nature rising above the dignity of the whole heavenly creation, above the ranks of angels, above the exalted status of archangels. Nor would there be any limit to its upward course until humanity was admitted to a seat at the right hand of the eternal Father, to be enthroned at last in the glory of him to whose nature it was wedded in the person of the Son.

Ascension

From a sermon by Saint Augustine, Bishop & Doctor

No one has ever ascended into heaven except the one who descended from heaven

Today our Lord Jesus Christ ascended into heaven; let our hearts ascend with him. Listen to the words of the Apostle: *If you have risen with Christ, set your hearts on the things that are above where Christ is, seated at the right hand of God; seek the things that are above, not the things that are on earth*[Col 3:1]. For just as he remained with us even after his ascension, so we too are already in heaven with him, even though what is promised us has not yet been fulfilled in our bodies.

Christ is now exalted above the heavens, but he still suffers on earth all the pain that we, the members of his body, have to bear. He showed this when he cried out from above: *Saul, Saul, why do you persecute me*[Acts 9:4]*?* and when he said: *I was hungry and you gave me food*[Mt 25:35-40].

Why do we on earth not strive to find rest with him in heaven even now, through the faith, hope and love that unites us to him? While in heaven he is also with us; and we while on earth are with him. He is here with us by his divinity, his power and his love. We cannot be in heaven, as he is on earth, by divinity, but in him, we can be there by love.

He did not leave heaven when he came down to us; nor did he withdraw from us when he went up again into heaven. The fact that he was in heaven even while he was on earth is borne out by his own statement: *No one has ever ascended into heaven except the one who descended from heaven, the Son of Man, who is in heaven*[Jn 3:13].

These words are explained by our oneness with Christ, for he is our head and we are his body. No one ascended into heaven except Christ because we also are Christ: he is the Son of Man by his union with us, and we by our union with him are the sons of God. So the Apostle says: *Just as the human body, which has many members, is a unity, because all the different members make one body, so is it also with Christ*[1 Cor 12:12]. He too has many members, but one body.

Out of compassion for us he descended from heaven, and although he ascended alone, we also ascend, because we are in him by grace. Thus, no one but Christ descended and no one but Christ ascended; not because there is no distinction between the head and the body, but because the body as a unity cannot be separated from the head.

Friday of the Sixth Week of Easter

From a sermon by Saint Leo the Great, Pope & Doctor

Our faith is increased by the Lord's ascension

At Easter, beloved brethren, it was the Lord's resurrection which was the cause of our joy; our present rejoicing is on account of his ascension into heaven. With all due solemnity we are commemorating that day on which our poor human nature was carried up, in Christ, above all the hosts of heaven, above all the ranks of angels, beyond the highest heavenly powers to the very throne of God the Father. It is upon this ordered structure of divine acts that we have been firmly established, so that the grace of God may show itself still more marvelous when, in spite of the withdrawal from men's sight of everything that is rightly felt to command their reverence, faith does not fail, hope is not shaken, charity does not grow cold.

For such is the power of great minds, such is the light of truly believing souls, that they put unhesitating faith in what is not seen with the bodily eye; they fix their desires on what is beyond sight. Such fidelity could never be born in our hearts, nor could anyone be justified by faith, if our salvation lay only in what was visible.

And so our Redeemer's visible presence has passed into the sacraments. Our faith is nobler and stronger because sight has been replaced by a doctrine whose authority is accepted by believing hearts, enlightened from on high. This faith was increased by the Lord's ascension and strengthened by the gift of the Spirit; it would remain unshaken by fetters and imprisonment, exile and hunger, fire and ravening beasts, and the most refined tortures ever devised by brutal persecutors. Throughout the world women no less than men, tender girls as well as boys, have given their life's blood in the struggle for this faith. It is a faith that has driven out devils, healed the sick and raised the dead.

Even the blessed apostles, though they had been strengthened by so many miracles and instructed by so much teaching, took fright at the cruel suffering of the Lord's passion and could not accept his resurrection without hesitation. Yet they made such progress through his ascension that they now found joy in what had terrified them before. They were able to fix their minds on Christ's divinity as he sat at the right hand of his Father, since what was presented to their bodily eyes no longer hindered them from turning all their attention to the realization that he had not left his Father when he came down to earth, nor had he abandoned his disciples when he ascended into heaven.

The truth is that the Son of Man was revealed as Son of God in a more perfect and transcendent way once he had entered into his Father's glory; he now began to be indescribably more present in his divinity to those from whom he was further removed in his humanity. A more mature faith enabled their minds to stretch upward to the Son in his equality with the Father; it no longer needed contact with Christ's tangible body, in which as man he is inferior to the Father. For while his glorified body retained the same nature, the faith of those who believed in him was now summoned to heights where, as the Father's equal, the only-begotten Son is reached not by physical handling but by spiritual discernment.

Saturday of the Sixth Week of Easter

From the treatise on John by Saint Augustine, Bishop & Doctor

Two kinds of life

The Church recognizes two kinds of life as having been commended to her by God. One is a life of faith, the other a life of vision; one is a life passed on pilgrimage in time, the other in a dwelling place in eternity; one is a life of toil, the other of repose; one is spent on the road, the other in our homeland; one is active, involving labor, the other contemplative, the reward of labor.

The first kind of life is symbolized by the apostle Peter, the second by John. All of the first life is lived in this world, and it will come to an end with this world. The second life will be imperfect till the end of this world, but it will have no end in the next world. And so Christ says to Peter: *Follow me;* but of John he says: *If I wish him to remain until I come, what is that to you? Your duty is to follow me*[Jn 21:19, 22].

You are to follow me by imitating my endurance of transient evils; John is to remain until my coming, when I will bring eternal blessings. A way of saying this more clearly might be: Your active life will be perfect if you follow the example of my passion, but to attain its full perfection John's life of contemplation must wait until I come.

Perfect patience is to follow Christ faithfully, even to death, but for perfect knowledge we must await his coming. Here, in the land of the dying, the sufferings of the world must be endured; there, in the land of the living, shall be seen the good things of the Lord.

Christ's words, *I wish him to remain until I come*[Jn 21:23], should not be taken to imply that John was to remain on earth until Christ's coming, but rather that he was to wait because it is not now but only when Christ comes that the life he symbolizes will find fulfillment. On the other hand, Christ says to Peter: *Your duty is to follow me*[Jn 21:19], because the life Peter symbolizes can attain its goal only by action here and now.

Yet we should make no mental separation between these great apostles. Both lived the life symbolized by Peter; both were to attain the life symbolized by John. Symbolically, one followed, the other remained, but living by faith they both endured the sufferings of this present life of sorrow and they both longed for the joys of the future life of happiness.

Nor were they alone in this. They were one with the whole Church, the bride of Christ, which will in time be delivered from the trials of this life and live for ever in the joy of the next. These two kinds of life were represented respectively by Peter and John, yet both apostles lived by faith in this present, passing life and in eternal life both have the joy of vision.

And so for the sake of all the saints inseparably united to the body of Christ, to guide them through the storms of this life, Peter, the chief of the apostles, received the keys of the kingdom of heaven with the power to bind and loose sins; and for the sake of those same saints, to plumb the depths of that other, hidden life, John the evangelist reclined on the breast of Christ.

For it is not only Peter but the whole Church that binds and looses from sin; and as for the sublime teaching of John about the Word, who in the beginning was God with God, and everything else he told us about Christ's divinity, and about the trinity and unity of the Godhead, which now, until the Lord comes, is all like a faint reflection in a mirror, but which will be seen face to face in the kingdom of heaven - it was not only John who drank in this teaching that came forth from the Lord's breast as from a fountain. All who belong to the Lord are to drink it in, each according to his capacity, and this is why the Lord himself has spread John's gospel throughout the world.

Sunday of the Seventh Week of Easter

From a homily on the Song of Songs by Saint Gregory of Nyssa, bishop

The glory you gave to me, I have given to them

When love has entirely cast out fear, and fear has been transformed into love, then the unity brought us by our Savior will be fully realized, for all men will be united with one another through their union with the one supreme Good. They will possess the perfection ascribed to the dove, according to our interpretation of the text: *One alone is my dove, my perfect one. She is the only child of her mother, her chosen one*[Song 6:9]

Our Lord's words in the gospel bring out the meaning of this text more clearly. After having conferred all power on his disciples by his blessing, he obtained many other gifts for them by his prayer to the Father. Among these was included the greatest gift of all, which was that they were no longer to be divided in their judgment of what was right and good, for they were all to be united to the one supreme Good. As the Apostle says, they were to be bound together with the bonds of peace in the unity that comes from the Holy Spirit. They were to be made one body and one spirit by the one hope to which they were all called. We shall do better, however, to quote the sacred words of the gospel itself. *I pray,* the Lord says, *that they all may be one; that as you, Father, are in me and I am in you, so they also may be one in us*[Jn 17:20-21].

Now the bond that creates this unity is glory. That the Holy Spirit is called glory no one can deny if he thinks carefully about the Lord's words: *The glory you gave to me, I have given to them.* In fact, he gave this glory to his disciples when he said to them: *Receive the Holy Spirit.* Although he had always possessed it, even before the world existed, he himself received this glory when he put on human nature. Then, when his human nature had been glorified by the Spirit, the glory of the Spirit was passed on to all his kin, beginning with his disciples. This is why he said: *The glory you gave to me, I have given to them, so that they may be one as we are one. With me in them and you in me, I want them to be perfectly one*[Jn 17:22-23].

Whoever has grown from infancy to manhood and attained to spiritual maturity possesses the mastery over his passions and the purity that makes it possible for him to receive the glory of the Spirit. He is that perfect dove upon whom the eyes of the bridegroom rest when he says: *One alone is my dove, my perfect one.*

Monday of the Seventh Week of Easter

From a catechetical instruction by Saint Cyril of Jerusalem, Bishop & Doctor

The living water of the Holy Spirit

The water that I shall give him will become in him a fountain of living water, welling up into eternal life[Jn 4:14]. This is a new kind of water, a living, leaping water, welling up for those who are worthy. But why did Christ call the grace of the Spirit water? Because all things are dependent on water; plants and animals have their origin in water. Water comes down from heaven as rain, and although it is always the same in itself, it produces many different effects, one in the palm tree, another in the vine, and so on throughout the whole of creation. It does not come down, now as one thing, now as another, but while remaining essentially the same, it adapts itself to the needs of every creature that receives it.

In the same way the Holy Spirit, whose nature is always the same, simple and indivisible, apportions grace to each man as he wills. Like a dry tree which puts forth shoots when watered, the soul bears the fruit of holiness when repentance has made it worthy of receiving the Holy Spirit. Although the Spirit never changes, the effects of his action, by the will of God and in the name of Christ, are both many and marvelous.

The Spirit makes one man a teacher of divine truth, inspires another to prophesy, gives another the power of casting out devils, enables another to interpret holy Scripture. The Spirit strengthens one man's self-control, shows another how to help the poor, teaches another to fast and lead a life of asceticism, makes another oblivious to the needs of the body, trains another for martyrdom. His action is different in different people, but the Spirit himself is always the same. *In each person,* Scripture says, *the Spirit reveals his presence in a particular way for the common good*[1 Cor 12:4-11].

The Spirit comes gently and makes himself known by his fragrance. He is not felt as a burden, for he is light, very light. Rays of light and knowledge stream before him as he approaches. The Spirit comes with the tenderness of a true friend and protector to save, to heal, to teach, to counsel, to strengthen, to console. The Spirit comes to enlighten the mind first of the one who receives him, and then, through him, the minds of others as well.

As light strikes the eyes of a man who comes out of darkness into the sunshine and enables him to see clearly things he could not discern before, so light floods the soul of the man counted worthy of receiving the Holy Spirit and enables him to see things beyond the range of human vision, things hitherto undreamed of.

Tuesday of the Seventh Week of Easter

From the treatise On the Holy Spirit by Saint Basil the Great, Bishop & Doctor

The work of the Holy Spirit

The titles given to the Holy Spirit must surely stir the soul of anyone who hears them, and make him realize that they speak of nothing less than the supreme Being. Is he not called the Spirit of God, the Spirit of truth who proceeds from the Father, the steadfast Spirit, the guiding Spirit? But his principal and most personal title is the Holy Spirit.

To the Spirit all creatures turn in their need for sanctification; all living things seek him according to their ability. His breath empowers each to achieve its own natural end.

The Spirit is the source of holiness, a spiritual light, and he offers his own light to every mind to help it in its search for truth. By nature the Spirit is beyond the reach of our mind, but we can know him by his goodness. The power of the Spirit fills the whole universe, but he gives himself only to those who are worthy, acting in each according to the measure of his faith.

Simple in himself, the Spirit is manifold in his mighty works. The whole of his being is present to each individual; the whole of his being is present everywhere. Though shared in by many, he remains unchanged; his self-giving is no loss to himself. Like the sunshine, which permeates all the atmosphere, sp over land and sea, and yet is enjoyed by each person as though it were for him alone, so the Spirit pours forth his grace in full measure, sufficient for all, and yet is present as though exclusively to everyone who can receive him. To all creatures that share in him he gives a delight limited only by their own nature, not by his ability to give.

The Spirit raises our hearts to heaven, guides the steps of the weak, and brings to perfection those who are making progress. He enlightens those who have been cleansed from every stain of sin and makes them spiritual by communion with himself.

As clear, transparent substances become very bright when sunlight falls on them and shine with a new radiance, so also souls in whom the Spirit dwells, and who are enlightened by the Spirit, become spiritual themselves and a source of grace for others.

From the Spirit comes foreknowledge of the future, understanding of the mysteries of faith, insight into the hidden meaning of Scripture, and other special gifts. Through the Spirit we become citizens of heaven, we are admitted to the company of the angels, we enter into eternal happiness, and abide in God. Through the Spirit we acquire a likeness to God; indeed, we attain what is beyond our most sublime aspirations – we become God.

Wednesday of the Seventh Week of Easter

From the dogmatic constitution on the Church of the Second Vatican Council

The mission of the Holy Spirit in the Church

When the Son completed the work with which the Father had entrusted him on earth, the Holy Spirit was sent on the day of Pentecost to sanctify the Church unceasingly, and thus enable believers to have access to the Father through Christ in the one Spirit. He is the Spirit of life, the fountain of water welling up to give eternal life. Through him the Father gives life to men, dead because of sin, until he raises up their mortal bodies in Christ.

The Spirit dwells in the Church and in the hearts of the faithful as in a temple. He prays in them and bears witness in them to their adoption as sons. He leads the Church into all truth and gives it unity in communion and in service. He endows it with different hierarchical and charismatic gifts, directs it by their means, and enriches it with his fruits.

By the power of the Gospel he enables the Church to grow young, perpetually renews it, and leads it to complete union with its Bridegroom. For the Spirit and the Bride say to the Lord Jesus: "Come!"

In this way the Church reveals itself as a people whose unity has its source in the unity of Father, Son and Holy Spirit.

The whole company of the faithful, who have an anointing by the Holy Spirit, cannot err in faith. They manifest this distinctive characteristic of theirs in the supernatural instinct of faith (*sensus fidei*) of the whole people when, from the bishops to the most ordinary lay person among the faithful, they display a universal agreement on matters of faith and morals.

This instinct of faith is awakened and kept in being by the Spirit of truth. Through it the people of God hold indefectibly to *the faith once delivered to the saints*[Jude 1:3] penetrate it more deeply by means of right judgment, and apply it more perfectly in their lives. They do all this under the guidance of the sacred teaching office: by faithful obedience to it they receive, not the word of men but in truth the word of God.

Moreover, the Holy Spirit not only sanctifies and guides God's people by the sacraments and the ministries, and enriches it with virtues, he also distributes special graces among the faithful of every state of life, *assigning* His gifts *to each as he chooses*[1 Cor 12:11]. By means of these special gifts he equips them and makes them eager for various activities and responsibilities that benefit the Church in its renewal or its increase, in accordance with the text: *To each is given the manifestation of the Spirit for a good purpose*[1 Cor 12:7].

These charisms, the simpler and more widespread as well as the most outstanding, should be accepted with a sense of gratitude and consolation, since in a very special way they answer and serve the needs of the Church.

Thursday of the Seventh Week of Easter

From a commentary on the gospel of John by Saint Cyril of Alexandria, Bishop & Doctor

If I do not go away, the Comforter will not come to you

After Christ had completed his mission on earth, it still remained necessary for us to become sharers in the divine nature of the Word. We had to give up our own life and be so transformed that we would begin to live an entirely new kind of life that would be pleasing to God. This was something we could do only by sharing in the Holy Spirit.

It was most fitting that the sending of the Spirit and his descent upon us should take place after the departure of Christ our Savior. As long as Christ was with them in the flesh, it must have seemed to believers that they possessed every blessing in him; but when the time came for him to ascend to his heavenly Father, it was necessary for him to be united through his Spirit to those who worshipped him, and to dwell in our hearts through faith. Only by his own presence within us in this way could he give us confidence to cry out, *Abba, Father*[Gal 4:6], make it easy for us to grow in holiness and, through our possession of the all-powerful Spirit, fortify us invincibly against the wiles of the devil and the assaults of men.

It can easily be shown from examples both in the Old Testament and the New that the Spirit changes those in whom he comes to dwell; he so transforms them that they begin to live a completely new kind of life. Saul was told by the prophet Samuel: *The Spirit of the Lord will take possession of you, and you shall be changed into another man*[1 Sam 10:6]. Saint Paul writes: *As we behold the glory of the Lord with unveiled faces, that glory, which comes from the Lord who is the Spirit, transforms us all into his own likeness, from one degree of glory to another*[2 Cor 3:18].

Does this not show that the Spirit changes those in whom he comes to dwell and alters the whole pattern of their lives? With the Spirit within them it is quite natural for people who had been absorbed by the things of this world to become entirely other-worldly in outlook, and for cowards to become men of great courage. There can be no doubt that this is what happened to the disciples. The strength they received from the Spirit enabled them to hold firmly to the love of Christ, facing the violence of their persecutors unafraid. Very true, then, was our Savior's saying that it was to their advantage for him to return to heaven: his return was the time appointed for the descent of the Holy Spirit.

From the treatise on the Trinity by Saint Hilary of Poitiers, Bishop & Doctor

The Father's gift in Christ

Our Lord commanded us to baptize in the name of the Father and of the Son and of the Holy Spirit. In baptism, then, we profess faith in the Creator, in the only-begotten Son and in the gift which is the Spirit. There is one Creator of all things, for in God there is one Father from whom all things have their being. And there is one only-begotten Son, our Lord Jesus Christ, through whom all things exist. And there is one Spirit, the gift who is in all. So all follow their due order, according to the proper operation of each: one power, which brings all things into being, one Son, through whom all things come to be, and one gift of perfect hope. Nothing is wanting to this flawless union: in Father, Son and Holy Spirit, there is infinity of endless being, perfect reflection of the divine image, and mutual enjoyment of the gift.

Our Lord has described the purpose of the Spirit's presence in us. Let us listen to his words: *I have yet many things to say to you, but you cannot bear them now*[Jn 16:12]. *It is to your advantage that I go away; if I go, I will send you the Advocate*[Jn 16:7]. And also: *I will ask the Father and he will give you another Counselor to be with you for ever, the Spirit of truth*[Jn 14:16-17]. *He will guide you into all the truth; for he will not speak on his own authority, but whatever he hears he will speak, and he will declare to you the things that are to come. He will glorify me, for he will take what is mine*[Jn 16:13-14].

From among many of our Lord's sayings, these have been chosen to guide our understanding, for they reveal to us the intention of the giver, the nature of the gift and the condition for its reception. Since our weak minds cannot comprehend the Father or the Son, we have been given the Holy Spirit as our intermediary and advocate, to shed light on that hard doctrine of our faith, the incarnation of God.

We receive the Spirit of truth so that we can know the things of God. In order to grasp this, consider how useless the faculties of the human body would become if they were denied their exercise. Our eyes cannot fulfill their task without light, either natural or artificial; our ears cannot react without sound vibrations, and in the absence of any odor our nostrils are ignorant of their function. Not that these senses would lose their own nature if they were not used; rather, they demand objects of experience in order to function. It is the same with the human soul. Unless it absorbs the gift of the Spirit through faith, the mind has the ability to know God but lacks the light necessary for that knowledge.

This unique gift which is in Christ is offered in its fullness to everyone. It is everywhere available, but it is given to each man in proportion to his readiness to receive it. Its presence is the fuller, the greater a man's desire to be worthy of it. This gift will remain with us until the end of the world, and will be our comfort in the time of waiting. By the favors it bestows, it is the pledge of our hope for the future, the light of our minds, and the splendor that irradiates our understanding.

Saturday of the Seventh Week of Easter

From a sermon by a sixth century African author

The Church in its unity speaks in the language of every nation

The disciples spoke in the language of every nation. At Pentecost God chose this means to indicate the presence of the Holy Spirit: whoever had received the Spirit spoke in every kind of tongue. We must realize, dear brothers, that this is the same Holy Spirit by whom love is poured out in our hearts. It was love that was to bring the Church of God together all over the world. And as individual men who received the Holy Spirit in those days could speak in all kinds of tongues, so today the Church, united by the Holy Spirit, speaks in the language of every people.

Therefore if somebody should say to one of us, "You have received the Holy Spirit, why do you not speak in tongues?" his reply should be, "I do indeed speak in the tongues of all men, because I belong to the body of Christ, that is, the Church, and she speaks all languages. What else did the presence of the Holy Spirit indicate at Pentecost, except that God's Church was to speak in the language of every people?"

This was the way in which the Lord's promise was fulfilled: *No one puts new wine into old wineskins. New wine is put into fresh skins, and so both are preserved*[Mk 2:22.] So when the disciples were heard speaking in all kinds of languages, some people were not far wrong in saying: *They have been drinking too much new wine*[Acts 2:13]. The truth is that the disciples had now become fresh wineskins, renewed and made holy by grace. The new wine of the Holy Spirit filled them, so that their fervor brimmed over and they spoke in manifold tongues. By this spectacular miracle they became a sign of the Catholic Church, which embraces the language of every nation.

Keep this feast, then, as members of the one body of Christ. It will be no empty festival for you if you really live what you are celebrating. For you are the members of that Church which the Lord acknowledges as his own, being himself acknowledged by her, that same Church which he fills with the Holy Spirit as she spreads throughout the world. He is like a bridegroom who never loses sight of his own bride; no one could ever deceive him by substituting some other woman.

To you men of all nations, then, who make up the Church of Christ, you, the members of Christ, you, the body of Christ, you, the bride of Christ – to all of you the Apostle addresses these words: *Bear with one another in love; do all you can to preserve the unity of the Spirit in the bond of peace*[Eph 4:2-3]. Notice that when Paul urges us to bear with one another, he bases his argument on love, and when he speaks of our hope of unity, he emphasizes the bond of peace. This Church is the house of God, built up of living stones, whose master is almighty God. It is his delight to dwell here. Take care, then, that he never has the sorrow of seeing it undermined by schism and collapsing in ruins.

Pentecost

From a treatise Against Heresies by Saint Irenaeus, Bishop, Doctor & Martyr

The sending of the Holy Spirit

When the Lord told his disciples to *go and teach all nations and baptize them in the name of the Father and of the Son and of the Holy Spirit*[Mt 28:19], he conferred on them the power of giving men new life in God.

He had promised through the prophets that in these last days he would pour out his Spirit on his servants and handmaids, and that they would prophesy. So when the Son of God became the Son of Man, the Spirit also descended upon him, becoming accustomed in this way to dwelling with the human race, to living in men and to inhabiting God's creation. The Spirit accomplished the Father's will in men who had grown old in sin, and gave them new life in Christ.

Luke says that the Spirit came down on the disciples at Pentecost, after the Lord's ascension, with power to open the gates of life to all nations and to make known to them the new covenant. So it was that men of every language joined in singing one song of praise to God, and scattered tribes, restored to unity by the Spirit, were offered to the Father as the firstfruits of all the nations.

This was why the Lord had promised to send the Advocate: he was to prepare us as an offering to God. Like dry flour, which cannot become one lump of dough, one loaf of bread, without moisture, we who are many could not become one in Christ Jesus without the water that comes down from heaven. And like parched ground, which yields no harvest unless it receives moisture, we who were once like a waterless tree could never have lived and borne fruit without this abundant rainfall from above. Through the baptism that liberates us from change and decay we have become one in body; through the Spirit we have become one in soul.

The Spirit of wisdom and understanding, the Spirit of counsel and strength, the Spirit of knowledge and the fear of God[Isa 11:2; Mt 3:16] came down upon the Lord, and the Lord in turn gave this Spirit to his Church, sending the Advocate from heaven into all the world into which, according to his own words, the devil too had been cast down like lightning.

If we are not to be scorched and made unfruitful, we need the dew of God. Since we have our accuser, we need an Advocate as well. And so the Lord in his pity for man, who had fallen into the hands of brigands, having himself bound up his wounds and left for his care two coins bearing the royal image, entrusted him to the Holy Spirit. Now, through the Spirit, the image and inscription of the Father and the Son have been given to us, and it is our duty to use the coin committed to our charge and make it yield a rich profit for the Lord.

Ordinary Time

Monday of the 1st Week in Ordinary Time

From a letter to the Corinthians by Saint Clement I, Pope & Martyr

The Word of God on high, fountain of wisdom

For his chosen ones scattered throughout the world, we shall make our constant prayer to the Creator of the universe. May he allow none of them to fall away, but preserve them all through his beloved Son, Jesus Christ, through whom he called us out of darkness into light, out of ignorance to the knowledge of his glorious name.

Give us grace, Lord, to hope in your Name, to which all creatures owe their being. Open the eyes of our heart to know you alone, *the Most High in the highest heavens, the holy One, whose dwelling is in the holy*[Isa 57:15]. *You abase the arrogance of the proud, frustrate the designs of the godless, exalt the lowly and humble the lofty. You give men wealth and take it away; you slay them, save them and give them new life*. Alone the Benefactor of *spirits and God of all flesh, your gaze penetrates the depths*, you observe the doings of men. Helper of those in peril, *Savior of those in despair*, you created and still keep watch over all that draws breath. You cause the peoples on the earth to multiply, and from them all choose those who love you through Jesus Christ, your beloved Son. Through him you have instructed us, sanctified us, honored us.

Lord, we entreat you to help us. Come to the aid of the afflicted, pity the lowly, raise up the fallen, show your face to the needy, heal the sick, convert the wayward, feed the hungry, deliver the captives, support the weak, encourage the fainthearted. Let all nations know that you alone are God; Jesus Christ is your Son, and *we are your people and the sheep of your pasture*[Ps 78:13].

Lord, you created the world according to the eternal decree now revealed in your works. Faithful throughout all generations, you are just in judgment, wonderful in power and majesty. You formed your creation with wisdom, established it with prudence. Everything we see proclaims your goodness. You are kind and compassionate, and never fail those who put their trust in you. Forgive us for our failings and for our sins.

Do not hold all the transgressions of your servants against them, but purify us by your truth, and *so guide our footsteps that by walking in holiness and justice and simplicity of heart we may do what is good and pleasing* in your sight and in the sight of our leaders.

Lord, *let the light of your face shine upon us, so that we may enjoy your blessings* in peace, protected by your strong hand, and freed from all sin by your outstretched arm; and deliver us from those who hate us unjustly.

Give peace and concord to us and to all mankind, even as you gave it to our ancestors *when they devoutly called upon you in faith and truth*. Lord, you alone are able to bestow these and even greater benefits upon us. We praise you through Jesus Christ, our high priest and the champion of our souls. Through him be glory and majesty to you now and throughout all generations, for ever and ever. Amen.

Tuesday of the 1st Week in Ordinary Time

From the Detailed Rules for Monks by St. Basil the Great, Bishop & Doctor

The ability to love is within each of us

Love of God is not something that can be taught. We did not learn from someone else how to rejoice in light or want to live, or to love our parents or guardians. It is the same – perhaps even more so – with our love for God: it does not come by another's teaching. As soon as the living creature (that is, man) comes to be, a power of reason is implanted in us like a seed, containing within it the ability and the need to love. When the school of God's law admits this power of reason, it cultivates it diligently, skillfully nurtures it, and with God's help brings it to
perfection.

For this reason, as by God's gift, I find you with the zeal necessary to attain this end, and you on your part help me with your prayers. I will try to fan into flame the spark of divine love that is hidden within you, as far as I am able through the power of the Holy Spirit.

First, let me say that we have already received from God the ability to fulfill all his commands. We have then no reason to resent them, as if something beyond our capacity were being asked of us. We have no reason either to be angry, as if we had to pay back more than we had received. When we use this ability in a right and fitting way, we lead a life of virtue and holiness. But if we misuse it, we fall into sin.

This is the definition of sin: the misuse of powers given us by God for doing good, a use contrary to God's commandments. On the other hand, the virtue that God asks of us is the use of the same powers based on a good conscience in accordance with God's command.

Since this is so, we can say the same about love. Since we received a command to love God, we possess from the first moment of our existence an innate power and ability to love. The proof of this is not to be sought outside ourselves, but each one can learn this from himself and in himself. It is natural for us to want things that are good and pleasing to the eye, even though at first different things seem beautiful and good to different people. In the same way, we love what is related to us or near to us, though we have not been taught to do so, and we spontaneously feel well disposed to our benefactors.

What, I ask, is more wonderful than the beauty of God? What thought is more pleasing and satisfying than God's majesty? What desire is as urgent and overpowering as the desire implanted by God in a soul that is completely purified of sin and cries out in its love: *I am wounded by love*? The radiance of divine beauty is altogether beyond the power of words to describe.

Wednesday of the 1st Week in Ordinary Time

From the treatise Against Heresies by Saint Irenaeus, Bishop, Doctor & Martyr

Knowledge of the Father consists in the self-revelation of the Son

No one can know the Father apart from God's Word, that is, unless the Son reveals him, and no one can know the Son unless the Father so wills. Now the Son fulfills the Father's good pleasure: the Father sends, the Son is sent, and he comes. The Father is beyond our sight and comprehension; but he is known by his Word, who tells us of him who surpasses all telling. In turn, the Father alone has knowledge of his Word. And the Lord has revealed both truths. Therefore, the Son reveals the knowledge of the Father by his revelation of himself. Knowledge of the Father consists in the self-revelation of the Son, for all is revealed through the Word.

The Father's purpose in revealing the Son was to make himself known to us all and so to welcome into eternal rest those who believe in him, establishing them in justice, preserving them from death. To believe in him means to do his will.

Through creation itself the Word reveals God the Creator. Through the world he reveals the Lord who made the world. Through all that is fashioned he reveals the craftsman who fashioned it all. Through the Son the Word reveals the Father who begot him as Son. All speak of these things in the same language, but they do not believe them in the same way. Through the law and the prophets the Word revealed himself and his Father in the same way, and though all the people equally heard the message not all equally believed it. Through the Word, made visible and palpable, the Father was revealed, though not all equally believed in him. But all saw the Father in the Son, for the Father of the Son cannot be seen, but the Son of the Father can be seen.

The Son performs everything as a ministry to the Father, from beginning to end, and without the Son no one can know God. The way to know the Father is the Son. Knowledge of the Son is in the Father, and is revealed through the Son. For this reason the Lord said: *No one knows the Son except the Father; and no one knows the Father except the Son, and those to whom the Son has revealed him*[Mt 11:27]. The word "revealed" refers not only to the future – as though the Word began to reveal the Father only when he was born of Mary; it refers equally to all time. From the beginning the Son is present to creation, reveals the Father to all, to those the Father chooses, when the Father chooses, and as the Father chooses. So, there is in all and through all one God the Father, one Word and Son, and one Spirit, and one salvation for all who believe in him.

Thursday of the 1st Week in Ordinary Time

From a Discourse Against the Pagans by Saint Athanasius, Bishop & Doctor

The Word of the Father gives order, direction and unity to creation

By his own wisdom and Word, who is our Lord and Savior Christ, the all-holy Father (whose excellence far exceeds that of any creature), like a skillful steersman guides to safety all creation, regulating and keeping it in being, as he judges right. It is right that creation should exist as he has made it and as we see it happening, because this is his will, which no one would deny. For if the movement of the universe were irrational, and the world rolled on in random fashion, one would be justified in disbelieving what we say. But if the world is founded on reason, wisdom and science, and is filled with orderly beauty, then it must owe its origin and order to none other than the Word of God.

He is God, the living and creative God of the universe, the Word of the good God, who is God in his own right. The Word is different from all created things: he is the unique Word belonging only to the good Father. This is the Word that created this whole world and enlightens it by his loving wisdom. He who is the good Word of the good Father produced the order in all creation, joining opposites together, and forming from them one harmonious sound. He is God, one and only-begotten, who proceeds in goodness from the Father as from the fountain of goodness, and gives order, direction and unity to creation.

By his eternal Word the Father created all things and implanted a nature in his creatures. He did not want to see them tossed about at the mercy of their own natures, and so be reduced to nothingness. But in his goodness he governs and sustains the whole of nature by his Word (who is himself also God), so that under the guidance, providence and ordering of that Word, the whole of nature might remain stable and coherent in his light. Nature was to share in the Father's Word, whose reality is true, and be helped by him to exist, for without him it would cease to be. For unless the Word, who is the very *image of the invisible God, the firstborn of all creation*[Col 1:15], kept it in existence it could not exist. For whatever exists, whether visible or invisible, remains in existence through him and in him, and he is also the head of the Church, as we are taught by the ministers of truth in their sacred writings.

The almighty and most holy Word of the Father pervades the whole of reality, everywhere unfolding his power and shining on all things visible and invisible. He sustains it all and binds it together in himself. He leaves nothing devoid of his power but gives life and keeps it in being throughout all of creation and in each individual creature.

Friday of the 1st Week in Ordinary Time

From a Discourse Against the Pagans by Saint Athanasius, Bishop & Doctor

The Word creates a divine harmony in creation

In the beginning was the Word, and the Word was with God, and the Word was God. All things were made through him, and without him nothing was made[Jn 1:1-3]. In these words John the theologian teaches that nothing exists or remains in being except in and through the Word.

Think of a musician tuning his lyre. By his skill he adjusts high notes to low and intermediate notes to the rest, and produces a series of harmonies. So too the wisdom of God holds the world like a lyre and joins things in the air to those on earth, and things in heaven to those in the air, and brings each part into harmony with the whole. By his decree and will he regulates them all to produce the beauty and harmony of a single, well-ordered universe. While remaining unchanged with his Father, he moves all creation by his unchanging nature, according to the Father's will. To everything he gives existence and life in accordance with its nature, and so creates a wonderful and truly divine harmony.

To illustrate this profound mystery, let us take the example of a choir of many singers. A choir is composed of a variety of men, women and children, of both old and young. Under the direction of one conductor, each sings in the way that is natural for him: men with men's voices, boys with boys' voices, old people with old voices, young people with young voices. Yet all of them produce a single harmony. Or consider the example of our soul. It moves our senses according to their several functions so that in the presence of a single object they all act simultaneously: the eye sees, the ear hears, the hand touches, the nose smells, the tongue tastes, and often the other parts of the body act as well as, for example, the feet may walk.

Although this is only a poor comparison, it gives some idea of how the whole universe is governed. The Word of God has but to give a gesture of command and everything falls into place; each creature performs its own proper function, and all together constitute one single harmonious order.

Saturday of the 1st Week in Ordinary Time

From a letter to the Corinthians by Saint Clement I, Pope & Martyr

From the first, faith has been God's means of justifying men

God's blessing must be our objective, and the way to win it our study. Search the records of ancient times. Why was our father Abraham blessed? Was it not because his upright and straightforward conduct was inspired by faith? As for Isaac's faith, it was so strong that, assured of the outcome, he willingly allowed himself to be offered in sacrifice. Jacob had the humility to leave his native land on account of his brother, and go and serve Laban. He was given the twelve tribes of Israel.

Honest reflection upon each of these examples will make us realize the magnitude of God's gifts. All the priests and levites who served the altar of God were descended from Jacob. The manhood of the Lord Jesus derived from him. Through the tribe of Judah, kings, princes and rulers sprang from him. Nor are his other tribes without their honor, for God promised Abraham: *Your descendants shall be as the stars of heaven*[Gen 26:4].

It is obvious, therefore, that none of these owed their honor and exaltation to themselves, or to their own labors, or to their deeds of virtue. No; they owed everything to God's will. So likewise with us, who by his will are called in Christ Jesus. We are not justified by our wisdom, intelligence, piety, or by any action of ours, however holy, but by faith, the one means by which God has justified men from the beginning. To him be glory for ever and ever. Amen.

What must we do then, brothers? Give up good works? Stop practicing Christian love? God forbid! We must be ready and eager for every opportunity to do good, and put our whole heart into it. Even the Creator and Lord of the universe rejoices in his works. By his supreme power he set the heavens in their place; by his infinite wisdom he gave them their order. He separated the land from the waters surrounding it and made his own will its firm foundation. By his command he brought to life the beasts that roam the earth. He created the sea and all its living creatures, and then by his power set bounds to it. Finally, with his own holy and undefiled hands, he formed man, the highest and most intelligent of his creatures, the copy of his own image. *Let us make man,* God said, *in our image and likeness. And God made man, male and female he made them*[Gen 1:26-27]. Then, when he had finished making all his creatures, God gave them his approval and blessing: *Increase and multiply*[Gen 1:28], he charged them.

We must recognize, therefore, that all upright men have been graced by good works, and that even the Lord himself took delight in the glory his works gave him. This should inspire us with a resolute determination to do his will and make us put our whole strength into the work of living a Christian life.

Sunday of the 2nd Week in Ordinary Time

From a Letter to the Ephesians by Saint Ignatius of Antioch, Bishop & Martyr

The harmony of unity

It is right for you to give glory in every way to Jesus Christ who has given glory to you; you must be made holy in all things by being united in perfect obedience, in submission to the bishop and the presbyters.

I am not giving you orders as if I were a person of importance. Even if I am a prisoner for the name of Christ, I am not yet made perfect in Jesus Christ. I am now beginning to be a disciple and I am speaking to you as my fellow-disciple. It is you who should be strengthening me by your faith, your encouragement, your patience, your serenity. But since love will not allow me to be silent about you, I am taking the opportunity to urge you to be united in conformity with the mind of God. For Jesus Christ, our life, without whom we cannot live, is the mind of the Father, just as the bishops, appointed over the whole earth, are in conformity with the mind of Jesus Christ.

It is fitting, therefore, that you should be in agreement with the mind of the bishop as in fact you are. Your excellent presbyters, who are a credit to God, are as suited to the bishop as strings to a harp. So in your harmony of mind and heart the song you sing is Jesus Christ. Every one of you should form a choir, so that, in harmony of sound through harmony of hearts, and in unity taking the note from God, you may sing with one voice through Jesus Christ to the Father. If you do this, he will listen to you and see from your good works that you are members of his Son. It is then an advantage to you to live in perfect unity, so that at all times you may share in God.

If in a short space of time I have become so close a friend of your bishop – in a friendship not based on nature but on spiritual grounds – how much more blessed do I judge you to be, for you are as united with him as the Church is to Jesus Christ, and Jesus Christ to the Father, so that all things are in harmony through unity. Let no one make any mistake: unless a person is within the sanctuary, he is deprived of God's bread. For if the prayer of one or two has such power, how much more has the prayer of the bishop and the whole Church.

Monday of the 2nd Week in Ordinary Time

From a letter to the Ephesians by Saint Ignatius of Antioch, Bishop & Martyr

Have Faith in Christ, and love

Try to gather together more frequently to give thanks to God and to praise him. For when you come together frequently, Satan's powers are undermined, and the destruction that he threatens is done away with in the unanimity of your faith. Nothing is better than peace, in which all warfare between heaven and earth is brought to an end.

None of this will escape you if you have perfect faith and love toward Jesus Christ. These are the beginning and the end of life: faith the beginning, love the end. When these two are found together, there is God, and everything else concerning right living follows from them. No one professing faith sins; no one possessing love hates. *A tree is known by its fruit*[Lk 6:44]. So those who profess to belong to Christ will be known by what they do. For the work we are about is not a matter of words here and now, but depends on the power of faith and on being found faithful to the end.

It is better to remain silent and to be than to talk and not be. Teaching is good if the speaker also acts. Now there was one teacher who *spoke, and it was made*[Ps 32:9], and even what he did in silence is worthy of the Father. He who has the word of Jesus can truly listen also to his silence, in order to be perfect, that he may act through his speech and be known by his silence. Nothing is hidden from the Lord, but even our secrets are close to him. Let us then do everything in the knowledge that he is dwelling within us that we may be his temples, and he God within us. He is, and will reveal himself, in our sight, according to the love we bear him in holiness.

Make no mistake, my brothers: those who corrupt families *will not inherit the kingdom of God*[1 Cor 6:9-10]. If those who do these things in accordance with the flesh have died, how much worse will it be if one corrupts through evil doctrine the faith of God for which Jesus Christ was crucified. Such a person, because he is defiled, will depart into the unquenchable fire, as will anyone who listens to him.

For the Lord received anointing on his head in order that he might breathe incorruptibility on the Church. Do not be anointed with the evil odor of the teachings of the prince of this world, that he may not lead you captive away from the life that is set before you. But why is it that we are not all wise when we have received the knowledge of God, which is Jesus Christ? Why do we perish in our stupidity, not knowing the gift the Lord has truly sent us?

My spirit is given over to the humble service of the cross which is a stumbling block to unbelievers but to us salvation and eternal life.

Tuesday of the 2nd Week in Ordinary Time

From a letter to the Corinthians by Saint Clement I, Pope & Martyr

Who can express the binding power of divine love?

Let the man truly possessed by the love of Christ keep his commandments. Who can express the binding power of divine love? Who can find words for the splendor of its beauty? Beyond all description are the heights to which it lifts us. Love unites us to God; *it cancels innumerable sins*[1 Pet 4:8], has no limits to its endurance, bears everything patiently. Love is neither servile nor arrogant. It does not provoke schisms or form cliques, but always acts in harmony with others. By it all God's chosen ones have been sanctified; without it, it is impossible to please him. Out of love the Lord took us to himself; because he loved us and it was God's will, our Lord Jesus Christ gave his life's blood for us – he gave his body for our body, his soul for our soul.

See then, beloved, what a great and wonderful thing love is, and how inexpressible its perfection. Who are worthy to possess it unless God makes them so? To him therefore we must turn, begging of his mercy that there may be found in us a love free from human partiality and beyond reproach. Every generation from Adam's time to ours has passed away; but those who by God's grace were made perfect in love have a dwelling now among the saints, and when at last the kingdom of Christ appears, they will be revealed. *Take shelter in your rooms for a little while,* says Scripture, *until my wrath subsides*[Isa 26:20]. *Then I will remember the good days, and will raise you from your graves*[Ezek 37:12].

Happy are we, beloved, if love enables us to live in harmony and in the observance of God's commandments, for then it will also gain for us the remission of our sins. Scripture pronounces *happy those whose transgressions are pardoned, whose sins are forgiven. Happy the man,* it says, *to whom the Lord imputes no fault, on whose lips there is no guile*[Ps 31:1-2]. This is the blessing given those whom God has chosen through Jesus Christ our Lord. To him be glory for ever and ever. Amen.

Wednesday of the 2nd Week in Ordinary Time

From the dogmatic constitution on the Church of the Second Vatican Council

See, I will save my people

In his wisdom and goodness the eternal Father created the whole world according to his supremely free and mysterious purpose and decreed that men should be raised up to share in the divine life. When they fell in Adam, he did not abandon them but always kept providing them with aids to salvation, in consideration of Christ, *who is the image of the invisible God, the firstborn of all creation*[Col 1:15]. Before the ages the Father *already knew* all the elect *and predestined them to be made into the likeness of his Son, so that he should be the firstborn among many brothers*[Rom 8:29].

God resolved to gather into holy Church all who believe in Christ. The Church, foreshadowed even from the beginning of the world, so marvelously prepared in the history of the people of Israel, established in these last times and revealed by the outpouring of the Holy Spirit, will be made perfect in glory at the end of time. Then, as we read in the Fathers of the Church, all the righteous from Adam onward – from Abel, the righteous, to the last of the elect – will be gathered in the universal Church in the presence of the Father.

Finally, those who have not yet received the Gospel are in their different ways related to God's people.

In the first place, there is that people which was given the covenants and the promises and from which Christ was born by human descent: the people which is by God's choice most dear on account of the patriarchs. God never repents of his gifts or his call.

God's plan of salvation embraces those also who acknowledge the Creator. Among these are especially the Mohammedans; they profess their faith as the faith of Abraham, and with us they worship the one, merciful God who will judge men on the last day.

God himself is not far from those others who seek the unknown God in darkness and shadows, for it is he who gives to all men life and inspiration and all things, and who as Savior desires all men to be saved.

Eternal salvation is open to those who, through no fault of their own, do not know Christ and his Church but seek God with a sincere heart, and under the inspiration of grace try in their lives to do his will, made known to them by the dictates of their conscience. Nor does Divine Providence deny the aids necessary for salvation to those who, without blame on their part, have not yet reached an explicit belief in God, but strive to lead a good life, under the influence of God's grace.

Whatever goodness and truth is found among them is seen by the Church as a preparation for the Gospel, and as given by him who shines on all men, so that they may at last have life.

Thursday of the 2nd Week in Ordinary Time

From a letter by Fulgentius of Ruspe, Bishop

Christ lives for ever to make intercession for us

Notice, at the conclusion of our prayer we never say, "through the Holy Spirit," but rather, "through Jesus Christ, your Son, our Lord." Through the mystery of the Incarnation, Jesus Christ *became man, the mediator of God and man. He is a priest for ever according to the order of Melchizedek. By shedding his own blood he entered once and for all into the Holy Places. He did not enter a place made by human hands, a mere type of the true one*[Heb Chapters 7-10]; but, he entered heaven itself, where he is at God's right hand interceding for us. Quite correctly, the Church continues to reflect this mystery in her prayer.

This mystery of Jesus Christ the high priest is reflected in the apostle Paul's statement: *Through him, then, let us always offer the sacrifice of praise to God, the fruit of lips that profess belief in his name*[Heb 13:15]. We were once enemies of the Father, but have been reconciled through the death of Christ. Through him then we offer our sacrifice of praise, our prayer to God. He became our offering to the Father, and through him our offering is now acceptable. It is for this reason that Peter the apostle urges us *to be built up as living stones into a spiritual house, a holy priesthood to offer spiritual sacrifices pleasing to God through Jesus Christ*[1 Pet 2:5]. This then is the reason why we offer prayer to God our Father, but through Jesus Christ our Lord.

When we speak of Christ's priesthood, what else do we mean than the incarnation? Through this mystery, the Son of God, *though his state was divine...emptied himself to assume the condition of a slave. As a slave, he humbled himself and in obedience he even accepted death*[Phil 2:6-11]. Even though he possessed equality with the Father, *he became a little less than the angels*. Always equal to the Father, the Son became a little less because he became a man. Christ lowered himself *when he emptied himself to assume the condition of a slave*.

By this condition, Christ, the only-begotten Son of God, though himself ever remaining God, became a priest. To him along with the Father, we offer our sacrifice. Yet, through him the sacrifice we now offer is holy, living and pleasing to God. Indeed, if Christ had not sacrificed himself for us, we could not offer any sacrifice. For it is in him that our human nature becomes a redemptive offering. When we offer our prayers through him, our priest, we confess that Christ truly possesses the flesh of our race. Clearly the Apostle refers to this when he says: *Every high priest is taken from among men. He is appointed to act on behalf of these same men in their relationship to God; he is to offer gifts and sacrifices to God*[Heb 5:1].

We do not, however, only say "your Son" when we conclude our prayer. We also say, "who lives and reigns with you in the unity of the Holy Spirit." In this way we commemorate the natural unity of the Father, Son and Holy Spirit. It is clear, then, that the Christ who exercises a priestly role on our behalf is the same Christ who enjoys a natural unity and equality with the Father and the Holy Spirit.

Friday of the 2nd Week in Ordinary Time

From the treatise On Spiritual Perfection by Diadochus of Photice, Bishop

All our love must be for God

No one who is in love with himself is capable of loving God. The man who loves God is the one who mortifies his self-love for the sake of the immeasurable blessings of divine love. Such a man never seeks his own glory but only the glory of God. If a person loves himself he seeks his own glory, but the man who loves God loves the glory of his Creator. Anyone alive to the love of God can be recognized from the way he constantly strives to glorify him by fulfilling all his commandments and by delighting in his own abasement. Because of his great majesty it is fitting that God should receive glory, but if he hopes to win God's favor it becomes man to be humble. If we possess this love for God, we too will rejoice in his glory as Saint John the Baptist did, and we shall never stop repeating: *His fame must increase, but mine must diminish*[Jn 3:30].

I know a man who, though lamenting his failure to love God as much as he desires, yet loves him so much that his soul burns with ceaseless longing for God to be glorified, and for his own complete effacement. This man has no feeling of self-importance even when he receives praise. So deep is his desire to humble himself that he never even thinks of his own dignity. He fulfills his priestly duty by celebrating the Liturgy, but his intense love for God is an abyss that swallows up all consciousness of his high office. His humility makes him oblivious of any honor it might bring him, so that in his own estimation he is never anything but a useless servant. Because of his desire for self-abasement, he regards himself as though degraded from his office. His example is one that we ourselves should follow by fleeing from all honor and glory for the sake of the immeasurable blessings of God's love, for he has loved us so much!

Anyone who loves God in the depths of his heart has already been loved by God. In fact, the measure of a man's love for God depends upon how deeply aware he is of God's love for him. When this awareness is keen it makes whoever possesses it long to be enlightened by the divine light, and this longing is so intense that it seems to penetrate his very bones. He loses all consciousness of himself and is entirely transformed by the love of God.

Such a man lives in this life and at the same time does not live in it, for although he still inhabits his body, he is constantly leaving it in spirit because of the love that draws him toward God. Once the love of God has released him from self-love, the flame of divine love never ceases to burn in his heart and he remains united to God by an irresistible longing. As the Apostle says: *If we are taken out of ourselves it is for the love of God; if we are brought back to our senses it is for your sake*[2 Cor 5:13].

Saturday of the 2nd Week in Ordinary Time

From the treatise Against Heresies by Saint Irenaeus, Bishop, Doctor & Martyr

The pure oblation of the Church

The oblation of the Church, which the Lord taught was to be offered throughout the whole world, has been regarded by God as a pure sacrifice, and is acceptable to him. Not that he needs sacrifice from us, but the one who makes the offering himself receives glory in his offering, provided that his gift is accepted. Through a gift both honor and love are shown to a king.

The Lord wants us to make our offering in all sincerity and freedom from sin. He declared this when he said: *When, therefore, you offer your gift at the altar and remember that your brother holds something against you, leave your gift before the altar, and first go and be reconciled with your brother; and then come back and offer your gift*[Mt 5:23-24].

We must offer God the first fruits of his creation, as Moses said: *You will not come empty-handed into the presence of the Lord your God*[Deut 16:16]. In showing gratitude to God for his gifts man is to be accounted pleasing to God, and so receive the honor that comes from God.

It is not oblations as such that have met with disapproval. There were oblations of old; there are oblations now. There were sacrifices among the people of Israel; there are sacrifices in the Church. Only the kind of oblation has been changed: now it is offered by freemen, not by slaves. There is one and the same Lord, but the character of an oblation made by slaves is distinctive, so too that of an oblation made by sons: their oblations bear the mark of freedom.

With God there is nothing without purpose, nothing without its meaning and reason. Thus the people of Israel used to dedicate tithes of their possessions. But those who have been given freedom devote what they possess to the Lord's use. They give it all to him, not simply what is of lesser value, cheerfully and freely because they hope for greater things, like the poor widow who put into God's treasury her whole livelihood.

We must make oblation to God, and in all things be found pleasing to God the Creator, in sound teaching, in sincere faith, in firm hope, in ardent love, as we offer the first-fruits of the creatures that are his. The Church alone offers this pure oblation to the Creator when it makes its offering to him from his creation, with thanksgiving.

We offer him what is his, and so we proclaim communion and unity and profess our belief in the resurrection of flesh and spirit. Just as bread from the earth, when it receives the invocation of God, is no longer common bread but the Eucharist, made up of two elements, one earthly and one heavenly, so also our bodies, in receiving the Eucharist, are no longer corruptible, for they have the hope of resurrection.

Sunday of the Third Week in Ordinary Time

From the constitution on the sacred Liturgy of the Second Vatican Council

Christ is present to his Church

Christ is always present to his Church, especially in the actions of the liturgy. He is present in the sacrifice of the Mass, in the person of the minister (it is the same Christ who formerly offered himself on the cross that now offers by the ministry of priests) and most of all under the eucharistic species. He is present in the sacraments by his power, in such a way that when someone baptizes, Christ himself baptizes. He is present in his word, for it is he himself who speaks when the holy Scriptures are read in the Church. Finally, he is present when the Church prays and sings, for he himself promised: *Where two or three are gathered in my name, I am there in their midst*[Mt 18:20].

Indeed, in this great work which gives perfect glory to God and brings holiness to men, Christ is always joining in partnership with himself his beloved Bride, the Church, which calls upon its Lord and through him gives worship to the eternal Father.

It is therefore right to see the liturgy as an exercise of the priestly office of Jesus Christ, in which through signs addressed to the senses man's sanctification is signified and, in a way proper to each of these signs, made effective, and in which public worship is celebrated in its fullness by the mystical body of Jesus Christ, that is, by the head and by his members.

Accordingly, every liturgical celebration, as an activity of Christ the priest and of his body, which is the Church, is a sacred action of a pre-eminent kind. No other action of the Church equals its title to power or its degree of effectiveness.

In the liturgy on earth we are given a foretaste and share in the liturgy of heaven, celebrated in the holy city of Jerusalem, the goal of our pilgrimage, where Christ *is seated at the right hand of God, as minister of the sanctuary and of the true tabernacle*[Heb 8:2]. With the whole company of heaven we sing a hymn of praise to the Lord; as we reverence the memory of the saints, we hope to have some part with them, and to share in their fellowship; *we wait for the Savior, our Lord Jesus Christ, until he, who is our life, appears, and we appear with him in glory*[Titus 2:3; Col 3-4].

By an apostolic tradition taking its origin from the very day of Christ's resurrection, the Church celebrates the paschal mystery every eighth day, the day that is rightly called the Lord's day. On Sunday the Christian faithful ought to gather together, so that by listening to the word of God and sharing in the Eucharist they may recall the passion, death and resurrection of the Lord Jesus and give thanks to God who *has given* them *a new birth with a lively hope through the resurrection of Jesus Christ from the dead*[1 Pet 1:3]. The Lord's day is therefore the first and greatest festival, one to be set before the loving devotion of the faithful and impressed upon it, so that it may be also a day of joy and of freedom from work. Other celebrations must not take precedence over it, unless they are truly of the greatest importance, since it is the foundation and the kernel of the whole liturgical year.

Monday of the Third Week in Ordinary Time

From the pastoral constitution on the Church in the Modern World
The Second Vatican Council

The sanctity of marriage and the family

Husband and wife, by the covenant of marriage, are no longer two, but one flesh. By their intimate union of persons and of actions they give mutual help and service to each other, experience the meaning of their unity, and gain an ever deeper understanding of it day by day.

This intimate union in the mutual self-giving of two persons, as well as the good of the children, demands full fidelity from both, and an indissoluble unity between them.

Christ the Lord has abundantly blessed this richly complex love which springs from the divine source of love and is founded on the model of his union with the Church.

In earlier times God met his people in a covenant of love and fidelity. So now the Savior of mankind, the Bridegroom of the Church, meets Christian husbands and wives in the sacrament of matrimony. Further, he remains with them in order that, as he loved the Church and gave himself up for her, so husband and wife may, in mutual self-giving, love each other with perpetual fidelity.

True married love is caught up into God's love; it is guided and enriched by the redeeming power of Christ and the saving action of the Church, in order that the partners may be effectively led to God and receive help and strength in the sublime responsibility of parenthood.

Christian partners are therefore strengthened, and as it were consecrated, by a special sacrament for the duties and the dignity of their state. By the power of this sacrament they fulfill their obligations to each other and to their family and are filled with the spirit of Christ. This spirit pervades their whole lives with faith, hope and love. Thus they promote their own perfection and each other's sanctification, and so contribute together to the greater glory of God.

Hence, with parents leading the way by example and family prayer, their children - indeed, all within the family circle - will find it easier to make progress in natural virtues, in salvation and in holiness. Husband and wife, raised to the dignity and the responsibility of parenthood, will be zealous in fulfilling their task as educators, especially in the sphere of religious education, a task that is primarily their own.

Children, as active members of the family, contribute in their own way to the holiness of their parents. With the love of grateful hearts, with loving respect and trust, they will return the generosity of their parents and will stand by them as true sons and daughters when they meet with hardship and the loneliness of old age.

Tuesday of the Third Week in Ordinary Time

From the Detailed Rules for Monks by Saint Basil the Great, Bishop & Doctor

How shall we repay the Lord for all his goodness to us?

What words can adequately describe God's gifts? They are so numerous that they defy enumeration. They are so great that any one of them demands our total gratitude in response.

Yet even though we cannot speak of it worthily, there is one gift which no thoughtful man can pass over in silence. God fashioned man in his own image and likeness; he gave him knowledge of himself; he endowed him with the ability to think which raised him above all living creatures; he permitted him to delight in the unimaginable beauties of paradise, and gave him dominion over everything upon earth.

Then, when man was deceived by the serpent and fell into sin, which led to death and to all the sufferings associated with death, God still did not forsake him. He first gave man the law to help him; he set angels over him to guard him; he sent the prophets to denounce vice and to teach virtue; he restrained man's evil impulses by warnings and roused his desire for virtue by promises. Frequently, by way of warning, God showed him the respective ends of virtue and of vice in the lives of other men. Moreover, when man continued in disobedience even after he had done all this, God did not desert him.

No, we were not abandoned by the goodness of the Lord. Even the insult we offered to our Benefactor by despising his gifts did not destroy his love for us. On the contrary, although we were dead, our Lord Jesus Christ restored us to life again, and in a way even more amazing than the fact itself, *for his state was divine, yet he did not cling to his equality with God, but emptied himself to assume the condition of a slave*[Phil 2:6-7.]

He bore our infirmities and endured our sorrows. He was wounded for our sake so that by his wounds we might be healed. He redeemed us from the curse by becoming a curse for our sake[Isa 53:4-5], and he submitted to the most ignominious death in order to exalt us to the life of glory. Nor was he content merely to summon us back from death to life; he also bestowed on us the dignity of his own divine nature and prepared for us a place of eternal rest where there will be joy so intense as to surpass all human imagination.

How, then, shall we repay the Lord for all his goodness to us? He is so good that he asks no recompense except our love: that is the only payment he desires. To confess my personal feelings, when I reflect on all these blessings I am overcome by a kind of dread and numbness at the very possibility of ceasing to love God and of bringing shame upon Christ because of my lack of recollection and my preoccupation with trivialities.

Wednesday of the Third Week in Ordinary Time

From a sermon on the Song of Songs by Saint Bernard, Abbot & Doctor

Where sin abounded grace has overflowed

Where can the weak find a place of firm security and peace, except in the wounds of the Savior? Indeed, the more secure is my place there the more he can do to help me. The world rages, the flesh is heavy, and the devil lays his snares, but I do not fall, for my feet are planted on firm rock. I may have sinned gravely. My conscience would be distressed, but it would not be in turmoil, for I would recall the wounds of the Lord: *he was wounded for our iniquities*[Isa 53:5-12]. What sin is there so deadly that it cannot be pardoned by the death of Christ? And so if I bear in mind this strong, effective remedy, I can never again be terrified by the malignancy of sin.

Surely the man who said: *My sin is too great to merit pardon*[Ps 24:6-11], was wrong. He was speaking as though he were not a member of Christ and had no share in his merits, so that he could claim them as his own, as a member of the body can claim what belongs to the head. As for me, what can I appropriate that I lack from the heart of the Lord who abounds in mercy? They pierced his hands and feet and opened his side with a spear. Through the openings of these wounds I may drink *honey from the rock and oil from the hardest stone*[Deut 32:13]*: that is, I may taste and see that the Lord is sweet*[Ps 33:9].

He was thinking thoughts of peace, and I did not know it, *for who knows the mind of the Lord, or who has been his counselor*[Rom 11:34]? But the piercing nail has become a key to unlock the door, that I may see the good will of the Lord. And what can I see as I look through the hole? Both the nail and the wound cry out that God was in Christ reconciling the world to himself. *The sword pierced his soul and came close to his heart*, so that he might be able to feel compassion for me in my weaknesses.

Through these sacred wounds we can see the secret of his heart, the great mystery of love, *the sincerity of his mercy with which he visited us from on high*. Where have your love, your mercy, your compassion shone out more luminously than in your wounds, sweet, gentle Lord of mercy? More mercy than this no one has than that he lay down his life for those who are doomed to death.

My merit comes from his mercy; for I do not lack merit so long as he does not lack pity. And if the Lord's mercies are many, then I am rich in merits. For even if I am aware of many sins, what does it matter? *Where sin abounded grace has overflowed*[Rom 5:20]. And if *the Lord's mercies are from all ages for ever*[Ps 24:6], I too *will sing of the mercies of the Lord for ever*[Ps 88:2]. Will I not sing of my own righteousness? No, *Lord, I shall be mindful only of your justice*[Ps 70:16]. Yet that too is my own; for God has made you my righteousness.

Thursday of the Third Week in Ordinary Time

From a sermon by John the Serene, Bishop

Love the Lord and walk in his ways

The Lord is my light and my salvation; whom shall I fear[Ps 26:1]*?* How great was that servant who knew how he was given light, whence it came, and what sort of man he was when he was favored by that light. The light he saw was not that which fades at dusk, but *the light which no eye has seen*. Souls brightened by this light do not fall into sin or stumble on vice.

Our Lord said: *Walk while you have the light in you*[Jn 12:35]. What other light did he mean but himself? For it was he who said: *I came as a light into the world*[Jn 12:46]*,* so that those who have eyes may not see and the blind may receive *the light.* The Lord then is our light, the sun of justice and righteousness, who has shone on his Catholic Church spread throughout the world. The prophet spoke as a figure of the Church when he cried: *The Lord is my light and my salvation; whom shall I fear?*

The spiritual man who has been thus illumined does not limp or leave the path, but bears all things. Glimpsing our true country from afar, he puts up with adversities; he is not saddened by the things of time, but finds his strength in God. He lowers his pride and endures, possessing patience through humility. That true light *which enlightens every man who comes into the world*[Jn 1:9] bestows itself on those who reverence it, shining where it wills, on whom it wills, and revealing itself according to the will of God the Son.

When this light begins to shine upon the man who sat *in darkness and the shadow of death*[Ps 22:4; Lk 1:76-79]*,* in the darkness of evil and the shadow of sin, he is shocked, he calls himself to account, repents of his misdeeds in shame, and says: *The Lord is my light and my salvation; whom shall I fear?* Great is this salvation, my brethren, which fears neither sickness nor lethargy and disregards pain. We should then in the fullest sense not only with our voice but with our very soul cry out, *The Lord is my light and my salvation; whom shall I fear?* If he enlightens and saves me, whom shall I fear? Even though the dark shadows of evil suggestions crowd about, *the Lord is my light*. They can approach, but cannot prevail; they can lay siege to our heart, but cannot conquer it. Though the blindness of concupiscence assails us, again we say: *The Lord is my light*. For he is our strength; he gives himself to us and we give ourselves to him. Hasten to this physician while you can, or you may not be able to find him when you want him.

Friday of the Third Week in Ordinary Time

From a commentary on the psalms by John Fisher, Bishop & Martyr

The wonderful works of God

First God freed Israel from the bondage of Egypt by performing many signs and wonders. He permitted them to cross the Red Sea dry-shod. He fed them in the desert with food from heaven in the form of manna and quail. When they were suffering from thirst, he produced an everflowing spring of water from the hardest rock. He gave them victory over all the enemies who made war against them. He forced the river to flow backward for a time. He divided the promised land and distributed it among them according to the number of their tribes and families.

Yet even though he treated them so lovingly and generously, the Israelites were ungrateful and seemed forgetful of all this. They abandoned the worship of God and more than once they were guilty of the abominable sin of idolatry.

Then he also took pity on us, *when we were pagans who went off to mute idols wherever we were led*[1 Cor 12:2]. He severed us from the wild olive tree of paganism and, breaking our natural branches, he grafted us onto the true olive tree of Judaism and made us share in the root of his grace and its richness. Finally, *he did not spare his own Son but gave him up for us all*[Rom 8:32]*, an offering and a sacrifice to God in a fragrant odor*[Eph 5:2] *that he might redeem us from all our iniquity and cleanse for himself an acceptable people*[Titus 2:14].

Now all these things are not merely certain arguments but also clear proof of his deep love and kindness for us. And yet we are the most ungrateful of men. Indeed, we have gone beyond the bounds of ingratitude: we give no thought to his love, nor do we recognize the extent of his kindnesses to us. Rather we reject the one who lavishes so many favors and even appear to despise him; and the remarkable mercy that he has continually shown to sinners does not move us to form our lives and conduct according to his most holy command.

Clearly these things are worthy to be written down in the second generation so as to preserve their memory for ever. Thus all who are still to be counted among Christians will know the great kindness of God toward us and never cease singing his divine praises.

Saturday of the Third Week in Ordinary Time

From the pastoral constitution on the Church in the Modern World
The Second Vatican Council

The mystery of death

In the face of death the enigma of human existence reaches its climax. Man is not only the victim of pain and the progressive deterioration of his body; he is also, and more deeply, tormented by the fear of final extinction. But the instinctive judgment of his heart is right when he shrinks from, and rejects, the idea of a total collapse and definitive end of his own person. He carries within him the seed of eternity, which cannot be reduced to matter alone, and so he rebels against death. All efforts of technology, however useful they may be, cannot calm his anxieties; the biological extension of his life-span cannot satisfy the desire inescapably present in his heart for a life beyond this life.

Imagination is completely helpless when confronted with death. Yet the Church, instructed by divine revelation, affirms that man has been created by God for a destiny of happiness beyond the reach of earthly trials. Moreover, the Christian faith teaches that bodily death, to which man would not have been subject if he had not sinned, will be conquered; the almighty and merciful Savior will restore man to the wholeness that he had lost through his own fault. God has called man, and still calls him, to be united in his whole being in perpetual communion with himself in the immortality of the divine life. This victory has been gained for us by the risen Christ, who by his own death has freed man from death.

Faith, presented with solid arguments, offers every thinking person the answer to his questionings concerning his future destiny. At the same time, it enables him to be one in Christ with his loved ones who have been taken from him by death and gives him hope that they have entered into true life with God.

Certainly, the Christian is faced with the necessity, and the duty, of fighting against evil through many trials, and of undergoing death. But by entering into the paschal mystery and being made like Christ in death, he will look forward, strong in hope, to the resurrection.

This is true not only of Christians but also of all men of good will in whose heart grace is invisibly at work. Since Christ died for all men, and the ultimate vocation of man is in fact one, that is, a divine vocation, we must hold that the Holy Spirit offers to all the possibility of being united with this paschal mystery in a way known only to God.

Such is the great mystery of man, enlightening believers through the Christian revelation. Through Christ and in Christ light is thrown on the enigma of pain and death which overwhelms us without his Gospel to teach us. Christ has risen, destroying death by his own death; he has given us the free gift of life so that as sons in the Son we may cry out in the Spirit, saying: *Abba, Father!*

Sunday of the Fourth Week in Ordinary Time

From a letter to the Church of Smyrna
Saint Ignatius of Antioch, Bishop and Martyr

Christ has called us to his kingdom and glory

From Ignatius, known as Theophorus, to the Church of God the Father and of Jesus Christ, his beloved, at Smyrna in Asia, wishing you all joy in an immaculate spirit and the Word of God. By his mercy you have won every gift and lack none, filled as you are with faith and love, beloved of God and fruitful in sanctity.

I celebrate the glory of Jesus Christ as God, because he is responsible for your wisdom, well aware as I am of the perfection of your unshakeable faith. You are like men who have been nailed body and soul to the cross of Jesus Christ, confirmed in love by his blood.

In regard to the Lord, you firmly believe that he was *of the race of David according to the flesh*[Rom 9:5], but God's son by the will and power of God; truly born of the Virgin and baptized by John, *that all justice might be fulfilled*[Mt 3:15]; truly nailed to a cross in the flesh for our sake under Pontius Pilate and the Tetrarch Herod, and of his most blessed passion we are the fruit. And thus, by his resurrection he raised up a standard over his saints and faithful ones for all time (both Jews and Gentiles alike) in the one body of his Church. For he endured all this for us, for our salvation; and he really suffered, and just as truly rose from the dead.

As for myself, I am convinced that he was united with his body even after the resurrection. When he visited Peter and his companions, he said to them: *Take hold of me, touch me and see that I am not a spirit without a body*[Lk 24:39]. Immediately they touched him and believed, clutching at his body and his very spirit. And for this reason they despised death and conquered it. In addition, after his resurrection, the Lord ate and drank with them like a real human being, even though in spirit he was united with his Father.

And so I am giving you serious instruction on these things, dearly beloved, even though I am aware that you believe them to be so.

Monday of the Fourth Week in Ordinary Time

From a commentary on the psalms by Saint Hilary of Poitiers, Bishop & Doctor

The hearts and minds of all believers were one

Behold, how good and pleasant it is for brothers to dwell in unity[Ps 132:1]! It is good and pleasant for brothers to dwell in unity, because when they do so their association creates the assembly of the Church. The term "brothers" describes the bond of affection arising from their singleness of purpose.

We read that when the apostles first preached, the chief instruction they gave lay in this saying: *The hearts and minds of all believers were one*[Acts 4:32]. So it is fitting for the people of God to be brothers under one Father, to be united under one Spirit, to live in harmony under one roof, to be limbs of one body.

It is pleasant and good for brothers to dwell in unity. The prophet suggested a comparison for this good and pleasant activity when he said: *It is like the ointment on the head which ran down over the beard of Aaron, down upon the collar of his garment*[Ps 132:2]. Aaron's oil was made of the perfumes used to anoint a priest. It was God's decision that his priest should have this consecration first, and that our Lord too should be anointed, but not visibly, *by those who are joined with him*[1 Cor 6:15-17]. Aaron's anointing did not belong to this world; it was not done with the horn used for kings, but *with the oil of gladness*[Heb 1:9]. So afterward Aaron was called the anointed one as the Law prescribed.

When this oil is poured out upon men of unclean heart, it snuffs out their lives, but when it is received as an anointing of love, it exudes the sweet odor of harmony with God. As Paul says, *we are the goodly fragrance of Christ*[2 Cor 2:14-16]. So just as it was pleasing to God when Aaron was anointed priest with this oil, so it is good and pleasant for brothers to dwell in unity.

Now the oil ran down from his head to his beard. A beard adorns a man of mature years. We must not be children before Christ except in the restricted scriptural sense of being children in wickedness but not in our way of thinking. Now Paul calls all who lack faith, children, because they are too weak to take solid food and still need milk. As he says: *I fed you with milk rather than the solid food for which you were not yet ready; and you are still not ready*[1 Cor 3:2].

Tuesday of the Fourth Week in Ordinary Time

From the treatise Against Heresies by Saint Irenaeus, Bishop, Doctor & Martyr

In Christ are the firstfruits of the resurrection

The Word of God became man, the Son of God became the Son of Man, in order to unite man with himself and make him, by adoption, a son of God. Only by being united to one who is himself immune could we be preserved from corruption and death, and how else could this union have been achieved if he had not first become what we are? How else could what is corruptible and mortal in us have been swallowed up in his incorruptibility and immortality, to enable us to receive adoptive sonship? Therefore, the Son of God, our Lord, the Word of the Father, is also the son of man; he became the son of man by a human birth from Mary, a member of the human race.

The Lord himself has given us a sign here below and in the heights of heaven, a sign that man did not ask for because he never dreamt that such a thing would be possible. A virgin was with a child and she bore a son who is called Emmanuel, which means "God with us." He came down to the earth here below in search of the sheep that was lost, the sheep that was in fact his own creature, and then ascended into the heights of heaven to offer to the Father and entrust to his care the human race that he had found again. The Lord himself became the first-fruits of the resurrection of mankind, and when its time of punishment for disobedience is over the rest of the body, to which the whole human race belongs, will rise from the grave as the head has done. By God's aid it will grow and be strengthened in all its joints and ligaments, each member having its own proper place in the body. There are many rooms in the Father's house because the body has many members.

God bore with man patiently when he fell because he foresaw the victory that would be his through the Word. Weakness allowed strength its full play, and so revealed God's kindness and great power.

Wednesday of the Fourth Week in Ordinary Time

From the treatise On Spiritual Perfection by Diadochus of Photice, Bishop

The mind has a spiritual sense which teaches us to distinguish between good and evil

The light of true knowledge makes it possible to discern without error the difference between good and evil. Then the path of justice, which leads to the Sun of Justice, brings the mind into the limitless light of knowledge, since it never fails to seek the love of God with all confidence.

Therefore, we must maintain great stillness of mind, even in the midst of our struggles. We shall then be able to distinguish between the different types of thoughts that come to us: those that are good, those sent by God, we will treasure in our memory; those that are evil and inspired y the devil we will reject. A comparison with the sea may help us. A tranquil sea allows the fisherman to gaze right to its depths. No fish can hide there and escape his sight. The stormy sea, however, becomes murky when it is agitated by the winds. The very depths that it revealed in its placidness, the sea now hides. The skills of the fisherman are useless.

Only the Holy Spirit can purify the mind: unless the strong man enters and robs the thief, the booty will not be recovered. So by every means, but especially by peace of soul, we must try to provide the Holy Spirit with a resting place. Then we shall have the light of knowledge shining within us at all times, and it will show up for what they are all the dark and hateful temptations that come from demons, and not only will it show them up: exposure to this holy and glorious light will also greatly diminish their power.

This is why the Apostle says: *Do not stifle the Spirit*[1 Thess 5:19]. The Holy Spirit is the Spirit of goodness: do not grieve him by your evil actions and thoughts, and so deprive yourself of the defense his light affords you. In his own being, which is eternal and life-giving, he is not stifled, but when he is grieved he turns away and leaves the mind in darkness, deprived of the light of knowledge.

The mind is capable of tasting and distinguishing accurately whatever is presented to it. Just as when our health is good we can tell the difference between good and bad food by our bodily sense of taste and reach for what is wholesome, so when our mind is strong and free from all anxiety, it is able to taste the riches of diving consolation, and to preserve, through love, the memory of this taste. This teaches us what is best with absolute certainty. As Saint Paul says: *My prayer is that your love may increase more and more in knowledge and insight, and so enable you to choose what is best*[Phil 1:9-10].

Thursday of the Fourth Week in Ordinary Time

From the Catecheses by Saint Cyril of Jerusalem, Bishop & Doctor

Even in time of persecution let the cross be your joy

The Catholic Church glories in every deed of Christ. Her supreme glory, however, is the cross. Well aware of this, Paul says: *God forbid that I glory in anything but the cross of our Lord Jesus Christ*[Gal 6:14]*!*

At Siloam, there was a sense of wonder, and rightly so. A man born blind recovered his sight. But of what importance is this, when there are so many blind people in the world? Lazarus rose from the dead, but even this only affected Lazarus. What of those countless numbers who have died because of their sins? Those five miraculous loaves fed five thousand people. Yet this is a small number compared to those all over the world who were starved by ignorance. After eighteen years a woman was freed from the bondage of Satan. But are we not all shackled by the chains of our own sins?

For us all, however, the cross is the crown of victory! It has brought light to those blinded by ignorance. It has released those enslaved by sin. Indeed, it has redeemed the whole of mankind!

Do not, then, be ashamed of the cross of Christ; rather, glory in it. Although it is a stumbling block to the Jews and folly to the Gentiles, the message of the cross is our salvation. Of course it is folly to those who are perishing, but to us who are being saved it is the power of God. For it was not a mere man who died for us, but the Son of God, God made man.

In the Mosaic law a sacrificial lamb banished the destroyer. But now *it is the Lamb of God who takes away the sin of the world*[Jn 1:29]. Will he not free us from our sins even more? The blood of an animal, a sheep, brought salvation. Will not the blood of the only-begotten Son bring us greater salvation?

He was not killed by violence, he was not forced to give up his life. His was a willing sacrifice. Listen to his own words: *I have the power to lay down my life and take it up again*[Jn 10:18]. Yes, he willingly submitted to his own passion. He took joy in his achievement; in his crown of victory he was glad and in the salvation of man he rejoiced. He did not blush at the cross for by it he was to save the world. No, it was not a lowly man who suffered but God incarnate. He entered the contest for the reward he would win by his patient endurance.

Certainly in times of tranquility the cross should give you joy. But maintain the same faith in times of persecution. Otherwise you will be a friend of Jesus in times of peace and his enemy during war. Now you receive the forgiveness of your sins and the generous gift of grace from your king. When war comes, fight courageously for him.

Jesus never sinned; yet he was crucified for you. Will you refuse to be crucified for him, who for your sake was nailed to the cross? You are not the one who gives the favor; you have received one first. For your sake he was crucified on Golgotha. Now you are returning his favor; you are fulfilling your debt to him.

Friday of the Fourth Week in Ordinary Time

From a homily by a spiritual writer of the fourth century

May you be filled to the complete fullness of Christ

Those who have been considered worthy to go forth as the sons of God and to be born again of the Holy Spirit from on high, and who hold within them the Christ who renews them and fills them with light, are directed by the Spirit in varied and different ways and in their spiritual repose they are led invisibly in their hearts by grace.

At times they are like men who mourn and lament over their fellow men, and pouring forth prayers for the whole human race, they plunge into tears and lamentation, on fire with spiritual love for mankind.

At other times they are enkindled by the Spirit with such love and exultation that, were it possible, they would clasp in their embrace all mankind, without discrimination, good and bad alike.

Sometimes they are cast down below all mankind in lowliness of spirit, so that they reckon theirs to be the lowest and most abject of conditions.

And sometimes they are held by the Spirit in ineffable joy.

At one time they are like a brave man who puts on the king's full armor and goes down into battle; he fights bravely against the enemy and defeats them. In like manner, the spiritual man takes up the heavenly arms of the Spirit and marches against the enemy and engaging in battle tramples the foe beneath his feet.

At another time the soul is at rest in deepest silence, tranquility and peace, existing in sheer spiritual pleasure and in ineffable repose and a perfect state.

Again, the soul is instructed by grace in a certain understanding in the ineffable wisdom and the inscrutable knowledge of the Spirit on matters which neither tongue nor lips can utter.

Then again, the soul becomes like any ordinary man.

In such varied ways does grace work within them and many are the means by which it leads the soul, renewing it according to God's will and training it in different ways so that it may be set before the heavenly Father pure and whole and blameless.

We, too, therefore must make our prayer to God and entreat in love and in great hope that he may bestow upon us the heavenly grace of the gift of the Spirit. We pray that we, too, may be guided by that Spirit and that he may lead us into the fullness of divine will and refresh us with the varied kinds of his repose, that by the help of this guidance, exercise of grace and spiritual advancement, we may be considered worthy to attain to the perfection of the fullness of Christ, as the Apostle says: *that you may be filled to the complete fullness of Christ*[Eph 3:14-19].

Saturday of the Fourth Week in Ordinary Time

From the pastoral constitution on the Church in the Modern World of the Second Vatican Council

Man and his activity

The activity of man, as it has its origin in man, has man also as its end. Man through his work not only introduces change into things and into society; he also perfects himself. He learns a great deal; he develops his powers; he advances above and beyond himself. This kind of gain, properly understood, is more valuable than any external possessions. Man's worth is greater because of what he is than because of what he has.

In the same way, all that men do to secure greater justice, more widespread brotherhood and a more humane structure of social relationships has more value than advance in technology. Technological development may provide the raw material for human progress, but of itself it is totally unable to bring it into being.

The criterion, therefore, for assessing man's activity is this: does it, in accordance with God's plan, fit in with the true good of the human race and allow man, individually and corporately, to develop and fulfill his vocation in its entirety?

Many of our contemporaries, however, seem to be afraid that a closer relationship between religion and man's activity will injure the autonomy of men or societies or the different sciences. If by the autonomy of earthly realities we mean that created things and even societies have their own distinctive laws and values, which must be gradually identified, used and regulated by men, this kind of autonomy is rightly demanded. Not only is it insisted on by modern man, it is also in harmony with the design of the Creator. By the very fact of creation everything is provided with its own stability, its own truth and goodness, its own laws and orderly functioning. Man must respect these, acknowledging the methods proper to each science or art.

One should therefore deplore certain attitudes of mind which are sometimes found even among Christians because of a failure to recognize the legitimate autonomy of science. These mental attitudes have given rise to conflict and controversy and led many to assume that faith and science are mutually opposed.

If, on the other hand, the autonomy of the temporal order is understood to mean that created things do not depend on God, and that man may use them without reference to the Creator, all who believe in God will realize how false is this teaching. For creation without the Creator fades into nothingness.

Sunday of the Fifth Week in Ordinary Time

From an explanation of Paul's letter to the Galatians by Saint Augustine, Bishop & Doctor

Let us understand the workings of God's grace

Paul writes to the Galatians to make them understand that by God's grace they are no longer under the law. When the Gospel was preached to them, there were some among them of Jewish origin known as circumcisers – though they called themselves Christians – who did not grasp the gift they had received. They still wanted to be under the burden of the law. Now God had imposed that burden on those who were slaves to sin and not on servants of justice. That is to say, God had given a just law to unjust men in order to show them their sin, not to take it away. For sin is taken away only by the gift of faith that works through love. The Galatians had already received this gift, but the circumcisers claimed that the Gospel would not save them unless they underwent circumcision and were willing to observe also the other traditional Jewish rites.

The Galatians, therefore, began to question Paul's preaching of the Gospel because he did not require Gentiles to follow Jewish observances as other apostles had done. Even Peter had yielded to the scandalized protests of the circumcisers. He pretended to believe that the Gospel would not save the Gentiles unless they fulfilled the burden of the law. But Paul recalled him from such dissimulation, as is shown in this very same letter. A similar issue arises in Paul's letter to the Romans, but with an evident difference. Through his letter to them Paul was able to resolve the strife and controversy that had developed between the Jewish and Gentile converts.

In the present letter Paul is writing to persons who were profoundly influenced and disturbed by the circumcisers. The Galatians had begun to believe them and to think that Paul had not preached rightly, since he had not ordered them to be circumcised. And so the Apostle begins by saying: *I am amazed that you are so quickly deserting him who called you to the glory of Christ, and turning to another gospel*[Gal 1:6].

After this there comes a brief introduction to the point at issue. But remember in the very opening of the letter Paul had said that he was an apostle *not from men nor by any man*[Gal 1:1], a statement that does not appear in any other letter of his. He is making it quite clear that the circumcisers, for their part, are not from God but from men, and that his authority in preaching the Gospel must be considered equal to that of the other apostles. For he was called to be an apostle *not from men nor by any man,* but through God the Father and his Son, Jesus Christ.

Monday of the Fifth Week in Ordinary Time

From a short discourse by Saint Bonaventure, Cardinal & Doctor

He who knows Jesus Christ can understand all sacred Scripture

The source of sacred Scripture was not human research but divine revelation. This revelation comes *from the Father of Light from whom the whole concept of fatherhood in heaven and on earth derives*[Eph 3:14-17]. From him, through Jesus Christ his Son, the Holy Spirit enters into us. Then, through the Holy Spirit who allots and apportions his gifts to each person as he wishes, we receive the gift of faith, *and through faith Christ lives in our hearts*[Eph 3:17]. So we come to know Christ and this knowledge becomes the main source of a firm understanding of the truth of all sacred Scripture. It is impossible, therefore, for anyone to achieve this understanding unless he first receives the gift of faith in Christ. This faith is the foundation of the whole Bible, a lamp to its understanding. As long as our earthly state keeps us from seeing the Lord, this same faith is the firm basis of all supernatural enlightenment, the light guiding us to it, and the doorway through which we enter upon it. What is more, the extent of our faith is the measure of the wisdom which God has given us. Thus, *no one should overestimate his wisdom; instead, he should soberly make his assessment according to the extent of the faith which God has given him*[Rom 12:3].

The outcome or the fruit of holy Scripture is by no means negligible: it is the fullness of eternal happiness. For these are the books which tell us of eternal life, which were written not only that we might believe but also that we might have everlasting life. When we do live that life we shall understand fully, we shall love completely, and our desires will be totally satisfied. Then, with all our needs fulfilled, we shall truly know *the love that surpasses understanding* and so *be filled with the fullness of God*[Eph 3:19]. The purpose of the Scriptures, which come to us from God, is to lead us to this fullness according to the truths contained in those sayings of the apostles to which I have referred. In order to achieve this, we must study holy Scripture carefully, and teach it and listen to it in the same way.

If we are to attain the ultimate goal of eternal happiness by the path of virtue described in the Scriptures, we have to begin at the very beginning. We must come with a pure faith to the Father of Light and acknowledge him in our hearts. We must ask him to give us, through his Son and in the Holy Spirit, a true knowledge of Jesus Christ, and along with that knowledge a love of him. Knowing and loving him in this way, confirmed in our faith and grounded in our love, we can know *the length and breadth and height and depth*[Eph 3:18] of his sacred Scripture. Through that knowledge we can come at last to know perfectly and love completely the most blessed Trinity, whom the saints desire to know and love and in whom all that is good and true finds its meaning and fulfillment.

Tuesday of the Fifth Week in Ordinary Time

From a homily on Genesis by Origen, Priest

The sacrifice of Abraham

Abraham took wood for the burnt offering and placed it upon Isaac his son, and he took fire and a sword in his hands, and together they went off[Gen 22:6]. Isaac himself carries the wood for his own holocaust: this is a figure of Christ. For he bore the burden of the cross, and yet to carry the wood for the holocaust is really the duty of the priest. He is then both victim and priest. This is the meaning of the expression: *together they went off*. For when Abraham, who was to perform the sacrifice, carried the fire and the knife, Isaac did not walk behind him, but with him. In this way he showed that he exercised the priesthood equally with Abraham.

What happens after this? *Isaac said to Abraham his father: Father*[Gen 22:7]. This plea from the son was at that instant the voice of temptation. For do you not think the voice of the son who was about to be sacrificed struck a responsive chord in the heart of the father? Although Abraham did not waver because of his faith, he responded with a voice full of affection and asked: *What is it, my son*[Gen 22:7]? Isaac answered him: *Here are the fire and the wood, but where is the sheep for the holocaust*[Gen 22:7]? And Abraham replied: *God will provide for himself a sheep for the holocaust, my son*[Gen 22:8].

The careful yet loving response of Abraham moves me greatly. I do not know what he saw in spirit, because he did not speak of the present but of the future: *God will provide for himself a sheep*[Gen 22:8]. His reply concerns the future, yet his son inquires about the present. Indeed, the Lord himself provided a sheep for himself in Christ.

Abraham extended his hand to take the sword and slay his son, and the angel of the Lord called to him from heaven and said: Abraham, Abraham. And he responded: Here I am. And the angel said: Do not put your hand upon the boy or do anything to him, for now I know that you fear God[Gen 22:10-12]. Compare these words to those of the Apostle when he speaks of God: *He did not spare his own Son but gave him up for us and all*[Rom 8:32]. God emulates man with magnificent generosity. Abraham offered to God his mortal son who did not die, and God gave up his immortal Son who died for all of us.

And Abraham, looking about him, saw a ram caught by the horns in a bush[Gen 22:13]. We said before that Isaac is a type of Christ. Yet this also seems true of the ram. To understand how both are figures of Christ – Isaac who was not slain and the ram who was – is well worth our inquiry.

Christ is the Word God, but *the Word became flesh*[Jn 1:14]. Christ therefore suffered and died, but in the flesh. In this respect, the ram is the type, just as John said: *Behold the lamb of God, behold him who takes away the sins of the world*[Jn 1:29]. The Word, however, remained incorruptible. This is Christ according to the spirit, and Isaac is the type. Therefore, Christ himself is both victim and priest according to the spirit. For he offers the victim to the Father according to the spirit. For he offers the victim to the Father according to the flesh, and he is himself offered on the altar of the cross.

Wednesday of the Fifth Week in Ordinary Time

From a letter by Saint Ambrose, Bishop & Doctor

We are heirs of God, coheirs with Christ

The person who puts to death by the Spirit the deeds of our sinful nature will live, says the Apostle. This is not surprising since one who has the Spirit of God becomes a child of God. So true is it that he is a child of God that he receives not a spirit that enslaves but the Spirit that makes us sons. So much so that the Holy Spirit bears witness to our spirit that we are sons of God. This is the witness of the Holy Spirit: he cries out in our hearts, *Abba, Father*, as we read in the letter to the Galatians.

There is also that other great testimony to the fact that we are sons of God: *we are heirs of God, coheirs with Christ*[Rom 8:17]. A coheir of Christ is one who is glorified along with Christ. The one who is glorified along with him is one who, by suffering for him, suffers along with him.

To encourage us in suffering, Paul adds that all our sufferings are small in comparison with the wonderful reward that will be revealed in us; our labors do not deserve the blessings that are to come. We shall be restored to the likeness of God, and counted worthy of seeing him face to face.

He enhances the greatness of the revelation that is to come by adding that creation also looks forward to this revealing of the sons of God. Creation, he says, is at present condemned to frustration, not of its own choice, but it lives in hope. Its hope is in Christ, as it awaits the grace of his ministry; or it hopes that it will share in the glorious freedom of the sons of God and be freed from its bondage to corruption, so that there will be one freedom, shared by creation and by the sons of God when their glory will be revealed.

At present, however, while this revealing is delayed, all creation groans as it looks forward to the glory of adoption and redemption; it is already in labor with that spirit of salvation, and is anxious to be freed from its subjection to frustration.

The meaning is clear: those who have the first-fruits of the Spirit are groaning in expectation of the adoption of sons. This adoption of sons is that of the whole body of creation, when it will be as it were a son of God and see the divine, eternal goodness face to face. The adoption of sons is present in the Church of the Lord when the Spirit cries out: *Abba, Father*, as you read in the letter to the Galatians. But it will be perfect when all who are worthy of seeing the face of God rise in incorruption, in honor and in glory. Then our humanity will know that it has been truly redeemed. So Paul glories in saying: *We are saved by hope*[Rom 8:24-25.] Hope saves, just as faith does, for of faith it is said: *Your faith has saved you*[Lk 7:50; Lk 17:11-19].

Thursday of the Fifth Week in Ordinary Time

From an explanation of Paul's letter to the Galatians by Saint Augustine, Bishop & Doctor

Let Christ be formed in you

The Apostle says, *Be like me*, for though born a Jew, by reason of spiritual discernment I now consider carnal things of small importance. And he adds, *For I am as you are*[2 Cor 11:22], that is to say: For I, like you, am a man. Then he tactfully reminds them of his love so that they will not look on him as an enemy: *Brothers, I beseech you*, he says, *you did me no wrong*[Gal 4:12], as if to say, "Do not imagine that I want to wrong you." And to have them imitate him as they would a parent, he addresses them as little children: *My little children, with whom I am again in labor until Christ be formed in you*[Gal 4:19]. Actually he is here speaking more in the person of Mother Church than his own. So too he says elsewhere: *I was gentle among you like a nurse fondling her little ones*[1 Thess 2:7].

Christ is formed in the believer by faith of the inner man, called to the freedom that grace bestows, meek and gentle, not boasting of nonexistent merits, but through grace making some beginning of merit. Hence he can be called "my least one" by him who said: *Inasmuch as you did it to the least of my brethren you did it to me*[Mt 25:40].

Christ is formed in him who receives Christ's mold, who clings to him in spiritual love. By imitating him he becomes, as far as is possible to his condition, what Christ is. John says: *He who remains in Christ should walk as he did*[1 Jn 2:6].

Children are conceived in order to be formed in their mother's womb, and when they have been so formed, mothers are in travail to give them birth. We can thus understand Paul's words: *With whom I am in labor until Christ be formed in you* [Gal 4:19]. By labor we understand his anxiety for those with whom he is in travail, that they be born unto Christ. And he is again in labor when he sees them in danger of being led astray. These anxieties, which can be likened to the pangs of childbirth, will continue until they *come to full age in Christ, so as not to be moved by every wind of doctrine*[Eph 4:14].

He is not therefore talking about the beginnings of faith by which they were born, but of strong and perfect faith when he says: *With whom I am again in labor until Christ be formed in you* [Gal 4:19]. He also refers elsewhere in different words to his being in labor, when he says: *There is the daily pressure upon me of my anxiety for all the churches. Who is weak and I am not weak? Who is made to fall, and I am not indignant*[2 Cor 11:28-29]?

Friday of the Fifth Week in Ordinary Time

From a sermon by Saint Leo the Great, Pope & Doctor

Recognize the dignity of your nature

Our Lord Jesus Christ, born true man without ever ceasing to be true God, began in his person a new creation and by the manner of his birth gave man a spiritual origin. What mind can grasp this mystery, what tongue can fittingly recount this gift of love? Guilt becomes innocence, old becomes new, strangers are adopted and outsiders are made heirs. Rouse yourself, man, and recognize the dignity of your nature. Remember that you were made in God's image; though corrupted in Adam, that image has been restored in Christ.

Use creatures as they should be used: the earth, the sea, the sky, the air, the springs and rivers. Give praise and glory to their Creator for all that you find beautiful and wonderful in them. See with your bodily eyes the light that shines on earth, but embrace with your whole soul and all your affections *the true light which enlightens every man who comes into this world*[Jn 1:9]. Speaking of this light the prophet said: *Draw close to him and let his light shine upon you and your face will not blush with shame*[Num 6:24-26]. If we are indeed the temple of God and if the Spirit of God lives in us, then what every believer has within himself is greater than what he admires in the skies.

Our words and exhortations are not intended to make you disdain God's works or think there is anything contrary to your faith in creation, for the good God has himself made all things good. What we do ask is that you use reasonably and with moderation all the marvelous creatures, which adorn this world; as the Apostle says: *The things that are seen are transient but the things that are unseen are eternal*[2 Cor 4:18].

For we are born in the present only to be reborn in the future. Our attachment, therefore, should not be to the transitory; instead, we must be intent upon the eternal. Let us think of how divine grace has transformed our earthly natures so that we may contemplate more closely our heavenly hope. We hear the Apostle say: *You are dead and your life is hidden with Christ in God. But when Christ your life appears, then you will also appear in glory with him*[Col 3:3-4], who lives and reigns with the Father and the Holy Spirit for ever and ever. Amen.

Saturday of the Fifth Week in Ordinary Time

From a sermon by Blessed Isaac of Stella, Abbot

The preeminence of charity

Why, brothers, are we so little concerned to seek one another's well-being, so that where we see a greater need, we might show a greater readiness to help and carry one another's burdens? For this is what the blessed apostle Paul urges us to do in the words: *Bear one another's burdens, and so fulfill the law of Christ*; and also: *Support each other in charity*[Gal 6:2]. For this surely is the law of Christ.

Why can I not patiently bear the weakness I see in my brother which, either out of necessity or because of physical or moral weakness, cannot be corrected? And why can I not instead generously offer him consolation, as it is written: *Their children shall be carried on their shoulders and consoled upon their knees*[Isa 49:22]? Is it because I lack that virtue which *suffers all things*[1 Cor 13:4-7], is patient enough to bear all, and generous enough to love?

This is indeed the law of Christ, who truly *bore our weaknesses* in his passion and *carried our sorrows*[Isa 53:4] out of pity, loving those he carried and carrying those he loved. Whoever attacks a brother in need, or plots against him in his weakness of whatever sort, surely fulfills the devil's law and subjects himself to it. Let us then be compassionate toward one another, loving all our brothers, bearing one another's weaknesses, yet ridding ourselves of our sins.

The more any way of life sincerely strives for the love of God and the love of our neighbor for God's sake, the more acceptable it is to God, no matter what be its observances or external form. For charity is the reason why anything should be done or left undone, changed or left unchanged; it is the initial principle and the end to which all things should be directed. Whatever is honestly done out of love and in accordance with love can never be blameworthy. May he then deign to grant us this love, for without it we cannot please him, and without him we can do absolutely nothing, God, who lives and reigns for ever. Amen.

Sunday of the Sixth Week in Ordinary Time

From a commentary on the Diatessaron by Saint Ephrem, Deacon & Doctor

God's word is an inexhaustible spring of life

Lord, who can comprehend even one of your words? We lose more of it than we grasp, like those who drink from a living spring. For God's word offers different facets according to the capacity of the listener, and the Lord has portrayed his message in many colors, so that whoever gazes upon it can see in it what suits him. Within it he has buried manifold treasures, so that each of us might grow rich in seeking them out.

The word of God is a tree of life that offers us blessed fruit from each of its branches. It is like that rock which was struck open in the wilderness, from which all were offered spiritual drink. As the Apostle says: *They ate spiritual food and they drank spiritual drink*1 Cor 10:4.

And so whenever anyone discovers some part of the treasure, he should not think that he has exhausted God's word. Instead he should feel that this is all that he was able to find of the wealth contained in it. Nor should he say that the word is weak and sterile or look down on it simply because this portion was all that he happened to find. But precisely because he could not capture it all he should give thanks for its riches.

Be glad then that you are overwhelmed, and do not be saddened because he has overcome you. A thirsty man is happy when he is drinking, and he is not depressed because he cannot exhaust the spring. So let this spring quench your thirst, and not your thirst the spring. For if you can satisfy your thirst without exhausting the spring, then when you thirst again you can drink from it once more; but if when your thirst is sated the spring is also dried up, then your victory would turn to your own harm.

Be thankful then for what you have received, and do not be saddened at all that such an abundance still remains. What you have received and attained is your present share, while what is left will be your heritage. For what you could not take at one time because of your weakness, you will be able to grasp at another if you only persevere. So do not foolishly try to drain in one draught what cannot be consumed all at once, and do not cease out of faintheartedness from what you will be able to absorb as time goes on.

Monday of the Sixth Week in Ordinary Time

From a sermon by Saint Bernard, Abbot & Doctor

On the search for wisdom

Let us work for the food which does not perish – our salvation. Let us work in the vineyard of the Lord to earn our daily wage in the wisdom which says: *Those who work in me will not sin*[1 Jn 3:6]. Christ tells us: *The field is the world*[Mt 13:38]. Let us work in it and dig up wisdom, its hidden treasure, a treasure we all look for and want to obtain.

If you are looking for it, really look. Be converted and come[Mt 7:7; Mt 18:3]. Converted from what? *From your own willfulness*. "But," you may say, "if I do not find wisdom in my own will, where shall I find it? My soul eagerly desires it. And I will not be satisfied when I find it, if it is not *a generous amount, a full measure, overflowing into my hands*[Lk 6:38]." You are right, for *blessed is the man who finds wisdom and is full of prudence*[Prov 3:13].

Look for wisdom while it can still be found. Call for it while it is near. Do you want to know how near it is? *The word is near you, in your heart and on your lips*[Rom 10:8], provided that you seek it honestly. Insofar as you find wisdom in your heart, prudence will flow from your lips, but be careful that it flows from and not away from them, or that you do not vomit it up. If you have found wisdom, you have found honey. But do not eat so much that you become too full and bring it all up. Eat so that you are always hungry. Wisdom says: *Those who eat me continue to hunger*[Sir 24:21-23]. Do not think you have too much of it, but do not eat too much or you will throw it up. If you do, what you seem to have will be taken away from you, because you gave up searching too soon. While wisdom is near and while it can be found, look for it and ask for its help. Solomon says: *A man who eats too much honey does himself no good; similarly, the man who seeks his own glorification will be crushed by that same renown*[Prov 25:27].

Happy is the man who has found wisdom. Even more happy is the man *who lives in wisdom,* for he perceives its abundance. There are three ways for wisdom or prudence to abound in you: if you confess your sins, if you give thanks and praise, and if your speech is edifying. *Man believes with his heart and so he is justified. He confesses with his lips and so he is saved*[Rom 10:10]. *In the beginning of his speech the just man is his own accuser*[Prov 18:17], next he gives glory to God, and thirdly, if his wisdom extends that far, he edifies his neighbor.

Tuesday of the Sixth Week in Ordinary Time

From the Discourses against the Arians by Saint Athanasius, Bishop & Doctor

We know the Father through creative and incarnate Wisdom

The only-begotten Son, the Wisdom of God, created the entire universe. Scripture says: *You have made all things by your wisdom, and the earth is full of your creatures*[Ps 103:24-25]. Yet simply to be was not enough: God also wanted his creatures to be good. That is why he was pleased that his own wisdom should descend to their level and impress upon each of them singly and upon all of them together a certain resemblance to their Model. It would then be manifest that God's creatures shared in his wisdom and that all his works were worthy of him.

For as the word we speak is an image of the Word who is God's Son, so also is the wisdom implanted in us an image of the Wisdom who is God's Son. It gives us the ability to know and understand and so makes us capable of receiving him who is the all-creative Wisdom, through whom we can come to know the Father. *Whoever has the Son has the Father also*[1 Jn 2:23], Scripture says, and *Whoever receives me receives the One who sent me*[Mt 10:40]. And so, since this image of the Wisdom of God has been produced in us and in all creatures, the true and creative Wisdom rightly takes to himself what applies to his image and says: *The Lord created me in his works*[Prov 8:22].

But because *the world was not wise enough to recognize God in his wisdom,* as we have explained it, *God determined to save those who believe by means of the "foolish" message that we preach*[1 Cor 1:20-21]. Not wishing to be known any longer, as in former times, through the mere image and shadow of his wisdom existing in creatures, he caused the true Wisdom himself to take flesh, to become man, and to suffer death on the cross so that all who believed in him might be saved by faith.

Yet this was the same Wisdom of God who had in the beginning revealed himself and his Father through himself by means of his image in creatures (which is why Wisdom too is said to be created). Later, as John declares, that Wisdom, who is also the Word, became flesh, and after destroying the power of death and saving our race, he revealed himself and his Father through himself with greater clarity. *Grant,* he prayed, *that they may know you, the only true God, and Jesus Christ whom you have sent*[Jn 17:3].

So now the whole earth is filled with the knowledge of God, since it is one and the same thing to know the Father through the Son, and to know the Son who comes from the Father. The Father rejoices in his Son, and with the same joy the Son delights in the Father and says: *I was his joy; every day I took delight in his presence*[Prov 8:30-36].

Wednesday of the Sixth Week in Ordinary Time

From a commentary on the Book of Proverbs by Procopius of Gaza, Bishop

The Wisdom of God has mingled wine and spread a table for us

Wisdom has built herself a house[Prov 9:1]. God the Father's Power, himself a person, has fashioned as his dwelling-place the whole world in which he lives by his activity, and also man who, created to resemble God's own image and likeness, has a nature which is partly seen and partly hidden from our eyes.

And she has set up seven pillars[Prov 9:1]. To man who was made in the image of Christ when the rest of creation was completed, Wisdom gave the seven gifts of the Spirit to enable him to believe in Christ and to keep his commandments. By means of these gifts the spiritual man grows and develops until, through firm faith and the supernatural graces he receives, he finally reaches maturity. Knowledge stimulates virtue and virtue reflects knowledge. The fear of the Lord, understanding and knowledge give the true orientation to his natural wisdom. Power makes him eager to seek understanding of the will of God as revealed in the laws by which the entire creation is governed. Counsel distinguishes these most sacred and eternal laws of God from anything opposed to them; for these laws are meant for man to ponder, to proclaim, and to fulfill. Insight disposes man to embrace these expressions of God's will and to reject whatever contravenes them.

She has mingled her wine in a bowl and spread her table[Prov 9:2]. Because the Word of God has mingled in man, as in a bowl, a spiritual and a physical nature, and has given him a knowledge both of creation and of himself as the Creator, it is natural for the things of God to have on man's mind the inebriating effect of wine. Christ himself, the bread from heaven, is his nourishment enabling him to grow in virtue, and it is Christ who quenches his thirst and gladdens him with his teaching. For all who desire to share in it, he has prepared this rich banquet, this spiritual feast.

She has sent forth her servants with the sublime message that all are to come to the bowl and drink[Prov 9:3-5]. Christ has sent forth his apostles, the servants of his divine will, to proclaim the message of the Gospel which, since it is spiritual, transcends both the natural and the written law. By this he calls us to himself in whom as in a bowl there was brought about by the mystery of the incarnation a marvelous mingling of the divine and human natures, although each still remains distinct. And through the apostles he cries out: *Is anyone foolish? Let him turn to me*[Prov 9:4]. If anyone is so foolish as to think in his heart that there is no God, let him renounce his disbelief and turn to me by faith. Let him know that I am the maker of all things and their Lord.

And to those who lack wisdom he says: *Come, eat my bread and drink the wine that I have prepared for you*[Prov 9:5]. To those who still lack the works of faith and the higher knowledge which inspires them he says: "Come, eat my body, the bread that is the nourishment of virtue, and drink my blood, the wine that cheers you with the joy of true knowledge and makes you divine. For in a wonderful way I have mingled my divinity with my blood for your salvation."

Thursday of the Sixth Week in Ordinary Time

From the Explanations of the Psalms by Saint Ambrose, Bishop & Doctor

Open your lips, and let God's word be heard

We must always meditate on God's wisdom, keeping it in our hearts and on our lips. Your tongue must speak justice, the law of God must be in your heart. Hence Scripture tells you: *You shall speak of these commandments when you sit in your house, and when you walk along the way, and when you lie down, and when you get up*[Deut 6:7]. Let us then speak of the Lord Jesus, for he is wisdom, he is the word, the Word indeed of God.

It is also written: *Open your lips, and let God's word be heard*[Ezek 3:27]. God's word is uttered by those who repeat Christ's teaching and meditate on his sayings. Let us always speak this word. When we speak about wisdom, we are speaking of Christ. When we speak about virtue, we are speaking of Christ. When we speak about justice, we are speaking of Christ. When we speak about peace, we are speaking of Christ. When we speak about truth and life and redemption, we are speaking of Christ.

Open your lips, says Scripture, *and let God's word be heard*. It is for you to open, it is for him to be heard. So David said: *I shall hear what the Lord says in me*[Ps 84:9]. The very Son of God says: *Open your lips, and I will fill them.* Not all can attain to the perfection of wisdom as Solomon or Daniel did, but the spirit of wisdom is poured out on all according to their capacity, that is, on all the faithful. If you believe, you have the spirit of wisdom.

Meditate, then, at all times on the things of God, and speak the things of God, *when you sit in your house*. By house we can understand the Church, or the secret place within us, so that we are to speak within ourselves. Speak with prudence, so as to avoid falling into sin, as by excess of talking. *When you sit in your house*, speak to yourself as if you were a judge. *When you walk along the way*, speak, so as never to be idle. You speak *along the way* if you speak in Christ, for Christ is the way. When you walk along the way, speak to yourself, speak to Christ. Hear him say to you: *I desire that in every place men should pray, lifting holy hands without anger or quarreling*[1 Tim 2:8]. When you lie down, speak so that the sleep of death may not steal upon you. Listen and learn how you are to speak as you lie down: *I will not give sleep to my eyes or slumber to my eyelids until I find a place for the Lord, a dwelling place for the God of Jacob*[Ps 131:4-5].

When you get up or rise again, speak of Christ, so as to fulfill what you are commanded. Listen and learn how Christ is to awaken you from sleep. Your soul says: *I hear my brother knocking at the door*[Rev 3:20]*;* . Then Christ says to you: *Open the door to me, my sister, my spouse*. Listen and learn how you are to awaken Christ. Your soul says: *I charge you, daughters of Jerusalem, awaken or reawaken the love of my heart*[Song 8:4-14]. Christ is that love.

Friday of the Sixth Week in Ordinary Time

From the Tractates on the first letter of John by Saint Augustine, Bishop & Doctor

Our heart longs for God

We have been promised that *we shall be like him, for we shall see him as he is*[1 Jn 3:2]. By these words, the tongue has done its best; now we must apply the meditation of the heart. Although they are the words of Saint John, what are they in comparison with the divine reality? and how can we, so greatly inferior to John in merit, add anything of our own? Yet we have received, as John has told us, an anointing by the Holy One which teaches us inwardly more than our tongue can speak. Let us turn to this source of knowledge, and because at present you cannot see, make it your business to desire the divine vision.

The entire life of a good Christian is in fact an exercise of holy desire. You do not yet see what you long for, but the very act of desiring prepares you, so that when he comes you may see and be utterly satisfied.

Suppose you are going to fill some holder or container, and you know you will be given a large amount. Then you set about stretching your sack or wineskin or whatever it is. Why? Because you know the quantity you will have to put in it and your eyes tell you there is not enough room. By stretching it, therefore, you increase the capacity of the sack, and this is how God deals with us. Simply by making us wait he increases our desire, which in turn enlarges the capacity of our soul, making it able to receive what is to be given to us.

So, my brethren, let us continue to desire, for we shall be filled. Take note of Saint Paul stretching as it were his ability to receive what is to come: *Not that I have already obtained this*, he said, *or am made perfect. Brethren, I do not consider that I have already obtained it*[Phil 3:12]. We might ask him, "If you have not yet obtained it, what are you doing in this life?" *This one thing I do*, answers Paul, *forgetting what lies behind, and stretching forward to what lies ahead*[Phil 3:13]*, I press on toward the prize to which I am called in the life above*[Phil 3:14]. Not only did Paul say he stretched forward, but he also declared that he pressed on toward a chosen goal. He realized in fact that he was still short of receiving *what no eye has seen, nor ear has heard, nor the heart of man conceived*[1 Cor 2:9].

Such is our Christian life. By desiring heaven we exercise the powers of our soul. Now this exercise will be effective only to the extent that we free ourselves from desires leading to infatuation with this world. Let me return to the example I have already used, of filling an empty container. God means to fill each of you with what is good; so cast out what is bad! If he wishes to fill you with honey and you are full of sour wine, where is the honey to go? The vessel must be emptied of its contents and then be cleansed. Yes, it must be cleansed even if you have to work hard and scour it. It must be made fit for the new thing, whatever it may be.

We may go on speaking figuratively of honey, gold or wine – but whatever we say we cannot express the reality we are to receive. The name of that reality is God. But who will claim that in that one syllable we utter the full expanse of our heart's desire? Therefore, whatever we say is necessarily less than the full truth. We must extend ourselves toward the measure of Christ so that when he comes he may fill us with his presence. *Then we shall be like him, for we shall see him as he is is*[1 Jn 3:2].

Saturday of the Sixth Week in Ordinary Time

From the pastoral constitution on the Church in the Modern World
The Second Vatican Council

The sanctity of marriage and the family

Husband and wife, by the covenant of marriage, are no longer two, but one flesh. By their intimate union of persons and of actions they give mutual help and service to each other, experience the meaning of their unity, and gain an ever deeper understanding of it day by day.

This intimate union in the mutual self-giving of two persons, as well as the good of the children, demands full fidelity from both, and an indissoluble unity between them.

Christ the Lord has abundantly blessed this richly complex love, which springs from the divine source of love and is founded on the model of his union with the Church.

In earlier times God met his people in a covenant of love and fidelity. So now the Savior of mankind, the Bridegroom of the Church, meets Christian husbands and wives in the sacrament of matrimony. Further, he remains with them in order that, as he loved the Church and gave himself up for her, so husband and wife may, in mutual self-giving, love each other with perpetual fidelity.

True married love is caught up into God's love; it is guided and enriched by the redeeming power of Christ and the saving action of the Church, in order that the partners may be effectively led to God and receive help and strength in the sublime responsibility of parenthood.

Christian partners are therefore strengthened, and as it were consecrated, by a special sacrament for the duties and the dignity of their state. By the power of this sacrament they fulfill their obligations to each other and to their family, and are filled with the spirit of Christ. This spirit pervades their whole lives with faith, hope and love. Thus they promote their own perfection and each other's sanctification, and so contribute together to the greater glory of God.

Hence, with parents leading the way by example and family prayer, their children – indeed, all within the family circle – will find it easier to make progress in natural virtues, in salvation and in holiness. Husband and wife, raised to the dignity and the responsibility of parenthood, will be zealous in fulfilling their task as educators, especially in the sphere of religious education, a task that is primarily their own.

Children, as active members of the family, contribute in their own way to the holiness of their parents. With the love of grateful hearts, with loving respect and trust, they will return the generosity of their parents and will stand by them as true sons and daughters when their parents meet with hardship and the loneliness of old age.

Sunday of the Seventh Week in Ordinary Time

From the chapters On Charity Saint Maximus the Confessor, Abbot

Without love everything is in vain

Charity is a right attitude of mind which prefers nothing to the knowledge of God. If a man possesses any strong attachment to the things of this earth, he cannot possess true charity. For anyone who really loves God prefers to know and experience God rather than his creatures. The whole set and longing of his mind is ever directed toward him.

For God is far superior to all his creation, since everything which exists has been made by God and for him. And so, in deserting God, who is beyond compare, for the inferior works of creation, a man shows that he values God, the author of creation, less than creation itself.

The Lord himself reminds us: *Whoever loves me will keep my commandments. And this is my commandment: that you love one another*[Jn 14:15; 15:14]. So the man who does not love his neighbor does not obey God's command. But one who does not obey his command cannot love God. A man is blessed if he can love all men equally. Moreover, if he truly loves God, he must love his neighbor absolutely. Such a man cannot hoard his wealth. Rather, like God himself, he generously gives from his own resources to each man according to his needs.

Since he imitates God's generosity, the only distinction he draws is the person's need. He does not distinguish between a good man and a bad one, a just man and one who is unjust. Yet his own goodness of will makes him prefer the man who strives after virtue to the one who is depraved.

A charitable mind is not displayed simply in giving money; it is manifested still more by personal service as well as by the communication of God's word to others: In fact, if a man's service toward his brothers is genuine and if he really renounces worldly concerns, he is freed from selfish desires. For he now shares in God's own knowledge and love. Since he does possess God's love, he does not experience weariness as he follows the Lord his God. Rather, following the prophet Jeremiah, he withstands every type of reproach and hardship without even harboring an evil thought toward any man.

For Jeremiah warns us: *Do not say: "We are the Lord's temple."*[Jer 7:4] Neither should you say: *"Faith alone in our Lord Jesus Christ can save me."*[Jas 2:24] By itself faith accomplishes nothing. For even the devils believe and shudder. No, faith must be joined to an active love of God which is expressed in good works. The charitable man is distinguished by sincere and long-suffering service to his fellow man: it also means using things aright.

Monday of the Seventh Week in Ordinary Time

From a homily on Ecclesiastes by Saint Gregory of Nyssa, Bishop

Christ is our head, and the wise man keeps his eyes upon him

We shall be blessed with clear vision if we keep our eyes fixed on Christ, for he, as Paul teaches, is our head, and there is in him no shadow of evil. Saint Paul himself and all who have reached the same heights of sanctity had their eyes fixed on Christ, and so have all who live and move and have their being in him.

As no darkness can be seen by anyone surrounded by light, so no trivialities can capture the attention of anyone who has his eyes on Christ. The man who keeps his eyes upon the head and origin of the whole universe has them on virtue in all its perfection; he has them on truth, on justice, on immortality and on everything else that is good, for Christ is goodness itself.

The wise man, then, turns his eyes toward the One who is his head, but the fool gropes in darkness[Eccl 2:14]. No one who puts his lamp under a bed instead of on a lamp-stand will receive any light from it. People are often considered blind and useless when they make the supreme Good their aim and give themselves up to the contemplation of God, but Paul made a boast of this and proclaimed himself a fool for Christ's sake. The reason he said, *We are fools for Christ's sake*[1 Cor 4:10] was that his mind was free from all earthly preoccupations. It was as though he said, "We are blind to the life here below because our eyes are raised toward the One who is our head."

And so, without board or lodging, he traveled from place to place, destitute, naked, exhausted by hunger and thirst. When men saw him in captivity, flogged, shipwrecked, led about in chains, they could scarcely help thinking him a pitiable sight. Nevertheless, even while he suffered all this at the hands of men, he always looked toward the One who is his head and he asked: *What can separate us from the love of Christ, which is in Jesus? Can affliction or distress? Can persecution, hunger, nakedness, danger or death*[Rom 8:35]? In other words, "What can force me to take my eyes from him who is my head and to turn them toward things that are contemptible?"

He bids us follow his example: *Seek the things that are above*[Col 3:1], he says, which is only another way of saying: "Keep your eyes on Christ."

Tuesday of the Seventh Week in Ordinary Time

From a homily on Ecclesiastes by Saint Gregory of Nyssa, Bishop

There is a time to be born and a time to die

There is a time to be born and a time to die[Eccl 3:2]. The fact that there is a natural link between birth and death is expressed very clearly in this text of Scripture. Death invariably follows birth and everyone who is born comes at last to the grave.

There is a time to be born and a time to die. God grant that mine may be a timely birth and a timely death! Of course no one imagines that the Speaker regards as acts of virtue our natural birth and death, in neither of which our own will plays any part. A woman does not give birth because she chooses to do so; neither does anyone die as a result of his own decision. Obviously, there is neither virtue nor vice in anything that lies beyond our control. So we must consider what is meant by a timely birth and a timely death.

It seems to me that the birth referred to here is our salvation, as is suggested by the prophet Isaiah. This reaches its full term and is not stillborn when, having been conceived by the fear of God, the soul's own birth pangs bring it to the light of day. We are in a sense our own parents, and we give birth to ourselves by our own free choice of what is good. Such a choice becomes possible for us when we have received God into ourselves and have become children of God, children of the Most High. On the other hand, if what the Apostle calls *the form of Christ* has not been produced in us, we abort ourselves. The man of God must reach maturity.

Now if the meaning of a timely birth is clear, so also is the meaning of a timely death. For Saint Paul every moment was a time to die, as he proclaims in his letters: *I swear by the pride I take in you that I face death every day*[1 Cor 15:31]. Elsewhere he says, *For your sake we are put to death daily* and *we felt like men condemned to death*[Rom 8:36].

How Paul died daily is perfectly obvious. He never gave himself up to a sinful life but kept his body under constant control. He carried death with him, Christ's death, wherever he went. He was always being crucified with Christ. It was not his own life he lived; it was Christ who lived in him. This surely was a timely death-a death whose end was true life.

I put to death and I shall give life[Deut 32:39], God says, teaching us that death to sin and life in the Spirit is his gift, and promising that whatever he puts to death he will restore to life again.

Wednesday of the Seventh Week on Ordinary Time

From the Commentary on Ecclesiastes by Saint Jerome, Priest & Doctor

Seek the things that are above

Every man to whom God has given wealth and possessions and power to enjoy them, and to accept his lot, and to take pleasure in his labor—that man has received a gift from God. For he will not notice the days of his life as they pass because God has filled his heart with joy[Eccl 5:18-19]. Compare him with the man who is anxious about his wealth and is full of vexation as he hoards up possessions that perish. Our text says that it is better to take delight in what you have. The first man at least has some pleasure in what he has, while the second suffers from excessive anxiety. And the reason is that the ability to enjoy riches is a gift from God; *he does not count the days of his life*[Eccl 5:20], for God allows him to enjoy life; without sadness or anxiety, he is filled with the delight of the moment. However, it is better to understand the text with the Apostle as referring to God's gift of spiritual food and drink; man is to contemplate goodness in his works, for it takes great work and study for us to contemplate true good. And this is our lot: to rejoice in study and work. This is a good goal, but not completely good *until Christ is revealed in our lives*[Col 3:4].

All the work of a man is to satisfy his mouth, yet his spirit will be hungry. For what has a wise man more than a fool, except the knowledge of how to live[Eccl 6:7-8]? All that men work for in this world is consumed by their mouths, chewed up by their teeth, and passed into the stomach for digestion. And even when something delights the taste, the pleasure lasts only as long as he can taste it.

But after all this, the mind of the eater gets no satisfaction, for he will want to eat again, and neither wise man nor fool can live without food, and even a poor man seeks nothing more than to keep his body alive and not die of starvation. Or again, it may be because the spirit gains nothing useful from feeding the body. Food is common to the wise and the foolish alike, and for the poor man food is wealth.

However, it is better to understand the text as referring to the man in Ecclesiastes, who is learned in the sacred Scripture, and knows that neither mouth nor spirit is satisfied so long as he still desires learning. In this the wise man has the advantage over the fool. For if he knows himself to be poor (and the poor are called blessed in the Gospel), he strives to understand the important things in life, and he walks *the straight and narrow way which leads to life*[Mt 7:14]. He is poor in wickedness, and he knows where Christ, who is our life, is to be found.

Thursday of the Seventh Week in Ordinary Time

From an instruction by Saint Columban, Abbot

The unfathomable depths of God

God is everywhere in his immensity, and everywhere close at hand. As he says of himself: *I am a God close at hand, not a God far off*[Jer 23:23]. The God we seek is not one who dwells at a distance from us, for we have him present with us, if only we are worthy. He dwells in us as the soul in the body, if only we are sound members of his, if we are dead to sin. Then in very truth he dwells in us, the one who said: *I will dwell in them and walk among them*[Ezek 37:27]. If we are worthy of his presence with us, then in truth we are made alive by him as his living members. As the Apostle says: *In him we live and move and have our being*[Acts 17:28].

Who, I ask, will search out the Most High in his own being, for he is beyond words or understanding? Who will penetrate the secrets of God? Who will boast that he knows the infinite God, who fills all things, yet encompasses all things, who pervades all things, yet reaches beyond all things, who holds all things in his hand, yet escapes the grasp of all things? *No one has ever seen him as he is*[Jn 1:18]. No one must then presume to search for the unsearchable things of God: his nature, the manner of his existence, his selfhood. These are beyond telling, beyond scrutiny, beyond investigation. With simplicity, but also with fortitude, only believe that this is how God is and this is how he well be, for God is incapable of change.

Who then is God? He is Father, Son and Holy Spirit, one God. Do not look for any further answers concerning God. Those who want to understand the unfathomable depths of God must first consider the world of nature. Knowledge of the Trinity is rightly compared with the depth of the sea. Wisdom asks: *Who will find out what is so very deep*[Eccl 7:24]? As the depths of the sea are invisible to human sight, so the Godhead of the Trinity is found to be beyond the grasp of human understanding. If any one, I say, wants to know what he should believe he must not imagine that he understands better through speech than through belief; the knowledge of God that he seeks will be all the further off than it was before.

Seek then the highest wisdom, not by arguments in words but by the perfection of your life, not by speech but by the faith that comes from simplicity of heart, not from the learned speculations of the unrighteous. If you search by means of discussions for the God who cannot be defined in words, he *will depart further from you* than he was before. If you search for him by faith, *wisdom will stand* where wisdom lives, *at the gates*[Prov 8:3]. Where wisdom is, wisdom will be seen, at least in part. But wisdom is also to some extent truly attained when the invisible God is the object of faith, in a way beyond our understanding, for we must believe in God, invisible as he is, though he is partially seen by a heart that is pure.

Friday of the Seventh Week in Ordinary Time

From a commentary on Ecclesiastes by Saint Gregory of Agrigentum, Bishop

Exult, my soul, in the Lord

Come, eat your bread in gladness and drink your wine with a cheerful heart, for your works have been pleasing to God. If we would interpret this text in its obvious and ordinary sense, it would be correct to call it a righteous exhortation, in which Ecclesiastes counsels us to embrace a simple way of life and to be led by doctrines which involve a genuine faith in God. Then we may eat our bread in gladness and drink our wine with a cheerful heart. We will not fall into slanderous speech nor be involved in anything devious; rather we should think that which is right, and, insofar as we can, we should help the poor and destitute with mercy and generosity, truly dedicated to those pursuits and good deeds which please God.

But a spiritual interpretation of the text leads us to a loftier meaning and teaches us to take this as the heavenly and mystical bread, which has come down from heaven, bringing life to the world, and to drink a spiritual wine with a cheerful heart, that wine which flowed from the side of the true vine at the moment of his saving passion. Of this the Gospel of our salvation says: *When Jesus had taken bread and had blessed it, he said to his holy disciples and apostles, Take, eat; this is my body which is broken for you for the forgiveness of sins; and in like manner, he took the cup and said, All of you, drink of this: this is my blood of the new covenant, which will be shed for you and for many for the forgiveness of sins*[Mt 26:26-28]. For whoever eats this bread and drinks this mystical wine enjoys true happiness and rejoices, exclaiming: *You have put gladness into my heart*[Ps 4:7].

Indeed, I think this is the bread and this is the wine that is referred to in the book of Proverbs by God's subsistent Wisdom, Christ our Savior, saying: *Come, eat my bread and drink the wine I have mixed for you*[Prov 9:5], hereby referring to our mystical sharing in the Word. For those worthy to receive this are ever clothed in the works of light, which shine like a bright light as the Lord says in the Gospel: *Let your light shine before men, so that they may see your good works and glorify your Father who is in heaven*[Mt 5:16]. And, indeed, oil appears to flow continually over their heads, the oil that is the Spirit of truth, guarding and preserving them from all the harm of sin.

Saturday of the Seventh Week in Ordinary Time

From a commentary on Ecclesiastes by Saint Gregory of Agrigentum, Bishop

Approach the Lord and receive his light

In the words of Ecclesiastes: *Light itself is delightful*[Eccl 11:7], and it is a great boon for the eye to have sight of the sun. Devoid of light, the world would be without beauty and life would be lifeless. That was why Moses, who saw God, said in anticipation: *And God saw the light and said that it was good*[Gen 1:4]. To reflect on the true and eternal light is even more fitting for us. This light is Christ who *enlightens every man who comes into the world*[Jn 1:9], the savior and redeemer of the world. He is the one who became man and sank to the very depths of the human condition. As David said: *Sing to God a hymn to his name, make a highway for him who rises to the west. His name is the Lord, rejoice before him*[Ps 67:5]*!*

This light he called delightful and foretold that it would be good to see the sun of glory. In the days of his incarnation, he said: *I am the light of the world. He who follows me will not walk in darkness but will possess the light of life*[Jn 8:12]. On another occasion he said: *This is the judgment: the light has come into the world*[Jn 3:19].

Sunlight, then, is a symbol. What we see with our eyes foretells the coming of the Sun of Justice. He was a most delightful light for those who were worthy to be instructed by him personally. He was also a radiance to those who saw him with their bodily eyes when he lived on earth as a man among men. It was not just any man they saw, for he was true God. He made the blind see, the lame walk, and the deaf hear. He cleansed the lepers, and by a simple command he raised the dead back to life.

Now it is our supreme delight to behold him and contemplate his divine splendor with the eyes of our spirit. When we participate in and associate with that beauty, we are enlightened and adorned and this is our delight. We take delight in being saturated with the sweetness of the Spirit, in being clothed in holiness, in achieving wisdom. Finally we are filled with a joy that comes from God and endures through all the days of our earthly life. In the wise words of Ecclesiastes: *A man may live for many years, but he will experience happiness throughout his days*[Eccl 11:8]. For all who gaze upon the Sun of Justice, he is their supreme delight. David spoke of them: *Let them be joyful before God and be jubilant with joy*[Ps 67:4]. Indeed he even said: *Rejoice in the Lord, you who are just, for praise befits those who are upright*[Ps 32:1].

Sunday of the Eighth Week in Ordinary Time

From the Moral Reflections on Job by Saint Gregory the Great, Pope & Doctor

The blameless and upright man who fears God

Some men are so guileless that they do not recognize what righteousness is. But the more they forsake the innocence of true simplicity, the more they fail to rise to moral rectitude; for in not knowing how to guide their actions by right living, they are too simple to remain innocent.

Hence Paul warns his disciples, saying: *I want you to be wise in what is good but guileless in evil*[Rom 16:19]. And again, *do not be like boys in your thinking, but be like infants in evil*[1 Cor 14:20]. Thus the Truth himself bids his disciples: *Be wise as serpents and simple as doves*[Mt 10:16]. In this command he has deliberately joined the two ideas together; the serpent's cunning complements the dove's simplicity, and the dove's simplicity moderates the serpent's cunning. This is why the Holy Spirit reveals his presence to men not only as a dove but also as fire. For the dove symbolizes simplicity, and the fire, intense dedication. Thus the dove and the fire, taken together, have a special significance: whoever is filled with the Spirit becomes so dedicated to this gentle simplicity that he is also aflame with the zeal of righteousness against the faults of sinners.

A blameless and upright man is one who fears God and turns away from evil[Job 1:8]. Whoever seeks our eternal country surely lives a blameless and upright life. He is blameless in his deeds, upright in his faith; blameless in the good actions he performs here on earth, upright in the lofty ideals he perceives deep within himself. Now there are some who are not simple in this good action, for they seek not an inner reward, but outward approval. Thus the wise man rightly said: *Woe to the sinner who walks the earth along two paths*[Sir 2:12]. The sinner indeed walks the face of the earth in two directions: externally, his actions seem to be holy, but inwardly his thoughts are worldly.

This is well said, then: *He fears God and turns away from evil*[Prov 14:16], because the holy Church of the elect sets out along the path of simplicity and righteousness in fear, but finishes in love. For it is the Church's task to turn completely away from evil; once she has begun by love of God, she rejects sin. If she still does good only out of fear, then inwardly she has not withdrawn from evil; for she commits sin by desiring to sin, if only she could sin without punishment.

Rightly therefore Job was said to fear God because he turned away from evil. For love is moved by fear when the mind rejects the thought of sin.

Monday of the Eighth Week in Ordinary Time

The Moral Reflections on Job by St Gregory the Great, Pope & Doctor

If we have received good from the hand of the Lord, why should we not endure evil?

When Paul perceived within himself the riches of internal wisdom, yet saw the corruptibility of his own body, he was led to say: *We have this treasure in earthen vessels*[2 Cor 4:7]. Now in the blessed Job the earthen vessel felt the gaping sores without, while this treasure of wisdom remained whole and intact within. For outwardly his body was in agony, but inwardly from the treasure of wisdom came forth holy thoughts: *If we have received good from the hand of the Lord, why should we not endure evil*[Job 2:10]? The *good* here refers either to the temporal or to the eternal gifts of God, and the *evil* to the scourges of the present time, about which the Lord says through the prophet: *I am the Lord and there is no other. I form the light and create the darkness. I make peace and create evil*[Isa 45:6-7] ["Create Evil": the evils of afflictions and punishments, but not the evil of sin].

I form the light and create the darkness[Isa 45:7], for though outwardly these scourges create the darkness of anguish, inwardly knowledge enkindles the light in the mind. *I make peace and create evil,* for peace with God is restored to us when those things which were rightly created for us, but are not ordinarily desired, are turned into scourges and become evil for us. It is through sin that we become opposed to God; therefore, it is fitting that we should return to his peace by way of scourges. In this manner, when everything created for good is turned into a source of pain for us, the mind of the chastened man may be humbly renewed and restored to peace with his Creator.

We ought particularly to observe in Job's words how skillfully he meets his wife's persuading: *If we have received good from the hand of the Lord, why should we not endure evil?* It is a great comfort in tribulation if, in times of adversity, we recall the gifts our Creator has given us. Nor will overwhelming sorrow break us, if we quickly call to mind the gifts which have sustained us. For it is written: *On the day of prosperity do not forget affliction, and on the day of affliction do not forget prosperity*[Sir 11:25-27]. For if a man receives God's gifts, but forgets his affliction, he can fall through his own excessive joy. On the other hand, when a man is bruised by the scourges, but is not at all consoled by the thought of the blessings he has been fortunate to receive, he is completely cast down.

Thus both attitudes must be united so that one may be supported by the other: the memory of the gift can temper the pain of the affliction, and the foreboding and fear of the affliction can modify the joy of the gift. And so the holy Job, to soothe his soul's depression in the midst of his wound, weighs the delightful gifts he has received even while he suffers from the scourges, saying: *If we have received good from the hand of the Lord, why should we not endure evil?*

Tuesday of the Eighth Week in Ordinary Time

From the Confessions of Saint Augustine, Bishop & Doctor

Whoever I may be, Lord, I lie exposed to your scrutiny

Lord, you know me. Let me know you. Let me come to know you *even as I am known*[1 Cor 13:12]. You are the strength of my soul; enter it and make it a place suitable for your dwelling, a possession *without spot or blemish*[Eph 5:27]. This is my hope and the reason I speak. In this hope I rejoice, when I rejoice rightly. As for the other things of this life, the less they deserve tears, the more likely will they be lamented; and the more they deserve tears, the less likely will men sorrow for them. *For behold, you have loved the truth, because the one who does what is true enters into the light*[Jn 3:21]. I wish to do this truth before you alone by praising you, and before a multitude of witnesses by writing of you.

O Lord, the depths of a man's conscience lie exposed before your eyes. Could anything remain hidden in me, even though I did not want to confess it to you? In that case I would only be hiding you from myself, not myself from you. But now my sighs are sufficient evidence that I am displeased with myself; that you are my light and the source of my joy; that you are loved and desired. I am thoroughly ashamed of myself; I have renounced myself and chosen you, recognizing that I can please neither you nor myself unless you enable me to do so.

Whoever I may be, Lord, I lie exposed to your scrutiny. I have already told of the profit I gain when I confess to you. And I do not make my confession with bodily words, bodily speech, but with the words of my soul and the cry of my mind which you hear and understand. When I am wicked, my confession to you is an expression of displeasure with myself. But when I do good, it consists in not attributing this goodness to myself. *For you, O Lord, bless the just man*[Ps 5:13], but first *you justify the wicked*. And so I make my confession before you in silence, and yet not in silence. My voice is silent, but my heart cries out.

You, O Lord, are my judge. *For though no one knows a man's innermost self except the man's own spirit within him*[1 Cor 2:11], yet there is something in a man which even his own spirit does not know. But you know all of him, for you have made him. As for me, I despise myself in your sight, knowing that I am but dust and ashes; yet I know something of you that I do not know of myself.

True, *we see now indistinctly as in a mirror, but not yet face to face*[1 Cor 13:12]. Therefore, so long as I am in exile from you, I am more present to myself than to you. Yet I do know that you cannot be overcome, while I am uncertain which temptations I can resist and which I cannot. Nevertheless, I have hope, because *you are faithful and do not allow us to be tempted beyond our endurance, but along with the temptation you give us the means to withstand it*[1 Cor 10:13].

I will confess, therefore, what I know of myself, and also what I do not know. The knowledge that I have of myself, I possess because you have enlightened me; while the knowledge of myself that I do not yet possess will not be mine until my darkness shall be made as the noonday sun before your face.

Wednesday of the Eighth Week in Ordinary Time

From the Confessions of Saint Augustine, Bishop & Doctor

All my hope lies in your great mercy

Where did I find you, that I came to know you? You were not within my memory before I learned of you. Where, then, did I find you before I came to know you, if not within yourself, far above me? We come to you and go from you, but no place in involved in this process. In every place, O Truth, you are present to those who seek your help, and at one and the same time you answer all, though they seek your counsel on different matters.

You respond clearly, but not everyone hears clearly. All ask what they wish, but do not always hear the answer they wish. Your best servant is he who is intent not so much on hearing his petition answered, as rather on willing whatever he hears from you.

Late have I loved you, O Beauty ever ancient, ever new, late have I loved you! You were within me, but I was outside, and it was there that I searched for you. In my unloveliness I plunged into the lovely things which you created. You were with me, but I was not with you. Created things kept me from you; yet if they had not been in you they would not have been at all. You called, you shouted, and you broke through my deafness. You flashed, you shone, and you dispelled my blindness. You breathed your fragrance on me; I drew in breath and now I pant for you. I have tasted you; now I hunger and thirst for more. You touched me, and I burned for your peace.

When once I shall be united to you with my whole being, I shall at last be free of sorrow and toil. Then my life will be alive, filled entirely with you. When you fill someone, you relieve him of his burden, but because I am not yet filled with you, I am a burden to myself. My joy when I should be weeping struggles with my sorrows when I should be rejoicing. I know not where victory lies. Woe is me! Lord, have mercy on me! My evil sorrows and good joys are at war with one another. I know not where victory lies. Woe is me! Lord, have mercy! Woe is me! I make no effort to conceal my wounds. You are my physician, I your patient. You are merciful; I stand in need of mercy.

Is not the life of man upon earth a trial[Job 7:1]? Who would want troubles and difficulties? You command us to endure them, not to love them. No person loves what he endures, though he may love the act of enduring. For even if he is happy to endure his own burden, he would still prefer that the burden not exist. I long for prosperity in times of adversity, and I fear adversity when times are good. Yet what middle ground is there between these two extremes where the life of man would be other than trial? Pity the prosperity of this world, pity it once and again, for it corrupts joy and brings the fear of adversity. Pity the adversity of this world, pity it again, then a third time; for it fills men with a longing for prosperity, and because adversity itself is hard for them to bear and can even break their endurance. *Is not the life of man upon earth a trial,* a continuous trial?

All my hope lies only in your great mercy.

Thursday of the Eighth Week in Ordinary Time

From the Moral Reflections on Job by Saint Gregory the Great, Pope & Doctor

The law of the Lord is manifold

How must we interpret this law of God? How, if not by love? The love that stamps the precepts of right-living on the mind and bids us put them into practice. Listen to Truth speaking of this law: *This is my commandment, that you love one another*[Jn 15:12]. Listen to Paul: *The whole law,* he declares, *is summed up in love*[Gal 5:14]*;* and again: *Help one another in your troubles, and you will fulfill the law of Christ*[Gal 6:2]. The law of Christ – does anything other than love more fittingly describe it? Truly we are keeping this law when, out of love, we go to the help of a brother in trouble.

But we are told that this law is manifold. Why? Because love's lively concern for others is reflected in all the virtues. It begins with two commands, but it soon embraces many more. Paul gives a good summary of its various aspects. *Love is patient,* he says*, and kind; it is never jealous or conceited; its conduct is blameless; it is not ambitious, not selfish, not quick to take offense; it harbors no evil thoughts, does not gloat over other people's sins, but is gladdened by an upright life*[1 Cor 13:4-8].

The man ruled by this love shows his patience by bearing wrongs with equanimity; his kindness by generously repaying good for evil. Jealousy is foreign to him. It is impossible to envy worldly success when he has no worldly desires. He is not conceited. The prizes he covets lie within; outward blessings do not elate him. His conduct is blameless, for he cannot do wrong in devoting himself entirely to love of God and his neighbor. He is not ambitious. The welfare of his own soul is what he cares about. Apart from that he seeks nothing. He is not selfish. Unable to keep anything he has in this world, he is as indifferent to it as if it were another's. Indeed, in his eyes nothing is his own but what will be so always. He is not quick to take offense. Even under provocation, thought of revenge never crosses his mind. The reward he seeks hereafter will be greater in proportion to his endurance. He harbors no evil thoughts. Hatred is utterly rooted out of a heart whose only love is goodness. Thoughts that defile a man can find no entry. He does not gloat over other people's sins. No; an enemy's fall affords him no delight, for loving all men, he longs for their salvation.

On the other hand, *he is gladdened by an upright life*. Since he loves others as himself, he takes as much pleasure in whatever good he sees in them as if the progress were his own. That is why this law of God is manifold.

Friday of the Eighth Week in Ordinary Time

From the Moral Reflections on Job by Saint Gregory the Great, Pope & Doctor

The interior witness

Whoever is mocked by his friend, as I am, shall call upon God, and he shall hear him[Job 12:4]. A weak-minded person is frequently diverted toward pursuing exterior happiness when the breath of popular favor accompanies his good actions. So he gives up his own personal choices, preferring to remain at the mercy of whatever he hears from others. Thus, he rejoices not so much to become but to be called blessed. Eager for praise, he gives up what he had begun to be; and so he is severed from God by the very means by which he appeared to be commendable in God.

But sometimes a soul firmly strives for righteousness and yet is beset by men's ridicule. He does what is admirable but he gets only mockery. He might have gone out of himself because of man's praise; hc returns to himself when repelled by their abuse. Finding no resting-place without, he cleaves more intensely to God within. All his hope is fixed on his Creator, and amid all the ridicule and abuse he invokes his interior witness alone. One who is afflicted in this way grows closer to God the more he turns away from human popularity. He straightway pours himself out in prayer, and, pressured from without, he is refined with a more perfect purity to penetrate what is within.

In this context, the words apply: *Whoever is mocked by his friend, as I am, shall call upon God, and he shall hear him*. For while the wicked reproach the just, they show them whom they should look to as the witness of their actions. Thus afflicted, the soul strengthens itself by prayer; it is united within to one who listens from on high precisely because it is cut off externally from the praise of men. Again, we should note how appropriately the words are inscrted: *as I am*. There are some people who are both oppressed by human mockery and are yet deprived of God's favorable hearing. For when the mockery is done to a man's own sin, it obviously does not produce the merit that is due to virtue.

The simplicity of the just man is laughed to scorn[Job 12:4]. It is the wisdom of this world to conceal the heart with stratagems, to veil one's thoughts with words, to make what is false appear true and what is true appear false. On the other hand it is the wisdom of the just never to pretend anything for show, always to use words to express one's thoughts, to love the truth as it is and to avoid what is false, to do what is right without reward and to be more willing to put up with evil than to perpetrate it, not to seek revenge for wrong, and to consider as gain any insult for truth's sake. But this guilelessness is laughed to scorn, for the virtue of innocence is held as foolishness by the wise of this world. Anything that is done out of innocence, they doubtless consider to be stupidity, and whatever truth approves of, in practice is called folly by their worldly wisdom.

Saturday in the Eighth Week in Ordinary Time

From a sermon by Saint Zeno of Verona, Bishop

Job was a type of Christ

Is Job a type of Christ? If I am right, he is, and the comparison will reveal the truth of my claim. But while Job was called a just man by God, God himself is the fountain of justice from whom all the saints drink. See what Scripture says: *The sun of justice will arise for you*[Mal 4:2]. Job was called truthful, but the Lord is, as he says in the Gospel, *the way, the truth and the life*[Jn 14:16]. And while Job was rich, the Lord is far richer, *for the earth is the Lord's and everything in it; the world and all who dwell in it*[Ps 23:1]. All rich men are his servants, and the whole world and all of nature as well.

But we may compare Job and Christ in many ways. As Job was tempted by the devil three times, so too Christ was tempted three times. The Lord set aside his riches out of love for us and chose poverty so that we might become rich, while Job lost all that he possessed. A violent wind killed Job's sons, while the sons of God, the prophets, were killed by the fury of the Pharisees. Job became ulcerated and disfigured, while the Lord, by becoming man, took on the defilement of the sins committed by all mankind. The wife of Job tempted him to sin, much as the synagogue tried to force the Lord to yield to corrupt leadership. Thus he was insulted by the priests, the servants of his altar, as Job was insulted by his friends. And as Job sat on a dunghill of worms, so all the evil of the world is really a dunghill which became the Lord's dwelling place, while men that abound in every sort of crime and base desire are really worms.

The restoration of health and riches to Job prefigures the resurrection, which gives health and eternal life to those who believe in Christ. Regaining lordship over all the world, Christ says: *All things have been given to me by my Father*[Lk 10:22]. And just as Job fathered other sons, so too did Christ, for the apostles, the sons of the Lord, succeeded the prophets.

Job died happily and in peace, but there is no death for the Lord. He is praised for ever, just as he was before time began, and as he always will be as time continues and moves into eternity.

Sunday of the Ninth Week in Ordinary Time

From the Confessions of Saint Augustine, Bishop & Doctor

Our heart is restless until it rests in you

You are great, Lord, and worthy of our highest praise; your power is great and there is no limit to your wisdom[Ps 144:3[1-21]]. Man, a tiny part of your creation, wishes to praise you. Though he bears about him his mortality, the evidence of his sin and the evidence that *you resist the proud*[1 Peter 5:5-6], yet this man, a tiny part of your creation, wishes to praise you. It is you who move man to delight in your praise. For you have made us for yourself, and our heart is restless until it rests in you.

Lord, help me to know and understand which is the soul's first movement, to call upon you for help or to praise you; or if it must first know you before it can call upon you. But if someone does not know you, how can he call upon you? For, not knowing you, he might call upon someone else instead of you. Or must you first be called upon in order to be known? But Scripture says: Unless *they believe in him, how shall they call upon him. And how shall they believe unless someone preaches to them*[Rom 10:14]?

Those who seek the Lord will praise him[Ps 21:27]. Seeking the Lord they will find him, and finding him they will praise him. Lord, let me seek you by calling upon you, and let me call upon you believing in you, for you have been preached to us. Lord, my faith calls upon you, the faith you have given me, the faith you have inspired in me by the incarnation of your Son and through the ministry of your preacher.

How shall I call upon my God, my Lord and my God? For when I call upon him, I am really calling him into myself. Where within me can my God come? How can God who made heaven and earth come into me? Lord my God, is there anything in me that can contain you? Can heaven and earth, which you have made and in which you have made me, contain you? Or is it true that whatever exists contains you since without you nothing would exist?

Since I do indeed exist and yet would not exist unless you were in me, why do I ask you to come to me? I am not now in hell, yet you are there. For the psalmist says: *If I descend into hell you are there*[Ps 138:8]. Therefore, my God, I would not exist at all, unless you were in me; or rather, I would not exist unless I were in you *from whom and by whom and in whom all things exist*[1 Cor 8:6]. Yes, Lord, it is so. To what place do I call you to come, since I am in you? Or from what place are you to come to me? Where can I go beyond the bounds of heaven and earth, that my God may come to me, for he has said: *I fill heaven and earth*[Jer 23:24]?

Who will help me to find rest in you? Who will send you into my heart to inebriate it, so that I will forget my evil ways and embrace you, my only good? What are you to me? Have mercy on me, that I may speak. What am I to you that you command me to love you, and grow angry and threaten me with terrible punishment if I do not? Is it then a small sorrow not to love you?

In your mercy, Lord my God, tell me what you are to me. *Say to my soul, I am your salvation*[Ps 34:3]. So speak that I may hear you. The ears of my heart are turned to you, Lord; open them and say to my soul: *I am your salvation*. I will run after your voice and I will lay hold of you. Do not hide your face from me. Let me see your face even if I die, for if I see it not, I shall die of longing.

Monday of the Ninth Week in Ordinary Time

From the teachings of Saint Dorotheus, Abbot

The reason for all disturbance is that no one finds fault with himself

Let us examine, my brothers, how it happens that many times a person hears something unpleasant and goes away untroubled, as if he had not heard it; and yet on some occasions he is disturbed and troubled as soon as he hears such words. What is the cause of this inconsistency? Is there one reason for it or many? I recognize a number of them, and one in particular is the source of all the others. As someone has put it: Occasionally this results from the condition in which the person happens to be.

If a person is engaged in prayer or contemplation, he can easily take a rebuke from his brother and be unmoved by it. On other occasions affection toward a brother is a strong reason; love bears all things with the utmost patience. Another reason may be contempt; if a person despises the one who is trying to trouble him and acts as if he is the vilest of all creatures and considers it beneath his dignity even to look at him, or to answer him, or to mention the affront and insults to anyone else, he will not be moved by his words.

The result of this is, as I have said, that no one is disturbed or troubled if he scorns and disregards what is said. But on the other hand, it is also possible that a person will be disturbed and troubled by his brother's words, either because he is not in a good frame of mind, or because he hates his brother. There are a great number of other reasons as well. Yet the reason for all disturbance, if we look to its roots, it that no one finds fault with himself.

This is the source of all annoyance and distress. This is why we sometimes have no rest. We must not be surprised when we are rebuked by holy men. We have no other path to peace but this.

We have seen that this is true in many cases, and, in our laziness and desire for rest, we hope or believe that we have entered upon a straight path when we are impatient with everyone, and yet cannot bear to blame ourselves.

This is the way we are. It does not matter how many virtues a man may have, even if they are beyond number and limit. If he has turned from the path of self-accusation, he will never find peace. He will always be troubled himself, or else he will be a source of trouble for others and all his labors will be wasted.

Tuesday of the Ninth Week in Ordinary Time

From the teachings of Saint Dorotheus, Abbot

On false spiritual peace

The man who finds fault with himself accepts all things cheerfully - misfortune, loss, disgrace, dishonor and any other kind of adversity. He believes that he is deserving of all these things and nothing can disturb him. No one could be more at peace than this man.

But perhaps you will offer me this objection: "Suppose my brother injures me, and on examining myself I find that I have not given him any cause. Why should I blame myself?"

Certainly if someone examines himself carefully and with fear of God, he will never find himself completely innocent. He will see that he has given some provocation by an action, a word or by his manner. If he does find that he is not guilty in any of these ways, certainly he must have injured that brother somehow at some other time. Or perhaps he has been a source of annoyance to some other brother. For this reason he deserves to endure the injury because of many other sins that he has committed on other occasions.

Someone else asks why he should accuse himself when he was sitting peacefully and quietly when a brother came upon him with an unkind or insulting word. He cannot tolerate it, and so he thinks that his anger is justified. If that brother had not approached him and said those words and upset him, he never would have sinned.

This kind of thinking is surely ridiculous and has no rational basis. For the fact that he has said anything at all in this situation breaks the cover on the passionate anger within him, which is all the more exposed by his excessive anxiety. If he wished, he would do penance. He has become like a clean, shiny grain of wheat that, when broken, is full of dirt inside.

The man who thinks that he is quiet and peaceful has within him a passion that he does not see. A brother comes up, utters some unkind word and immediately all the venom and mire that lie hidden within him are spewed out. If he wishes mercy, he must do penance, purify himself and strive to become perfect. He will see that he should have returned thanks to his brother instead of returning the injury, because his brother has proven to be an occasion of profit to him. It will not be long before he will no longer be bothered by these temptations. The more perfect he grows, the less these temptations will affect him. For the more the soul advances, the stronger and more powerful it becomes in bearing the difficulties that it meets.

Wednesday of the Ninth Week in Ordinary Time

From the Moral Reflections on Job by Saint Gregory the Great, Pope & Doctor

True doctrine dispels arrogance

Listen, Job, to what I say and ponder all my words[Job 33:1]. The teaching of the arrogant has this characteristic: they do not know how to introduce their teaching humbly and they cannot convey correctly to others the things they understand correctly themselves. With their words they betray what they teach; they give the impression that they live on lofty heights from which they look down disdainfully on those whom they are teaching; they regard the latter as inferiors, to whom they do not deign to listen as they talk; indeed they scarcely deign to talk to them at all - they simply lay down the law.

To teachers of this kind the Lord through the prophet says rightly: *But you will rule them with severity and with power*[Ps 2:9]. There is no doubt that such as are prone not to correct their subjects with quiet reasoning, but to compel them to change by rough and domineering methods, rule with severity and power.

On the contrary true doctrine all the more effectively shuns the voice of arrogance through reflection, in which it pursues the arrogant teacher himself with the arrows of its words. It ensures that the pride which it attacks in the hearts of those listening to the sacred words will not in fact be preached by arrogant conduct. For true doctrine tries both to teach by words and to demonstrate by living example - humility, which is the mother and mistress of virtues. Its goal is to express humility among the disciples of truth more by deeds than by words.

Accordingly, when addressing the Thessalonians, Paul is oblivious of his own eminent dignity as an apostle; he actually says: *We became as little children in your midst*[1 Thess 2:7]. Similarly, the apostle Peter enjoins: *Be always prepared to satisfy everybody who asks a reason for the hope which is in you*[1 Pet 3:15]; and by adding the words, *with a good conscience, speak gently and respectfully*[1 Pet 3:16], Peter draws attention to the manner in which sacred doctrine should be taught.

When he tells his disciples: *These things command and teach with all power*[1 Tim 4:11], Paul really recommends the credibility that goes hand in hand with good behavior rather than the domineering exercise of power. When one practices first and preaches afterwards, one is really teaching with power. Doctrine loses credibility, if conscience tethers the tongue. Paul, therefore, in the saying quoted above, does not refer to the power of lofty rhetoric but to the confidence elicited by good deeds. Of the Lord, too, it is said: *He taught with authority unlike the Scribes and the Pharisees*[Mt 7:29]. He alone in a unique and sovereign way spoke from the power of his goodness because no evil weakness led him into sin. For he had from the power of his own divine nature what he gave to us through the sinlessness of his human nature.

Thursday of the Ninth Week in Ordinary Time

From the Moral Reflections on Job by Saint Gregory the Great, Pope & Doctor

The Church moves forward like the advancing dawn

Since the daybreak or the dawn is changed gradually from darkness into light, the Church, which comprises the elect, is fittingly styled daybreak or dawn. While she is being led from the night of infidelity to the light of faith, she is opened gradually to the splendor of heavenly brightness, just as dawn yields to the day after darkness. The Song of Songs says aptly: *Who is this who moves forward like the advancing dawn*[Song 6:10]*?* Holy Church, inasmuch as she keeps searching for the rewards of eternal life, has been called the dawn. While she turns her back on the darkness of sins, she begins to shine with the light of righteousness.

This reference to the dawn conjures up a still more subtle consideration. The dawn intimates that the night is over; it does not yet proclaim the full light of day. While it dispels the darkness and welcomes the light, it holds both of them, the one mixed with the other, as it were. Are not all of us who follow the truth in this life daybreak and dawn? While we do some things which already belong to the light, we are not free from the remnants of darkness. In Scripture the Prophet says to God: *No living being will be justified in your sight*[Ps 142:2]. Scripture also says: *In many ways all of us give offense.*

When he writes, *the night is passed,* Paul does not add, *the day is come,* but rather, *the day is at hand*[Rom 13:12-14]. Since he argues that after the night has passed, the day as yet is not come but is rather at hand, he shows that the period before full daylight and after darkness is without doubt the dawn, and that he himself is living in that period.

It will be fully day for the Church of the elect when she is no longer darkened by the shadow of sin. It will be fully day for her when she shines with the perfect brilliance of interior light. This dawn is aptly shown to be an ongoing process when Scripture says: *And you showed the dawn its place*[Job 38:12]. A thing which is shown its place is certainly called from one place to another. What is the place of the dawn but the perfect clearness of eternal vision? When the dawn has been brought there, it will retain nothing belonging to the darkness of night. When the Psalmist writes: *My soul thirsts for the living God; when shall I go and see the face of God*[Ps 41:3]*?,* does he not refer to the effort made by the dawn to reach its place? Paul was hastening to the place which he knew the dawn would reach when he said he wished to die and to be with Christ. He expressed the same idea when he said: *For me to live is Christ, and to die is gain*[Phil 1:21].

Friday of the Ninth Week in Ordinary Time

From a sermon by Baldwin of Canterbury, Bishop

The Lord sees our thoughts and the intentions of our hearts

The Lord knows the thoughts and intentions of our hearts. Without a doubt, every one of them is known to him, while we know only those which he lets us read by the grace of discernment. The spirit of man does not know all that is in man, nor all of the thoughts which he has, willingly or unwillingly. Man does not always perceive his thoughts as they really are. Having clouded vision, he does not discern them clearly with his mind's eye.

Often under the guise of devotion a suggestion occurs to our mind – coming from our own thoughts or from another person or from the tempter – and in God's eyes we do not deserve any reward for our virtue. For there are certain imitations of true virtues as also of vices which play tricks with the heart and bedazzle the mind's vision. As a result, the appearance of goodness often seems to be in something which is evil, and equally the appearance of evil seems to be in something good. This is part of our wretchedness and ignorance, causing us anguish and anxiety.

It has been written: *There are paths which seem to man to be right, but which in the end lead him to hell*[Prov 14:12]. To avoid this peril, Saint John gives us these words of advice: *Test the spirits to see if they are from God*[1 Jn 4:1]. Now no one can test the spirits to see if they are from God unless God has given him discernment of spirits to enable him to investigate spiritual thoughts, inclinations and intentions with honest and true judgment. Discernment is the mother of all the virtues; everyone needs it either to guide the lives of others or to direct and reform his own life.

In the sphere of action, a right thought is one ruled by the will of God, and intentions are holy when directed single-mindedly toward him. In a word, we could see clearly through any action of ours, or into our entire lives, if we had a simple eye. A simple eye is an eye, and it is simple. This means that we see by right thinking what is to be done, and by our good intention we carry it out with simple honesty, because deceitful action is wrong. Right thinking does not permit mistakes; a good intention rules out pretense. This then is true discernment, a combination of right thinking and good intention.

Therefore, we must do all our actions in the light of discernment as if in God and in his presence.

Saturday of the Ninth Week in Ordinary Time

From the Exposition of John by Saint Thomas Aquinas, Priest & Doctor

The way to come to true life

Christ himself is the way, and therefore he says: *I am the way*[Jn 14:6]. This certainly is eminently right for *through him we have access to the Father*[Eph 2:18].

Since this way is not separate from its end, but joined to it, he adds *the truth and the life;* thus he is himself at once both the way and the goal. In his human nature he is the way, and in his divine nature he is the goal. Therefore, speaking as man he says: *I am the way;* and speaking as God he adds: *the truth and the life.* These two words are an apt description of this goal.

For this goal is the object of human desire, and a man desires two things above all. In the first place he wants to know the truth, which is peculiar to him; and secondly he wants to continue to exist, which is common to all things. Christ is the way by which we come to know truth, though he is also that truth: *Lead me, O Lord, in truth, and I shall enter into your way*[Ps 85:11]. Christ is also the way to come to life, though he is also that life: *You have made known the ways of life*[Acts 2:28].

Therefore, he designated the end of this way by truth and life, about which we have spoken above with reference to Christ. First, he himself is life, for *life was in him;* then, he is truth, because *he was the light of men*[Jn 1:4-12], and light is truth.

If, then, you are looking for the way by which you should go, take Christ, because he himself is the way: *This is the way; walk in it.* And Augustine says: *Make man your way and you shall arrive at God.* It is better to limp along the way than stride along off the way. For a man who limps along the way, even if he only makes slow progress, comes to the end of the way; but one who is off the way, the more quickly he runs, the further away is he from his goal.

If you are looking for a goal, hold fast to Christ, because he himself is the truth, where we desire to be. *My mouth shall reflect on the truth*[Prov 8:7]. If you are looking for a resting place, hold fast to Christ, because he himself is the life. *Whoever finds me finds life, and receives salvation from the Lord*[Prov 8:35].

Therefore hold fast to Christ if you wish to be safe. You will not be able to go astray, because he is the way. He who remains with him does not wander in trackless places; he is on the right way. Moreover he cannot be deceived, because he is the truth, and he teaches every truth. And he says: *For this I was born and for this I have come, to bear witness to the truth*[Jn 18:37]. Nor can he be disturbed, because he is both life and the giver of life. For he says: *I have come that they may have life, and have it more abundantly*[Jn 10:10].

Sunday of the Tenth Week in Ordinary Time

From the beginning of a letter to the Romans by Saint Ignatius of Antioch, Bishop & Martyr

I wish you to please God and not men

Ignatius, called Theophorus, to the church which has found mercy in the generosity of the Father on high and of Jesus Christ, his only Son; to the church which is loved and enlightened by the Father, who wills all that exists in accordance with the love of Jesus Christ our God; to the Church which rules over the land of the Romans, a church worthy of God, worthy of honor and of praise, worthy to be called blessed, worthy to receive the answer to its prayer, pure, and preeminent in love among Christian communities, observing the law of Christ and bearing the Father's name. I greet this church in the name of Jesus Christ, Son of the Father. To those who were in union, body and soul, with his every command, and filled inalienably with the grace of God, and cleansed wholly from all foreign stain, I wish every blameless joy in Jesus Christ out Lord.

Through my prayers I have been granted the favor of seeing you, my holy brothers, face to face, as indeed I have constantly asked. I now hope to embrace you as a prisoner in Christ Jesus, provided that it is God's will for me to be found worthy to the end. For a good start has been made, if only I may gain the grace to secure my prize without hindrance. For I fear that your love may harm me. It is easy for you to do as you wish, but hard for me to attain to God if you should not allow me to be martyred.

I wish you to please God and not men - as indeed you are doing. I shall never again have such an opportunity to get to God, nor will you, if you keep silent, ever have the credit for a greater achievement. If you keep silent about me, I become a word of God; but if you love me in the flesh, I become a meaningless cry. Grant me no more than to be made a sacrifice to God while there is still an altar at hand. Thus you may form a choir of love and sing praise to the Father in Christ Jesus for so graciously summoning the bishop of Syria from the sun's rising to come to the place of its setting. It is a fine thing for me to set with the sun, leaving the world and going to God, that I may rise in him.

Monday of the Tenth Week in Ordinary Time

From a letter to the Romans by Saint Ignatius of Antioch, Bishop & Martyr

Let me not only be called a Christian, but prove to be one

You have never begrudged the martyrs their triumph but rather trained them for it. And so I am asking you to be consistent with the lessons you teach them. Just beg for me the courage and endurance not only to speak but also to will what is right, so that I may not only be called a Christian, but prove to be one. For if I prove myself to be a Christian by martyrdom, then people will call me one, and my loyalty to Christ will be apparent when the world sees me no more. Nothing you can see is truly good. For our Lord Jesus Christ, now that he has returned to his Father, has revealed himself more clearly. Our task is not one of producing persuasive propaganda; Christianity shows its greatness when it is hated by the world.

I am writing to all the churches to declare to them all that I am glad to die for God, provided you do not hinder me. I beg you not to show me a misplaced kindness. Let me be the food of beasts that I may come to God. I am his wheat, and I shall be ground by the teeth of beasts, that I may become Christ's pure bread.

I would rather that you coaxed the beasts to become my tomb and to leave no scrap of me behind; then when I have died I will be a burden to no one. I shall be a true disciple of Christ when the world no longer sees my body. Pray to Christ for me that by these means I may become a sacrifice to God. I do not give you orders like Peter and Paul. They were apostles, I am a condemned criminal; they were free, I am still a slave. But if I suffer, I shall become the freedman of Jesus Christ and I shall rise again to freedom in him.

Now as a prisoner I am learning to give up my own wishes. All the way from Syria to Rome I am fighting wild beasts, by land and by sea, by day and by night, chained as I am to ten leopards, I mean the detachment of soldiers who guard me; the better you treat them, the worse they become. I am more and more trained in discipleship by their ill-usage of me, *but I am not therefore justified*[1 Cor 4:4]. How happy I will be with the beasts which are prepared for me! I hope that they will make short work of me. I shall even coax them to devour me quickly and not to be afraid of touching me, as sometimes happens; in fact, if they hold back, I shall force them to it. Bear with me, for I know what is good for me. Now I am beginning to be a disciple. May nothing visible or invisible rob me of my prize, which is Jesus Christ! The fire, the cross, packs of wild beasts, lacerations, rendings, wrenching of bones, mangling of limbs, crushing of the whole body, the horrible tortures of the devil – let all these things come upon me, if only I may gain Jesus Christ!

Tuesday of the Tenth Week of Ordinary Time

From a letter to the Romans by Saint Ignatius of Antioch, Bishop & Martyr

My earthly desires have been crucified

The delights of this world and all its kingdoms will not profit me. I would prefer to die in Jesus Christ than to rule over all the earth. I seek him who died for us, I desire him who rose for us. I am in the throes of being born again. Bear with me, my brothers; do not keep me from living, do not wish me to die. I desire to belong to God; do not give me over to the world, and do not seduce me with perishable things. Let me see the pure light; when I am there, I shall be truly a man at last. Let me imitate the sufferings of my God. If anyone has God in him, let him understand what I want and have sympathy for me, knowing what drives me on.

The prince of this world would snatch me away and destroy my desire to be with God. So let none of you who will be there give him help; side rather with me, that is, with God. Do not have Jesus Christ on your lips and the world in your hearts. Give envy no place among you. And if, when I get there, I should beg for your intervention, pay no attention to me; no, believe instead what I am writing to you now. For I write to you while I yet live, but I long for death. My earthly desires have been crucified, and there no longer burns in me the love of perishable things, but a living water speaks within me, saying: "Come to the Father."

I take no delight in corruptible food or in the pleasures of this life. I want the bread of God, which is the flesh of Jesus Christ, who was of David's seed, and for drink I want his blood, the sign of his imperishable love.

I no longer wish to live, as men count life. And I shall have my way, if you wish it so. Wish it, then, so that you too may have God's favor. With these few words I beg you to believe me. Jesus Christ will make plain to you the truth of what I say; he is the true voice that speaks the Father's truth. Pray for me that I may reach my goal. I have written to you not prompted by merely human feelings and values, but by God's purpose for me. If I am to suffer, it will be because you loved me well; if I am rejected, it will be because you hated me.

Remember in your prayers the church of Syria: it now has God for its shepherd instead of me. Jesus Christ alone will be its bishop, along with your love. For myself, I am ashamed to be counted among its members, for I do not deserve it, being the least of all, born out of due time. Yet, if I attain to God, by his mercy I shall be something. I greet you from my heart, and so do the churches that have welcomed me in love not as a mere passerby but as the representative of Jesus Christ. Yes, even the churches that were not on my route humanly speaking, though spiritually on the same journey, were there to meet me in city after city.

Wednesday of the Tenth Week of Ordinary Time

From a homily on Joshua by Origen, Priest

The crossing of the Jordan

The ark of the covenant led the people of God across the Jordan. The priests and the levites halted, and the waters, as though out of reverence to the ministers of God, stopped flowing. They piled up in a single mass, thus allowing the people of God to cross in safety. As a Christian, you should not be amazed to hear of these wonders performed for men of the past. The divine Word promises much greater and more lofty things to you who have passed through Jordan's stream by the sacrament of baptism: he promises you a passage even through the sky. Listen to what Paul says concerning the just: *We shall be caught up in the clouds to meet Christ in heaven, and so we shall always be with the Lord*[1 Thess 4:17]. There is absolutely nothing for the just man to fear; the whole of creation serves him. Listen to another promise that God makes him through the prophet: *If you pass through fire, the flame shall not burn you, for I am the Lord your God*[Isa 43:2]. The just man is everywhere welcome, and everything renders him due service.

So you must not think that these events belong only to the past, and that you who now hear the account of them do not experience anything of the kind. It is in you that they all find their spiritual fulfillment. You have recently abandoned the darkness of idolatry, and you now desire to come and hear the divine law. This is your departure from Egypt. When you became a catechumen and began to obey the laws of the Church, you passed through the Red Sea; now at the various stops in the desert, you give time every day to hear the law of God and to see the face of Moses unveiled by the glory of God. But once you come to the baptismal font and, in the presence of the priests and deacons, are initiated into those sacred and august mysteries which only those know who should, then, through the ministry of the priests, you will cross the Jordan and enter the promised land. There Moses will hand you over to Jesus, and he himself will be your guide on your new journey.

Mindful, then, of all the mighty works of God, remembering that he divided the sea for you and held back the waters of the river, you will turn to them and say: *Why was it, sea, that you fled? Jordan, why did you turn back? Mountains, why did you skip like rams, and you hills, like young sheep*[Ps 113:5]? And the word of the Lord will reply: *The earth is shaken at the face of the Lord, at the face of the God of Jacob, who turns stones into a pool and rock into springs of water*[Ps 113:7-8].

Thursday of the Tenth Week in Ordinary Time

From a homily on Joshua by Origen, Priest

The capture of Jericho

Once Jericho was surrounded it had to be stormed. How then was Jericho stormed? No sword was drawn against it, no battering ram was aimed at it, no javelins were hurled. The priests merely sounded their trumpets, and the walls of Jericho collapsed.

In the Scriptures Jericho is often represented as an image of the world. There can be no doubt that the man whom the Gospel describes as going down from Jerusalem to Jericho and falling into the hands of brigands is an image of Adam being driven out of paradise into the exile of this world. Likewise the blind men in Jericho, to whom Jesus came to give sight, signified the people in this world who were blinded by ignorance, to whom the Son of God came.

Jericho will fall, then; this world will perish. Indeed in the sacred books the end of the world was proclaimed long ago. How will the world be brought to an end, and by what means will it be destroyed? The answer of Scripture is: *By the sound of trumpets*. If you ask what trumpets, then let Paul reveal the secret. Listen to what he says: *The trumpet will sound, and the dead who are in Christ will rise incorruptible. The voice of the archangel and the trumpet of God will give the signal, and the Lord himself will come down from heaven*[1 Thess 4:16-17]. Then the Lord Jesus will conquer Jericho with trumpets and destroy it, saving only the harlot and her household.

Jesus our Lord *will come,* says Paul, and he will come with the sound of trumpets. He will save only the woman who received his spies, that is, his apostles, in faith and obedience, and hid them on the roof of her house; and he will join this harlot to the house of Israel. But let us not bring up her past sins again or impute them to her. She was a harlot once, but now she is joined to Christ, chaste virgin to one chaste husband. Listen to what the Apostle says of her: *He has determined to present you to Christ as a chaste virgin to her one and only husband*[2 Cor 11:2]. Indeed, Paul himself had been born of her: *Misled by our folly and disbelief,* he said, *we too were once slaves to our passions and to pleasures of every kind*[Titus 3:3].

If you wish to learn more fully about how this harlot ceased to be a harlot then listen to Paul once again: *And such were you also, but you have been cleansed and made holy in the name of our Lord Jesus Christ and in the Spirit of our God*[1 Cor 6:11]. To assure her escape when Jericho was destroyed, the harlot was given that most effective symbol of salvation, the scarlet cord. For it is by the blood of Christ that the entire Church is saved, in the same Jesus Christ our Lord, to whom belongs glory and dominion for ever and ever. Amen.

Friday of the Tenth Week in Ordinary Time

From The Explanation of the Psalms by Saint Ambrose, Bishop & Doctor

The appeal of the Book of Psalms

Though all Scripture is fragrant with God's grace, the Book of Psalms has a special attractiveness.

Moses wrote the history of Israel's forefathers in prose, but after leading the people through the Red Sea - a wonder that remained in their memory - he broke into a song of triumph in praise of God when he saw King Pharaoh drowned along with his forces. His genius soared to a higher level, to match an accomplishment beyond his own powers.

Miriam too raised her timbrel and sang encouragement for the rest of the women, saying: *Let us sing to the Lord, for he has triumphed gloriously; he has cast horse and rider into the sea*[Ex 15:1].

In the Book of Psalms there is profit for all, with healing power for our salvation. There is instruction from history, teaching from the law, prediction from prophecy, chastisement from denunciation, persuasion from moral preaching. All who read it may find the cure for their own individual failings. All with eyes to see can discover in it a complete gymnasium for the soul, a stadium for all the virtues, equipped for every kind of exercise; it is for each to choose the kind he judges best to help him gain the prize.

If you wish to read and imitate the deeds of the past, you will find the whole history of the Israelites in a single psalm: in one short you can amass a treasure for the memory. If you want to study the power of the law, which is summed up in the bond of charity (*Whoever loves his neighbor has fulfilled the law*[Rom 13:8]), you may read in the psalms of the great love with which one man faced serious dangers singlehandedly in order to remove the shame of the whole people. You will find the glory of charity more than a match for the parade of power.

What am I to say of the grace of prophecy? We see that what others hinted at in riddles was promised openly and clearly to the psalmist alone: the Lord Jesus was to be born of his seed, according to the word of the Lord, *I will place upon your throne one who is the fruit of your flesh*[Ps 131:11].

In the psalms, then, not only is Jesus born for us, he also undergoes his saving passion in his body, he lies in death, he rises again, he ascends into heaven, he sits at the right hand of the Father. What no man would have dared to say was foretold by the psalmist alone, and afterward proclaimed by the Lord himself in the Gospel.

Saturday of the Tenth Week in Ordinary Time

From The Explanation of the Psalms by Saint Ambrose, Bishop & Doctor

I will sing in spirit, and with understanding

What is more pleasing than a psalm? David expresses it well: *Praise the Lord, for a song of praise is good: let there be praise of our God with gladness and grace*[Ps 146:1]. Yes, a psalm is a blessing on the lips of the people, a hymn in praise of God, the assembly's homage, a general acclamation, a word that speaks for all, the voice of the Church, a confession of faith in song. It is the voice of complete assent, the joy of freedom, a cry of happiness, the echo of gladness. It soothes the temper, distracts from care, lightens the burden of sorrow. It is a source of security at night, a lesson in wisdom by day. It is a shield when we are afraid, a celebration of holiness, a vision of serenity, a promise of peace and harmony. It is like a lyre, evoking harmony from a blend of notes. Day begins to the music of a psalm. Day closes to the echo of a psalm.

In a psalm instruction vies with beauty. We sing for pleasure. We learn for our profit. What experience is not covered by a of the psalms? I come across the words: *A song for the beloved*, and I am aflame with desire for God's love. I go through God's revelation in all its beauty, the intimations of resurrection, the gifts of his promise. I learn to avoid sin. I see my mistake in feeling ashamed of repentance for my sins.

What is a psalm but a musical instrument to give expression to all the virtues? The psalmist of old used it, with the aid of the Holy Spirit, to make earth reecho the music of heaven. He used the dead gut of strings to create harmony from a variety of notes, in order to send up to heaven the song of God's praise. In doing so he taught us that we must first die to sin, and then create in our lives on earth a harmony through virtuous deeds, if the grace of our devotion is to reach up to the Lord.

David thus taught us that we must sing an interior song of praise, like St. Paul, who tells us: *I shall pray in spirit, and also with understanding; I shall sing in spirit, and also with understanding*[1 Cor 14:15]. We must fashion our lives and shape our actions in the light of the things that are above. We must not allow pleasure to awaken bodily passions, which weigh our soul down instead of freeing it. The holy prophet told us that his songs of praise were to celebrate the freeing of his soul, when he said: *I shall sing to you, God, on the lyre, holy one of Israel; my lips will rejoice when I have sung to you, and my soul also, which you have set free*[Ps 70:22-23].

Sunday of the Eleventh Week in Ordinary Time

From a treatise on the Lord's Prayer by St. Cyprian of Carthage, Bishop & Martyr

Let your prayer come from a humble heart

When we pray, our words should be calm, modest and disciplined. Let us reflect that we are standing before God. We should please him both by our bodily posture and the manner of our speech. It is characteristic of the vulgar to shout and make a noise, not those who are modest. On the contrary, they should employ a quiet tone in their prayer.

Moreover, in the course of his teaching, the Lord instructed us to pray in secret. Hidden and secluded places, even our own rooms, give witness to our belief that God is present everywhere; that he sees and hears all; that in the fullness of his majesty, he penetrates hidden and secret places. This is the teaching of Jeremiah: *Am I God when I am near, and not God when I am far away? Can anyone hide in a dark corner without my seeing him? Do I not fill heaven and earth*[Jer 23:23]*?* Another passage of Scripture says: *The eyes of the Lord are everywhere, observing both good and wicked men*[Prov 15:3].

The same modesty and discipline should characterize our liturgical prayer as well. When we gather to celebrate the divine mysteries with God's priest, we should not express our prayer in unruly words; the petition that should be made to God with moderation is not to be shouted out noisily and verbosely. For God hears our heart not our voice. He sees our thoughts; he is not to be shouted at. The Lord showed us this when he asked: *Why do you think evil in your hearts*[Mt 9:4]*?* The book of Revelation testifies to this also: *And all the churches shall know that I am the one who searches the heart and the desires*[Rev 2:23].

Anna maintained this rule; in her observance of it she is an image of the Church. In the First Book of Kings we are told that she prayed quietly and modestly to God in the recesses of her heart. Her prayer was secret but her faith was evident. She did not pray with her voice, but with her heart, for she knew that in this way the Lord would hear her. She prayed with faith and obtained what she sought. Scripture makes this clear in the words: *She was speaking in her heart; her lips were moving but her voice could not be heard; and the Lord heard her prayer*[1 Sam 1:13]. The psalmist also reminds us: *Commune within your own hearts, and in the privacy of your room express your remorse*[Ps 4:5]. This is the teaching of the Holy Spirit. Through Jeremiah he suggests this: *Say in your hearts: Lord, it is you that we have to worship*[Jer Chapters 7-11].

My friends, anyone who worships should remember the way in which the tax-collector prayed in the temple alongside the Pharisee. He did not raise his eyes immodestly to heaven or lift up his hands arrogantly. Instead he struck his breast and confessing the sins hidden within his heart he implored the assistance of God's mercy. While the Pharisee was pleased with himself, the tax-collector deserved to be cleansed much more because of the manner in which he prayed. For he did not place his hope of salvation in the certainty of his own innocence; indeed, no one is innocent. Rather he prayed humbly, confessing his sins. And the Lord who forgives the lowly heard his prayer.

Monday of the Eleventh Week in Ordinary Time

From a Treatise on the Lord's Prayer by St. Cyprian of Carthage, Bishop & Martyr

Our prayer is communal

Above all, he who preaches peace and unity did not want us to pray by ourselves in private or for ourselves alone. We do not say "My Father, who art in heaven," nor "Give me this day my daily bread." It is not for himself alone that each person asks to be forgiven, not to be led into temptation or to be delivered from evil. Rather, we pray in public as a community, and not for one individual but for all. For the people of God are all one.

God is then the teacher of harmony, peace and unity, and desires each of us to pray for all men, even as he bore all men in himself alone. The three young men shut up in the furnace of fire observed this rule of prayer. United in the bond of the Spirit they uttered together the same prayer. The witness of holy Scripture describes this incident for us, so that we might imitate them in our prayer. Then all three began to sing in unison, blessing God. Even though Christ had not yet taught them to pray, nevertheless, they spoke as with one voice.

It is for this reason that their prayer was persuasive and efficacious. For their simple and spiritual prayer of peace merited the presence of the Lord. So too, after the ascension we find the apostles and the disciples praying together in this way. Scripture relates: They all joined together in continuous prayer, with the women including Mary, the mother of Jesus, and his brothers.

They all joined together in continuous prayer. The urgency and the unity of their prayer declares that God, who fashions a bond of unity among those who live in his home, will admit into his divine home for all eternity only those who pray in unity.

My dear friends, the Lord's Prayer contains many great mysteries of our faith. In these few words there is great spiritual strength, for this summary of divine teaching contains all of our prayers and petitions. And so, the Lord commands us: Pray then like this: Our Father, who art in heaven.

We are new men; we have been reborn and restored to God by his grace. We have already begun to be his sons and we can say "Father." John reminds us of this: He came to his own home, and his own people did not receive him. But to all who received him, who believe in his name, he gave the power to become children of God. Profess your belief that you are sons of God by giving thanks. Call upon God who is your Father in heaven.

Tuesday of the Eleventh Week in Ordinary Time

From a treatise on the Lord's Prayer by St. Cyprian of Carthage, Bishop & Martyr

May your name be hallowed

How merciful the Lord is to us, how kind and richly compassionate! He wished us to repeat this prayer in God's sight, to call the Lord our Father and, as Christ is God's Son, be called in turn sons of God! None of us would ever have dared to utter this name unless he himself had allowed us to pray in this way. And therefore, dear friends, we should bear in mind and realize that when we call God our Father we ought also to act like sons. If we are pleased to call him Father, let him in turn be pleased to call us sons.

We should live like the temples of God we are, so that it can be seen that God lives in us. No act of ours should be unworthy of the spirit. Now that we have begun to live in heaven and in the spirit, all our thoughts and actions should be heavenly and spiritual; for, as the Lord God himself has said: *Those who honor me I will honor, and those who despise me shall be despised*[1 Sam 2:30]. And the blessed Apostle wrote in his letter: *You are not your own; you were bought with a great price. So glorify and bear God in your body*[1 Cor 6:19-20].

We go on to say, *May your name be hallowed*[Mt 6:9-13]. It is not that we think to make God holy by our prayers; rather we are asking God that his name may be made holy in us. Indeed, how could God be made holy, he who is the source of holiness? Still, because he himself said: *Be holy, for I am holy*[1 Pet 1:6], we pray and beseech him that we who have been hallowed in baptism may persevere in what we have begun. And we pray for this every day, for we have need of daily sanctification; sinning every day, we cleanse our faults again and again by constant sanctification.

The Apostle Paul instructs us in these words concerning the sanctification which God's loving kindness confers on us: *Neither the immoral, nor idolaters, nor adulterers, nor homosexuals, nor thieves, nor the greedy, nor drunkards, nor revilers, nor robbers will inherit the kingdom of God. And such indeed you were. But you have been washed, you have been sanctified, you have been justified in the name of the Lord Jesus Christ and in the Spirit of our God. We were sanctified,* he says, *in the name of the Lord Jesus Christ and in the Spirit of our God*[1 Cor 6:9-11]. Hence we make our prayer that this sanctification may remain in us. But further, our Lord who is also our judge warns those who have been cured and brought back to life by him to sin no more lest something worse happen to them. Thus we offer constant prayers and beg night and day that this sanctification and new life which is ours by God's favor may be preserved by his protection.

From a treatise on the Lord's Prayer by St. Cyprian of Carthage, Bishop & Martyr

Your kingdom come. Your will be done.

The prayer continues: *Your kingdom come.* We pray that God's kingdom will become present for us in the same way that we ask for his name to be hallowed among us. For when does God not reign, when could there be in him a beginning of what always was and what will never cease to be? What we pray for is that the kingdom promised to us by God will come, the kingdom won by Christ's blood and passion. Then we who formerly were slaves in this world will reign from now on under the dominion of Christ, in accordance with his promise: *Come, O blessed of my Father, receive the kingdom which was prepared for you from the foundation of the world*[Mt 25:34].

However, my dear friends, it could also be that the kingdom of God whose coming we daily wish for is Christ himself, since it is his coming that we long for. He is our resurrection, since we rise again in him; so too he can he thought of as the kingdom of God because we are to reign in him. And it is good that we pray for God's kingdom; for though it is a heavenly kingdom, it is also an earthly one. But those who have already renounced the world are made greater by holding positions of authority in that kingdom.

After this we add: *Your will be done on earth as it is in heaven;* we pray not that God should do his will, but that we may carry out his will. How could anyone prevent the Lord from doing what he wills? But in our prayer we ask that God's will be done in us, because the devil throws up obstacles to prevent our mind and our conduct from obeying God in all things. So if his will is to be done in us we have need of his will, that is, his help and protection. No one can be strong by his own strength or secure save by God's mercy and forgiveness. Even the Lord, to show the weakness of the human nature which he bore, said: *Father, if it be possible, let this cup pass from me*[Mt 26:39], and then, by way of giving example to his disciples that they should do God's will and not their own, he added: *Nevertheless, not as I will, but as you will*[Mt 26:39].

All Christ did, all he taught, was the will of God. Humility in our daily lives, an unwavering faith, a moral sense of modesty in conversation, justice in acts, mercy in deed, discipline, refusal to harm others, a readiness to suffer harm, peaceableness with our brothers, a whole hearted love of the Lord, loving in him what is of the Father, fearing him because he is God, preferring nothing to him who preferred nothing to us, clinging tenaciously to his love, standing by his cross with loyalty and courage whenever there is any conflict involving his honor and his name, manifesting in our speech the constancy of our profession and under torture confidence for the fight, and in dying the endurance for which we will be crowned - this is what it means to wish to be a coheir with Christ, to keep God's command; this is what it means to do the will of the Father.

Thursday in the Eleventh Week in Ordinary Time

From a treatise on the Lord's Prayer by St. Cyprian of Carthage, Bishop & Martyr

After the gift of bread we ask pardon for our sins

As the Lord's Prayer continues, we ask: *Give us this day our daily bread*. We can understand this petition in a spiritual and in a literal sense. For in the divine plan both senses may help toward our salvation. For Christ is the bread of life; this bread does not belong to everyone, but is ours alone. W hen we say, our Father, we understand that he is the father of those who know him and believe in him. In the same way we speak of our daily bread, because Christ is the bread of those who touch his body.

Now, we who live in Christ and receive his eucharist, the food of salvation, ask for this bread to be given us every day. Otherwise we may be forced to abstain from this communion because of some serious sin. In this way we shall be separated from the body of Christ, as he taught us in the words: *I am the bread of life which has come down from heaven. Anyone who eats my bread will live for ever and the bread that I will give is my flesh for the life of the world*[Jn 6:51]. Christ is saying, then, that anyone who eats his bread will live for ever. Clearly they possess life who approach his body and share in the Eucharistic communion. For this reason we should be apprehensive and pray that no one has to abstain from this communion, lest he be separated from the body of Christ and be far from salvation. Christ has warned of this: *If you do not eat the flesh of the Son of man and drink his blood you will have no life in you*[Jn 6:53]. We pray for our daily bread, Christ, to be given to us. With this help, we who live and abide in him will never be separated from his body and his grace.

After this we ask pardon for our sins, in the words: *and forgive us our trespasses*. The gift of bread is followed by a prayer for forgiveness. To be reminded that we are sinners and forced to ask forgiveness for our faults is prudent and sound. Even while we are asking God's forgiveness, our hearts are aware of our state! This command to pray daily for our sins reminds us that we commit sin every day. No one should complacently think himself innocent, lest his pride lead to further sin. Such is the warning that John gives us in his letter: *If we say we have no sin, we deceive ourselves, and the truth is not in us. If we confess our sins, the Lord is faithful and just, and will forgive our sins*[1 Jn 1:8-9]. His letter includes both points, that we should beg for forgiveness for our sins, and that we receive pardon when we do. He calls the Lord faithful, because he remains loyal to his promise, by forgiving us our sins. He both taught us to pray for our sins and our faults, and also promised to show us a father's mercy and forgiveness.

Friday of the Eleventh Week in Ordinary Time

From a treatise on the Lord's Prayer by St. Cyprian of Carthage, Bishop & Martyr

We are God's children; let us abide in his peace

Christ clearly laid down an additional rule to bind us by a certain contractual condition: we ask that our debts be forgiven insofar as we forgive our own debtors. Thus we are made aware that we cannot obtain what we ask regarding our own trespasses unless we do the same for those who trespass against us. This is why he says elsewhere: *The measure you give will be the measure you get*[Lk 6:38]. And the servant who, after his master forgives all his debt, refuses to forgive his fellow servant is thrown into prison. Because he refused to be kind to his fellow servant, he lost the favor his master had given him.

Along with his other precepts Christ lays this down even more forcefully with a most vigorous condemnation. He says: *When you stand up to pray, if you have anything against anyone, let it go, so that your heavenly Father may also forgive you*[Mk 11:25]*; but if you do not forgive men their trespasses, neither will your Father forgive you your trespasses*[Mt 6:14-15]. You will have no excuse on the day of judgment, for then you will be judged just as you have judged, and you will suffer whatever you have done to others.

God bids us to be peace-loving, harmonious *and of one mind in his house*[1 Pet 3:8]; he wants us to live with the new life he gave us at our second birth. As sons of God, we are to abide in peace; as we have one Spirit, we should be one in mind and heart. Thus God does not receive the sacrifice of one who lives in conflict; and he orders us to turn back from the altar and be first reconciled with our brother, that God too may be appeased by the prayers of one who is at peace. The greatest offering we can make to God is our peace, harmony among fellow Christians, a people united with the unity of the Father, the Son and the Holy Spirit.

When Cain and Abel first offered their sacrifices, God considered not so much the gifts as the spirit of the giver: God was pleased with Abel's offering because he was pleased with his spirit. Thus Abel the just man, the peacemaker, in his blameless sacrifice taught men that when they offer their gift at the altar they should approach as he did, in the fear of God, simplicity of heart, ruled by justice and peaceful harmony. Since this was the character of Abel's offering, it was only right that he himself should afterward become a sacrifice. As martyrdom's first witness and possessing the Lord's qualities of justice and peace, he foreshadowed the Lord's passion in the glory of his own death. Such, then, are the men who are crowned by the Lord and will be justified with him on the day of judgment.

But St. Paul and the sacred Scriptures tell us that the quarrelsome man and the troublemaker, who is never at peace with his brothers, cannot escape the charge of internal dissension even though he may die for Christ's name. For it is written: *He who hates his brother is a murderer*[1 Jn 3:15], nor can he attain the kingdom of heaven. God cannot abide a murderer. He cannot be united with Christ, who has preferred to imitate Judas rather than Christ.

Saturday of the Eleventh Week in Ordinary Time

From a treatise on the Lord's Prayer by St. Cyprian of Carthage, Bishop & Martyr

Prayer should be expressed in deeds as well as words

Dear friends, why does the fact that God has taught us such a prayer as this astonish us? Did he not express all of our prayers in his own words of life? Indeed this was already foretold by Isaiah. Filled with the Holy Spirit, he spoke of the majesty and fidelity of God: *The Lord will speak a final brief word of justice, a word throughout the world*[Rom 9:28]. Our Lord Jesus Christ came for all mankind. He gathered together male and female, the learned and the unlearned, the old and the young and taught them his saving doctrine. He did not want his disciples to be burdened by memorizing his teaching; he made a complete summary of his commands such as was necessary for a trusting faith, and could be quickly learned.

Thus he summarized his teaching on the mystery of eternal life and its meaning with an admirable, divine brevity: *And eternal life is this: to know you, the only true God, and Jesus Christ whom you sent*[Jn 17:3]. Again, in quoting the first and the greatest precept of the law and the prophets, he spoke in the same way: *Listen, Israel, the Lord your God is one Lord, and you shall love the Lord your God with all your heart, with all your soul, and with all your strengthDeut 6:4-5. This is the first commandment. The second is like it: You must love your neighbor as yourself. On these two commandments depends all that is contained in the law and the prophets*[Mt 22:37-40]. On another occasion the Lord said: *Always treat others as you would like them to treat you: that is the meaning of the law and the prophets*[Mt 7:12].

God taught us to pray not only by his words, but also by his actions. He taught us by his own example for he often prayed on our behalf. The Scripture says: *He withdrew to the wilderness and prayed*[Lk 5:16]. And again: *He went into the hills to pray and he spent the whole night in prayer to God*[Lk 6:12].

Was the sinless Lord praying for himself? No, he was praying and interceding on our behalf. He explained this to Peter: *Behold Satan demanded that he might sift you like wheat, but I have prayed for you that your faith may not fail*[Lk 22:31-32]. Later on he prayed to the Father for everyone: *I am not praying for these only, but also for those who will believe in me through their preaching, that they may be one; just as you, Father, are in me, and I in you, that they also may be one in us*[Jn 17:20-21]. God loves us; for the sake of our salvation he is generous toward us. He is not satisfied with redeeming us by his blood. He also prays to the Father on our behalf. Consider the love exemplified in that prayer. The Father and Son are one; we too are to abide in that oneness.

Sunday of the Twelfth Week in Ordinary Time

From a treatise on the Trinity by Faustus Luciferanus, Priest

Christ, king and priest for ever

Our Savior received a bodily anointing and so became a true king and a true priest. Both king and priest he was of his very self; a savior could be nothing less. Hear in his own words how he himself became a king: *I have been appointed king by God on Zion his holy mountain*[Ps 2:6]. Hear in the Father's words that he was a priest: *You are a priest for ever in the line of Melchizedek*[Ps 109:4; Heb 7:17]. Aaron was the first under the law to be made a priest by being anointed with chrism, yet the Father does not say, "in the line of Aaron," lest it be believed that the Savior's priesthood could be passed on by inheritance, for at that time Aaron's priesthood was transmitted by lineal descent. But the Savior's priesthood is not inherited because this priest lives on for ever. Therefore Scripture says: *You are a priest for ever in the line of Melchizedek*[Ps 109:4; Heb 7:17].

There is, therefore, a savior in the flesh who is both a king and a priest, though his anointing was not physical but spiritual. Among the Israelites, those kings and priests who were actually anointed with oil were either kings or priests. No man could be both king and priest; he had to be one or the other. Only Christ was both king and priest; because he had come to fulfill the law, he alone possessed the twofold perfection of kingship and priesthood.

Those who had been anointed with the oil of kingship or priesthood, although they received only one of these anointings, were called messiahs. Our Savior, however, who is the Christ, was anointed by the Holy Spirit so that the passage in Scripture might be fulfilled: *God, your God, has anointed you with the oil of gladness and raised you above your companions*[Heb 1:9]. The difference, then, between the one Christ and the many christs is in the anointing, since he was anointed with the oil of gladness, which signifies nothing other than the Holy Spirit.

This we know to be true from the Savior himself. When he took the book of Isaiah, he opened it and read: *The Spirit of the Lord is upon me because he has anointed me*[Isa 61:1; Lk 4:18]. He then said that the prophecy was fulfilled in the hearing of those listening.

Peter, the prince of the apostles, also taught that the chrism which made the Savior a christ was the Holy Spirit; that is to say, the power of God. When in the Acts of the Apostles Peter spoke to that faithful and merciful man, the centurion, he said among other things: *After the baptism which John preached, Jesus of Nazareth, whom God anointed with the Holy Spirit and with power, started out in Galilee and traveled about performing powerful miracles, and freeing all who were possessed by the devil*[Acts 10:36-38].

So you see that Peter too said that Jesus in his humanity was anointed with the Holy Spirit and with power. Thus Jesus in his humanity truly became the Christ. By the anointing of the Holy Spirit, he was made both king and priest for ever.

Monday of the Twelfth Week in Ordinary Time

From a treatise on Christian Perfection by Saint Gregory of Nyssa, Bishop

The Christian is another Christ

No one has known Christ better than Paul, nor surpassed him in the careful example he gave of what anyone should be who bears Christ's name. So precisely did he mirror his Master that he became his very image. By a painstaking imitation, he was transformed into his model and it seemed to be no longer Paul who lived and spoke, but Christ himself. He shows his keen awareness of this grace when he refers to the Corinthians' desire for proof that Christ was speaking in him; as he says: *It is no longer I who live: it is Christ who lives in me*[Gal 2:20].

Paul teaches us the power of Christ's name when he calls him the power and wisdom of God, our peace, the unapproachable light where God dwells, our expiation and redemption, our great high priest, our paschal sacrifice, our propitiation; when he declares him to be the radiance of God's glory, the very pattern of his nature, the creator of all ages, our spiritual food and drink, the rock and the water, the bedrock of our faith, the cornerstone, the visible image of the invisible God. He goes on to speak of him as the mighty God, the head of his body, the Church, the firstborn of the new creation, the first fruits of those who have fallen asleep, the firstborn of the dead, the eldest of many brothers; he tells us that Christ is the mediator between God and man, the only-begotten Son crowned with glory and honor, the Lord of glory, the beginning of all things, the king of justice and of peace, the king of the whole universe, ruling a realm that has no limits.

Paul calls Christ by many other titles too numerous to recall here. Their cumulative force will give some conception of the marvelous content of the name "Christ," revealing to us his inexpressible majesty, insofar as our minds and thoughts can comprehend it. Since, by the goodness of God, we who are called "Christians" have been granted the honor of sharing this name, the greatest, the highest, the most sublime of all names, it follows that each of the titles that express its meaning should be clearly reflected in us. If we are not to lie when we call ourselves "Christians," we must bear witness to it by our way of living.

Tuesday of the Twelfth Week in Ordinary Time

From a treatise on Christian Perfection by St Gregory of Nyssa, Bishop

Christ should be manifest in our whole life

The life of the Christian has three distinguishing aspects: deeds, words and thought. Thought comes first, then words, since our words express openly the interior conclusions of the mind. Finally, after thoughts and words, comes action, for our deeds carry out what the mind has conceived. So when one of these results in our acting or speaking or thinking, we must make sure that all our thoughts, words and deeds are controlled by the divine ideal, the revelation of Christ. For then our thoughts, words and deeds will not fall short of the nobility of their implications.

What then must we do, we who have been found worthy of the name of Christ? Each of us must examine his thoughts, words and deeds, to see whether they are directed toward Christ or are turned away from him. This examination is carried out in various ways. Our deeds or our thoughts or our words are not in harmony with Christ if they issue from passion. They then bear the mark of the enemy who smears the pearl of the heart with the slime of passion, dimming and even destroying the luster of the precious stone.

On the other hand, if they are free from and untainted by every passionate inclination, they are directed toward Christ, the author and source of peace. He is like a pure, untainted stream. If you draw from him the thoughts in your mind and the inclinations of your heart, you will show a likeness to Christ, your source and origin, as the gleaming water in a jar resembles the flowing water from which it was obtained.

For the purity of Christ and the purity that is manifest in our hearts are identical. Christ's purity, however, is the fountainhead; ours has its source in him and flows out of him. Our life is stamped with the beauty of his thought. The inner and the outer man are harmonized in a kind of music. The mind of Christ is the controlling influence that inspires us to moderation and goodness in our behavior. As I see it, Christian perfection consists in this: sharing the titles which express the meaning of Christ's name, we bring out this meaning in our minds, our prayers and our way of life.

Wednesday of the Twelfth Week in Ordinary Time

From a treatise on Spiritual Friendship by Saint Aelred, Abbot

True, perfect, and eternal friendship

Jonathan, outstanding among all young men, took no heed of his royal lineage or his hope of the throne, but allied himself with David the servant and made him his equal in friendship before the Lord. The king had made David a fugitive, forced him to hide in the desert, and condemned him to death. And yet Jonathan preferred David to himself, exalting him, humbling himself. *You,* he said, *will be king and I will follow after you*[1 Sam 23:17].

What a splendid picture of true friendship! What an astonishing situation! Here was the king, raging against his servant and stirring up the whole country as if David were aiming at the crown. He accuses the priests of treason and puts them to death on a mere suspicion. He combs and searches woods and valleys, besieges the mountains and rocky crags with troops, and every man is sworn to wreak vengeance upon the source of the King's indignation. Only Jonathan, who alone should have had greater cause for envy, thought it right to resist his father. Putting himself at the service of his friend, he offered help and advice in his time of need. Jonathan set friendship above a kingdom. *You are to be the king,* he said, *and I will be second to you*[1 Sam 23:17]. And still the father tried to incite his son to envy David. He covered him with abuse and frightened him by threatening to deprive him of the kingdom and strip him of his rank.

Even when the king pronounced sentence of death upon David, Jonathan still did not desert his friend. *Why should David die? How has he sinned? What has he done? When he risked his life and killed the Philistine, you rejoiced. Why then should he die*[1 Sam 20:32]*?* So maddened was the king at these words that he tried to pin Jonathan to the wall with his spear, heaping upon him further abuse and threats: *Bastard son of a wayward woman,* he screamed, *I know well that, to your undoing and that of your shameful mother's, you love him*[1 Sam 20:30]. With this he spewed forth the full measure of his venom over Jonathan and uttered the words that were his final attempt to arouse bitter envy and jealous ambition: *As long as the son of Jesse lives, your kingdom shall never be established*[1 Sam 20:31].

Who would not be moved to envy by these words? Whose love, whose favor, whose abiding friendship would not be corrupted, weakened and destroyed by such an utterance? But in his great love, this young man kept faith with his friend. He was steadfast in the face of threats, unmoved by insults; forgetting renown, he thought only of service. He spurned a kingdom for the sake of friendship. *You,* he said, *will be king, and I will be second to you.*

This is what truly perfect, stable and lasting friendship is, a tie that envy cannot spoil, nor suspicion weaken, nor ambition destroy. A friendship so tempted yielded not an inch, was buffeted but did not collapse. In the face of so many insults, it remained unshaken. *Go,* therefore, *and do likewise*[Lk 10:37].

Thursday of the Twelfth Week in Ordinary Time

From a homily by Saint Gregory of Nyssa, Bishop

God is like an inaccessible rock

Consider the feelings of a man who looks down into the depths of the sea from the top of a mountain. This is similar to my own experience when the voice of the Lord from on high, as from a mountaintop, reached the unfathomable depths of my intellect. Along the seacoast, you may often see mountains facing the sea. It is as though they had been sliced in two, with a sheer drop from top to bottom. At the top a projection forms a ledge overhanging the depths below. If a man were to look down from that ledge, he would be overcome by dizziness. In this same way my soul grows dizzy when it hears the great voice of the Lord saying: *Blessed are the clean of heart, for they shall see God*[Mt 5:8].

The vision of God is offered to those who have purified their hearts. Yet, *no man has seen God at any time*[Ex 33:20; Jn 1:18]. These are the words of the great Saint John and they are confirmed by Saint Paul's lofty thought, in the words: God is *he whom no one has seen or can see*[1 Tim 6:16]. He is that smooth, steep and sheer rock, on which the mind can find no secure resting place to get a grip or lift ourselves up. In the view of Moses, he is inaccessible. In spite of every effort, our minds cannot approach him. We are cut off by the words: *No man can see God and live* [Ex 33:20]. And yet, to see God is eternal life. But John, Paul and Moses, pillars of our faith, all testify that it is impossible to see God. Look at the dizziness that affects the soul drawn to contemplating the depths of these statements. If God is life, then he who does not see God does not see life. Yet God cannot be seen; the apostles and prophets, inspired by the Holy Spirit, have testified to this. Into what straits is man's hope driven!

Yet God does raise and sustain our flagging hopes. He rescued Peter from drowning and made the sea into a firm surface beneath his feet. He does the same for us; the hands of the Word of God are stretched out to us when we are out of our depth, buffeted and lost in speculation. Grasped firmly in his hands, we shall be without fear: *Blessed are the pure of heart,* he says, *for they shall see God.*

Friday of the Twelfth Week in Ordinary Time

From a homily by Saint Gregory of Nyssa, Bishop

The hope of seeing God

The happiness God promises certainly knows no limits. When one has gained such a blessing, what is left to desire? In seeing God one possesses all things. In the language of Scripture, to see is to have. *May you see the good things of Jerusalem* is the same as *May you possess the good things of JerusalemPs 127:5*. When the prophet says: *May the wicked man be carried off and not see the glory of the Lord*[Isa 26:10], he means: *May he not share in the glory of the Lord.*

One who has seen God has, in the act of seeing, gained all that is counted good: life without end, everlasting freedom from decay, undying happiness, a kingdom that has no end, lasting joy, true light, a voice to sing pleasingly in the spirit, unapproachable glory, perpetual rejoicing, in a word, the totality of blessing.

Such is the wonderful hope held out by the beatitudes. As we have seen, the condition for seeing God is purity of heart, and now once more my mind is in confusion, as from an attack of giddiness, wondering if purity of heart is something impossible, something beyond the capacity of human nature. If the vision of God is dependent on purity of heart, and if Moses and Paul did not attain this vision - they state that neither they nor anyone else can see God - then the promise of the beatitude spoken by the Word seems to be something impossible of realization.

What do we gain from knowing the means by which God may be seen if we have not the power to see him? It is like saying that one is blessed if one is in heaven because in heaven things are seen that are not seen on earth. If we were told beforehand how to get to heaven, it would be helpful to know that one is blessed if one is in heaven. But as long as the way to heaven is impossible what do we gain by knowing about the happiness of heaven? This only saddens and annoys us when we realize the good things we are deprived of, because it is impossible to get there.

Surely the Lord does not encourage us to do something impossible to human nature because the magnitude of what he commands is beyond the reach of our human strength? The truth is different. He does not command those creatures to whom he has not given wings to become birds, nor those to whom he has assigned a life on land to live in water. If then in the case of all other creatures the command is according to the capacity of those who receive it, and does not oblige them to anything beyond their nature, we shall come to the conclusion that we are not to give up hope of gaining what is promised by the beatitude. John and Paul and Moses, then, and any others like them, did not fail to achieve that sublime happiness that comes from the vision of God; not Paul, who said: *There is stored up for me a crown of righteousness, which the judge who judges justly will give me*[2 Tim 4:8], nor John, who leaned on the breast of Jesus, nor Moses, who heard God saying to him, *I know you above all others*[Ex 33:17].

If it is clear that those who taught that the contemplation of God was beyond their powers are themselves blessed, and if blessedness consists in the vision of God and is granted to the pure in heart, then purity of heart, leading to blessedness, is certainly not among the things that are impossible.

Hence it can be said that those who with Paul teach that the vision of God is beyond our powers are right in what they say, and that the voice of the Lord does not contradict them when he promises that the pure in heart will see God.

Saturday of the Twelfth Week in Ordinary Time

From a homily by Saint Gregory of Nyssa, Bishop

God can be found in man's heart

In our human life bodily hearth is a good thing, but this blessing consists not merely in knowing the causes of good health but in actually enjoying it. If a man eulogizes good health and then eats food that has unhealthy effects, what good is his praise of health when he finds himself on a sickbed? Similarly, from the Lord's saying: *Blessed are the pure of heart, for they shall see God*[Mt 5:8], we are to learn that blessedness does not lie in knowing something about God, but rather in possessing God within oneself.

I do not think these words mean that God will be seen face to face by the man who purifies the eye of his soul. Their sublime import is brought out more clearly perhaps in that other saying of the Lord's: *The kingdom of God is within you*[Lk 17:20-21]. This teaches us that the man who cleanses his heart of every created thing and every evil desire will see the image of the divine nature in the beauty of his own soul. I believe the lesson summed up by the Word in that short sentence was this: You men have within you a desire to behold the supreme good. Now when you are told that the majesty of God is exalted above the heavens, that his glory is inexpressible, his beauty indescribable, and his nature transcendent, do not despair because you cannot behold the object of your desire. If by a diligent life of virtue you wash away the film of dirt that covers your heart, then the divine beauty will shine forth in you.

Take a piece of iron as an illustration. Although it might have been black before, once the rust has been scraped off with a whetstone, it will begin to shine brilliantly and to reflect the rays of the sun. So it is with the interior man, which is what the Lord means by the heart. Once a man removes from his soul the coating of filth that has formed on it through his sinful neglect, he will regain his likeness to his Archetype, and be good. For what resembles the supreme Good is itself good. If he then looks into himself, he will see the vision he has longed for. This is the blessedness of the pure of heart: in seeing their own purity they see the divine Archetype mirrored in themselves.

Those who look at the sun in a mirror, even if they do not look directly at the sky, see its radiance in the reflection just as truly as do those who look directly at the sun's orb. It is the same, says the Lord, with you. Even though you are unable to contemplate and see the inaccessible light, you will find what you seek within yourself, provided you return to the beauty and grace of that image which was originally placed in you. For God is purity; he is free from sin and a stranger to all evil. If this can be said of you, then God will surely be within you. If your mind is untainted by any evil, free from sin, and purified from all stain, then indeed are you blessed, because your sight is keen and clear. Once purified, you see things that others cannot see. When the mists of sin no longer cloud the eye of your soul, you see that blessed vision clearly in peace and purity of your own heart. That vision is nothing else than the holiness, the purity, the simplicity and all the other glorious reflections of God's nature, through which God himself is seen.

Sunday in the Thirteenth Week in Ordinary Time

From a homily by Pope Paul VI

We proclaim Christ to the whole world

Not to preach the Gospel would be my undoing, for Christ himself sent me as his apostle and witness. The more remote, the more difficult the assignment, the more *my love of God spurs me on*. I am bound to proclaim that Jesus is *Christ, the Son of the living God*. Because of him we come to know the God we cannot see. *He is the firstborn of all creation; in him all things find their being*[Col 1:15-17]. Man's teacher and redeemer, he was born for us, died for us, and for us he rose from the dead.

All things, all history converges in Christ. A man of sorrow and hope, he knows us and loves us. As our friend he stays by us throughout our lives; at the end of time he will come to be our judge; but we also know that he will be the complete fulfillment of our lives and our great happiness for all eternity.

I can never cease to speak of Christ for he is our truth and our light; *he is the way, the truth and the life*[Jn 14:6]. He is our bread, our source of living water who allays our hunger and satisfies our thirst. He is our shepherd, our leader, our ideal, our comforter and our brother.

He is like us but more perfectly human, simple, poor, humble, and yet, while burdened with work, he is more patient. He spoke on our behalf; he worked miracles; and he founded a new kingdom: in it the poor are happy; peace is the foundation of a life in common; where the pure of heart and those who mourn are uplifted and comforted; the hungry find justice; sinners are forgiven; and all discover that they are brothers.

The image I present to you is the image of Jesus Christ. As Christians you share his name; he has already made most of you his own. So once again I repeat his name to you Christians and I proclaim to all men: Jesus Christ is the beginning and the end, the alpha and the omega, Lord of the new universe, the great hidden key to human history and the part we play in it. He is the mediator – the bridge, if you will – between heaven and earth. Above all he is the Son of man, more perfect than any man, being also the Son of God, eternal and infinite. He is the son of Mary his mother on earth, more blessed than any woman. She is also our mother in the spiritual communion of the mystical body.

Remember: it is Jesus Christ I preach day in and day out. His name I would see echo and re-echo for all time even to the ends of the earth.

Monday of the Thirteenth Week in Ordinary Time

From a sermon by Saint Augustine, Bishop & Doctor

He is the Lord our God, and we are the people of his pasture

The words we have sung contain our declaration that we are God's flock: *For he is the Lord our God who made us*[Ps 99:3]. He is our God, *and we are the people of his pasture and the sheep of his hands*[Ps 94:7]. Human shepherds did not make the sheep they own; they did not create the sheep they pasture. Our Lord God, however, because he is God and Creator, made for himself the sheep which he has and pastures. No one else created the sheep he pastures, nor does anyone else pasture the sheep he created.

In this song we have declared that we are his flock, the people of his pasture, and the sheep of his hands. Let us listen therefore to the words he addresses to us as his sheep. Earlier he addressed the shepherds, but now he speaks to the sheep. We listened to those earlier words of his and we - the shepherds - trembled, but you listened without a qualm.

What is to happen when we hear these words today? Are we in turn to be without a qualm while you tremble? By no means! We are shepherds, and the shepherd listens and trembles not only at what is said to the shepherds but also at what is said to the sheep. If he does listen without a qualm to what is said to his sheep, he is not concerned for them. And further, on that occasion we asked you in your charity to remember two points about us: first, that we are Christians, and second, that we are placed in charge. Because we are placed in charge, we are ranked among the shepherds, if we are good; but because we are Christians, we too are members of the flock with you. Therefore, whether the Lord is addressing the shepherds or the sheep, we must listen to all his words and tremble; our hearts must always remain concerned.

And so, my brothers, let us listen to the words with which the Lord upbraids the wicked sheep and to the promises he makes to his own flock. *You are my sheep*[Jn 10:26-29], he says. Even in the midst of this life of tears and tribulations, what happiness, what great joy it is to realize that we are God's flock! To him were spoken the words: *You are the shepherd of Israel*[Ezek 34:1-16]. Of him it was said: *The guardian of Israel will not slumber, nor will he sleep*[Ps 120:4]. He keeps watch over us when we are awake; he keeps watch over us when we sleep. A flock belonging to a man feels secure in the care of its human shepherd; how much safer should we feel when our shepherd is God. Not only does he lead us to pasture, but he even created us.

You are my sheep, says the Lord God. See, I judge between one sheep and another, and between rams and goats[Ezek 34:17]. What are goats doing here in the flock of God? In the same pastures, at the same springs, goats - though destined for the left - mingle with those on the right. They are tolerated now, but will be separated later. In this way the patience of the flock develops and becomes like God's own patience. For it is he who will do the separating, placing some on the left and others on the right.

Tuesday of the Thirteenth Week in Ordinary Time

From a sermon by Saint Augustine, Bishop & Doctor

If I wanted to please men, I would not be a servant of Christ

This is our glory: the witness of our conscience[2 Cor 1:12]. There are men who rashly judge, who slander, whisper and murmur, who are eager to suspect what they do not see, and eager to spread abroad things they have not even a suspicion of. Against men of this sort, what defense is there save the witness of our own conscience?

My brothers, we do not seek, nor should we seek, our own glory even among those who approval we desire. What we should seek is their salvation, so that if we walk as we should they will not go astray in following us. They should imitate us if we are imitators of Christ; and if we are not, they should still imitate him. He cares for his flock, and he alone is to be found with those who care for their flocks, because they are all in him.

And so we seek no advantage for ourselves when we aim to please men. We want to take our joy in men - and we rejoice when they take pleasure in what is good, not because this exalts us, but because it benefits them.

It is clear who is intended by the apostle Paul: *If I wanted to please men, I would not be a servant of Christ*[Gal 1:10]. And similarly when he says: *Be pleasing to all men in all things, even as I in all things please all men*[1 Cor 10:33]. Yet his words are as clear as water, limpid, undisturbed, unclouded. And so you should, as sheep, feed on and drink of his message; do not trample on it or stir it up.

You have listened to our Lord Jesus Christ as he taught his apostles: *Let your actions shine before men so that they may see you good deeds, and give glory to your Father who is in heaven*[Mt 5:16], for it is the Father who made you thus. *We are the people of his pasture, the sheep of his hands*[Ps 94:7]. If then you are good, praise is due to him who made you so; it is no credit to you, for if you were left to yourself, you could only be wicked. Why then do you try to pervert the truth, in wishing to be praised when you do good, and blaming God when you do evil? For though he said: *Let your works shine before men* [Mt 5:16], in the same Sermon on the Mount he also said: *Do not parade your good deeds before men*[Mt 6:1]. So if you think there are contradictions in Saint Paul, you will find the same in the Gospels; but if you refrain from troubling the waters of your heart, you will recognize here the peace of the Scriptures and with it you will have peace.

And so, my brothers, our concern should be not only to live as we ought, but also to do so in the sight of men; not only to have a good conscience but also, so far as we can in our weakness, so far as we can govern our frailty, to do nothing which might lead our weak brother into thinking evil of us. Otherwise, as we feed on the good pasture and drink the pure water, we may trample on God's meadow, and weaker sheep will have to feed on trampled grass and drink from troubled waters.

Wednesday of the Thirteenth Week in Ordinary Time

From the book Way of Perfection by Saint Teresa of Avila, Virgin & Doctor

Your kingdom come

When asking a favor of some person of importance would anyone be so ill-mannered and thoughtless as not first to consider how best to address him in order to make a good impression and give him no cause for offense? Surely he would think over his petition carefully and his reason for making it, especially if it were for something specific and important as our good Jesus tells us our petitions should be. It seems to me that this point deserves serious attention. My Lord, could you not have included all in one word by saying "Father, give us whatever is good for us?" After all, to one who understands everything so perfectly, what need is there to say more?

O Eternal Wisdom, between you and your Father that was enough; that was how you prayed in the garden. You expressed your desire and fear but surrendered yourself to his will. But as for us, my Lord, you know that we are less submissive to the will of your Father and need to mention each thing separately in order to stop and think whether it would be good for us, and otherwise not ask for it. You see, the gift our Lord intends for us may be by far the best, but if it is not what we wanted we are quite capable of flinging it back in his face. That is the kind of people we are; ready cash is the only wealth we understand.

Therefore, the good Jesus bids us repeat these words, this prayer for his kingdom to come in us: *Hallowed be your name, your kingdom come*[Mt 6:9-13]. See how wise our Master is! But what do we mean when we pray for this kingdom? That is what I am going to consider now, for it is important that we should understand it. Our good Jesus placed these two petitions side by side because he realized that in our inadequacy we could never fittingly hallow, praise, exalt or glorify this holy name of the eternal Father unless he enabled us to do so by giving us his kingdom here on earth. But since we must know what we are asking for and how important it is to pray for it without ceasing and to do everything in our power to please him who is to give it to us, I should now like to give you my own thoughts on the matter.

Of the many joys that are found in the kingdom of heaven, the greatest seems to me to be the sense of tranquility and well-being that we shall experience when we are free from all concern for earthly things. Glad because others are glad and for ever at peace, we shall have the deep satisfaction of seeing that by all creatures the Lord is honored and praised, and his name blessed. No one ever offends him, for there everyone loves him. Loving him is the soul's one concern. Indeed it cannot help but love him, for it knows him. Here below our love must necessarily fall short of that perfection and constancy, but even so how different it would be, how much more like that of heaven, if we really knew our Lord!

Thursday of the Thirteenth Week in Ordinary Time

From a sermon on Psalm Forty-One addressed to the newly baptized by Saint Jerome, Priest & Doctor

I will enter God's marvelous dwelling place

As the deer longs for running water, so my soul longs for you, my God[Ps 41:2]. Just as the deer longs for running water, so do our newly baptized members, our young deer, so to speak, also yearn for God. By leaving Egypt and the world, they have put Pharaoh and his entire army to death in the waters of baptism. After slaying the evil, their hearts long for the springs of running water in the Church. These springs are the Father, the Son and the Holy Spirit. Jeremiah testifies that the Father is like a fountain when he says: *They have forsaken me, the fountain of living water, to dig for themselves cisterns, broken cisterns that can hold no water*[Jer 2:13]. In another passage we read about the Son: *They have forsaken the fountain of wisdom*[Bar 3:12]. And again, John says of the Holy Spirit: *Whoever drinks the water I will give him, that water shall become in him a fountain of water, springing up into eternal life*[Jn 4:14]. The evangelist explains that the Savior said this of the Holy Spirit. The testimony of these texts establishes beyond doubt that the three fountains of the Church constitute the mystery of the Trinity.

These are the waters that the heart of the believer longs for, these are the waters that the heart of the newly baptized yearns for when he says: *My heart thirsts for God, the living fountain*[Ps 41:2-3]. This is not a weak, faint desire to see God; rather the newly baptized actually burn with desire and thirst for God. Before they received baptism, they used to ask one another: *When shall I go and see the face of God*[Ps 41:2-3]*?* Now their quest has been answered. they have come forward and they stand in the presence of God. They have come before the altar and have looked upon the mystery of the Savior.

Having received the body of Christ, and being reborn in the life-giving waters, they speak up boldly and say: *I shall go into God's marvelous dwelling place, his house*[Ps 131:7]. The house of God is the Church, his marvelous dwelling place, filled with joyful voices giving thanks and praise, filled with all the sounds of festive celebration.

This is the way you should speak, you newly baptized, for you have now put on Christ. Under our guidance, by the word of God you have been lifted out of the dangerous waters of this world like so many little fish. In us the nature of things has been changed. Fish taken out of the sea die; but the apostles have fished for us and have taken us out of the sea of this world so we could be brought from death to life. As long as we were in the world, our eyes looked down into the abyss and we lived in filth. After we were rescued from the waves, we began to look upon the sun and look up at the true light. Confused in the presence of so much joy, we say: *Hope in God, for I shall again praise him, in the presence of my savior and my God*[Ps 42:6].

Friday of the Thirteenth Week in Ordinary Time

From a book on the Predestination of the Saints by Saint Augustine, Bishop & Doctor

In his human nature Jesus Christ is descended from the line of David

The greatest glory of predestination and grace is the Savior himself, *the mediator between God and men, the man Christ Jesus*[1 Tim 2:5]. What, I ask you, did his human nature do in the way of good works or of faith to merit beforehand this glory? Give me an answer to this question: How did his humanity merit to be taken up by the Word, coeternal with the Father, into unity with his person and so to be the only-begotten Son of God? What goodness, of whatever kind, did he possess beforehand? What had he done, what faith had he shown, what request had he made, that he should attain to that point of preeminence, beyond all human power of description? Was it not through the action of the Word in taking this humanity to himself that, from the moment when he came into existence, this human being came into existence as the only Son of God?

We must keep before our eyes the very source of grace, taking its origin in Christ, our head, and flowing through all his members according to the capacity of each. The grace which makes any man a Christian from the first moment of his coming to believe is the same grace which made this man the Christ from his coming to be as man. The Spirit through whom men are reborn is the same Spirit through whom Christ was born. The Spirit by whom we receive forgiveness of sins is the same Spirit who brought it about that Christ knew no sin. Clearly, God knew that he would do all this. The predestination of the saints is the same predestination that reached its greatest glory in the Saint above all other saints. Who can deny this among those who understand correctly the utterances of Truth? For we have been taught that inasmuch as the Son of God became man, the Lord of glory himself was the object of predestination.

Jesus then was predestined. He who was to be the son of David in his human nature was to be the Son of God in power through the action of the Spirit of holiness, for he was born of the Holy Spirit and of the Virgin Mary. This unique taking to himself of a human nature by God the Word came about in such a way, too mysterious for our understanding, that with truth and accuracy the Word could be called at one and the same time the Son of God and the son of man: son of man because of the human nature that was taken, and Son of God because it was the only-begotten God who took that human nature. We are not to believe in God as a quaternity but as a trinity.

Human nature was in this case predestined to so marvelous, so sublime, so perfect a dignity that it could not be raised higher; just as the divine nature itself could not demean itself any lower than by taking human nature with all its weakness, even to dying on a cross. Just as one Christ was predestined to be our head, so we, the many, were predestined to be his members. Let there be no mention here of human merits; they were lost through Adam. Let God's grace reign supreme, as it does through Jesus Christ, our Lord, the only Son of God, the one Lord. If anyone can find in Christ, our head, any merits preceding his unique birth, he may look also for merits in ourselves preceding our rebirth as his many members.

Saturday of the Thirteenth Week in Ordinary Time

From a catechetical instruction by Saint Cyril of Jerusalem, Bishop & Doctor

Acknowledge your sins at a time of God's favor

If there is any slave of sin here present, he should at once prepare himself through faith for the rebirth into freedom that makes us God's adopted children. He should lay aside the wretchedness of slavery to sin, and put on the joyful slavery of the Lord, so as to be counted worthy to inherit the kingdom of heaven. By acknowledging your sins strip away your former self, seduced as it is by destructive desires, and put on the new self, renewed in the likeness of its Creator. Through faith receive the pledge of the Holy Spirit, so that you may be welcomed into the everlasting dwelling places. Draw near, to be marked with the supernatural seal, so that you may be easily recognized by your master. Become a member of Christ's holy and spiritual flock, so that one day you may be set apart on his right hand, and so gain the life prepared as your inheritance.

Those whose sins still cling to them like a goatskin will stand on his left hand because they did not approach Christ's fountain of rebirth to receive God's grace. By rebirth I mean, not rebirth of the body, but the spiritual rebirth of the soul. Our bodies are brought into being by parents who can be seen, but our souls are reborn through faith: *the Spirit breathes where he wills*. At the end, if you are made worthy, you may hear the words: *Well done, good and faithful servant,* when, that is, you are found with no stain of hypocrisy on your conscience.

If anyone here present is thinking of putting God's grace to the test, he is deceiving himself, and he does not understand the nature of things. You are but a man; there is one who searches out men's thoughts and hearts. You must keep your soul innocent and free from deceit.

The present is a time for the acknowledgment of sins. Acknowledge what you have done, in word or deed, by night or day. Acknowledge your sins at a time of God's favor, and on the day of salvation you will receive the treasures of heaven.

Wash yourself clean, so that you may hold a richer store of grace. Sins are forgiven equally for all, but communion in the Holy Spirit is given in the measure of each one's faith. If you have done little work, you will receive little; if you have achieved a great deal, great will be your reward. The race you are running is for your own advantage; look after your own interests.

If you have a grudge against anyone, forgive him. You are drawing near to receive forgiveness for your own sins; you must yourself forgive those who have sinned against you.

Sunday of the Fourteenth Week in Ordinary Time

From a sermon by Saint Augustine, Bishop & Doctor

A sacrifice to God is a contrite spirit

I acknowledge my transgression[Ps 50:5], says David. If I admit my fault, then you will pardon it. Let us never assume that if we live good lives we will be without sin; our lives should be praised only when we continue to beg for pardon. But men are hopeless creatures, and the less they concentrate on their own sins, the more interested they become in the sins of others. They seek to criticize, not to correct. Unable to excuse themselves, they are ready to accuse others. This was not the way that David showed us how to pray and make amends to God, when he said: *I acknowledge my transgression, and my sin is ever before me* [Ps 50:5]. He did not concentrate on others' sins; he turned his thoughts upon himself. He did not merely stroke the surface, but he plunged inside and went deep down within himself. He did not spare himself, and therefore was not impudent in asking to be spared.

Do you want God to be appeased? Learn what you are to do that God may be pleased with you. Consider the psalm again: *If you wanted sacrifice, I would indeed have given it; in burnt offerings you will take no delight*[Ps 50:18]. Are you then to be without sacrifice? Are you to offer nothing? Will you please God without an offering? Consider what you read in the same psalm: *If you wanted sacrifice, I would indeed have given it; in burnt offerings you will take no delight*. But continue to listen, and say with David: *A sacrifice to God is a contrite spirit; God does not despise a contrite and humble heart*[Ps 50:19]. Cast aside your former offerings, for now you have found out what you are to offer. In the days of your fathers you would have made offerings of cattle – these were the sacrifices. *If you wanted sacrifice, I would indeed have given it*. These then, Lord, you do not want, and yet you do want sacrifice.

You will take no delight in burnt offerings, David says. If you will not take delight in burnt offerings, will you remain without sacrifice? Not at all. *A sacrifice to God is a contrite spirit; God does not despise a contrite and humble heart*.

You now have the offering you are to make. No need to examine the herd, no need to outfit ships and travel to the most remote provinces in search of incense. Search within your heart for what is pleasing to God. Your heart must be crushed. Are you afraid that it might perish so? You have the reply: *Create a clean heart in me, O God*[Ps 50:12]. For a clean heart to be created, the unclean one must be crushed.

We should be displeased with ourselves when we commit sin, for sin is displeasing to God. Sinful though we are, let us at least be like God in this, that we are displeased at what displeases him. In some measure then you will be in harmony with God's will, because you find displeasing in yourself what is abhorrent to your Creator.

Monday of the Fourteenth Week in Ordinary Time

From a letter to the Corinthians by Saint Clement I, Pope & Martyr

Seek the good of all, not personal advantage

The command has been written: *Cling to the saints, for those who cling to them will be sanctified*. There is a passage in Scripture as well which states: *With the innocent man you will be innocent, and with the chosen one you will be chosen also; likewise with the perverse you will deal perversely*. Devote yourselves, then, to the innocent and the just; they are God's chosen ones. Why are there strife and passion, schisms and even war among you? Do we not possess the same Spirit of grace which was given to us and the same calling in Christ? Why do we tear apart and divide the body of Christ? Why do we revolt against our own body? Why do we reach such a degree of insanity that we forget that we are members of one another? Do not forget the words of Jesus our Lord: *Woe to that man; it would be better for him if he had not been born rather than scandalize one of my chosen ones*[Mt 26:24]. *Indeed it would be better for him to have a great millstone round his neck and to be drowned in the sea than that he lead astray one of my chosen ones*[Mt 18:6]. Your division has led many astray, has made many doubt, has made many despair, and has brought grief upon us all. And still your rebellion continues.

Pick up the letter of blessed Paul the apostle. What did he write to you at the beginning of his ministry? Even then you had developed factions. So Paul, inspired by the Holy Spirit, wrote to you concerning himself and Cephas and Apollos. But that division involved you in less sin because you were supporting apostles of high reputation and a person approved by them.

We should put an end to this division immediately. Let us fall down before our master and implore his mercy with our tears. Then he will be reconciled to us and restore us to the practice of brotherly love that befits us. For this is the gate of justice that leads to life, as it is written: *Open to me the gates of justice. When I have entered there, I shall praise the Lord. This is the gate of the Lord; the just shall enter through it*[Ps 117:19]. There are many gates which stand open, but the gate of justice is the gateway of Christ. All who enter through this gate are blessed, pursuing their way in holiness and justice, performing all their tasks without discord. A person may be faithful; he may have the power to utter hidden mysteries; he may be discriminating in the evaluation of what is said and pure in his actions. But the greater he seems to be, the more humbly he ought to act, and the more zealous he should be for the common good rather than his own interest.

Tuesday of the Fourteenth Week in Ordinary Time

From a discourse on the psalms by Saint Augustine, Bishop & Doctor

Whether they like it or not, those who are outside the Church are our brothers

We entreat you, brothers, as earnestly as we are able, to have charity, not only for one another, but also for those who are outside the Church. Of these some are still pagans, who have not yet made an act of faith in Christ. Others are separated, insofar as they are joined with us in professing faith in Christ, our head, but are yet divided from the unity of his body. My friends, we must grieve over these as over our brothers. Whether they like it or not, they are our brothers; and they will only cease to be so when they no longer say *our Father.*

The prophet refers to some men saying: *When they say to you: You are not our brothers, you are to tell them: You are our brothers.* Consider whom he intended by these words. Were they the pagans? Hardly; for nowhere either in Scripture or in our traditional manner of speaking do we find them called our brothers. Nor could it refer to the Jews, who do not believe in Christ. Read Saint Paul and you will see that when he speaks of "brothers," without any qualification, he refers always to Christians. For example, he says: *Why do you judge your brother or why do you despise your brother*[Rom 14:10]*?* And again: *You perform iniquity and commit fraud, and this against your brothers.*

Those then who tell us: *You are not our brothers,* are saying that we are pagans. That is why they want to baptize us again, claiming that we do not have what they can give. Hence their error of denying that we are their brothers. Why then did the prophet tell us: *Say to them: You are our brothers?* It is because we acknowledge in them that which we do not repeat. By not recognizing our baptism, they deny that we are their brothers; on the other hand, when we do not repeat their baptism but acknowledge it to be our own, we are saying to them: *You are our brothers.*

If they say, "Why do you seek us? What do you want of us?" we should reply: *You are our brothers.* They may say, "Leave us alone. We have nothing to do with you." But we have everything to do with you, for we are one in our belief in Christ; and so we should be in one body, under one head.

And so, dear brothers, we entreat you on their behalf, in the name of the very source of our love, by whose milk we are nourished, and whose bread is our strength, in the name of Christ our Lord and his gentle love. For it is time now for us to show them great love and abundant compassion by praying to God for them. May he one day give them a clear mind to repent and to realize that they have nothing whatever to say against the truth; they have nothing now but the sickness of their hatred, and the stronger they think they are, the weaker they become. We entreat you then to pray for them, for they are weak, given to the wisdom of the flesh, to fleshly and carnal things, but yet they are our brothers. They celebrate the same sacraments as we, not indeed with us, but still the same. They respond with the same Amen, not with us, but still the same. And so pour out your hearts for them in prayer to God.

Wednesday of the Fourteenth Week in Ordinary Time

From the ancient document entitled "The Teaching of the Twelve Apostles"
Didache

The Eucharist

Celebrate the Eucharist as follows: Say over the cup: "We give you thanks, Father, for the holy vine of David, your servant, which you made known to us through Jesus your servant. To you be glory for ever."

Over the broken bread say: "We give you thanks, father, for the life and the knowledge which you have revealed to us through Jesus your servant. To you be glory for ever. As this broken bread scattered on the mountains was gathered and became one, so too, may your Church be gathered together from the ends of the earth into your kingdom. For glory and power are yours through Jesus Christ for ever."

Do not let anyone eat or drink of your eucharist except those who have been baptized in the name of the Lord. For the statement of the Lord applies here also: *Do not give to dogs what is holy*[Mt 7:6].

When you finish the meal, offer thanks in this manner: "We thank you, Holy Father, for your name which you enshrined in our hearts. We thank you for the knowledge and faith and immortality which you revealed to us through your servant Jesus. To you be glory for ever. Almighty ruler, you created all things for the sake of your name; you gave men food and drink to enjoy so that they might give you thanks. Now you have favored us through Jesus your servant with spiritual food and drink as well as with eternal life. Above all we thank you because you are mighty. To you be glory for ever.

"Remember, Lord, your Church and deliver her from all evil. Perfect her in your love; and, once she has been sanctified, gather her together from the four winds into the kingdom which you have prepared for her. For power and glory are yours for ever.

"May grace come and this world pass away! Hosanna to the God of David. If anyone is holy, let him come. If anyone is not, let him repent. Maranatha. Amen."

On the Lord's day, when you have been gathered together, break bread and celebrate the Eucharist. But first confess your sins so that your offering may be pure. If anyone has a quarrel with his neighbor, that person should not join you until he has been reconciled. Your sacrifice must not be defiled. In this regard, the Lord has said: *In every place and time offer me a pure sacrifice. I am a great king, says the Lord, and my name is great among the nations*[Didache 14:1-3; Mal 1:6-14].

Thursday of the Fourteenth Week in Ordinary Time

From an exposition of psalm 118 by Saint Ambrose, Bishop & Doctor

God's temple is holy; you are his temple

My Father and I will come and make our home with him[Jn 14:23]. Let your door stand open to receive him, unlock your soul to him, offer him a welcome in your mind, and then you will see the riches of simplicity, the treasures of peace, the joy of grace. Throw wide the gate of your heart, stand before the sun of the everlasting light *that shines on every man*[Jn 1:9]. This true light shines on all, but if anyone closes his window he will deprive himself of eternal light. If you shut the door of your mind, you shut out Christ. Though he can enter, he does not want to force his way in rudely, or compel us to admit him against our will.

Born of a virgin, he came forth from the womb as the light of the whole world in order to shine on all men. His light is received by those who long for the splendor of perpetual light that night can never destroy. The sun of our daily experience is succeeded by the darkness of night, but the sun of holiness never sets, because wisdom cannot give place to evil.

Blessed then is the man at whose door Christ stands and knocks. Our door is faith; if it is strong enough, the whole house is safe. This is the door by which Christ enters. So the Church says in the Song of Songs: *The voice of my brother is at the door*. Hear his knock, listen to him asking to enter: *Open to me, my sister, my betrothed, my dove, my perfect one, for my head is covered with dew, and my hair with the moisture of the night*[Song 5:2].

When does God the Word most often knock at your door? - When his head is covered with the dew of night. He visits in love those in trouble and temptation, to save them from being overwhelmed by their trials. His head is covered with dew or moisture when those who are his body are in distress. That is the time when you must keep watch so that when the bridegroom comes he may not find himself shut out, and take his departure. If you were to sleep, if your heart were not wide awake, he would not knock but go away; but if your heart is watchful, he knocks and asks you to open the door to him.

Our soul has a door; it has gates. *Lift up you heads, O gates, and be lifted up, eternal gates, and the King of glory will enter*[Ps 23:9]. If you open the gates of your faith, the King of glory will enter your house in the triumphal procession in honor of his passion. Holiness too has its gates. We read in Scripture what the Lord Jesus said through his prophet: *Open for me the gates of holiness*[Ps 117:19].

It is the soul that has its door, its gates. Christ comes to this door and knocks; he knocks at these gates. Open to him; he wants to enter, to find his bride waiting and watching.

Friday of the Fourteenth Week in Ordinary Time

From a letter to the Corinthians by Saint Clement I, Pope & Martyr

We are blessed if we fulfill the commands of the Lord in the harmony of love

Beloved, see what a marvelous thing love is; its perfection is beyond our expression. Who can truly love save those to whom God grants it? We ought to beg and beseech him in his mercy that our love may be genuine, unmarred by any too human inclination. From Adam down to the present time all generations have passed away; but those who were perfected in love by God's grace have a place among the saints who will be revealed when the kingdom of Christ comes to us. As it is written: *Enter your chambers for a little while, until my wrath and anger pass away; and I shall remember a good day and raise you from your graves*[Isa 26:20-21]. We are blessed, beloved, if we fulfill the commands of the Lord in harmonious, loving union, so that through love our sins may be forgiven. For it is written: *Blessed are those whose transgressions are forgiven, whose sins are covered. Blessed is the man to whom the Lord imputes not iniquity, and in whose mouth there is no deceit*[Ps 31:1-2]. This is the blessing that has been given to those who have been chosen by God through our Lord Jesus Christ, to whom be glory for ever. Amen.

We should pray then that we may be granted forgiveness for our sins and for whatever we may have done when led astray by our adversary's servants. And for those who were the leaders of the schism and the sedition, they too should look to the common hope. For those who live in pious fear and in love are willing to endure torment rather than have their neighbor suffer; and they more willingly suffer their own condemnation than the loss of that harmony that has been so nobly and righteously handed down to us. For it is better for a man to confess his sins than to harden his heart.

Who then among you is generous, who is compassionate, who is filled with love? He should speak out as follows: If I have been the cause of sedition, conflict and schisms, then I shall depart; I shall go away wherever you wish, and I shall do what the community wants, if only the flock of Christ live in peace with the presbyters who are set over them. Whoever acts thus would win great glory for himself in Christ, and he would be received everywhere, *for the earth is the Lord's and the fullness thereof*[Ps 23:1]. Thus have they acted in the past and will continue to act in the future who live without regret as citizens in the city of God.

Saturday of the Fourteenth Week in Ordinary Time

From a discourse on the psalms by Saint Augustine, Bishop & Doctor

Jesus Christ, the true Solomon

The temple that Solomon built to the Lord was a type and figure of the future Church as well as of the body of the Lord. For this reason Christ says in the Gospel: *Destroy this temple and in three days I will raise it up again*[Jn 2:19]. For just as Solomon built the ancient temple, so the true Solomon, the true peacemaker, our Lord Jesus Christ, built a temple for himself. Now Solomon means peacemaker; Jesus, however, is the true peacemaker, of whom Saint Paul says: *He is our peace, uniting the two into one*[Eph 2:14-15]. The true peacemaker brought together in himself two walls coming from different angles and himself became the cornerstone. One wall was formed of the circumcised believers and the other of the uncircumcised gentiles who had faith. And of these two peoples he made one Church, with himself as the cornerstone and, therefore, the true peacemaker.

And so when Solomon the king of Israel, the son of David and Bathsheba, built his temple, he acted as a figure of Christ, the true Solomon and peacemaker. But I do not think it was Solomon of old, the type of Christ, who really built God's dwelling. As the beginning of the psalm tells us: *Unless the Lord build the house, in vain have the builders labored on it*[Ps 126:1]. Thus it is the Lord who builds the house; it is the Lord Jesus who builds his own dwelling. Many may toil on its building, but unless he builds it, *in vain have the builders labored on it*.

And who are those who labor on it? All those who preach God's word in the Church, who are ministers of his sacraments. All of us now rush, work and build, and before us other men rushed, worked and built; still, *unless the Lord build the house, in vain have the builders labored on it*. The apostles, and Paul specifically, saw some of them fail, and said: *You observe the days, the years, the months and the seasons; I fear that I may have toiled for you to no purpose*[Gal 4:10-11]. For realizing that he was the result of the Lord's building from within, he was sorrowful because he had toiled for them to no avail. Hence, we are the ones who speak from without, but he builds from within. We notice the fact that you are listening, but he alone knows what you are thinking, for he sees our thoughts. He is the one who builds, admonishes, instills fear, opens the mind, and bends the perceptions to the act of belief. Yet we too, his ministers, labor, and are as it were his workmen.

Sunday of the Fifteenth Week in Ordinary Time

From the beginning of the treatise On the Mysteries by Saint Ambrose, Bishop & Doctor

Catechesis on the rites preceding baptism

We gave a daily instruction on right conduct when the s were taken from the history of the patriarchs or the maxims of Proverbs. These s were intended to instruct and train you, so that you might grow accustomed to the ways of our forefathers, entering into their paths and walking in their footsteps, in obedience to God's commands.

Now the season reminds us that we must speak of the mysteries, setting forth the meaning of the sacraments. If we had thought fit to teach these things to those not yet initiated through baptism, we should be considered traitors rather than teachers. Then, too, the light of the mysteries is of itself more effective where people do not know what to expect than where some instruction has been given beforehand.

Open then your ears. Enjoy the fragrance of eternal life, breathed on you by means of the sacraments. We explained this to you as we celebrated the mystery of "the opening" when we said: *Effetha, that is, be opened*[Mk 7:32-34]. Everyone who was to come for the grace of baptism had to understand what he was to be asked, and must remember what he was to answer. This mystery was celebrated by Christ when he healed the man who was deaf and dumb, in the Gospel which we proclaimed to you.

After this, the holy of holies was opened up for you; you entered into the sacred place of regeneration. Recall what you were asked; remember what you answered. You renounced the devil and his works, the world and its dissipation and sensuality. Your words are recorded, not on a monument to the dead but in the book of the living.

There you saw the levite, you saw the priest, you saw the high priest. Do not consider their outward form but the grace given by their ministries. You spoke in the presence of angels, as it is written: *The lips of a priest guard knowledge, and men seek the law from his mouth, for he is the angel of the Lord almighty*[Mal 2:7-9]. There is no room for deception, no room for denial. He is an angel whose message is the kingdom of Christ and eternal life. You must judge him, not by his appearance but by his office. Remember what he handed on to you, weigh up his value, and so acknowledge his standing.

You entered to confront your enemy, for you intended to renounce him to his face. You turned toward the east, for one who renounces the devil turns toward Christ and fixes his gaze directly on him.

Monday of the Fifteenth Week in Ordinary Time

From the treatise On the Mysteries by St Ambrose, Bishop & Doctor

We are born again of water and the Holy Spirit

What did you see in the baptistry? Water certainly, but not water alone. You saw the levites ministering there, the high priest asking questions and consecrating. First of all, the Apostle taught you that we must fix our eyes, *not on the things that are seen but on the things that are unseen, for the things that are seen are for a time, but the things that are unseen are eternal*[2 Cor 4:18]. In another place you may read that *the invisible things* of God, *from the creation of the world, can be understood through the things that have been created, and his everlasting power and godhead*[Rom 1:20] can be known through his works. The Lord himself says: *If you do not believe me, believe at least my works*[Jn 10:38]. Then believe that the presence of the godhead is there. You believe in its activity, and refuse to believe in its presence? How could there be activity if there were no presence beforehand?

Consider how ancient the mystery is, prefigured as it was in the creation of the world itself. In the very beginning, when God made heaven and earth, *the spirit*, God tells us, *moved over the waters*[Gen 1:2]. Was the spirit not active as he moved over the waters? When the prophet tells you that *by the word of the Lord the heavens were established, and by the spirit of his mouth all their array*[Ps 32:6], realize that the spirit was active in this making of the world. The fact that he moved over the waters, and the fact that he was active, both rest on prophetic testimony. Moses tells us that the spirit moved over the waters; David testifies that the spirit was active.

Listen to another testimony. All flesh had become corrupt because of its sins. God said: *My spirit will not remain in men, for they are flesh*[Gen 6:3]. God thus shows that the spiritual grace is repelled by uncleanness of the flesh and by the stain of more serious sin. So God resolved to restore the gift he had given. He sent the flood and ordered Noah, the righteous man, into the ark. When the flood began to subside Noah sent first a raven, then a dove, which, as we read, came back with an olive branch. You see water, you see wood, you look on a dove, and you hesitate to believe the mystery?

The water is that in which the flesh is dipped, to wash away all its sin. In it all wickedness is buried. The wood is that to which the Lord Jesus was fastened when he suffered for us. The dove is the one in whose likeness the Holy Spirit descended, as you have learned from the New Testament: the Spirit who breathes into you peace of soul, tranquility of mind.

Tuesday of the Fifteenth Week in Ordinary Time

From the treatise On the Mysteries by St Ambrose, Bishop & Doctor

All this was a sign of what was to come

The Apostle teaches you *that our fathers were all covered by the cloud, all passed through the sea, all were baptized into Moses in the cloud and in the sea*[1 Cor 10:1]. Further, Moses in his canticle says: *You sent your spirit, and the sea overwhelmed them*[Exod 15:10]. You observed that in this crossing by the Hebrews there was already a symbol of holy baptism. The Egyptian perished; the Hebrew escaped. What else is the daily lesson of this sacrament than that guilt is drowned, and error destroyed, while goodness and innocence pass over unharmed?

You are taught that our fathers were covered by the cloud, a cloud of blessing that cooled the fire of bodily passions. A cloud of blessing: it is with a cloud of blessing that the Holy Spirit overshadows those whom he comes to visit. The Holy Spirit came at last upon the Virgin Mary, and the power of the Most High overshadowed her, when she conceived for all mankind him who is redemption. This great miracle was prefigured through Moses. If then the Spirit was prefigured, is he not now present in truth, for Scripture tells you that *the law was given through Moses, but grace and truth came through Jesus Christ*[Jn 1:17]?

Marah was a spring of bitter water. When Moses threw wood into it, its water became sweet. Water, you see, is of no avail for future salvation without the proclamation of the Lord's cross. But when it has been consecrated through the saving mystery of the cross, it is then ready for use in the laver of the Spirit and in the cup of salvation. Therefore, as Moses in his role of prophet threw wood into the spring of Marah, so also the priest sends out into the fountain of baptism the proclamation of the Lord's cross, and the water becomes sweet, ready for the giving of grace.

Do not then believe only what the eyes of your body tell you. What is not seen is here more truly seen, for what is seen belongs to time but what is not seen belongs to eternity. What is not comprehended by the eyes but is seen by the mind and the soul is seen in a truer and deeper sense.

Finally, learn from the s we have gone through from the books of the Kings. Naaman was a Syrian; he was a leper, and could not be healed by anyone. Then a girl from among the captives said that there was a prophet in Israel who could cleanse him from the disease of leprosy. Taking gold and silver, we are told, he went to see the king of Israel. The king, on learning the reason for his coming, rent his garments, saying that it was really to find an excuse against him, for what he was being asked was beyond the power of a king.

Elisha, however, told the king to send the Syrian to him, and he would learn that there was a God in Israel. When he came, Elisha ordered him to bathe seven times in the river Jordan. Then Naaman began to reflect that the rivers of his own country had better waters, and that he had often bathed in them, and never been cleansed of his leprosy. This gave him pause, and he refused to obey the prophet's instructions. But on the advice and persuasion of his servants he yielded and bathed, and was instantly made clean. He realized then that it is not waters that make clean but grace.

Here was a man who doubted before being made whole. You are already made whole, and so ought not to have any doubt.

Wednesday of the Fifteenth Week in Ordinary Time

From the treatise On the Mysteries by Saint Ambrose, Bishop & Doctor

Water does not sanctify without the Holy Spirit

You were told before not to believe only what you saw. This was to prevent you from saying: Is this the great mystery *that eye has not seen nor ear heard nor man's heart conceived*[1 Cor 2:9]*?* I see the water I used to see every day; does this water in which I have often bathed without being sanctified really have the power to sanctify me? Learn from this that water does not sanctify without the Holy Spirit.

You have read that the three witnesses in baptism – the water, the blood and the Spirit – are one. This means that if you take away one of these the sacrament is not conferred. What is water without the cross of Christ? Only an ordinary element without sacramental effect. Again, without water there is no sacrament of rebirth: *Unless a man is born again of water and the Spirit he cannot enter into the kingdom of God*[Jn 3:5]. The catechumen believes in the cross of the Lord with which he too is signed, but unless he is baptized in the name of the Father, and of the Son and of the Holy Spirit he cannot receive the forgiveness of sins or the gift of spiritual grace.

The Syrian Naaman bathed seven times under the old law, but you were baptized in the name of the Trinity. You proclaimed your faith in the Father – recall what you did – and the Son and the Spirit. Mark the sequence of events. In proclaiming this faith you died to the world, you rose again to God, and, as though buried to sin, you were reborn to eternal life. Believe, then, that the water is not without effect.

The paralytic at the pool was waiting for someone. Who was this if not the Lord Jesus, born of a virgin? At his coming it is not a question of a shadow healing an individual, but Truth himself healing the universe. He is the one whose coming was expected, the one of whom God the Father spoke when he said to John the Baptist: *He on whom you see the Spirit coming down from heaven and resting, this is the one who baptizes in the Holy Spirit*[Jn 1:33]. He is the one witnessed to by John: *I saw the Spirit coming down from heaven as a dove and resting on him*[Jn 1:32]. Why did the Spirit come down as a dove if not to let you see and understand that the dove sent out by holy Noah from the ark was a figure of this dove? In this way you were to recognize a type of this sacrament.

Is there any room left for doubt? The Father speaks clearly in the Gospel: *This is my beloved Son, in whom I am well pleased*[Mt 3:17]*;* the Son too, above whom the Holy Spirit showed himself in the form of a dove; and also the Holy Spirit, who came down as a dove. David too speaks clearly: *The voice of the Lord is above the waters; the God of glory has thundered; the Lord is above the many waters*[Jn 28:3]. Again, Scripture bears witness for you that fire came down from heaven in answer to Gideon's prayers, and that when Elijah prayed, God sent fire which consumed the sacrifice.

Do not consider the merits of individuals but the office of the priests. If you do look at merits, consider the merits of Peter and also of Paul in the same way you consider the merits of Elijah; they have handed on to us this sacrament which they received from the Lord Jesus. Visible fire was sent upon them to give them faith; in us who believe an invisible fire is at work. That visible fire was a sign, our invisible fire is for our instruction.

Believe then that the Lord Jesus is present when he is invoked by the prayers of the priests. He said: *Where two or three are gathered, there I am also*[Mt 18:20]. How much more does he give his loving presence where the Church is, where the sacraments are!

You went down into the water. Remember what you said: I believe in the Father and the Son and the Holy Spirit. Not: I believe in a greater, a lesser and a least. You are committed by this spoken understanding of yours to believe the same of the Son as of the Father, and the same of the Holy Spirit as of the Son, with this one exception: you proclaim that you must believe in the cross of the Lord Jesus alone.

Thursday of the Fifteenth Week in Ordinary Time

From the treatise On the Mysteries by Saint Ambrose, Bishop & Doctor

Instruction on the postbaptismal rites

After this you went up to the priest. Consider what followed. Was it not what David spoke of when he said: *Like oil on the head, running down on the beard, the beard of Aaron*[Ps 132:2]? This is the oil spoken of also by Solomon: *Your name is oil poured out, so that the maidens loved you and attracted you*[Song 1:3]. How many souls, reborn today, have loved you, Lord Jesus, and have said: *Draw us after you; we shall make haste to follow you, in the fragrance of your garments*[Song 1:4], to breathe the fragrance of resurrection.

Understand why this is done: *Because the eyes of the wise man are in his head*[Eccl 2:14]. The oil flows down on the beard, that is, on the grace of youth; it flows on Aaron's beard, in order to make you *a chosen race*, a race of priests, bought at a great price. We are all anointed with spiritual grace to share in God's kingdom and in priesthood.

Then you received white garments as a sign that you had cast off the clothing of sin and put on the chaste covering of innocence, as the psalmist prophesied: *You will sprinkle me with hyssop and I shall be cleansed, you will wash me and I shall be made whiter than snow*[Ps 50:9]. One who is baptized is seen to be made clean in terms of the law and of the Gospel. In terms of the law, because Moses used a bunch of hyssop to sprinkle the blood of the lamb; in terms of the Gospel, because Christ's garments were white as snow when in the Gospel he revealed the glory of his resurrection. The sinner who is forgiven is made whiter than snow. The Lord promised the same through Isaiah: *If your sins are as scarlet, I will make them white as snow*[Isa 1:18].

Wearing the garments given her in the rebirth by water, the Church says, in the words of the Song of Songs: *I am black but beautiful, daughters of Jerusalem*[Song 1:5-7]. Black because of the frailty of humanity, beautiful through grace; black because she is made up of sinners, beautiful through the sacrament of faith. When they see these garments the daughters of Jerusalem cry out in wonder: *Who is this who comes up, all in white*[Song 8:5]? She was black, how is she suddenly made white?

When Christ sees his Church clothed in white - for her sake he himself had put on *filthy clothing*, as you may read in the prophecy of Zechariah - when he sees the soul washed clean by the waters of rebirth, he cries out: *How beautiful you are, my beloved, how beautiful you are; your eyes are like the eyes of a dove*[Song 4:1], for it was in the likeness of a dove that the Holy Spirit came down from heaven.

Remember, then, that you received a spiritual seal, *the spirit of wisdom and understanding, the spirit of knowledge and reverence, the spirit of holy fear*[Isa 11:2]. Keep safe what you received. God the Father sealed you, Christ the Lord strengthened you and sent the Spirit into your hearts as the pledge of what is to come, as you learned in the from the Apostle.

Friday of the Fifteenth Week in Ordinary Time

From the treatise On the Mysteries by Saint Ambrose, Bishop & Doctor

To the newly baptized on the Eucharist

Fresh from the waters and resplendent in these garments, God's holy people hasten to the altar of Christ, saying: *I will go in to the altar of God, to God who gives joy to my youth*[Ps 42:4]. They have sloughed off the old skin of error, *their youth renewed like an eagle's*[Ps 102:5], and they make haste to approach that heavenly banquet. They come and, seeing the sacred altar prepared, cry out: *You have prepared a table in my sight*[Ps 22:5]. David puts these words into their mouths: *The Lord is my shepherd and nothing will be lacking to me. He has set me down there in a place of pasture. He has brought me beside refreshing water*[Ps 22:1-2]. Further on, we read: *For though I should walk in the midst of the shadow of death, I shall not be afraid of evils, for you are with me. Your rod and your staff have given me comfort. You have prepared in my sight a table against those who afflict me. You have made my head rich in oil, and your cup, which exhilarates, how excellent it is*[Ps 22:3-5].

It is wonderful that God rained manna on our fathers and they were fed with daily food from heaven. And so it is written: *Man ate the bread of angels*[Ps 77:25]. Yet those who ate that bread all *died* in the desert. But the food that you receive, that *living bread which came down from heaven*[Jn 6:51], supplies the very substance of eternal life, and whoever will eat it will never die, for it is the body of Christ.

Consider now which is the more excellent: the bread of angels or the flesh of Christ, which is indeed the body that gives life. The first was manna from heaven, the second is above the heavens. One was of heaven, the other is of the Lord of the heavens; one subject to corruption if it was kept till the morrow, the other free from all corruption, for if anyone tastes of it with reverence he will be incapable of corruption. For our fathers, water flowed from the rock; for you, blood flows from Christ. Water satisfied their thirst for a time; blood cleanses you for ever. The Jew drinks and still thirsts, but when you drink you will be incapable of thirst. What happened in symbol is now fulfilled in reality.

If what you marvel at is a shadow, how great is the reality whose very shadow you marvel at. Listen to this, which shows that what happened in the time of our fathers was but a shadow. *They drank,* it is written, *from the rock that followed them, and the rock was Christ. All this took place as a symbol for us*[1 Cor 10:4]. You know now what is more excellent: light is preferable to its shadow, reality to its symbol, the body of the Giver to the manna he gave from heaven.

Saturday of the Fifteenth Week in Ordinary Time

From the treatise On the Mysteries by Saint Ambrose, Bishop & Doctor

The sacrament that you receive is effected by the words of Christ

We see that grace can accomplish more than nature, yet so far we have been considering instances of what grace can do through a prophet's blessing. If the blessing of a human being had power even to change nature, what do we say of God's action in the consecration itself, in which the very words of the Lord and Savior are effective? If the words of Elijah had power even to bring down fire from heaven, will not the words of Christ have power to change the natures of the elements? You have read that in the creation of the whole world *he spoke and they came to be; he commanded and they were created*[Ps 32:9]. If Christ could by speaking create out of nothing what did not yet exist, can we say that his words are unable to change existing things into something they previously were not? It is no lesser feat to create new natures for things than to change their existing natures.

What need is there for argumentation? Let us take what happened in the case of Christ himself and construct the truth of this mystery from the mystery of the incarnation. Did the birth of the Lord Jesus from Mary come about in the course of nature? If we look at nature we regularly find that conception results from the union of man and woman. It is clear then that the conception by the Virgin was above and beyond the course of nature. And this body that we make present is the body born of the Virgin. Why do you expect to find in this case that nature takes its ordinary course in regard to the body of Christ when the Lord himself was born of the Virgin in a manner above and beyond the order of nature? This is indeed the true flesh of Christ, which was crucified and buried. This is then in truth the sacrament of his flesh.

The Lord Jesus himself declares: *This is my body*[Lk 22:9]. Before the blessing contained in these words a different thing is named; after the consecration a body is indicated. He himself speaks of his blood. Before the consecration something else is spoken of; after the consecration blood is designated. And you say: "Amen," that is: "It is true." What the mouth utters, let the mind within acknowledge; what the word says, let the heart ratify.

So the Church, in response to grace so great, exhorts her children, exhorts her neighbors, to hasten to these mysteries: *Neighbors,* she says, *come and eat; brethren, drink and be filled*. In another passage the Holy Spirit has made clear for you what you are to eat, what you are to drink. *Taste,* the prophet says, *and see that the Lord is good; blessed is the man who puts his trust in him*[Ps 33:9]. Christ is in that sacrament, for it is the body of Christ. It is therefore not bodily food but spiritual. Thus the Apostle too says, speaking of its symbol: *Our fathers ate spiritual food and drank spiritual drink*[1 Cor 10:4]. For the body of God is spiritual; the body of Christ is that of a divine spirit, for Christ is a spirit. We read: *The spirit before our face is Christ the Lord*. And in the letter of Saint Peter we have this: *Christ died for you*[1 Pet 3:18]. Finally, it is this food that gives strength to our hearts, this drink which *gives joy to the heart of man*[Ps 103:15], as the prophet has written.

Sunday of the Sixteenth Week in Ordinary Time

From the beginning of a letter to the Magnesians by Saint Ignatius of Antioch, Bishop & Martyr

We should be Christians in deed, as well as in name

Ignatius, also called Theophorus, to the church at Magnesia on the Maeander, a church blessed with the grace of God the Father in Christ Jesus, our Savior, in whom I salute you. I send you every good wish in God the Father and in Jesus Christ.

I was delighted to hear of your love of God, so well-ordered and devout, and so I decided to address you in the faith of Jesus Christ. Honored as I am with a name of the greatest splendor, though I am still in chains I sing with the praises of the churches, and pray that they be united with the flesh and the spirit of Jesus Christ, who is our eternal life; a union in faith and love, to which nothing must be preferred; and above all a union with Jesus and the Father, for if in him we endure all the power of the prince of this world, and escape unharmed, we shall make our way to God.

I have had the honor of seeing you in the person of Damas your bishop, a man of God, and in the persons of your worthy presbyters, Bassus and Apollonius, and my fellow-servant, the deacon Zotion; may I continue to take delight in him for he is obedient to the bishop as to the grace of God, and to the presbyters as to the law of Jesus Christ.

Now it hardly becomes you to presume on your bishop's youth, but rather, having regard to the power of God the Father, to show him every mark of respect. This, I understand, is what your holy presbyters do, not taking advantage of his youthful condition but deferring to him with the prudence which comes from God, or rather not to him but to the Father of Jesus Christ, to the bishop of all. So then, for the honor of him who loves us, it is proper to obey without hypocrisy; for a man does not so much deceive the bishop he can see as try to deceive the bishop he cannot see. In such a case he has to reckon not with a man, but with God who knows the secrets of the heart.

We should then really live as Christians and not merely have the name; for many invoke the bishop's name but do everything apart from him. Such men, I think, do not have a good conscience, for they do not assemble lawfully as commanded.

All things have an end, and two things, life and death, are side by side set before us, and each man will go *to his own place*[2 Cor 5:10]. Just as there are two coinages, one of God and the other of the world, each with its own image, so unbelievers bear the image of this world, and those who have faith with love bear the image of God the Father through Jesus Christ. Unless we are ready through his power to die in the likeness of his passion, his life is not in us.

Monday of the Sixteenth Week in Ordinary Time

From a letter to the Magnesians by Saint Ignatius of Antioch, Bishop & Martyr

One prayer, one hope in love and in holy joy

In the persons I mentioned, I saw and loved in faith your whole community; and so I urge you to strive to do all things in the harmony of God. The bishop is to preside as God's representative, the presbyters are to perform the rule of the apostolic council, and the deacons, who are so dear to me, are to be entrusted with the service of Jesus Christ, who was with the Father before time began and has now at last manifested himself to us. Follow the ways of God, and have respect for one another; let no one judge his neighbor as the world does, but love one another always in Jesus Christ. Let there be nothing among you that could divide you, but live in accord with the bishop and those who are over you as a sign and a pattern of eternal life.

The Lord did nothing either of himself or through his apostles without his Father, with whom he is united; so too, you should undertake nothing without the bishop and the presbyters. Do not attempt to persuade yourselves that what you do on your own account is right and proper, but when you meet together there must be one petition, one prayer, one mind, one hope in love and in holy joy, for Jesus Christ is one and perfect before all else. You must all be quick to come together, as to one temple of God, one altar, to the one Jesus Christ, who came forth from the one Father, while still remaining one with him, and returned to him.

Do not be led astray by false doctrines or by old and idle tales. For if we still live by the law, we admit that we have not received grace. But the holy prophets lived according to Jesus Christ, and that is why they were persecuted. They were inspired by his grace to bring full conviction to an unbelieving world that there is one God, manifested now through Jesus Christ his Son, his Word, who came forth from the Father and was in all things pleasing to the one who sent him.

Those who lived by the ancient customs attained a fresh hope; they no longer observed Saturday, but Sunday, the Lord's day, for on that day life arose for us through Christ and through his death. Some deny this mystery, but through it we have received our faith and because of it we persevere, that we may prove to be disciples of our only teacher, Jesus Christ. Even the prophets awaited him as their teacher, since they were his disciples in spirit. That is why Christ, whom they rightly awaited, raised them from the dead when he appeared. How then can we live without him?

Tuesday of the Sixteenth Week in Ordinary Time

From a letter to the Magnesians by Saint Ignatius of Antioch, Bishop & Martyr

You have Christ within you

Let us not be insensible of Christ's loving kindness. For if he had acted as we do, we would have been lost indeed. Therefore let us become his disciples and learn to live in the Christian way; those who are called by any other name are not of God. Cast out the evil leaven that has become old and sour, and replace it with the new leaven, which is Jesus Christ. He must be the salt of your lives, so that none of you may become corrupt, since it is by your wholesomeness that you will be judged. It is absurd to profess Christ with the lips and at the same time to practice Judaism; for Christianity did not develop into faith in Judaism, but Judaism into faith in Christianity. It was in this that men of every tongue believed and were brought together unto God.

I do not write this to you, my dear friends, because I have heard that any one of you is thus disaffected, but because, though I am a lesser man than yourselves, I would have you all guard against falling into the snares of false doctrine. Have a firm faith in the reality of the Lord's birth, and passion and resurrection which took place when Pontius Pilate was procurator. All these deeds were truly and certainly accomplished by Jesus Christ, who is our hope; may none of you ever be turned away from him!

May you be my joy in all things, if I am worthy of it. For although I am in chains, I do not deserve to be compared with any of you who live in freedom. I know that you are not inflated with pride, for you have Jesus Christ within you. And I know that you blush when I praise you, as the Scripture says: *The just man is his own accuser*[Prov 18:17]. Take care, then, to be firmly grounded in the teachings of the Lord and his apostles so that *you may prosper in all your doings*[3 Jn 1:2] both in body and in soul, in faith and in love, in the Son, and in the Father and in the Spirit, in the beginning and in the end, along with your most worthy bishop and his spiritual crown, your presbyters, and with the deacons, who are men of God. Be obedient to the bishop and to one another, as Jesus Christ was in the flesh to the Father, and the apostles to Christ and to the Father and to the Spirit, so that there may be unity in flesh and in spirit.

I have exhorted you only briefly, for I am aware that you are filled with God. Remember me in your prayers, that I may attain to God. And remember the church in Syria, from which I am unworthy to be called. How I need your united prayer and love in God! Remember, then, the Church in Syria, that it may be strengthened through your prayers.

The Ephesians at Smyrna, where I write these lines, send their greetings. They have come together here like yourselves for the glory of God; they have consoled me in every way and so has Polycarp, their bishop. The other churches, too, greet you for the glory of Jesus Christ. Farewell; may you abide in God's harmony, possessing that undivided spirit which is Jesus Christ.

Wednesday of the Sixteenth Week in Ordinary Time

From the Imitation of Christ ~ Thomas a Kempis, Priest

The kingdom of God is the peace and joy of the Spirit

Turn to the Lord with your whole heart and leave behind this wretched world. Then your soul shall find rest. For the kingdom of God is the peace and joy of the Holy Spirit. If you prepare within your heart a fitting dwelling place, Christ will come to you and console you.

His glory and beauty *are within you,* and he delights in dwelling there. The Lord frequently visits the heart of man. There he shares with man pleasant conversations, welcome consolation, abundant peace and a wonderful intimacy.

So come, faithful soul. Prepare your heart for your spouse to dwell within you. For he says: *If anyone loves me, he will keep my word and we shall come to him and make our dwelling within him*[Jn 14:23].

Make room for Christ. When you possess Christ you are a rich man, for he is sufficient for you. He himself, shall provide for you and faithfully administer all your cares. You will not have to place your hope in men. Put all your trust in God; let him be both your fear and your love. He will respond on your behalf and will do whatever is in your best interest.

You have here no *lasting city*[Heb 13:14-16]. For wherever you find yourself, you will always be a pilgrim from another city. Until you are united intimately with Christ, you will never find your true rest.

Let your thoughts be with the Most High and direct your prayers continually to Christ. If you do not know how to contemplate the glory of heaven, take comfort in the passion of Christ, and dwell willingly in his sacred wounds. Endure with Christ, suffer for him, if you wish to reign with him.

Once you have entered completely into the depths of Jesus, and have a taste of his powerful love, then you will not care about your own convenience or inconvenience. Rather you will rejoice all the more in insults and injuries, for the love of Jesus makes a man scorn his own needs.

Thursday of the Sixteenth Week in Ordinary Time

From the Explanations of the Psalms by Saint Ambrose, Bishop & Doctor

We are sealed with the glory of your face

Why do you turn away your face[Ps 87:15]? We think that God is turning his face away from us when we find ourselves in such distress that our senses are clouded in darkness and we cannot see the glory of him who is truth. We are convinced that if God would pay attention to our condition and be pleased to visit our souls, nothing could plunge us in gloom. If a person's face is more enlightening than other parts of his body - so that when we look at someone we either see him as a stranger or recognize him as someone we know, whom our glance will not allow to pass unrecognized - how much more does the face of God enlighten those on whom he directs his gaze.

In his usual way Saint Paul has something striking to say on this subject. He employs his gift for making Christ better understood to bring him closer to us through the use of appropriate ideas and expressions. He tells us: *God, who commanded light to shine out of darkness, has caused light to shine in our hearts, so that we might receive the revelation of God's glory in the face of Jesus Christ*[2 Cor 4:6]. We know, then, the place where Christ is shining within us. He is the eternal splendor enlightening our minds and hearts. He was sent by the Father to shine on us in the glory of his face, and so enable us to see what is eternal and heavenly, where before we were imprisoned in the darkness of this world.

There should be no need for me to speak of Christ when even Peter the apostle said to the man born lame: *Look at us.* He looked at Peter and was enlightened by the grace of faith. He would not have received healing had he not believed with faith.

Such was the glory possessed by the apostles. Yet Zacchaeus, hearing that the Lord Jesus was passing by, climbed a tree, for he was small in stature and could not see him because of the crowd. He saw Christ and discovered the light. He saw Christ and gave up what was his own, though he was a man who took what belonged to others.

Why do you turn away your face? We may say it in another way. Even if, Lord, you turn your face away from us, yet *we are sealed with the glory of your face*[Eph 1:13-14.] Your glory is in our hearts and shines in the deep places of our spirit. Indeed, no one can live if you should turn away your face.

Friday of the Sixteenth Week in Ordinary Time

From the Confessions by Saint Augustine, Bishop & Doctor

Christ died for all

The true Mediator was he whom you revealed to humble men in your secret mercy, and whom you sent so they might learn that same humility by following his example. This was *the Mediator between God and man, the man Christ Jesus*[1 Tim 2:5], who intervened between sinful mortals and the immortal Just One, himself mortal like men, and like God, just. Thus, since life and peace are the compensation for righteousness, he could, by a justice united with God, annul the death of sinners now justified, since he willed to share death with them.

Good Father, how you loved us, *sparing not your only Son but delivering him up for us sinners*[Rom 8:32]! How you loved us, for whose sake he, *thinking it no robbery to be equal with you, was made subject to death on the cross*[Phil 2:6-11]. He alone, free among the dead, *had the power to lay down his life and the power to take it up again*[Jn 10:18]. For our sake he became in your sight both victor and victim - victor, indeed, because he was victim. For our sake, too, he became before you both priest and sacrifice - priest, indeed, because he was a sacrifice, changing us from slaves to sons by being your Son and serving us.

Rightly then have I firm hope that you will heal all my infirmities through him who sits at your right hand and *intercedes for us*[Rom 8:34]. Otherwise I should despair. For great and numerous are these infirmities of mine, great indeed and numerous, but your medicine is mightier. We might have thought your Word remote from any union with man, and so have despaired of ourselves, if he had not *become flesh and dwelt among us*[Jn 1:14].

Crushed by my sins and the weight of my misery, I had taken thought in my heart and contemplated flight into the desert. But you stopped me and gave me comfort with the words: *Christ died for all, that those who live might no longer live for themselves but for him who died for them*[2 Cor 5:15].

Behold, Lord, I cast upon you my concern that I may live and *I shall meditate on the wonders of your law*[Ps 118:27]. You know my ignorance and my weakness; teach me and heal me. Your only Son, in whom *are hidden all the treasures of wisdom and knowledge*[Col 2:3], redeemed me with his blood. *Let not arrogant men speak evil of me*[Titus 3:2]. For I meditate on my ransom, and I eat it and drink it and try to share it with others; though poor I want to be filled with it in the company of those who eat and are filled; and *they shall praise the Lord who seek him*[Ps 21:26].

Saturday of the Sixteenth Week in Ordinary Time

From a homily on the second letter to the Corinthians by Saint John Chrysostom, Bishop & Doctor

Our heart is enlarged

Our heart is enlarged[2 Cor 6:11-18]. For as heat makes things expand, so it is the work of love to expand the heart, for its power is to heat and make fervent. It is this that opened Paul's lips and enlarged his heart. *For I do not love only in words;* he means, *but my loving heart too is in unison with my words; and so I speak with confidence, without restraint or reserve*. There was nothing more capacious than the heart of Paul, for he loved all the faithful with as intimate a love as any lover could have for a loved one, his love not being divided and lessened but remaining whole and entire for each of them. And what marvel is it that his love for the faithful was such, since his heart embraced the unbelievers, too, throughout the whole world?

So he did not just say, "I love you," but with greater emphasis: *Our mouth is open, our heart is enlarged;* we hold you all in it, and not only that, but with room for you to move freely. For those who are loved enter fearlessly into the heart of their lover. And therefore he says: *You are not constrained because of us, but you are constrained in your own affections*[2 Cor 6:12]. See how this reproach is tempered with much forbearance, as is the way with those who love much. For he did not say: *You do not love me,* but *you do not love me in the same measure;* for he did not want to charge them more harshly.

Indeed one may see with what a wonderful love for the faithful he is always inflamed, as one finds proof of it in all his writings. To the Romans he says: *I desire to see you, and I have often planned to come to you*[Rom 1:11-13], and *if by any means at last I may succeed in reaching you*[Rom 1:10]. To the Galatians he says: *My little children, with whom I am again in labor*[Gal 4:19]; to the Ephesians: *For this cause I bend my knees on your behalf*[Eph 3:14-21]; and to the Thessalonians: *What is my hope and my joy and my crown of glory? Is it not yourselves*[1 Thess 2:19]? For he used to say that he carried them about in his heart and in his chains.

Again he writes to the Colossians: *I want you to know how greatly I strive for you and for all who have not seen my face*[Col 2:1]; and to the Thessalonians: *Like a nurse taking care of her children, being desirous of you, we were ready to share with you not only the Gospel but also our own selves*[1 Thess 2:7-12]. So too he says: *You are not restricted by us*[2 Cor 6:12]. And so Paul does not merely say that he loves them but also that they love him, so that in this way he may draw them to him. Indeed, to the Corinthians he bears witness of this love when he says: *Titus came, telling us of your longing, your mourning, your zeal for me*[2 Cor 7:7].

Sunday of the Seventeenth Week in Ordinary Time

From a homily on the Second Letter to the Corinthians
By St. John Chyrsostom, Bishop & Doctor

I rejoice exceedingly in all my tribulations

Again Paul turns to speak of love, softening the harshness of his rebuke. For after convicting and reproaching them for not loving him as he had loved them, breaking away from his love and attaching themselves to troublemakers, he again takes the edge off the reproach by saying: *Open your hearts to us*[2 Cor 6:11-13], that is, *love us*. He asks for a favor which will be no burden to them but will be more profitable to the giver than to the receiver. And he did not use the word "love" but said, more appealingly: *Open your hearts to us.*

Who, he said, has cast us out of your minds, thrust us from your hearts? How is it that you feel constraint with us? For, since he has said earlier: *You are restricted in your own affection*[2 Cor 6:12], he now declares himself more openly and says: *Open your hearts to us,* thus once more drawing them toward him. For nothing so much wins love as the knowledge that one's lover desires most of all to be himself loved.

For I said before, he tells them, *that you are in our hearts to die together or live together*[2 Cor 7:3]. This is love at its height, that even though in disfavor, he wishes both to die and to live with them. For you are in our hearts, not just somehow or other, but in the way I have said. It is possible to love and yet to draw back when danger threatens; but my love is not like that.

I am filled with consolation. What consolation? That which comes from you because you, being changed for the better, have consoled me by what you have done. It is natural for a lover both to complain that he is not loved in return and to fear that he may cause distress by complaining too much. Therefore, he says: *I am filled with consolation, I rejoice exceedingly*[2 Cor 7:4].

It is as if he said, I was much grieved on your account, but you have made it up for me in full measure and given me comfort; for you have not only removed the cause for any grief but filled me with a richer joy.

Then he shows the greatness of that joy by saying not only *I rejoice exceedingly* but also the words which follow: *in all my tribulations*[2 Cor 7:4]. So great, he says, was the delight that you gave me that it was not even dimmed by so much tribulation, but overcame by its strength and keenness all those sorrows which had invaded my heart, and took away from me all awareness of them.

Monday of the Seventeenth Week in Ordinary Time

From a Sermon by Saint Caesarius of Arles, Bishop

Divine and human mercy

Blessed are the merciful, for they shall receive mercy[Mt 5:7]. My brothers and sisters, sweet is the thought of mercy, but even more so is mercy itself. It is what all men hope for, but unfortunately, not what all men deserve. For while all men wish to receive it, only a few are willing to give it.

How can a man ask for himself what he refuses to give to another? If he expects to receive any mercy in heaven, he should give mercy on earth. Do we all desire to receive mercy? Let us make mercy our patroness now, and she will free us in the world to come. Yes, there is mercy in heaven, but the road to it is paved by our merciful acts on earth. As Scripture says: *Lord, your mercy is in heaven*[Ps 35:6].

There is, therefore, an earthly as well as heavenly mercy, that is to say, a human and a divine mercy. Human mercy has compassion on the miseries of the poor. Divine mercy grants forgiveness of sins. Whatever human mercy bestows here on earth, divine mercy will return to us in our homeland. In this life God feels cold and hunger in all who are stricken with poverty; for, remember, he once said: *What you have done to the least of my brothers you have done to me*[Mt 25:40]. Yes, God who sees fit to give his mercy in heaven wishes it to be a reality here on earth.

What kind of people are we? When God gives, we wish to receive, but when he begs, we refuse to give. Remember, it was Christ who said: *I was hungry and you gave me nothing to eat*[Mt 25:42]. When the poor are starving, Christ too hungers. Do not neglect to improve the unhappy conditions of the poor, if you wish to ensure that your own sins be forgiven you. Christ hungers now, my brethren; it is he who deigns to hunger and thirst in the persons of the poor. And what he will return in heaven tomorrow is what he receives here on earth today.

What do you wish for, what do you pray for, my dear brothers and sisters, when you come to church? Is it mercy? How can it be anything else? Show mercy, then, while you are on earth, and mercy will be shown to you in heaven. A poor person asks you for something; you ask God for something. He begs for a morsel of food; you beg for eternal life. Give to the beggar so that you may merit to receive from Christ. For he it is who says: *Give and it will be given to you*[Lk 6:38]. It baffles me that you have the impudence to ask for what you do not want to give. Give when you come to church. Give to the poor. Give them whatever your resources will allow.

Tuesday of the Seventeenth Week in Ordinary Time

From a sermon on charity by Saint Basil the Great, Bishop & Doctor

Sow integrity for yourselves

Man should be like the earth and bear fruit; he should not let inanimate matter appear to surpass him. The earth bears crops for your benefit, not for its own, but when you give to the poor, you are bearing fruit which you will gather in for yourself, since the reward for good deeds goes to those who perform them. Give to a hungry man, and what you give becomes yours, and indeed it returns to you with interest. As the sower profits from wheat that falls onto the ground, so will you profit greatly in the world to come from the bread that you place before a hungry man. Your husbandry must be the sowing of heavenly seed: *Sow integrity for yourselves*[Titus 2:7], says Scripture.

You are going to leave your money behind you here whether you wish to or not. On the other hand, you will take with you to the Lord the honor that you have won through good works. In the presence of the universal judge, all the people will surround you, acclaim you as a public benefactor, and tell of your generosity and kindness.

Do you not see how people throw away their wealth on theatrical performances, boxing contests, mimes and fights between men and wild beasts, which are sickening to see, and all for the sake of fleeting honor and popular applause? If you are miserly with your money, how can you expect any similar honor? Your reward for the right use of the things of this world will be everlasting glory, a crown of righteousness, and the kingdom of heaven; God will welcome you, the angels will praise you, all men who have existed since the world began will call you blessed.

Do you care nothing for these things, and spurn the hopes that lie in the future for the sake of your present enjoyment? Come, distribute your wealth freely, give generously to those who are in need. Earn for yourself the psalmist's praise: *He gave freely to the poor; his righteousness will endure for ever*[2 Cor 9:9].

How grateful you should be to your own benefactor; how you should beam with joy at the honor of having other people come to your door, instead of being obliged to go to theirs! But you are now ill-humored and unapproachable; you avoid meeting people, in case you might be forced to loosen your purse-strings even a little. You can say only one thing: "I have nothing to give you. I am only a poor man." A poor man you certain are, and destitute of all real riches; you are poor in love, generosity, faith in God and hope of eternal happiness.

Wednesday of the Seventeenth Week in Ordinary Time

From a catechetical instruction by Saint Cyril of Jerusalem, Bishop & Doctor

The Church as the assembly of the people of God

The Church is called Catholic or universal because it has spread throughout the entire world, from one end of the earth to the other. Again, it is called Catholic because it teaches fully and unfailingly all the doctrines which ought to be brought to men's knowledge, whether concerned with visible or invisible things, with the realities of heaven or the things of earth. Another reason for the name Catholic is that the Church brings under religious obedience all classes of men, rulers and subjects, learned and unlettered. Finally, it deserves the title Catholic because it heals and cures unrestrictedly every type of sin that can be committed in soul or in body, and because it possesses within itself every kind of virtue that can be named, whether exercised in actions or in words or in some kind of spiritual charism.

It is most aptly called a church, which means an "assembly of those called out," because it "calls out" all men and gathers them together, just as the Lord says in Leviticus: *Assemble all the congregation at the door of the tent of meeting*[Lev 8:3]. It is worth noting also that the word "assemble" is used for the first time in the Scriptures at this moment when the Lord appoints Aaron high priest. So in Deuteronomy God says to Moses: *Assemble the people before me and let them hear my words, so that they may learn to fear me*[Deut 4:10]. There is a further mention of the assembly in the passage about the tablets of the Law: *And on them were written all the words which the Lord had spoken to you on the mountain out of the midst of the fire, on the day of the assembly*[Deut 9:10]; it is as though he had said, even more clearly, "on the day when you were called out by God and gathered together." So too the psalmist says: *I will give thanks to you in the great assembly, O Lord; in the mighty throng I will praise you*[Ps 34:18].

Long ago the psalmist sang: *Bless God in the assembly; bless the Lord, you who are Israel's sons*[Ps 67:26]. But now the Savior has built a second holy assembly, our Christian Church, from the Gentiles. It was of this that he spoke to Peter: *On this rock I will build my Church, and the powers of death shall not prevail against it*[Mt 16:18].

Now that the single church which was in Judea has been rejected, the churches of Christ are already multiplying throughout the world, and of them it is said in the psalms: *Sing a new song to the Lord, let his praise be sung in the assembly of the saints*[Ps 149:1]. Taking up the same theme the prophet says to the Jews: *I have no pleasure in you, says the Lord of hosts*[Mal 1:10]; and immediately he adds: *For from the rising of the sun to its setting my name is glorified among the nations*[Mal 1:11]. Of this holy Catholic Church Paul writes to Timothy: *That you may know how one ought to behave in the household of God, which is the Church of the living God, the pillar and bulwark of the truth*[1 Tim 3:15].

Thursday of the Seventeenth Week in Ordinary Time

From a catechetical instruction by Saint Cyril of Jerusalem, Bishop & Doctor

The Church is the bride of Christ

The Catholic Church is the distinctive name of this holy Church which is the mother of us all. She is the bride of our Lord Jesus Christ, the only-begotten Son of God (for Scripture says: *Christ loved the Church and gave himself up for her*[Eph 5:25]*)*. She is the type and she bears the image of *the Jerusalem above that is free and is the mother of us all*[Gal 4:26], that Jerusalem which once was barren but now has many children.

The first assembly, that is, the assembly of Israel, was rejected, and now in the second, that is, in the Catholic Church, *God has appointed first, apostles, second, prophets, third, teachers then workers of miracles, then healers, helpers, administrators and speakers in various kinds of tongues*[1 Cor 12:28], as Paul says; and together with these is found every sort of virtue - wisdom and understanding, self-control and justice, mercy and kindness, and invincible patience in persecution. *With the weapons of righteousness in the right hand and in the left, in glory and dishonor*[2 Cor 6:7,] this Church in earlier days, when persecution and afflictions abounded, crowned her holy martyrs with the varied and many-flowered wreaths of endurance. But now when God has favored us with times of peace, she receives her due honor from kings and men of high station, and from every condition and race of mankind. And while the rulers of the different nations have limits to their sovereignty, the holy Catholic Church alone has a power without boundaries throughout the entire world. For, as Scripture says: *God has made peace her borders*[Ps 147:14]

Instructed in this holy Catholic Church and bearing ourselves honorably, we shall gain the kingdom of heaven and inherit eternal life. For the sake of enjoying this at the Lord's hands, we endure all things. The goal set before us is no trifling one; we are striving for eternal life. In the Creed, therefore, after professing our faith, "in the resurrection of the body," that is, of the dead, which I have already discussed, we are taught to believe "in life everlasting," and for this as Christians we are struggling.

Now real and true life is none other than the Father, who is the fountain of life and who pours forth his heavenly gifts on all creatures through the Son in the Holy Spirit, and the good things of eternal life are faithfully promised to us men also, because of his love for us.

Friday of the Seventeenth Week in Ordinary Time

From the beginning of a letter to Polycarp by Saint Ignatius of Antioch, Bishop & Martyr

We must bear with everything for God, so that he in turn may bear with us

Ignatius, also called Theophorus, to Polycarp, who is bishop of the Church of Smyrna, or rather who has for his bishop God the Father and the Lord Jesus Christ, greetings and all good wishes.

Recognizing your devotion to God, firmly built as if upon a solid rock, I am full of thanksgiving to him for allowing me to see your blessed countenance - may I forever enjoy the sight of it in God! I beseech you by the grace with which you are endowed to press forward on your course and to exhort all men to salvation. Justify your episcopal dignity by your unceasing concern for the spiritual and temporal welfare of your flock; let unity, the greatest of all goods, be your preoccupation. Cary the burdens of all men as the Lord carries yours; have patience with all in charity, as indeed you do. Give yourself to prayer continually, ask for wisdom greater than you now have, keep alert with an unflagging spirit. Speak to each man individually, following God's example; bear the infirmities of all, like a perfect athlete of God. The greater the toil, the richer the reward.

If you love only your good disciples, you gain no merit; rather you must win over the more troublesome of them by kindness. The same salve does not heal all wounds; convulsions should be allayed with poultices. *Be prudent as the serpent* in all things, and *innocent as the dove*[Mt 10:16] always. You are both body and soul; treat gently the manifestations of human fault, even as you pray for the knowledge of things invisible, and then you will lack nothing but abound in every blessing. Do as the circumstances require, like the pilot looking to the wind and the storm-tossed sailor to the harbor, that you may win your way to God with your people. Exercise self-discipline, for you are God's athlete; the prize is immortality and eternal life, as you know full well. In everything I am your devoted friend - I and my chains, which you have kissed.

Do not be overwhelmed by those who seem trustworthy and yet teach heresy. Remain firm, like the anvil under the hammer. The good athlete must take punishment in order to win. And above all we must bear with everything for God, so that he in turn may bear with us. Increase your zeal. Read the signs of the times. Look for him who is outside time, the eternal one, the unseen, who became visible for us; he cannot be touched and cannot suffer, yet he became subject to suffering and endured so much for our sake.

Do not neglect windows; after the Lord, it is you who must be their guardian. Nothing must be done without your approval, and you must do nothing without God's approval, as indeed is the case; stand firm. Services should be held often; seek out everyone by name. Do not look down upon slaves, whether men or women; yet they too should not be arrogant, but should give better service for the glory of God so as to gain from him a better freedom. They should not be anxious for their freedom to be bought at the community's expense, for they might then prove to be the slaves of their own desires.

Saturday of the Seventeenth Week in Ordinary Time

From a letter to Polycarp by Saint Ignatius of Antioch, Bishop & Martyr

Let everything be done for God's honor

Avoid evil practices; indeed, preach against them. Tell my sisters to love the Lord and be content with their husbands in the flesh and in the spirit, and in the same way bid my brothers in Christ's name to love their wives as the Lord loves his Church. If anyone can remain chaste in honor of the Savior's flesh, then let him do so without boasting. For if he boasts of it, he is lost; and if he thinks himself for this reason better than the bishop, he is lost. Those who marry should be united with the bishop's approval, so that the marriage may follow God's will and not merely the prompting of the flesh. Let everything be done for God's honor.

Hear your bishop, that God may hear you. My life is a sacrifice for those who are obedient to the bishop, the presbyters and the deacons; and may it be my lot to share with them in God. Work together in harmony, struggle together, run together, suffer together, rest together, rise together, as stewards, advisors and servants of God. Seek to please him whose soldiers you are and from whom you draw your pay; let none of you prove a deserter. Let your baptism be your armor, your faith your helmet, your charity your spear, your patience your panoply. Let your good works be your deposits, so that you may draw out well-earned savings. So be patient and gentle with one another, as God is with you. May I have joy in you for ever!

Since I have heard that the church of Antioch in Syria is in peace through your prayers, I too am more tranquil in my reliance upon God. If only I may find my way to God through my passion and at the resurrection prove to be your disciple! My most blessed Polycarp, you should convene a godly council and appoint someone whom you consider dear and especially diligent to be called God's courier and to have the honor of going into Syria and advancing God's glory by speaking of your untiring charity. A Christian is not his own master; his time is God's. This is God's work, and it will be yours as well when you have performed it. I have trust in the grace of God that you are ready to act generously when it comes to God's work. Since I knew so well your zeal for the truth, I have limited my appeal to these few words.

I could not write to all the churches because I am sailing at once from Troas to Neapolis as is required of me. I want you, therefore, as one who knows God's purpose, to write to the churches of the East and bid them to do the same. Those who can should send representatives, while the rest should send letters through your delegates. Thus your community will be honored for a good work which will be remembered for ever, as their bishop deserves.

I wish all of you well for ever in Jesus Christ; through him may you all remain in God's unity and in his care. Farwell in the Lord!

Sunday of the Eighteenth Week in Ordinary Time

From the beginning of a letter attributed to Barnabas

Hope of life is the beginning and end of our faith

Greetings, sons and daughters. In the name of the Lord who loves us, peace be to you. Because the Lord has granted you an abundance of blessings, I rejoice immeasurably in your blessed and glorious company.

You have received abundantly that indwelling grace which is the Spirit's gift, and for this reason I hope in my own salvation and I give thanks all the more when I see the bountiful fullness of the Lord's Spirit pouring over you. I have longed so much for you that when I saw you I was overwhelmed.

I am now convinced and fully aware that I have learned much by speaking with you, for the Lord accompanied me on the road to righteousness, and so I am driven in all ways to love you more than my own life. For surely there is a great store of faith and charity within you because of your hope for life in Christ. Therefore, I have been thinking that if my concern for you inspires me to pass on to you a portion of what I have received, then I will be rewarded for ministering to souls such as yours. Consequently, I am writing you, that you may have perfect knowledge along with your faith.

The Lord has given us these three basic doctrines: hope for eternal life, the beginning and end of our faith; justice, the beginning and end of righteousness; and love, which bears cheerful and joyous witness to the works of righteousness. Now the Lord has made the past and present known to us through his prophets, and he has given us the ability to taste the fruits of the future beforehand. Thus, when we see prophecies fulfilled in their appointed order, we ought to grow more fully and deeply in awe of him. Let me suggest a few things – not as a teacher, but as one of you – which should bring you joy in the present situation.

When evil days are upon us and the worker of malice gains power, we must attend to our own souls and seek to know the ways of the Lord. In those times reverential fear and perseverance will sustain our faith, and we will find need of forbearance and self-restraint as well. Provided that we hold fast to these virtues and look to the Lord, then wisdom, understanding, knowledge and insight will make joyous company with them.

Truly, the Lord has revealed to us through the prophets that he has no need of sacrifice, burnt offerings or oblations. He says in one place: *Your endless sacrifices, what are they to me? says the Lord. I have had my fill of holocausts; I do not want the fat of your lambs, nor the blood of your bulls and goats, nor your presence in my sight. Indeed, who has made these demands of you? No more will you trample my courts. Your sacrifices of fine flour are in vain; your incense is loathsome to me; I cannot bear your feasts of the new moon, nor your sabbaths.*[Isa 1:11-13]

Monday of the Eighteenth Week in Ordinary Time

From a letter attributed to Barnabas

The new law of our Lord

God has abolished the sacrifices of the old law so that the new law of our Lord Jesus Christ, which does not bind by slavish compulsion, might have an offering not made by man. On another occasion he says to them: *When I brought your forefathers out of Egypt, I gave them no commands about burnt offerings and sacrifices. I said not a word about them. What I did command was this: Do not contrive any evil against one another, and do not love perjury*[Jer 7:22-24].

We are not stupid; surely we ought to understand our Father's kindly purpose in this. He does not want us to go astray as they did, nor to ask how we are to approach him. Here is what he says to us: *The sacrifice acceptable to God is a broken heart; the fragrance pleasing to the Lord is a soul that gives glory to its Maker*[Ps 50:18-19]. You see, my brothers, we must carefully seek after our own salvation; otherwise, one who is bent on deceiving us will insinuate himself and turn us aside from the path that leads to life.

God spoke of this once again when he said to them: *On such a day you are keeping a fast that will not carry your cry to heaven. Is it that sort of fast that I require, a day of mortification like that*[Isa 58:5]*?* But to us he says: *Is it not this that I demand of you as a fast—loose the fetters of injustice, untie the knots of all contracts that involve extortion, set free those who have been crushed, tear up every unjust agreement. Share your food with the starving; when you meet a naked man, give him clothing; welcome the homeless into your house*[Isa 58:6-11].

Accordingly, we must flee from all vanity and show an utter hatred for the deeds of the evil way. Do not turn inward and live only for yourselves as though already assured of salvation; join together rather and seek the common good. For, as Scripture says: *Shame on those who are wise in their own judgment and think themselves clever*[Isa 5:21]. Rather, let us become spiritual; let us be a perfect dwelling place for God. As far as we can, we should dwell upon the fear of God and strive to keep his commandments, finding our delight in his observances. The Lord will *judge the world without respect to persons*[1 Pet 1;17]; everyone will receive his just deserts; if he has been good, his good works will go before him; if wicked, the wages of sin will lie in wait for him. We must never relax our efforts as though our calling were already realized. Never let us fall asleep in a state of sin, lest the prince of wickedness gain power over us and snatch us away from the kingdom of the Lord.

My brothers, grasp this further point: You see the Israelites rejected, even after the many signs and wonders worked among them; let us then see to it that we are not found among those of whom Scripture says: *Many are called, but few are chosen*[Mt 22:14].

Tuesday of the Eighteenth Week in Ordinary Time

From a letter attributed to Barnabas

The new creation

The Lord was willing to hand over his body for destruction so that by the shedding of his blood we might be made holy through the remission of our sins. According to Scripture this refers to both Israel and us. *He was wounded for our transgressions and bruised by our iniquities; by his wounds we are healed. He was led like a sheep to the slaughter, like a lamb that is dumb before its shearer*[Isa 53:5-12]. What a debt of gratitude, then, do we owe to the Lord for letting us see the meaning of the past, for instructing us about the present and not leaving us in ignorance about the future. In the words of Scripture: *Not unjustly are nets spread for birds*[Prov 1:17]. This means that a man is justly condemned if, knowing the right way, he heads into the way of darkness.

The Lord was ready to undergo suffering for our souls' sake, even though he is Lord of the whole earth, the one to whom God said at the foundation of the world: *Let us make man in our own image and likeness*[Gen 1:26]. But, in that case, my brothers, how could he allow himself to suffer at the hands of men? This is the explanation. The prophets inspired by his grace foretold what he would do; he allowed himself to suffer because he had to be seen in the flesh, in order that he might destroy the power of death and manifest the resurrection from the dead. In this way he would carry out the promises that had been made to our forefathers, and while still on earth prepare for himself a new people; he would also show that, after the resurrection, he was to be our judge. Furthermore, by teaching Israel and working such great signs and wonders, he proclaimed the good news and showed the depths of his love for that people.

Having thus renewed us by forgiving our sins, he refashioned us; he gave us the souls of children, as though we had been born anew. For it is to us that Scripture refers when the Father says to the Son: *Let us make man according to our own image and likeness; and let him rule over the beasts on the earth and the birds in the air and the fish in the sea*[Gen 1:26.] The Lord saw the beauty of our fashioning and added: *Increase and multiply and fill the earth*[Gen 1:28].

All this God said to his Son. But let me now point out to you how he also speaks to us. It is indeed a second act of creation that the Lord has performed in these last days; that is why he says: *Behold, I am making the last things like the first*[Rev 21:1-8.] It was this that the prophet had in mind when he said: *Enter into a land flowing with milk and honey, and rule over it*[Deut 27:3]. It is true, you see, that we have been completely remade. This is what God means by the words of another prophet: *Behold, says the Lord, I will take the stony hearts out of this people,* that is, the people whom the Spirit of the Lord foreknew, *and put hearts of flesh into them*[Ezek 36:26]. For he willed to appear in the flesh and live among us.

And so, my brothers, the dwelling place of our hearts is a temple sacred to the Lord. Again, the Lord says: *Let me give thanks to you in the assembly of the people*[Ps 34:18]. So it is we whom he has led into a fertile land.

Wednesday of the Eighteenth Week in Ordinary Time

From a letter attributed to Barnabas

The way of light

Consider now the way of light; any man who is bent on reaching his appointed goal must be very careful in all he does. Now these are the directions that have been given to us for this journey: love your Creator; reverence your Maker; give glory to him who redeemed you when you were dead; be single-minded but rich in spiritual treasure; avoid those who travel down death's highway; hate whatever is displeasing to God; detest all hypocritical pretense; do not abandon God's commandments. Do not put on airs, but be modest whatever you do; claim no credit for yourself. Plot no evil against your neighbor, and do not give pride an entrance into your heart.

Love your neighbor more than your own life. Do not kill an unborn child through abortion, nor destroy it after birth. Do not refrain from chastising son or daughter, but bring them up from childhood in the fear of the Lord. Do not set your heart on what belongs to your neighbor and do not give in to greed. Do not associate with the arrogant but cultivate those who are humble and virtuous.

Accept as a blessing whatever comes your way in the knowledge that nothing ever happens without God's concurrence. Avoid duplicity in thought or in word, for such deception is a deadly snare.

Share with your neighbor whatever you have, and do not say of anything, this is mine. If you both share an imperishable treasure, how much more must you share what is perishable. Do not be hasty in speech; the mouth is a deadly snare. For your soul's good, make every effort to live chastely. Do not hold out your hand for what you can get, only to withdraw it when it comes to giving. Cherish as the apple of your eye anyone who speaks to you of the word of the Lord.

Night and day you will bear in mind the hour of judgment; every day you will seek out the company of God's faithful, either by preaching the word, earnestly exhorting them, ever considering how you can save souls by your eloquence, or else by working with your hands to make reparation for your past sins.

Never hesitate to give, and when you do give, never grumble; then you will know the one who will repay you. Preserve the traditions you have received, adding nothing and taking nothing away. The evildoer will ever be hateful to you. Be fair in your judgments. Never stir up dissension, but act as peacemaker and reconcile the quarrelsome. Confess your sins, and do not begin to pray with a guilty conscience.

Such then is the way of light.

Thursday of the Eighteenth Week in Ordinary Time

From a treatise by Baldwin of Canterbury, Bishop

Love is as strong as death

Death is strong, for it can rob us of the gift of life. Love too is strong, for it can restore us to a better life.

Death is strong, for it can strip us of this robe of flesh. Love too is strong, for it can take death's spoils away and give them back to us.

Death is strong, for no man can withstand it. Love too is strong, for it can conquer death itself, soothe its sting, calm its violence, and bring its victory to naught. The time will come when death is reviled and taunted: *O death, where is your sting? O death, where is your victory*[1 Cor 15:55-57]?

Love is as strong as death[Song 8:6-7] because Christ's love is the very death of death. Hence it is said: *I will be your death, O death! I will be your sting, O hell*[Hos 13:14]! Our love for Christ is also as strong as death, because it is itself a kind of death: destroying the old life, rooting out vice, and laying aside dead works.

Our love for Christ is a return, though very unequal, for his love of us, and it is a likeness modeled on his. For *he first loved us* and, through the example of love he gave us, he became a seal upon us by which we are made like him. We lay aside the likeness of the earthly man and put on the likeness of the heavenly man; we love him as he has loved us. For in this matter *he has left us an example so that we might follow in his steps*[1 Pet 2:21].

That is why he says: *Set me as a seal upon your heart*[Song 8:6]. It is as if he were saying: "Love me as I love you. Keep me in your mind and memory, in your desires and yearnings, in your groans and sobs. Remember, man, the kind of being I made you; how far I set you above other creatures; the dignity I conferred upon you; the glory and honor with which I crowned you; how I made you only a little less than the angels and set all things under your feet. Remember not only how much I have done for you but all the hardship and shame I have suffered for you. Yet look and see: Do you not wrong me? Do you not fail to love me? Who loves you as I do? Who created and redeemed you but I?

Lord, take away my heart of stone, a heart so bitter and uncircumcised, and give me a new heart, a heart of flesh, a pure heart. You cleanse the heart and love the clean heart. Take possession of my heart and dwell in it, contain it and fill it, you who are higher than the heights of my spirit and closer to me than my innermost self! You are the pattern of all beauty and the seal of all holiness. Set the seal of your likeness upon my heart! In your mercy set your seal upon my heart, *God of my heart and the God who is my portion for ever*[Ps 72:26]! Amen.

Friday of the Eighteenth Week in Ordinary Time

From a Spiritual Canticle by Saint John of the Cross, Priest & Doctor

I give myself as your spouse for ever

The soul united to God and transformed in him draws from within God a divine breath, much like the most high God himself. And God, abiding in the soul, breathes forth the life of the soul as its exemplar. This I take to be what Paul meant when he said: *Because you are children of God, God has sent the Spirit of his Son into your hearts, crying, "Abba, Father"*[Gal 4:6]; this is what takes place in those who have achieved perfection.

One should not wonder that the soul is capable of so sublime an activity. For if God so favors her that she is made God-like by union with the most Holy Trinity, I ask you then, why it should seem so incredible that the soul, at one with the Trinity and in the greatest possible likeness to it, should share the understanding, knowledge and love which God achieves in himself.

How this is possible no other power or wisdom can express, save by explaining how the Son of God obtained this sublime state for us and won for us the power to be the children of God, as he asked of the Father: *Father, I desire that where I am those you have given me may also be with me, that they may see the glory you have given me*[Jn 17:24], that is, that they may share with certainty the very task I perform.

And then he said: *"Not for them alone do I ask but also for those who will come to believe in me through their teaching, that all may be one as you, Father, are one in me and I in you, that they may be one in us; that the world may believe that you have sent me. And the glory you have given me I have given them that they may be one as we are. I in them, you in me, that they may be made perfect, and the world will know that you sent me and as you have loved me, so I have loved them."*[Jn 17:20-23]

The Father thus gives them the same love he shares with the Son, though not by nature as with the Son, but through unity and transformation of love. One should not think that the Son is asking the Father to make the saints one with him in essence and nature as the Son is with the Father, but rather that they be united with him in love, just as the Father and Son are one in the essential unity of love. Accordingly, souls possess the same goods by participation that the Son possesses by nature. As a result, they are truly divine by participation, equals and companions of God.

Thus Peter said: *May grace and peace be perfected in you in the knowledge of God and Christ Jesus our Lord. For all things of his divine power, which are given to us for our life and goodness, are given through the knowledge of him who called us to his own glory and power, by which he has given us great and precious promises, that by these we may be made partakers of the divine nature*[2 Pet 1:2-4]. So the soul, in this union which God has ordained, joins in the work of the Trinity, not yet fully as in the life to come, but nonetheless even now in a real and perceptible way.

O my soul, created to enjoy such exquisite gifts, what are you doing, where is your life going? How wretched is the blindness of Adam's children, if indeed we are blind to such a brilliant light and deaf to so insistent a voice.

Saturday of the Eighteenth Week in Ordinary Time

From the treatise Against Heresies by Saint Irenaeus, Bishop, Doctor & Martyr

It is mercy that I want, not sacrifice

That they might be saved God demanded of these men of old not sacrifices and holocausts, but faith, obedience and righteousness. God expressed his will when he taught them in the words of Hosea: *I desire mercy more than sacrifices, the knowledge of God more than holocausts*[Hos 6:6]. Our Lord's warning to them was the same: *If you had known what was meant by the words "I desire mercy and not sacrifice," you would never have condemned the guiltless*[Mt 12:7]. He bore witness that the prophets had spoken the truth; he also brought home to his listeners the folly of their own sin.

Moreover, he instructed his disciples to offer to God the first fruits of creation, not because God had any need, but so that they themselves should not be unproductive and ungrateful. This is why he took bread, a part of his creation, gave thanks and said: *This is my body.* In the same way he declared that the cup, an element of the same creation as ourselves, was his blood; he taught them that this was the new sacrifice of the new covenant. The Church has received this sacrifice from the apostles; throughout the world she offers to God, who feeds us, the first-fruits of his own gifts, under the new covenant. It was foretold by Malachi, one of the twelve prophets, in the words: *I take no pleasure in you, says the Lord Almighty, and no sacrifice will I accept from your hands. For, from the rising of the sun to its setting, the Gentiles glorify my name, and in every place incense and a spotless sacrifice are offered to my name; my name is great among the Gentiles, says the Lord Almighty*[Mal 1:10-11].

But what name is glorified among the Gentiles if not that of our Lord, through whom glory is given both to the Father and to man. And since this name belongs to his own Son, who became man by the Fathers' will, the Father calls this name his own. If a king were to paint a picture of his son, he could claim it as his own on two counts: because it is his son's picture, and because he himself made it. In the same way, the Father declares that the name of Jesus Christ, which is glorified in the Church throughout the world, is his own, because it is his Son's name and because he wrote it to save mankind.

And so, since the Son's name belongs to the Father and since the Church makes its offerings through Jesus Christ to almighty God, for these two reasons the prophet is right when he says: *In every place incense and a pure sacrifice are offered to my name*[Mal 1:11]. In the book of Revelation, John speaks of incense as *the prayer of the saints*[Rev 8:4].

Sunday of the Nineteenth Week in Ordinary Time

From a dialogue On Divine Providence by Saint Catherine of Siena, Virgin & Doctor

The bonds of love

My sweet Lord, look with mercy upon your people and especially upon the mystical body of your Church. Greater glory is given to your name for pardoning a multitude of your creatures than if I alone were pardoned for my great sins against your majesty. It would be no consolation for me to enjoy your life if your holy people stood in death. For I see that sin darkens the life of your bride the Church – my sin and the sins of others.

It is a special grace I ask for, this pardon for the creatures you have made in your image and likeness. When you created man, you were moved by love to make him in your own image. Surely only love could so dignify your creatures. But I know very well that man lost the dignity you gave him; he deserved to lose it, since he had committed sin.

Moved by love and wishing to reconcile the human race to yourself, you gave us your only-begotten Son. He became our mediator and our justice by taking on all our injustice and sin out of obedience to your will, eternal Father, just as you willed that he take on our human nature. What an immeasurably profound love! Your Son went down from the heights of his divinity to the depths of our humanity. Can anyone's heart remain closed and hardened after this?

We image your divinity, but you image our humanity in that union of the two which you have worked in a man. You have veiled the Godhead in a cloud, in the clay of our humanity. Only your love could so dignify the flesh of Adam. And so by reason of this immeasurable love I beg, with all the strength of my soul, that you freely extend your mercy to all your lowly creatures.

Monday of the Nineteenth Week in Ordinary Time

From a treatise On the Incarnation of the Lord by Theodoret of Cyr, Bishop

I will heal their wounds

Of his own free will Jesus ran to meet those sufferings that were foretold in the Scriptures concerning him. He had forewarned his disciples about them several times; he had rebuked Peter for being reluctant to accept the announcement of his passion, and he had made it clear that it was by means of his suffering that the world's salvation was to be accomplished. This was why he stepped forward and presented himself to those who came in search of him, saying: *I am the one you are looking for*[Jn 18:8]. For the same reason he made no reply when he was accused, and refused to hide when he could have done so; although in the past he had slipped away on more than one occasion when they had tried to apprehend him.

Jesus also wept over Jerusalem because by her unwillingness to believe she was bent on her own ruin, and upon the temple, once so renowned, he passed sentence of utter destruction. Patiently he put up with being struck in the face by a man who was doubly a slave, in body and in spirit. He allowed himself to be slapped, spat upon, insulted, tortured, scourged and finally crucified. He accepted two robbers as his companions in punishment, on his right and on his left. He endured being reckoned with murderers and criminals. He drank the vinegar and the bitter gall yielded by the unfaithful vineyard of Israel. He submitted to crowning with thorns instead of with vine twigs and grapes; he was ridiculed with the purple cloak, holes were dug in his hands and his feet, and at last he was carried to the grave.

All this he endured in working out our salvation. For since those who were enslaved to sin were liable to the penalties of sin, he himself, exempt from sin though he was and walking in the path of perfect righteousness, underwent the punishment of sinners. By his cross he blotted out the decree of the ancient curse: for, as Paul says: *Christ redeemed us from the curse of the law by becoming a curse for us; for it is written: "Cursed be everyone who hangs on a tree."*[Gal 3:13] And by his crown of thorns he put an end to that punishment meted out to Adam, who after his sin had heard the sentence: *Cursed is the ground because of you; thorns and thistles shall it bring forth for you*[Gen 3:17-18].

In tasting the gall Jesus took on himself the bitterness and toil of man's mortal, painful life. By drinking the vinegar he made his own the degradation men had suffered, and in the same act gave us the grace to better our condition. By the purple robe he signified his kingship, by the reed he hinted at the weakness and rottenness of the devil's power. By taking the slap in the face, and thus suffering the violence, corrections and blows that were due to us, he proclaimed our freedom.

His side was pierced as Adam's was; yet there came forth not a woman who, being beguiled, was to be the death-bearer, but a fountain of life that regenerates the world by its two streams: the one to renew us in the baptismal font and clothe us with the garment of immortality, the other to feed us, the reborn, at the table of God, just as babes are nourished with milk.

Tuesday of the Nineteenth Week in Ordinary Time

From a treatise On the Incarnation of the Lord by Saint Theodoret of Cyr, Bishop

By his wounds we are healed

Our Savior's passion is a healing remedy for us, as the prophet teaches when he cries out: *He bears our sins and suffers pain for us, and we esteemed him stricken, smitten by God and afflicted. But for our sins he was wounded, for our iniquities he was bruised; upon him fell the chastisement that brought us peace, and by his wounds we are healed. We had all gone astray like sheep*, and therefore he *was led like a lamb to the slaughter, and was dumb like a sheep before its shearer*[Isa 53:4-7].

When a shepherd sees that his sheep have scattered, he keeps one of them under his control and leads it to the pastures he chooses, and thus he draws the other sheep back to him by means of this one. And so it was when God the Word saw that the human race had gone astray: he took the *form of a slave* and united it to himself, and by means of it won over the whole race of men to him, enticing the sheep that were grazing in bad pastures and exposed to wolves, and leading them to the pastures of God.

This was the purpose for which our Savior assumed our nature, this was why Christ the Lord accepted the sufferings that brought us salvation, was sent to his death and was committed to the tomb. He broke the grip of the age-old tyranny and promised incorruptibility to those who were prisoners of corruption. For when he rebuilt that temple which had been destroyed and raised it up again, he thereby gave trustworthy and firm promises to those who had died and were awaiting his resurrection.

Jesus tells us: "Just as my human nature, which I took from you, has won its resurrection in virtue of the God-head that dwelt in it and with which it was united, just as this nature has shed decay and suffering and passed over to incorruptibility and immortality; so, in the same way, you too will be set free from the grievous slavery of death; you too will cast aside your corruptible nature and your sufferings and you will be clothed with impassibility."

To this end he imparted the gift of baptism to all mankind through his apostles. *Go*, he said, *make disciples of all nations, baptizing them in the name of the Father and of the Son and of the Holy Spirit*[Mt 28:19-20]. Baptism is a kind of symbol and type of the Lord's death, which is why Paul says: *If we have shared with God's Son in a death like his, we shall certainly share in his resurrection*[Rom 6:5].

Wednesday of the Nineteenth Week in Ordinary Time

From a discourse on the psalms by Saint Augustine, Bishop & Doctor

Come, let us go up to the mountain of the Lord

As we have heard, so also have we seen[1 Jn 1:3]. Truly blessed Church! You have both heard and seen. You have heard the promises, and you see their fulfillment; you have heard in prophecy, and you see their fulfillment; you have heard in prophecy, and you see in the Gospel. Yes, all that has now been brought to completion was prophesied in times past. Raise up your eyes, then, and cast your gaze around the world. See God's people, your heritage, spread to the ends of the earth. See the Scripture now fulfilled: *All the kings of the earth will adore him, all the nations will serve him*[Ps 71:11]. See fulfilled what has been said: *Be exalted above the heavens, O God, and your glory above all the earth*[Ps 56:11-12]. See him whose hands and feet were pierced by nails, whose bones were numbered as they hung upon the wood, and for whose garments they cast lots. See him reigning, whom they saw hanging upon the cross; see him enthroned in heaven, whom they despised when he walked on the earth. See the word fulfilled: *All the ends of the earth shall turn to the Lord, and all nations shall worship in his sight*[Ps 21:28]. See all this and shout with joy: *As we have heard, so also have we seen*[1 Jn 1:3].

Deservedly then the Church is itself called from among the Gentiles: *Hear, O daughter, and see, and forget your people and your father's house*[Ps 44:11]. Hear and see. First you hear what you do not see; later you will see what you have heard. For he says: *A people I did not know served me, as soon as they heard me they obeyed*[Ps 17:45]. If they *obeyed as soon as they heard,* it follows that they did not see. What then of the passage: *Those who were not told of him will see, and they who have not heard will understand*[Isa 52:15; Rom 15:21]? Those to whom the prophets were not sent were the first to hear and understand the prophets, whereas those who at first did not hear them were astonished when they heard them later. Those to whom the prophets were sent remained behind, possessing the books of Scripture but not understanding the truth, possessing the tables of the law but not keeping their inheritance. *As we have heard, so also have we seen*[1 Jn 1:3] also applies to us.

In the city of the Lord of hosts, in the city of our God[Ps 47:9], that is where we have heard; there too we have seen. *God has made this city firm for ever*[Heb 11:10]. No one should say boastfully: *See, here is Christ; see, he is there*[Mt 24:23-28]. Such a claim only leads to factions. But God has promised unity. The kings were gathered together in unity, not scattered through schisms. Yet perhaps that city which had gained possession of the world will at some time be overthrown? No, *God has made it firm for ever* [Heb 11:10]. If God has made its foundation firm for ever, how can you fear that this foundation may collapse?

Thursday of the Nineteenth Week in Ordinary Time

From a treatise on Christian Perfection by St Gregory of Nyssa, Bishop

We possess Christ, our peace, our light

He is our peace, for he has made both one[Eph 2:14]. Since we think of Christ as our peace, we may call ourselves true Christians only if our lives express Christ by our own peace. As the Apostle says: *He has put enmity to death*[Eph 2:16]. We must never allow it to be rekindled in us in any way but must declare that it is absolutely dead. Gloriously has God slain enmity, in order to save us; may we never risk the life of our souls by being resentful or by bearing grudges. We must not awaken that enmity or call it back to life by our wickedness, for it is better left dead.

No, since we possess Christ who is peace, we must put an end to this enmity and live as we believe he lived. He broke down the separating wall, uniting what was divided, bringing about peace by reconciling in his single person those who disagreed. In the same way, we must be reconciled not only with those who attack us from outside, but also with those who stir up dissension within; flesh then will no longer be opposed to the spirit, nor the spirit to the flesh. Once we subject the wisdom of the flesh to God's law, we shall be re-created as one single man at peace. Then, having become one instead of two, we shall have peace within ourselves.

Now peace is defined as harmony among those who are divided. When, therefore, we end that civil war within our nature and cultivate peace within ourselves, we become peace. By this peace we demonstrate that the name of Christ, which we bear, is authentic and appropriate.

When we consider that Christ is the true light, having nothing in common with deceit, we learn that our own life also must shine with the rays of that true light. Now these rays of the Sun of Justice are the virtues which pour out to enlighten us so that *we may put away the works of darkness and walk honorably as in broad daylight*[Rom 13:12-14]. When we reject the deeds of darkness and do everything in the light of day, we become light and, as light should, we give light to others by our actions.

If we truly think of Christ as our source of holiness, we shall refrain from anything wicked or impure in thought or act and thus show ourselves to be worthy bearers of his name. For the quality of holiness is shown not by what we say but by what we do in life.

Friday of the Nineteenth Week in Ordinary Time

From a sermon on Baptism by Saint Pacian, Bishop

We follow the new way through the Spirit of Christ

The sin of Adam had come into all men. *Through one man,* the Apostle says, *sin entered and through sin, death. Thus it has come to all men*[Rom 5:12-21]. Therefore, the justice of Christ must enter into men; and as the old Adam ruined his descendants through sin, so Christ must bring new life to all men through justice. The Apostle stresses this theme when he says: *As through the disobedience of one man, many were made sinners, so too, through the obedience of one man, many were made just. And, as sin brought death to the offender, so grace through justice brings birth to life eternal*[Rom 5:19-21].

Someone may say to me: "But the sin of Adam is justifiably transmitted to his posterity. Since they were descended from him, and since we are not descended from Christ, how can we be saved because of him?" Do not think in physical terms about descent, then you will see how Christ is our father. In these times of salvation, Christ received body and soul from Mary. He came to save this soul, not to leave it in hell. He united it with his spirit and made it his own. And this is the marriage of the Lord, the union of two in one flesh, so that according to that great mystery, two become one flesh, Christ and his Church.

From this marriage the Christian people are born, by the descent of the spirit of the Lord. The essential nature of the soul, engendered by heavenly seed, grows in the womb of our mother, the Church, and at birth is given life by Christ. Therefore, the Apostle says: *The first Adam was a living soul, the new Adam a life-giving spirit*[1 Cor 15:45]. Thus Christ continues in the Church through his priests, as the same Apostle says: *In Christ, I have begotten you*[1 Cor 4:15]. And so, the seed of Christ, that is, the Spirit of God, brings forth the new man, nourished in the womb of his mother, welcomed at his birth at the font through the hands of the priests, while faith presides over the ceremony.

Christ must, therefore, be received in order to beget, for the apostle John says: *To all who received him he gave the power to become sons of God*[Jn 1:12]. But these things cannot be accomplished except by the sacrament of the font, the chrism and the priest. For sin is washed away by the waters of the font; the Holy Spirit is poured forth in the chrism; and we obtain both of these gifts through the hands and the mouth of the priest. Thus the whole man is reborn and renewed in Christ. *Just as Christ rose from the dead, so we shall walk in the newness of life*[Rom 6:4], that is, we put away the errors of our old lives and we follow the new way through the Spirit in Christ.

Saturday of the Nineteenth Week in Ordinary Time

From a sermon on Baptism by Saint Pacian, Bishop

Who, O God, is like you? You take away guilt

As we have borne the image of the earthly man, so we shall bear the image of him who is from heaven; since the first man who came from the earth, is earthly, but the second man who came from heaven, is heavenly[1 Cor 15:45-49]. And so, dearly beloved, we shall not die anymore. Even if we fall asleep in this body, we shall live in Christ, as he said: *Whoever believes in me, even if he die, shall live*[Jn 11:25].

As the Lord is our witness, we are certain that Abraham, Isaac, Jacob and all the saints of God are alive. For concerning them the Lord says: *They are all alive. For God is a God of the living, and not of the dead*[Lk 20:38]. And the Apostle says of himself: *For me, to live is Christ and to die is gain. I would rather die and be with Christ*[Phil 1:21]. And again: *But while we are still in this body we are away from God, for we are guided by faith, and not by appearance*[2 Cor 5:6-8]. This is what we believe, dearest brothers. For the rest: *If we place our hope in this world, we are the most miserable of men*[1 Cor 15:19-26]. Life in this world, whether it be that of beasts, wild animals or birds, as you yourselves see, is either similar to ours or more tedious. What is peculiar to man, and what Christ gives through his Spirit, is eternal life, but only if we sin no more. Thus death is acquired by sin but avoided by right living; life is lost through sin and preserved through good living. *The wages of sin is death; the gift of God is eternal life through Jesus Christ our Lord*[Rom 6:23].

It is Christ who redeemed us, as the Apostle says: *Forgiving us all our sins and destroying what was recorded against us by disobedience, he bore our burden in public view, fixed it to the cross, stripped his own flesh, exposed the powers of this world and freely conquered them in himself*[Col 2:13-14]. He released our shackles and destroyed our chains, as David had said: *The Lord lifts up what has been torn down*[Ps 144:14]*; the Lord frees those in shackles; the Lord gives light to the blind*[Lk 4:18]. And again: *You have destroyed my chains; I will offer sacrifice to you with praise*[Ps 115:16-17]. And so when we come to the sign of the Lord in the sacrament of baptism we are freed of these chains and liberated by the blood of Christ and by his name.

Therefore, beloved, we are washed clean but once; we are freed only once; we are received into the immortal kingdom once and for all. Once and for all *are they happy whose sins are forgiven and whose stains are blotted out*[Ps 31:1]. Hold fast to what you have received; preserve it joyfully; sin no more. Keep yourselves as children cleansed by that sacrament and made spotless for the day of the Lord.

Sunday of the Twentieth Week in Ordinary Time

From a homily on Matthew by Saint John Chrysostom, Bishop & Doctor

Salt of the earth and light of the world

You are the salt of the earth[Mt 5:13-16]. It is not for your own sake, he says, but for the world's sake that the word is entrusted to you. I am not sending you into two cities only or ten or twenty, not to a single nation, as I sent the prophets of old, but across land and sea, to the whole world. And that world is in a miserable state. For when he says: *You are the salt of the earth* [Mt 5:13-16], he is indicating that all mankind had lost its savor and had been corrupted by sin. Therefore, he requires of these men those virtues which are especially useful and even necessary if they are to bear the burdens of many. For the man who is kindly, modest, merciful and just will not keep his good works to himself but will see to it that these admirable fountains send out their streams for the good of others. Again, the man who is clean of heart, a peacemaker and ardent for truth will order his life so as to contribute to the common good.

Do not think, he says, that you are destined for easy struggles or unimportant tasks. *You are the salt of the earth* [Mt 5:13-16]. What do these words imply? Did the disciples restore what had already turned rotten? Not at all. Salt cannot help what is already corrupted. That is not what they did. But what had first been renewed and freed from corruption and then turned over to them, they salted and preserved in the newness the Lord had bestowed. It took the power of Christ to free men from the corruption caused by sin; it was the task of the apostles through strenuous labor to keep that corruption from returning.

Have you noticed how, bit by bit, Christ shows them to be superior to the prophets? He says they are to be teachers not simply for Palestine but for the whole world. Do not be surprised, then, he says, that I address you apart from the others and involve you in such a dangerous enterprise. Consider the numerous and extensive cities, peoples and nations I will be sending you to govern. For this reason I would have you make others prudent, as well as being prudent yourselves. For unless you can do that, you will not be able to sustain even yourselves.

If others lose their savor, then your ministry will help them regain it. But if you yourselves suffer that loss, you will drag others down with you. Therefore, the greater the undertakings put into your hands, the more zealous you must be. For this reason he says: *But if the salt becomes tasteless, how can its flavor be restored? It is good for nothing now, but to be thrown out and trampled by men's feet* [Mt 5:13-16].

When they hear the words: *When they curse you and persecute you and accuse you of every evil*[Mt 5:11], they may be afraid to come forward. Therefore he says; "Unless you are prepared for that sort of thing, it is in vain that I have chosen you. Curses shall necessarily be your lot but they shall not harm you and will simply be a testimony to your constancy. If through fear, however, you fail to show the forcefulness your mission demands, your lot will be much worse, for all will speak evil of you and despise you. That is what being trampled by men's feet means."

Then he passes on to a more exalted comparison: *You are the light of the world*[Mt 5:14-16]. Once again, "of the world": not of one nation or twenty cities, but of the whole world. The light he means is an intelligible light, far superior to the rays of the sun we see, just as the salt is a spiritual salt. First salt, then light, so that you may learn how profitable sharp words may be and how useful serious doctrine. Such teaching holds in check and prevents dissipation; it leads to virtue and sharpens the mind's eye. *A city set on a hill cannot be hidden; nor do men light a lamp and put it under a basket*[Mt 5:14-16]. Here again he is urging them to a careful manner of life and teaching them to be watchful, for they live under the eyes of all and have the whole world for the arena of their struggles.

Monday of the Twentieth Week in Ordinary Time

From the Moral Reflections on Job by Saint Gregory the Great, Pope & Doctor

Struggles without, fears within

Holy men beset by tribulation must endure the assaults of those who use violence and verbal attacks. The former they resist with the shield of patience, but against the latter they launch the sharp arrows of true doctrine. In both types of fighting they win the day through the wonderful arts that virtue bestows, for with wisdom they teach the wayward while showing a courageous contempt for outward hostility; the straying sheep they set on the right path by their teaching; the attacker they suffer and overcome. For they have nothing but patient scorn for the enemy who moves against them, but they sympathize with their weaker fellows and bring them back to the safe way, opposing the former lest they lead others astray and fearing for the latter lest they completely lose sight of the truly upright life.

Let us see how a soldier in God's camp fights against both types of enemy. Paul says: *Struggles without, fears within*[2 Cor 11:23-28]. He lists the attacks he must endure from without: *Dangers from floods, dangers from robbers, dangers from my own people, dangers from the pagans, dangers in the city, dangers in the desert, dangers on the seas, dangers from false brothers*. He also tells us what weapons he uses against his enemies in this war: *Toil and hardship, many sleepless nights, hunger and thirst, frequent fasts, cold and nakedness.*

When beset by so many struggles, he guards the camp, he tells us, with great watchfulness. Immediately he adds: *Besides these outward difficulties there is that daily weight upon me: my anxiety for all the churches*. Thus he himself fights courageously and devotes himself compassionately to protecting his neighbors. He tells us of the evils he endures but also of the blessings he brings to others.

Let us reflect, then, on how difficult it is simultaneously to endure attacks from without and to protect the weak from within. He endures the attacks without, inasmuch as he suffers flogging and chains; inwardly he experiences fear, since he is afraid that his sufferings may be a stumbling-block not to himself but to his disciples. For this reason he writes to them: *Let no one be shaken by these trials, for you know that they are our lot*[1 Thess 3:3-4]. Amid his own sufferings it was the fall of others he feared, lest the disciples, seeing him flogged for the faith, might refuse to acknowledge their own faith.

What an immensely loving heart! He thinks nothing of what he himself suffers and is concerned only that the disciples may be led astray interiorly. He scorns his own bodily wounds and brings healing to the inner wounds of others. It is characteristic of holy men that their own painful trials do not make them lose their concern for the well-being of others. They are grieved by the adversity they must endure, yet they look out for others and teach them needed lessons; they are like gifted physicians who are themselves stricken and lie ill. They suffer wounds themselves but bring others the medicine that restores health.

Tuesday of the Twentieth Week in Ordinary Time

From a homily in praise of the Virgin Mother by Saint Bernard, Abbot & Doctor

Prepared by the Most High, prefigured by the patriarchs

It was fitting that the Virgin should give birth only to God; and it was also fitting that God should be born only of the Virgin. Accordingly, the Creator of mankind, in order that he might become a man by being born of a human being, had to seek out from among all mankind and designate as his mother a woman he knew would be worthy of him and pleasing to him. And so he chose a sinless virgin, that he might be born sinless and free of all stain. He chose a humble virgin, from whom he might come forth meek and humble of heart, to display a most necessary and salutary model of these virtues for all mankind. Thus he allowed a virgin to conceive, in whom he had earlier inspired a vow of virginity, and required of her the merit of humility.

Otherwisc how could the angel afterward pronounce her full of grace, if she had the slightest good quality which did not come from grace? Thus she, who was to conceive and bring forth the holy of holies, must be sanctified physically and so she received the gift of virginity; that she might be sanctified spiritually, she received the gift of humility.

The Virgin then, adorned like a queen with the jewels of virtue, shone with the glory of body and soul; and seen on high as radiantly beautiful, she so attracted the inhabitants of heaven that she moved the heart of the King with desire for her and brought down from above the heavenly message. Scripture says: *The angel was sent to a virgin*[Lk 1:26-27]. For she was truly virgin in body, virgin in mind, a virgin by her special calling, sanctified, as the Apostle reminds us, in both mind and body. This came about by no unforeseen or accidental occurrence; she was chosen from eternity, foreknown and prepared by the Most High for himself, guarded by the angels, prefigured by the patriarchs, and promised by the prophets.

Wednesday of the Twentieth Week in Ordinary Time

From a sermon by Saint Augustine, Bishop & Doctor

He who perseveres to the end will be saved

Whenever we suffer some affliction, we should regard it both as a punishment and as a correction. Our holy Scriptures themselves do not promise us peace, security and rest. On the contrary, the Gospel makes no secret of the troubles and temptations that await us, but it also says that *he who perseveres to the end will be saved*[Mt 24:13]. What good has there ever been in this life since the time when the first man received the just sentence of death and the curse from which Christ our Lord has delivered us?

So we must not grumble, my brothers, for as the Apostle says: *Some of them murmured and were destroyed by serpents!*[1 Cor 10:9-11]. Is there any affliction now endured by mankind that was not endured by our fathers before us? What sufferings of ours even bear comparison with what we know of their sufferings? And yet you hear people complaining about this present day and age because things were so much better in former times. I wonder what would happen if they could be taken back to the days of their ancestors - would we not still hear them complaining? You may think past ages were good, but it is only because you are not living in them.

It amazes me that you who have now been freed from the curse, who have believed in the Son of God, who have been instructed in the holy Scriptures - that *you* can think the days of Adam were good. And your ancestors bore the curse of Adam, of that Adam to whom the words were addressed: *With sweat on your brow you shall eat your bread; you shall till the earth from which you were taken, and it will yield you thorns and thistles*[Gen 3:19]. This is what he deserved and what he had to suffer; this is the punishment meted out to him by the just judgment of God. How then can you think that the past ages were better than your own? From the time of that first Adam to the time of his descendants today, man's lot has been labor and sweat, thorns and thistles. Have we forgotten the flood and the calamitous times of famine and war whose history has been recorded precisely in order to keep us from complaining to God on account of our own times? Just think what those past ages were like! Is there one of us who does not shudder to hear or read of them? Far from justifying complaints about our own time, they teach us how much we have to be thankful for.

Thursday of the Twentieth Week in Ordinary Time

From a treatise On the Hail Mary by Saint Baldwin of Canterbury, Bishop

A flower rises from the root of Jesse

Every day we devoutly greet the most Blessed Virgin Mary with the angel's greeting and we usually add: *Blessed is the fruit of your womb*[Lk 1:41-45]. After she was greeted by the Virgin, Elizabeth added this phrase as if she were echoing the salutation of the angel: *Blessed are you among women and blessed is the fruit of your womb.* This is the fruit of which Isaiah spoke: *On that day the shoot of the Lord shall be splendid and radiant - the sublime fruit of earth*[Isa 4:2]. What is this fruit but the holy one of Israel, the seed of Abraham, the shoot of the Lord, the flower arising from the root of Jesse, the fruit of life, whom we have shared?

Blessed surely in seed and blessed in the shoot, blessed in the flower, blessed in the gift, finally blessed in thanksgiving and praise, Christ, the seed of Abraham, was brought forth from the seed of David into the flesh.

He alone among men is found perfected in every good quality, for the Spirit was given to him without measure so that he alone could fulfill all justice. For his justice is sufficient for all nations, according to the Scriptures. *As the earth brings forth its buds, and as the garden germinates its own seed, so the Lord God shall bring forth justice and praise before all the nations*[Isa 61:11]. For this is the shoot of justice, which the flower of glory adorns with its blessings when it has grown. But how great is this glory? How can anyone think of anything more glorious, or rather, how can anyone conceive of this at all? For the flower rises from the root of Jesse. You ask: "How far?" Surely it rises even to the highest place, because *Jesus Christ is in the glory of God the Father*[Phil 2:11]. His magnificence is elevated abovc the heavens so that he, the issue of the Lord, is splendid and glorious, the sublime fruit of earth.

But what is our benefit from this fruit? What other than the fruit of blessing from the blessed fruit? From this seed, this shoot, this flower, surely the fruit of blessing comes forth. It has come even to us; first as a seed it is planted through the grace of pardon, then germinated with the increase of perfection, and finally it flowers in the hope or the attainment of glory. For the fruit was blessed by God, and in God, so that God may be glorified through it. For us, too, the fruit was blessed, so that blessed by God we may be glorified in him through the promise spoken to Abraham. God made the fruit a blessing for all nations.

Friday of the Twentieth Week in Ordinary Time

From the Explanations of the Psalms by Saint Ambrose, Bishop & Doctor

The man Christ Jesus, the one mediator between God and men

Brother cannot redeem brother, but a man will redeem man. No one can give to God the ransom for himself nor the price of his soul's redemption[Ps 48:8-10]. Christ is saying: *What have I to fear in the day of evil*[Ps 48:6]? What can do me harm if I do not need a redeemer but am myself the redeemer of all mankind? Shall I free others, yet tremble for myself? See, I shall make all things new, so as to surpass even the love and devotion of brothers. Where a brother, born of the womb, cannot redeem, suffering as he does from the infirmity of a common nature, yet a man will redeem, that man of whom it is written: The Lord *will send them a man who will save them*[Isa 19:20]; the man who said of himself: *You seek to kill me, a man who has spoken the truth to you*[Jn 8:40]

He is a man, yet who will recognize him? Why will no one recognize him? Because, as there is one God, so there is *one mediator between God and men, the man Christ Jesus*[1 Tim 2:5-6]. He alone will redeem man, showing love greater even than that of brothers. He poured out his blood for strangers, as no one is able to do for a brother. He did not spare his own body in redeeming us from sin, but *gave himself as the redemption of all*[1 Tim 2:5-6], and Paul the apostle is a true witness to him: *I speak the truth and do not lie*[Rom 9:11].

But why will this man be the only redeemer? Because no one can equal him in the love he showed in laying down his life for his own poor servants. Nor can anyone equal him in sinlessness, for all men are ruled by sin, and all are victims of the fall of the first Adam. He alone is chosen to redeem, for he alone cannot be subject to that age-old sin. So let us understand by "the man" the one who took upon himself the condition of man in order to crucify in his own flesh the sin of all, and to cancel by his own blood the debt owed by all: the Lord Jesus.

You may ask: How can we say that a brother cannot redeem when the man we are discussing has said: *I shall declare your name to my brothers*[Heb 2:12]? But it was not as our brother but as the man Christ Jesus, in whom God dwelt, that he forgave our sins. For it is written that *God was in Christ, reconciling the world to himself*[2 Cor 5:19]. God was in the man Christ Jesus, of whom alone it was said: *The Word became flesh and dwelt among us*[Jn 1:14]. It was not, therefore, as a brother but as the Lord that he dwelt among us in the flesh.

Saturday of the Twentieth Week in Ordinary Time

From The Explanation of the Psalms by Saint Ambrose, Bishop & Doctor

Christ has reconciled the world to God by his own blood

In reconciling the world to God, Christ stood in no need of reconciliation for himself. What sin of his was there to atone for, sinless as he was? When he was asked for the temple-tax, a sin-offering imposed by the law, he said to Peter: *Simon, from whom do the kings of the earth receive tribute or tax? From their own sons or from strangers? Peter replied: From strangers. The Lord said to him: Then the sons are free. But so as not to give scandal to them, cast a hook and take the first fish that comes; open its mouth, and you will find a shekel. Take it, and give it to them for me and for you*[Mt 17:24-27].

Christ shows that he does not need to atone for sin on his own behalf: he is no slave of sin but, as Son of God, is free from all sin. The Son sets free, a slave remains in his sin. Christ is therefore free of all sin, and does not pay the price of his own redemption. His blood could pay the ransom for all the sins of the whole world. The one who has no debt to pay for himself is the right person to set others free.

It is not only that Christ has no ransom to pay or atonement to make for his own sins; if we apply his words to every individual man they can be taken to mean that individuals do not need to make atonement for themselves, for Christ is the atonement for all, the redemption for all.

Is any man's blood fit to redeem him, seeing that it was Christ who shed his blood for the redemption of all? Is anyone's blood comparable to Christ's? Is anyone great enough to make atonement for himself over and above the atonement which Christ has offered in himself, Christ who alone has reconciled the world to God by his blood? What greater victim, what more excellent sacrifice, what better advocate can there be than he who because the propitiation for the sins of all, and gave his life for us as our redemption?

We do not need, then, to look for an atonement or redemption made by each individual, because the price paid for all is the blood of Christ, that blood by which the Lord Jesus has redeemed us, he who alone has reconciled us to the Father. He has labored even to the end, shouldering our burdens himself. *Come to me,* he says, *all you that labor, and I will refresh you*[Mt 11:28].

Sunday of the Twenty-First Week in Ordinary Time

From the pastoral constitution on the Church in the modern world of the Second Vatican Council

The foreshadowing of the new age

We do not know the time when earth and humanity will reach their completion, nor do we know the way in which the universe will be transformed. The world as we see it, disfigured by sin, is passing away. But we are assured that God is preparing a new dwelling place and a new earth. In this new earth righteousness is to make its home, and happiness will satisfy, and more than satisfy, all the yearnings for peace that arise in human hearts. On that day, when death is conquered, the sons of God will be raised up in Christ; what was sown as something weak and perishable will be clothed in incorruption. Love and the fruits of love will remain, and the whole of creation, made by God for man, will be set free from the frustration that enslaves it.

We are warned indeed that a man gains nothing if he wins the whole world at the cost of himself. Yet our hope in a new earth should not weaken, but rather stimulate our concern for developing this earth, for on it there is growing up the body of a new human family, a body even now able to provide some foreshadowing of the new age. Hence, though earthly progress is to be carefully distinguished from the growth of Christ's kingdom, yet in so far as it can help toward the better ordering of human society it is of great importance to the kingdom of God.

The blessings of human dignity, brotherly communion and freedom – all the good fruits on earth of man's co-operation with nature in the Spirit of the Lord and according to his command – will be found again in the world to come, but purified of all stain, resplendent and transfigured, when Christ hands over to the Father an eternal and universal kingdom: "a kingdom of truth and life, a kingdom of holiness and grace, a kingdom of justice, love and peace." On this earth the kingdom is already present in sign; when the Lord comes it will reach its completion.

Monday of the Twenty-First Week in Ordinary Time

From an exposition on John by Saint Thomas Aquinas, Priest & Doctor

The remnant of Israel shall be led to pasture. They shall lie down to rest

I am the Good Shepherd[Jn 10:11-18]. Surely it is fitting that Christ should be a shepherd, for just as a flock is guided and fed by a shepherd so the faithful are fed by Christ with spiritual food and with his own body and blood. The Apostle said: *You were once like sheep without a shepherd, but now you have returned to the guardian and ruler of your souls*[1 Pet 2:25]. The prophet has said: *As a shepherd he pastures his flock*[Isa 40:11-16].

Christ said that the shepherd enters through the gate and that he is himself the gate as well as the shepherd. Then it is necessary that he enter through himself. By so doing, he reveals himself, and through himself he knows the Father. But we enter through him because through him we find happiness.

Take heed: no one else is the gate but Christ. Others reflect his light, but no one else is the true light. John the Baptist *was not the light, but he bore witness to the light*[Jn 1:8]. It is said of Christ, however: *He was the true light that enlightens every man*[Jn 1:9]. For this reason no one says that he is the gate; this title is Christ's own. However, he has made others shepherds and given that office to his members; for Peter was a shepherd, and so were the other apostles and all good bishops after them. Scripture says: *I shall give you shepherds according to my own heart*[Jer 3:15]. Although the bishops of the Church, who are her sons, are all shepherds, nevertheless Christ refers only to one person in saying: *I am the Good Shepherd,* because he wants to emphasize the virtue of charity. Thus, no one can be a good shepherd unless he is one with Christ in charity. Through this we become members of the true shepherd.

The duty of a good shepherd is charity; therefore Christ said: *The good shepherd gives his life for his sheep*[Jn 10-11-18]. Know the difference between a good and a bad shepherd: the good shepherd cares for the welfare of his flock, but the bad shepherd cares only for his own welfare.

The Good Shepherd doe not demand that shepherds lay down their lives for a real flock of sheep. But every spiritual shepherd must endure the loss of his bodily life for the salvation of the flock, since the spiritual good of the flock is more important than the bodily life of the shepherd, when danger threatens the salvation of the flock. This is why the Lord says: *The good shepherd lays down his life,* that is, his physical life, *for his sheep*[Jn 10-11-18]; this he does because of his authority and love. Both, in fact, are required: that they should be ruled by him, and that he should love them. The first without the second is not enough.

Christ stands out for us as the example of this teaching: *If Christ laid down his life for us, so we also ought to lay down our lives for our brothers*[1 Jn 3:16].

Tuesday of the Twenty-First Week in Ordinary Time

From a homily by Saint John Chrysostom, Bishop & Doctor

Five paths of repentance

Would you like me to list also the paths of repentance? They are numerous and quite varied, and all lead to heaven.

A first path of repentance is the condemnation of your own sins: *Be the first to admit your sins and you will be justified*[1 Jn 1:9]. For this reason, too, the prophet wrote: *I said: I will accuse myself of my sins to the Lord, and you forgave the wickedness of my heart*[Ps 31:5]. Therefore, you too should condemn your own sins; that will be enough reason for the Lord to forgive you, for a man who condemns his own sins is slower to commit them again. Rouse your conscience to accuse you within your own house, lest it become your accuser before the judgment seat of the Lord.

That, then, is one very good path of repentance. Another and no less valuable one is to put out of our minds the harm done us by our enemies, in order to master our anger, and to forgive our fellow servants' sins against us. Then our own sins against the Lord will be forgiven us. Thus you have another way to atone for sin: *For if you forgive your debtors, your heavenly Father will forgive you*[Mt 6;12-15].

Do you want to know of a third path? It consists of prayer that is fervent, careful and comes from the heart.

If you want to hear of a fourth, I will mention almsgiving, whose power is great and far-reaching.

If, moreover, a man lives a modest, humble life, that, no less than the other things I have mentioned, takes sin away. Proof of this is the tax-collector who had no good deeds to mention, but offered his humility instead and was relieved of a heavy burden of sins.

Thus I have shown you five paths of repentance: condemnation of your own sins, forgiveness of our neighbor's sins against us, prayer, almsgiving and humility.

Do not be idle, then, but walk daily in all these paths; they are easy, and you cannot plead your poverty. For, though you live out your life amid great need, you can always set aside your wrath, be humble, pray diligently and condemn your own sins; poverty is no hindrance. Poverty is not an obstacle to our carrying out the Lord's bidding, even when it comes to that path of repentance which involves giving money (almsgiving, I mean). The widow proved that when she put her two mites into the box!

Now that we have learned how to heal these wounds of ours, let us apply the cures. Then, when we have regained genuine health, we can approach the holy table with confidence, go gloriously to meet Christ, the king of glory, and attain the eternal blessings through the grace, mercy and kindness of Jesus Christ, our Lord.

Wednesday of the Twenty-First Week in Ordinary Time

From an instruction by Saint Columban, Abbot

Whoever thirsts, let him come to me and drink his fill

My dear brethren, listen to my words. You are going to hear something that must be said. You quench your soul's thirst with drafts of the divine fountain. I now wish to speak of this. Revive yourself, but do not extinguish your thirst. Drink, I say, but do not entirely quench your thirst, for the fountain of life, the fountain of love calls us to him and says: *Whoever thirsts, let him come to me and drink*[Jn 7:37].

Understand well what you drink. Jeremiah would tell us; the fountain of life would himself tell us; *For they abandoned me, the fountain of living water, says the Lord*[Jer 2:12]. The Lord himself, our God Jesus Christ, is the fountain of life, and accordingly he invites us to himself as to a fountain, that we may drink. Whoever loves him, drinks him; he drinks who is filled with the Word of God, he drinks who loves him fully and really desires him. He drinks who is on fire with the love of wisdom.

Consider the source of the fountain; bread comes down to us from the same place, since the same one is the bread and the fountain, the only-begotten Son, our God, Christ the Lord, for whom we should always hunger. We may even eat him out of love for him, and devour him out of desire, longing for him eagerly. Let us drink from him, as from a fountain, with an abundance of love. May we drink him with the fullness of desire, and may we take pleasure in his sweetness and savor.

For the Lord is sweet and agreeable; rightly then let us eat and drink of him yet remain ever hungry and thirsty, since he is our food and drink, but can never be wholly eaten and consumed. Though he may be eaten, he is never consumed; one can drink of him and he is not diminished because our bread is eternal and our fountain is sweet and everlasting. Hence the prophet says: *You who thirst, go to the fountain*[Isa 55:1]. He is the fountain for those who are thirsty but are never fully satisfied. Therefore he calls to himself the hungry whom he raised to a blessed condition elsewhere. They were never satisfied in drinking; the more they drank, the greater their thirst.

It is right, brothers, that we must always long for, seek and love the Word of God on high, the fountain of wisdom. According to the Apostle's words *all the hidden treasures of wisdom and knowledge are in him*[Col 2:3], and he calls the thirsty to drink.

If you thirst, drink of the fountain of life; if you are hungry, eat the bread of life. Blessed are they who hunger for this bread and thirst for this fountain, for in so doing they will desire ever more to eat and drink. For what they eat and drink is exceedingly sweet and their thirst and appetite for more is never satisfied. Though it is ever tasted it is ever more desired. Hence the prophet-king says: *Taste and see how sweet, how agreeable is the Lord*[Ps 33:9].

Thursday of the Twenty-First Week in Ordinary Time

From an instruction by Saint Columban, Abbot

You, O God, are everything to us

Brethren, let us follow that vocation by which we are called from life to the fountain of life. He is the fountain, not only of living water, but of eternal life. He is the fountain of light and spiritual illumination; for from him come all these things: wisdom, life and eternal light. The author of life is the fountain of life; the creator of light is the fountain of spiritual illumination. Therefore, let us seek the fountain of light and life and the living water by despising what we see, by leaving the world and by dwelling in the highest heavens. Let us seek these things, and like rational and shrewd fish may we drink the living water which *wells up to eternal life*[Jn 4:14].

Merciful God, good Lord, I wish that you would unite me to that fountain, that there I may drink of the living spring of the water of life with those others who thirst after you. There in that heavenly region may I ever dwell, delighted with abundant sweetness, and say: "How sweet is the fountain of living water which never fails, the water welling up to eternal life."

O God, you are yourself that fountain ever and again to be desired, ever and again to be consumed. Lord Christ, always give us this water to be for us the *source of the living water which wells up to eternal life*[Jn 4:14]. I ask you for your great benefits. Who does not know it? You, King of glory, know how to give great gifts, and you have promised them; there is nothing greater than you, and you bestowed yourself upon us; you gave yourself for us.

Therefore, we ask that we may know what we love, since we ask nothing other than that you give us yourself. For you are our all: our life, our light, our salvation, our food and our drink, our God. Inspire our hearts, I ask you, Jesus, with that breath of your Spirit; wound our souls with your love, so that the soul of each and every one of us may say in truth: *Show me my soul's desire,* for I am wounded by your love.

These are the wounds I wish for, Lord. Blessed is the soul so wounded by love. Such a soul seeks the fountain of eternal life and drinks from it, although it continues to thirst and its thirst grows ever greater even as it drinks. Therefore, the more the soul loves, the more it desires to love, and the greater its suffering, the greater its healing. In this same way may our God and Lord Jesus Christ, the good and saving physician, wound the depths of our souls with a healing wound - the same Jesus Christ who reigns in unity with the Father and the Holy Spirit, for ever and ever. Amen.

Friday of the Twenty-First Week in Ordinary Time

From a commentary on Joel by Saint Jerome, Priest & Doctor

Return to me

Return to me with all your heart and show a spirit of repentance *with fasting, weeping and mourning*[Joel 2:12]; so that while you fast now, later you may be satisfied, while you weep now, later you may laugh, while you mourn now, you may some day enjoy consolation. It is customary for those in sorrow or adversity to tear their garments. The gospel records that the high priest did this to exaggerate the charge against our Lord and Savior; and we read that Paul and Barnabas did so when they heard words of blasphemy. I bid you not to tear your garments but rather to *rend your hearts*[Joel 2:13] which are laden with sin. Like wine skins, unless they have been cut open, they will burst of their own accord. After you have done this, return to the Lord your God, from whom you had been alienated by your sins. Do not despair of his mercy, no matter how great your sins, for great mercy will take away great sins.

For the Lord is *gracious and merciful*[Joel 2:13] and prefers the conversion of a sinner rather than his death. Patient and generous in his mercy, he does not give in to human impatience but is willing to wait a long time for our repentance. So extraordinary is the Lord's mercy in the face of evil, that if we do penance for our sins, he regrets his own threat and does not carry out against us the sanctions he had threatened. So by the changing of our attitude, he himself is changed. But in this passage we should interpret "evil" to mean, not the opposite of virtue, but affliction, as we read in another place: *Sufficient for the day are its own evils*[Mt 6:34]. And, again: *If there is evil in the city, God did not create it*.

In like manner, given all that we have said above - that God is kind and merciful, patient, generous with his forgiveness, and extraordinary in his mercy toward evil - lest the magnitude of his clemency make us lax and negligent, he adds this word through his prophet: *Who knows whether he will not turn and repent and leave behind him a blessing*[Joel 2:14]? In other words, he says: "I exhort you to repentance, because it is my duty, and I know that God is inexhaustibly merciful, as David says: *Have mercy on me, God, according to your great mercy, and in the depths of your compassion, blot out all my iniquities*[Ps 50:3]. But since we cannot know the depth of the riches and of the wisdom and knowledge of God, I will temper my statement, expressing a wish rather than taking anything for granted, and I will say: *Who knows whether he will not turn and repent*[Joel 2:14]?" Since he says, *Who*, it must be understood that it is impossible or difficult to know for sure.

To these words the prophet adds: *Offerings and libations for the Lord our God*[Lev 23:37]. What he is saying to us in other words is that, God having blessed us and forgiven us our sins, we will then be able to offer sacrifice to God.

Saturday of the Twenty-First Week in Ordinary Time

From a homily on Matthew by Saint John Chrysostom, Bishop & Doctor

Do not adorn the church and ignore your afflicted brother

Do you want to honor Christ's body? Then do not scorn him in his nakedness, nor honor him here in the church with silken garments while neglecting him outside where he is cold and naked. For he who said: *This is my body*, and made it so by his words, also said: *You saw me hungry and did not feed me, and inasmuch as you did not do it for one of these, the least of my brothers, you did not do it for me*[Mt 25:42-46]. What we do here in the church requires a pure heart, not special garments; what we do outside requires great dedication.

Let us learn, therefore, to be men of wisdom and to honor Christ as he desires. For a person being honored finds greatest pleasure in the honor he desires, not in the honor we think best. Peter thought he was honoring Christ when he refused to let him wash his feet; but what Peter wanted was not truly an honor, quite the opposite! Give him the honor prescribed in his law by giving your riches to the poor. For God does not want golden vessels but golden hearts.

Now, in saying this I am not forbidding you to make such gifts; I am only demanding that along with such gifts and before them you give alms. He accepts the former, but he is much more pleased with the latter. In the former, only the giver profits; in the latter, the recipient does too. A gift to the Church may be taken as a form of ostentation, but an alms is pure kindness.

Of what use is it to weigh down Christ's table with golden cups, when he himself is dying of hunger? First, fill him when he is hungry; then use the means you have left to adorn his table. Will you have a golden cup made but not give a cup of water? What is the use of providing the table with cloths woven of gold thread, and not providing Christ himself with the clothes he needs? What profit is there in that? Tell me: If you were to see him lacking the necessary food but were to leave him in that state and merely surround his table with gold, would he be grateful to you or rather would he not be angry? What if you were to see him clad in worn-out rags and stiff from the cold, and were to forget about clothing him and instead were to set up golden columns for him, saying that you were doing it in his honor? Would he not think he was being mocked and greatly insulted?

Apply this also to Christ when he comes along the roads as a pilgrim, looking for shelter. You do not take him in as your guest, but you decorate floor and walls and the capitals of the pillars. You provide silver chains for the lamps, but you cannot bear even to look at him as he lies chained in prison. Once again, I am not forbidding you to supply these adornments; I am urging you to provide these other things as well, and indeed to provide them first. No one has ever been accused for not providing ornaments, but for those who neglect their neighbor a hell awaits with an inextinguishable fire and torment in the company of the demons. Do not, therefore, adorn the church and ignore your afflicted brother, for he is the most precious temple of all.

Sunday of the Twenty-Second Week in Ordinary Time

From a sermon by Saint Augustine, Bishop & Doctor

The Lord has had pity on us

Happy are we if we do the deeds of which we have heard and sung. Our hearing them means having them planted in us, while our doing them shows that the seed has borne fruit. By saying this, I wish to caution you, dearly beloved, not to enter the Church fruitlessly, satisfied with mere hearing of such mighty blessings and failing to do good works. For *we have been saved by his grace,* says the Apostle, *and not by our works, lest anyone may boast; for it is by his grace that we have been saved*[Eph 2:8-9]. It is not as if a good life of some sort came first, and that thereupon God showed his love and esteem for it from on high, saying: "Let us come to the aid of these men and assist them quickly because they are living a good life." No, our life was displeasing to him; whatever we did by ourselves was displeasing to him; but what he did in us was not displeasing to him. He will, therefore, condemn what we have done, but he will save what he himself has done in us.

We were not good, but God had pity on us and sent his Son to die, not for good men but for bad ones, not for the just but for the wicked. Yes, *Christ died for the ungodly*[Rom 5:6]. Notice what is written next: *One will hardly die for a righteous man, though perhaps for a good man one will dare even to die*[Rom 5:7]. Perhaps someone can be found who will dare to die for a good man; but for the unjust man, for the wicked one, the sinner, who would be willing to die except Christ alone who is so just that he justifies even the unjust?

And so, my brothers, we had no good works, for all our works were evil. Yet although men's actions were such, God in his mercy did not abandon men. He sent his Son to redeem us, not with gold or silver but at the price of his blood poured out for us. Christ, the spotless lamb, became the sacrificial victim, led to the slaughter for the sheep that were blemished – if indeed one can say that they were blemished and not entirely corrupt. Such is the grace we have received! Let us live so as to be worthy of that great grace, and not do injury to it. So mighty is the physician who has come to us that he has healed all our sins! If we choose to be sick once again, we will not only harm ourselves, but show ingratitude to the physician as well.

Let us then follow Christ's paths which he has revealed to us, above all the path of humility, which he himself became for us. He showed us that path by his precepts, and he himself followed it by his suffering on our behalf. In order to die for us – because as God he could not die – *the Word became flesh and dwelt among us*[Jn 1:14]. The immortal One took on mortality that he might die for us, and by dying put to death our death.

This is what the Lord did, this the gift he granted to us. The mighty one was brought low, the lowly one was slain, and after he was slain, he rose again and was exalted. For he did not intend to leave us dead in hell, but to exalt in himself at the resurrection of the dead those whom he had already exalted and made just by the faith and praise they gave him. Yes, he gave us the path of humility. If we keep to it we shall confess our belief in the Lord and have good reason to sing: *We shall praise you, God, we shall praise you and call upon your name*[Ps 85:9].

Monday of the Twenty-Second Week in Ordinary Time

From the Imitation of Christ ~ Thomas a Kempis, Priest

I taught my prophets

My son, says the Lord, listen to my words, the most delightful of all words, surpassing all the knowledge of the philosophers and wise men of this world. *My words are spirit and life*[Jn 6:63] and cannot be comprehended by human senses alone.

They are not to be interpreted according to the vain pleasure of the listener, but they must be listened to in silence and received with all humility and great affection.

And I said: *Blessed is the man whom you teach, Lord, and whom you instruct in your law; for him you soften the blow of the evil day*[Ps 93:12-13], and you do not desert him on the earth.

The Lord says, I have instructed my prophets from the beginning and even to the present time I have not stopped speaking to all men, but many are deaf and obstinate in response.

Many hear the world more easily than they hear God; they follow the desires of the flesh more readily than the pleasure of God.

The world promises rewards that are temporal and insignificant, and these are pursued with great longing; I promise rewards that are eternal and unsurpassable, yet the hearts of mortals respond sluggishly.

Who serves and obeys me in all matters with as much care as the world and its princes are served?

Blush, then, you lazy, complaining servant, for men are better prepared for the works of death than you are for the works of life. They take more joy in vanity than you in truth.

Yet they are often deceived in their hope, while my promise deceives no one, and leaves empty-handed no one who confides in me. What I have promised I shall give; what I have said I will fulfill for any man who remains faithful in my love unto the very end. I am the rewarder of all good men, the one who rigorously tests the devoted.

Write my words in your heart and study them diligently, for they will be absolutely necessary in the time of temptation. Whatever you fail to understand in my words will become clear to you on the day of your visitation.

I am accustomed to visit my elect in a double fashion, that is, with temptation and with consolation. And I read to them two lessons each day: one to rebuke them for their faults; the other to exhort them to increase their virtue.

He who possesses my words yet spurns them earns his own judgment on the last day[Rom 2:5-8].

Tuesday of the Twenty-Second Week in Ordinary Time

From the Imitation of Christ ~ Thomas a Kempis, Priest

The truth of the Lord endures for ever

You thunder your judgments upon me, O Lord; you shake all my bones with fear and dread, and my soul becomes severely frightened. I am bewildered when I realize that *even the heavens are not pure in your sight*[Job 15:15].

If you discovered iniquity in the angels[2 Pet 2:4-10] and did not spare them, what will become of me? The stars fell from heaven, and I, mere dust, what should I expect? Those whose works seemed praiseworthy fell to the depths, and I have seen those who once were fed with the bread of angels delighting in the husks of swine.

There is no holiness where you have withdrawn your hand, O Lord; no profitable wisdom if you cease to rule over it; no helpful strength if you cease to preserve it. For if you forsake us, we sink and perish; but if you visit us, we rise up and live again. We are unstable, but you make us firm; we grow cool, but you inflame us.

All superficial glory has been swallowed up in the depths of your judgment upon me.

What is all flesh in your sight? *Can the clay be glorified in opposition to its Maker*[Rom 9:20-21]*?*

How can anyone be aroused by empty talk if his heart is subject in the truth to God?

The whole world cannot swell with pride the man who is subject to truth; nor will he be swayed by the flattery of all his admirers, if he has established all his trust in God.

For those who do all the talking amount to nothing; they fail with their din of words, but *the truth of the Lord endures for ever*[1 Pet 1:25].

Wednesday of the Twenty-Second Week in Ordinary Time

From a commentary on John by Origen, Priest

Christ spoke of his body as a temple

Destroy this temple and in three days I will raise it up[Jn 2:18-19]. It seems to me that Jesus meant the Jews in this episode to stand for sensual men and those desirous of carnal and sensual things. These Jews were angry at his expulsion of the people who were turning his Father's house into a market. So they asked for a sign to justify these actions, a sign that would show that the Word of God, whom they refused to accept, was acting rightly. The Savior's reply combines a statement about the temple with a prophecy about his own body, for in answer to their question: *What sign can you give to justify your conduct*[Jn 2:18-19]? he says: *Destroy this temple and in three days I will raise it up*[Jn 2:18-19].

Indeed, I think that both the temple and the body of Jesus can be seen in a single perspective as a type of the Church. For the Church is being built out of living stones; it is in process of becoming a *spiritual dwelling for a holy priesthood, raised on the foundations of apostles and prophets, with Christ as its chief cornerstone*[1 Pet 2:4-8]. Hence it bears the name "temple." On the other hand, it is written: *You are the body of Christ, and individually members of it*[1 Cor 12:27]. Thus even the harmonious alignment of the stones should seem to be destroyed and fragmented and, as described in the twenty-first psalm, all the bones which go to make up Christ's body should seem to be scattered by insidious attacks in persecutions or times of trouble, or by those who in days of persecution undermine the unity of the temple, nevertheless the temple will be rebuilt and the body will rise again on the third day, after the day of evil which threatens it and the day of consummation which follows. For the third day will dawn upon a new heaven and a new earth when these bones that form the whole house of Israel are raised up on that great day of the Lord, when death has been defeated. So the resurrection of Christ, accomplished after his suffering on the cross, embraces the mystery of the resurrection of his whole body.

For just as that physical body of Christ was crucified and buried, and afterward raised up, so in the same way the whole body of Christ's holy ones has been crucified and lives no longer with its own life. For each of them, like Paul, makes his boast of nothing else but the cross of our Lord Jesus Christ, by which he has himself been crucified to the world, and the world to him. But each Christian has not only been crucified with Christ and crucified to the world; he has been buried with Christ too, as Paul tells us: *We have been buried with Christ*[Rom 6:4]. But as though already in possession of some pledge of the resurrection, Paul goes on to say: *And we have risen with him*[Rom 6:4].

Thursday of the Twenty-Second Week in Ordinary Time

From the beginning of a sermon on the beatitudes by Saint Leo the Great, Pope & Doctor

I shall put my laws within them

Dearly beloved, when our Lord Jesus Christ was preaching the Gospel of the kingdom and healing various illnesses throughout the whole of Galilee, the fame of his mighty works spread into all of Syria, and great crowds from all parts of Judea flocked to the heavenly physician. Because human ignorance is slow to believe what it does not see, and equally slow to hope for what it does not know, those who were to be instructed in the divine teaching had first to be aroused by bodily benefits and visible miracles so that, once they had experienced his gracious power, they would no longer doubt the wholesome effect of his doctrine.

In order, therefore, to transform outward healings into inward remedies, and to cure men's souls now that he had healed their bodies, our Lord separated himself from the surrounding crowds, climbed to the solitude of a neighboring mountain, and called the apostles to himself. From the height of this mystical site he then instructed them in the most lofty doctrines, suggesting both by the very nature of the place and by what he was doing that it was he who long ago had honored Moses by speaking to him. Then, his words evidenced a terrifying justice, but now they reveal a sacred compassion, in order to fulfill what was promised in the words of the prophet Jeremiah: *Behold the days are coming, says the Lord, when I shall establish a new covenant with the house of Israel and with the house of Judah. After those days, says the Lord, I shall put my laws within them and write them on their hearts*[Jer 31:31-33].

And so it was that he who had spoken to Moses spoke also to the apostles. Writing in the hearts of his disciples, the swift hand of the Word composed the ordinances of the new covenant. And this was not done as formerly, in the midst of dense clouds, amid terrifying sounds and lightning, so that the people were frightened away from approaching the mountain. Instead, there was a tranquil discourse which clearly reached the ears of all who stood nearby so that the harshness of the law might be softened by the gentleness of grace, and the spirit of adoption might dispel the terror of slavery.

Concerning the content of Christ's teaching, his own sacred words bear witness; thus whoever longs to attain eternal blessedness can now recognize the steps that lead to that high happiness. *Blessed*, he says, *are the poor in spirit, for theirs is the kingdom of heaven*[Mt 5:3]. It might have been unclear to which poor he was referring, if after the words *Blessed are the poor*, he had not added anything about the kind of poor he had in mind. For then the poverty that many suffer because of grave and harsh necessity might seem sufficient to merit the kingdom of heaven. But when he says: *Blessed are the poor in spirit*, he shows that the kingdom of heaven is to be given to those who are distinguished by their humility of soul rather than by their lack of worldly goods.

Friday of the Twenty-Second Week in Ordinary Time

From a sermon on the beatitudes by Saint Leo the Great, Pope & Doctor

Blessed are the poor in spirit

It cannot be doubted that the poor can more easily attain the blessing of humility than those who are rich. In the case of the poor, the lack of worldly goods is often accompanied by a quiet gentleness, whereas the rich are more prone to arrogance. Nevertheless, many wealthy people are disposed to use their abundance not to swell their own pride but to perform works of benevolence. They consider their greatest gain what they spend to alleviate the distress of others.

This virtue is open to all men, no matter what their class or condition, because all can be equal in their willingness to give, however unequal they may be in earthly fortune. Indeed, their inequality in regard to worldly means is unimportant, provided they are found equal in spiritual possessions. Blessed, therefore, is that poverty which is not trapped by the love of temporal things and does not seek to be enriched by worldly wealth, but desires rather to grow rich in heavenly goods.

The apostles were the first after the Lord himself to provide us with an example of this generous poverty, when they all equally left their belongings at the call of the heavenly master. By an immediate conversion they were turned from the catching of fish to become fishers of men, and by their own example they won many others to the imitation of their own faith. In these first sons of the Church there was but one heart and one soul among all who believed. Abandoning all their worldly property and possessions in their dedicated poverty, they were enriched with eternal goods, and in accordance with the apostolic preaching, they rejoiced to have nothing of this world and to possess all things with Christ.

Therefore, when the apostle Peter was on his way up to the temple and was asked for alms by the lame man, he replied: *Silver and gold I have not; but what I have I give you. In the name of Jesus Christ of Nazareth, arise and walk*[Acts 3:6]. What is more sublime than this humility? And what could be richer than this poverty? Though Peter cannot assist with money, he can confer gifts of nature. With a word Peter brought healing to the man who had been lame from birth; he who did not give a coin with the emperor's image refashioned the image of Jesus in this man.

And by the riches of this treasure, not only did he help the man who recovered the power to walk, but also five thousand others who believed the preaching of the apostle because of this miraculous cure. Thus Peter, who in his poverty had no money to give to the beggar, bestowed such a bounty of divine grace that in restoring to health the feet of one man, he healed the hearts of many thousands of believers. He had found all of them lame; but he made them leap for joy in Christ.

Saturday of the Twenty-Second Week in Ordinary Time

From a sermon on the beatitudes by Saint Leo the Great, Pope & Doctor

The blessedness of Christ's reign

After preaching the blessings of poverty, the Lord went on to say: *Blessed are they who mourn, for they shall be comforted*[Mt 5:4]. But the mourning for which he promises eternal consolation, dearly beloved, has nothing to do with ordinary worldly distress; for the tears which have their origin in the sorrow common to all mankind do not make anyone blessed. There is another cause for the sighs of the saints, another reason for their blessed tears. Religious grief mourns for sin, one's own or another's; it does not lament because of what happens as a result of God's justice, but because of what is done by human malice. Indeed, he who does wrong is more to be lamented than he who suffers it, for his wickedness plunges the sinner into punishment, whereas endurance can raise the just man to glory.

Next the Lord says: *Blessed are the meek, for they shall inherit the earth*[Mt 5:5]. To the meek and gentle, the lowly and the humble, and to all who are ready to endure any injury, he promises that they will possess the earth. Nor is this inheritance to be considered small or insignificant, as though it were distinct from our heavenly dwelling; for we know that it is the kingdom of heaven which is also the inheritance promised to the meek. The earth that is promised to the meek and which will be given to the gentle for their own possession is none other than the bodies of the saints. Through the merit of their humility their bodies will be transformed by a joyous resurrection and clothed in the glory of immortality. No longer opposed in any way to their spirits, their bodies will remain in perfect harmony and unity with the will of the soul. Then, indeed, the outer man will be the peaceful and unblemished possession of the inner man.

Then, truly will the meek inherit the earth in perpetual peace, and nothing will be taken from their rights; for *this perishable nature shall put on the imperishable and this mortal nature shall put on immortality*[1 Cor 15:53-55]. Their risk will turn into reward; what was a burden will have become an honor.

Sunday of the Twenty-Third Week in Ordinary Time

From a sermon on the beatitudes by Saint Leo the Great, Pope & Doctor

Christian wisdom

The Lord then goes on to say: *Blessed are those who hunger and thirst for righteousness, for they shall be filled*[Mt 5:6]. This hunger is not for any bodily food, this thirst is not for any earthly drink: it is a longing to be blessed with righteousness, and, by penetrating the secret of all mysteries, to be filled with the Lord himself.

Happy is the soul that longs for the food of righteousness and thirsts for this kind of drink; it would not seek such things if it had not already savored their delight. When the soul hears the voice of the Spirit saying to it through the prophet: *Taste and see that the Lord is good*[Ps 33:9], it has already received a portion of God's goodness, and is on fire with love, the love that gives joy of the utmost purity. It counts as nothing all that belongs to time; it is entirely consumed with desire to eat and drink the food of righteousness. The soul lays hold of the true meaning of the first and great commandment: *You shall love the Lord God with your whole heart, and your whole mind and your whole strength*[Mt 22:37-40], for to love God is nothing else than to love righteousness.

Finally, just as concern for one's neighbor is added to love of God, so the virtue of mercy is added to the desire for righteousness, as it is said: *Blessed are the merciful, for God will be merciful to them*[Mt 5:7].

Remember, Christian, the surpassing worth of the wisdom that is yours. Bear in mind the kind of school in which you are to learn your skills, the rewards to which you are called. Mercy itself wishes you to be merciful, righteousness itself wishes you to be righteous, so that the Creator may shine forth in his creature, and the image of God be reflected in the mirror of the human heart as it imitates his qualities. The faith of those who live their faith is a serene faith. What you long for will be given you; what you love will be yours for ever.

Since it is by giving alms that everything is pure for you, you will also receive that blessing which is promised next by the Lord: *Blessed are the pure of heart, for they shall see God*[Mt 5:8]. Dear friends, great is the happiness of those for whom such a reward is prepared. Who are the clean of heart if not those who strive for those virtues we have mentioned above? What mind can conceive, what words can express the great happiness of seeing God? Yet human nature will achieve this when it has been transformed so that it sees the Godhead *no longer in a mirror or obscurely but face to face*[1 Cor 13:12] – the Godhead that no man has been able to see. In the inexpressible joy of this eternal vision, human nature will possess *what eye has not seen or ear heard, what man's heart has never conceived*[1 Cor 2:9].

Monday of the Twenty-Third Week in Ordinary Time

From a sermon on the beatitudes by Saint Leo the Great, Pope & Doctor

Those who love your law shall have abundant peace

The blessedness of seeing God is justly promised to the pure of heart. For the eye that is unclean would not be able to see the brightness of the true light, and what would be happiness to clear minds would be a torment to those that are defiled. Therefore, let the mists of worldly vanities be dispelled, and the inner eye be cleansed of all the filth of wickedness, so that the soul's gaze may feast serenely upon the great vision of God.

It is to the attainment of this goal that the next words refer: *Blessed are the peacemakers, for they shall be called sons of God*[Mt 5:9]. This blessedness, dearly beloved, does not derive from any casual agreement or from any and every kind of harmony, but it pertains to what the Apostle says: *Be at peace before the Lord*[1 Thess 5:23-28], and to the words of the prophet: *Those who love your law shall enjoy abundant peace; for them it is no stumbling block*[Ps 118:165].

Even the most intimate bonds of friendship and the closest affinity of minds cannot truly lay claim to this peace if they are not in agreement with the will of God. Alliances based on evil desires, covenants of crime and pacts of vice – all lie outside the scope of this peace. Love of the world cannot be reconciled with love of God, and the man who does not separate himself from the children of this generation cannot join the company of the sons of God. But those who keep God ever in their hearts, and are *anxious to preserve the unity of the spirit in the bond of peace*[Eph 4:3], never dissent from the eternal law as they speak the prayer of faith. *Your will be done on earth as it is in heaven*[Mt 6:10].

These then are the peacemakers; they are bound together in holy harmony and are rightly given the heavenly title of *sons of God, coheirs with Christ*[Rom 8:17]. And this is the reward they will receive for their love of God and neighbor: when their struggle with all temptation is finally over, there will be no further adversities to suffer or scandal to fear; but they will rest in the peace of God undisturbed, through our Lord who lives and reigns with the Father and the Holy Spirit for ever and ever. Amen.

Tuesday of the Twenty-Third Week in Ordinary Time

From a sermon by Saint Bernard, Abbot & Doctor

I shall stand upon my watchtower to see what the Lord will say to me

We read in the gospel that when the Lord was teaching his disciples and urged them to share in his passion by the mystery of eating his body, some said: *This is a hard saying*[Jn 6:60]; and from that time they no longer followed him. When he asked the disciples whether they also wished to go away, they replied: *Lord, to whom shall we go? You have the words of eternal life*[Jn 6:68].

I assure you, my brothers, that even to this day it is clear to some that the words which Jesus speaks are *spirit and life* [Jn 6:63], and for this reason they follow him. To others these words seem hard, and so they look elsewhere for some pathetic consolation. Yet wisdom cries out in the streets, in the broad and spacious way that leads to death, to call back those who take this path.

Finally, he says: *For forty years I have been close to this generation, and I said: They have always been fainthearted*[Ps 94:8-11]. You also read in another psalm: *God has spoken once*. Once, indeed, because for ever. His is a single, uninterrupted utterance, because it is continuous and unending.

He calls upon sinners to return to their true spirit and rebukes them when their hearts have gone astray, for it is in the true heart that he dwells and there he speaks, fulfilling what he taught through the prophet: *Speak to the heart of Jerusalem*[Isa 40:2].

You see, my brothers, how the prophet admonishes us for our advantage: *If today you hear his voice, harden not your hearts*[Ps 94:8; Heb 3:15]. You can read almost the same words in the gospel and in the prophet. For in the gospel the Lord says: *My sheep hear my voice*[Jn 10:27]. And in the psalm blessed David says: *You are his people (meaning, of course, the Lord's) and the sheep of his pasture*[Ps 99:3]*. If today you hear his voice, harden not your hearts*.

Hear also the prophet Habakkuk in today's . Far from hiding the Lord's reprimands, he dwells on them with attentive and anxious care. He says: *I will stand upon my watchtower and take up my post on the ramparts, keeping watch to see what he will say to me and what answers I will make to those who try to confute me*[Hab2:1]. I beg you, my brothers, stand upon our watch-tower, for now is the time for battle. Let all our dealings be in the heart, where Christ dwells, in right judgment and wise counsel, but in such a way as to place no confidence in those dealings, nor rely upon our fragile defenses.

Wednesday of the Twenty-Third Week in Ordinary Time

From a sermon by Saint Bernard, Abbot & Doctor

The stages of contemplation

Let us take our stand on secure ground, leaning with all our strength on Christ, the most solid rock, according to the words: *He set my feet on a rock and guided my steps*[Ps 39:2-4]. Thus firmly established, let us begin to contemplate, to see what he is saying to us and what reply we ought to make to his charges.

The first stage of contemplation, my dear brothers, is constantly to consider what God wants, what is pleasing to him, and what is acceptable in his eyes. *We all offend in many things*[Jas3:2]; our strength cannot match the rectitude of God's will, being neither one with it nor wholly in accord with it; let us then humble ourselves *under the powerful hand of the most high God*[Ps 90:1-2] and be concerned to show ourselves unworthy before his merciful gaze, saying: *Heal me, Lord, and I shall be healed; save me and I shall be saved*[Jer 17:14]. And again, *Lord, have mercy on me; heal my soul because I have sinned against you*[Ps 40:5].

Once the eye of the soul has been purified by such considerations, we no longer abide within our own spirit in a sense of sorrow, but abide rather in the Spirit of God with great delight. No longer do we consider what is the will of God for us, but rather what it is in itself. For our *life is in his will*. Thus we are convinced that what is according to his will is in every way more advantageous and fitting for us. And so, concerned as we are to preserve the life of our soul, we should be equally concerned, insofar as we can, not to deviate from his will.

Thus having made some progress in our spiritual exercise under the guidance of the Spirit who searches the deep things of God, let us reflect how sweet is the Lord and how good he is in himself; in the words of the prophet let us pray to see God's will; no longer shall we frequent our own hearts but his temple. At the same time we shall say: *My soul is humbled within me, therefore I shall be mindful of you*[St. Bernard].

The whole of the spiritual life consists of these two elements. When we think of ourselves, we are perturbed and filled with a salutary sadness. And when we think of the Lord, we are revived to find consolation in the joy of the Holy Spirit. From the first we derive fear and humility, from the second hope and love.

Thursday of the Twenty-Third Week in Ordinary Time

From a discourse on the psalms by Saint Bruno, Priest

If I should forget you, Jerusalem

How beautiful are your tabernacles! My soul longs to reach the courts of the Lord[Ps 83:2-3], the fullness of the heavenly Jerusalem, the city of the Lord. He then explains why he desires to enter the courts of the Lord. It is because *they are blessed who dwell in your house* [Ps 83:5], the heavenly Jerusalem, Lord, God of the heavenly powers, my King and my God. It is as if he were to say: Who does not long to enter your courts since you are God, the Creator and King and Lord of hosts, and all *who dwell in your house are blessed*? For him courts and house are the same. When he says *blessed,* he means that they enjoy as much happiness as can be conceived. Clearly they are blessed because out of their devoted love *they will praise you for ever*[Ps 44:18], that is, for all eternity. For they would not offer praise for all eternity unless they were blessed for all eternity.

Now even though we may have faith, hope and love, none of us can attain this state of blessedness by ourselves. Rather, *blessed is the man* - he alone attains blessedness - *whose help is from you*[Ps 83:6] in rising to the heights of happiness on which he has set his heart. In other words, he alone can be said to come to true blessedness who, having resolved in his heart to rise to this state of happiness by the many stages of the virtues and good works, receives the help of your grace. No one can rise up by himself as the Lord testifies: *No one ascends into heaven,* of his own power, *except the Son of Man who is in heaven*[Jn 3:13].

Thus he contemplates this journey, living as he does in a *vale of tears* [Ps 83:67], for this life is lowly and full of tears and sorrow. The life of heaven, by contrast, is called a mountain full of joy.

But since the psalmist said: *Blessed is the man whose help comes from you* [Ps 83:6], someone might ask: Does God really help us in this? And the answer is that God does help the blessed. For our lawgiver Christ, who gave us the law, gives now and will continue to give his blessings, the abundant gifts of grace, by which he will bless his own, that is, raise them to beatitude. By these blessings, then, they will rise from *strength to strength*[Ps 83:7-8]. One day in the heavenly Zion they will see Christ as the God of gods, as the one who, being God, will deify his own. Or, again, those who are to be the new Zion will see in spirit the God of gods - the Trinity. In other words, then their minds will see God, who cannot be seen in this life. For then God will be *all in all*[1 Cor 15:28].

Friday of the Twenty-Third Week in Ordinary Time

From a sermon by Blessed Isaac of Stella, Abbot

Christ will forgive no sin without the Church

The prerogative of receiving the confession of sin and the power to forgive sin are two things that belong properly to God alone. We must confess our sins to him and look to him for forgiveness. Since only he has the power to forgive sins, it is to him that we must make our confession. But when the Almighty, the Most High, wedded a bride who was weak and of low estate, he made that maid-servant a queen. He took her from her place behind him, at his feet, and enthroned her at his side. She had been born from his side, and therefore he betrothed her to himself. And as all that belongs to the Father belongs also to the Son because by nature they are one, so also the bridegroom gave all he had to the bride and he shared in all that was hers. He made her one both with himself and with the Father. Praying for his bride, the Son said to the Father: *I want them to be one with us, even as you and I are one*[Jn 17:21-23].

And so the bridegroom is one with the Father and one with the bride. Whatever he found in his bride alien to her own nature he took from her and nailed to his cross when he bore her sins and destroyed them on the tree. He received from her and clothed himself in what was hers by nature and gave her what belonged to him as God. He destroyed what was diabolical, took to himself what was human, and conferred on her what was divine. So all that belonged to the bride was shared in by the bridegroom, and he who had done no wrong and on whose lips was found no deceit could say: *Have pity on me, Lord, for I am weak*[Ps 6:2-3]. Thus, sharing as he did in the bride's weakness, the bridegroom made his own her cries of distress, and gave his bride all that was his. Therefore, she too has the prerogative of receiving the confession of sin and the power to forgive sin, which is the reason for the command: *Go, show yourself to the priest*[Lk 17:14].

The Church is incapable of forgiving any sin without Christ, and Christ is unwilling to forgive any sin without the Church. The Church cannot forgive the sin of one who has not repented, who has not been touched by Christ; Christ will not forgive the sin of one who despises the Church. *What God has joined together, man must not separate*[Mk 10:9]. *This is a great mystery, but I understand it as referring to Christ and the Church*[Eph 5:32].

Do not destroy the whole Christ by separating head from body, for Christ is not complete without the Church, nor is the Church complete without Christ. The whole and complete Christ is head and body. This is why he said: *No one has ever ascended into heaven except the Son of Man whose home is in heaven*[Jn 3:13]. He is the only man who can forgive sin.

Saturday of the Twenty-Third Week in Ordinary Time

From a sermon by Saint Athanasius, Bishop & Doctor

You gave us life in the beginning; give us new life

God, the Word of the all-good Father, did not disregard the human race, his own creation, when it was sinking back into corruption, but rather by the offering of his own body he destroyed the death men had incurred, and by his teaching he corrected their negligence. So he restored by his power all that belongs to man's estate.

Anyone can find confirmation of this from the Savior's own disciples who spoke of him, for in their writings one reads: *The charity of Christ constrains us as we judge that if one died on behalf of all, then all died; and he died for all in order that we may live no longer for ourselves but for him who died for us and rose from the dead*[2 Cor 5:14-21], our Lord Jesus Christ. And again: *We see Jesus, who for a little while was made lower than the angels, crowned with glory and honor because he suffered death, that by God's grace he might taste death for everyone*[Heb 2:9]. Then the writer goes on to show why it had to be God the Word and no other who became man: *Indeed it was fitting that in bringing many sons to glory, God, for whom and through whom all things exist, should make perfect the one who leads them to salvation*[Heb 2:9]. By this he means that the task of bringing men back from the corruption into which they had fallen belonged to no other save God the Word who had made them in the beginning. Further, Scripture shows that the Word assumed a body for the purpose of offering it in sacrifice on behalf of other bodies like his own, for the writer continues: *Since the children have blood and flesh in common, he likewise shared in them himself so that by his own death he might destroy the one who had power over death, that is, the devil, and might deliver those who all their life long were enslaved by fear of death*[Heb 2:14-15]

For by the sacrifice of his own body he both put an end to the law that stood against us and made a new beginning of life for us by giving us the hope of resurrection. Hence Paul, the Christ-bearer, declares: *As through a man came death, so through a man has come the resurrection of the dead. For as all died in Adam, so also in Christ all shall be made to live*[1 Cor 15:20-22].

No longer, then, do we die as men condemned, but as men being raised even now, we await the general resurrection of all, which God, whose work and gift it is, *will reveal at the appointed time*[1 Cor 4:5].

Sunday of the Twenty-Fourth Week in Ordinary Time

From the beginning of a sermon on Pastors by Saint Augustine, Bishop & Doctor

I am a Christian as well as a leader

You have often learned that all our hope is in Christ and that he is our true glory and our salvation. You are members of the flock of the Good Shepherd, who watches over Israel and nourishes his people. Yet there are shepherds who want to have the title of shepherd without wanting to fulfill a pastor's duties; let us then recall what God says to his shepherds through the prophet. You must listen attentively; I must listen with fear and trembling.

The word of the Lord came to me and said: Son of man, prophesy against the shepherds of Israel and speak to the shepherds of Israel[Ezek 34:2]. We just heard this a moment ago, my brothers, and I have decided to speak to you on this passage. The Lord will help me to speak the truth if I do not speak on my own authority. For if I speak on my own authority, I will be a shepherd nourishing myself and not the sheep. However, if my words are the Lord's, then he is nourishing you no matter who speaks. *Thus says the Lord God: Shepherds of Israel, who have been nourishing only themselves! Should not the shepherds nourish the sheep* [Ezek 34:2-4]? In other words, true shepherds take care of their sheep, not themselves. This is the principle reason why God condemns those shepherds: they took care of themselves rather than their sheep. Who are they who nourish themselves? They are the shepherds the Apostle described when he said: *They all seek what is theirs and not what is Christ's*[Phil 2:21].

I must distinguish carefully between two aspects of the role the lord has given me, a role that demands a rigorous accountability, a role based on the Lord's greatness rather than on my own merit. The first aspect is that I am a Christian; the second, that I am a leader. I am a Christian for my own sake, whereas I am a leader for your sake; the fact that I am a Christian is to my own advantage, but I am a leader for your advantage.

Many persons come to God as Christians but not as leaders. Perhaps they travel by an easier road and are less hindered since they bear a lighter burden. In addition to the fact that I am a Christian and must give God an account of my life, I as a leader must give him an account of my stewardship as well.

Monday of the Twenty-Fourth Week in Ordinary Time

From a sermon On Pastors by Saint Augustine, Bishop & Doctor

The shepherds who feed themselves

Let us consider the unflattering words of God which Scripture addresses to shepherds who feed themselves and not the sheep. *You consume their milk and cover yourselves with their wool; you kill the fatlings, but my sheep you do not pasture. You have failed to strengthen what was weak, to heal what was sick, and to bind up what was injured. You did not call back what went astray, nor seek out what was lost. What was strong you have destroyed, and my sheep have been scattered because there is no shepherd*[Ezek 34:3-5].

This is spoken to the shepherds who feed themselves and not the sheep; it speaks of their concern and their neglect. What is their concern? *You consume their milk and cover yourselves with their wool.* And so the Apostle asks: *Who plants a vineyard and does not eat from its fruit? Who pastures a flock and does not drink from the milk of the flock*[1 Cor 9:7]*?* Thus we learn that the milk of the flock is whatever temporal support and sustenance God's people give to those who are placed over them. It is of this that the Apostle was speaking in the passage just quoted.

Although he chose to support himself by the labor of his own hands and not to ask for milk from the sheep, the Apostle did say that he had the right to receive the milk, for the Lord had established that they who preach the Gospel should live from the Gospel. Paul also says that others of his fellow apostles made use of this right, a right granted them, and not unlawfully usurped. But Paul went further by not taking what was rightfully his. He forgave the debt, whereas the others did not demand what was not due them. Therefore Paul went further. Perhaps his action was foreshadowed by the Good Samaritan who, when he brought the sick man to the inn, said: *If you spend any more, I will repay you on my way back*[Lk 10:33-35].

What more can I say concerning those shepherds who do not need the milk of the flock? They are more merciful; or rather, they carry out a more abundant ministry of mercy. They are able to do so, and they do it. Let them receive praise, but do not condemn the others. The Apostle himself did not seek what was given. However, he wanted the sheep to be fruitful, not sterile and unable to give milk.

Tuesday of the Twenty-Fourth Week in Ordinary Time

From a sermon On Pastors by Saint Augustine, Bishop & Doctor

Paul's example

Once when Paul was in great need, in chains for his confession of the truth, his fellow Christians sent him what was necessary for his wants and needs. He thanked them with these words: *You have done well to share in my need. It is true that I have leaned to be self-sufficient in whatever circumstances I find myself. I know what it is to have plenty and I have learned how to endure privation. I can do all things in him who strengthens me. Still you have done well to send things for my use*[Phil 4:11-14].

Just as this indicates in what sense they had done well, it also shows what Paul himself sought, namely, to avoid being numbered among those who feed themselves and not the sheep. For he does not so much rejoice at his own deliverance from need as he does at their generosity. What then was he seeking? *I do not set my heart upon gifts*[Phil 4:17], he says; *all I seek for is the fruit of my labor*. Not that I may be filled, he says, but that you may not remain empty.

As for those who cannot support themselves with their own hands as Paul did, let them take from the milk of the sheep, let them receive what is necessary for their needs, but let them not neglect the weakness of the sheep. Let them not seek any benefit for themselves, lest they appear to be preaching the Gospel for the sake of their own need and privation; rather, let them provide the light of the true word for the sake of men's enlightenment. For they are like lamps, as it has been said: *Let your belts be fastened and your lamps burning*[Lk 12:35], *and: No one lights a lamp and puts it under a bushel basket; rather, he puts it on a lamp-stand, that it may give light to all who are in the house; so let your light shine before men in order that they may see your good works and glorify your Father who is in heaven*[Mt 5:15-16].

Now if a lamp has been lighted for you in your house, would you not add oil to keep it from going out? Of course, if the lamp received the oil and failed to shine, it was obviously not fit to be put on the lamp-stand and should have been discarded at once. But for the light to be kept alive it must receive fuel which is to be provided out of charity. Only let not the Gospel be for sale, with preachers demanding a price for it and making their living from it. If they sell it like that, they are selling for a pittance something that is of great value. Let them receive support in their need from the people, but payment for their stewardship from the Lord. No, it is not right for the people to give payment to those who serve them out of love of the Gospel. Payment is to be expected only from the one who also grants salvation.

Why then are they rebuked? Why are they accused? Because, when they took the milk and covered themselves with the wool, they neglected the sheep. They sought only to serve their own cause and not Christ's.

Wednesday of the Twenty-Fourth Week in Ordinary Time

From a sermon On Pastors by Saint Augustine, Bishop & Doctor

Let each one seek not what is his but what is Christ's

I have explained what it means to consume milk. Now let us consider what it means to clothe with wool. One who gives milk gives sustenance, while one who gives wool gives honor. These are precisely the two things that pastors, who feed themselves and not the sheep, look for from the people — the benefit of having their wants supplied as well as the favor of honor and praise.

Yes, clothing can well be taken to mean honor, since it covers nakedness. For every man without exception is weak. And who is any man placed over you except someone just like yourself. Your pastor is in the flesh, he is mortal, he eats, sleeps and awakens; he was born and he is going to die. In himself he is, when you think of it, simply a man. But it is true that you make him something more by giving him honor; it is as if you were covering what is weak.

Consider the nature of the clothing that the apostle Paul received from God's good people. He said: *You have received me like an angel of God. I testify that if it were possible you would have torn out your eyes and given them to me*[Gal 4:14-15]. Indeed great honor was shown to him. But did he then spare sinners because of that honor, perhaps out of fear that it would be refused and that he would receive less praise when he gave blame? Had he done so, he would be among those shepherds who feed themselves and not the sheep. He would then say to himself: "What has this to do with me? Let everyone do what he will; my sustenance is safe, and my honor too. I have enough milk and wool, so let each one do as he likes." But then are things really secure for you if each one does as he pleases? I do not want to make you a leader over the people but one of them. *If one member suffers, all the members suffer with him*[1 Cor 12:26].

In recalling how they treated him, the Apostle does not want to appear forgetful of the honor they did him. Therefore he gives testimony that they received him like an angel of God, that if it were possible, they were willing to tear out their eyes and give them to him. Yet he still comes to the sheep that is ill, to the one that is diseased, to cut the wound and not to spare the diseased part. He says: *Have I then become your enemy by preaching the truth*[Gal 4:16]? He took from the milk of the sheep, as I mentioned a short time ago, and he was clothed with their wool, but he did not neglect his sheep. He did not seek what was his but what was Christ's.

Thursday of the Twenty-Fourth Week in Ordinary Time

From a sermon On Pastors by Saint Augustine, Bishop & Doctor

Be an example for the faithful

After the Lord had shown what wicked shepherds esteem, he also spoke about what they neglect. The defects of the sheep are widespread. There are very few healthy and sound sheep, few that are solidly sustained by the food of truth, and few that enjoy the good pasture God gives them. But the wicked shepherds do not spare such sheep. It is not enough that they neglect those that are ill and weak, those that go stray and are lost. They even try, so far as it is in their power, to kill the strong and healthy. Yet such sheep live; yes, by God's mercy they live. As for the wicked shepherds themselves, they kill the sheep. "How do they kill them?" you ask. By their wicked lives and by giving bad example. Or was God's servant, who was high among the members of the chief shepherd, told this in vain: *Show yourself as an example of good works toward all men*[Titus 2:7], and, *Be an example to the faithful*[1 Tim 4:12]?

Even the strong sheep, if he turns his eyes from the Lord's laws and looks at the man set over him, notices when his shepherd is living wickedly and begins to say in his heart: "If my pastor lives like that, why should I not live like him?" The wicked shepherd kills the strong sheep. But if he kills the strong one what does he do to the rest? After all, by his wicked life he kills even the sheep he had not strengthened but had found strong and hardy.

I appeal to your love, and again I say, even if the sheep have life and if they are strong in the word of the Lord, and if they hold fast to what they have heard from their Lord, *Do what they say but not what they do*[Mt 23:3]. Still, as far as he himself is concerned, the shepherd who lives a wicked life before the people kills the sheep under his care. Let such a shepherd not deceive himself because the sheep is not dead, for though it still lives, he is a murderer - just as when the lustful man looks on a woman with desire, even though she is chaste, he has committed adultery. For the Lord said in plain truth: *Whoever has looked upon a woman with desire has already committed adultery with her in his heart*[Mt 5:28]. He has not entered her bedroom, yet he has ravished her within the bedroom of his heart.

Therefore anyone who lives wickedly before those who have been placed under his care kills, as far as he himself is concerned, even the strong. Whoever imitates him, dies; whoever does not, has life. But as for him, he kills both of them. *You kill what is healthy and you do not pasture my sheep*[Ezek 34:2-10].

Friday of the Twenty-Fourth Week in Ordinary Time

From a sermon On Pastors by Saint Augustine, Bishop & Doctor

Prepare your soul for temptation

You have already been told about the wicked things shepherds desire. Let us now consider what they neglect. *You have failed to strengthen what was weak, to heal what was sick, and to bind up what was injured*[Ezek 34:4], that is, what was broken. *You did not call back the straying sheep, nor seek out the lost. What was strong you have destroyed* [Ezek 34:4]. Yes, you have cut it down and killed it. The sheep is weak, that is to say, its heart is weak and so, incautious and unprepared, it may give in to temptations.

The negligent shepherd fails to say to the believer: *My son, come to the service of God, stand fast in fear and in righteousness, and prepare your soul for temptation*[Sir 2:1.] A shepherd who does say this strengthens the one who is weak and makes him strong. Such a believer will then not hope for the prosperity of this world. For if he has been taught to hope for worldly gain, he will be corrupted by prosperity. When adversity comes, he will be wounded or perhaps destroyed.

The builder who builds in such manner is not building the believer on a rock but upon sand. *But the rock was Christ*[1 Cor 10:4]. Christians must imitate Christ's sufferings, not set their hearts on pleasures. He who is weak will be strengthened when told: "Yes, expect the temptations of this world, but the Lord will deliver you from them all if your heart has not abandoned him. For it was to strengthen your heart that he came to suffer and die, came to be spit upon and crowned with thorns, came to be accused of shameful things, yes, came to be fastened to the wood of the cross. All these things he did for you, and you did nothing. He did them not for himself, but for you."

But what sort of shepherds are they who for fear of giving offense not only fail to prepare the sheep for the temptations that threaten, but even promise them worldly happiness? God himself made no such promise to this world. On the contrary, God foretold hardship upon hardship in this world until the end of time. And you want the Christian to be exempt from these troubles? Precisely because he is a Christian, he is destined to suffer more in this world.

For the Apostle says: *All who desire to live a holy life in Christ will suffer persecution*[2 Tim 3:12]. But you, shepherd, seek what is yours and not what is Christ's, you disregard what the Apostle says: *All who want to live a holy life in Christ will suffer persecution*[2 Tim 3:12]. You say instead: "If you live a holy life in Christ, all good things will be yours in abundance. If you do not have children, you will embrace and nourish all men, and none of them shall die." Is this the way you build up the believer? Take note of what you are doing and where you are placing him. You have built him on sand. The rains will come, the river will overflow and rush in, the winds will blow, and the elements will dash against that house of yours. It will fall, and its ruin will be great.

Lift him up from the sand and put him on the rock. Let him be in Christ, if you wish him to be a Christian. Let him turn his thoughts to sufferings, however unworthy they may be in comparison to Christ's. Let him center his attention on Christ, who was without sin, and yet made restitution for what he had not done. Let him consider Scripture, which says to him: *He chastises every son whom he acknowledges*[Heb 12:6]. Let him prepare to be chastised, or else not seek to be acknowledged as a son.

Saturday of the Twenty-Fourth Week in Ordinary Time

From a sermon On Pastors by Saint Augustine, Bishop & Doctor

Offer the bandage of consolation

Scripture says: *God chastises every son whom he acknowledges*[Heb 12:6]. But the bad shepherd says: "Perhaps I will be exempt." If he is exempt from the suffering of his chastisements, then he is not numbered among God's sons. You will say: "Does God indeed punish every son?" Yes, every one, just as he chastised his only Son. His only Son, born of the substance of the Father, equal to the Father *in the form of God*[Phil 2:5-6], the Word through whom all things were made, he could not be chastised. For this reason he was clothed with flesh so that he might know chastisement. God punishes his only Son who is without sin; does he then leave unpunished an adopted son who is with sin? The Apostle says that we have been called to adoption. We have been adopted as sons, that we might be coheirs with the only Son, and also that we might be his inheritance: *Ask of me and I will give you the nations as your inheritance*[Ps 2:8]. Christ gave us the example by his own sufferings.

But clearly one who is weak must neither be deceived with false hope nor broken by fear. Otherwise he may fail when temptations come. Say to him: *Prepare your soul for temptation*[Sir 2:1]. Perhaps he is starting to falter, to tremble with fear, perhaps he is unwilling to approach. You have another passage of Scripture for him: *God is faithful. He does not allow you to be tempted beyond your strength*[1 Cor 10:13]. Make that promise while preaching about the sufferings to come, and you will strengthen the man who is weak. When someone is held back because of excessive fear, promise him God's mercy. It is not that temptations will be lacking, but that God will not permit anyone to be tempted beyond what he can bear. In this manner you will be binding up the broken one.

When they hear of the trials that are coming, some men arm themselves more and, so to speak, are eager to drain the cup. The ordinary medicine of the faithful seems to them but a small thing; for their part they seek the glorious death of the martyrs. Others hear of the temptations to come, and when they do arrive, as arrive they must, they become broken and lame. Yet it is right that such things befall the Christian, and no one esteems them except the one who desires to be a true Christian.

Offer the bandage of consolation, bind up what has been broken. Say this: "Do not be afraid. God in whom you have believed does not abandon you in temptations. God is faithful. He does not allow you to be tempted beyond your strength. It is not I who say this, but the Apostle, and he says further: *Are you willing to accept his trial, the trial of Christ who speaks in me?* When you hear this you are hearing it from Christ himself, you are hearing it from the shepherd who gives pasture to Israel. For of him it was said: *You will give us tears to drink in measure*. The Apostle says: *He does not allow you to be tempted beyond your strength*. This is also what the prophet intends by adding the words: *in measure*. God rebukes but also encourages, he brings fear and he brings consolation, he strikes and he heals. Do not reject him."

Sunday of the Twenty-Fifth Week in Ordinary Time

From a sermon On Pastors by Saint Augustine, Bishop & Doctor

On weak Christians

You have failed to strengthen the weak[Ezek 34:4], says the Lord. He is speaking to wicked shepherds, false shepherds, shepherds who seek their own concerns and not those of Christ. They enjoy the bounty of milk and wool, but they take no care at all of the sheep, and they make no effort to heal those who are ill. I think there is a difference between one who is weak (that is, not strong) and one who is ill, although we often say that the weak are also suffering from illness.

My brothers, when I try to make that distinction, perhaps I could do it better and with greater precision, or perhaps someone with more experience and insight could do so. But when it comes to the words of Scripture, I say what I think so that in the meantime you will not be deprived of all profit. In the case of the weak sheep, it is to be feared that the temptation, when it comes, may break him. The sick person, however, is already ill by reason of some illicit desire or other, and this is keeping him from entering God's path and submitting to Christ's yoke.

There are men who want to live a good life and have already decided to do so, but are not capable of bearing sufferings even though they are ready to do good. Now it is a part of the Christian's strength not only to do good works but also to endure evil. Weak men are those who appear to be zealous in doing good works but are unwilling or unable to endure the sufferings that threaten. Lovers of the world, however, who are kept from good works by some evil desire, lie sick and listless, and it is this sickness that deprives them of any strength to accomplish good works.

The paralytic was like that. When his bearers could not bring him in to the Lord, they opened the roof and lowered him down to the feet of Christ. Perhaps you wish to do this in spirit: to open the roof and to lower a paralytic soul down to the Lord. All its limbs are lifeless, it is empty of every good work, burdened with its sins, and weak from the illness brought on by its evil desires. Since all its limbs are helpless, and the paralysis is interior, you cannot come to the physician. But perhaps the physician himself is concealed within; for the true understanding of Scripture is hidden. Reveal therefore what is hidden, and thus you will open the roof and lower the paralytic to the feet of Christ.

As for those who fail to do this and those who are negligent, you have heard what was said to them: *You have failed to heal the sick; you have failed to bind up what was broken* [Ezek 34:4]. Of this we have already spoken. Man was broken by terrible temptations. But there is at hand a consolation that will bind what was broken: *God is faithful. He does not allow you to be tempted beyond your strength, but with the temptation he will also provide the way of escape, that you may be able to endure it*[1 Cor 10:13].

Monday of the Twenty-Fifth Week in Ordinary Time

From a sermon On Pastors by Saint Augustine, Bishop & Doctor

Welcome or unwelcome, insist upon the message

The straying sheep you have not recalled; the lost sheep you have not sought[Ezek 34:4]. In one way or another, we go on living between the hands of robbers and the teeth of raging wolves, and in light of these present dangers we ask your prayers. The sheep moreover are insolent. The shepherd seeks out the straying sheep, but because they have wandered away and are lost they say that they are not ours. " Why do you want us? Why do you seek us?" they ask, as if their straying and being lost were not the very reason for our wanting them and seeking them out. "If I am straying," he says, "if I am lost, why do you want me?" You are straying, that is why I wish to recall you. You have been lost, I wish to find you. "But I wish to stray," he says: "I wish to be lost."

So you wish to stray and be lost? How much better that I do not also wish this. Certainly, I dare say, I am unwelcome. But I listen to the Apostle who says: *Preach the word; insist upon it, welcome and unwelcome*[2 Tim 4:2]. Welcome to whom? Unwelcome to whom? By all means welcome to those who desire it; unwelcome to those who do not. However unwelcome, I dare to say: "You wish to stray, you wish to be lost; but I do not want this." For the one whom I fear does not wish this. And should I wish it, consider his words of reproach: *The straying sheep you have not recalled; the lost sheep you have not sought*[Ezek 34:4]. Shall I fear you rather than him? *Remember, we must all present ourselves before the judgment seat of Christ*[2 Cor 5:10].

I shall recall the straying; I shall seek the lost. Whether they wish it or not, I shall do it. And should the brambles of the forests tear at me when I seek them, I shall force myself through all straits; I shall put down all hedges. So far as the God whom I fear grants me the strength, I shall search everywhere. I shall recall the straying; I shall seek after those on the verge of being lost. If you do not want me to suffer, do not stray, do not become lost. It is enough that I lament your straying and loss. No, I fear that in neglecting you, I shall also kill what is strong. Consider the passage that follows: *And what was strong you have destroyed*. Should I neglect the straying and lost, the strong one will also take delight in straying and in being lost.

Tuesday of the Twenty-Fifth Week in Ordinary Time

From a sermon On Pastors by Saint Augustine, Bishop & Doctor

The Church, like a vine, spreads everywhere in her growth

They were scattered on every mountain and on every hill and over the entire face of the earth[Ezek 34:6]. What is the meaning of the phrase: *They were scattered over the entire face of the earth?* Some men continually strive for all the goods of the world, the goods that are so evident on the face of the earth; yes, they love and prize them. They do not want to die, to have their lives buried in Christ. *Over the entire face of the earth:* such men love earthly things; moreover such straying sheep are to be found over the entire face of the earth. They dwell indifferent places, but one mother, pride, has given birth to them all, just as one mother, our Catholic Church, has given birth to all faithful Christians scattered over the whole world.

Small wonder that pride gives birth to division, and love to unity. But our catholic mother is herself a shepherd; she seeks the straying sheep everywhere, strengthens the weak, heals the sick, and binds up the injured. They may not know one another, but she knows all of them because she reaches out to all her sheep.

Thus she is like a vine that is spread out everywhere in its growth. The straying sheep are like useless branches which because of their sterility are deservedly cut off, not to destroy the vine but to prune it. When these branches were cut down, they were left lying there. But the vine grew and flourished, and it knew both the branches that remained upon it and those that had been cut off and left lying beside it.

She calls the stray sheep back, however, because the Apostle said in reference to the broken branches: *God has the power to graft them on again*[Rom 11:23]. Call them sheep straying from the flock or branches cut off from the vine, God is equally capable of calling back the sheep or of grafting the branches on again, for he is equally the chief shepherd and the true farmer. *And they were scattered over the entire face of the earth, and there was no one to search for them, no one to call them back*[Ezek 34:6], that is to say, no one among those wicked shepherds. *There was no one to search for them,* that is, no one among men.

Therefore, shepherds, hear the word of the Lord: I live, says the Lord God[Ezek 34:9-15]. Notice the beginning of this passage; it is as if God were taking an oath, giving testimony to his own life. *I live, says the Lord.* The shepherds are dead, but the sheep are safe, for the Lord lives. *I live, says the Lord God.* Which shepherds are dead? Those who seek what is theirs and not what is Christ's. But will there be shepherds who seek what is Christ's and not what is theirs, and will they be found? There will indeed be such shepherds, and they will indeed be found; they are not lacking, nor will they be lacking in the future.

Wednesday of the Twenty-Fifth Week in Ordinary Time

From a sermon On Pastors by Saint Augustine, Bishop & Doctor

Do whatever they tell you, but do not follow what they do

Shepherds, hear the word of the Lord[Ezek 34:9]. But what are the shepherds to hear? *Thus says the Lord God: Behold I myself am over the shepherds, and I will claim my sheep from their hands*[Ezek 34:10].

Hear and learn, you sheep of God. God calls for an accounting of his sheep from the wicked shepherds and inquires into the death of his sheep at their hands. For in another passage he speaks through the same prophet: *Son of man, I have appointed you a watchman for the house of Israel. You shall hear the word from my mouth and you shall point out the way to them in my name. When I say to the sinner: You shall die, and you do not speak to warn the wicked man from his wicked way, because of his wickedness he shall die, but you shall be held responsible for his death. If, however, you warn the wicked man to turn away from his wickedness, and he fails to do so, he shall die in his iniquity, but you shall have saved your soul*[Ezek 3:17-19].

Dear brothers, what does this mean? Do you see how dangerous it is to keep silent? The sinner dies and rightly so; he dies in his wickedness and in his sin, for his failure to heed you has killed him. He could have found the Lord, the living shepherd who says: *I live*. But he was heedless; and the one appointed for this task, the watchman, did not warn him. The wicked one then justly suffers death and the watchman rightly suffers damnation. But the Lord says, if you say to the wicked man: *You shall surely die*, and if he fails to heed the sword of judgment with which I have threatened him, that sword will overtake and kill him, and he will die in his sin; but you will have saved your soul. Therefore it is our task not to keep silent, and it is your task, even if we ourselves are silent, to hear the words of the shepherd from the Scriptures.

I have said that he will take the sheep from the bad shepherds and give them to shepherds who are good. Let us consider whether he does so. I see him taking the seep from the bad shepherds, when he says: *Behold, I myself am over the shepherds, and I will claim my sheep from their hands; and I will turn away from them so that they may not pasture my sheep, and the shepherds shall no longer give pasture*[Ezek 34:9-10]. For when I say: "Let them pasture my sheep," they give pasture to themselves and not to my sheep. Therefore, *I will turn away from them so that they may not pasture my sheep*[Ezek 34:10].

How does the Lord turn away from them to keep them from pasturing his sheep? *Do whatever they tell you, but do not follow what they do*[Mt 23:3]. It is as if he said: "The words they say are mine, but their deeds are their own." If you do not follow the example of the bad shepherds, they are not giving you pasture. But if you do what they say, it is I who am feeding you.

Thursday of the Twenty-Fifth Week in Ordinary Time

From a sermon On Pastors by Saint Augustine, Bishop & Doctor

In good pastures I shall feed my sheep

I shall lead them forth from the Gentiles, and I shall gather them from foreign lands; I shall bring them into their own land, and I shall feed them on the mountains of Israel[Ezek 34:13]. It was God who brought forth the mountains of Israel, that is to say, the authors of the divine Scriptures. Feed there that you may feed in safety. Whatever you hear from that source, you should savor. Whatever is foreign to it, reject. Hear the voice of the shepherd, lest you wander about in the mist. Gather at the mountains of holy Scripture. There, are the things that will delight your hearts; there, you will find nothing poisonous, nothing hostile; there the pastures are most plentiful. There, you will be healthy sheep; you will feed safely on the mountain of Israel.

And I shall feed them in streams and in every inhabited place in the land[Ezek 34:13]. From the mountains which we have shown you, there have issued the streams of the gospel message because *their voice has gone forth into the whole world*[Ps 18:5], and every habitable place has become pleasant and fertile for the grazing sheep.

In good pastures and on the high mountains of Israel, I shall feed them. And their grazing ground shall be there[Ezek 34:14], that is, the place where they will rest, where they will say: "I am happy"; where they will say: "It is true, it is clear, we are not deceived." They will find rest in the glory of God, when they find rest in those grazing grounds. *And they will sleep,* that is, find rest, *and they will rest in good pleasures*[Ezek 34:14-15].

And they will be fed in rich pastures on the mountains of Israel [Ezek 34:14]. I have already spoken of the mountains of Israel, the good mountains to which we raise our eyes and from which may come our help. But our help is from the Lord, who made heaven and earth. Let us not then place our hope in the good mountains themselves, but let us rely on his word which says: *I will feed my sheep on the mountains of Israel*. Let us not merely remain on the mountains themselves, for he added immediately: *I will feed my sheep*. Raise your eyes, therefore, to the mountains, whence your help comes; but take note that he says: *I will feed*. For you help is *from the Lord, who made heaven and earth*[Ps 123:8].

He concludes by saying: *And I will feed them with judgment* [Ezek 34:16]. Observe that he alone so feeds his sheep, in feeding them with judgment. For what man can judge rightly concerning another? Our whole daily life is filled with rash judgments. He of whom we had despaired is converted suddenly and becomes very good. He from whom we had anticipated a great deal suddenly fails and becomes very bad. Neither our fear nor our hope is certain.

What any man is today, that man himself scarcely knows. Still in some way he does know what he is today. What he will be tomorrow, however, he does not know. Hence the Lord, who assigns to each what is owed to him, feeds his sheep with judgment, giving some things to one group, other things to another, and to each his due. For he knows what he is doing. With judgment he feeds those whom he, being judged himself, redeemed. Therefore, he himself feeds his sheep with judgment.

Friday of the Twenty-Fifth Week in Ordinary Time

From a sermon On Pastors by Saint Augustine, Bishop & Doctor

All good shepherds are one in the one shepherd

Christ is your shepherd and judge; he judges between his own sheep and other sheep. *My sheep,* he says, *hear my voice and follow me*[Jn 10:27-28].

In this statement I find that all good shepherds are one in the one shepherd. It is not that good shepherds are lacking; they are there in the one shepherd. When we speak of "many" we refer to those who are divided from each other. Here only one is spoken of, because in this passage unity is commended. The reason why shepherds are not mentioned here, but only one shepherd, is not because the Lord has failed to find anyone to whom to entrust his sheep; he entrusted the sheep to Peter because he had found Peter. Indeed, in the case of Peter he also commended the unity of the flock. There were many apostles, and yet to one only did he say: *Feed my sheep* [Jn 21:15-17]. Do not imagine that there will be no more good shepherds, or that we shall find them lacking, or that the Lord's mercy will not produce and establish them.

Certainly, if there are good sheep there are also good shepherds; good sheep give rise to good shepherds. But all good shepherds are one in the one good shepherd; they form a unity. If only they feed the sheep, Christ is feeding the sheep. The friends of the bridegroom do not speak with their own voice, but they take great joy in listening to the bridegroom's voice. Christ himself is the shepherd when they act as shepherds. "I feed them," he says, because his voice is in their voice, his love in their love.

When he entrusted his sheep to Peter as one person to another, Christ chose to make Peter one with himself. He wanted to entrust him with the sheep in such a way that he himself might be the head and Peter might represent the body, that is, the Church. As bridegroom and bride, Christ and the Church were to be two in one flesh.

Accordingly, what does he say before he entrusts the sheep to Peter as to someone who is not separate from himself? *Peter, do you love me? He answered: I love you. And again: Do you love me? He answered: I love you. And a third time: Do you love me? He answered: I love you*[Jn 21:15-17]. He receives an assurance of love in order to establish unity. Christ is the one shepherd who is one with the other shepherds, and in whom they themselves are one.

Shepherds are not mentioned, but they are not passed over. Shepherds have cause for pride, but *if anyone boasts it should be in the Lord*[2 Cor 10:17]. This means that Christ should be the shepherd, that they should be shepherds for Christ, shepherds in Christ, not shepherds for themselves, apart from Christ. When the prophet said: *I will feed my sheep,* it was not because of a lack of shepherds, as though he were foretelling those evil times to come and saying: "I have no one to whom I can entrust my sheep." At a time when Peter himself, and the apostles too, were alive in the body, Christ, the one in whom alone all are one, said this: *I have other sheep that are not of this sheepfold; I must bring them in as well, so that there may be one flock and one shepherd*[Jn 10:16].

All shepherds should therefore be one in the one good shepherd. All should speak with the one voice of the one shepherd, so that the sheep may hear and follow their shepherd; not this or that shepherd, but the one shepherd. All should speak with one voice in Christ, not with different voices. *Brethren, I beg all of you to say the same thing, and to have no dissensions among you*[1 Cor 1:10]. The sheep should hear this voice, a voice purified from all schism, freed from all heresy, and so follow their shepherd, who says: *My sheep hear my voice and follow me.*

Saturday of the Twenty-Fifth Week in Ordinary Time

From a discourse on the psalms by Saint Hilary of Poitiers, Bishop

The river whose streams gladden the city of God

The river of God is brimming with water. You have provided their food, for this is your way of preparing them[Ps 64:10]. There can be no doubt about the river referred to, for the prophet says: *There is a river whose streams gladden the city of God*[Ps 45:5]*; and in the gospel the Lord himself says: Streams of living water welling up to eternal life will flow from the heart of anyone who drinks the water I shall give him*[Jn 4:14]*.* He was speaking of the Holy Spirit, whom those who believed in him were to receive. The river of God is brimming with water; that is to say, we are inundated by the gifts of the Holy Spirit and from that fountain of life the river of God pours into us in a full flood.

We also have food prepared for us. And who is this food? It is he in whom we are prepared for life with God, for by receiving his holy body we receive a place in the communion of his holy body. This is what is meant by the words of the psalm: *You have provided their food, for this is your way of preparing them*[Ps 64:10]. For as well as refreshing us now, that food also prepares us for the life to come.

We who have been reborn through the sacrament of baptism experience intense joy when we feel within us the first stirrings of the Holy Spirit. We begin to have an insight into the mysteries of faith, we are able to prophesy and to speak with wisdom. We become steadfast in hope and receive the gift of healing. Demons are made subject to our authority. These gifts enter us like a gentle rain, and once having done so, little by little, they bring forth fruit in abundance.

Sunday of the Twenty-Sixth Week in Ordinary Time

From the beginning of a letter to the Philippians by Saint Polycarp, Bishop & Martyr

It is by grace that you are saved

From Polycarp and his fellow presbyters to the pilgrim church of God at Philippi: May you have mercy and peace in abundance from Almighty God and Jesus Christ our Savior.

I rejoice with you greatly in the Lord Jesus Christ because you have assumed the pattern of true love and have rightly helped on their way those who were in chains. Such chains are becoming to the faithful; they are the rich crown of the chosen ones of our Lord and God. I am glad, too, that your deep-rooted faith, proclaimed of old, still abides and continues to bear fruit in the life-giving power of our Lord Jesus Christ. He, for our sins, did not refuse to go down to death, and *God raised him up after destroying the pains of hell*[Acts 2:24]*. With a glorious joy that no words can express you believe in Christ without seeing him*[1 Pet 1:8]. This is the joy in which many wish to share *knowing that it is by grace that you are saved and not by works*[Eph 2:8-9 (nota bene: the "works" spoken of here refer to the Jewish 603 other "rules." This is not in conflict with Jas 2:14-17)], for so God has willed through Jesus Christ.

So prepare yourselves for the struggle, serve the Lord in fear [Sir 2:1; 1 Pet 1:3-9] and truth. Put aside empty talk and popular errors; *your faith must be in him who raised our Lord Jesus Christ from the dead and gave him a share in his own glory*[1 Pet 1:21] and a seat at his right hand. To him everything was made subject in heaven and on earth; all things obey him, who will come as judge of the living and the dead. All who refuse to believe in him must answer to God for the blood of his Son.

He who raised him from the dead will raise us too if we do his will and keep his commandments, loving what he loved, refraining from all wrongdoing, fraud, avarice, malice and slander. We must abstain from false witness, *not returning evil for evil, nor curse for curse*[1 Pet 3:9], nor blow for blow, nor denunciation for denunciation. Always remember the words of the Lord, who taught: *Do not judge and you will not be judged; forgive and you will be forgiven; be merciful and you will find mercy; the amount you measure out to others will be the amount measured out to you*[Lk 6:37-38]*. Blessed are the poor and those who suffer persecution, for theirs is the kingdom of God*[Mt 5:3-12].

Monday of the Twenty-Sixth Week in Ordinary Time

From a letter to the Philippians by Saint Polycarp, Bishop & Martyr

Let us put on the armor of righteousness

It is not out of presumption that I write to you, my brothers, on what righteousness means, but rather because you asked me to do so. For neither I nor anyone like me can equal the wisdom of the blessed and glorious Paul. When he was in your city, he fully and courageously taught the men of that time the word of truth; when he was absent, he wrote you letters. By carefully studying these letters, you can strengthen yourselves in the faith that has been given to you. This faith is *the mother of us all,* followed by hope, preceded by love - love of God, of Christ, of our neighbor. Whoever lives within this framework has fulfilled the commandment of righteousness. For anyone who has love is far from sin.

Now the source of all evil is the desire to possess[1 Tim 6:10]. Mindful that we *brought nothing into this world and can take nothing out of it*[1 Tim 6:7], let us put on the armor of righteousness. We must begin by teaching ourselves how to walk in the commandment of the Lord. Then you should teach your wives to walk in the faith that has been handed down to them, in love and in chastity. They must love their husbands with complete fidelity, but they must cherish all others equally, and with self-control; they must raise their children in the discipline that comes from fear of God. We must teach widows to be discreet in all that concerns the faith of the Lord; they must pray without ceasing for all men, shunning all calumny, gossip, false witness, greed, in a word, every sort of evil. They must bear in mind that they are God's sacrificial altar. He sees everything clearly, nothing escapes his vigilance, be it calculation, thought or some secret desire of the heart.

God, as we know, *is not mocked*[Gal 6:7]. Let us walk in a way that is worthy of his commands and his purposes. Deacons, in the same way, must be blameless in the sight of his goodness, for they are servants of God and of Christ, not of men. They must avoid calumny, hypocritical talk and greed. Merciful and diligent, they must control all their desires, walking according to the truth of the Lord who became the servant of all. If we please him in this life, we shall receive the life to come; for he has promised us that he will raise us from the dead, and that, if we lead lives worthy of him, we shall reign along with him. This is what our faith tells us.

Tuesday of the Twenty-Sixth Week in Ordinary Time

From a letter to the Philippians by Saint Polycarp, Bishop & Martyr

Jesus has set us a personal example

Presbyters should be sympathetic and merciful to everyone, bringing back those who have wandered, visiting the sick; they must not neglect widows and orphans, or the poor, *ever providing for what is good in the sight of God and of men*[2 Cor 8:21]. They should refrain entirely from anger, human respect and prejudice; avarice should be wholly alien to them. Nor should they be rash in believing something said against another, nor too severe in judging others, since they know that we are all debtors through sin.

If, then, we pray to the Lord to forgive us, we must in turn forgive. For we live under the eye of our Lord and God, and *we must all stand before the judgment seat of God, each to give an account of himself*[2 Cor 5:10]. Let us then serve God with fear and awe. The Lord's command is also the command of the apostles who preached the Gospel to us, to say nothing of the prophets who foretold the Lord's coming. Our observance of what is good should be meticulous, avoiding anything that might cause another to stumble; we must shun false brothers and those who assume the Lord's name hypocritically and lead the unwary into error.

For anyone who does not confess that Jesus has come in the flesh is the antichrist[1 Jn 4:3]. And anyone who refuses to admit the testimony of the cross is of the devil. Whoever perverts the Lord's words to suit his own desires and denies that there is a resurrection or a judgment is the firstborn of Satan. So let us abandon the folly of the masses and their false teaching, and return to the teaching that was handed down to us from the beginning. We must be alert in prayer, constant in fasting; and in our prayers let us beg God, who sees everything, *not to lead us into temptation*[Mt 6:13]. As the Lord has said: *The spirit is willing, but the flesh is weak*[Mt 26:41].

So let us persevere in the pledge of our righteousness and in our hope, that is, in Christ Jesus. *In his mouth no hint of guilt was discovered; he committed no sin and yet bore our sins in his own body on the tree*[1 Pet 2:22-23]. Rather, he endured everything for our sake so that we might live in him. Let us then imitate his constancy; if we should suffer because of his name, let us give him that glory. For this is the personal example he has given us, this is the object of our faith.

Wednesday of the Twenty-Sixth Week in Ordinary Time

From a letter to the Philippians by Saint Polycarp, Bishop & Martyr

Let us run our race in faith and righteousness

I ask you all to respond to the call of righteousness and to practice boundless patience. Your own eyes have seen it not only in blessed Ignatius, Zosimus and Rufus, but in others from among you as well, to say nothing of Paul and the other apostles. Be assured that all these men *did not run their race in vain*[Phil 2:16]. No, they ran it in faith and in righteousness and are now with the Lord in the place that they have earned, even as they were once with him in suffering. *Their love was not for this present world*[1 Jn 2:15-17]; rather, it was for him who died for our sakes and, on account of us, was raised up again by God.

Be steadfast, then, and follow the Lord's example, strong and unshaken in faith, loving the community as you love one another. United in the truth, show the Lord's own gentleness in your dealings with one another, and look down on no one. If you can do good, do not put it off, because *almsgiving frees one from death*[Tob 12:9]. Be subject to one another, and *make sure that your behavior among the pagans is beyond reproach*[1 Pet 2:12]. Thus you will be praised *for the good you have done,* and the Lord will not be blasphemed because of you. *But woe to that man on whose account the Lord's name is blasphemed*[Mt 18:6-7]. Therefore, teach everyone to live soberly, just as you live yourselves.

I am greatly saddened on account of Valens who at one time was presbyter among you; he does not understand the position to which he was called. So I urge all of you to be chaste and honest, to avoid avarice and to refrain from every form of evil. If a man cannot control himself in these ways, how can he teach someone else to do so? If he does not avoid greed, he will be defiled by idolatrous practices and will be reckoned as one of the pagans who know nothing of the Lord's judgment. Or, as Paul teaches: *Do we not know that the holy ones will judge the world*[1 Cor 6:2]?

However, I have never seen or heard of anything of that sort among you, for whom blessed Paul labored and whom he commends at the beginning of his letter. For he boasted about you in all the churches which at that time were the only ones that had come to know God; we ourselves had not yet come to that knowledge.

Brothers, I am deeply sorry for Valens and for his wife; may the Lord grant them true repentance. As for yourselves, be self-controlled in this respect. *Do not look on such people as enemies*[Polycarp], but invite them back as frail members who have gone astray, so that the entire body of which you are a part will be saved. In doing this you are contributing to your own spiritual development.

Thursday of the Twenty-Sixth Week in Ordinary Time

From a letter to the Philippians by Saint Polycarp, Bishop & Martyr

May Christ build you up in faith and in truth

I am sure that you are well grounded in the Scriptures and nothing of their message escapes you. I, however, have not been so fortunate. As these same Scriptures put it: *Be angry and do not sin and Do not let the sun set on your anger*[Eph 4:26]. Blessed is the man who bears this in mind, as I am sure you do.

May God the father of our Lord Jesus Christ and the eternal high priest himself, the Son of God, Jesus Christ, build you up in faith and in truth and in great gentleness. May you never know anger, but be patient, long-suffering, persevering and chaste. May he grant you a place among his saints; and may he give the same to us along with you, as well as to all on earth who put their faith in our Lord Jesus Christ and in his *Father who has raised him from the dead*[Polycarp].

Keep all the saints in your prayers. Pray, too, for our rulers, for our leaders, and for all those in power, even for those who persecute and hate you, and for those who are enemies of the cross. In this way, your good works will be seen by all men, and you will be perfected in him.

Both you and Ignatius have written me to ask whether anyone going to Syria will deliver your letter as well as ours. If the opportunity offers itself, I will do it; if I cannot, I will send a representative.

As you request, we have returned to you the letters Ignatius sent us and as many other letters as we had; they are being enclosed with this letter. You will derive great benefit from them, for they are full of faith and patience, and great edification in all that refers to our Lord. Send us any certain information you may possess about Ignatius and his companions.

I am sending this letter to you by Crescens, whom I commended to you when I was present, and do so again. He has lived blamelessly among us, as I am sure he will among you. When his sister comes to you, she too will come with our commendation.

May you find protection in the Lord Jesus Christ, and may his grace be with all who are yours. Amen.

Friday of the Twenty-Sixth Week in Ordinary Time

From a treatise on the letter to the Philippians by Saint Ambrose, Bishop & Doctor

Rejoice in the Lord always

Dear brethren, God's love is calling us to the joys of eternal happiness for the salvation of our souls. You have just listened to the from the Apostle in which he says: *Rejoice in the Lord always*[Phil 4:4]. The joys of this world lead to eternal misery, but the joys that are according to the Lord's will, bring those who persevere in them to joys that are enduring and everlasting. The Apostle therefore says: *Again I say: rejoice*[Phil 4:4].

He urges us to find ever increasing joy in God and in keeping his commandments. The more we try in this world to give ourselves completely to God our Lord by obeying his commands, the greater will be our happiness in the life to come, and the greater the glory that will be ours in the presence of God.

Let your moderation be known to all men[Phil 4:5]. That is to say, your holiness of life must be evident, not only in the sight of God, but also in the sight of men. It must give an example of moderation and self-control to all your contemporaries on earth and serve also as a memorial of goodness before God and men.

The Lord is near; have no anxiety[Phil 4:4-7]. The Lord is always near to all who call upon his help with sincerity, true faith, sure hope, and perfect love. He knows what you need, even before you ask him. He is always ready to come to the aid of all his faithful servants in every need. There is no reason for us to be in a state of great anxiety when evils threaten; we must remember that God is very near us as our protector. *The Lord is at hand for those who are troubled in heart, and he will save those who are downcast in spirit. The tribulations of the just are many, and the Lord will rescue them from them*[Ps 33:19-20]. If we do our best to obey and keep his commandments, he does not delay in giving us what he has promised.

But in every prayer and entreaty let your petitions be made known to God, with thanksgiving[Phil 4:6]. In time of trouble we must not grumble or be downhearted; God forbid! We must rather be patient and cheerful, *giving thanks to God always in everything*[Eph 5:20].

Saturday of the Twenty-Sixth Week in Ordinary Time

From a book on Christian formation by Saint Gregory of Nyssa, Bishop

Fight the good fight of faith

Whoever is in Christ is a new creation; the old has passed away[2 Cor 5:17]. Now by the "new creation" Paul means the indwelling of the Holy Spirit in a heart that is pure and blameless, free of all malice, wickedness or shamefulness. For when a soul has come to hate sin and has delivered itself as far as it can to the power of virtue, it undergoes a transformation by receiving the grace of the Spirit. Then is it healed, restored and made wholly new. Indeed the two texts: *Purge out the old leaven that you may be a new one, and: Let us celebrate the festival, not with the old leaven but with the unleavened bread of sincerity and truth*[1 Cor 5:7-8], support those passages which speak about the new creation.

Yet the tempter spreads many a snare to trap the soul, and of itself human nature is too weak to defeat him. This is why the Apostle bids us to arm ourselves with heavenly weapons, when he says: *Put on the breastplate of righteousness and have your feet shod with the gospel of peace and have truth around your waist as a belt*[Eph 6:14]. Can you not see how many forms of salvation the Apostle indicates, all leading to the same path and the same goal? Following them to the heights of God's commandments, we easily complete the race of life. For elsewhere the Apostle says: *Let us run with fidelity the race that has been set before us, with our eyes on Jesus, the origin and the goal of our faith*[Heb 12:1-3].

So a man who openly despises the accolades of this world and rejects all earthly glory must also practice self-denial. Such self-denial means that you never seek your own will but God's, using God's will as a sure guide; it also means possessing nothing apart from what is held in common. In this way it will be easier for you to carry out your superior's commands promptly, in joy and in hope; this is required of Christ's servants who are redeemed for service to the brethren. For this is what the Lord wants when he says: *Whoever wishes to be first and great among you must be the last of all and a servant to all*[Mt 20:26].

Our service of mankind must be given freely. One who is in such a position must be subject to everyone and serve his brothers as if he were paying off a debt. Moreover, those who are in charge should work harder than the others and conduct themselves with greater submission than their own subjects. Their lives should serve as a visible example of what service means, and they should remember that those who are committed to their trust are held in trust from God.

Those, then, who are in a position of authority must look after their brothers as conscientious teachers look after the young children who have been handed over to them by their parents. If both disciples and masters have this loving relationship, then subjects will be happy to obey whatever is commanded, while superiors will be delighted to lead their brothers to perfection. If you try to outdo one another in showing respect, your life on earth will be like that of the angels.

Sunday of the Twenty-Seventh Week in Ordinary Time

From the Pastoral Guide by Saint Gregory the Great, Pope & Doctor

Let the pastor be discreetly silent, and to the point when he speaks

A spiritual guide should be silent when discretion requires and speak when words are of service. Otherwise he may say what he should not or be silent when he should speak. Indiscreet speech may lead men into error and an imprudent silence may leave in error those who could have been taught. Pastors who lack foresight hesitate to say openly what is right because they fear losing the favor of men. As the voice of truth tells us, such leaders are not zealous pastors who protect their flocks, rather they are like mercenaries who flee by taking refuge in silence when the wolf appears.

The Lord reproaches them through the prophet: *They are dumb dogs that cannot bark*[Isa 56:10]. On another occasion he complains: *You did not advance against the foe or set up a wall in front of the house of Israel, so that you might stand fast in battle on the day of the Lord*[Ezek 13:5]. To advance against the foe involves a bold resistance to the powers of this world in defense of the flock. To stand fast in battle on the day of the Lord means to oppose the wicked enemy out of love for what is right.

When a pastor has been afraid to assert what is right, has he not turned his back and fled by remaining silent? Whereas if he intervenes on behalf of the flock, he sets up a wall against the enemy in front of the house of Israel. Therefore, the Lord again says to his unfaithful people: *Your prophets saw false and foolish visions and did not point out your wickedness, that you might repent of your sins*[Lam 2:14]. The name of prophet is sometimes given in the sacred writings to teachers who both declare the present to be fleeting and reveal what is to come. The word of God accuses them of seeing false visions because they are afraid to reproach men for their faults and thereby lull the evildoer with an empty promise of safety. Because they fear reproach, they keep silent and fail to point out the sinner's wrongdoing.

The word of reproach is a key that unlocks a door, because reproach reveals a fault of which the evildoer is himself often unaware. That is why Paul says of the bishop: *He must be able to encourage men in sound doctrine and refute those who oppose it*[Titus 1:9]. For the same reason God tells us through Malachi: *The lips of the priest are to preserve knowledge, and men shall look to him for the law, for he is the messenger of the Lord of hosts*[Mal 2:7]. Finally, that is also the reason why the Lord warns us through Isaiah: *Cry out and be not still; raise your voice in a trumpet call*[Isa 58: *1*].

Anyone ordained a priest undertakes the task of preaching, so that with a loud cry he may go on ahead of the terrible judge who follows. If, then, a priest does not know how to preach, what kind of cry can such a dumb herald utter? It was to bring this home that the Holy Spirit descended in the form of tongues on the first pastors, for he causes those whom he has filled, to speak out spontaneously.

Monday of the Twenty-Seventh Week in Ordinary Time

From a treatise on Cain and Abel by Saint Ambrose, Bishop & Doctor

Pray especially for the whole body of the Church

Offer God a sacrifice of praise and fulfill your vows to the Most High[Ps 49:14-15]. If you praise God you offer your vow and fulfill the promise you have made. So the Samaritan leper, healed by the Lord's word of command, gained greater credit than the other nine; he alone returned to Christ, praising God and giving thanks. Jesus said of him: *There was no one to come back and thank God except this foreigner. He tells him: Stand up and go on your way, for your faith has made you whole*[Lk 17:18-19].

The Lord Jesus, in his divine wisdom, taught you about the goodness of the Father, who knows how to give good things, so that you might ask for the things that are good from Goodness itself. He urges you to pray earnestly and frequently, not offering long and wearisome prayers, but praying often, and with perseverance. Lengthy prayers are usually filled with empty words, while neglect of prayer results in indifference to prayer.

Again, Christ urges you, when you ask forgiveness for yourself, to be especially generous to others, so that your actions may commend your prayer. The Apostle, too, teaches you how to pray: you must avoid anger and contentiousness, so that your prayer may be serene and wholesome. He tells you also that every place is a place of prayer, though our Savior says: *Go into your room*[Mt 6:6].

But by "room" you must understand, not a room enclosed by walls that imprison your body, but the room that is within you, the room where you hide your thoughts, where you keep your affections. This room of prayer is always with you, wherever you are, and it is always a secret room, where only God can see you.

You are told to pray especially for the people, that is, for the whole body, for all its members, the family of your mother the Church; the badge of membership in this body is love for each other. If you pray only for yourself, you pray for yourself alone. If each one prays for himself, he receives less from God's goodness than the one who prays on behalf of others. But as it is, because each prays for all, all are in fact praying for each one.

To conclude, if you pray only for yourself, you will be praying, as we said, for yourself alone. But if you pray for all, all will pray for you, for you are included in all. In this way there is a great recompense; through the prayers of each individual, the intercession of the whole people is gained for each individual. There is here no pride, but an increase of humility and a richer harvest from prayer.

Tuesday of the Twenty-Seventh Week in Ordinary Time

From the letter to the Trallians by Saint Ignatius of Antioch, Bishop & Martyr

I wish to forewarn you, for you are my dearest children

Ignatius, also called Theophorus, to the holy church at Tralles in the province of Asia, dear to God the Father of Jesus Christ, elect and worthy of God, enjoying peace in body and in the Spirit through the passion of Jesus Christ, who is our hope through our resurrection when we rise to him. In the manner of the apostles, I too send greetings to you with the fullness of grace and extend my every best wish.

Reports of your splendid character have reached me: how you are beyond reproach and ever unshaken in your patient endurance – qualities that you have not acquired but are yours by nature. My informant was your own bishop Polybius, who by the will of God and Jesus Christ visited me here in Smyrna. He so fully entered into my joy at being in chains for Christ that I came to see your whole community embodied in him. Moreover, when I learned from him of your God-given kindliness toward me, I broke out in words of praise for God. It is on him, I discovered, that you pattern your lives.

Your submission to your bishop, who is in the place of Jesus Christ, shows me that you are not living as men usually do but in the manner of Jesus himself, who died for us that you might escape death by belief in his death. Thus one thing is necessary, and you already observe it, that you do nothing without your bishop; indeed, be subject to the clergy as well, seeing in them the apostles of Jesus Christ our hope, for if we live in him we shall be found in him.

Deacons, too, who are ministers of the mysteries of Jesus should in all things be pleasing to all men. For they are not mere servants with food and drink, but emissaries of God's Church; hence they should guard themselves against anything deserving reproach as they would against fire.

Similarly, all should respect the deacons as Jesus Christ, just as all should regard the bishop as the image of the Father, and the clergy as God's senate and the college of the apostles. Without these three orders you cannot begin to speak of a church. I am confident that you share my feelings in this matter, for I have had an example of your love in the person of your bishop who is with me now. His whole bearing is a great lesson, and his very gentleness wields a mighty influence.

By God's grace there are many things I understand, but I keep well within my limitations for fear that boasting should be my undoing. At the moment, then, I must be more apprehensive than ever and pay no attention at all to those who flatter me; their praise is as a scourge. For though I have a fierce desire to suffer martyrdom, I know not whether I am worthy of it. Most people are unaware of my passionate longing, but it assails me with increasing intensity. My present need, then, is for that humility by which the prince of this world is overthrown.

And so I strongly urge you, not I so much as the love of Jesus Christ, to be nourished exclusively on Christian fare, abstaining from the alien food that is heresy. And this you will do if you are neither arrogant nor cut off from God, from Jesus Christ, and from the bishop and the teachings of the apostles. Whoever is within the sanctuary is pure; but whoever is not is unclean. That is to say, whoever acts apart from the bishop and the clergy and the deacons is not pure in his conscience. In writing this, it is not that I am aware of anything of the sort among you; I only wish to forewarn you, for you are my dearest children.

Wednesday of the Twenty-Seventh Week in Ordinary Time

From a letter to the Trallians by Saint Ignatius of Antioch, Bishop & Martyr

Renew yourselves in the faith that is the body of Christ and in the love that is his blood

Make yourselves gentle, and be born again in the faith which is the body of the Lord and in the love which is the blood of Jesus Christ. No one must bear a grudge against his neighbor. Never give the pagans the slightest pretext, so that the great majority who serve God will not be mocked because of the folly of a few. *Woe to him on account of whose folly my name is blasphemed*[St. Ignatius of Antioch].

So turn a deaf ear to the talk of anyone whose language has nothing to do with Jesus Christ. Descended from David, he was truly born of Mary, he really ate and drank. He was really persecuted under Pontius Pilate, and truly died by crucifixion, while heavenly and earthly beings and those under the earth looked on. He truly rose from the dead, being raised by his Father. Those who believe in him will be raised like him by the Father. We shall rise again in Christ without whom we do not have true life.

Avoid, then, those poisonous growths that bear deadly fruit; the mere taste of them is sudden death. Such growths are not of the Father's planting; if they were they would be recognized as branches of the cross, their fruit would be imperishable. The cross of Christ's passion is his invitation to you who are the members of his body. The head cannot come to life without the members, since God, the very ground of unity, has foretold such a union.

I send you greetings from Smyrna and from all God's churches which are here with me. They have been a comfort to me in every way, both physically and spiritually. The chains which I wear for the sake of Jesus Christ, praying all the time that I may come to God, are my plea. Continue to live together in that harmony of yours and persevere in prayer together. It is fitting that everyone, and especially the presbyters, should comfort the bishop and thereby honor the Father and Jesus Christ, and his apostles.

I beg you, if you love me, listen to me, so that this letter of mine may not witness against you. And pray for me, too, lest I be found unfit, for in God's mercy I need your love to make me worthy of the destiny that is mine.

The communities of Smyrna and Ephesus send greetings. In all your prayers remember the church in Syria. I am unworthy to claim membership in it, being the least of them all. And now, farewell in Jesus Christ. Be submissive to your bishop, as you would to God's command, and also to the clergy. As individuals, love one another with undivided affection. My life is being sacrificed for you, not only at this moment, but also when I shall come before God. Though I am still in danger, God the Father, through Jesus Christ, is my pledge that my prayer and yours will be heard. My desire is that, through him, you may be found without fault.

Thursday of the Twenty-Seventh Week in Ordinary Time

From a letter to the Philadelphians by Saint Ignatius of Antioch, Bishop & Martyr

One bishop with the presbyters and deacons

Ignatius, also called Theophorus, to the church of God the Father and the Lord Jesus Christ located at Philadelphia in the province of Asia. You have found mercy and have been strengthened in the peace of God; you are now filled with gladness because of the passion of our Lord, and by his mercy you are made believers in his resurrection. I greet you in the blood of Jesus Christ. You are my abiding and unshakable joy, especially if your members remain united with the bishop and with his presbyters and deacons, all appointed in accordance with the mind of Christ who by his own will has strengthened them in the firmness which the Spirit gives.

I know that this bishop has obtained his ministry, which serves the community, neither by his own efforts, nor from men nor even out of vainglory, but from the love of God the Father and of the Lord Jesus Christ. I am deeply impressed by his gentleness, and by his silence he is more effective than the empty talkers. He is in harmony with the commandments as is a lute with its strings. I call him blessed, then, for his sentiments toward God, since I know these to be virtuous and perfect, and for his stability and calm, in which he imitates the gentleness of the living God.

As sons of the light of truth, flee divisions and evil doctrines; where your shepherd is, follow him as his flock.

For all who belong to God and Jesus Christ are with the bishop; all who repent and return to the unity of the Church will also belong to God, that they may live according to Jesus Christ. Do not be deceived, my brothers. If anyone follows a schismatic, *he will not obtain the inheritance of God's kingdom;* if anyone lives by an alien teaching, he does not assent to the passion of the Lord.

Be careful, therefore, to take part only in the one eucharist; for there is only one flesh of our Lord Jesus Christ and one cup to unite us with his blood, one altar and one bishop with the presbyters and deacons, who are his fellow servants. Then, whatever you do, you will do according to God.

My brothers, I overflow with love for you and with a joyous heart I make you strong - although it is not so much I but Jesus Christ. Although imprisoned for his sake, I fear more because of my imperfection. But your prayers will perfect me in the eyes of God so that I might yet receive the inheritance promised me by the merciful God. I seek refuge in the person of Christ through the Gospels and I appeal to the true ministry of the Church through the apostles.

Friday of the Twenty-Seventh Week in Ordinary Time

From the first instruction by Saint Vincent of Lerins, Priest

The development of doctrine

Is there to be no development of religion in the Church of Christ? Certainly, there is to be development and on the largest scale.

Who can be so grudging to men, so full of hate for God, as to try to prevent it? But it must truly be development of the faith, not alteration of the faith. Development means that each thing expands to be itself, while alteration means that a thing is changed from one thing into another.

The understanding, knowledge and wisdom of one and all, of individuals as well as of the whole Church, ought then to make great and vigorous progress with the passing of the ages and the centuries, but only along its own line of development, that is, with the same doctrine, the same meaning and the same import.

The religion of souls should follow the law of development of bodies. Though bodies develop and unfold their component parts with the passing of the years, they always remain what they were. There is a great difference between the flower of childhood and the maturity of age, but those who become old are the very same people who were once young. Though the condition and appearance of one and the same individual may change, it is one and the same nature, one and the same person.

The tiny members of unweaned children and the grown members of young men are still the same members. Men have the same number of limbs as children. Whatever develops at a later age was already present in seminal form; there is nothing new in old age that was not already latent in childhood.

There is no doubt, then, that the legitimate and correct rule of development, the established and wonderful order of growth, is this: in older people the fullness of years always brings to completion those members and forms that the wisdom of the Creator fashioned beforehand in their earlier years.

If, however, the human form were to turn into some shape that did not belong to its own nature, or even if something were added to the sum of its members or subtracted from it, the whole body would necessarily perish or become grotesque or at least be enfeebled. In the same way, the doctrine of the Christian religion should properly follow these laws of development, that is, by becoming firmer over the years, more ample in the course of time, more exalted as it advances in age.

In ancient times our ancestors sowed the good seed in the harvest field of the Church. It would be very wrong and unfitting if we, their descendants, were to reap, not the genuine wheat of truth but the intrusive growth of error.

On the contrary, what is right and fitting is this: there should be no inconsistency between first and last, but we should reap true doctrine from the growth of true teaching, so that when, in the course of time, those first sowings yield an increase it may flourish and be tended in our day also.

Saturday of the Twenty-Seventh Week in Ordinary Time

From a homily on the Gospels by St. Gregory the Great, Pope & Doctor

The performance of our ministry

Let us listen to what the Lord says as he sends the preachers forth: *The harvest is great but the laborers are few. Pray therefore the Lord of the harvest to send laborers into his harvest*[Lk 10:2]. We can speak only with a heavy heart of so few laborers for such a great harvest, for although there are many to hear the good news there are only a few to preach it. Look about you and see how full the world is of priests, yet in God's harvest a laborer is rarely to be found; for although we have accepted the priestly office, we do not fulfill its demands.

Beloved brothers, consider what has been said: *Pray the Lord of the harvest to send laborers into his harvest*[Mt 9:38]. Pray for us so that we may have the strength to work on your behalf; that our tongue may not grow weary of exhortation, and that after we have accepted the office of preaching, our silence may not condemn us before the just judge. For frequently the preacher's tongue is bound fast on account of his own wickedness; while on the other hand it sometimes happens that because of the people's sins, the word of preaching is withdrawn from those who preside over the assembly. With reference to the former situation, the psalmist says: *But God asks the sinner: Why do you recite my commandments*[Ps 49:16]? And with reference to the latter, the Lord tells Ezekiel: *I will make your tongue cleave to the roof of you mouth, so that you shall be dumb and unable to reprove them, for they are a rebellious house*[Ezek 3:26]. He clearly means this: the word of preaching will be taken away from you because as long as this people irritates me by their deeds, they are unworthy to hear the exhortation of truth. It is not easy to know for whose sinfulness the preacher's word is withheld, but it is indisputable that the shepherd's silence while often injurious to himself will always harm his flock.

There is something else about the life of the shepherds, dearest brothers, which discourages me greatly. But lest what I claim should seem unjust to anyone, I accuse myself of the very same thing, although I fall into it unwillingly - compelled by the urgency of these barbarous times. I speak of our absorption in external affairs; we accept the duties of office, but by our actions we show that we are attentive to other things. We abandon the ministry of preaching and, in my opinion, are called bishops to our detriment, for we retain the honorable office but fail to practice the virtues proper to it. Those who have been entrusted to us abandon God, and we are silent. They fall into sin, and we do not extend a hand of rebuke.

But how can we who neglect ourselves be able to correct someone else? We are wrapped up in worldly concerns, and the more we devote ourselves to external things, the more insensitive we become in spirit.

For this reason the Church rightfully says about her own feeble members: *They made me keeper of the vineyards, but my own vineyard I have not kept*[Song 1:6]. We are set to guard the vineyards but do not guard our own, for we get involved in irrelevant pursuits and neglect the performance of our ministry.

Sunday of the Twenty-Eighth Week in Ordinary Time

From a commentary on Haggai by Saint Cyril of Alexandria, Bishop & Doctor

My name is great among the nations

When our Savior came, he appeared as a divine temple, glorious beyond any comparison, far more splendid and excellent than the older temple. He exceeded the old as much as worship in Christ and the gospels exceeds the cult of the laws, as much as truth exceeds its shadows.

Furthermore, I might point out that originally there was just one temple at Jerusalem, in which one people, the Israelites, offered their sacrifices. Since the only-begotten Son became like us, and as Scripture says, though he was *Lord and God, he has shone upon us*[Ps117:27], the rest of the world has been filled with places of worship. Now there are countless worshippers who honor the universal God with spiritual offerings and fragrant sacrifices. This, surely, is what Malachi foretold, speaking, as if in the person of God: *I am a great king, says the Lord; my name is honored among the nations, and everywhere there is offered to my name the fragrance of a pure sacrifice*[Mal 1:11].

With justice, therefore, do we say that the final temple, the Church, will be more glorious. To those who are so solicitous for the Church and labor for its construction, Haggai declares that a gift will be made, a gift from heaven given by the Savior. That gift is Christ himself, the peace of all men; *through him we have access in the one Spirit to the Father*[Eph 2:18]. The prophet goes on to say: *I will give peace to this place and peace of soul to save all who lay the foundation to rebuild the temple*. Christ too says somewhere: *My peace I give you.* Paul will teach how profitable this is for those who love: *The peace of Christ,* he says, *which surpasses all understanding will keep your minds and hearts*[Phil 4:7]. Isaiah, the seer, made the same prayer: *O Lord our God, give us peace, for you have given us everything*[Isa 26:12]. Once a man has been found worthy of Christ's peace, he can easily save his soul and guide his mind to carry out exactingly the demands of virtue.

Haggai, therefore, declares that peace will be given to all who build. One builds the Church either as a teacher of the sacred mysteries, as one set over the house of God, or as one who works for his own good by setting himself forth as a living and spiritual stone *in the holy temple, God's dwelling place in the Spirit*[Eph 2:21-22]. The results of these efforts will profit such men so that each will be able to gain his own salvation without difficulty.

Monday of the Twenty-Eighth Week in Ordinary Time

From a treatise against Fabianus by Fulgentius of Ruspe, Bishop

We are made holy by our sharing in Christ's body and blood

In our offering of the holy sacrifice we fulfill the command of our Savior, as recorded by the apostle Paul: *The Lord Jesus, on the night in which he was betrayed, took bread, and after he had given thanks, broke it and said: This is my body, which is for you. Do this in remembrance of me. In the same way, after the supper, he took the cup saying: This cup is the new covenant in my blood. Do this, whenever you drink it, in remembrance of me. For as often as you eat this bread and drink this cup, you shall proclaim the death of the Lord until he comes*[1 Cor 11:23-26].

This sacrifice is offered, then, to proclaim the Lord's death; it is offered in remembrance of him who laid down his life for our sake. As he says: *Greater love than this no one has, that one lay down his life for his friends*[Jn 15:13]. Because Christ died for us out of love, we ask, when we make remembrance of his death at the time of sacrifice, that we too may be granted love through the coming of the Holy Spirit. We pray that by the love which Christ had for us when he braved the cross, we may receive the grace of the Spirit and be crucified to the world, and the world to us. *The death Christ died, he died to sin, once for all, but the life he lives, he lives to God*[Rom 6:10-11]. Let us imitate our Lord's death, and also *live a new life*. Strengthened with the gift of his love, let us die to sin and live for God.

For God's love has been poured out in our hearts through the Holy Spirit, who has been given to us[Rom 5:5]. Indeed our sharing in the Lord's body and blood when we eat his bread and drink his cup teaches us that we should die to the world, and that we should keep our *life hidden with Christ in God, crucifying our flesh with its vices and evil desires*[Col 3:3].

That is why all the faithful who love God and their neighbor truly drink the cup of the Lord's love even though they may not drink the cup of his bodily suffering. And becoming inebriated from it, they put to death whatever in their nature is rooted in earth. They clothe themselves with the Lord Jesus Christ and do not indulge fleshly desires. They do not fix their gaze on visible things, but contemplate things which the eye cannot see. Thus they drink the Lord's cup by preserving the holy bond of love; without it, even if a man should deliver *his body to be burned*[1 Cor 13:1-3], he gains nothing. But the gift of love enables us to become in reality what we celebrate as mystery in the sacrifice.

Tuesday of the Twenty-Eighth Week in Ordinary Time

From an instruction by St. Columban, Abbot

Light everlasting in the temple of the eternal high priest

How blessed, how fortunate, are *those servants whom the Lord will find watchful when he comes*[Lk 12:37]. Blessed is the time of waiting when we stay awake for the Lord, the Creator of the universe, who fills all things and transcends all things.

How I wish he would awaken me, his humble servant, from the sleep of slothfulness, even though I am of little worth. How I wish he would enkindle me with that fire of divine love. The flames of his love burn beyond the stars; the longing for his overwhelming delights and the divine fire ever burn within me!

How I wish I might deserve to have my lantern always burning at night in the temple of my Lord, to give light to all who enter the house of my God. Give me, I pray you, Lord, in the name of Jesus Christ, your Son and my God, that love that does not fail so that may lantern, burning within me and giving light to others, may be always lighted and never extinguished.

Jesus, our most loving Savior, be pleased to light our lanterns, so that they might burn for ever in your temple, receiving eternal light from you, the eternal light, to lighten our darkness and to ward off from us the darkness of the world.

Give your light to my lantern, I beg you, my Jesus, so that by its light I may see that holy of holies which receives you as the eternal priest entering among the columns of your great temple. May I ever see you only, look on you, long for you; may I gaze with love on you alone, and have my lantern shining and burning always in your presence.

Loving Savior, be pleased to show yourself to us who knock, so that in knowing you we may love only you, love you alone, desire you alone, contemplate only you day and night, and always think of you. Inspire in us the depth of love that is fitting for you to receive as God. So may your love pervade our whole being, possess us completely, and fill all our senses, that we may know no other love but love for you who are everlasting. May our love be so great that the many waters of sky, land and sea cannot extinguish it in us: *many waters could not extinguish love*[Song 8:7].

May this saying be fulfilled in us also, at least in part, by your gift, Jesus Christ, our Lord, to whom be glory for ever and ever. Amen.

Wednesday of the Twenty-Eighth Week in Ordinary Time

From an inquiry addressed to Thalassius by Saint Maximus the Confessor, Abbot

The light that illumines all men

The lamp set upon the lamp-stand is Jesus Christ, the true light from the Father, the light that enlightens every man who comes into the world. In taking our own flesh he has become, and is rightly called, a lamp, for he is the connatural wisdom and word of the Father. He is proclaimed in the Church of God in accordance with orthodox faith, and he is lifted up and resplendent among the nations through the lives of those who live virtuously in observance of the commandments. So he gives light to all in the house (that is, in this world), just as he himself, God the Word, says: *No one lights a lamp and puts it under a bushel, but on a stand, and it gives light to all in the house*[Mt 5:15]. Clearly he is calling himself the lamp, he who was by nature God, and became flesh according to God's saving purpose.

I think the great David understood this when he spoke of the Lord as a lamp, saying: *Your word is a lamp to my feet and a light to my path*[Ps 118:105]. For God delivers us from the darkness of ignorance and sin, and hence he is greeted as a lamp in Scripture.

Lamp-like indeed, he alone dispelled the gloom of ignorance and the darkness of evil and became the way of salvation for all men. Through virtue and knowledge, he leads to the Father those who are resolved to walk by him, who is the way of righteousness, in obedience to the divine commandments. He has designated holy Church the lamp-stand, over which the word of God sheds light through preaching, and illumines with the rays of truth whoever is in this house which is the world, and fills the minds of all men with divine knowledge.

This word is most unwilling to be kept under a bushel; it wills to be set in a high place, upon the sublime beauty of the Church. For while the word was hidden under the bushel, that is, under the letter of the law, it deprived all men of eternal light. For then it could not give spiritual contemplation to men striving to strip themselves of a sensuality that is illusory, capable only of deceit, and able to perceive only decadent bodies like their own. But the word wills to be set upon a lamp-stand, the Church, where rational worship is offered in the spirit, that it may enlighten all men. For the letter, when it is not spiritually understood, bears a carnal sense only, which restricts its expression and does not allow the real force of what is written to reach the hearer's mind.

Let us, then, not light the lamp by contemplation and action, only to put it under a bushel - that lamp, I mean, which is the enlightening word of knowledge - lest we be condemned for restricting by the letter the incomprehensible power of wisdom. Rather let us place it upon the lamp-stand of holy Church, on the heights of true contemplation, where it may kindle for all men the light of divine teaching.

Thursday of the Twenty-Eighth Week in Ordinary Time

From a treatise on John by Saint Augustine, Bishop & Doctor

See, I will save my people

No one comes to me unless the Father draws him[Jn 6:44]. Do not think that you are drawn against you will; the will is drawn also by love. We must not be afraid of men who weigh words but are far from understanding what belongs above all to divine truth. They may find fault with this passage of Scripture and say to us: "How can I believe of my own free will if I am drawn to believe?" I answer: "It is not enough that you are moved by the will, for you are drawn also by desire."

What does this mean, to be drawn by desire? *Take delight in the Lord, and he will give you the desires of your heart*[Ps 36:4]. The heart has its own desires; it takes delight, for example, in the bread from heaven. The poet could say: "Everyone is drawn by his own desire," not by necessity but by desire, not by compulsion but by pleasure. We can say then with greater force that one who finds pleasure in truth, in happiness, in justice, in everlasting life, is drawn to Christ, for Christ is all these things.

Are our bodily senses to have their desires, but not the will? If the will does not have its desires, how can Scripture say: *The children of men will find their hope under the shadow of your wings, they will drink their fill from the plenty of your house, and you will give them drink from the running stream of your delights, for with you is the fountain of life, and in your light we shall see light*[Ps 35:8-10].

Show me one who loves; he knows what I mean. Show me one who is full of longing, one who is hungry, one who is a pilgrim and suffering from thirst in the desert of this world, eager for the fountain in the homeland of eternity; show me someone like that, and he knows what I mean. But if I speak to someone without feeling, he does not understand what I am saying.

You have only to show a leafy branch to a sheep, and it is drawn to it. If you show nuts to a boy, he is drawn to them. He runs to them because he is drawn, drawn by love, drawn without any physical compulsion, drawn by a chain attached to his heart. "Everyone is drawn by his own desire." This is a true saying, and earthly delights and pleasures, set before those who love them, succeed in drawing them. If this is so, are we to say that Christ, revealed and set before us by the Father, does not draw us? What does the soul desire more than truth? Why then does the soul have hungry jaws, a spiritual palate as it were, sensitive enough to judge the truth, if not in order to eat and drink wisdom, justice, truth, eternal life?

Blessed are those who hunger and thirst for justice, that is, here on earth. *They shall be satisfied*[Mt 5:6] that is, in heaven. Christ says: I give each what he loves, I give each the object of his hope; he will see what he believed in, though without seeing it. What he now hungers for, he will eat; what he now thirsts for, he will drink to the full. When? At the resurrection of the dead, for *I will raise him up on the last day*[Jn 6:40].

Friday of the Twenty-Eighth Week in Ordinary Time

From The City of God by Saint Augustine, Bishop & Doctor

In every place there is sacrifice and a clean oblation offered to my name

Every work that effects our union with God in holy fellowship is a true sacrifice; every work, that is, which is referred to that final end, that ultimate good, by which we are able to be in the true sense happy. As a consequence even that mercy by which aid is given to man is not a sacrifice unless it is done for the sake of God. Sacrifice, though performed or offered by man, is something divine; that is why the ancient Latins gave it this name of "sacrifice," of something sacred. Man himself, consecrated in the name of God and vowed to God, is therefore a sacrifice insofar as he dies to the world in order to live for God. This too is part of mercy, the mercy that each one has for himself. Scripture tells us: *Have mercy on your soul by pleasing God*.

Works of mercy, then, done either to ourselves or to our neighbor and referred to God are true sacrifices. Works of mercy, however, are performed for no other reason than to free us from wretchedness and by this means to make us happy (and we cannot be happy except through that good of which Scripture speaks: *It is good for me to cling to God*). It clearly follows that the whole redeemed city, that is, the assembly and fellowship of the saints, is offered to God as a universal sacrifice through the great high priest, who in the nature of a slave offered even himself for us in his passion, in order that we might be the body of so great a head. He offered this nature of a slave; he was offered in that nature, because in that nature he is the mediator, in that nature he is the high priest, in that nature he is the sacrifice.

The Apostle urges us to present our bodies *as a living sacrifice, holy and pleasing to God, and as our spiritual worship*[Rom 12:1], and not to follow the pattern of this world but to be transformed by the renewal of our minds and hearts, so that we may discern what is the will of God, what is good and pleasing and perfect, the total sacrifice that is ourselves. *By the grace of God that has been given me, he says, I say to all who are among you: Do not think more highly of yourselves than you should, but judge yourselves with moderation according to the measure of faith God has given to each of you. As we have in the same body many members, yet all the members do not have the same functions, so we are many, but are one body in Christ; we are each of us members of one another, having different gifts according to the grace that has been given us*[Rom 12:3-6].

This is the sacrifice of Christians, *the many who are one body in Christ*. This is the sacrifice which the Church celebrates in the sacrament of the altar, that sacrament known to the faithful; in that sacrament it is made clear to the Church that in the sacrifice she offers, she herself is offered.

Saturday of the Twenty-Eighth Week in Ordinary Time

From the pastoral constitution on the Church in the modern world of the Second Vatican Council

I am the Alpha and the Omega, the first and the last

The way in which the earthly and the heavenly city interpenetrate each other can be recognized only by faith; indeed, it remains a mystery of human history, that is, of a history always troubled by sin until the glory of the sons of God is fully revealed.

As she pursues her appointed goal of bringing salvation to men, the Church not only communicates the divine life to mankind but also in some measure reflects the light of that life over the whole world. She does this especially through her work of restoring and enhancing the dignity of the human person, of strengthening the fabric of human society, and of enriching the daily activity of men with a deeper meaning and importance. The Church believes that in this way she can make a great contribution, through individual members and the community as a whole, toward bringing a greater humanity to the family of man and to its history.

While the Church helps the world and herself receives much from the world, she has one object in view: the coming of God's kingdom and the salvation of the whole human race. Every good that the people of God in the course of its earthly pilgrimage can confer on the family of men derives from the fact that the Church is the universal sacrament of salvation, revealing, and at the same time bringing into operation, the mystery of God's love for man.

The Word of God, through whom all things were made, was himself made flesh so that as perfect man he might save all men and bring all things into unity. The Lord is the final end of human history, the point toward which the aspirations of history and civilization are moving, the focus of the human race, the joy of all hearts and the fulfillment of their desires. He it is whom the Father raised from the dead, lifted up on high and set at his right hand, appointing him judge of the living and the dead. In his Spirit we have been brought to life and gathered into unity, and so make our pilgrim way toward the goal of human history, a goal in complete harmony with the loving plan of God *to make all things one in Christ, the things in heaven and the things on earth*[Eph 1:10].

The Lord himself says: *See, I am coming soon; I bring my recompense with me, to give to everyone what his deeds deserve. I am Alpha and Omega, the first and the last, the beginning and the end*[Rev 22:12-13].

Sunday of the Twenty-Ninth Week in Ordinary Time

From a letter to Proba by Saint Augustine, Bishop & Doctor

Let us exercise our desire in prayer

Why in our fear of not praying as we should, do we turn to so many things, to find what we should pray for? Why do we not say instead, in the words of the psalm: *I have asked one thing from the Lord, this is what I will seek: to dwell in the Lord's house all the days of my life, to see the graciousness of the Lord, and to visit his temple*[Ps 26:4]. There, the days do not come and go in succession, and the beginning of one day does not mean the end of another; all days are one, simultaneously and without end, and the life lived out in these days has itself no end.

So that we might obtain this life of happiness, he who is true life itself taught us to pray, not in many words as though speaking longer could gain us a hearing. After all, we pray to one who, as the Lord himself tells us, knows what we need before we ask for it.

Why he should ask us to pray, when he knows what we need before we ask him, may perplex us if we do not realize that our Lord and God does not want to know what we want (for he cannot fail to know it) but wants us rather to exercise our desire through our prayers, so that we may be able to receive what he is preparing to give us. His gift is very great indeed, but our capacity is too small and limited to receive it. That is why we are told: *Enlarge your desires, do not bear the yoke with unbelievers*[2 Cor 6:14].

The deeper our faith, the stronger our hope, the greater our desire, the larger will be our capacity to receive that gift, which is very great indeed. *No eye has seen it*[1 Cor 2:9]; it has no color. *No ear has heard it*[1 Cor 2:9]; it has no sound. *It has not entered man's hear*[1 Cor 2:9]*t*; man's heart must enter into it.

In this faith, hope and love we pray always with unwearied desire. However, at set times and seasons we also pray to God in words, so that by these signs we may instruct ourselves and mark the progress we have made in our desire, and spur ourselves on to deepen it. The more fervent the desire, the more worthy will be its fruit. When the Apostle tells us: *Pray without ceasing*[1 Thess 5:16-18], he means this: Desire unceasingly that life of happiness which is nothing if not eternal, and ask it of him who alone is able to give it.

Monday of the Twenty-Ninth Week in Ordinary Time

From a letter to Proba by Saint Augustine, Bishop & Doctor

Let us turn our mind to the task of prayer at appointed hours

Let us always desire the happy life from the Lord God and always pray for it. But for this very reason we turn our mind to the task of prayer at appointed hours, since that desire grows lukewarm, so to speak, from our involvement in other concerns and occupations. We remind ourselves through the words of prayer to focus our attention on the object of our desire; otherwise, the desire that began to grow lukewarm may grow chill altogether and may be totally extinguished unless it is repeatedly stirred into flame.

Therefore, when the Apostle says: *Let your petitions become known before God*[Phil 4:6-7], this should not be taken in the sense that they are in fact becoming known to God who certainly knew them even before they were made, but that they are becoming known to us before God through submission and not before men through boasting.

Since this is the case, it is not wrong or useless to pray even for a long time when there is the opportunity. I mean when it does not keep us from performing the other good and necessary actions we are obliged to do. But even in these actions, as I have said, we must always pray with that desire. To pray for a longer time is not the same as to pray by multiplying words, as some people suppose. Lengthy talk is one thing, a prayerful disposition which lasts a long time is another. For it is even written in reference to the Lord himself that he spent the night in prayer and that he prayed at great length. Was he not giving us an example by this? In time, he prays when it is appropriate; and in eternity, he hears our prayers with the Father.

The monks in Egypt are said to offer frequent prayers, but these are very short and hurled like swift javelins. Otherwise their watchful attention, a very necessary quality for anyone at prayer, could be dulled and could disappear through protracted delays. They also clearly demonstrate through this practice that a person must not quickly divert such attention if it lasts, just as one must not allow it to be blunted if it cannot last.

Excessive talking should be kept out of prayer but that does not mean that one should not spend much time in prayer so long as fervent attitude continues to accompany his prayer. To talk at length in prayer is to perform a necessary action with an excess of words. To spend much time in prayer is to knock with a persistent and holy fervor at the door of the one whom we beseech. This task is generally accomplished more through sighs than words, more through weeping than speech. He *places our tears in his sight*[Ps 55:9], and *our sighs are not hidden from him*, for he has established all things through his Word and does not seek human words.

Tuesday of the Twenty-Ninth Week in Ordinary Time

From a letter to Proba by Saint Augustine, Bishop & Doctor

On the Lord's Prayer

We need to use words so that we may remind ourselves to consider carefully what we are asking, not so that we may think we can instruct the Lord or prevail on him.

Thus, when we say: *Hallowed be your name*[Mt 6:9-13], we are reminding ourselves to desire that his name, which in fact is always holy, should also be considered holy among men. I mean that it should not be held in contempt. But this is a help for men, not for God.

And as for our saying: *Your kingdom come*, it will surely come whether we will it or not. But we are stirring up our desires for the kingdom so that it can come to us and we can deserve to reign there.

When we say: *Your will be done on earth as it is in heaven* [Mt 6:9-13], we are asking him to make us obedient so that his will may be done in us as it is done in heaven by his angels.

When we say: *Give us this day our daily bread* [Mt 6:9-13], in saying *this day* we mean "in this world." Here we ask for a sufficiency by specifying the most important part of it; that is, we use the word "bread" to stand for everything. Or else we are asking for the sacrament of the faithful, which is necessary in this world, not to gain temporal happiness but to gain the happiness that is everlasting.

When we say: *Forgive us our trespasses as we forgive those who trespass against us* [Mt 6:9-13], we are reminding ourselves of what we must ask and what we must do in order to be worthy in turn to receive.

When we say: *Lead us not into temptation* [Mt 6:9-13], we are reminding ourselves to ask that his help may not depart from us; otherwise we could be seduced and consent to some temptation, or despair and yield to it.

When we say: *Deliver us from evil* [Mt 6:9-13], we are reminding ourselves to reflect on the fact that we do not yet enjoy the state of blessedness in which we shall suffer no evil. This is the final petition contained in the Lord's Prayer, and it has a wide application. In this petition the Christian can utter his cries of sorrow, in it he can shed his tears, and through it he can begin, continue and conclude his prayer, whatever the distress in which he finds himself. Yes, it was very appropriate that all these truths should be entrusted to us to remember in these very words.

Whatever be the other words we may prefer to say (words which the one praying chooses so that his disposition may become clearer to himself or which he simply adopts so that his disposition may be intensified), we say nothing that is not contained in the Lord's Prayer, provided of course we are praying in a correct and proper way. But if anyone says something which is incompatible with this prayer of the Gospel, he is praying in the flesh, even if he is not praying sinfully. And yet I do not know how this could be termed anything but sinful, since those who are born again through the Spirit ought to pray only in the Spirit.

Wednesday of the Twenty-Ninth Week in Ordinary Time

From a letter to Proba by Saint Augustine, Bishop & Doctor

You will find everything in the Lord's Prayer

We read, for example: *May you receive glory among all the nations as you have among us*[1Chr 16:23-36], and *May your prophets prove themselves faithful*[Sir 36:20-21]. What does this mean but *Hallowed be your name*[Mt 6:9-13]?

We read: *Lord of power and might, touch our hearts and show us your face, and we shall be saved*[Ps 79:4]. What does this mean but *Your kingdom come*[Mt 6:9-13]?

We read: *Direct my ways by your word, and let no sin rule over me*[Ps 118:133.] What does this mean but *Your will be done on earth as it is in heaven*[Mt 6:9-13]?

We read: *Do not give me poverty or riches*[Prov 30:8-9]. What does this mean but *Give us this day our daily bread*[Mt 6:9-13]?

We read: *Lord, remember David and all his patient suffering*[Ps 131:1], and *Lord, if I have done this, if there is guilt on my hands, if I have repaid evil for evil*[Ps 7:4-5]....What does this mean but *Forgive us our trespasses as we forgive those who trespass against us*[Mt 6:9-13]?

We read: *Rescue me, God, from my enemies, deliver me from those who rise up against me*[Ps 17:48-49]. What does this mean but *Deliver us from evil*[Mt 6:9-13]?

If you study every word of the petitions of Scripture, you will find, I think, nothing that is not contained and included in the Lord's Prayer. When we pray, then, we may use different words to say the same things, but we may not say different things.

We should not hesitate to make these prayers for ourselves, for our friends, for strangers, and even for enemies, though the emotions in our heart may vary with the strength or weakness of our relationships with individuals.

You now know, I think, the attitudes you should bring to prayer, as well as the petitions you should make, and this not because of what I have taught you but thanks to the teaching of the one who has been pleased to teach us all.

We must search out the life of happiness, we must ask for it from the Lord our God. Many have discussed at great length the meaning of happiness, but surely we do not need to go to them and their long drawn out discussions. Holy Scripture says concisely and with truth: *Happy is the people whose God is the Lord*[Ps 143:15]. We are meant to belong to that people, and to be able to see God and live with him for ever, and so *the object of this command is love from a pure heart, from a good conscience and a sincere faith*[1 Tim 1:5].

In these three qualities, "a good conscience" stands for "hope." Faith, hope and love bring safely to God the person who prays, that is, the person who believes, who hopes, who desires, and who ponders what he is asking of the Lord in the Lord's Prayer.

Thursday of the Twenty-Ninth Week in Ordinary Time

From a letter to Proba by Saint Augustine, Bishop & Doctor

We do not know what it is right to pray for

You may still want to ask why the Apostle said: *We do not know what it is right to pray for*[Rom 8:26], because, surely, we cannot believe that either he or those to whom he wrote did not know the Lord's Prayer.

He showed that he himself shared this uncertainty. Did he know what it was right to pray for when he was given a thorn in the flesh, an angel of Satan to bruise him, so that he might not be puffed up by the greatness of what was revealed to him? Three times he asked the Lord to take it away from him, which showed that he did not know what he should ask for in prayer. At last, he heard the Lord's answer, explaining why the prayer of so great a man was not granted, and why it was not expedient for it to be granted: *My grace is sufficient for you, for power shines forth more perfectly in weakness*[2 Cor 12:9].

In the kind of affliction, then, which can bring either good or ill, we do not know what it is right to pray for; yet, because it is difficult, troublesome and against the grain for us, weak as we are, we do what every human would do, we pray that it may be taken away from us. We owe, however, at least this much in our duty to God: if he does not take it away, we must not imagine that we are being forgotten by him but, because of our loving endurance of evil, must await greater blessings in its place. In this way, *power shines forth more perfectly in weakness*[2 Cor 12:9]. These words are written to prevent us from having too great an opinion of ourselves if our prayer is granted, when we are impatient in asking for something that it would be better not to receive; and to prevent us from being dejected, and distrustful of God's mercy toward us, if our prayer is not granted, when we ask for something that would bring us greater affliction, or completely ruin us through the corrupting influence of prosperity. In these cases we do not know what it is right to ask for in prayer.

Therefore, if something happens that we did not pray for, we must have no doubt at all that what God wants is more expedient than what we wanted ourselves. Our great Mediator gave us an example of this. After he had said: *Father, if it is possible, let this cup be taken away from me*[Mt 26:39], he immediately added, *Yet not what I will, but what you will, Father*[Mt 26:39], so transforming the human will that was his through his taking a human nature. As a consequence, and rightly so, *through the obedience of one man the many are made righteous*[Rom 5:19].

Friday of the Twenty-Ninth Week in Ordinary Time

From a letter to Proba by Saint Augustine, Bishop & Doctor

The Spirit pleads for us

The person who asks for and seeks this one thing from the Lord makes his petition confidently and serenely. He has no fear that, when he receives it, it may harm him, for if this is absent, anything else he duly receives brings no benefit at all. This is the one, true and only life of happiness, that, immortal and incorruptible in body and spirit, we should contemplate the Lord's graciousness for ever. It is for the sake of this one thing that everything else is sought and without impropriety requested. The person who has this will have all that he wants; in heaven, he will be unable to want, because he will be unable to possess anything that is unfitting.

In heaven is the fountain of life, that we should now thirst for in prayer as long as we live in hope and do not yet see the object of our hope, *under the protection of* his *wings in* whose *presence is all our desire*[Ps 90:4], so that we may drink our fill *from the plenty of his house*[Ps 35:9-10] and be given drink from *the running stream of his delights*[Ps 35:9-10], for with him is *the fountain of life, and in* his *light we shall see light*[Ps 35:9-10], when our desire will be satisfied with good things, and there will be nothing to ask for with sighs but only what we possess with joy.

Yet, since this is that peace that surpasses all understanding, even when we ask for it in prayer we do not know how to pray for what is right. Certainly we do not know something if we cannot think of it as it really is; whatever comes to mind we reject, repudiate, find fault with; we know that this is not what we are seeking, even if we do not yet know what kind of thing it really is.

There is then within us a kind of instructed ignorance, instructed, that is, by the Spirit of God who helps our weakness. When the Apostle said: *If we hope for something we do not see, we look forward to it with patience*[Rom 8:25], he added, *In the same way the Spirit helps our weakness; we do not know what it is right to pray for, but the Spirit himself pleads with sighs too deep for words. He who searches hearts knows what the Spirit means, for he pleads for the saints according to God's will*[Rom 8:26-27].

We must not understand by this that the Holy Spirit of God pleads for the saints as if he were someone different from what God is: in the Trinity the Spirit is the unchangeable God and one God with the Father and the Son. Scripture says: *He pleads for the saints*[Rom 8:26] because he moves the saints to plead, just as it says: *The Lord your God tests you, to know if you love him*[Deut 13:3-5], in this sense, that he does it to enable you to know. So the Spirit moves the saints to plead with sighs too deep for words by inspiring in them a desire for the great and as yet unknown reality that we look forward to with patience. How can words express what we desire when it remains unknown? If we were entirely ignorant of it we would not desire it; again, we would not desire it or seek it with sighs, if we were able to see it.

Saturday of the Twenty-Ninth Week in Ordinary Time

From a sermon by Saint Peter Chrysologus, Bishop & Doctor

The Word, the Wisdom of God, was made flesh

The holy Apostle has told us that the human race takes its origin from two men, Adam and Christ; two men equal in body but unequal in merit, wholly alike in their physical structure but totally unlike in the very origin of their being. *The first man, Adam,* he says, *became a living soul, the last Adam a life-giving spirit*[1 Cor 15:45-49].

The first Adam was made by the last Adam, from whom he also received his soul, to give him life. The last Adam was formed by his own action; he did not have to wait for life to be given him by someone else, but was the only one who could give life to all. The first Adam was formed from valueless clay, the second Adam came forth from the precious womb of the Virgin. In the case of the first Adam, earth was changed into flesh; in the case of the second Adam, flesh was raised up to be God.

What more need be said? The second Adam stamped his image on the first Adam when he created him. That is why he took on himself the role, and the name, of the first Adam, in order that he might not lose what he had made in his own image. The first Adam, the last Adam; the first had a beginning, the last knows no end. The last Adam is indeed the first; as he himself says: *I am the first and the last*[Rev 22:13].

I am the first, that is, I have no beginning. *I am the last,* that is, I have no end. *But what was spiritual,* says the Apostle, *did not come first; what was living came first, then what is spiritua*[1 Cor 15:45-49]*l*. The earth comes before its fruit, but the earth is not so valuable as its fruit. The earth exacts pain and toil; its fruit bestows subsistence and life. The prophet rightly boasted of this fruit: *Our earth has yielded its fruit*[Ps 66:7]. What is this fruit? The fruit referred to in another place: *I will place upon your throne one who is the fruit of your body*[Ps 131:11]. *The first man,* says the Apostle, *was made from the earth and belongs to the earth; the second man is from heaven, and belongs to heaven*[1 Cor 15:45-49].

The man made from the earth is the pattern of those who belong to the earth; the man from heaven is the pattern of those who belong to heaven. How is it that these last, though they do not belong to heaven by birth, will yet belong to heaven, men who do not remain what they were by birth but persevere in being what they have become by rebirth? The reason is, brethren, that the heavenly Spirit, by the mysterious infusion of his light, gives fertility to the womb of the virginal font. The Spirit brings forth as men belonging to heaven those whose earthly ancestry brought them forth as men belonging to the earth, and in a condition of wretchedness; he gives them the likeness of their Creator. Now that we are reborn, refashioned in the image of our Creator, we must fulfill what the Apostle commands: *So, as we have worn the likeness of the man of earth, let us also wear the likeness of the man of heaven*[1 Cor 15:45-49].

Now that we are reborn, as I have said, in the likeness of our Lord, and have indeed been adopted by God as his children, let us put on the complete image of our Creator so as to be wholly like him, not in the glory that he alone possesses, but in innocence, simplicity, gentleness, patience, humility, mercy, harmony, those qualities in which he chose to become, and to be, one with us.

Sunday of the Thirtieth Week in Ordinary Time

From a letter to the Corinthians by Saint Clement I, Pope & Martyr

In his goodness to all, God gives order and harmony to the world

Let us fix our gaze on the Father and Creator of the whole world, and let us hold on to his peace and blessings, his splendid and surpassing gifts. Let us contemplate him in our thoughts and with our mind's eye reflect upon the peaceful and restrained unfolding of his plan; let us consider the care with which he provides for the whole of his creation.

By his direction the heavens are in motion, and they are subject to him in peace. Day and night fulfill the course he has established without interfering with each other. The sun, the moon and the choirs of stars revolve in harmony at his command in their appointed paths without deviation. By his will the earth blossoms in the proper seasons and produces abundant food for men and animals and all the living things on it without reluctance and without any violation of what he has arranged.

Yet unexplored regions of the abysses and inexpressible realms of the deep are subject to his laws. The mass of the boundless sea, joined together by his ordinance in a single expanse, does not overflow its prescribed limits but flows as he commanded it. For he said: *Thus far shall you come, and your waves will be halted here*[Job 38:11]. The ocean, impassable for men, and the worlds beyond it are governed by the same edicts of the Lord.

The seasons, spring, summer, autumn and winter, follow one another in harmony. The quarters from which the winds blow function in due season without the least deviation. And the ever-flowing springs, created for our health as well as our enjoyment, unfailingly offer their breasts to sustain human life. The tiniest of living creatures meet together in harmony and peace. The great Creator and Lord of the universe commanded all these things to be established in peace and harmony, in his goodness to all, and in overflowing measure to us who seek refuge in his mercies through our Lord Jesus Christ; to him be glory and majesty for ever and ever. Amen

Monday of the Thirtieth Week in Ordinary Time

From a letter to the Corinthians by Saint Clement I, Pope & Martyr

We must not turn our backs and flee from God's will

Dear friends take care that God's blessings, which are many, do not become the condemnation of us all; we must live lives worthy of him and in mutual harmony do what is good and acceptable in his sight. He tells us: *The Spirit of the Lord is a lantern, searching the hidden places of our inmost being*[Prov 20:27].

We must remember how near he is and that no thought of ours, no conversation we hold is hidden from him. It is right, therefore, that we should not turn our backs and flee from God's will. We should rather give offense to stupid and foolish men, puffed up and taking pride in their boastful speech, than give offense to God.

Let us reverence the Lord Jesus, whose blood was shed for us. Let us respect those in authority, let us honor the presbyters. Let us train the young in the fear of God. Let us lead our wives toward all that is good. Let them show by their conduct that they are lovers of chastity; by their gentleness let them reveal a pure and sincere disposition; by their silence let them manifest the control they have over their tongues; let them bestow an equal charity, without respect for persons, on all who have a holy fear of God.

Your children must share in the way of discipleship in Christ. They must learn how effective humility is before God, what chaste love can accomplish with God, how good and noble is the fear of God, for it brings salvation to all who possess it and who live holy lives with a pure heart. The one whose Spirit is in us is the searcher of our thoughts and of the counsels of our hearts. At his will, he shall take that Spirit from us.

All this is strengthened by the faith that comes to us in Christ. He himself addresses us through the Holy Spirit and says: *Come, my children, listen to me: I will teach you the fear of the Lord. Is there a man who wants life, desiring to see good days? Keep your tongue from evil, and your lips from speaking what is false. Turn away from evil and do good. Seek peace and go in pursuit of it*[Ps 33:12-15].

The Father is merciful in all he does and full of generosity; he is loving to those who fear him. In goodness and gentleness he gives his graces to those who approach him with undivided hearts. We must then put away all duplicity and not be distrustful in the face of his excelling and ennobling gifts.

Tuesday of the Thirtieth Week in Ordinary Time

From a letter to the Corinthians by Saint Clement I, Pope & Martyr

God is faithful in his promises

Consider, beloved, how the Lord keeps reminding us of the resurrection that is to come, of which he has made the Lord Jesus Christ the first-fruits by raising him from the dead. Let us look, beloved, at the resurrection that occurs at its appointed time. Day and night show us a resurrection; the night lies in sleep, day rises again; the day departs, night takes its place. Let us think about the harvest; how does the sowing take place, and in what manner? The sower goes out and casts each seed onto the ground. Dry and bare, they fall into the earth and decay. Then the greatness of the Lord's providence raises them up again from decay, and out of one many are produced and yield fruit.

In this hope, then, let our hearts be bound fast to him who is faithful in his promises and just in his judgments. He forbade us to tell lies; still less will he himself tell a lie. Nothing is impossible for God except to tell a lie. Then let our faith in him be awakened; let us reflect that everything is close to him.

By the word of his power he established all things, and by his word he can reduce them to ruin. *Who shall say to him: What have you done? Who shall stand up against the power of his might*[Dan 4:32]? He will accomplish everything when he wills and as he wills, and nothing that he has decreed shall pass away. All things stand in his presence, and nothing lies hidden from his counsel, *if the heavens tell forth the glory of God, the firmament reveals the work of his hands, day speaks to day, and night shares knowledge with night; there are no words, no speeches, and their voices are not heard*[Ps 18:2-5].

Since all things lie open to his eyes and ears, let us hold him in awe and rid ourselves of impure desires to do works of evil, so that we may be protected by his mercy from the judgment that is to come. Which of us can escape his mighty hand? What world will give asylum to one who deserts him? *Where will I go, where will I hide from his face? If I go up to heaven, you are there; if I go to the limits of the earth, your right hand is there; if I lie down in the deep, your spirit is there*[Ps 138:7-15]. Where, then, can one go, where can one escape to, from the presence of him whose hands embrace the universe?

Let us then approach him in holiness of soul, raising up to him hands pure and undefiled, out of love for our good and merciful Father who made us a chosen portion for himself.

Wednesday of the Thirtieth Week in Ordinary Time

From a letter to the Corinthians by Saint Clement I, Pope & Martyr

Let us follow the way of truth

Let us put on unity of mind, thinking humble thoughts, exercising self-control, keeping ourselves far from all backbiting and slander, being righteous in deed, and not in word only. Scripture says: *He who says much hears much in his own turn. Or does the easy talker think that he is righteous*[Pope St. Clement]?

It is our duty then to be eager to do good, for everything is from God. He warns us: *See, the Lord is coming, and the reward he brings is before him, for paying each according to his work*[Rom 2:6]. He urges us, who believe in him with all our heart, not to be idle or careless in any good work. Our boasting and our confidence must rest on him. Let us be subject to his will. Let us look carefully at the whole host of his angels; they stand ready and serve his will. Scripture says: *Ten thousand times ten thousand stood before him, and a thousand thousand served him, and cried out: Holy, holy, holy is the Lord of hosts; the whole creation is full of his glory*[Dan 7:10; Rev 4:8-11].

We, too, dutifully gathered together in unity of mind, should cry out to him continuously as with one voice, so as to share in his great and glorious promises. It is written: *Eye has not seen, ear has not heard, man's heart has not conceived, what great things have been prepared for those who wait for him*[1 Cor 2:9].

Beloved, how blessed, how wonderful, are God's gifts! Life with immortality, glory with righteousness, truth with confidence, self-control with holiness: all these are the gifts that fall within our understanding. What then are those gifts that are in store for those who wait for him? Only the most holy Creator and Father of the ages knows their greatness and their splendor.

We should then strive with the greatest zeal to be found among the number of those who await him, so that we may share in the promised gifts. How will this be, beloved? If our mind is fixed on God through faith, if we are diligent in seeking what is pleasing and acceptable to him, if we fulfill what is according to his blameless will and follow the way of truth, casting away from ourselves all that is unholy.

Thursday of the Thirtieth Week in Ordinary Time

From a discourse Against the Arians by Saint Athanasius, Bishop & Doctor

Wisdom's likeness and image is created in God's works

An impress of Wisdom has been created in us and in all his works. Therefore, the true Wisdom which shaped the world claims for himself all that bears his image, and rightly says: The Lord created me in his works. These words are really spoken by the wisdom that is in us, but the Lord himself here adopts them as his own. Wisdom himself is not created, because he is the Creator, but by reason of the created image of himself found in his works, he speaks thus as though he were speaking of himself. Our Lord said: He who receives you receives me, and he could say this because the impress of himself is in us. In the same way, although Wisdom is not to be numbered among created things, yet because his form and likeness is in his works, he speaks as if he were a creature, and says: The Lord created me in his works, when his purpose first unfolded.

The likeness of Wisdom has been stamped upon creatures in order that the world may recognize in it the Word who was its maker and through the Word come to know the Father. This is Paul's teaching: What can be known about God is clear to them, for God has shown it to them. Ever since the creation of the world his invisible nature has been there for the mind to perceive in things that have been made. Accordingly the Word is not a creature, for the passage that begins: The Lord created me . . . is to be understood as referring to that wisdom which is truly in us and is said to be so.

But if this fails to persuade our opponents, let them tell us whether there is any wisdom in created things. If there is none, why does the apostle Paul allege as the cause of men's sins: By God's wisdom, the world failed to come to a knowledge of God through wisdom? And if there is no created wisdom, how is it that the expression a multitude of wise men is found in Scripture? And again, Scripture testifies that the wise man is wary and turns away from evil, and by wisdom is a house built. Further, Ecclesiastes says: A wise man's wisdom will light up his face. He also rebukes presumptuous persons with the warning: Do not say, "How is it that former days were better than these?" For it is not in wisdom that you ask this.

So there is a wisdom in created things, as the son of Sirach too bears witness: The Lord has poured it out upon all his works, to be with men as his gift, and with wisdom he has abundantly equipped those who love him. This quality of being "poured out" belongs not to the essence of that self-existent Wisdom who is the Only-begotten, but to that wisdom which reflects the only begotten one in the world. Why then is it beyond belief if the creative and archetypal Wisdom, whose likeness is the wisdom and understanding poured out in the world, should say, as though speaking directly of himself: The Lord created me in his works? For the wisdom in the world is not creative, but is itself created in God's works, and in the light of this wisdom the heavens declare the glory of God, and the firmament proclaims the work of his hands.

Friday of the Thirtieth Week in Ordinary Time

From a work by Baldwin of Canterbury, Bishop

The word of God is both living and powerful

The word of God is both living and powerful and much more piercing than a two-edged sword[Heb 4:12]. The word of God is plainly shown in all its strength and wisdom to those who seek out Christ, who is the word, the power and the wisdom of God. This word was with the Father in the beginning, and in its own time was revealed to the apostles, then preached by them and humbly received in faith by believers. So, the word is in the Father, as well as on our lips and in our hearts.

This word of God is living; the Father gave it life in itself, just as he has life in himself. For this reason it not only is alive, but it is life, as he says of himself: *I am the way, the truth and the life*[Jn 14:6]. Since he is life, he is both living and life-giving. For, *as the Father raises up the dead and gives them life, so also the Son gives life to those he chooses*[Jn 5:21]. He is life-giving when he calls the dead from the grave and says: *Lazarus, come forth*[Jn 11:43].

When this word is preached, in the very act of preaching it gives to its own voice which is heard outwardly a certain power which is perceived inwardly so much so that the dead are brought back to life and by these praises the sons of Abraham are raised from the dead. This word then is alive in the heart of the Father, on the lips of the preacher, and in the hearts of those who believe and love him. Since this word is so truly alive, undoubtedly it is full of power.

It is powerful in creation, powerful in the government of the universe, powerful in the redemption of the world. For what is more powerful, more effective? Who shall speak of its power; who shall make all its praises heard? It is powerful in what it accomplishes, powerful when preached. It does not come back empty; it bears fruit in all to whom it is sent.

It is powerful and *more piercing than any two-edged sword* when it is believed and loved. For what is impossible to the believer? What is difficult for a lover? When this word is spoken, its message pierces the heart like the sharp arrows of a strong man, like nails driven deep; it enters so deeply that it penetrates to the innermost recess. This word is much more piercing than any two-edged sword, inasmuch as it is stronger than any courage or power, sharper than any shrewdness of human ingenuity, keener than all human wisdom, or the subtlety of learned argument.

Saturday of the Thirtieth Week in Ordinary Time

From a dialogue On Divine Providence by Saint Catherine of Siena, Virgin & Doctor

How good and comforting is your spirit dwelling in all men, O Lord

With a look of mercy that revealed his indescribable kindness, God the Father spoke to Catherine:

Beloved daughter, everything I give to man comes from the love and care I have for him. I desire to show my mercy to the whole world and my protective love to all those who want it.

But in his ignorance man treats himself very cruelly. My care is constant, but he turns my life-giving gifts into a source of death. Yes, I created him with loving care and formed him in my image and likeness. I pondered, and I was moved by the beauty of my creation.

I gave him a memory to recall my goodness, for I wanted him to share in my own power. I gave him an intellect to know and understand my will through the wisdom of my Son, for I am the giver of every good gift and I love him with a father's constant love. Through the Holy Spirit I gave him a will to love what he would come to know with his intellect.

In my loving care I did all this, so that he could know me and perceive my goodness and rejoice to see me for ever. But as I have recounted elsewhere, heaven had been closed off because of Adam's disobedience. Immediately after his sin all manner of evil made its advance throughout the world.

So that I might commute the death consequent upon this disobedience, I attended to you with loving care - out of provident concern I handed over my only-begotten Son to make satisfaction for your needs. I demanded supreme obedience from him so that the human race might be freed of the poison which had infected the entire earth because of Adam's disobedience. With eager love he submitted to a shameful death on the cross and by that death he gave you life, not merely human but divine.

Sunday of the Thirty-First Week in Ordinary Time

From the pastoral constitution on the Church in the Modern World of the Second Vatican Council

The promotion of peace

Peace is not the mere absence of war or the simple maintenance of a balance of power between forces, nor can it be imposed at the dictate of absolute power. It is called, rightly and properly, *a work of justice*. It is the product of order, the order implanted in human society by its divine founder, to be realized in practice as men hunger and thirst for ever more perfect justice.

The common good of the human race is subject to the eternal law as its primary principle, but its requirements in practice keep changing with the passage of time. The result is that peace is never established finally and for ever; the building up of peace has to go on all the time. Again, the human will is weak and wounded by sin; the search for peace therefore demands from each individual constant control of the passions, and from legitimate authority untiring vigilance.

Even this is not enough. Peace here on earth cannot be maintained unless the good of the human person is safeguarded, and men are willing to trust each other and share their riches of spirit and talent. If peace is to be established it is absolutely necessary to have a firm determination to respect other persons and peoples and their dignity, and to be zealous in the practice of brotherhood.

Peace is therefore the fruit also of love; love goes beyond what justice can achieve. Peace on earth, born of love for one's neighbor, is the sign and the effect of the peace of Christ that flows from God the Father. In his own person the incarnate Son, the Prince of Peace, reconciled all men to God through his death on the cross. In his human nature he destroyed hatred and restored unity to all mankind in one people and one body. Raised on high by the resurrection, he sent the Spirit of love into the hearts of men.

All Christians are thus urgently summoned to *live the truth in love*, and to join all true peacemakers in prayer and work for peace. Moved by the same spirit, we cannot but praise those who renounce violence in defense of rights, and have recourse to means of defense otherwise available to the less powerful as well, provided that this can be done without injury to the rights and obligations of others or of the community.

Monday of the Thirty-First Week in Ordinary Time

From the pastoral constitution on the Church in the modern world of the Second Vatican Council

Reeducation for peace

Men must not be content simply to support the efforts of others in the work for peace; they must also scrutinize their own attitudes. Statesmen, responsible as they are for the common good of their own nation and at the same time for the well-being of the whole world, are very much dependent on the opinions and convictions of the general public. Their efforts to secure peace are of no avail as long as men are divided or set against each other by feelings of hostility, contempt and distrust, by racial hatred or by inflexible ideologies. There is then a very great and urgent need to reeducate men and to provide fresh inspiration in the field of public opinion.

Those engaged in education, especially among young people, and those who influence public opinion, should consider it a very serious responsibility to work for the reeducation of mankind to a new attitude toward peace. We must all undergo a change of heart. We must look out on the whole world and see the tasks that we can all do together to promote the well-being of the family of man. We must not be misled by a false sense of hope. Unless antagonism and hatred are abandoned, unless binding and honest agreements are concluded, safeguarding universal peace in the future, mankind, already in grave peril, may well face in spite of its marvelous advance in knowledge that day of disaster when it knows no other peace than the awful peace of death.

In saying this, however, the Church of Christ, living as it does in the midst of these anxious times, continues unwaveringly in hope. Time and again, in season and out of season, it seeks to proclaim to our age the message of the Apostle: *Now is the hour of God's favor*[2 Cor 6:2], the hour for change of heart; *now is the day of salvation*[2 Cor 6:2].

To build peace, the causes of human discord which feed the fires of war must first be eliminated, and among these especially the violations of justice. Many of these causes are due to gross economic inequality and delay in providing necessary remedies. Others arise from a spirit of domination and from a contempt for others, and, among more fundamental causes, from human envy, distrust, pride and other forms of selfishness. Since man cannot bear so many violations of due order, the result is that, even where war does not rage, the world is constantly plagued by human conflict and acts of violence.

The same evils are also found in relations between nations. It is therefore absolutely necessary that international institutions should cooperate more effectively, more resolutely and with greater coordination of effort, in order to overcome or prevent these evils, and to check unbridled acts of violence. There must also be constant encouragement for the creation of organizations designed to promote peace.

Tuesday of the Thirty-First Week in Ordinary Time

From the pastoral constitution on the Church in the Modern World of the Second Vatican Council

The Christian duty of working for peace

Christians should cooperate, willingly and wholeheartedly, in building an international order based on genuine respect for legitimate freedom and on a brotherhood of universal friendship. This is all the more urgent because the greater part of the world still experiences such poverty that in the voices of the poor Christ himself can be heard, crying out for charity from his followers. There are nations - many of them with a majority of Christians - which enjoy an abundance of goods, while others are deprived of the necessities of life, and suffer from hunger, disease and all kinds of afflictions. This scandal must be removed from among men, for the glory of Christ's Church and its testimony to the world are the spirit of poverty and the spirit of love.

Christians, especially young Christians, deserve praise and support when they offer themselves voluntarily in the service of other people and other nations. Indeed, it is the duty of all God's people , with bishops giving a lead by word and example, to do all in their power to relieve the sufferings of our times, following the age-old custom of the Church in giving not only what they can spare but also what they need for themselves.

Without being uniform or inflexible, a method of collecting and distributing contributions should be established in each diocese and nation and on a world-wide level. Wherever it seems appropriate, there should be joint action between Catholics and other Christians. The spirit of charity, far from forbidding prudence and orderliness in social and charitable action, in fact demands them. Those intending to serve the developing countries must therefore undergo appropriate and systematic training.

In order to foster and encourage cooperation among men, the Church must be present and active in the community of nations. It must work through its own public organizations with the full and sincere cooperation of all Christians in their one desire to serve all mankind.

This end will be more effectively achieved if the faithful are themselves conscious of their human and Christian responsibilities and seek to awaken among those in their own walk of life a readiness to cooperate with the international community. Special care should be taken to give this kind of formation to young people in their religious and secular education.

Finally, it is to be hoped that, in carrying out their responsibilities in the international community, Catholics will seek to cooperate actively and constructively with other Christians, who profess the same Gospel of love, and with all men who hunger and thirst for true peace.

Wednesday of the Thirty-First Week in Ordinary Time

From a catechetical instruction by Saint Cyril of Jerusalem, Bishop & Doctor

The power of faith transcends man's strength

The one word faith can have two meanings. One kind of faith concerns doctrines. It involves the soul's ascent to and acceptance of some particular matter. It also concerns the soul's good, according to the words of the Lord: *Whoever hears my voice and believes in him who sent me has eternal life, and will not come to be judged*[Jn 5:24]. And again: *He who believes in the Son is not condemned, but has passed from death to life*[Jn 5:24].

How great is God's love for men! Some good men have been found pleasing to God because of years of work. What they achieved by working for many hours at a task pleasing to God is freely given to you by Jesus in one short hour. For if you believe that Jesus Christ is Lord and that God raised him from the dead, you will be saved and taken up to paradise by him, just as he brought the thief there. Do not doubt that this is possible. After all, he saved the thief on the holy hill of Golgotha because of one hour's faith; will he not save you too since you have believed?

The other kind of faith is given by Christ by means of a special grace. *To one wise sayings are given through the Spirit, to another perceptive comments by the same Spirit, to another faith by the same Spirit, to another gifts of healing*[1 Cor 12:7-11]. Now this kind of faith, given by the Spirit as a special favor, is not confined to doctrinal matters, for it produces effects beyond any human capability. If a man who has this faith says to this mountain *move from here to there, it will move.* For when anybody says this in faith, believing it will happen and having no doubt in his heart, he then receives that grace.

It is of this kind of faith, moreover, that it is said: *If you have faith like a grain of mustard seed*[Mt 17:20]. The mustard seed is small in size but it holds an explosive force; although it is sown in a small hole, it produces great branches, and when it is grown birds can nest there. In the same way faith produces great effects in the soul instantaneously. Enlightened by faith, the soul pictures God and sees him as clearly as any soul can. It circles the earth; even before the end of this world it sees the judgment and the conferring of promised rewards. So may you have the faith which depends on you and is directed to God, that you may receive from him that faith too which transcends man's capacity.

Thursday of the Thirty-First Week in Ordinary Time

From a catechetical instruction by Saint Cyril of Jerusalem, Bishop & Doctor

On the creed

In learning and professing the faith, you must accept and retain only the Church's present tradition, confirmed as it is by the Scriptures. Although not everyone is able to read the Scriptures, some because they have never learned to read, others because their daily activities keep them from such study, still so that their souls will not be lost through ignorance, we have gathered together the whole of the faith in a few concise articles.

Now I order you to retain this creed for your nourishment throughout life and never to accept any alternative, not even if I myself were to change and say something contrary to what I am now teaching, not even if some angel of contradiction, changed into an angel of light, tried to lead you astray. For *even if we, or an angel from heaven, should preach to you a gospel contrary to that which you have now received, let him be accursed in your sight*[Gal 1:8-9].

So for the present be content to listen to the simple words of the creed and to memorize them; at some suitable time you can find the proof of each article in the Scriptures. This summary of the faith was not composed at man's whim; the most important sections were chosen from the whole Scripture to constitute and complete a comprehensive statement of the faith. Just as the mustard seed contains in a small grain many branches, so this brief statement of the faith keeps in its heart, as it were, all the religious truth to be found in Old and New Testament alike. That is why, my brothers, you must consider and preserve the traditions you are now receiving. Inscribe them across your heart.

Observe them scrupulously, so that no enemy may rob any of you in an idle and heedless moment; let no heretic deprive you of what has been given to you. Faith is rather like depositing in a bank the money entrusted to you, and God will surely demand an account of what you have deposited. In the words of the Apostle: *I charge you before the God who gives life to all things, and before Christ who bore witness under Pontius Pilate in a splendid declaration*[1 Tim 6:13], to keep unblemished this faith you have received, until the coming of our Lord Jesus Christ.

You have now been given life's great treasure; when he comes, the Lord will ask for what he has entrusted to you. *At the appointed time he will reveal himself, for he is the blessed and sole Ruler, King of kings, Lord of lords. He alone is immortal, dwelling in unapproachable light. No man has seen or ever can see him. To him be glory, honor and power for ever and ever. Amen*[1 Tim 6:15-16].

.

Friday of the Thirty-First Week in Ordinary Time

From a sermon by Saint Gregory Nazianzen, Bishop & Doctor

It is a holy thought to pray for the dead

What is man that you are mindful of him[Ps 8:5]? What is this new mystery surrounding me? I am both small and great, both lowly and exalted, mortal and immortal, earthly and heavenly. I am to be buried with Christ and to rise again with him, to become a coheir with him, a son of God, and indeed God himself.

This is what the great mystery means for us; this is why God became man and became poor for our sake: it was to raise up our flesh, to recover the divine image, to re-create mankind, so that all of us might become one in Christ who perfectly became in us everything that he is himself. So we are no longer to be *male and female, barbarian and Scythian, slave and free*[Col 3:11] – distinctions deriving from the flesh – but are to bear within ourselves only the seal of God, by whom and for whom we were created. We are to be so formed and molded by him that we are recognized as belonging to his one family.

If only we could be what we hope to be, by the great kindness of our generous God! He asks so little and gives so much, in this life and in the next, to those who love him sincerely. In a spirit of hope and out of love for him, let us then *bear and endure all things*[1 Cor 13:7] and give thanks for everything that befalls us, since even reason can often recognize these things as weapons to win salvation. And meanwhile let us commend to God our own souls and the souls of those who, being more ready for it, have reached the place of rest before us although they walked the same road as we do.

Lord and Creator of all, and especially of your creature man, you are the God and Father and ruler of your children; you are the Lord of life and death, you are the guardian and benefactor of our souls. You fashion and transform all things in their due season through your creative Word, as you know to be best in your deep wisdom and providence. Receive now those who have gone ahead of us in our journey from this life.

And receive us too at the proper time, when you have guided us in our bodily life as long as may be for our profit. Receive us prepared indeed by fear of you, but not troubled, not shrinking back on that day of death or uprooted by force like those who are lovers of the world and the flesh. Instead, may we set out eagerly for that everlasting and blessed life which is in Christ Jesus our Lord. To him be glory for ever and ever. Amen.

Saturday of the Thirty-First Week in Ordinary Time

From a treatise on death as a blessing by Saint Ambrose, Bishop & Doctor

Let us show Christ crucified in our lives

The Apostle tells us: *The world is crucified to me, and I to the world*[Gal 6:14]. We are to understand that this death by crucifixion takes place in this life, and that this death is a blessing. So he goes on to urge us *to bear the death of Jesus with us in our bodies, for whoever bears the death of Jesus in his body will bear also in his body the life of the Lord Jesus*[2 Cor 4:10-18].

Death must be active within us if life also is to be active within us. "Life" is life after death, a life that is a blessing. This blessing of life comes after victory, when the contest is over, when the law of our fallen nature no longer rebels against the law of our reason, when we no longer need to struggle against the body that leads to death, for the body already shares in victory. It seems to me that this "death" is more powerful than "life." I accept the authority of the Apostle when he says: *Death is therefore active within us, but life also is active within you*[2 Cor 4:10-18]. Yet the "death" of this one man was building up life for countless multitudes of peoples! He therefore teaches us to seek out this kind of death even in this life, so that the death of Christ may shine forth in our lives – that blessed death by which our outward self is destroyed and our inmost self renewed, and our earthly dwelling crumbles away and a home in heaven opens before us.

The person who cuts himself off from this fallen nature of ours and frees himself from its chains is imitating death. These are the bonds spoken of by the Lord through Isaiah: *Loose the bonds of injustice, untie the thongs of the yoke, set free the oppressed and break every yoke of evil*[Isa 58:6].

The Lord allowed death to enter this world so that sin might come to an end. But he gave us the resurrection of the dead so that our nature might not end once more in death; death was to bring guilt to an end, and the resurrection was to enable our nature to continue forever.

"Death" in this context is a passover to be made by all mankind. You must keep facing it with perseverance. It is a passover from corruption, from mortality to immortality, from rough seas to a calm harbor. The word "death" must not trouble us; the blessings that come from a safe journey should bring us joy. What is death but the burial of sin and the resurrection of goodness? Scripture says: *Let my soul die among the souls of the just*[Num 23:10]; that is, let me be buried with the just, so that I may cast off my sins and put on the grace of the just, of those who bear the death of Christ with them, in their bodies and in their souls.

Sunday of the Thirty-Second Week in Ordinary Time

From a homily written in the second century

Christ willed to save those who were perishing

Brethren, we ought to regard Jesus Christ both as God and judge of the living and the dead. We should not hold our Savior in low esteem, for if we esteem him but little, we may hope to obtain but little from him. Moreover, people who hear these things and think them of small importance commit sin, and we ourselves sin if we do not realize what we have been called from, who has called us, and to what place, and how much suffering Jesus Christ endured on our account.

How then shall we repay him? What fruit can we bear that would be worthy of what he has given us? For how many benefits are we not in his debt! He has enlightened our minds; he has called us sons as a father does; he saved us when we were about to perish. How then shall we praisc him, how repay him for his gifts? Spiritually blind, we worshipped stones and pieces of wood, gold and silver and bronze, things made by men, and our whole life was death. Darkness enfolded us, and nothing but gloom met our eyes. Then, by his will, we escaped from the cloud that enveloped us and recovered our sight. For he saw our many errors and the damnation that awaited us, and knowing that apart from him we had no hope of salvation, he pitied us, and in his mercy saved us. He called us when we were not his people and willed us to become his people.

Rejoice, O barren woman who never bore a child; break into shouts of joy, you who never knew a mother's pangs; for the deserted wife shall have more children than she who has a husband[Isa 54:1]. When he says: *Rejoice, O barren woman who never bore a child*, he is speaking of us, for our Church was barren until children were given her. When he says: *Break into shouts of joy, you who never knew a mother's pangs*, he means that we should not grow weary like women in labor, but tirelessly and in all simplicity offer our prayers to God. He declares that *the deserted wife shall have more children than she who has a husband*, because faith has now made our people who seemed to have been deserted by God more numerous than those who were thought to possess him.

Another text says: *I have come not to call the righteous, but sinners to repentence*[Lk 5:32], for it is those who are perishing who must be saved. It is a great and wonderful work to uphold those who are falling, rather than those who already stand firm. Christ willed to save people who were in danger of losing their souls, and he has been the salvation of many. When we were on the point of perishing, he came and called us.

Monday of the Thirty-Second Week in Ordinary Time

From a homily written in the second century

Let us confess our faith in God by our deeds

Great is the mercy that Jesus Christ has shown us. The first benefit that we owe to his mercy is that we who are living do not sacrifice to dead gods or worship them, but have, through Christ, attained a knowledge of the Father. What else is knowledge of the Father but the recognition of his through whom this knowledge comes to us? He himself declares: *Everyone who acknowledges me, I in my turn will acknowledge in the presence of the Father*[Mt 10:32]. This then will be our reward if we acknowledge him through whom we have been saved. But how shall we show that we acknowledge him? By doing what he says, by not disobeying his commands, and by honoring him not only with our lips but with our whole heart and our whole mind. For he says in Isaiah: *This people pays me lip service, but its heart is far from me*[Isa 29:13].

Let us not only call him Lord, for that will not save us. *Not everyone who says to me, Lord, Lord, will be saved,* he warns, *but only the man who does what is right*[Mt 7:21-23]. So then, brothers, let us show our faith in him by our deeds, by loving one another, by not committing adultery, by not finding fault with one another, or being envious. Instead, let us be chaste, merciful and kind. We should also have compassion for one another, and not be covetous. We have to prove that we believe in him by performing such actions as these and by avoiding whatever is contrary to them, since we fear God rather than men. Should we fail to do so, we have the Lord's warning: *If you do not keep my commandments, even though I had pressed you to my heart, I will thrust you away from me and say to you: Out of my sight, you whose deeds are evil; you are complete strangers to me*[Lev 26:14-33].

Therefore, my brothers, let us enter the lists in the knowledge that the contest is imminent. Many men travel far to contend for a crown that soon fades, yet not all of them win, but only those who have strained every nerve and competed fairly. Let us so contend that we may all be crowned. Let us run a straight course in the race of the Christian life, setting out in great numbers to take part in it, and then striving for the crown with all our might. Even if we are not all able to win, at least let us draw near to victory.

Now we must surely know that even when the contest is for a wreath that lasts but a day, if anyone is found to be breaking the rules, he is flogged and driven off the racecourse. What do you suppose, then, will be the fate of the man who breaks the rules in the contest of the Christian life? Of those who have not kept the seal of their baptism unbroken Scripture says: *The worm does not die and the fire is never extinguished. They will be a spectacle to all men*[Mk 9:46-48].

Tuesday of the Thirty-Second Week in Ordinary Time

From a homily written in the second century

Sincere repentance

We should repent of our sins while we are still on earth. When a potter is making a vessel and it becomes misshapen or breaks in his hands, he shapes it again; but once placed in the oven, it is beyond repair. Now the clay in the craftsman's hands is an image of ourselves, and it teaches us that, while still in this world, we must wholeheartedly repent of sins committed in the body and make it possible for the Lord to save us while there is time. When we have left this world, we shall no longer be able to repent and confess our sins. We must do the will of the Father, keep our bodies pure, and observe the commandments of the Lord, for this is the way to obtain eternal life. The Lord says in the gospel: *If you have not been observant in small matters, who will entrust you with anything important? For I tell you that the man who is faithful in the smallest things is faithful in the greatest things as well*[Lk 16:10-13]. In other words, in order to obtain eternal life, we must remain pure and keep the seal of our baptism undefiled.

Nor must any of you say that our bodies will not share in the judgment, nor rise again. In what were you saved? In what did you receive your sight? Think for a moment. Was it not in this very body? Our bodies are the temple of God, and as such we must guard them, for even as we were called in the body, so shall we also be judged in the body. Since Christ, our Lord and Savior, who in the beginning was spirit, became flesh and in this way called us, it is in this flesh of ours that we shall also receive our reward.

Therefore, let us love one another, so that we may all attain to the kingdom of God. While we can still be healed, let us surrender ourselves into the hands of our divine physician and give him his recompense – the recompense of true sorrow for our sins. Since he who knows all things sees what is in our hearts, let us praise him with our hearts as well as our lips. He will then receive us as his sons. The Lord himself has said: *Those who do my Father's will are my brothers*[Mt 12:48-50].

Wednesday of the Thirty-Second Week in Ordinary Time

From a homily written in the second century

In hope we endure

For the sake of eternal life, my brothers, let us do the will of the Father who called us, resisting the temptations that lead us into sin and striving earnestly to advance in virtue. Let us revere God for fear of the evils that spring from impiety. If we are zealous in doing good, we shall have peace, but there is no peace for those who, governed by human respect, prefer present enjoyment to the future promises. They realize neither the torment that is laid up for them on account of these momentary pleasures, nor the joy of the promises to come. And indeed it could be endured if their conduct affected only themselves, but as it is, they persist in corrupting the innocent, unaware that they incur a double condemnation, for themselves and their disciples.

So let us serve God with a pure heart, and then we shall be living as we should. If we fail to serve him because of our disbelief, we shall only be miserable. *Wretched are those of wavering faith*, says the prophet, *the people who doubt in their hearts and say: We heard all this even when our parents were alive and day after day we have waited in vain for any proof of it. O foolish ones! Think of a tree, and see how you resemble it. A vine, for example, first sheds its leaves and then the bud appears; after that there comes the sour grape and finally a cluster of ripened fruit. So it is with my people. They have had their tumults and afflictions, but afterward will come their reward*.

Therefore, my brothers, in order to obtain the reward, we must endure in hope with unwavering faith. He who made the promise to repay every man as his deeds deserve will be faithful to it. If we do what is right in God's sight, we shall enter into his kingdom and receive the promise *which no ear has heard, no eye seen, no human heart conceived*[1 Cor 2:9-11].

So let us live loving and upright lives, in hourly expectation of the kingdom of God, since we do not know when God will come. Let us repent at once of our great folly and wickedness, and from now on always be ready to do good. We should blot out past sins by being truly sorry for them, and then we shall be saved. We must have no desire to curry favor with men, nor should we think only of making ourselves acceptable to our fellow Christians. We should live upright lives in order to win the respect of non-Christians as well. The Name must not be blasphemed on our account.

Thursday of the Thirty-Second Week in Ordinary Time

From a homily written in the second century

The living Church is the body of Christ

My name is constantly blasphemed by unbelievers[Isa 52:5], says the Lord. *Woe to the man who causes my name to be blasphemed*. Why is the Lord's name blasphemed? Because we say one thing and do another. When they hear the words of God on our lips, unbelievers are amazed at their beauty and power, but when they see that those words have no effect in our lives, their admiration turns to scorn, and they dismiss such words as myths and fairy tales.

They listen, for example, when we tell them that God has said: *It is no credit to you if you love those who love you, but only if you love your enemies, and those who hate you*[Lk 6:32-36]. They are full of admiration at such extraordinary virtue, but when they observe that we not only fail to love people who hate us, but even those who love us, they laugh us to scorn, and the Name is blasphemed.

Therefore, brothers, if we do the will of God the Father, we shall be members of the first spiritual Church that was created before the sun and the moon; but if we fail to do the will of the Lord, we shall be among those to whom it is said in Scripture: *My house has been made into a robbers' den*[Mt 21:13]. We must choose then, if we want to be saved, to be members of the Church of life.

You surely cannot be ignorant of the fact that the living Church is the body of Christ; for Scripture says: *God made man male and female*[Gen 1:27]. Now the male signifies Christ, and the female signifies the Church, which, according to both the Old and the New Testament, is no recent creation, but has existed from the beginning. At first the Church was purely spiritual, even as our Jesus was spiritual, but it appeared in the last days to save us.

For the spiritual Church was made manifest in the body of Christ, in order to show us that if we uphold its honor in the outward, visible form, and do not defile it, we shall, through the Holy Spirit, be made its members in the true, spiritual sense. For the body of the Church is a copy of the Spirit, and no one who defaces the copy can have any part in what the copy represents. In other words, brothers, you must preserve the honor of the body in order to share in the Spirit. For if we say that the body is the Church and the Spirit is Christ, it follows that anyone who dishonors his body, dishonors the Church. Such a man will have no part in the Sprit, which is Christ. But if the Holy Spirit is joined to it, this body can receive an immortal life that is wonderful beyond words, for the blessings God has made ready for his chosen ones surpass all human powers of description.

Friday of the Thirty-Second Week in Ordinary Time

From a homily written in the second century

Let us return to God who has called us

With regard to self-control, I believe I have given you good advice. No one who follows it will have reason for regret but will save his own soul and mine as well, since I have been his counselor. Indeed there is no small reward for converting an erring soul and saving it from perishing. Moreover, whether it is our duty to speak or to listen, we have it in our power to make some recompense to the God who created us, by speaking or listening with faith and love.

We must remain firm in our faith, therefore, and live upright and holy lives, for we shall then feel at ease and confident when we present our petitions to God, who says: *While you are still speaking I will say: "See, I am here!"*[Isa 65:24] In these words the Lord makes a wonderful promise, and shows us that he is more ready to give than we are to ask. We all have a share in this extraordinary goodness, so the great blessings we receive should never make us envy one another. In fact, the degree of pleasure these words bring to those who live by them is equaled only by the condemnation they will bring on those who disregard them.

So you see, my brothers, that we have been given every inducement to amend our lives. We have been called by God, and now it is up to us to return to him while we still have time and one who is ready to receive us. For if we renounce sinful pleasures and practice self control by refusing to yield to our evil desires, we shall share in the mercy of Jesus.

You must know, however, that the day of judgment, like a flaming furnace, is already approaching. Sun, moon and stars will be consumed, and the whole earth will become like lead melting in the fire. All that each man has done, whether openly or in secret, will then be brought to light. Therefore, a very good way of atoning for our sins is by being generous to the poor. Fasting is better than prayer, but almsgiving surpasses both, for *love covers a multitude of sins*[1 Pet 4:8]. Nevertheless, prayer delivers the soul from death if it proceeds from a good conscience. Happy the man who is found rich in these virtues; by relieving the poor, he himself will be relieved of his sins.

To make sure that none of us is lost, we must repent from the bottom of our hearts. Since we have been commanded to go out and rescue idolaters and to instruct them, is it not even more important to save souls who already know God? If we are all to be saved, we shall have to help one another and support the weak in their struggle to live a good life. When one of us does wrong, it is for the others to warn him and persuade him of his error.

Saturday of the Thirty-Second Week in Ordinary Time

From a homily written in the second century

Our salvation depends on the integrity of our lives

Let us be sure that when the day of judgment comes, our place will be among those who give thanks to God and have served him, and not with the ungodly who face condemnation. As for myself, I am only a sinner, not yet beyond the reach of temptation; but even amidst all the devil's machinations, I still strive to make progress and hope to attain at least some virtue, for I fear the judgment that awaits me.

My brothers and sisters, you have heard the word of God who is the very fountainhead of truth. Therefore, I now read you an appeal to heed what is written, and thereby save both yourselves and your reader. The reward I ask is that you repent with your whole heart, to save yourselves and find life. If we do this, we shall set an example for all young people, for whom the glory and goodness of God is a challenge to be generous in his service.

Let me say also that when we are given a warning and corrected for doing something wrong, we should not be so foolish as to take offense and be angry. There are times when we are unconscious of the sins we commit because our hearts are fickle, lacking in faith. Futile desires becloud our minds. We need to pull ourselves up, therefore, because our very salvation is at stake. Those who keep God's commandments will have reason to rejoice. For a short time in this world they may have to suffer, but they will rise again and their reward will endure for ever. No one who holds God in reverence should grieve over the hardships of this present time, for a time of blessedness awaits him. He will live again in heaven in the company of all those who have gone before him; for all eternity he will rejoice, never to know sorrow again.

So do not be disturbed at the sight of wicked men possessing great wealth while the servants of God suffer want. We, my brothers and sisters, must have faith. Competing as we are in the arena of the living God, we are receiving the training in this present life that will make us worthy to be crowned in the life to come. No honest man becomes rich overnight; he has to wait for the reward of his labors. If God gave virtue an immediate recompense, we should straightway find ourselves engaging in commerce, instead of perfecting ourselves in his service. Although to all outward appearance we might be irreproachable, we should not be seeking God, but our own advantage, and bringing down on our sinful souls the divine judgment that would soon make us feel the full weight of our chains.

To the one invisible God, the Father of truth, who sent forth the Savior, the author of immortality, and through him revealed to us the truth and the heavenly life - to him be glory throughout all ages, for ever and ever. Amen.

Sunday of the Thirty-Third Week in Ordinary Time

From a discourse on the Psalms by Saint Augustine, Bishop & Doctor

Let us not resist the first coming, so that we may not dread the second

All the trees of the forest will exult before the face of the Lord, for he has come, he has come to judge the earth[1 Chr 16:33]. He has come the first time, and he will come again. At his first coming, his own voice declared in the gospel: *Hereafter you shall see the Son of Man coming upon the clouds*[Mt 26:64]. What does he mean by *hereafter?* Does he not mean that the Lord will come at a future time when all the nations of the earth will be striking their breasts in grief? Previously he came through his preachers, and he filled the whole world. Let us not resist his first coming, so that we may not dread the second.

What then should the Christian do? He ought to use the world, not become its slave. And what does this mean? It means having, as though not having. So says the Apostle: *My brethren, the appointed time is short: from now on let those who have wives live as though they had none; and those who mourn as though they were not mourning; and those who rejoice as though they were not rejoicing; and those who buy as though they had no goods; and those who deal with this world as though they had no dealings with it. For the form of this world is passing away. But I wish you to be without anxiety* [1 Cor 7:29-32]. He who is without anxiety waits without fear until his Lord comes. For what sort of love of Christ is it to fear his coming? Brothers, do we not have to blush for shame? We love him, yet we fear his coming. Are we really certain that we love him? Or do we love our sins more? Therefore let us hate our sins and love him who will exact punishment for them. He will come whether we wish it or not. Do not think that because he is not coming just now, he will not come at all. He will come, you know not when; and provided he finds you prepared, your ignorance of the time of his coming will not be held against you.

All the trees of the forest will exult[1 Chr 16:33]. He has come the first time, and he will come again to judge the earth; he will find those rejoicing who believed in his first coming, *for he has come.*

He will judge the world with equity and the peoples in his truth[Ps 9:8-9.] What are equity and truth? He will gather together with him for the judgment his chosen ones, but the others he will set apart; for he will place some on his right, others on his left. What is more equitable, what more true than that they should not themselves expect mercy from the judge, who themselves were unwilling to show mercy before the judge's coming. Those, however, who were willing to show mercy will be judged with mercy. For it will be said to those placed on his right: *Come, blessed of my Father, take possession of the kingdom which has been prepared for you from the beginning of the world*[Mt 25:34]. And he reckons to their account their works of mercy: *For I was hungry and you gave me to eat; I was thirsty and you gave me to drink*[Mt 25:35-40].

What is imputed to those placed on his left side? That they refused to show mercy. And where will they go? *Depart into the everlasting fire*[Mt 25:41]. The hearing of this condemnation will cause much wailing. But what has another psalm said? *The just man will be held in everlasting remembrance; he will not fear the evil report*[Ps 111:7-8]. What is the evil report? *Depart into the everlasting fire, which was prepared for the devil and his angels*[Mt 25:41]. Whoever rejoices to hear the good report will not fear the bad. This is equity, this is truth.

Or do you, because you are unjust, expect the judge not to be just? Or because you are a liar, will the truthful one not be true? Rather, if you wish to receive mercy, be merciful before he comes; forgive whatever has been done against you; give of your abundance. Of whose possessions do you give, if not from his? If you were to give of your own, it would be largess; but since you give of his, it is restitution. *For what have you that you have not received*[1 Cor 4:7]*?* These are the sacrifices most pleasing to God: mercy, humility, praise, peace, charity. Such as these, then, let us bring and, free from fear, we shall await the coming of the judge *who will judge the world in equity and the peoples in his truth*[Ps 9:8].

Monday of the Thirty-Third Week in Ordinary Time

From a treatise on Forgiveness by Fulgentius of Ruspe, Bishop

He who overcomes shall not be harmed by the second death

In a moment, in the twinkling of an eye as the final trumpet sounds, for the trumpet shall indeed sound, the dead shall rise incorruptible and we shall be changed[1 Cor 15:52]. In saying "we," Paul is indicating that the gift of that future change will also be given to those who during their time on earth are united to him and his companions by upright lives within the communion of the Church. He hints at the nature of the change when he says: *This corruptible body must put on incorruptibility, this mortal body immortality*[1 Cor 15:53]. In order, then, that men may obtain the transformation which is the reward of the just, they must first undergo here on earth a change which is God's free gift. Those who in this life have been changed from evil to good are promised that future change as a reward.

Through justification and the spiritual resurrection, grace now effects in them an initial change that is God's gift. Later on, through the bodily resurrection, the transformation of the just will be brought to completion, and they will experience a perfect, abiding, unchangeable glorification. The purpose of this change wrought in them by the gifts of both justification and glorification is that they may abide in an eternal, changeless state of joy.

Here on earth they are changed by the first resurrection, in which they are enlightened and converted, thus passing from death to life, sinfulness to holiness, unbelief to faith, and evil actions to holy life. For this reason the second death has no power over them. It is of such men that the Book of Revelation says: *Happy the man who shares in the first resurrection; over such as he the second death has no power*[Rev 20:6]. Elsewhere the same book says: *He who overcomes shall not be harmed by the second death*[Rev 2:11]. As the first resurrection consists of the conversion of the heart, the second death consists of unending torment.

Let everyone, therefore, who does not wish to be condemned to the endless punishment of the second death now hasten to share in the first resurrection. For if any during this life are changed out of fear of God and pass from an evil life to a good one, they pass from death to life and later they shall be transformed from a shameful state to a glorious one.

Tuesday of the Thirty-Third Week in Ordinary Time

From a discourse by Saint Andrew of Crete, Bishop

Behold, your king is coming to you, the Holy One, the Savior

Let us say to Christ: *Blessed is he who comes in the name of the Lord, the king of Israel*[Jn 12:12-13]. Let us wave before him like palm branches the words inscribed above him on the cross. Let us show him honor, not with olive branches but with the splendor of merciful deeds to one another. Let us spread the thoughts and desires of our hearts under his feet like garments, so that entering with the whole of his being, he may draw the whole of our being into himself and place the whole of his in us. Let us say to Zion in the words of the prophet: Have courage, daughter of Zion, do not be afraid. Behold, your king comes to you, humble and mounted on a colt, the foal of a beast of burden.

He is coming who is everywhere present and pervades all things; he is coming to achieve in you his work of universal salvation. He is coming who came to call to repentance not the righteous but sinners, coming to recall those who have strayed into sin. Do not be afraid, then: *God is in the midst of you, and you shall not be shaken*[Ps 45:2-6]

Receive him with open, outstretched hands, for it was on his own hands that he sketched you. Receive him who laid your foundations on the palms of his hands. Receive him, for he took upon himself all that belongs to us except sin, to consume what is ours in what is his. Be glad, city of Zion, our mother, and fear not. *Celebrate your feasts.* Glorify him for his mercy, who has come to us in you. Rejoice exceedingly, daughter of Jerusalem, sing and leap for joy. *Be enlightened, be enlightened,* we cry to you, as holy Isaiah trumpeted, *for the light has come to you and the glory of the Lord has risen over you*[Isa 60:19-21].

What kind of *light* is this? It is that which *enlightens every man coming into the world*[Jn 1:9]. It is the everlasting light, the timeless light revealed in time, the light manifested in the flesh although hidden by nature, the light that shone round the shepherds and guided the Magi. It is the light that was in the world from the beginning, through which the world was made, yet the world did not know it. It is that light which came to its own, and its own people did not receive it.

And what is this *glory of the Lord?* Clearly it is the cross on which Christ was glorified, he, the radiance of the Father's glory, even as he said when he faced his passion: *Now is the Son of Man glorified, and God is glorified in him, and will glorify him at once*[Jn 13:31]. The glory of which he speaks here is his lifting up on the cross, for Christ's glory is his cross and his exultation upon it, as he plainly says: *When I have been lifted up, I will draw all men to myself*[Jn 12:32].

Wednesday of the Thirty-Third Week in Ordinary Time

From a sermon by Saint Augustine, Bishop & Doctor

The heart of the just man will rejoice in the Lord

The just man will rejoice in the Lord and put his hope in him; the hearts of all good men will be filled with joy[Ps 63:11]. We must surely have sung these words with our hearts as well as with our voices. Indeed, the tongue of the Christian expresses his deepest feelings when it addresses such words to God. *The just man will rejoice*, not in the world, but *in the Lord. Light has dawned for the just*, Scripture says in another place, *and joy for the upright of heart*. Were you wondering what reason he has for joy? Here you are told: *The just man will rejoice in the Lord*. Another text runs: *Delight in the Lord, and he will give you your heart's desires*[Ps 36:4].

What are we instructed to do then, and what are we enabled to do? To rejoice in the Lord. But who can rejoice in something he does not see? Am I suggesting that we see the Lord then? No, but we have been promised that we shall see him. *Now, as long as we are in the body, we walk by faith, for we are absent from the Lord*[2 Cor 5:6-8; Phil 1:21-23]. We walk by faith, and not by sight. When will it be by sight? *Beloved*, says John, *we are now the sons of God; what we shall be has not yet been revealed, but we know that when it is revealed we shall be like him, because we shall see him as he is*[1 Jn 3:2]. When this prophecy is fulfilled, then it will be by sight.

That will be the great joy, the supreme joy, joy in all its fullness. Then we shall no longer drink the milk of hope, but we shall feed on the reality itself. Nevertheless, even now, before that vision comes to us, or before we come to that vision, let us rejoice in the Lord; for it is no small reason for rejoicing to have a hope that will some day be fulfilled.

Therefore, since the hope we now have inspires love, the *just man rejoices* [Ps 63 11], Scripture says, *in the Lord*[Ps 63 11]; but because he does not yet see, it immediately goes on to say, and *hopes in him* [Ps 63 11].

Yet already we have the firstfruits of the Spirit, and have we not also other reasons for rejoicing? For we are drawing near to the one we love, and not only are we drawing near – we even have some slight feeling and taste of the banquet we shall one day eagerly eat and drink.

But how can we rejoice in the Lord if he is far from us? Pray God he may not be far. If he is, that is your doing. Love, and he will draw near; love, and he will dwell within you. *The Lord is at hand; have no anxiety*[Phil 4:4-8]. Are you puzzled to know how it is that he will be with you if you love? *God is love*[1 Jn 4:7-12].

"What do you mean by love?" you will ask me. It is that which enables us to be loving. What do we love? A good that words cannot describe, a good that is for ever giving, a good that is the Creator of all good. Delight in him from whom you have received everything that delights you. But in that I do not include sin, for sin is the one thing that you do not receive from him. With that one exception, everything you have comes from him.

Thursday of the Thirty-Third Week in Ordinary Time

From a commentary on the Song of Songs by Saint Gregory of Nyssa, Bishop

A prayer to the Good Shepherd

Where do you pasture your sheep, O good Shepherd, you who carry on your shoulders the whole flock? For it is but one sheep, this entire human race whom you lift onto your shoulders. Show me the place where there are green pastures, let me know restful waters, lead me out to nourishing grass and call me by name so that I can hear your voice, for I am your own sheep. And through that voice calling me, give me eternal life.

Tell me, you whom my soul loves[Song 1:7]. This is how I address you, because your true name is above all other names; it is unutterable and incomprehensible to all rational creatures. And so the name I use for you is simply the statement of my soul's love for you, and this is an apt name for making your goodness known. Very dark though I am, how could I not love you who so loved me, that you laid down your life for the sheep you tend? No greater love can be conceived than this, that you should purchase my salvation at the cost of your life.

Show me, then, says the bride, where you tend your sheep, so that I may find the saving pasture and be filled with heavenly nourishment. For whoever does not eat this food cannot enter eternal life. Let me run to you, the spring, and drink the divine draught that you cause to pour forth for the thirsty, offering water from your side opened by the spear. Whoever drinks of this becomes *a fountain of water springing up to eternal life*[Jn 4:14].

If you feed me thus, then you will surely make me lie down *at noonday*, and I shall at once *sleep in peace*[Ps 4:9], resting in a light that knows no shadow. Indeed, there is no shadow at noon, for the sun shines directly over that summit where you make those you tend lie down, and take your children with you to your bed. No one is judged worthy of this noonday rest who is not a child of light and of the day. But if anyone makes himself equally distant from the shadows of daybreak and those of nightfall, that is, from the origin of evil and its conclusion, the sun of righteousness makes him lie down at noontide.

Show me, then, says the bride, how I should lie down; show me the path to this noonday repose, lest my ignorance of your truth cause me to stray from your good guidance and consort with flocks which are strangers to your.

Thus speaks the bride, anxious about the beauty God has given her, and seeking to learn how her comeliness may continue for ever.

Friday of the Thirty-Third Week in Ordinary Time

From a treatise On the Kingdom of Jesus by Saint John Eudes, Priest

The mystery of Christ in us and in the Church

We must strive to follow and fulfill in ourselves the various stages of Christ's plan as well as his mysteries, and frequently beg him to bring them to completion in us and in the whole Church. For the mysteries of Jesus are not yet completely perfected and fulfilled. They are complete, indeed, in the person of Jesus, but not in us, who are his members, nor in the Church, which is his mystical body. The Son of God wills to give us a share in his mysteries and somehow to extend them to us. He wills to continue them in us and in his universal Church. This is brought about first through the graces he has resolved to impart to us and then through the works he wishes to accomplish in us through these mysteries. This is his plan for fulfilling his mysteries in us.

For this reason Saint Paul says that Christ is being brought to fulfillment in his Church and that all of us contribute to this fulfillment, and thus he achieves the fullness of life, that is, the mystical stature that he has in his mystical body, which will reach completion only on judgment day. In another place Paul says: *I complete in my own flesh what is lacking in the sufferings of Christ*[Col 1:24].

This is the plan by which the Son of God completes and fulfills in us all the various stages and mysteries. He desires us to perfect the mystery of his incarnation and birth by forming himself in us and being reborn in our souls through the blessed sacraments of baptism and the eucharist. He fulfills his hidden life in us, hidden with him in God.

He intends to perfect the mysteries of his passion, death and resurrection, by causing us to suffer, die and rise again with him and in him. Finally, he wishes to fulfill in us the state of his glorious and immortal life, when he will cause us to live a glorious, eternal life with him and in him in heaven.

In the same way he would complete and fulfill in us and in his Church his other stages and mysteries. He wants to give us a share in them and to accomplish and continue them in us. So it is that the mysteries of Christ will not be completed until the end of time, because he has arranged that the completion of his mysteries in us and in the Church will only be achieved at the end of time.

Saturday of the Thirty-Third Week in Ordinary Time

From a conference by Saint Thomas Aquinas, Priest & Doctor

I shall be satisfied when your glory is seen

It is fitting that the end of all our desires, namely eternal life coincides with the words at the end of the creed, "Life everlasting. Amen."

The first point about eternal life is that man is united with God. For God himself is the reward and end of all our labors: *I am your protector and your supreme reward*[Gen 15:1]. This union consists in seeing perfectly: *At present we are looking at a confused reflections in a mirror, but then we shall see face to face*[1 Cor 13:12].

Next it consists in perfect praise, according to the words of the prophet: *Joy and happiness will be found in it, thanksgiving and words of praise.*

It also consists in the complete satisfaction of desire, for there the blessed will be given more than they wanted or hoped for. The reason is that in this life no one can fulfill his longing, nor can any creature satisfy man's desire. Only God satisfies, he infinitely exceeds all other pleasures. That is why man can rest in nothing but God. As Augustine says: *You have made us for yourself, Lord, and our heart can find no rest until it rests in you*[St. Augustine, Confessions].

Since in their heavenly home the saints will possess God completely, obviously their longing will be satisfied, and their glory will be even greater. That is why the Lord says: *Enter into the joy of your Lord*[Mt 25:23]. Augustine adds: *The fullness of joy will not enter into those who rejoice, but those who rejoice will enter into joy. I shall be satisfied when your glory is seen*[Augustine], and again: *He who satisfies your desire with good things*[Augustine].

Whatever is delightful is there in superabundance. If delights are sought, there is supreme and most perfect delight. It is said of God, the supreme good: *Boundless delights are in your right hand*[Ps 15:11].

Again, eternal life consists of the joyous community of all the blessed, a community of supreme delight, since everyone will share all that is good with all the blessed. Everyone will love everyone else as himself, and therefore will rejoice in another's good as in his own. So it follows that the happiness and joy of each grows in proportion to the joy of all.

Sunday of the Thirty-Fourth Week in Ordinary Time (Christ the King)

From a notebook On Prayer by Origen, Priest

Your kingdom come

The kingdom of God, in the words of our Lord and Savior, *does not come for all to see; nor shall they say: Behold, here it is, or behold, there it is*[Lk 17:20-21]*; but the kingdom of God is within us, for the word of God is very near, in our mouth and in our heart*[Rom 10:8]. Thus it is clear that he who prays for the coming of God's kingdom prays rightly to have it within himself, that there it may grow and bear fruit and become perfect. For God reigns in each of his holy ones. Anyone who is holy obeys the spiritual laws of God, who dwells in him as in a well-ordered city. The Father is present in the perfect soul, and with him Christ reigns, according to the words: *We shall come to him and make our home with him*[Jn 14:23].

Thus the kingdom of God within us, as we continue to make progress, will reach its highest point when the Apostle's words are fulfilled, and Christ, having subjected all his enemies to himself, will hand over his *kingdom to God the Father, that God may be all in all*[1 Cor 15:24]. Therefore, let us pray unceasingly with that disposition of soul which the Word may make divine, saying to our Father who is in heaven: *Hallowed be your name; your kingdom come*[Mt 6:9-13].

Note this too about the kingdom of God. It is not a *sharing of justice with iniquity,* nor *a society of light with darkness,* nor a *meeting of Christ with Belial*[2 Cor 6:14]. The kingdom of God cannot exist alongside the reign of sin.

Therefore, if we wish God to reign in us, in no way *should sin reign in our mortal body*[Rom 6:12]; rather we should *mortify our members which are upon the earth*[Col 3:5] and bear fruit in the Spirit. There should be in us a kind of spiritual paradise where God may walk and be our sole ruler with his Christ. In us the Lord will sit at the right hand of that spiritual power which we wish to receive. And he will sit there until all his enemies who are within us become *his footstool*[Heb 10:13], and every principality, power and virtue in us is cast out.

All this can happen in each one of us, and the last enemy, death, can be destroyed; then Christ will say in us: *O death, where is your sting? O hell, where is your victory*[1 Cor 15:55-57]*?* And so, what is *corruptible* in us must be clothed with holiness and *incorruptibility;* and what is *mortal* must be clothed, now that death has been conquered, in the Father's *immortality*[1 Cor 15:53-55]. Then God will reign is us, and we shall enjoy even now the blessings of rebirth and resurrection.

Monday of the Thirty-Fourth Week in Ordinary Time

From a sermon by Saint Leo the Great, Pope & Doctor

Each man's profit matches his toil

The Lord says: *Unless your justice exceeds that of the scribes and Pharisees, you will not enter into the kingdom of heaven*[Mt 5:20]. How indeed can justice exceed unless *compassion rises above judgment*[Jas 2:13]*?* What is as right or as worthy as a creature, fashioned in the image and likeness of God, imitating his Creator who, by the remission of sins, brought about the reparation and sanctification of believers? With strict vengeance removed and the cessation of all punishment, the guilty man was restored to innocence, and the end of wickedness became the beginning of virtue. Can anything be more just than this?

This is how Christian justice can exceed that of the scribes and Pharisees, not by canceling out the law but by rejecting earthly wisdom. This is why, in giving his disciples a rule for fasting, the Lord said: *Whenever you fast do not become sad like the hypocrites. For they disfigure their faces in order to seem to be fasting. Amen I say to you, they have received their reward*[Mt 6:16]. What reward but that of human praise? Such a desire often puts on a mask of justice, for where there is no concern for conscience, untruthful reputation gives pleasure. The result is that concealed injustice enjoys a false reputation.

For the man who loves God it is sufficient to please the one he loves; and there is no greater recompense to be sought than the loving itself; for love is from God by the very fact that God himself is love. The good and chaste soul is so happy to be filled with him that it desires to take delight in nothing else. For what the Lord says is very true: *Where your treasure is, there also will your heart be*[Mt 6:21]. What is a man's treasure but the heaping up of profits and the fruit of his toil. *For whatever a man sows this too will he reap*[Gal 6:7], and each man's gain matches his toil; and where delight and enjoyment are found, there the heart's desire is attached. Now there are many kinds of wealth and a variety of grounds for rejoicing; every man's treasure is that which he desires. If it is based on earthly ambitions, its acquisition makes men not blessed but wretched.

But those who enjoy the things that are above and eternal rather than earthly and perishable, possess an incorruptible, hidden store of which the prophet speaks: *Our treasure and salvation have come, wisdom and instruction and piety from the Lord: these are the treasures of justice*[Isa 33:6]. Through these, with the help of God's grace, even earthly possessions are transformed into heavenly blessings; it is a fact that many people use the wealth which is either rightfully left to them or otherwise acquired, as a tool of devotion. By distributing what might be superfluous to support the poor, they are amassing imperishable riches, so that what they have discreetly given cannot be subject to loss. They have properly placed those riches where their heart is; it is a most blessed thing to work to increase such riches rather than to fear that they may pass away.

Tuesday of the Thirty-Fourth Week in Ordinary Time

From a treatise on John by Saint Augustine, Bishop & Doctor

To the source you will come, the light itself you will see

We Christians are the light, at least by comparison with unbelievers. Thus the Apostle says: For *once you were darkness, but now you are light in the Lord; walk then as sons of the light*[Eph 5:8-14]. And elsewhere he says: *The night is far spent, the day is drawing near. Let us therefore lay aside the works of darkness and put on the armor of light; let us walk uprightly as in the day*[Rom 13:12-13].

Nevertheless, since the days in which we are now living are still dark compared to the light which we shall see, hear what the apostle Peter says. He speaks of a voice that came from the Supreme Glory and said to the Lord Jesus Christ: *You are my beloved Son in whom I am well pleased*[Mt 17:5]. *This voice,* he says, *we heard coming from heaven, when we were with him on the holy mountain*[2 Pet 1:18]. Because we ourselves were not present there and did not hear that voice from heaven, Peter says to us: *And we possess a more certain prophetic word to which you do well to attend, as to a lamp shining in a dark place, until the day dawns and the morning star rises in your hearts*[2 Pet 1:19].

When, therefore, our Lord Jesus Christ shall come and, as the apostle Paul says, *brings to light things hidden in darkness and make plain the secrets of the heart, so that everyone may receive his commendation from God*[1 Cor 4:5], then lamps will no longer be needed. When that day is at hand, the prophet will not be read to us, the book of the Apostle will not be opened, we shall not require the testimony of John, we shall have no need of the Gospel itself. Therefore all Scriptures will be taken away from us, those Scriptures which in the night of this world burned like lamps so that we might not remain in darkness.

When all these things are removed as no longer necessary for our illumination, and when the men of God by whom they were ministered to us shall themselves together with us behold the true and dear light without such aids, what shall we see? With what shall our minds be nourished? What will give joy to our gaze? Where will that gladness come from, *which eye has not seen, and ear has not heard, which has not even been conceived by the heart of man*[1 Cor 2:9]? What shall we see?

I implore you to love with me and, by believing, to run with me; let us long for our heavenly country, let us sigh for our heavenly home, let us truly feel that here we are strangers. What shall we then see? Let the gospel tell us: *In the beginning was the Word and the Word was with God and the Word was God*[Jn 1:1]. You will come to the fountain, with whose dew you have already been sprinkled. Instead of the ray of light which was sent through slanting and winding ways into the heart of your darkness, you will see the light itself in all its purity and brightness. It is to see and experience this light that you are now being cleansed. *Dearly beloved,* John himself says, *we are the sons of God, and it has not yet been disclosed what we shall be; but we know that when he appears we shall be like him, because we shall see him as he is*[1 Jn 3:2].

I feel that your spirits are being raised up with mine to the heavens above; but the *body which is corruptible weighs down the soul, and this earthly tent burdens the thoughtful mind*[Wis 9:15]. I am about to lay aside this book, and you are soon going away, each to his own business. It has been good for us to share the common light, good to have enjoyed ourselves, good to have been glad together. When we part from one another, let us not depart from him.

Wednesday of the Thirty-Fourth Week in Ordinary Time

From a homily attributed to Saint Macarius, Bishop

Woe to the soul that does not have Christ dwelling in it

When God was displeased with the Jews, he delivered Jerusalem to the enemy, and they were conquered by those who hated them; there were no more sacrifices or feasts. Likewise angered at a soul who had broken his commands, God handed it over to its enemies, who corrupted and totally dishonored it. When a house has no master living in it, it becomes dark, vile and contemptible, choked with filth and disgusting refuse. So too is a soul which has lost its master, who once rejoiced there with his angels. This soul is darkened with sin, its desires are degraded, and it knows nothing but shame.

Woe to the path that is not walked on, or along which the voices of men are not heard, for then it becomes the haunt of wild animals. Woe to the soul if the Lord does not walk within it to banish with his voice the spiritual beasts of sin. Woe to the house where no master dwells, to the field where no farmer works, to the pilotless ship, storm-tossed and sinking. Woe to the soul without Christ as its true pilot; drifting in the darkness, buffeted by the waves of passion, storm-tossed at the mercy of evil spirits, its end is destruction. Woe to the soul that does not have Christ to cultivate it with care to produce the good fruit of the Holy Spirit. Left to itself, it is choked with thorns and thistles; instead of fruit it produces only what is fit for burning. Woe to the soul that does not have Christ dwelling in it; deserted and foul with the filth of the passions, it becomes a haven for all the vices.

When a farmer prepares to till the soil be must put on clothing and use tools that are suitable. So Christ our heavenly king, came to till the soil of mankind devastated by sin. He assumed a body and, using the cross as his plowshare, cultivated the barren soul of man. He removed the thorns and thistles which are the evil spirits and pulled up the weeds of sin. Into the fire be cast the straw of wickedness. And when he had plowed the soul with the wood of the cross, he planted in it a most lovely garden of the Spirit, that could produce for its Lord and God the sweetest and most pleasant fruit of every kind.

Thursday of the Thirty-Fourth Week in Ordinary Time

From a homily on Matthew by Saint John Chrysostum, Bishop & Doctor

If we are sheep, we overcome; if wolves, we are overcome

As long as we are sheep, we overcome and, though surrounded by countless wolves, we emerge victorious; but if we turn into wolves, we are overcome, for we lose the shepherd's help. He, after all, feeds the sheep not wolves, and will abandon you if you do not let him show his power in you.

What he says is this: "Do not be upset that, as I send you out among the wolves, I bid you be as sheep and doves. I could have managed things quite differently and sent you, not to suffer evil nor to yield like sheep to the wolves, but to be fiercer than lions. But the way I have chosen is right. It will bring you greater praise and at the same time manifest my power." That is what he told Paul: *My grace is enough for you, for in weakness my power is made perfect*[2 Cor 12:9]. "I intend," he says, "to deal the same way with you." For, when he says, *I am sending you out like sheep*[Mt 10:16], he implies: "But do not therefore lose heart, for I know and am certain that no one will be able to overcome you."

The Lord, however, does want them to contribute something, lest everything seem to be the work of grace, and they seem to win their reward without deserving it. Therefore he adds: *You must be clever as snakes and innocent as doves* [Mt 10:16]. But, they may object, what good is our cleverness amid so many dangers? How can we be clever when tossed about by so many waves? However great the cleverness of the sheep as he stands among the wolves - so may wolves! - what can it accomplish? However great the innocence of the dove, what good does it do him, with so many hawks swooping upon him? To all this I say: Cleverness and innocence admittedly do these irrational creatures no good, but they can help you greatly.

What cleverness is the Lord requiring here? The cleverness of a snake. A snake will surrender everything and will put up no great resistance even if its body is being cut in pieces, provided it can save its head. So you, the Lord is saying, must surrender everything but your faith: money, body, even life itself. For faith is the head and the root; keep that, and though you lose all else, you will get it back in abundance. The Lord therefore counseled the disciples to be not simply clever or innocent; rather he joined the two qualities so that they become a genuine virtue. He insisted on the cleverness of the snake so that deadly wounds might be avoided, and he insisted on the innocence of the dove so that revenge might not be taken on those who injure or lay traps for you. Cleverness is useless without innocence.

Do not believe that this precept is beyond your power. More than anyone else, the Lord knows the true natures of created things; he knows that moderation, not a fierce defense, beats back a fierce attack.

Friday of the Thirty-Fourth Week in Ordinary Time

From a sermon on man's mortality by Saint Cyprian, Bishop & Martyr

Let us banish the fear of death and think of the eternal life that follows it

Our obligation is to do God's will, and not our own. We must remember this if the prayer that our Lord commanded us to say daily is to have any meaning on our lips. How unreasonable it is to pray that God's will be done, and then not promptly obey it when he calls us from this world! Instead we struggle and resist like self-willed slaves and are brought into the Lord's presence with sorrow and lamentation, not freely consenting to our departure, but constrained by necessity. And yet we expect to be rewarded with heavenly honors by him to whom we come against our will! Why then do we pray for the kingdom of heaven to come if this earthly bondage pleases us? What is the point of praying so often for its early arrival if we would rather serve the devil here than reign with Christ.

The world hates Christians, so why give your love to it instead of following Christ, who loves you and has redeemed you? John is most urgent in his epistle when he tells us not to love the world by yielding to sensual desires. *Never give your love to the world,* he warns, *or to anything in it. A man cannot love the Father and love the world at the same time. All that the world offers is the lust of the flesh, the lust of the eyes and earthly ambition. The world and its allurements will pass away, but the man who has done the will of God shall live for ever*[1 Jn 2:15-17]. Our part, my dear brothers, is to be single-minded, firm in faith, and steadfast in courage, ready for God's will, whatever it may be. Banish the fear of death and think of the eternal life that follows it. That will show people that we really live our faith.

We ought never to forget, beloved, that we have renounced the world. We are living here now as aliens and only for a time. When the day of our homecoming puts an end to our exile, frees us from the bonds of the world, and restores us to paradise and to a kingdom, we should welcome it. What man, stationed in a foreign land, would not want to return to his own country as soon as possible? Well, we look upon paradise as our country, and a great crowd of our loved ones awaits us there, a countless throng of parents, brothers and children longs for us to join them. Assured though they are of their own salvation, they are still concerned about ours. What joy both for them and for us to see one another and embrace! O the delight of that heavenly kingdom where there is no fear of death! O the supreme and endless bliss of everlasting life!

There is the glorious band of apostles, there, the exultant assembly of prophets, there, the innumerable host of martyrs, crowned for their glorious victory in combat and in death. There, in triumph, are the virgins who subdued their passions by the strength of continence. There, the merciful are rewarded, those who fulfilled the demands of justice by providing for the poor. In obedience to the Lord's command, they turned their earthly patrimony into heavenly treasure.

My dear brothers, let all our longing be to join them as soon as we may. May God see our desire, may Christ see this resolve that springs from faith, for he will give the rewards of his love more abundantly to those who have longed for him more fervently.

Saturday of the Thirty-Fourth Week in Ordinary Time

From a sermon by Saint Augustine, Bishop & Doctor

Let us sing alleluia to the good God who delivers us from evil

Let us sing alleluia here on earth, while we still live in anxiety, so that we may sing it one day in heaven in full security. Why do we now live in anxiety? Can you expect me not to feel anxious when I read: *Is not man's life on earth a time of trial*[Job 7:1]? Can you expect me not to feel anxious when the words still ring in my ears: *Watch and pray that you will not be put to the test*[Mt 26:41]? Can you expect me not to feel anxious when there are so many temptations here below that prayer itself reminds us of them, when we say: *Forgive us our trespasses, as we forgive those who trespass against us*[Mt 6:12-14]? Every day we make our petitions, every day we sin. Do you want me to feel secure when I am daily asking pardon for my sins, and requesting help in time of trial? Because of my past sins I pray: *Forgive us our trespasses, as we forgive those who trespass against us* [Mt 6:12-14], and then, because of the perils still before me, I immediately go on to add: *Lead us not into temptation* [Mt 6:12-14]. How can all be well with people who are crying out with me: *Deliver us from evil* [Mt 6:12-14]? And yet, brothers, while we are still in the midst of this evil, let us sing alleluia to the good God who delivers us from evil.

Even here amidst trials and temptations let us, let all men, sing alleluia. *God is faithful*, says holy Scripture, *and he will not allow you to be tried beyond your strength*[1 Cor 10:13]. So let us sing alleluia, even here on earth. Man is still a debtor, but God is faithful. Scripture does not say that he will not allow you to be tried, but that *he will not allow you to be tried beyond your strength. Whatever the trial, he will see your through it safely, and so enable you to endure*[1 Cor 10:13]. You have entered upon a time of trial but you will come to no harm - God's help will bring you through it safely. You are like a piece of pottery, shaped by instruction, fired by tribulation. When you are put into the oven therefore, keep your thoughts on the time when you will be taken out again; for God is faithful, and *he will guard both your going in and your coming out*[Ps 120:8].

But in the next life, when this body of ours has become immortal and incorruptible, then all trials will be over. *Your body is indeed dead, and why? Because of sin* [Rom 8:10]. Nevertheless, *your spirit lives, because you have been justified*[Rom 8:10]. Are we to leave our dead bodies behind then? By no means. Listen to the words of holy Scripture: *If the Spirit of him who raised Christ from the dead dwells within you, then he who raised Christ from the dead will also give life to your own mortal bodies*[Rom 8:11]. At present your body receives its life from the soul, but then it will receive it from the Spirit.

O the happiness of the heavenly alleluia, sung in security, in fear of no adversity! We shall have no enemies in heaven, we shall never lose a friend. God's praises are sung both there and here, but here they are sung in anxiety, there, in security; here they are sung by those destined to die, there, by those destined to live for ever; here they are sung in hope, there, in hope's fulfillment; here they are sung by wayfarers, there, by those living in their own country.

So, then, my brothers, let us sing now, not in order to enjoy a life of leisure, but in order to lighten our labors. You should sing as wayfarers do - sing, but continue your journey. Do not be lazy, but sing to make your journey more enjoyable. Sing, but keep going. What do I mean by keep going? Keep on making progress. This progress, however, must be in virtue; for there are some, the Apostle warns, whose only progress is in vice. If you make progress, you will be continuing your journey, but be sure that your progress is in virtue, true faith and right living. Sing then, but keep going.

Trinity Sunday

From the first letter to Serapion by Saint Athanasius, Bishop & Doctor

Light, radiance and grace are in the Trinity and from the Trinity

It will not be out of place to consider the ancient tradition, teaching and faith of the Catholic Church, which was revealed by the Lord, proclaimed by the apostles and guarded by the fathers. For upon this faith the Church is built, and if anyone were to lapse from it, he would no longer be a Christian either in fact or in name.

We acknowledge the Trinity, holy and perfect, to consist of the Father, the Son and the Holy Spirit. In this Trinity there is no intrusion of any alien element or of anything from outside, nor is the Trinity a blend of creative and created being. It is a wholly creative and energizing reality, self-consistent and undivided in its active power, for the Father makes all things through the Word and in the Holy Spirit, and in this way the unity of the holy Trinity is preserved. Accordingly, in the Church, one God is preached, one God who is *above all things and through all things and in all things*[Eph 4:6]. God is *above all things* as Father, for he is principle and source; he is *through all things* through the Word; and he is *in all things* in the Holy Spirit.

Writing to the Corinthians about spiritual matters, Paul traces all reality back to one God, the Father, saying: *Now there are varieties of gifts, but the same Spirit; and varieties of service, but the same Lord; and there are varieties of service, but the same Lord; and there are varieties of working, but it is the same God who inspires them all in everyone*[1 Cor 12:4-11].

.Even the gifts that the Spirit dispenses to individuals are given by the Father through the Word. For all that belongs to the Father belongs also to the Son, and so the graces given by the Son in the Spirit are true gifts of the Father. Similarly, when the Spirit dwells in us, the Word who bestows the Spirit is in us too, and the Father is present in the Word. This is the meaning of the text: *My Father and I will come to him and make our home with him*[Jn 14:23]. For where the light is, there also is the radiance; and where the radiance is, there too are its power and its resplendent grace.

This is also Paul's teaching in his second letter to the Corinthians: *The grace of our Lord Jesus Christ and the love of God and the fellowship of the Holy Spirit be with you all*[2 Cor 13:14]. For grace and the gift of the Trinity are given by the Father through the Son in the Holy Spirit. Just as grace is given from the Father through the Son, so there could be no communication of the gift to us except in the Holy Spirit. But when we share in the Spirit, we possess the love of the Father, the grace of the Son and the fellowship of the Spirit himself.

Corpus Christi

From a work by Thomas Aquinas, Priest & Doctor

O precious and wonderful banquet!

Since it was the will of God's only-begotten Son that men should share in his divinity, he assumed our nature in order that by becoming man he might make men gods. Moreover, when he took our flesh he dedicated the whole of its substance to our salvation. He offered his body to God the Father on the altar of the cross as a sacrifice for our reconciliation. He shed his blood for our ransom and purification, so that we might be redeemed from our wretched state of bondage and cleansed from all sin. But to ensure that the memory of so great a gift would abide with us for ever, he left his body as food and his blood as drink for the faithful to consume in the form of bread and wine.

O precious and wonderful banquet, that brings us salvation and contains all sweetness! Could anything be of more intrinsic value? Under the old law it was the flesh of calves and goats that was offered, but here Christ himself, the true God, is set before us as our food. What could be more wonderful than this? No other sacrament has greater healing power; through it sins are purged away, virtues are increased, and the soul is enriched with an abundance of every spiritual gift. It is offered in the Church for the living and the dead, so that what was instituted for the salvation of all may be for the benefit of all. Yet, in the end, no one can fully express the sweetness of this sacrament, in which spiritual delight is tasted at its very source, and in which we renew the memory of that surpassing love for us which Christ revealed in his passion.

It was to impress the vastness of this love more firmly upon the hearts of the faithful that our Lord instituted this sacrament at the Last Supper. As he was on the point of leaving the world to go to the Father, after celebrating the Passover with his disciples, he left it as a perpetual memorial of his passion. It was the fulfillment of ancient figures and the greatest of all his miracles, while for those who were to experience the sorrow of his departure, it was destined to be a unique and abiding consolation.

The Most Sacred Heart of Jesus

From a work by Saint Bonaventure, Cardinal & Doctor

With you is the source of life

Take thought now, redeemed man, and consider how great and worthy is he who hangs on the cross for you. His death brings the dead to life, but at his passing heaven and earth are plunged into mourning and hard rocks are split asunder.

It was a divine decree that permitted one of the soldiers to open his sacred side with a lance. This was done so that the Church might be formed from the side of Christ as he slept the sleep of death on the cross, and so that the Scripture might be fulfilled: *They shall look on him whom they pierced*[Zech 12:10;Jn 19:37; Rev 1:7]. The blood and water which poured out at that moment were the price of our salvation. Flowing from the secret abyss of our Lord's heart as from a fountain, this stream gave the sacraments of the Church the power to confer the life of grace, while for those already living in Christ it became a spring of living water welling up to life everlasting.

Arise, then, beloved of Christ! Imitate the dove *that nests in a hole in the cliff*[Jer 48:28], keeping watch at the entrance *like the sparrow that finds a home*[Ps 83:4]. There like the turtledove hide your little ones, the fruit of your chaste love. Press your lips to the fountain, *draw water from the wells of your Savior*[Isa 12:3]; for *this is the spring flowing out of the middle of paradise, dividing into four rivers*[Bonaventure], inundating devout hearts, watering the whole earth and making it fertile.

Run with eager desire to this source of life and light, all you who are vowed to God's service. Come, whoever you may be, and cry out to him with all the strength of your heart. "O indescribable beauty of the most high God and purest radiance of eternal light! Life that gives all life, light that is the source of every other light, preserving in everlasting splendor the myriad flames that have shone before the throne of your divinity from the dawn of time! Eternal and inaccessible fountain, clear and sweet stream flowing from a hidden spring, unseen by mortal eye! None can fathom your depths nor survey your boundaries, none can measure your breadth, nothing can sully your purity. From you flows *the river which gladdens the city of God*[Ps 45:5] and makes us cry out with joy and thanksgiving in hymns of praise to you, for we know by our own experience that *with you is the source of life, and in your light we see light*[Ps 35:10].

The Immaculate Heart of Mary

From a sermon by St. Lawrence Justinian, Bishop

Mary stored up all these things in her heart

While Mary contemplated all she had come to know through, listening and observing, she grew in faith, increased in merits, and was more illuminated by wisdom and more consumed by the fire of charity. The heavenly mysteries were opened to her, and she was filled with joy; she became fruitful by the Spirit, was being directed toward God, and watched over protectively while on earth. So remarkable are the divine graces that they elevate one from the lowest depths to the highest summit, and transform one to a greater holiness. How entirely blessed was the mind of the Virgin which, through the indwelling and guidance of the Spirit, was always and in every way open to the power of the Word of God. She was not led by her own senses, nor by her own will; thus she accomplished outwardly through her body what wisdom from within gave to her faith. It was fitting for divine Wisdom, which created itself a home in the Church, to use the intervention of the most blessed Mary in guarding the law, purifying the mind, giving an example of humility and providing a spiritual sacrifice.

Imitate her, O faithful soul. Enter into the deep recesses of your heart so that you may be purified spiritually and cleansed from your sins. God places more value on good will in all we do than on the works themselves. Therefore, whether we give ourselves to God in the work of contemplation or whether we serve the needs of our neighbor by good works, we accomplish these things because the love of Christ urges us on. The acceptable offering of the spiritual purification is accomplished not in a man-made temple but in the recesses of the heart where the Lord Jesus freely enters.

Proper of Saints

January 2nd

Saints Basil the Great and Gregory Nazianzen, Bishops & Doctors

From a sermon by Saint Gregory Nazianzen, bishop

Two bodies, but a single spirit

Basil and I were both in Athens. We had come, like streams of a river, from the same source in our native land, had separated from each other in pursuit of learning, and were now united again as if by plan, for God so arranged it.

I was not alone at that time in my regard for my friend, the great Basil. I knew his irreproachable conduct, and the maturity and wisdom of his conversation. I sought to persuade others, to whom he was less well known, to have the same regard for him. Many fell immediately under his spell, for they had already heard of him by reputation and hearsay.

What was the outcome? Almost alone of those who had come to Athens to study he was exempted from the customary ceremonies of initiation for he was held in higher honor than his status as a first-year student seemed to warrant.

Such was the prelude to our friendship, the kindling of that flame that was to bind us together. In this way we began to feel affection for each other. When, in the course of time, we acknowledged our friendship and recognized that our ambition was a life of true wisdom, we became everything to each other: we shared the same lodging, the same table, the same desires, the same goal. Our love for each other grew daily warmer and deeper.

The same hope inspired us: the pursuit of learning. This is an ambition especially subject to envy. Yet between us there was no envy. On the contrary, we made capital out of our rivalry. Our rivalry consisted, not in seeking the first place for oneself but in yielding it to the other, for we each looked on the other's success as his own.

We seemed to be two bodies with a single spirit. Though we cannot believe those who claim that "everything is contained in everything," yet you must believe that in our case each of us was in the other and with the other.

Our single object and ambition was virtue, and a life of hope in the blessings that are to come; we wanted to withdraw from this world before we departed from it. With this end in view we ordered our lives and all our actions. We followed the guidance of God's law and spurred each other on to virtue. If it is not too boastful to say, we found in each other a standard and rule for discerning right from wrong.

Different men have different names, which they owe to their parents or to themselves, that is, to their own pursuits and achievements. But our great pursuit, the great name we wanted, was to be Christians, to be called Christians.

January 4th

St. Elizabeth Ann Seton

From a conference to her spiritual daughters

Our daily work is to do the will of God

I will tell you what is my own great help. I once read or heard that an interior life means but the continuation of our Savior's life in us; that the great object of all his mysteries is to merit for us the grace of his interior life and communicate it to us, it being the end of his mission to lead us into the sweet land of promise, a life of constant union with himself. And what was the first rule of our dear Savior's life? You know it was to do his Father's will. Well, then, the first end I propose in our daily work is to do the will of God; secondly, to do it in the manner he wills; and thirdly, to do it because it is his will.

I know what his will is by those who direct me; whatever they bid me do, if it is ever so small in itself, is the will of God for me. Then do it in the manner he wills it, not sewing an old thing as if it were new, or a new thing as if it were old; not fretting because the oven is too hot, or in a fuss because it is too cold. You understand – not flying and driving because you are hurried, not creeping like a snail because no one pushes you. Our dear Savior was never in extremes. The third object is to do his will *because* God wills it, that is, to be ready to quit at any moment and to do anything else to which you may be called....

You think it very hard to lead a life of such restraint unless you keep your eye of faith always open. Perseverance is a great grace. To go on gaining and advancing every day, we must be resolute, and bear and suffer as our blessed forerunners did. Which of them gained heaven without a struggle?...

What are our real trials? By what name shall we call them? One cuts herself out a cross of pride; another, one of causeless discontent; another, one of restless impatience or peevish fretfulness. But is the whole any better than children's play if looked at with the common eye of faith? Yet we know certainly that our God calls us to a holy life, that he gives us every grace, every abundant grace; and though we are so weak of ourselves, this grace is able to carry us through every obstacle and difficulty.

But we lack courage to keep a continual watch over nature, and therefore, year after year, with our thousand graces, multiplied resolutions, and fair promises, we run around in a circle of misery and imperfections. After a long time in the service of God, we come nearly to the point from whence we set out, and perhaps with even less ardor for penance and mortification than when we began our consecration to him.

You are now in your first setout. Be above the vain fears of nature and efforts of your enemy. You are children of eternity. Your immortal crown awaits you, and the best of Fathers waits there to reward your duty and love. You may indeed sow here in tears, but you may be sure there to reap in joy.

January 5th

St. John Neumann, Bishop

From a letter to Cardinal Barnabo by John Neumann, bishop

I have labored with all my powers to fulfill the duties of my office

Indeed, I have apparently delayed too long in writing to the Holy See the letter promised by the Archbishop of Baltimore in the name of the council. However, this delay was not without reason. For the council was scarcely finished and I was discussing the division of the Diocese of Philadelphia and my translation to a new see with one of the Fathers of the council, when the Father intimated to me [that he did not know] whether that could more probably be hoped for, since the Holy See thought that I would resign from the episcopate, or wished to resign. In the same way when the Archbishop of Baltimore informed me of the designation of a coadjutor, he added that in the event that I should persevere in the desire to resign, the Holy See would permit me to give the title of the ecclesiastical property to the same coadjutor.

I was no little disturbed by the fear that I had done something that so displeased the Holy Father that my resignation would appear desirable to him. If this be the case, I am prepared without any hesitation to leave the episcopacy. I have taken this burden out of obedience, and I have labored with all my powers to fulfill the duties of my office, and with God's help, as I hope, not without fruit.

When the care of temporal things weighed upon my mind and it seemed to me that my character was little suited for the very cultured world of Philadelphia, I made known to my fellow bishops during the Baltimore council of 1858 that it seemed opportune to me to request my translation to one or the other see that was to be erected (namely in the City of Pottsville or in Wilmington, North Carolina). But to give up the episcopal career never entered my mind, although I was conscious of my unworthiness and ineptitude; for things had not come to such a pass that I had one or the other reason out of the six for which a bishop could safely ask the Holy Father permission to resign. For a long time I have doubted what should be done…

Although my coadjutor has proposed to me that he would take the new see if it is erected, I have thought it much more opportune and I have asked the Fathers that he be appointed to the See of Philadelphia, since he is much more highly endowed with facility and alacrity concerning the administration of temporal things. Indeed, I am much more accustomed to the country, and will be able to care for the people and faithful living in the mountains, in the coal mines and on the farms, since I would be among them.

If, however, it should be displeasing to His Holiness to divide the diocese, I am, indeed, prepared either to remain in the same condition in which I am at present, or if God so inspires His Holiness to give the whole administration of the diocese to the Most Reverend James Wood, I am equally prepared to resign from the episcopate and to go where I may more securely prepare myself for death and for the account which must be rendered to the Divine Justice.

I desire nothing but to fulfill the wish of the Holy Father whatever it may be.

January 7th

St. Raymond of Penyafort, Priest

From a letter by St. Raymond, Priest

May the God of love and peace set your hearts at rest

The preacher of God's truth has told us that all who want to live righteously in Christ will suffer persecution. If he spoke the truth and did not lie, the only exception to this general statement is, I think, the person who either neglects, or does not know how, *to live temperately, justly and righteously in this world*[Titus 2:12].

May you never be numbered among those whose house is peaceful, quiet and free from care; those on whom the Lord's chastisement does not descend; those who live out their days in prosperity, and in the twinkling of an eye will go down to hell.

Your purity of life, your devotion, deserve and call for a reward; because you are acceptable and pleasing to God your purity of life must be made purer still, by frequent buffetings, until you attain perfect sincerity of heart. If from time to time you feel the sword falling on you with double or treble force, this also should be seen as sheer joy and the mark of love.

The two-edged sword consists in conflict without, fears within. It falls with double or treble force within, when the cunning spirit troubles the depths of your heart with guile and enticements. You have learned enough already about these kinds of warfare, or you would not have been able to enjoy peace and interior tranquility in all its beauty.

The sword falls with double and treble force externally when, without cause being given, there breaks out from within the Church persecution in spiritual matters, where wounds are more serious, especially when inflicted by friends.

This is that enviable and blessed cross of Christ, which Andrew, that manly saint, received with joyful heart: the cross in which alone we must make our boast, as Paul, God's chosen instrument, has told us.

Look then on Jesus, the author and preserver of faith: in complete sinlessness he suffered, and at the hands of those who were his own, and was numbered among the wicked. As you drink the cup of the Lord Jesus (how glorious it is!), give thanks to the Lord, the giver of all blessings.

May the God of love and peace set your hearts at rest and speed you on your journey; may he meanwhile shelter you from disturbance by others in the hidden recesses of his love, until he brings you at last into that place of complete plentitude where you will repose for ever in the vision of peace, in the security of trust and in the restful enjoyment of his riches.

January 13th

St. Hilary, Bishop & Doctor

From a sermon On the Trinity by St. Hilary of Poitiers, Bishop & Doctor

May I serve you by making you known

I am well aware, almighty God and Father, that in my life I owe you a most particular duty. It is to make my every thought and word speak of you.

In fact, you have conferred on me this gift of speech, and it can yield no greater return than to be at your service. It is for making you known as Father, the Father of the only-begotten God, and preaching this to the world that knows you not and to the heretics who refuse to believe in you.

In this matter the declaration of my intention is only of limited value. For the rest, I need to pray for the gift of your help and your mercy. As we spread our sails of trusting faith and public avowal before you, fill them with the breath of your Spirit, to drive us on as we begin this course of proclaiming your truth. We have been promised, and he who made the promise is trustworthy: *Ask, and it will be given to you; seek, and you will find; knock, and it will be opened to you*[Mt 7:7-8].

Yes, in our poverty we will pray for our needs. We will study the sayings of your prophets and apostles with unflagging attention, and knock for admittance wherever the gift of understanding is safely kept. But yours it is, Lord, to grant our petitions, to be present when we seek you and to open when we knock.

There is an inertia in our nature that makes us dull; and in our attempt to penetrate your truth we are held within the bounds of ignorance by the weakness of our minds. Yet we do comprehend divine ideas by earnest attention to your teaching and by obedience to the faith which carries us beyond mere human apprehension.

So we trust in you to inspire the beginnings of this ambitious venture, to strengthen its progress, and to call us into a partnership in the spirit with the prophets and the apostles. To that end, may we grasp precisely what they meant to say, taking each word in its real and authentic sense. For we are about to say what they already have declared as part of the mystery of revelation: that you are the eternal God, the Father of the eternal, only-begotten God; that you are one and not born from another; and that the Lord Jesus is also one, born of you from all eternity. We must not proclaim a change in truth regarding the number of gods. We must not deny that he is begotten of you who are the one God; nor must we assert that he is other than the true God, born of you who are truly God the Father.

Impart to us, then, the meaning of the words of Scripture and the light to understand it, with reverence for the doctrine and confidence in its truth. Grant that we may express what we believe. Through the prophets and apostles we know about you, the one God the Father, and the one Lord Jesus Christ. May we have the grace, in the face of heretics who deny you, to honor you as God, who is not alone, and to proclaim this as truth.

January 17th

St. Anthony, Abbot

From the Life of St. Anthony by St. Athanasius, Bishop & Doctor

Saint Anthony receives his vocation

When Anthony was about eighteen or twenty years old, his parents died, leaving him with an only sister. He cared for her as she was very young, and also looked after their home.

Not six months after his parents' death, as he was on his way to church for his usual visit, he began to think of how the apostles had left everything and followed the Savior, and also of those mentioned in the book of Acts who had sold their possessions and brought the apostles the money for distribution to the needy. He reflected too on the great hope stored up in heaven for such as these. This was all in his mind when, entering the church just as the Gospel was being read, he heard the Lord's words to the rich man: *If you want to be perfect, go and sell all you have and give the money to the poor--you will have riches in heaven. Then come and follow me*[Mt 19:21].

It seemed to Anthony that it was God who had brought the saints to his mind and that the words of the Gospel had been spoken directly to him. Immediately he left the church and gave away to the villagers all the property he had inherited, about 200 acres of very beautiful and fertile land, so that it would cause no distraction to his sister and himself. He sold all his other possessions as well, giving to the poor the considerable sum of money he collected. However, to care for his sister he retained a few things.

The next time he went to church he heard the Lord say in the Gospel: *Do not be anxious about tomorrow.* Without a moment's hesitation he went out and gave the poor all that he had left. He placed his sister in the care of some well-known and trustworthy virgins and arranged for her to be brought up in the convent. Then he gave himself up to the ascetic life, not far from his own home. He kept a careful watch over himself and practiced great austerity. He did manual work because he had heard the words: *If anyone will not work, do not let him eat*[2 Thes 3:10]. He spent some of his earnings on bread and the rest he gave to the poor.

Having learned that we should always be praying, even when we are by ourselves, he prayed without ceasing. Indeed, he was so attentive when Scripture was read that nothing escaped him and because he retained all he heard, his memory served him in place of books.

Seeing the kind of life he lived, the villagers and all the good men he knew called him the friend of God, and they loved him as both son and brother.

January 20th

St. Fabian, Pope & Martyr

From a letter about the death of St. Fabian, pope, by St. Cyprian and the Roman Church

Fabian offers us a model of courage

Informed of the death of Pope Fabian, Saint Cyprian sent this letter to the priests and deacons of Rome:

"My dear brothers, while the news of the death of my good colleague was still uncertain, and opinions were divided, I received your letter delivered through the courtesy of the subdeacon Crementius, in which I was most fully informed of Fabian's glorious death. I was quite happy that his virtuous demise corresponded with the integrity of his administration. Hence I too offer you congratulations that you honor his memory with so striking and praiseworthy a testimony. Through you we can see quite clearly what an honor for you is the glorious heritage of one who was your superior, and what an example of faith and courage it offers us. For just as the defection of a superior has such a harmful effect on the stability of those who follow him, so contrariwise it is helpful and encouraging when a bishop offers himself as a model for his brothers by the constancy of his faith."

Apparently before Cyprian received this letter, the Church of Rome had given the community at Carthage testimony of its loyalty in time of persecution.

"Our church stands firmly in the faith, although some have lapsed because they fear the loss of their outstanding positions or other personal sufferings. Although these have separated from us, we have not given them up; in the past we have urged them and now we continue to encourage them to do penance, in the hope that they may receive pardon from him who can give it; whereas if they were abandoned by us, they might become worse.

"And so you see, brothers, you should act in the same manner; in this way those who have lapsed, having changed their attitude because of your encouragement, might admit their Christianity if ever they are arrested again. Yet you do have other responsibilities, and we hereby make suggestions. If any of those who have fallen into this temptation should become ill and, after doing penance, should desire to receive communion, they should certainly be assisted. Widows, the destitute who cannot support themselves, and those who are in prison or who have been evicted from their homes should surely have someone to help them; likewise catechumens who are ill ought not to be disappointed in receiving assistance.

"Your brothers who are in chains send you their greetings, and also the priests, and the entire Church which lies awake in great anxiety to pray for all those who invoke the name of the Lord. And so we ask you in turn to remember us."

January 20th

St. Sebastian, Martyr

From an exposition of psalm 118 by St. Ambrose, Bishop & Doctor

Faithful witnessing to Christ

To enter the kingdom of God we must endure many tribulations[Acts 14:22]. If there are many persecutions, there are many testings; where there are many crowns of victory, there are many trials of strength. It is then to your advantage if there are many persecutors; among many persecutions you may more easily find a path to victory.

Take the example of the martyr Sebastian, whose birthday in glory we celebrate today. He was a native of Milan. At a time when persecution either had ceased or had not yet begun or was of a milder kind, he realized that there was only slight, if any, opportunity for suffering. He set out for Rome, where bitter persecutions were raging because of the fervor of the Christians. There he endured suffering; there he gained his crown. He went to the city as a stranger and there established a home of undying glory. If there had been only one persecutor, he would not have gained a martyr's crown.

The persecutors who are visible are not the only ones. There are also invisible persecutors, much greater in number. This is more serious. Like a king bent on persecution, sending orders to persecute to his many agents, and establishing different persecutors in each city or province, the devil directs his many servants in their work of persecution, whether in public or in the souls of individuals. Of this kind of persecution Scripture says: *All who wish to live a holy life in Christ Jesus suffer persecution*[2 Tim 3:12]. "All" suffer persecution; there is no exception. Who can claim exemption if the Lord himself endured the testing of persecution? How many there are today who are secret martyrs for Christ, giving testimony to Jesus as Lord! The Apostle knew this kind of martyrdom, this faithful witnessing to Christ; he said: *This is our boast, the testimony of our conscience*[2 Cor 1:12].

January 21st

St. Agnes, Virgin & Martyr

From a treatise On Virgins by St. Ambrose, Bishop & Doctor

Too young to be punished, yet old enough for a martyr's crown

Today is the birthday of a virgin; let us imitate her purity. It is the birthday of a martyr; let us offer ourselves in sacrifice. It is the birthday of Saint Agnes, who is said to have suffered martyrdom at the age of twelve. The cruelty that did not spare her youth shows all the more clearly the power of faith in finding one so young to bear it witness.

There was little or no room in that small body for a wound. Though she could scarcely receive the blow, she could rise superior to it. Girls of her age cannot bear even their parents' frowns and, pricked by a needle, weep as for a serious wound. Yet she shows no fear of the blood-stained hands of her executioners. She stands undaunted by heavy, clanking chains. She offers her whole body to be put to the sword by fierce soldiers. She is too young to know of death, yet is ready to face it. Dragged against her will to the altars, she stretches out her hands to the Lord in the midst of the flames, making the triumphant sign of Christ the victor on the altars of sacrilege. She puts her neck and hands in iron chains, but no chain can hold fast her tiny limbs.

A new kind of martyrdom! Too young to be punished, yet old enough for a martyr's crown; unfitted for the contest, yet effortless in victory, she shows herself a master in valor despite the handicap of youth. As a bride she would not be hastening to join her husband with the same joy she shows as a virgin on her way to punishment, crowned not with flowers but with holiness of life, adorned not with braided hair but with Christ himself.

In the midst of tears, she sheds no tears herself. The crowds marvel at her recklessness in throwing away her life untasted, as if she had already lived life to the full. All are amazed that one not yet of legal age can give her testimony to God. So she succeeds in convincing others of her testimony about God, though her testimony in human affairs could not yet be accepted. What is beyond the power of nature, they argue, must come from its creator.

What menaces there were from the executioner, to frighten her; what promises made, to win her over; what influential people desired her in marriage! She answered: "To hope that any other will please me does wrong to my Spouse. I will be his who first chose me for himself. Executioner, why do you delay? If eyes that I do not want can desire this body, then let it perish." She stood still, she prayed, she offered her neck.

You could see fear in the eyes of the executioner, as if he were the one condemned; his right hand trembled, his face grew pale as he saw the girl's peril, while she had no fear for herself. One victim, but a twin martyrdom, to modesty and to religion; Agnes preserved her virginity, and gained a martyr's crown.

January 22nd

St. Vincent, Deacon & Martyr

From a sermon by St .Augustine, Bishop & Doctor

Vincent conquers in him who conquered the world

To you, he said, *has been granted on Christ's behalf not only that you should believe in him but also that you should suffer for him*[Phil 1:29].

Vincent had received both these gifts and held them as his own. For how could he have them if he had not received them? And he displayed his faith in what he said, his endurance in what he suffered.

No one ought to rely on his own feelings when he speaks out, nor be confident in his own strength when he undergoes temptation. For whenever we speak prudently as we should, our wisdom comes from him, and whenever we endure evils courageously, our long-suffering comes from him.

Call to mind how Christ our Lord in the Gospel exhorted his disciples. It is the very king of martyrs equipping his troops with spiritual arms, explaining their battles, offering them support, and promising them their reward. He once said to his disciples: *In this world you will suffer persecution*, and then, to allay their fears, he added*, but rest assured, I have conquered the world*[Jn 16:33].

There is no need to wonder then, my dearly beloved brothers, that Vincent conquered in him who conquered the world. Christ said: *In this world you will suffer persecution* [Jn 16:33], but in such wise that the persecution will not overwhelm, and the attack will not overcome you. Against Christ's army the world arrays a twofold battleline. It offers temptation to lead us astray; it strikes terror into us to break our spirit. Hence if our personal pleasures do not hold us captive, and if we are not frightened by brutality, then the world is overcome. At both of these approaches Christ rushes to our aid, and the Christian is not conquered. If you were to consider in Vincent's martyrdom only human endurance, then his act is unbelievable from the outset. But first recognize the power to be from God, and he ceases to be a source of wonder.

Such savagery was being vented upon the martyr's body while such serenity issued from his lips, such harsh cruelties were being inflicted on his limbs while such assurance rang out in his words, that we should think that, by some miracle, as Vincent suffered, one person was speaking while another was being tortured. And this, my brothers, was true; it was really the truth; another person was speaking. Christ in the Gospel promised this to those who were to be his witnesses, to those whom he was preparing for contests of this kind. For he said: *Do not give thought to how or what you are to speak. For it is not you who speak, but the Spirit of your Father who speaks within you*[Mt 10:19]. Thus it was Vincent's body that suffered, but the Spirit who spoke. And at his voice, impiety was not only vanquished but human frailty was given consolation.

January 24th

St. Francis de Sales, Bishop & Doctor

From The Introduction to the Devout Life
by St. Francis de Sales, Bishop & Doctor

Devotion must be practiced in different ways

When God the Creator made all things, he commanded the plants to bring forth fruit each according to its own kind; he has likewise commanded Christians, who are the living plants of his Church, to bring forth the fruits of devotion, each one in accord with his character, his station and his calling.

I say that devotion must be practiced in different ways by the nobleman and by the working man, by the servant and by the prince, by the widow, by the unmarried girl and by the married woman. But even this distinction is not sufficient; for the practice of devotion must be adapted to the strength, to the occupation and to the duties of each one in particular.

Tell me, please, my Philothea, whether it is proper for a bishop to want to lead a solitary life like a Carthusian; or for married people to be no more concerned than a Capuchin about increasing their income; or for a working man to spend his whole day in church like a religious; or on the other hand for a religious to be constantly exposed like a bishop to all the events and circumstances that bear on the needs of our neighbor. Is not this sort of devotion ridiculous, unorganized and intolerable? Yet this absurd error occurs very frequently, but in no way does true devotion, my Philothea, destroy anything at all. On the contrary, it perfects and fulfills all things. In fact if it ever works against, or is inimical to, anyone's legitimate station and calling, then it is very definitely false devotion.

The bee collects honey from flowers in such a way as to do the least damage or destruction to them, and he leaves them whole, undamaged and fresh, just as he found them. True devotion does still better. Not only does it not injure any sort of calling or occupation, it even embellishes and enhances it.

Moreover, just as every sort of gem, cast in honey, becomes brighter and more sparkling, each according to its color, so each person becomes more acceptable and fitting in his own vocation when he sets his vocation in the context of devotion. Through devotion your family cares become more peaceful, mutual love between husband and wife becomes more sincere, the service we owe to the prince becomes more faithful, and our work, no matter what it is, becomes more pleasant and agreeable.

It is therefore an error and even a heresy to wish to exclude the exercise of devotion from military divisions, from the artisans' shops, from the courts of princes, from family households. I acknowledge, my dear Philothea, that the type of devotion which is purely contemplative, monastic and religious can certainly not be exercised in these sorts of stations and occupations, but besides this threefold type of devotion, there are many others fit for perfecting those who live in a secular state.

Therefore, in whatever situations we happen to be, we can and we must aspire to the life of perfection.

January 25th

The Conversion of St. Paul, Apostle

From a homily by St. John Chrysostom, Bishop & Doctor

For love of Christ, Paul bore every burden

Paul, more than anyone else, has shown us what man really is, and in what our nobility consists, and of what virtue this particular animal is capable. Each day he aimed ever higher; each day he rose up with greater ardor and faced with new eagerness the dangers that threatened him. He summed up his attitude in the words: *I forget what is behind me and push on to what lies ahead*[Phil 3:13]. When he saw death imminent, he bade others share his joy: *Rejoice and be glad with me*[Phil 2:18]! And when danger, injustice and abuse threatened, he said: *I am content with weakness, mistreatment and persecution*[2 Cor 12:10]. These he called the weapons of righteousness, thus telling us that he derived immense profit from them.

Thus, amid the traps set for him by his enemies, with exultant heart he turned their every attack into a victory for himself; constantly beaten, abused and cursed, he boasted of it as though he were celebrating a triumphal procession and taking trophies home, and offered thanks to God for it all: *Thanks be to God who is always victorious in us*[2 Cor 2:14-16]! This is why he was far more eager for the shameful abuse that his zeal in preaching brought upon him than we are for the most pleasing honors, more eager for death than we are for life, for poverty than we are for wealth; he yearned for toil far more than others yearn for rest after toil. The one thing he feared, indeed dreaded, was to offend God; nothing else could sway him. Therefore, the only thing he really wanted was always to please God.

The most important thing of all to him, however, was that he knew himself to be loved by Christ. Enjoying this love, he considered himself happier than anyone else; were he without it, it would be no satisfaction to be the friend of principalities and powers. He preferred to be thus loved and be the least of all, or even to be among the damned, than to be without that love and be among the great and honored.

To be separated from that love was, in his eyes, the greatest and most extraordinary of torments; the pain of that loss would alone have been hell, and endless, unbearable torture.

So too, in being loved by Christ he thought of himself as possessing life, the world, the angels, present and future, the kingdom, the promise and countless blessings. Apart from that love nothing saddened or delighted him; for nothing earthly did he regard as bitter or sweet.

Paul set no store by the things that fill our visible world, any more than a man sets value on the withered grass of the field. As for tyrannical rulers or the people enraged against him, he paid them no more heed than gnats.

Death itself and pain and whatever torments might come were but child's play to him, provided that thereby he might bear some burden for the sake of Christ.

January 26th

Saints Timothy and Titus, Bishops

From a homily by St. John Chrysostom, Bishop & Doctor

I have fought the good fight

Though housed in a narrow prison, Paul dwelt in heaven. He accepted beatings and wounds more readily than others reach out for rewards. Sufferings he loved as much as prizes; indeed he regarded them as his prizes, and therefore called them a grace or gift. Reflect on what this means. *To depart and be with Christ*[Phil 1:23] was certainly a reward, while remaining in the flesh meant struggle. Yet such was his longing for Christ that he wanted to defer his reward and remain amid the fight; those were his priorities.

Now, to be separated from the company of Christ meant struggle and pain for Paul; in fact, it was a greater affliction than any struggle or pain would be. On the other hand, to be with Christ was a matchless reward. Yet, for the sake of Christ, Paul chose the separation.

But, you may say: "Because of Christ, Paul found all this pleasant." I cannot deny that, for he derived intense pleasure from what saddens us. I need not think only of perils and hardships. It was true even of the intense sorrow that made him cry out: *Who is weak that I do not share the weakness? Who is scandalized that I am not consumed with indignation*[2 Cor 11:29]*?*

I urge you not simply to admire but also to imitate this splendid example of virtue, for, if we do, we can share his crown as well.

Are you surprised at my saying that if you have Paul's merits, you will share that same reward? Then listen to Paul himself: *I have fought the good fight, I have run the race, I have kept the faith. Henceforth a crown of justice awaits me, and the Lord, who is a just judge, will give it to me on that day – and not to me alone, but to those who desire his coming*[2 Tim 4:7-8]. You see how he calls all to share the same glory?

Now, since the same crown of glory is offered to all, let us eagerly strive to become worthy of these promised blessings.

In thinking of Paul we should not consider only his noble and lofty virtues or the strong and ready will that disposed him for such great graces. We should also realize that he shares our nature in every respect. If we do, then even what is very difficult will seem to us easy and light; we shall work hard during the short time we have on earth and someday we shall wear the incorruptible, immortal crown. This we shall do by the grace and mercy of our Lord Jesus Christ, to whom all glory and power belongs now and always through endless ages. Amen.

January 27th

St. Angela Merici, Virgin

From the Spiritual Testament by St. Angela Merici, Virgin

He has disposed all things pleasantly

Mothers and sisters most dear to me in Christ: in the first place strive with all your power and zeal to be open. With the help of God, try to receive such good counsel that, led solely by the love of God and an eagerness to save souls, you may fulfill your charge.

Only if the responsibilities committed to you are rooted firmly in this twofold charity will they bear beneficial and saving fruit. As our Savior says: *A good tree is not able to produce bad fruit*[Mt 7:18].

He says: A good tree, that is, a good heart as well as a soul inflamed with charity, can do nothing but good and holy works. For this reason Saint Augustine said: *Love, and do what you will*[Augustine], namely, possess love and charity and then do what you will. It is as if he had said: Charity is not able to sin.

I also beg you to be concerned about every one of your daughters. Bear them, so to speak, engraved upon your heart - not merely their names, but their conditions and states, whatever they may be. This will not be difficult for you if you embrace them with a living love.

Mothers of children, even if they have a thousand, carry each and everyone fixed in their hearts, and because of the strength of their love they do not forget any of them. In fact, it seems that the more children they have the more their love and care for each one is increased. Surely those who are mothers in spirit can and must act all the more in the same way, because spiritual love is more powerful than the love that comes from a blood relationship.

Therefore, mothers most dear to me, if you love these your daughters with a living and unaffected charity, it will be impossible for you not to have each and every one of them engraved upon your memory and in your mind.

I beg you again, strive to draw them by love, modesty, charity, and not by pride and harshness. Be sincerely kind to every one according to the words of our Lord: *Learn of me, for I am meek and humble of heart*[Mt 11:29]. Thus you are imitating God, of whom it is said: *He has disposed all things pleasantly*[St. Angela Merici]. And again Jesus said: *My yoke is easy and my burden is light*[Mt 11:28-30].

You also ought to exercise pleasantness toward all, taking great care especially that what you have commanded may never be done by reason of force. For God has given free will to everyone, and therefore he forces no one but only indicates, calls, persuades. Sometimes, however, something will have to be done with a stronger command, yet in a suitable manner and according to the state and necessities of individuals; but then also we should be impelled only by charity and zeal for souls.

January 28th

St. Thomas Aquinas, Priest & Doctor

From a conference by St. Thomas Aquinas, Priest & Doctor

The cross exemplifies every virtue

Why did the Son of God have to suffer for us? There was a great need, and it can be considered in a twofold way: in the first place, as a remedy for sin, and secondly, as an example of how to act.

It is a remedy, for, in the face of all the evils which we incur on account of our sins, we have found relief through the passion of Christ. Yet, it is no less an example, for the passion of Christ completely suffices to fashion our lives. Whoever wishes to live perfectly should do nothing but disdain what Christ disdained on the cross and desire what he desired, for the cross exemplifies every virtue.

If you seek the example of love: *Greater love than this no man has, than to lay down his life for his friends*[Jn 15:13]. Such a man was Christ on the cross. And if he gave his life for us, then it should not be difficult to bear whatever hardships arise for his sake.

If you seek patience, you will find no better example than the cross. Great patience occurs in two ways: either when one patiently suffers much, or when one suffers things which one is able to avoid and yet does not avoid. Christ endured much on the cross, and did so patiently, because *when he suffered he did not threaten; he was led like a sheep to the slaughter and he did not open his mouth*[1 Pet 2:23]. Therefore Christ's patience on the cross was great. *In patience let us run for the prize set before us, upon Jesus, the author and perfecter of our faith who, for the joy set before him, bore his cross and despised the shame*[Heb 12:2].

If you seek an example of humility, look upon the crucified one, for God wished to be judged by Pontius Pilate and to die.

If you seek an example of obedience, follow him who became obedient to the Father even unto death. *For just as by the disobedience of one man*, namely, Adam, *many were made sinners, so by the obedience of one man, many were made righteous*[Rom 5:19].

If you seek an example of despising earthly things, follow him who is *the King of kings and the Lord of lords, in whom are hidden all the treasures of wisdom and knowledge*[Col 2:3]. Upon the cross he was stripped, mocked, spat upon, struck, crowned with thorns, and given only vinegar and gall to drink.

Do not be attached, therefore, to clothing and riches, because *they divided my garments among themselves*[Ps 21:18-19; Jn 19:24]. Nor to honors, for he experienced harsh words and scourgings. Nor to greatness of rank, for *weaving a crown of thorns they placed it on my head*[Mt 27:29]. Nor to anything delightful, for *in my thirst they gave me vinegar to drink*[Ps 68:21-22;Mt 27:34].

January 31st

St. John Bosco, Priest

From a letter by St. John Bosco, Priest

I have always labored out of love

First of all, if we wish to appear concerned about the true happiness of our foster children and if we would move them to fulfill their duties, you must never forget that you are taking the place of the parents of these beloved young people. I have always labored lovingly for them, and carried out my priestly duties with zeal. And the whole Salesian society has done this with me.

My sons, in my long experience very often I had to be convinced of this great truth. It is easier to become angry than to restrain oneself, and to threaten a boy than to persuade him. Yes, indeed, it is more fitting to be persistent in punishing our own impatience and pride than to correct the boys. We must be firm but kind, and be patient with them.

I give you as a model the charity of Paul which he showed to his new converts. They often reduced him to tears and entreaties when he found them lacking docility and even opposing his loving efforts.

See that no one finds you motivated by impetuosity or willfulness. It is difficult to keep calm when administering punishment, but this must be done if we are to keep ourselves from showing off our authority or spilling out our anger.

Let us regard those boys over whom we have some authority as our own sons. Let us place ourselves in their service. Let us be ashamed to assume an attitude of superiority. Let us not rule over them except for the purpose of serving them better.

This was the method that Jesus used with the apostles. He put up with their ignorance and roughness and even their infidelity. He treated sinners with a kindness and affection that caused some to be shocked, others to be scandalized, and still others to hope for God's mercy. And so he bade us to be gentle and humble of heart.

They are our sons, and so in correcting their mistakes we must lay aside all anger and restrain it so firmly that it is extinguished entirely.

There must be no hostility in our minds, no contempt in our eyes, no insult on our lips. We must use mercy for the present and have hope for the future, as is fitting for true fathers who are eager for real correction and improvement.

In serious matters it is better to beg God humbly than to send forth a flood of words that will only offend the listeners and have no effect on those who are guilty.

February 2nd

Presentation of the Lord

From a sermon by St. Sophronius, Bishop

Let us receive the light whose brilliance is eternal

In honor of the divine mystery that we celebrate today, let us all hasten to meet Christ. Everyone should be eager to join the procession and to carry a light.

Our lighted candles are a sign of the divine splendor of the one who comes to expel the dark shadows of evil and to make the whole universe radiant with the brilliance of his eternal light. Our candles also show how bright our souls should be when we go to meet Christ.

The Mother of God, the most pure Virgin, carried the true light in her arms and brought him to those who lay in darkness. We too should carry a light for all to see and reflect the radiance of the true light as we hasten to meet him.

The light has come and has shone upon a world enveloped in shadows; the Dayspring from on high has visited us and given light to those who lived in darkness. This, then, is our feast, and we join in procession with lighted candles to reveal the light that has shone upon us and the glory that is yet to come to us through him. So let us hasten all together to meet our God.

The true light has come, *the light that enlightens every man who is born into this world*[Jn 1:9]. Let all of us, my brethren, be enlightened and made radiant by this light. Let all of us share in its splendor, and be so filled with it that no one remains in the darkness. Let us be shining ourselves as we go together to meet and to receive with the aged Simeon the light whose brilliance is eternal. Rejoicing with Simeon, let us sing a hymn of thanksgiving to God, the Father of the light, who sent the true light to dispel the darkness and to give us all a share in his splendor.

Through Simeon's eyes we too have seen the salvation of God which he prepared for all the nations and revealed as the glory of the new Israel, which is ourselves. As Simeon was released from the bonds of this life when he had seen Christ, so we too were at once freed from our old state of sinfulness.

By faith we too embraced Christ, the salvation of God the Father, as he came to us from Bethlehem. Gentiles before, we have now become the people of God. Our eyes have seen God incarnate, and because we have seen him present among us and have mentally received him into our arms, we are called the new Israel. Never shall we forget this presence; every year we keep a feast in its honor.

February 3rd

St. Blase, Bishop & Martyr

From a sermon by St. Augustine, Bishop & Doctor

Suffer for my sheep

The Son of man has come not to be served, but to serve, and to give his own life as a ransom for many[Mt 20:28; Mk 10:45]. Consider how the Lord served, and see what kind of servants he bids us to be. He gave *his own life as a ransom for many*; he ransomed us.

But who of us is fit to ransom anyone? By his blood, by his death we were ransomed from death; and we who lay prostrate were raised up by his humiliation. And yet we, too, have a duty to contribute our meager offerings to his members, for we have become his members. He is the head; we are the body.

In his letter, the apostle John holds up the Lord as our model. Jesus said: *Whoever wishes to be the greater among you will be your servant, just as the Son of Man has come not to be served but to serve and to give his own life as ransom for many*[Mt 20:27-28]. So in his exhortation to us to act likewise, John says: *Christ laid down his life for us; so we, too, ought to lay down our lives for our brothers*[1 Jn 3:16].

After his resurrection our Lord asked: *Peter, do you love me*[Jn 21:15-19]*?* and Peter replied: *I do love you*. The question and the answer were repeated three times. And each time the Lord added: *Feed my sheep*. In other words, if you want to show that you love me, *then feed my sheep*. What will you give me if you love me, since you look for everything to come from me? Now you know what you are to do if you love me: *Feed my sheep*. Thus we have the same question and answer once, twice, three times. *Do you love me? I do love you. Feed my sheep*. Three times Peter had denied in fear; three times he confessed out of love. By his replies and his profession of love, Peter condemned and wiped out his former fear. And so the Lord, after entrusting his sheep to him for the third time, immediately added: *When you were a young man, you would gird yourself and go wherever you wished. But when you are old, another will gird you and take you where you do not wish to go. This he spoke signifying by what death he was about to glorify God*[Jn 21:15-19]. Thus he foretold Peter's own sufferings and crucifixion. By this the Lord suggested that *feed my sheep* meant suffer for my sheep.

February 3rd

St. Ansgar, Bishop

From the decree on the Missionary Activity of the Church of the Second Vatican Council

We must boldly proclaim the mystery of Christ

Every disciple of Christ is responsible in his own measure for the spread of the faith, but Christ the Lord is always calling from among his followers those whom he wills, so that they may be with him and be sent by him to preach to the nations.

Through the Holy Spirit, who distributes gifts as he wills for the good of all, Christ implants in the hearts of individuals the vocation to be a missionary, and at the same time he raises up in the Church institutes which make their own the task of sp the Gospel that belongs to the whole Church.

A special vocation marks out those priests, religious and lay people who are prepared to undertake the missionary task in their own country or abroad, and have the right natural disposition for it, with suitable gifts and talents. Sent by lawful authority, they go out in obedience and faith to those who are far from Christ. They have been set apart for the task to which they have been called as ministers of the Gospel, *to make the Gentiles an acceptable offering, sanctified in the Holy Spirit*[Rom 15:16].

Those whom God calls must answer his call in such a way that, without regard for purely human counsel, they may devote themselves wholly to the work of the Gospel. This response cannot be given except with the inspiration and strength of the Holy Spirit.

The person who is sent enters into the life and mission of him who *emptied himself, taking the nature of a slave*[Phil 2:5-11]. He must be ready therefore to be true to his vocation for life, to deny himself, renouncing all that he had before, and to become all things to all men.

In preaching the Gospel to the nations he must boldly proclaim the mystery of Christ, whose ambassador he is, so that in Christ he may have the courage to speak as he ought, and not be ashamed of the scandal of the cross. He must follow in the footsteps of his Master, who was gentle and humble of heart, and reveal to others that his yoke is easy and his burden light.

By a life that is truly according to the Gospel, by much endurance, by forbearance, by kindness and sincere love, he must bear witness to his Lord, even, if need be, by the shedding of his blood.

He will pray to God for strength and courage, so that he may come to see that for one who experiences great hardship and extreme poverty there can be abundant joy.

February 5th

St. Agatha, Virgin & Martyr

From a homily on St. Agatha by St. Methodius of Sicily, Bishop

The gift of God, the source of all goodness

My fellow Christians, our annual celebration of a martyr's feast has brought us together. She achieved renown in the early Church for her noble victory; she is well known now as well, for she continues to triumph through her divine miracles, which occur daily and continue to bring glory to her name.

She is indeed a virgin, for she was born of the divine Word, God's only Son, who also experienced death for our sake. John, a master of God's word, speaks of this: *He gave the power to become children of God to everyone who received him*[Jn 1:12].

The woman who invites us to this banquet is both a wife and virgin. To use the analogy of Paul, she is the bride who has been betrothed to one husband, Christ. A true virgin, she wore the glow of a pure conscience and the crimson of the Lamb's blood for her cosmetics. Again and again she meditated on the death of her eager lover. For her, Christ's death was recent, his blood was still moist. Her robe is the mark of her faithful witness to Christ. It bears the indelible marks of his crimson blood and the shining threads of her eloquence. She offers to all who come after her these treasures of her eloquent confession.

Agatha, the name of our saint, means "good." She was truly good, for she lived as a child of God. She was also given as the gift of God, the source of all goodness to her bridegroom, Christ, and to us. For she grants us a share in her goodness.

What can give greater good than the Sovereign Good? Whom could anyone find more worthy of celebration with hymns of praise than Agatha?

Agatha, her goodness coincides with her name and way of life. She won a good name by her noble deeds, and by her name she points to the nobility of those deeds. Agatha, her mere name wins all men over to her company. She teaches them by her example to hasten with her to the true Good; God alone.

February 6th

Sts. Paul Miki and his Companions, Martyrs

From an account of the martyrdom of St. Paul Miki and his companions, by a contemporary writer

You shall be my witnesses

The crosses were set in place. Father Pasio and Father Rodriguez took turns encouraging the victims. Their steadfast behavior was wonderful to see. The Father Bursar stood motionless, his eyes turned heavenward. Brother Martin gave thanks to God's goodness by singing psalms. Again and again he repeated: "Into your hands, Lord, I entrust my life." Brother Francis Branco also thanked God in a loud voice. Brother Gonsalvo in a very loud voice kept saying the Our Father and Hail Mary.

Our brother, Paul Miki, saw himself standing now in the noblest pulpit he had ever filled. To his "congregation" he began by proclaiming himself a Japanese and a Jesuit. He was dying for the Gospel he preached. He gave thanks to God for this wonderful blessing and he ended his "sermon" with these words: "As I come to this supreme moment of my life, I am sure none of you would suppose I want to deceive you. And so I tell you plainly: there is no way to be saved except the Christian way. My religion teaches me to pardon my enemies and all who have offended me. I do gladly pardon the Emperor and all who have sought my death. I beg them to seek baptism and be Christians themselves."

Then he looked at his comrades and began to encourage them in their final struggle. Joy glowed in all their faces, and in Louis' most of all. When a Christian in the crowd cried out to him that he would soon be in heaven, his hands, his whole body strained upward with such joy that every eye was fixed on him.

Anthony, hanging at Louis' side, looked toward heaven and called upon the holy names – "Jesus, Mary!" He began to sing a psalm: "Praise the Lord, you children!" (He learned it in catechism class in Nagasaki. They take care there to teach the children some psalms to help them learn their catechism).

Others kept repeating "Jesus, Mary!" Their faces were serene. Some of them even took to urging the people standing by to live worthy Christian lives. In these and other ways they showed their readiness to die.

Then, according to Japanese custom, the four executioners began to unsheathe their spears. At this dreadful sight, all the Christians cried out, "Jesus, Mary!" And the storm of anguished weeping then rose to batter the very skies. The executioners killed them one by one. One thrust of the spear, then a second blow. It was over in a very short time.

February 8th

St. Jerome Emiliani

From a letter to his brothers by St. Jerome Emiliani

Place your trust in God alone

Sons of the Society of the Servants of the Poor, and dearly beloved brothers in Christ: Greetings from your poor father. I urge you to persevere in your love for Christ and your faithful observance of the law of Christ. In word and work I set an example for you when I was with you. And so the Lord is glorified in you through me.

Our goal is God, the source of all good. As we say in our prayer, we are to place our trust in God and in no one else. In his kindness, our Lord wished to strengthen your faith, for without it, as the evangelist points out, Christ could not have performed many of his miracles. He also wished to listen to your prayer, and so he ordained that you experience poverty, distress, abandonment, weariness and universal scorn. It was also his desire to deprive you of my physical presence, even though I am with you in spirit as your poor, dear, beloved father.

God alone knows the reasons for all this, yet we can recognize three causes. In the first place, our blessed Lord is telling you that he desires to include you among his beloved sons, provided that you remain steadfast in his ways, for this is the way he treats his friends and makes them holy.

The second reason is that he is asking you to grow continually in your confidence in him alone and not in others. For God, as I said before, does not work in those who refuse to place all their confidence and hope in him alone. But he does impart the fullness of his love upon those who possess a deep faith and hope; for them he does great things. So if you have been endowed with faith and hope, he will do great things for you; he will raise up the lowly. In depriving you of myself and everyone else you have loved, he will offer you an opportunity to choose one of these alternatives: either you will forsake your faith and return to the ways of the world, or you will remain steadfast in your faith and pass the test.

Now there is a third reason. God wishes to test you like gold in the furnace. The dross is consumed by the fire, but the pure gold remains and its value increases. It is in this manner that God acts with his good servant, who puts his hope in him and remains unshaken in times of distress. God raises him up and, in return for the things he has left out of love for God, he repays him a hundred-fold in this life and with eternal life hereafter.

This is the way God has dealt with all his saints. So it was with his people Israel after their period of trial in Egypt. He not only led them out of Egypt with many miracles and fed them with manna in the desert, he also gave them the promised land. If then you remain constant in faith in the face of trial, the Lord will give you peace and rest for a time in this world, and for ever in the next.

February 10th

St. Scholastica, Virgin

From the books of Dialogues by St. Gregory the Great, Pope & Doctor

She who loved more could do more

Scholastica, the sister of Saint Benedict, had been consecrated to God from her earliest years. She was accustomed to visiting her brother once a year. He would come down to meet her at a place on the monastery property, not far outside the gate.

One day she came as usual and her saintly brother went with some of his disciples; they spent the whole day praising God and talking of sacred things. As night fell they had supper together.

Their spiritual conversation went on and the hour grew late. The holy nun said to her brother: "Please do not leave me tonight; let us go on until morning talking about the delights of the spiritual life." "Sister," he replied, "what are you saying? I simply cannot stay outside my cell."

When she heard her brother refuse her request, the holy woman joined her hands on the table, laid her head on them and began to pray. As she raised her head from the table, there were such brilliant flashes of lightning, such great peals of thunder and such a heavy downpour of rain that neither Benedict nor his brethren could stir across the threshold of the place where they had been seated. Sadly he began to complain: "May God forgive you, sister. What have you done?" "Well," she answered, "I asked you and you would not listen; so I asked my God and he did listen. So now go off, if you can, leave me and return to your monastery."

Reluctant as he was to stay of his own will, he remained against his will. So it came about that they stayed awake the whole night, engrossed in their conversation about the spiritual life.

It is not surprising that she was more effective than he; since, as John says, *God is love*[1 Jn 4:7-12], it was absolutely right that she could do more, as she loved more.

Three days later, Benedict was in his cell. Looking up to the sky, he saw his sister's soul leave her body in the form of a dove, and fly up to the secret places of heaven. Rejoicing in her great glory, he thanked almighty God with hymns and words of praise. He then sent his brethren to bring her body to the monastery and lay it in the tomb he had prepared for himself.

Their minds had always been united in God; their bodies were to share a common grave.

February 11th

Our Lady of Lourdes

From a letter by St. Marie Bernadette Soubirous, Virgin

The lady spoke to me

I had gone down one day with two other girls to the bank of the river Gave when suddenly I heard a kind of rustling sound. I turned my head toward the field by the side of the river but the trees seemed quite still and the noise was evidently not from them. Then I looked up and caught sight of the cave where I saw a lady wearing a lovely white dress with a bright belt. On top of each of her feet was a pale yellow rose, the same color as her rosary beads.

At this I rubbed my eyes, thinking I was seeing things, and I put my hands into the fold of my dress where my rosary was. I wanted to make the sign of the cross but for the life of me I couldn't manage it and my hand just fell down. Then the lady made the sign of the cross herself and at the second attempt I managed to do the same, though my hands were trembling. Then I began to say the rosary while the lady let her beads slip through her fingers, without moving her lips. When I stopped saying the Hail Mary, she immediately vanished.

I asked my two companions if they had noticed anything, but they said no. Of course they wanted to know what I was doing and I told them that I had seen a lady wearing a nice white dress, though I didn't know who she was. I told them not to say anything about it, and they said I was silly to have anything to do with it. I said they were wrong and I came back next Sunday, feeling myself drawn to the place....

The third time I went the lady spoke to me and asked me to come every day for fifteen days. I said I would and then she said that she wanted me to tell the priests to build a chapel there. She also told me to drink from the stream. I went to the Gave, the only stream I could see. Then she made me realize she was not speaking of the Gave and she indicated a little trickle of water close-by. When I got to it I could only find a few drops, mostly mud. I cupped my hands to catch some liquid without success and then I started to scrape the ground. I managed to find a few drops of water but only at the fourth attempt was there sufficient for any kind of drink. The lady then vanished and I went back home.

I went back each day for fifteen days and each time, except one Monday and one Friday, the lady appeared and told me to look for a stream and wash in it and to see that the priests build a chapel there. I must also pray, she said, for the conversion of sinners. I asked her many times what she meant by that, but she only smiled. Finally with outstretched arms and eyes looking up to heaven she told me she was the Immaculate Conception.

During the fifteen days she told me three secrets but I was not to speak about them to anyone and so far I have not.

February 14th

Saints Cyril, Monk, & Methodius, Bishop

From an Old Slavonic Life of Constantine

Build up your Church and gather all into unity

Constantine, already burdened by many hardships, became ill. At one point during his extended illness, he experienced a vision of God and began to sing this verse: "My spirit rejoiced and my heart exulted because they told me we shall go into the house of the Lord."

Afterward he remained dressed in the vestments that were to be venerated later, and rejoiced for an entire day, saying: "From now on, I am not the servant of the emperor or of any man on earth, but of almighty God alone. Before, I was dead, now I am alive and I shall live for ever. Amen."

The following day, he assumed the monastic habit and took the religious name Cyril. He lived the life of a monk for fifty days.

When the time came for him to set out from this world to the peace of his heavenly homeland, he prayed to God with his hands outstretched and his eyes filled with tears: "O Lord, my God, you have created the choirs of angels and spiritual powers; you have stretched forth the heavens and established the earth, creating all that exists from nothing. You hear those who obey your will and keep your commands in holy fear. Hear my prayer and protect your faithful people, for you have established me as their unsuitable and unworthy servant.

"Keep them free from harm and the worldly cunning of those who blaspheme you. Build up your Church and gather all into unity. Make your people known for the unity and profession of their faith. Inspire the hearts of your people with your word and your teaching. You called us to preach the Gospel of your Christ and to encourage them to lives and works pleasing to you.

"I now return to you, your people, your gift to me. Direct them with your powerful right hand, and protect them under the shadow of your wings. May all praise and glorify your name, the Father, Son and Holy Spirit. Amen."

Once he had exchanged the gift of peace with everyone, he said: "Blessed be God, who did not hand us over to our invisible enemy, but freed us from his snare and delivered us from perdition." He then fell asleep in the Lord at the age of forty-two.

The Patriarch commanded all those in Rome, both the Greeks and Romans, to gather for his funeral. They were to chant over him together and carry candles; they were to celebrate his funeral as if he had been a pope. This they did.

February 17th

Seven Founders of the Order of Servites

From an account of the origin of the Servite Order

Let us praise famous men

There were seven men worthy of all our praise and veneration, whom our Lady brought into one community to form this order of hers and of her servants. They were like seven stars joined together to form a constellation.

When I entered this order I found only one of the seven still alive, Brother Alexis, whom our Lady was pleased to preserve from death down to our own time so that we might listen to his account of the founding of the order. As I saw myself and observed at first hand, Brother Alexis led so good a life that all who met him were moved by the force of his example. Moreover, he was a living testimony to that special kind of religious perfection characteristic of that first community.

But where did these men stand before they formed their own community? Let us consider this in four respects.

First, as regards the Church. Some of them had never married, having vowed themselves to perpetual celibacy; some were married men at the time; some had lost their wives after marriage and now were widowers.

Second, regarding their status in the city of Florence. They belonged to the merchant class and engaged in buying and selling the goods of this world. But once they found the pearl of great price, our order, they not only gave all they had to the poor but cheerfully offered themselves to God and our Lady in true and loyal service.

Third, concerning their devotion and reverence to our Lady. In Florence there was an ancient guild dedicated to the Blessed Virgin. Because of its age and the number and holiness of its members, both men and women, the guild had acquired a title of preeminence and was called the Major Guild of Our Blessed Lady. These seven men were devoted to our Lady and belonged to this guild before they established their own community.

Fourth, as for their spiritual perfection. They loved God above all things and dedicated their whole lives to him by honoring him in their every thought, word and deed.

But when by God's inspiration and the special urging of our Lady they had firmly resolved to form a community together, they set in order everything that concerned their homes and families, left to their families what they needed and gave all the rest to the poor. Then they sought the advice of virtuous men of good judgment, and described their plans to them.

They climbed the heights of Monte Senario and built on its summit a little house that would suit their purpose, and there they lived in common. As time passed, they began to realize that they were called not simply to sanctify themselves but to receive others into their community, and so increase the membership of this new order our Lady had inspired them to found. They recruited new members; some they accepted, and thus established our present order. In the beginning our Lady was the chief architect of this new order which was founded on the humility of its members, built up by their mutual love, and preserved by their poverty.

February 21st

St. Peter Damian, Bishop & Doctor

From a letter by St. Peter Damian, Bishop & Doctor

Let us rejoice in the joy that follows sadness

You asked me to write you some words of consolation, my brother. Embittered by so many tribulations, you are seeking some comfort for your soul. You asked me to offer you some soothing suggestions.

But there is no need for me to write. Consolation is already within your reach, if your good sense has not been dulled. *My son, come to the service of God. Stand in justice and fear. Prepare your soul; it is about to be tested*[Sir 2:1]. These words of Scripture show that you are a son of God and, as such, should take possession of your inheritance. What could be clearer than this exhortation?

Where there is justice as well as fear, adversity will surely test the spirit. But it is not the torment of a slave. Rather it is the discipline of a child by its parent.

Even in the midst of his many sufferings, the holy man Job could say: *Whip me, crush me, cut me in slices*[Job 6:9-11]*!* And he would always add: *This at least would bring me relief, yet my persecutor does not spare me*[Job 6:9-11].

But for God's chosen ones there is great comfort; the torment lasts but a short time. Then God bends down, cradles the fallen figure, whispers words of consolation. With hope in his heart, man picks himself up and walks again toward the glory of happiness in heaven.

Craftsmen exemplify this same practice. By hammering gold, the smith beats out the dross. The sculptor files metal to reveal a shining vein underneath. *The potter's furnace puts vessels to the test. And the fire of suffering tests the mettle of just men*[Sir 27:5; 1 Pet 1:7-9]. The apostle James echoes this thought: *Think it a great joy, dear brothers and sisters, when you stumble onto the many kinds of trials and tribulations*[Jas 1:2-17].

When men suffer pain for the evil they have perpetrated in life, they should take some reassurance. They also know that for their good deeds undying rewards await them in the life to come.

Therefore, my brother, scorned as you are by men, lashed as it were by God, do not despair. Do not be depressed. Do not let your weakness make you impatient. Instead, let the serenity of your spirit shine through your face. Let the joy of your mind burst forth. Let words of thanks break from your lips.

The way that God deals with men can only be praised. He lashes them in this life to shield them from the eternal lash in the next. He pins people down now; at a later time he will raise them up. He cuts them before healing; he throws them down to raise them anew.

The Scriptures reassure us: let your understanding your patience. In serenity look forward to the joy that follows sadness. Hope leads you to that joy and love enkindles your zeal. The well-prepared mind forgets the suffering inflicted from without and glides eagerly to what it has contemplated within itself.

February 22nd

Chair of St. Peter, Apostle

From a sermon by St. Leo the Great, Pope & Doctor

The Church of Christ rises on the firm foundation of Peter's faith

Out of the whole world one man, Peter, is chosen to preside at the calling of all nations, and to be set over all the apostles and all the fathers of the Church. Though there are in God's people many bishops and many shepherds, Peter is thus appointed to rule in his own person those whom Christ also rules as the original ruler. Beloved, how great and wonderful is this sharing in his power that God in his goodness has given to this man. Whatever Christ has willed to be shared in common by Peter and the other leaders of the Church, it is only through Peter that he has given to others what he has not refused to bestow on them.

The Lord now asks the apostles as a whole what men think of him. As long as they are recounting the uncertainty born of human ignorance, their reply is always the same.

But when he presses the disciples to say what they think themselves, the first to confess his faith in the Lord is the one who is first in rank among the apostles.

Peter says: *You are the Christ, the Son of the living God.* Jesus replies: *Blessed are you, Simon Bar-Jona, for flesh and blood has not revealed it to you, but my Father who is in heaven*[Mt 16:17-19]. You are blessed, he means, because my Father has taught you. You have not been deceived by earthly opinion, but have been enlightened by inspiration from heaven. It was not flesh and blood that pointed me out to you, but the one whose only-begotten Son I am.

He continues: *And I say to you.* In other words, as my Father has revealed to you my godhead, so I in my turn make known to you your pre-eminence. *You are Peter:* though I am the inviolable rock, *the cornerstone that makes both one,* the foundation apart from which no one can lay any other, yet you also are a rock, for you are given solidity by my strength, so that which is my very own because of my power is common between us through your participation.

And upon this rock I will build my Church, and the gates of hell shall not prevail against it[Mt 16:17-19]. On this strong foundation, he says, I will build an everlasting temple. The great height of my Church, which is to penetrate the heavens, shall rise on the firm foundation of this faith.

The gates of hell shall not silence this confession of faith; the chains of death shall not bind it. Its words are the words of life. As they lift up to heaven those who profess them, so they send down to hell those who contradict them.

Blessed Peter is therefore told: *To you I will give the keys of the kingdom of heaven. Whatever you bind on earth is also bound in heaven. Whatever you loose on earth shall be loosed also in heaven*[Mt 16:17-19].

The authority vested in this power passed also to the other apostles, and the institution established by this decree has been continued in all the leaders of the Church. But it is not without good reason that what is bestowed on all is entrusted to one. For Peter received it separately in trust because he is the prototype set before all the rulers of the Church.

February 23rd

St. Polycarp, Bishop & Martyr

From a letter on the martyrdom of St. Polycarp by the Church of Smyrna

A rich and pleasing sacrifice

When the pyre was ready, Polycarp took off all his clothes and loosened his undergarment. He made an effort also to remove his shoes, though he had been unaccustomed to this, for the faithful always vied with each other in their haste to touch his body. Even before his martyrdom he had received every mark of honor in tribute to his holiness of life.

There and then he was surrounded by the material for the pyre. When they tried to fasten him also with nails, he said: "Leave me as I am. The one who gives me strength to endure the fire will also give me strength to stay quite still on the pyre, even without the precaution of your nails." So they did not fix him to the pyre with nails but only fastened him instead. Bound as he was, with hands behind his back, he stood like a mighty ram, chosen out for sacrifice from a great flock, a worthy victim made ready to be offered to God.

Looking up to heaven, he said: "Lord, almighty God, Father of your beloved and blessed Son Jesus Christ, through whom we have come to the knowledge of yourself, God of angels, of powers, of all creation, of all the race of saints who live in your sight, I bless you for judging me worthy of this day, this hour, so that in the company of the martyrs I may share the cup of Christ, your anointed one, and so rise again to eternal life in soul and body, immortal through the power of the Holy Spirit. May I be received among the martyrs in your presence today as a rich and pleasing sacrifice. God of truth, stranger to falsehood, you have prepared this and revealed it to me and now you have fulfilled your promise.

"I praise you for all things, I bless you, I glorify you through the eternal priest of heaven, Jesus Christ, your beloved Son. Through him be glory to you, together with him and the Holy Spirit, now and for ever. Amen."

When he had said "Amen" and finished the prayer, the officials at the pyre lit it. But, when a great flame burst out, those of us privileged to see it witnessed a strange and wonderful thing. Indeed, we have been spared in order to tell the story to others. Like a ship's sail swelling in the wind, the flame became as it were a dome encircling the martyr's body. Surrounded by the fire, his body was like bread that is baked, or gold and silver white-hot in a furnace, not like flesh that has been burnt. So sweet a fragrance came to us that it was like that of burning incense or some other costly and sweet-smelling gum.

March 4th

St. Casimir

From the Life of St. Casimir written by a contemporary

By fulfilling the commands of the Most High he stored up treasure for himself

By the power of the Holy Spirit, Casimir burned with a sincere and unpretentious love for almighty God that was almost unbelievable in its strength. So rich was his love and so abundantly did it fill his heart, that it flowed out from his inner spirit toward his fellow men. As a result nothing was more pleasant, nothing more desirable for him, than to share his belongings, and even to dedicate and give his entire self to Christ's poor, to strangers, to the sick, to those in captivity and to all who suffer. To widows, orphans and the afflicted, he was not only a guardian and patron but a father, son and brother. One would have to compose a long account to record here all his works of love and dedication for God and for mankind. Indeed, it is difficult to imagine or to express his passion for justice, his exercise of moderation, his gift of prudence, his fundamental spiritual courage and stability, especially in a most permissive age, when men tended to be headstrong and by their very natures inclined to sin.

Daily he urged his father to practice justice throughout his kingdom and in the governance of his people; and whenever anything in the country had been overlooked because of human weakness or simple neglect, he never failed to point it out quietly to the king.

He actively took up the cause of the needy and unfortunate and embraced it as his own; for this reason the people called him the patron of the poor. Though the son of a king and descendant of a noble line, he was never unapproachable in his conversation or dealings with anyone, no matter how humble or obscure.

He always preferred to be counted among the meek and poor of spirit, among those who are promised the kingdom of heaven, rather than among the famous and powerful men of this world. He had no ambition for the power that lies in human rank and he would never accept it from his father. He was afraid the barbs of wealth, which our Lord Jesus Christ spoke of as thorns, would wound his soul, or that he would be contaminated by contact with worldly goods.

Many who acted as his personal servants or secretaries are still alive today; these men, of the highest integrity, who had personal knowledge of his private life, testify that he preserved his chastity to the very end of his life.

March 7th

Saints Perpetua and Felicity, Martyrs

From the story of the death of the holy martyrs of Carthage

Called and chosen for the glory of the Lord

The day of the martyrs' victory dawned. They marched from their cells into the amphitheater, as if into heaven, with cheerful looks and graceful bearing. If they trembled it was for joy and not for fear.

Perpetua was the first to be thrown down, and she fell prostrate. She got up and, seeing that Felicity was prostrate, went over and reached out her hand to her and lifted her up. Both stood up together. The hostility of the crowd was appeased, and they were ordered to the gate called Sanavivaria. There Perpetua was welcomed by a catechumen named Rusticus. Rousing herself as if from sleep (so deeply had she been in spiritual ecstasy), she began to look around. To everyone's amazement she said: "When are we going to be led to the beast?" When she heard that it had already happened she did not at first believe it until she saw the marks of violence on her body and her clothing. Then she beckoned to her brother and the catechumen, and addressed them in these words: "Stand firm in faith, love one another and do not be tempted to do anything wrong because of our sufferings."

Saturus, too, in another gate, encouraged the soldier Pudens, saying: "Here I am, and just as I thought and foretold I have not yet felt any wild beast. Now believe with your whole heart: I will go there and be killed by the leopard in one bite." And right at the end of the games, when he was thrown to the leopard he was in fact covered with so much blood from one bite that the people cried out to him: "Washed and saved, washed and saved!" And so, giving evidence of a second baptism, he was clearly saved who had been washed in this manner.

Then Saturus said to the soldier Pudens: "Farewell, and remember your faith as well as me; do not let these things frighten you; let them rather strengthen you." At the same time he asked for the little ring from Pudens' finger. After soaking it in his wound he returned it to Pudens as a keepsake, leaving him a pledge and a remembrance of his blood. Half dead, he was thrown along with the others into the usual place of slaughter.

The people, however, had demanded that the martyrs be led to the middle of the amphitheatre. They wanted to see the sword thrust into the bodies of the victims, so that their eyes might share in the slaughter. Without being asked they went where the people wanted them to go; but first they kissed one another, to complete their witness with the customary kiss of peace.

The others stood motionless and received the deathblow in silence, especially Saturus, who had gone up first and was first to die; he was helping Perpetua. But Perpetua, that she might experience the pain more deeply, rejoiced over her broken body and guided the shaking hand of the inexperienced gladiator to her throat. Such a woman – one before whom the unclean spirit trembled – could not perhaps have been killed, had she herself not willed it.

Bravest and happiest martyrs! You were called and chosen for the glory of our Lord Jesus Christ.

March 8th

St. John of God, Religious

From a letter by St. John of God, Religious

Christ is faithful and provides all things

If we look forward to receiving God's mercy, we can never fail to do good so long as we have the strength. For if we share with the poor, out of love for God, whatever he has given to us, we shall receive according to his promise a hundredfold in eternal happiness. What a fine profit, what a blessed reward! Who would not entrust his possessions to this best of merchants, who handles our affairs so well? With outstretched arms he begs us to turn toward him, to weep for our sins, and to become the servants of love, first for ourselves, then for our neighbors. Just as water extinguishes a fire, so love wipes away sin.

So many poor people come here that I very often wonder how we can care for them all, but Jesus Christ provides all things and nourishes everyone. Many of them come to the house of God, because the city of Granada is large and very cold, especially now in winter. More than a hundred and ten are now living here, sick and healthy, servants and pilgrims. Since this house is open to everyone, it receives the sick of every type and condition: the crippled, the disabled, lepers, mutes, the insane, paralytics, those suffering from scurvy and those bearing the afflictions of old age, many children, and above all countless pilgrims and travelers, who come here, and for whom we furnish the fire, water, and salt, as well as the utensils to cook their food. And for all of this no payment is requested, yet Christ provides.

I work here on borrowed money, a prisoner for the sake of Jesus Christ. And often my debts are so pressing that I dare not go out of the house for fear of being seized by my creditors. Whenever I see so many poor brothers and neighbors of mine suffering beyond their strength and overwhelmed with so many physical or mental ills which I cannot alleviate, then I become exceedingly sorrowful; but I trust in Christ, who knows my heart. And so I say: "Woe to the man who trusts in men rather than in Christ." Whether you like it or not, you will grow apart from men, but Christ is faithful and always with you, for Christ provides all things. Let us always give thanks to him. Amen.

March 9th

St. Frances of Rome, Religious

From the Life of St. Frances of Rome by Mary Magdalene Anguillaria, superior of the Oblates of the Tower of Specchi

The patience and charity of Saint Frances

God not only tested the patience of Frances with respect to her material wealth, but, as I have said before and will reiterate, he also tested her own body in a variety of ways, especially through long and serious illnesses which she had to undergo. And yet no one ever observed in her a tendency toward impatience. She never exhibited any displeasure when she complied with an order, no matter how foolish.

Through the premature deaths of her sons whom she loved dearly, Frances proved her constancy. With peace of soul she always reconciled herself to the will of God and gave him thanks for all that happened. With the same constancy she endured the slander of those who abused and reviled her and her way of life. She did not show the least hint of aversion toward them, even though she knew that they judged her rashly and spoke falsely of her way of life. Rather, returning good for evil, she habitually prayed to God for them.

God had not chosen her to be holy merely for her own advantage. Rather, the gifts he conferred upon her were to be for the spiritual and physical advantage of her neighbor. For this reason he made her so lovable that anyone with whom she spoke would immediately feel captivated by love for her and ready to help her in everything she wanted. Divine power was present and working in her words, so that in a few sentences she could bring consolation to the afflicted and the anxious, calm the restless, pacify the angry, reconcile enemies and extinguish long-standing hatreds and animosities. Again and again she would prevent a planned revenge from being carried out. She seemed able to subdue the passions of every type of person with a single word and lead them to do whatever she asked.

For this reason people flocked to Frances from all directions, as to a safe refuge. No one left her without being consoled, although she openly rebuked them for their sins and fearlessly reproved them for what was evil and displeasing to God. Many different diseases were rampant in Rome. Fatal diseases and plagues were everywhere, but the saint ignored the risk of contagion and displayed the deepest kindness toward the poor and the needy. Here empathy would first bring them to atone for their sins. Then she would help them by her eager care, and urge them lovingly to accept their trials, however difficult, from the hand of God. She would encourage them to endure their sufferings for love of Christ, since he had previously endured so much for them.

Frances was not satisfied with caring for the sick she could bring into her home. She would seek them out in their cottages and in public hospitals, and would refresh their thirst, smooth their beds, and bind their sores. The more disgusting and sickening the stench, the greater was the love and care with which she treated them. She used to go to the Campo Santo with food and rich delicacies to be distributed to the needy. On her return home she would bring pieces of worn-out clothes and unclean rags which she would wash lovingly and mend carefully, as if they were to be used for God himself. Then she would fold them carefully and perfume them. For thirty years Frances continued this service to the sick and the stranger.

While she was in her husband's house, she made frequent visits to Saint Mary's and Saint Cecilia's hospitals in Trastevere, and to the hospital of the Holy Spirit in Sassia and to a fourth hospital in the Campo Santo. During epidemics like this it was not only difficult to find doctors to care for the body but even priests to provide remedies for the soul. She herself would seek them out and bring them to those who were disposed to receive the sacraments of penance and the Eucharist. In order to have a priest more readily available to assist her in her apostolate, she supported, at her own expense, a priest who would go to the hospitals and visit the sick whom she had designated.

March 17th

St. Patrick, Bishop

From the Confession of St. Patrick, Bishop

Through me many peoples have been reborn in God

I give unceasing thanks to my God, who kept me faithful *in the day of my testing*[1 Jas 3; 1 Pet 1:7; 1 Cor 10:13; 1 Pet 4:12-13]. Today I can offer him sacrifice with confidence, giving myself as *a living victim*[Rom 12:1] to Christ, my Lord, *who kept me safe through all my trials*[2 Tim 4:18]. I can say now: *Who am I, Lord*[2 Sam 7:18], and what is my calling, that you worked through me with such divine power? You did all this so that today *among the Gentiles*[1 Pet 2:12] I might constantly *rejoice* and *glorify your name*[Ps 85:12] wherever I may be, both in prosperity and in adversity. You did it so that, whatever happened to me, I might accept good and evil equally, always giving thanks to God. God showed me how to have faith in him for ever, as one who is never to be doubted. He answered my prayer in such a way that *in the last days*[2 Tim 3], ignorant though I am, I might be bold enough to take up so holy and so wonderful a task, and imitate in some degree those whom the Lord had so long ago foretold as heralds of his Gospel, *bearing witness to all nations*[Mt 28:19-20; Mk 16:15; Lk 24:47; Jn 20:21].

How did I get this wisdom[Prov 4:5-9], that was not mine before? I did not know *the number of my days*[Ps 38:5], or have knowledge of God. How did so great and salutary a gift come to me, the gift of knowing and loving God, though at the cost of homeland and family? I came to the Irish peoples to preach the Gospel and endure the taunts of unbelievers, putting up with reproaches about my earthly pilgrimage, suffering many persecutions, *even bondage*, and losing my birthright of freedom for the benefit of others.

If I am worthy, *I am ready*[Phil 1:21] also to give up *my life*, without hesitation and most willingly, for his name. I want to *spend myself* in that country, *even in death*[Phil 1:21], if the Lord should grant me this favor. I am deeply in his debt, for he gave me the great grace that through me many peoples should be reborn in God, and then made perfect by confirmation and everywhere among them clergy ordained for a people so recently coming to believe, one people gathered by the Lord *from the ends of the earth*[Jn 12:32]. As God had prophesied of old through the prophets: *The nations shall come to you from the ends of the earth*[Jer 16:19], and say: *"How false are the idols made by our fathers: they are useless."* In another prophecy he said: *I have set you as a light among the nations, to bring salvation to the ends of the earth*[Isa 49:6].

It is among that people that I want to *wait for the promise*[Acts 1:4] made by him, who assuredly never tells a lie. He makes this promise in the Gospel: *They shall come from the east and west, and sit down with Abraham, Isaac and Jacob*[Mt 8:11]. This is our faith: believers are to come from the whole world.

March 18th

St. Cyril of Jerusalem, Bishop & Doctor

From a catechetical instruction by St. Cyril of Jerusalem, Bishop & Doctor

Prepare for the Holy Spirit

Let the heavens sing for joy and the earth exults[Ps 95:11]! For these people who are about to be sprinkled with hyssop will be cleansed spiritually. His power will purify them, for during His passion the hyssop touched his lips. Let the heavenly angels rejoice! Let those who are to be wedded to a spiritual spouse prepare themselves. *A voice cries in the wilderness: Prepare the way of the Lord*[Isa 40:3-8]. And so, children of justice, follow John's exhortation: *Make straight the way of the Lord*[Isa 40:3-5; Jn 1:23]. Remove all obstacles and stumbling blocks so that you will be able to go straight along the road to eternal life. Through a sincere faith prepare yourselves so that you may be free to receive the Holy Spirit. Through your penance begin to wash your garments; then, summoned to the spouse's bedchamber, you will be found spotless.

Heralds proclaim the bridegroom's invitation. All mankind is called to the wedding feast, for he is a generous lover. Once the crowd has assembled, the bridegroom decides who will enter the wedding feast. This is a figure for baptism.

Give your name at his gate and enter. I hope that none of you will later hear the words: *Friend, how did you enter without a wedding garment*[Mt 22:12]? Rather, may all of you hear the words: *Well done, my good and faithful servant. You have been faithful in small things, I shall put you in charge of many things. Enter into the joy of your Lord*[Mt 25:23].

Up to this point in the history of salvation you have stood outside the gate. Now I hope you will all hear the words: *The king has brought me into his chambers*[Song 1:4]. *My soul rejoices in my God. He has clothed me in the garment of salvation and in the cloak of joy. He has made me a bridegroom by placing a crown on my head. He has made me a bride by adorning me with jewels and golden ornaments*[Isa 61:10].

I do not say these things so that your souls will be found without stain or wrinkle or any other defect. Indeed, before you have received this grace, how could this happen to you who are called to receive forgiveness of sin? Rather, I ask that once you have received his grace you do nothing to deserve damnation. Even more, I ask you to hasten toward the fulfillment of his grace.

My brothers, this is a truly great occasion. Approach it with caution. You are standing in front of God and in the presence of the host of angels. The Holy Spirit is about to impress his seal on each of your souls. You are about to be pressed into the service of a great king.

And so prepare yourselves to receive the sacrament. The gleaming white garments you are about to put on are not the preparation I am speaking of, but rather the devotion of a clean conscience.

March 19th

St. Joseph, Husband of Mary

From a sermon by St. Bernardine of Siena, Priest

The faithful foster-father and guardian

There is a general rule concerning all special graces granted to any human being. Whenever the divine favor chooses someone to receive a special grace, or to accept a lofty vocation, God adorns the person chosen with all the gifts of the Spirit needed to fulfill the task at hand.

This general rule is especially verified in the case of Saint Joseph, the foster-father of our Lord and the husband of the Queen of our world, enthroned above the angels. He was chosen by the eternal Father as the trustworthy guardian and protector of his greatest treasures, namely, his divine Son and Mary, Joseph's wife. He carried out this vocation with complete fidelity until at last God called him, saying: *Good and faithful servant, enter into the joy of your Lord*.

What then is Joseph's position in the whole Church of Christ? Is he not a man chosen and set apart? Through him and, yes, under him, Christ was fittingly and honorably introduced into the world. Holy Church in its entirety is indebted to the Virgin Mother because through her it was judged worthy to receive Christ. But after her we undoubtedly owe special gratitude and reverence to Saint Joseph.

In him the Old Testament finds its fitting close. He brought the noble line of patriarchs and prophets to its promised fulfillment. What the divine goodness had offered as a promise to them, he held in his arms.

Obviously, Christ does not now deny to Joseph that intimacy, reverence and very high honor which he gave him on earth, as a son to his father. Rather we must say that in heaven Christ completes and perfects all that he gave at Nazareth.

Now we can see how the last summoning words of the Lord appropriately apply to Saint Joseph: *Enter into the joy of your Lord*. In fact, although the joy of eternal happiness enters into the soul of a man, the Lord preferred to say to Joseph: *Enter into joy*. His intention was that the words should have a hidden spiritual meaning for us. They convey not only that this holy man possesses an inward joy, but also that it surrounds him and engulfs him like an infinite abyss.

Remember us, Saint Joseph, and plead for us to your foster-child. Ask your most holy bride, the Virgin Mary, to look kindly upon us, since she is the mother of him who with the Father and the Holy Spirit lives and reigns eternally. Amen.

March 23rd

St. Turibius de Mongrovejo, Bishop

From the decree on the pastoral office of bishops in the Church of the Second Vatican Council

Ready for every good work

In exercising their duty of teaching, bishops are to proclaim the Gospel of Christ before men, a task that stands out among their principal duties. In the strength of the Spirit they are to call men to faith, or confirm them in a living faith. They are to set before them the mystery of Christ in its entirety, that is, those truths which are necessary in order to know Christ, as well as the divinely revealed way of glorifying God and so attaining to eternal happiness.

Moreover, they are to make it clear that earthly realities and human institutions are themselves directed, in the plan of God the creator, toward man's salvation, and are thus able to make no small contribution to the building up of the body of Christ.

They should therefore insist on the value placed by the Church's teaching on the human person, his freedom and also his physical life; on the family, its unity and stability, and the procreation and education of children; on civil society, with its laws and its professions; on work and leisure, the arts and technological developments; on poverty and affluence. They should also set forth the principles for resolving the very serious problems relating to the possession, increase and proper distribution of material goods, to peace and war, and to friendly relations among all peoples.

They should present Christian teaching in a way appropriate to the needs of the times, that is, in a way that meets the difficulties and problems that people today find a special burden and source of anxiety. They should also safeguard this teaching, instructing the faithful how to defend it and propagate it themselves. In handing on this teaching they should manifest the Church's motherly concern for all, believers and unbelievers alike. They should show a special solicitude for the poor and less fortunate, to whom the Lord has sent them to preach the good news.

In discharging their duty as father and shepherd, bishops should be among their people as those who serve, good shepherds who know their sheep and whose sheep know them. They should be outstanding in their spirit of love and concern for all, true fathers whose God-given authority all obey with joyful heart. They should unite and mold the entire family of their flock so that all are made aware of their responsibilities and are able to live and work in loving communion with each other.

To do this effectively, bishops should order their lives in keeping with the needs of the times, and so be *ready for every good work, enduring all for the sake of God's chosen ones*[Titus 3:1.]

March 25th

Annunciation

From a letter by St. Leo the Great, Pope & Doctor

The mystery of man's reconciliation with God

Lowliness is assured by majesty, weakness by power, mortality by eternity. To pay the debt of our sinful state, a nature that is incapable of suffering was joined to one that could suffer. Thus, in keeping with the healing that we needed, one and the same mediator between God and men, the man Jesus Christ, was able to die in one nature, and unable to die in the other.

He who is true God was therefore born in the complete and perfect nature of a true man, whole in his own nature, whole in ours. By our nature we mean what the Creator had fashioned in us from the beginning, and took to himself in order to restore it.

For in the Savior there was no trace of what the deceiver introduced and man, being misled, allowed to enter. It does not follow that because he submitted to sharing in our human weakness he therefore shared in our sins.

He took the nature of a servant without stain of sin, enlarging our humanity without diminishing his divinity. He emptied himself; though invisible he made himself visible, though Creator and Lord of all things he chose to be one of us mortal men. Yet this was the condescension of compassion, not the loss of omnipotence. So he who in the nature of God had created man, became in the nature of a servant, man himself.

Thus the Son of God enters this lowly world. He comes down from the throne of heaven, yet does not separate himself from the Father's glory. He is born in a new condition, by a new birth.

He was born in a new condition, for, invisible in his own nature, he became visible in ours. Beyond our grasp, he chose to come within our grasp. Existing before time began, he began to exist at a moment in time. Lord of the universe, he hid his infinite glory and took the nature of a servant. Incapable of suffering as God, he did not refuse to be a man, capable of suffering. Immortal, he chose to be subject to the laws of death.

He who is true God is also true man. There is no falsehood in this unity as long as the lowliness of man and the pre-eminence of God coexist in mutual relationship.

As God does not change by his condescension, so man is not swallowed up by being exalted. Each nature exercises its own activity, in communion with the other. The Word does what is proper to the Word, the flesh fulfils what is proper to the flesh.

One nature is resplendent with miracles, the other falls victim to injuries. As the Word does not lose equality with the Father's glory, so the flesh does not leave behind the nature of our race.

One and the same person – this must be said over and over again – is truly the Son of God and truly the son of man. He is God in virtue of the fact that *in the beginning was the Word, and the Word was with God, and the Word was God*[Jn 1:1]. He is man in virtue of the fact that *the Word was made flesh, and dwelt among us*[Jn 1:14].

April 2nd

St. Francis of Paola, Hermit

From a letter by St. Francis of Paola, Hermit

Be converted with a sincere heart

May our Lord Jesus Christ, a most generous giver, reward you for your labor.

Avoid evil, cast danger aside. Though we are unworthy, we and your brothers never cease to pray to God the Father and to his Son Jesus Christ and also to the Virgin Mary that you may receive everything you need for your spiritual and physical well-being.

I earnestly admonish you, therefore, my brothers, to look after your spiritual well-being with judicious concern. Death is certain; life is short and vanishes like smoke.

Fix your minds, then, on the passion of our Lord Jesus Christ. Inflamed with love for us, he came down from heaven to redeem us. For our sake he endured every torment of body and soul and shrank from no bodily pain. He himself gave us an example of perfect patience and love. We, then, are to be patient in adversity.

Put aside your hatred and animosity. Take pains to refrain from sharp words. If they escape your lips, do not be ashamed to let your lips produce the remedy, since they have caused the wounds. Pardon one another so that later on you will not remember the injury. The recollection of an injury is itself wrong. It adds to our anger, nurtures our sin and hates what is good. It is a rusty arrow and poison for the soul. It puts all virtue to flight. It is like a worm in the mind: it confuses our speech and tears to shreds our petitions to God. It is foreign to charity: it remains planted in the soul like a nail. It is wickedness that never sleeps, sin that never fails. It is indeed a daily death.

Be peace-loving. Peace is a precious treasure to be sought with great zeal. You are well aware that our sins arouse God's anger. You must change your life, therefore, so that God in his mercy will pardon you. What we conceal from men is known to God. Be converted, then, with a sincere heart. Live your life that you may receive the blessing of the Lord. Then the peace of God our Father will be with you always.

April 4th

St. Isidore, Bishop & Doctor

From the Book of Maxims by St. Isidore, Bishop

The scholar who is learned about the kingdom of heaven

Prayer purifies us, instructs us. Both are good when both are possible. Otherwise, prayer is better than .

If a man wants to be always in God's company, he must pray regularly and read regularly. When we pray, we talk to God; when we read, God talks to us.

All spiritual growth comes from and reflection. By we learn what we did not know; by reflection we retain what we have learned.

The holy Scriptures confers two benefits. It trains the mind to understand them; it turns man's attention from the follies of the world and leads him to the love of God.

Two kinds of study are called for here. We must first learn how the Scriptures are to be understood, and then see how to expound them with profit and in a manner worthy of them. A man must first be eager to understand what he is before he is fit to proclaim what he has learned.

The conscientious reader will be more concerned to carry out what he has read than merely to acquire knowledge of it. For it is a less serious fault to be ignorant of an objective than it is to fail to carry out what we do know. In we aim at knowing, but we must put into practice what we have learned in our course of study.

No one can understand holy Scripture without constant , according to the words: *Love her and she will exalt you. Embrace her and she will glorify you*[Prov 4:8].

The more you devote yourself to a study of the sacred utterances, the richer will be your understanding of them, just as the more the soil is tilled, the richer the harvest.

Some people have great mental powers but cannot be bothered with ; what could have taught them is devalued by their neglect. Others have a desire to know but are hampered by their slow mental processes; yet application to will teach them things which the clever fail to learn through laziness.

The man who is slow to grasp things but really tries hard is rewarded; equally he who does not cultivate his God-given intellectual ability is condemned for despising his gifts and sinning by sloth.

Learning unsupported by grace may get into our ears; it never reaches the heart. It makes a great noise outside but serves no inner purpose. But when God's grace touches our innermost minds to bring understanding, his word which has been received by the ear sinks deep into the heart.

April 5th

St. Vincent Ferrer, Priest

From the treatise On the Spiritual Life by St. Vincent Ferrer, Priest

On teaching

When you treat virtuous and sinful acts in your sermons and exhortations, use simple language and sensible idioms. Give apt and precise examples whenever you can. Each sinner in your congregation should feel moved as though you were preaching to him alone. Your words should sound as though they were coming, not from a proud or angry soul, but from a charitable and loving heart. Your tone of voice should be that of a father who suffers with his sinful children, as though they were seriously ill or were lying in a huge pit; and he struggles to free them, raise them up, and cherish them like a mother, as one who is happy over their progress and the hope they have of heaven's glory.

This way of preaching has proven profitable to congregations; for an abstract discourse on the virtues and vices hardly inspires those who listen.

When hearing confession, you should always radiate the warmest charity. Whether you are gently encouraging the fainthearted or putting the fear of God into the hardhearted, the penitent should feel that you are motivated only by pure love. Therefore, speak in a pleasant friendly, way before you use words that will prod his conscience.

Finally, if you truly want to help the soul of your neighbor, you should approach God first with all your heart. Ask him simply to fill you with charity, the greatest of all virtues; with it you can accomplish what you desire.

April 7th

St. John Baptist de la Salle, Priest

From a meditation by St. John Baptist de la Salle, Priest

Let the love of God impel you

The apostle Paul states that God has placed apostles, prophets and doctors in the Church. If you meditate on this you will be convinced that you too have been given your special place. Paul testifies to this. He declares that there are different kinds of ministry and work, and that the same Holy Spirit is manifested in a variety of gifts for the good of all, that is, the good of the Church.

Therefore you should not doubt that you have been given the same kind of grace to teach boys, to instruct them in the Gospel, and to form them in religion. This is a great gift which God gave you when he called you to this holy work.

In your teaching, the boys in your charge must see by the way you teach that you are true ministers of God, full of true charity and sincere in carrying out your task. It is most important for you to realize that you are ministers not only of God but also of Jesus Christ and the Church.

Saint Paul also urges us to regard as ministers of Christ not only all who preach the Gospel but also those who write the message that Christ dictates not with ink but with the spirit of the living God, not on tablets of stone but on the fleshy tablets of the heart - on the hearts of boys. Be driven by the love of God then, because Jesus Christ died for all, that those who live may live not for themselves but for him who died and rose for them. Let your students be moved by your untiring care for them and feel as though God were encouraging them through you, because you perform your duties as ambassadors of Christ.

Above all, let your charity and zeal show how you love the Church. Your work is for the Church, which is the body of Christ. By your diligence show your love for those whom God has given you, just as Christ loved the Church.

Take care that your boys enter into the building up of this temple so that one day they may become worthy to stand, glorious and without spot or wrinkle, before the tribunal of Jesus Christ. See to it that the abundant grace God has given them may be shown in the years to come, as well as the grace given you to teach them and to bring them up to inherit the kingdom of God and our Lord Jesus Christ.

April 11th

St. Stanislaus, Bishop and Martyr

From a letter by St. Cyprian, Bishop & Martyr

The contest of faith

As we do battle and fight in the contest of faith, God, his angels and Christ himself watch us. How exalted is the glory, how great the joy of engaging in a contest with God presiding, of receiving a crown with Christ as judge.

Dear brethren, let us arm ourselves with all our might, let us prepare ourselves for the struggle by innocence of heart, integrity of faith, dedication to virtue

The blessed Apostle teaches us how to arm and prepare ourselves: *Put round you the belt of truth; put on the breastplate of righteousness; for shoes wear zeal for the Gospel of peace; take up the shield of faith to extinguish all the burning arrows of the evil one; take the helmet of salvation, and the sword of the spirit, which is the word of God*[Eph 6:14-17].

Let us take this armor and defend ourselves with these spiritual defenses from heaven, so that we may be able to resist the threats of the devil, and fight back against him on the evil day.

Let us put on the breastplate of righteousness so that our hearts may be safeguarded, proof against the arrows of the enemy. Let our feet be protected by the shoes of the teaching of the Gospel so that when we begin to trample on the serpent and crush it, we may not be bitten and tripped up by it.

Let us with fortitude bear the shield of faith to protect us by extinguishing all the burning arrows that the enemy may launch against us.

Let us wear on our head the helmet of the spirit to defend our ears against the proclamations of death, our eyes against the sight of accursed idols, our forehead so that God's sign may be kept intact, our lips so that our tongue may proclaim victoriously its faith in Christ its Lord.

Let us arm our right hand with the sword of the spirit so that it may courageously refuse the daily sacrifices, and like the hand - mindful of the eucharist – that receives the body of the Lord, stretch out to embrace him, and so gain from the Lord the future prize of a heavenly crown.

Dear brethren, have all this firmly fixed in your hearts. If the day of persecution finds us thinking on these things and meditating upon them, the soldier of Christ, trained by Christ's commands and instructions, does not begin to panic at the thought of battle, but is ready for the crown of victory.

April 13th

St. Martin I, Pope & Martyr

From a letter by St. Martin, Pope & Martyr

Why am I anxious? The Lord is near

At all times in our letters we have desired to encourage you in your charity and to alleviate any anxiety you may have for us, as we have for all the saints and all our brothers who share this concern for us in the Lord. But now I am writing to you of things which do oppress us, and I speak the truth in the name of Christ our God.

Removed from all the turmoil of the world and cast aside by our sins, we are separated from life itself. For the people who live in this region are all pagans, and Christians who are known to live in the area have taken on pagan ways, showing none of that charity which human beings, even barbarians, regularly display in numerous compassionate deeds.

Indeed, I have been amazed and continue to be amazed at the lack of perception and the callousness of those who were once connected with me, both my friends and my relatives. They have all completely forgotten about my unhappy state, and do not care to know where I am, whether I am alive or dead.

What sort of conscience, I ask, do we have, we who are to be brought before the tribunal of Christ, where all who are formed out of the same lump of clay will be the accusers and all will have to justify their lives? What is this terror - or fear, if you will, though there is no reason for it - that men seem to have for fulfilling God's commandments even in the slightest degree? Have the evil spirits so succeeded in concealing me by this enforced exile? Have I been shown so clearly to be an enemy to the entire assembly of the Church, an adversary to all my people?

But *God wishes all men to be saved and to come to a knowledge of the truth*[1 Tim 2:4] through the prayers of Peter. Hence I pray that God will strengthen their hearts in the orthodox faith, help them to stand firm against every heretic and enemy of the Church, and guard them unshaken. And this I ask especially for their shepherd, now designated to be over them, that none may fall or go astray or renounce anything, however trifling, which they professed in writing in the sight of the Lord and his holy angels. In this way, together with me in my humiliation, they will receive the crown of justice in the true faith from the hand of our Lord and Savior Jesus Christ. For the Lord himself will take care of this lowly body of mine as befits his providence, whether this means unending suffering or some small consolation. Why am I anxious? *The Lord is near*[Ps 144:18]. But my hope is in his compassion that he will not delay in putting an end to this course which he has assigned to me.

Greet in the Lord all your people and all who for love of God have had compassion for my chains. May God on high shield you with his mighty arm from all temptation and preserve you for his kingdom.

April 21st

St. Anselm, Bishop and Doctor

From the Proslogion by St. Anselm, Bishop & Doctor

Let me know you and love you, so that I may find my joy in you

My soul, have you found what you are looking for? You were looking for God, and you have discovered that he is the supreme being, and that you could not possibly imagine anything more perfect. You have discovered that this supreme being is life itself, light, wisdom, goodness, eternal blessedness and blessed eternity. He is everywhere, and he is timeless.

Lord my God, you gave me life and restored it when I lost it. Tell my soul that so longs for you what else you are besides what it has already understood, so that it may see you clearly. It stands on tiptoe to see more, but apart from what it has seen already, it sees nothing but darkness. Of course it does not really see darkness, because there is no darkness in you, but it sees that it can see no further because of the darkness in itself.

Surely, Lord, inaccessible light is your dwelling place, for no one apart from yourself can enter into it and fully comprehend you. If I fail to see this light it is simply because it is too bright for me. Still, it is by this light that I do see all that I can, even as weak eyes, unable to look straight at the sun, see all that they can by the sun's light.

The light in which you dwell, Lord, is beyond my understanding. It is so brilliant that I cannot bear it, I cannot turn my mind's eye toward it for any length of time. I am dazzled by its brightness, amazed by its grandeur, overwhelmed by its immensity, bewildered by its abundance.

O supreme and inaccessible light, O complete and blessed truth, how far you are from me, even though I am so near to you! How remote you are from my sight, even though I am present to yours! You are everywhere in your entirety, and yet I do not see you; in you I move and have my being, and yet I cannot approach you; you are within me and around me, and yet I do not perceive you.

O God, let me know you and love you so that I may find my joy in you; and if I cannot do so fully in this life, let me at least make some progress every day, until at last that knowledge, love and joy come to me in all their plenitude. While I am here on earth let me learn to know you better, so that in heaven I may know you fully; let my love for you grow deeper here, so that there I may love you fully. On earth then I shall have great joy in hope, and in heaven complete joy in the fulfillment of my hope.

O Lord, through your Son you command us, no, you counsel us to ask, and you promise that you will hear us so that our joy may be complete. Lord, I am making the request that you urge us to make through your Wonder-Counselor. Give me then what you promise to give through your Truth. You, O God, are faithful; grant that I may receive my request, so that my joy may be complete.

Meanwhile, let this hope of mine be in my thoughts and on my tongue; let my heart be filled with it, my voice speak of it; let my soul hunger for it, my body thirst for it, my whole being yearn for it, until I enter into the joy of the Lord, who is Three in One, blessed for ever. Amen.

April 23rd

St. George, Martyr

From a sermon by St. Peter Damian, Bishop & Doctor

Invincibly defended by the banner of the cross

Dear brothers, our joy in today's feast is heightened by our joy in the glory of Easter, just as the splendor of a precious jewel enhances the beauty of its gold setting.

Saint George was a man who abandoned one army for another: he gave up the rank of tribune to enlist as a soldier for Christ. Eager to encounter the enemy, he first stripped away his worldly wealth by giving all he had to the poor. Then, free and unencumbered, bearing the shield of faith, he plunged into the thick of the battle, an ardent soldier for Christ.

Clearly what he did serves to teach us a valuable lesson: if we are afraid to strip ourselves of our worldly possessions, then we are unfit to make a strong defense of the faith.

As for Saint George, he was consumed with the fire of the Holy Sprit. Armed with the invincible standard of the cross, he did battle with an evil king and acquitted himself so well that, in vanquishing the king, he overcame the prince of all wicked spirits, and encouraged other soldiers of Christ to perform brave deeds in his cause.

Of course, the supreme invisible arbiter was there, who sometimes permits evil men to prevail so that his will may be accomplished. And although he surrendered the body of his martyr into the hands of murderers, yet he continued to take care of his soul, which was supported by the unshakable defense of its faith.

Dear brothers, let us not only admire the courage of this fighter in heaven's army but follow his example. Let us be inspired to strive for the reward of heavenly glory, keeping in mind his example, so that we will not be swayed from our path, though the world seduce us with its smiles or try to terrify us with naked threats of its trials and tribulations.

We must now cleanse ourselves, as Saint Paul tells us, from all defilement of body and spirit, so that one day we too may deserve to enter that temple of blessedness to which we now aspire.

Anyone who wishes to offer himself to God in the tent of Christ, which is the Church, must first bathe in the spring of holy baptism; then he must put on the various garments of the virtues. As it says in the Scriptures: *Let your priests be clothed in justice*[Ps 131:9]. He who is reborn in baptism is a new man. He may no longer wear the things that signify mortality. He has discarded the old self and must put on the new. He must live continually renewed in his commitment to a holy sojourn in this world.

Truly we must be cleansed of the stains of our past sins and be resplendent in the virtue of our new way of life. Then we can be confident of celebrating Easter worthily and of truly following the example of the blessed martyrs.

April 24th

St. Fidelis of Sigmaringen, Priest and Martyr

From a eulogy for St. Fidelis of Sigmaringen, Priest & Martyr

Faithful in name and in truth

Pope Benedict XIV praised Fidelis as a confessor of the Catholic faith in these words: "He practiced the fullness of charity in bringing consolation and relief to his neighbors as well as strangers. With a father's love he embraced all those who were in trouble. He supported great numbers of poor people with the alms he had collected from every quarter.

"With wealth collected from the powerful and from princes, he comforted widows and orphans in their loneliness. He was always helping prisoners in their spiritual and bodily needs. He showed constant zeal in visiting and comforting the sick whom he would win back to God and prepare for their last struggle.

"The most outstanding example of this meritorious way of life occurred when the Austrian army, stationed in the area of Raetia, was almost totally destroyed by an epidemic. To show compassion he used to bring food for the weak and the dying."

In addition to this charity, he was faithful in truth as well as in name. His zeal for defending the Catholic faith was unsurpassed and he preached it tirelessly. A few days before he shed his blood to bear witness to his preaching, he gave his last sermon. These are the words he left as a testament: "O Catholic faith, how solid, how strong you are! How deeply rooted, *how firmly founded on a solid rock*[Mt 7:24-25]! Heaven and earth will pass away, but you can never pass away. From the beginning the whole world opposed you, but you mightily triumphed over everything. *This is the victory that overcomes the world, our faith*[1 Jn 5:4]. It has subjected powerful kings to the rule of Christ; it has bound nations to his service.

"What made the holy apostles and martyrs endure fierce agony and bitter torments, except faith, and especially faith in the resurrection?

"What is it that today makes true followers of Christ cast luxuries aside, leave pleasures behind, and endure difficulties and pain? It is living faith *that expresses itself through love*[Gal 5:6]. It is this that makes us put aside the goods of the present in the hope of future goods. It is because of faith that we exchange the present for the future."

April 25th

St. Mark, Evangelist

From the treatise Against Heresies by St. Irenaeus, Bishop, Doctor & Martyr

Preaching truth

The Church, which has spread everywhere, even to the ends of the earth, received the faith from the apostles and their disciples. By faith, we believe in one God, the almighty Father *who made heaven and earth and the sea and all that is in them*[Ps 145:6]. We believe in one Lord Jesus Christ, the Son of God, who became man for our salvation. And we believe in the Holy Spirit who through the prophets foretold God's plan: the coming of our beloved Lord Jesus Christ, his birth from the Virgin, his passion, his resurrection from the dead, his ascension into heaven, and his final coming from heaven in the glory of his Father, to *recapitulate all things*[Eph 1:10] and to raise all men from the dead, so that, by the decree of his invisible Father, he may make a just judgment in all things and so that *every knee should bow in heaven and on earth and under the earth*[Phil 2:10] to Jesus Christ our Lord and our God, our Savior and our King, and *every tongue confess him* [Phil 2:11].

The Church, spread throughout the whole world, received this preaching and this faith and now preserves it carefully, dwelling as it were in one house. Having one soul and one heart, the Church holds this faith, preaches and teaches it consistently as though by a single voice. For though there are different languages, there is but one tradition.

The faith and the tradition of the churches founded in Germany are no different from those founded among the Spanish and the Celts, in the East, in Egypt, in Libya and elsewhere in the Mediterranean world. Just as God's creature, the sun, is one and the same the world over, so also does the Church's preaching shine everywhere to enlighten all men who want to come to a knowledge of the truth.

Now of those who speak with authority in the churches, no preacher however forceful will utter anything different - for no one is above the Master - nor will a less forceful preacher diminish what has been handed down. Since our faith is everywhere the same, no one who can say more augments it, nor can anyone who says less diminish it.

April 28th

St. Peter Chanel, Priest & Martyr

From a eulogy for St. Peter, Priest & Martyr

The blood of martyrs is the seed of Christians

As soon as Peter embraced religious life in the Society of Mary, he was sent at his own request to the missions of Oceania, and landed on the island of Futuna in the Pacific Ocean, where the name of Christ had never before been preached. A lay-brother who was constantly at his side gave the following account of his life in the missions.

"Because of his labors he was often burned by the heat of the sun, and famished with hunger, and he would return home wet with perspiration and completely exhausted. Yet he always remained in good spirits, courageous and energetic, as if he were returning from a pleasure jaunt, and this would happen almost every day.

"He could never refuse anything to the Futunians, even to those who persecuted him; he always made excuses for them and never rejected them, even though they were often rude and troublesome. He displayed an unparalleled mildness toward everyone on all occasions without exception. It is no wonder then that the natives used to call him the 'good-hearted man.' He once told a fellow religious: 'In such a difficult mission one has to be holy.'"

Quietly he preached Christ and the Gospel, but there was little response. Still with invincible perseverance he pursued his missionary task on both the human and religious level, relying on the example and words of Christ: *There is one who sows and another who reaps*[Jn 4:37]. And he constantly prayed for help from the Mother of God, to whom he was especially devoted.

By his preaching of Christianity he destroyed the cult of the evil spirits, which the chieftains of the Futunians encouraged in order to keep the tribe under their rule. This was the reason they subjected Peter to a most cruel death, hoping that by killing him the seeds of the Christian religion which he had sowed would be annihilated.

On the day before his martyrdom he had said: "It does not matter if I die. Christ's religion is so deeply rooted on this island that it cannot be destroyed by my death."

The blood of this martyr benefited, in the first place, the natives of Futuna, for a few years later they were all converted to the faith of Christ. But it benefited as well the other islands of Oceania, where Christian churches, which claim Peter as their first martyr, are now flourishing.

April 29th

St. Catherine of Siena, Virgin & Doctor

From the dialogue On Divine Providence
by St. Catherine of Siena, Virgin & Doctor

I tasted and I saw

Eternal God, eternal Trinity, you have made the blood of Christ so precious through his sharing in your divine nature. You are a mystery as deep as the sea; the more I search, the more I find, and the more I find the more I search for you. But I can never be satisfied; what I receive will ever leave me desiring more. When you fill my soul I have an even greater hunger, and I grow more famished for your light. I desire above all to see you, the true light, as you really are.

I have tasted and seen the depth of your mystery and the beauty of your creation with the light of my understanding. I have clothed myself with your likeness and have seen what I shall be. Eternal Father, you have given me a share in your power and the wisdom that Christ claims as his own, and your Holy Spirit has given me the desire to love you. You are my Creator, eternal Trinity, and I am your creature. You have made of me a new creation in the blood of your Son, and I know that you are moved with love at the beauty of your creation, for you have enlightened me.

Eternal Trinity, Godhead, mystery deep as the sea, you could give me no greater gift than the gift of yourself. For you are a fire ever burning and never consumed, which itself consumes all the selfish love that fills my being. Yes, you are a fire that takes away the coldness, illuminates the mind with its light and causes me to know your truth. By this light, reflected as it were in a mirror, I recognize that you are the highest good, one we can neither comprehend nor fathom. And I know that you are beauty and wisdom itself. The food of angels, you gave yourself to man in the fire of your love.

You are the garment which covers our nakedness, and in our hunger you are a satisfying food, for you are sweetness and in you there is no taste of bitterness, O triune God!

April 30th

St. Pius V, Pope

From a treatise on John by St. Augustine, Bishop & Doctor

The Church is founded upon the rock which Peter acknowledged

God never ceases to provide the human race with consolations in misfortune. But in addition to these, in the fullness of time, when he himself knew it should be done, he sent his own only-begotten Son through whom he created all things. While remaining God, his Son was to become man and be *the mediator between God and men, the man Jesus Christ*[1 Tim 2:5].

Those who believed in him through baptism were freed from the guilt of all their sins, freed from eternal damnation to live in faith, hope and love. On their journey among the trials and dangers of this world, they received the consolations of God, both in body and in spirit. They were to walk in his sight, keeping to the path which Christ made for them.

But even while walking on this path they are not without sin, since it develops subtly out of human weakness. Therefore Christ gave the saving remedy of charity to help them in their prayers, for he taught them to say: *Forgive us our sins as we forgive those who sin against us*[Lk 11:4].

Such is the practice which the Church in blessed hope carries out in this life of suffering. Now the apostle Peter, because of the primacy of his apostleship, stood as a symbol of the entire Church.

In himself he was by nature one man, by grace one Christian, by a more abundant grace an apostle and the chief of the apostles. But Christ said to him: *To you I shall give the keys of the kingdom of heaven and whatever you will bind upon the earth will be bound also in heaven and whatever you will forgive upon the earth will be forgiven also in heaven*[Mt 16:19]. Now these words applied to the entire Church. In this life it is shaken by various trials, as if by rains, floods and tempests, but it does not fall because it is founded upon the rock from which Peter received his name.

The Lord said: *Upon this rock I shall build my Church*[Mt 16:18] because Peter has first said: *You are Christ, the Son of the living God*[Mt 16:16]. The Lord was really saying: *I shall build my Church upon the rock which you have acknowledged*. For the *rock was Christ*, and upon this foundation even Peter himself was raised up. *Another foundation indeed no one can lay except that which was laid, which is Jesus Christ*.

The Church, which is founded upon Christ, received from him the keys of the kingdom of heaven, that is, the power of binding and forgiving sins, in the person of Peter. Therefore this Church, by loving and following Christ, is set free from evil. But this is even more the case with those who fight in behalf of truth even to the death.

May 1st

St. Joseph the Worker

From the Pastoral constitution on the Church in the Modern World of the Second Vatican Council

The worldwide activity of man

By his labor and abilities man has always striven to improve the quality of his life. Today, particularly by means of science and technology, he has extended his mastery over almost the whole of nature, and still continues to extend it. Through the development of the many means of communication among nations, the human family is coming to see itself, and establish itself, as a single worldwide community. As a result, where formerly man looked especially to supernatural forces for blessings, he now secures many of these benefits for himself, thanks to his own efforts.

In the face of this vast enterprise now engaging the whole human race, men are asking themselves a series of questions. What is the meaning and value of all this activity? How should these benefits be used? Where are the efforts of individuals and communities finally leading us?

The Church is the guardian of the deposit of God's word, from which are drawn the principles of the religious and moral order. Without always having a ready answer to every question, the Church desires to integrate the light of revelation with the skilled knowledge of mankind, so that it may shine on the path which humanity has lately entered.

Those who believe in God take it for granted that, taken by itself, man's activity, both individual and collective - that great struggle in which men in the course of the ages have sought to improve the conditions of human living - is in keeping with God's purpose.

Man, created in God's image, has been commissioned to master the earth and all it contains, and so rule the world in justice and holiness. He is to acknowledge God as the creator of all, and to see himself and the whole universe in relation to God, in order that all things may be subject to man, and God's name be an object of wonder and praise over all the earth.

This commission extends to even the most ordinary activities of everyday life. Where men and women, in the course of gaining a livelihood for themselves and their families, offer appropriate service to society, they can be confident that their personal efforts promote the work of the Creator, confer benefit on their fellowmen, and help to realize God's plan in history.

So far from thinking that the achievements gained by man's abilities and strength are in opposition to God's power, or that man with his intelligence is in some sense a rival to his Creator, Christians are, on the contrary, convinced that the triumphs of the human race are a sign of God's greatness and the effect of his wonderful providence.

The more the power of men increases, the wider is the scope of their responsibilities, as individuals and as communities.

It is clear, then, that the Christian message does not deflect men from the building up of the world, or encourage them to neglect the good of their fellowmen, but rather places on them a stricter obligation to work for these objectives.

May 2nd

St. Athanasius, Bishop & Doctor

From a discourse by St. Athanasius, Bishop & Doctor

On the incarnation of the Word

The Word of God, incorporeal, incorruptible and immaterial, entered our world. Yet is was not as if he had been remote from it up to that time. For there is no part of the world that was ever without his presence; together with his Father, he continually filled all things and places.

Out of his loving-kindness for us he came to us, and we see this in the way he revealed himself openly to us. Taking pity on mankind's weakness, and moved by our corruption, he could not stand aside and see death have the mastery over us; he did not want creation to perish and his Father's work in fashioning man to be in vain. He therefore took to himself a body, no different from our own, for he did not wish simply to be in a body or only to be seen.

If he had wanted simply to be seen, he could indeed have taken another, and nobler, body. Instead, he took our body in its reality.

Within the Virgin he built himself a temple, that is, a body; he made it his own instrument in which to dwell and to reveal himself. In this way he received from mankind a body like our own, and, since all were subject to the corruption of death, he delivered this body over to death for all, and with supreme love offered it to the Father. He did so to destroy the law of corruption passed against all men, since all died in him. The law, which had spent its force on the body of the Lord, could no longer have any power against his fellowmen. Moreover, this was the way in which the Word was to restore mankind to immortality, after it had fallen into corruption, and summon it back from death to life. He utterly destroyed the power death had against mankind - as fire consumes chaff - by means of the body he had taken and the grace of the resurrection.

This is the reason why the Word assumed a body that could die, so that this body, sharing in the Word who is above all, might satisfy death's requirement in place of all. Because of the Word dwelling in that body, it would remain incorruptible, and all would be freed for ever from corruption by the grace of the resurrection.

In death the Word made a spotless sacrifice and oblation of the body he had taken. By dying for others, he immediately banished death for all mankind.

In this way the Word of God, who is above all, dedicated and offered his temple, the instrument that was his body, for us all, as he said, and so paid by his own death the debt that was owed. The immortal Son of God, united with all men by likeness of nature, thus fulfilled all justice in restoring mankind to immortality by the promise of the resurrection.

The corruption of death no longer holds any power over mankind, thanks to the Word, who has come to dwell among them through his one body.

May 3rd

Saints Philip and James, Apostles

From the treatise On the Prescription of Heretics by Tertullian, Priest

The preaching of the Apostles

Our Lord Jesus Christ himself declared what he was, what he had been, how he was carrying out his Father's will, what obligations he demanded of men. This he did during his earthly life, either publicly to the crowds or privately to his disciples. Twelve of these he picked out to be his special companions, appointed to teach the nations.

One of them fell from his place. The remaining eleven were commanded by Christ, as he was leaving the earth to return to the Father after his resurrection, to go and teach the nations and to baptize them into the Father, the Son and the Holy Spirit.

The apostles cast lots and added Matthias to their number, in place of Judas, as the twelfth apostle. The authority for this action is to be found in a prophetic psalm of David. After receiving the power of the Holy Spirit which had been promised to them, so that they could work miracles and proclaim the truth, they first bore witness to their faith in Jesus Christ and established churches throughout Judea. They then went out into the whole world and proclaimed to the nations the same doctrinal faith.

They set up churches in every city. Other churches received from them a living transplant of faith and the seed of doctrine, and through this daily process of transplanting they became churches. They therefore qualify as apostolic churches by being the offspring of churches that are apostolic.

Every family has to be traced back to its origins. That is why we can say that all these great churches constitute that one original Church of the apostles; for it is from them that they all come. They are all primitive, all apostolic, because they are all one. They bear witness to this unity by the peace in which they all live, the brotherhood which is their name, the fellowship to which they are pledged. The principle on which these associations are based is common tradition by which they share the same sacramental bond.

The only way in which we can prove what the apostles taught – that is to say, what Christ revealed to them – is through those same churches. They were founded by the apostles themselves, who first preached to them by what is called the living voice and later by means of letters.

The Lord had said clearly in former times: *I have many more things to tell you, but you cannot endure them now*[Jn 16:12]. But he went on to say: *When the Spirit of truth comes, he will lead you into the whole truth*[Jn 16:13]. Thus Christ shows us that the apostles had full knowledge of the truth, for he had promised that they would receive the *whole truth* through the Spirit of truth. His promise was certainly fulfilled, since the Acts of the Apostles prove that the Holy Spirit came down on them.

May 12th

Saints Nereus and Achilleus, Martyrs

From a commentary on the psalms by St. Augustine, Bishop & Doctor

The sufferings of Christ are not in Christ alone

Jesus Christ is one man with head and body, the Savior of the body and the members of the body, two in one flesh, in one voice, in one passion, and, when wickedness has passed away, in one state of rest. The sufferings of Christ are therefore not in Christ alone; yes, but the sufferings of Christ are only in Christ.

If by Christ you mean both head and body, the sufferings of Christ are only in Christ. But if by Christ you mean only the head, then the sufferings of Christ are not in Christ alone. For if the sufferings of Christ are in Christ alone, how can the apostle Paul, as a member of Christ, say this: *That I may fill up in my flesh what is lacking of the sufferings of Christ*[Col 1:24]?

If then you are among the members of Christ, whatever human being you are, whoever you are that hears this, whoever you are that does not hear this (but if you are among the members of Christ you do hear this), whatever you suffer at the hands of those who are not among the members of Christ was lacking to the sufferings of Christ.

Your sufferings are added because they were lacking. You fill up a measure, you do not pour something that overflows. You suffer as much as needed to be added from your sufferings to the total suffering of Christ, who suffered as our head, and suffers in his members, that is, in ourselves.

Each one of us in his own measure pays his debt to what may be called this commonwealth of ours. In proportion to our store of strength we contribute as it were a tax of suffering. The final reckoning of all suffering will not take place until the world has come to an end.

Do not then imagine, brethren, that all the just who suffered persecution at the hands of the wicked, even those who were sent to foretell the coming of the Lord before he came, did not belong to the members of Christ. God forbid that one who belongs to the city which has Christ for king should not belong to the members of Christ.

In the blood of Abel, the just one, the whole city speaks, and so on until the blood of Zechariah. From then, it is the same city that goes on speaking in the blood of John, in the blood of the apostles, in the blood of the martyrs, in the blood of Christ's faithful people.

May 12th

St. Pancras, Martyr

From a Sermon by St. Bernard, Abbot & Doctor

I am with him in tribulation

I am with him in tribulation[Jn 16:33], says God. Shall I then seek anything here below apart from tribulation? *For me it is good to cling to God*[Ps 62:8-9], and also *to put my hope in the Lord God*[Ps 32:20-22], because he has said: *I will rescue him and glorify him*[Ps 90:15].

I am with him in tribulation [Ps 90:15]. *My delight,* he says, *is to be with the sons of men*[Prov 8:31] - Emmanuel, God with us. He himself descended to be near those who are saddened in spirit, to be with us in our tribulation. One day *we shall be caught up together in the clouds to meet the Lord in the air; and so we shall always be with the Lord*[1 Thes 4:17] - provided, however, that we are concerned here below to have him with us, as our companion on the journey, who will restore us to our true country or, better, as one who is now our way and our true country hereafter.

It is good for me to be sad, O Lord, as long as you are with me, rather than to be a king apart from you, to feast without you, to boast without you. It is better for me to embrace you in tribulation, to have you with me in the furnace, than to be without you in heaven. *For what do I have in heaven apart from you? What have I desired on earth*[Ps 72:25]*? Gold is tested in the furnace*[Prov 27:21]*, and the just by the trial of tribulation.* There, yes there, you are present with them, Lord. You are there in the midst of those gathered in your name, as you were once with three young men in the fiery furnace.

Why are we afraid, why do we hesitate, why do we flee from this furnace? The fire rages, but the Lord is with us in tribulation. *If God is with us who can be against us*[Rom 8:31-33]*?* And if he then rescues us, who will steal us from his hand? Lastly, if he honors us, who can dishonor us? If he honors us, who can humiliate us?

I will fill him with length of days[Ps 90:16]. It is as if he said more clearly: I know what he desires, I know what he thirsts for, and what he likes. He likes neither silver nor gold, pleasure nor curiosity, nor any of the honors of the world. All this he considers as loss; all this he despises, counting it as dung. He has totally emptied himself, and he does not allow himself to be concerned with things he knows can never satisfy him. He knows in whose image he has been made, of what greatness he is capable; he does not strive to raise himself up only to be cut down from the highest state.

So *I will fill him with length of days* [Ps 90:16], for only the true light can refresh, only the eternal can fill him. Indeed this length of days has no end, this light knows no setting, and this fullness can never turn to disgust.

May 14th

St. Matthias, Apostle

From a homily of St. John Chrysostom on the Acts of the Apostles

Make known to us, Lord, the one you choose Acts 1:15-26

In those days, Peter, stood up in the midst of the disciples and said Acts 1:15-26... As the fiery spirit to whom the flock was entrusted by Christ and as the leader in the band of the apostles, Peter always took the initiative in speaking: *My brothers, we must choose from among our number*. He left the decision to the whole body, at once augmenting the honor of those elected and avoiding any suspicion of partiality. For such great occasions can easily lead to trouble.

Did not Peter then have the right to make the choice himself? Certainly he had the right, but he did not want to give the appearance of showing special favor to anyone. Besides he was not yet endowed with the Spirit. *And they nominated two,* we read, *Joseph, who was called Barsabbas and surnamed Justus, and Matthias*. He himself did not nominate them; all present did. But it was he who brought the issue forward, pointing out that it was not his own idea but had been suggested to him by a scriptural prophecy. So he was speaking not as a teacher but as an interpreter.

So, he goes on, *we must choose from those men who lived in our company*. Notice how insistent he is that they should be eyewitnesses. Even though the Spirit would come to ratify the choice, Peter regards this prior qualification as most important.

Those who lived in our company, to continue the passage, *all through the time when the Lord Jesus came and went among us*. He refers to those who had dwelt with Jesus, not just those who had been his disciples. For of course from the very beginning many had followed him. Notice how it is written that Peter himself was *one of the two who had listened to John, and followed Jesus*.

All through the time when the Lord Jesus came and went among us, to continue further, *beginning with the baptism of John* – rightly so, because no one knew what had happened before that time, although they were to know of it later through the Spirit.

Up to the day, Peter added, *on which he was taken up from us – one of these must be made a witness along with us of his resurrection*. He did not say "a witness of the rest of his actions" but only *a witness of the resurrection!* That witness would be more believable who could declare that he who ate and drank and was crucified also rose from the dead. He needed to be a witness not of the times before or after that event, and not of the signs and wonders, but only of the resurrection itself. For the rest happened by general admission, openly; but the resurrection took place secretly, and was known to these men only.

And they all prayed together, saying: *You, Lord, know the hearts of men; make your choice known to us*. *You*, not *we*. Appropriately they said that he knew the hearts of men, because the choice was to be made by him, not by others.

They spoke with such confidence, because someone had to be appointed. They did not say "choose" but *make known to us* the chosen one; *the one you choose,* they said, fully aware that everything was preordained by God. *They then drew lots*. For they did not think themselves worthy to make the choice of their own accord, and therefore they wanted some sign for their instruction.

May 18th

St. John I, Pope & Martyr

From a letter by St. John of Avila, priest

The Life of Jesus revealed in us

Praise to the God and Father of our Lord Jesus Christ, the Father of mercy and God of all consolation who consoles us in all our trials and enables us to console others who are being tried, for we urge them on as God urges us on. As we share generously in the sufferings of Christ, so do we share generously in his consolation[2 Cor 1:3-5].

The words are those of Saint Paul the apostle. He was beaten with rods three times, flogged five times, stoned once and left for dead; he suffered every persecution men can inflict, his body was twisted by pain and toil. And all this was his lot not just on one or two occasions, for he writes: *We are constantly being handed over to death for Jesus' sake, so that his life may be revealed in us*[2 Cor 4:11].

In all these tribulations he does not murmur or complain about God, as weaker men do. He is not saddened as those who love status and pleasure are. He does not beg God to be relieved of them, as men do who are unaware of their true value and therefore will have no part of them. He does not make light of them, as men do who set little value upon them. On the contrary, fully aware of the value of these tribulations and rising above his own weakness, Paul blesses God amid his sufferings and thanks him as though he had bestowed a fine reward. He thinks it an honor to be able to suffer for him who subjected himself to so very much shame in order to free us from the dreadful effects of sin; who exalted us by giving us his Spirit and making us adopted sons of God; and who gave us, in his own person and through his own efforts, a proof and pledge of heavenly joy.

Dear brothers and sisters, I pray God may open your eyes and let you see what hidden treasures he bestows on us in the trials from which the world thinks only to flee. Shame turns into honor when we seek God's glory. Present affliction becomes the source of heavenly glory. To those who suffer wounds in fighting his battles God opens his arms in loving, tender friendship, which is more delightful by far than anything our earthly efforts might produce. If we have any sense, we shall yearn for these open arms of God. Can anyone but a man in whom all desire is dead fail to desire him who is wholly lovable, wholly desirable?

If you long for these festivals of heavenly joy, if you want to behold them and take part in them, be assured that there is no better way to reach them than the way of suffering. This is the way Christ and his disciples have always traveled. He calls it a narrow way, but it leads straight to life. That is why he tells us that if we want to join him, we shall travel the way he took. It is surely not right that the Son of God should go his way on the path of shame while the sons of men walk the way of worldly honor: *The disciple is not above his teacher, nor the servant greater than his master*[Mt 10:24].

God grant that our hearts may find no rest and seek no other food in this world, save in hardship and suffering beside the Lord's cross.

May 20th

St. Bernadine of Siena, Priest

From a sermon by St. Bernardine of Siena, priest

The name of Jesus is the glory of preachers

The name of Jesus is the glory of preachers, because the shining splendor of that name causes his word to be proclaimed and heard. And how do you think such an immense, sudden and dazzling light of faith came into the world, if not because Jesus was preached? Was it not through the brilliance and sweet savor of this name that God *called us into his marvelous light*[1 Pet 2:9]? When we have been enlightened, and in that same light behold the light of heaven, rightly may the apostle Paul say to us: *Once you were darkness, but now you are light in the Lord; walk as children of light*[Eph 5:8].

So this name must be proclaimed, that it may shine out and never be suppressed. But it must not be preached by someone with sullied mind or unclean lips, but stored up and poured out from a chosen vessel.

That is why our Lord said of Saint Paul: *He is a chosen instrument of mine, the vessel of my choice, to carry my name before the Gentiles and kings and the sons of Israel*[Acts 9:15]. In this chosen vessel there was to be a drink more pleasing than earth ever knew, offered to all mankind for a price they could pay, so that they would be drawn to taste of it. Poured into other chosen vessels, it would grow and radiate splendor. For our Lord said: *He is to carry my name.*

When a fire is lit to clear a field, it burns off all the dry and useless weeds and thorns. When the sun rises and darkness is dispelled, robbers, night-prowlers and burglars hide away. So when Paul's voice was raised to preach the Gospel to the nations, like a great clap of thunder in the sky, his preaching was a blazing fire carrying all before it. It was the sun rising in full glory. Infidelity was consumed by it, false beliefs fled away, and the truth appeared like a great candle lighting the whole world with its brilliant flame.

By word of mouth, by letters, by miracles and by the example of his own life, Saint Paul bore the name of Jesus wherever he went. He praised the name of Jesus *at all times*, but never more than when *bearing witness to his faith.*

Moreover, the Apostle did indeed carry this name *before the Gentiles and kings and the sons of Israel* as a light to enlighten all nations. And this was his cry wherever he journeyed: *The night is passing away, the day is at hand. Let us then cast off the works of darkness and put on the armor of light; let us conduct ourselves honorably as in the day*[Rom 13:12-14]. Paul himself showed forth the burning and shining light set upon a candlestick, everywhere proclaiming *Jesus, and him crucified.*

And so the Church, the bride of Christ, strengthened by his testimony, rejoices with the psalmist, singing: *O God, from my youth you have taught me, and I still proclaim your wondrous deeds*[Ps 70:17]. The psalmist exhorts her to do this, as he says: *Sing to the Lord, and bless his name, proclaim his salvation day after day*[Ps 95:2]. And this salvation is Jesus, her savior.

May 25th

St. Venerable Bede, Priest & Doctor

From a letter on the death of the Venerable Bede, by Cuthbert

I desire to see Christ

On Tuesday before the feast of the Ascension, Bede's breathing became labored and a slight swelling appeared in his legs. Nevertheless, he gave us instruction all day long and dictated cheerfully during the whole time. Among other things he repeated several times: "Learn your lesson quickly, for I do not know how long I shall be with you nor whether my Maker will soon take me from you." It seemed to us, however, that he knew very well that his end was near, and so he spent the whole night giving thanks to God.

At daybreak on Wednesday he told us to finish the writing we had begun. We worked until nine o'clock, when we went in procession with the relics as the custom of that day required. But one of our community, a boy named Wilbert, stayed with him and said to him: "Dear master, there is still one more chapter to finish in that book you were dictating. Do you think it would be too hard for you to answer any more questions?" Bede replied: "Not at all; it will be easy. Take up your pen and ink, and write quickly," and he did so.

At three o'clock, Bede said to me: "I have a few treasures in my private chest, some pepper, napkins, and a little incense. Run quickly and bring the priests of our monastery, and I will distribute among them these little presents that God has given me."

When the priests arrived he spoke to them and asked each one to offer Masses and prayers for him regularly. They gladly promised to do so. The priests were sad, however, and they all wept, especially because Bede had said that he thought they would not see his face much longer in this world. Yet they rejoiced when he said: "If it so please my Maker, it is time for me to return to him who created me and formed me out of nothing when I did not exist. I have lived a long time, and the righteous Judge has taken good care of me during my whole life. The time has come for my departure, and I long to die and be with Christ. My soul yearns to see Christ, my King, in all his glory." He said many other things which profited us greatly, and so he passed the day joyfully till evening.

When evening came, young Wilbert said to Bede, "Dear master, there is still one sentence that we have not written down." Bede said: "Quick, write it down." In a little while, Wilbert said: "There; now it is written down." Bede said: "Good. You have spoken the truth; it is finished. Hold my head in your hands, for I really enjoy sitting opposite the holy place where I used to pray; I can call upon my Father as I sit there."

And so Bede, as he lay upon the floor of his cell, sang: "Glory be to the Father, and to the Son, and to the Holy Spirit." And when he had named the Holy Spirit, he breathed his last breath. We believe most firmly that Bede has now entered into the joy of the heaven he longed for, since his labors here on earth were always dedicated to the glory of God.

May 25th

St. Gregory VII, Pope

From a letter by St. Gregory VII, pope

The Church must be free, chaste and catholic

I beg and implore in the Lord Jesus, who redeemed us by his death, that by careful investigation you may become aware of the trials and distresses brought on me by the enemies of Christianity and understand why and how I endure them.

By God's will Mother Church placed me in my unworthiness (and God knows that I was unwilling, too) upon the apostolic throne, and with all my powers I have tried to see that the holy Church, the bride of God, our lady and mother, might return to the beauty which is rightly hers and remain free, chaste and catholic. But, because this so greatly displeases our ancient foe, he has armed his minions against us so that they might overturn all our efforts. What he has been unable to do from the days of Constantine the Great he now does against us and particularly against the Apostolic See. Do not be surprised that, as the time goes on, he will fight all the harder to wipe out the Christian religion.

But now, my dearest brothers, listen carefully to what I tell you. All those throughout the world who are numbered as Christian and who truly acknowledge the Christian faith know and believe that the blessed Peter, the prince of the apostles, is the father of all Christians and, after Christ, the first shepherd, and that the holy Roman Church is the mother and teacher of all the churches. Therefore, if you believe this and hold to it without hesitation, I ask you and enjoin upon you by Almighty God - I, your brother and your unworthy teacher as I am - to support and assist your father and your mother if you wish to have, through them, the remission of all your sins, along with blessing and grace in this world and in the life to come.

May almighty God, from whom all good things come, continually enlighten your minds and fill them with love for him and for your neighbor, so that by your devotion you may deserve to make this father and mother of whom I have spoken your debtors and enter without shame into their company. Amen.

May 25th

St. Mary Magdalene de Pazzi, Virgin

From the writings On Revelation and On Trials by St. Mary Magdalene de Pazzi, virgin

Come, Holy Spirit

You, the Word, are most wonderful, working through the Holy Spirit to fill the soul with yourself, so that it is joined to God, grasps God, tastes God and absorbs nothing but God.

The Holy Spirit comes into the soul signed with the precious seal of the blood of the Word and of the slain Lamb; or rather that very blood urges it to come, although the Spirit moves itself and desires to come.

This Spirit which moves in itself is the substance of the Father and of the Word, and it proceeds from the essence of the Father and the good will of the Word; it comes into the soul like a fountain, and the soul is immersed in it. Just as two rushing rivers intermingle in such a way that the smaller loses its name and is absorbed into the larger, so the divine Spirit acts upon the soul and absorbs it. It is proper that the soul, which is lesser, should lose its name and surrender to the Spirit, as it will if it turns entirely toward the Spirit and is united.

This Spirit, dispenser of the treasures which lay in the lap of the Father, and guardian of the deliberations which pass between the Father and the Son, flows into the soul so sweetly and imperceptibly that few esteem its greatness.

It moves itself by its own weight and lightness into all places that are fitting and disposed to receive it. Its word is heard by all in the most attentive silence; through the impetus of love, the unmoved yet most perfect mover infuses itself into all.

You do not, O Holy Spirit, stand still in the unmoved Father or in the Word, and yet you are always in the Father and in the Word and in yourself and in all blessed spirits and creatures. You are the friend of the created because of the blood shed by the only-begotten Word, who in the greatness of his love made himself the friend of the created. You find rest in creatures who are prepared to receive you, so that in the transmission of your gifts they take on, through purity, their own particular likeness to you. You find rest in those creatures who absorb the effects of the blood of the Word and make themselves a worthy dwelling place for you.

Come, Holy Spirit. Let the precious pearl of the Father and the Word's delight come. Spirit of truth, you are the reward of the saints, the comforter of souls, light in the darkness, riches to the poor, treasure to lovers, food for the hungry, comfort to those who are wandering; to sum up, you are the one in whom all treasures are contained.

Come! As you descended upon Mary, that the Word might become flesh, work in us through grace as you worked in her through nature and grace.

Come! Food of every chaste thought, fountain of all mercy, sum of all purity.

Come! Consume in us whatever prevents us from being consumed in you.

May 26th

St. Philip Neri, Priest

From a sermon by St. Augustine, Bishop & Doctor

Rejoice in the Lord always

The Apostle tells us to rejoice, but in the Lord, not in the world. *Whoever wishes to be a friend of this world*, says Scripture, *will be reckoned an enemy of God*[Jas 4:4]. As a man cannot serve two masters, so one cannot rejoice both in the world and in the Lord.

Let joy in the Lord prevail, then, until joy in the world is no more. Let joy in the Lord go on increasing; let joy in the world go on decreasing until it is no more. This is said, not because we are not to rejoice while we are in this world, but in order that, even while we are still in this world, we may already rejoice in the Lord.

You may object: I am in the world; if I rejoice I certainly rejoice where I am. What is this? Do you mean that because you are in the world you are not in the Lord? Listen again to the Apostle, speaking now to the Athenians: in the Acts of the Apostles he says this of God and the Lord our creator: *In him we live and move and have our being*[Acts 17:28]. If he is everywhere, where is he not? Surely this was what he was exhorting us to realize. *The Lord is near, do not be anxious about anything*[Phil 4:5-7, Jas 5:8-9].

This is a great truth, that he ascended above all the heavens, yet is near to those on earth. Who is this stranger and neighbor if not the one who became our neighbor out of compassion?

The man lying on the road, left half-dead by robbers, the man treated with contempt by the priest and the levite who passed by, the man approached by the passing Samaritan to take care of him and help him, that man is the whole human race. When the immortal one, the holy one, was far removed from us because we were mortal and sinners, he came down to us, so that he, the stranger, might become our neighbor.

He did not treat us as our sins deserved[Ps 102:10]. For we are now sons of God. How do we show this? The only Son of God died for us, so that he might not remain alone. He who died as the only Son did not want to remain as the only Son. For the only Son of God made many sons of God. He bought brothers for himself by his blood; he made them welcome by being rejected; he ransomed them by being sold; he honored them by being dishonored; he gave them life by being put to death.

So, brethren, *rejoice in the Lord*, not in the world. That is, rejoice in the truth, not in wickedness; rejoice in the hope of eternity, not in the fading flower of vanity. That is the way to rejoice. Wherever you are on earth, however long you remain on earth, *the Lord is near, do not be anxious about anything*[Phil 4:5-7, Jas 5:8-9].

May 27th

St. Augustine of Canterbury, Bishop

From a letter by St. Gregory the Great, Pope & Doctor

The nation of Angles was bathed with the light of holy faith

Glory to God in the highest and peace to his people on earth[Lk 2:14], because the grain of wheat has fallen into the earth and has died. Christ has died in order to reign in heaven. Not only that: by his death we live; by his weakness we are strengthened; by his passion we are freed from suffering; impelled by his love, we are seeking in Britain brothers whom we do not know; through his help we have found those for whom we were searching, although we were not acquainted with them.

Who, dear brother, is capable of describing the great joy of believers when they have learned what the grace of Almighty God and your own cooperation achieved among the Angles? They abandoned the errors of darkness and were bathed with the light of holy faith. With full awareness they trampled on the idols which they had previously adored with savage fear. They are now committed to Almighty God. The guidelines given them for their preaching restrain them from falling into evil ways. In their minds they are submissive to the divine precepts and consequently feel uplifted. They bow down to the ground in prayer lest their minds cling too closely to earthly things. Whose achievement is this? It is the achievement of him who said: *My Father is at work until now and I am at work as well*[Jn 5:17].

God chose illiterate preachers and sent them into the world in order to show the world that conversion is brought about not by men's wisdom but rather by his own power. So in like manner God worked through weak instruments and wrought great things among the Angles. Dear brother, in this heavenly gift there is something which should inspire us with great fear and great joy.

For I know through your love for that people, specially chosen for you, that Almighty God has performed great miracles. But it is necessary that the same heavenly gift should cause you to rejoice with fear and to fear with gladness. You should be glad because by means of external miracles the souls of the Angles have been led to interior grace. But you should tremble lest, on account of these signs, the preacher's own weak soul be puffed up with presumption; lest, while seeming externally raised aloft in honor, it fall internally as a result of vainglory.

We should remember that when the disciples on their joyous return from their preaching mission said to their heavenly master: *Lord, in your name even devils were subjected to us*[Lk 10:17], he immediately retorted: *Do not rejoice about this but rather that your names are written in heaven*[Lk 10:17-21].

May 31st

The Visitation of the Blessed Virgin Mary

From a homily by St. Bede the Venerable, priest

Mary proclaims the greatness of the Lord working in her soul

My soul proclaims the greatness of the Lord, and my spirit rejoices in God my savior[Lk 1:46]. With these words Mary first acknowledges the special gifts she has been given. Then she recalls God's universal favors, bestowed unceasingly on the human race.

When a man devotes all his thoughts to the praise and service of the Lord, he proclaims God's greatness. His observance of God's commands, moreover, shows that he has God's power and greatness always at heart. His spirit rejoices in God his savior and delights in the mere recollection of his creator who gives him hope for eternal salvation.

These words are often for all God's creations, but especially for the Mother of God. She alone was chosen, and she burned with spiritual love for the son she so joyously conceived. Above all other saints, she alone could truly rejoice in Jesus, her savior, for she knew that he who was the source of eternal salvation would be born in time in her body, in one person both her own son and her Lord.

For the Almighty has done great things for me, and holy is his name[Lk 1:49]. Mary attributes nothing to her own merits. She refers all her greatness to the gift of the one whose essence is power and whose nature is greatness, for he fills with greatness and strength the small and the weak who believe in him.

She did well to add: *and holy is his name*[Lk 1:49], to warn those who heard, and indeed all who would receive his words, that they must believe and call upon his name. For they too could share in everlasting holiness and true salvation according to the words of the prophet: *and it will come to pass, that everyone who calls on the name of the Lord will be saved*[Acts 2:21]. This is the name she spoke of earlier: *and my spirit rejoices in God my Savior*[Lk 1:46].

Therefore it is an excellent and fruitful custom of holy Church that we should sing Mary's hymn at the time of evening prayer. By meditating upon the incarnation, our devotion is kindled, and by remembering the example of God's Mother, we are encouraged to lead a life of virtue. Such virtues are best achieved in the evening. We are weary after the day's work and worn out by our distractions. The time for rest is near, and our minds are ready for contemplation.

June 1st

St. Justin, Martyr

From the Acts of the martyrdom of St. Justin and his companion saints

I have accepted the true doctrines of the Christians

The saints were seized and brought before the prefect of Rome, whose name was Rusticus. As they stood before the judgment seat, Rusticus the prefect said to Justin: "Above all, have faith in the gods and obey the emperors." Justin said: "We cannot be accused or condemned for obeying the commands of our Savior, Jesus Christ.

Rusticus said: "What system of teaching do you profess?" Justin said: "I have tried to learn about every system, but I have accepted the true doctrines of the Christians, though these are not approved by those who are held fast by error."

The prefect Rusticus said: "Are those doctrines approved by you, wretch that you are?" Justin said: "Yes, for I follow them with their correct teaching."

The prefect Rusticus said: "What sort of teaching is that?" Justin said: "Worship the God of the Christians. We hold him to be from the beginning the one creator and maker of the whole creation, of things seen and things unseen. We worship also the Lord Jesus Christ, the Son of God. He was foretold by the prophets as the future herald of salvation for the human race and the teacher of distinguished disciples. For myself, since I am a human being, I consider that what I say is insignificant in comparison with his infinite godhead. I acknowledge the existence of a prophetic power, for the one I have just spoken of as the Son of God was the subject of prophecy. I know that the prophets were inspired from above when they spoke of his coming among men."

Rusticus said: "You are a Christian, then?" Justin said: "Yes, I am a Christian."

The prefect said to Justin: "You are called a learned man and think you know what is true teaching. Listen: if you were scourged and beheaded, are you convinced that you would go up to heaven?" Justin said: "I hope that I shall enter God's house if I suffer in that way. For I know that God's favor is stored up until the end of the whole world for all who have lived good lives."

The prefect Rusticus said: "Do you have an idea that you will go up to heaven to receive some suitable rewards?" Justin said: "It is not an idea that I have; it is something I know well and hold to be most certain."

The prefect Rusticus said: "Now let us come to the point at issue, which is necessary and urgent. Gather round then and with one accord offer sacrifice to the gods." Justin said: "No one who is right-thinking stoops from true worship to false worship."

The prefect Rusticus said: "If you do not do as you are commanded you will be tortured without mercy." Justin said: "We hope to suffer torment for the sake of our Lord Jesus Christ, and so be saved. For this will bring us salvation and confidence as we stand before the more terrible and universal judgment-seat of our Lord and Savior."

In the same way the other martyrs also said: "Do what you will. We are Christians; we do not offer sacrifice to idols."

The prefect Rusticus pronounced sentence, saying: "Let those who have refused to sacrifice to the gods and to obey the command of the emperor be scourged and led away to suffer capital punishment according to the ruling of the laws." Glorifying God, the holy martyrs went out to the accustomed place. They were beheaded, and so fulfilled their witness of martyrdom in confessing their faith in their Savior.

June 2nd

Saints Marcellinus and Peter, Martyrs

From the exhortation to Martyrdom by Origen, priest

Those who share in the sufferings of Christ will also share in his consolation

If passing from unbelief to faith means that we have *passed from death to life*[Jn 5:25], we should not be surprised to find that *the world hates us*. Anyone who has not *passed from death to life* [Jn 5:25], is incapable of loving those who have departed from death's dark dwelling place to enter a dwelling *made of living stones*[1 Pet 2:4-5] and filled with the light of life. Jesus *laid down his life for us*[1 Jn 3:16]; so we too should lay down our lives, I will not say for him, but for ourselves and also, surely, for those who will be helped by the example of our martyrdom.

Now is the time for Christians to rejoice, since Scripture says that *we should rejoice in our sufferings, knowing that suffering trains us to endure with patience, patient endurance makes us pleasing to God, and being pleasing to God gives us ground for a hope that will not be disappointed. Only let the love of God be poured forth in our hearts through the Holy Spirit*[Rom 5:3-5].

The more we share in the sufferings of Christ, the more we share, through him, in his consolation[1 Pet 4:12-13; 2 Cor 1:7]. We should be extremely eager to share in Christ's sufferings and to let them be multiplied in us if we desire the superabundant consolation that will be given to those who mourn. This consolation will not perhaps be the same for all, for if it were, Scripture would not say: *The more we share in the sufferings of Christ, the more we share in his consolation*[1 Pet 4:12-13; 2 Cor 1:7.]. Sharing in his consolation will be proportionate to our sharing in his suffering. We learn this from one who could say with all confidence: *We know that as you share in the sufferings, so you will share in the consolation as well*[1 Pet 4:12-13; 2 Cor 1:7.].

God says through the prophet: *At an acceptable time I heard you; on the day of salvation I helped you*[2 Cor 6:2]. What time could be more acceptable than when, for our fidelity to God in Christ, we are made a public spectacle and led away under guard, not defeated but triumphant?

In Christ and with Christ the martyrs disarm the principalities and powers and share in his triumph over them, for their share in Christ's sufferings makes them sharers also in the mighty deeds those sufferings accomplished. What could more appropriately be called the day of salvation than the day of such a glorious departure from this world? But I entreat you *not to give offense to anyone, so that our ministry may not be blamed. Be very patient and show in every way that you are servants of God*[2 Cor 6:3-10]. Say: *And now, what do I wait for? Is it not the Lord*[Ps 38:8]?

June 3rd

Saints Charles Lwanga and his Companions, Martyrs

From the homily at the canonization of the martyrs of Uganda by Pope Paul VI

The glory of the martyrs - a sign of rebirth

The African martyrs add another page to the martyrology – the Church's roll of honor – an occasion both of mourning and of joy. This is a page worthy in every way to be added to the annals of that Africa of earlier times which we, living in this era and being men of little faith, never expected to be repeated.

In earlier times there occurred those famous deeds, so moving to the spirit, of the martyrs of Scilli, of Carthage, and of that "white robed army" of Utica commemorated by Saint Augustine and Prudentius; of the martyrs of Egypt so highly praised by Saint John Chrysostom, and of the martyrs of the Vandal persecution. Who would have thought that in our days we should have witnessed events as heroic and glorious?

Who could have predicted to the famous African confessors and martyrs such as Cyprian, Felicity, Perpetua and – the greatest of all – Augustine, that we would one day add names so dear to us as Charles Lwanga and Matthias Mulumba Kalemba and their twenty companions? Nor must we forget those members of the Anglican Church who also died for the name of Christ.

These African martyrs herald the dawn of a new age. If only the mind of man might be directed not toward persecutions and religious conflicts but toward a rebirth of Christianity and civilization!

Africa has been washed by the blood of these latest martyrs, the first of this new age (and, God willing, let them be the last, although such a holocaust is precious indeed). Africa is reborn free and independent.

The infamous crime by which these young men were put to death was so unspeakable and so expressive of the times. It shows us clearly that a new people needs a moral foundation, needs new spiritual customs firmly planted, to be handed down to posterity. Symbolically, this crime also reveals that a simple and rough way of life – enriched by many fine human qualities yet enslaved by its own weakness and corruption – must give way to a more civilized life wherein the higher expressions of the mind and better social conditions prevail.

June 5th

St. Boniface, Bishop & Martyr

From a letter by St. Boniface, Bishop and Martyr

The careful shepherd watches over Christ's flock

In her voyage across the ocean of this world, the Church is like a great ship being pounded by the waves of life's different stresses. Our duty is not to abandon ship but to keep her on her course.

The ancient fathers showed us how we should carry out this duty: Clement, Cornelius and many others in the city of Rome, Cyprian at Carthage, Athanasius at Alexandria. They all lived under emperors who were pagans; they all steered Christ's ship – or rather his most dear spouse, the Church. This they did by teaching and defending her, by their labours and sufferings, even to the shedding of blood.

I am terrified when I think of all this. *Fear and trembling came upon me and the darkness* of my sins *almost covered me*[Ps 54:5-6] I would gladly give up the task of guiding the Church which I have accepted if I could find such an action warranted by the example of the fathers or by holy Scripture.

Since this is the case, and since the truth can be assaulted but never defeated or falsified, with our tired mind let us turn to the words of Solomon: *Trust in the Lord with all your heart and do not rely on your own prudence. Think on him in all your ways, and he will guide your steps*[Prov 3:5-6]. In another place he says: *The name of the Lord is an impregnable tower. The just man seeks refuge in it and he will be saved*[Prov 18:10].

Let us stand fast in what is right and prepare our souls for trial. Let us wait upon God's strengthening aid and say to him: *O Lord, you have been our refuge in all generations*[Ps 89:1].

Let us trust in him who has placed this burden upon us. What we ourselves cannot bear let us bear with the help of Christ. For he is all-powerful and he tells us: *My yoke is easy and my burden is light*[Mt 11:28-30].

Let us continue the fight on the day of the Lord. *The days of anguish and of tribulation*[Zeph 1:15] have overtaken us; if God so wills, *let us die for the holy laws of our fathers*[Boniface], so that we may deserve to obtain an eternal inheritance with them.

Let us be neither dogs that do not bark nor silent onlookers nor paid servants who run away before the wolf. Instead let us be careful shepherds watching over Christ's flock. Let us preach the whole of God's plan to the powerful and to the humble, to rich and to poor, to men of every rank and age, as far as God gives us the strength, in season and out of season, as Saint Gregory writes in his book of Pastoral Instruction.

June 6th

St. Norbert, Bishop

From the life of St. Norbert, Bishop

At ease in the company of the humble and great

(The words in quotation marks below have been taken from the biography of Saint Norbert, written by a Premonstratensian canon who was a contemporary of the saint: PL 170, 1262. 1269, 1294, 1295. Pope Innocent's Apostolic Letter was issued under leaden seal to Saint Norbert on June 5, 1133: Acta Sanctorum, 21, in Appendice p.50)

Norbert is deservedly numbered by historians among those who made an effective contribution to the reform movement under Pope Gregory VII. He established a clergy dedicated to the ideals of the Gospel and the apostolic Church. They were chaste and poor. They wore "the clothing and the symbols of the new man; that is to say, they wore the religious habit and exhibited the dignity proper to the priesthood." Norbert asked them "to live according to the norms of the Scriptures with Christ as their model." They were "to be clean in all matters pertaining to the altar and divine worship, to correct their faults and failings in their chapter meeting, and to care for and give shelter to the poor."

The priests lived in community, where they continued the work of the apostles. Inspired by the practice of the early Church, Norbert exhorted the faithful to join the monastic life in some capacity. So many men and women responded to the invitation that many asserted that no man since the apostles themselves had inspired so many to embrace the monastic life.

When Norbert was appointed an archbishop, he urged his brothers to carry the faith to the lands of the Wends. In his own diocese he tried unsuccessfully to convince the clergy of the need for reform and was confronted with noisy protests both in the street and in the church.

One of the principal goals of Norbert's life was to foster harmony between the Apostolic See and the German empire. At the same time he wanted to maintain Rome's freedom in the matter of ecclesiastical appointments. Apparently his efforts were so successful that Pope Innocent II thanked him profusely in a letter in which he called him a "devoted son," and Lothair made him chancellor of the realm.

Norbert did all these things with a steadfast faith: "Faith was the outstanding virtue of Norbert's life, as charity had been the hallmark of Bernard of Clairvaux's." Affable and charming, amiable to one and all, "he was at ease in the company of the humble and the great alike." Finally, he was a most eloquent preacher; after long meditation "he would preach the word of God," and with his fiery eloquence purged vices, refined virtues and filled souls of good will with the warmth of wisdom." He spent many hours in contemplation of the divine mysteries and fearlessly spread the spiritual insights which were the fruit of his meditation.

June 9th

St. Ephrem, Deacon & Doctor

From a sermon by St. Ephrem, Deacon & Doctor

The divine plan for the world is the mirror of the spiritual world

Lord, shed upon our darkened souls the brilliant light of your wisdom so that we may be enlightened and serve you with renewed purity. Sunrise marks the hour for men to begin their toil, but in our souls, Lord, prepare a dwelling for the day that will never end. Grant that we may come to know the risen life and that nothing may distract us from the delights you offer. Through our unremitting zeal for you, Lord, set upon us the sign of your day that is not measured by the sun.

In your sacrament we daily embrace you and receive you into our bodies; make us worthy to experience the resurrection for which we hope. We have had your treasure hidden within us ever since we received baptismal grace; it grows ever richer at your sacramental table. Teach us to find our joy in your favor! Lord, we have within us your memorial, received at your spiritual table; let us possess it in its full reality when all things shall be made new.

We glimpse the beauty that is laid up for us when we gaze upon the spiritual beauty your immortal will now creates within our mortal selves.

Savior, your crucifixion marked the end of your mortal life; teach us to crucify ourselves and make way for our life in the Spirit. May your resurrection, Jesus, bring true greatness to our spiritual self and may your sacraments be the mirror wherein we may know that self.

Savior, your divine plan for the world is a mirror for the spiritual world; teach us to walk in that world as spiritual men.

Lord, do not deprive our souls of the spiritual vision of you nor our bodies or your warmth and sweetness. The mortality lurking in our bodies spreads corruption through us; may the spiritual waters of your love cleanse the effects of mortality from our hearts. Grant, Lord, that we may hasten to our true city and, like Moses on the mountaintop, possess it now in vision.

June 11th

St. Barnabas, Apostle

From a treatise on the Gospel of St. Matthew by St. Chromatius, Bishop

You are the light of the world

You are the light of the world. A city set on a hill cannot be hidden. Nor do men light a lamp only to put it under a bushel basket; they put it on a stand where it gives light to all in the house[Mt 5:14-16]. The Lord called his disciples the salt of the earth because they seasoned with heavenly wisdom the hearts of men, rendered insipid by the devil. Now he calls them the light of the world as well, because they have been enlightened by him, the true and everlasting light, and have themselves become a light in the darkness.

Since he is the Sun of Justice, he fittingly calls his disciples the light of the world. The reason for this is that through them, as through shining rays, he has poured out the light of the knowledge of himself upon the entire world. For by manifesting the light of truth, they have dispelled the darkness of error from the hearts of men.

Moreover, we too have been enlightened by them. We have been made light out of darkness as the Apostle says: *For once you were darkness, but now you are light in the Lord; walk as children of light*[Eph 5:8]. He says another time: *For you are not sons of the night and of darkness, but you are all sons of light and of the day*[1 Thes 5:5].

Saint John also rightly asserts in his letter: *God is light*[1 Jn 1:5], and whoever abides in God is in the light just as God himself is in the light. Therefore, because we rejoice in having been freed from the darkness of error, we should always walk in the light as children of light. This is why the Apostle says: *Among them you shine as lights in the world, holding fast to the word of life*[Phil 2:15].

If we fail to live in the light, we shall, to our condemnation and that of others, be veiling over and obscuring by our infidelity the light men so desperately need. As we know from Scripture, the man who received the talent should have made it produce a heavenly profit, but instead he preferred to hide it away rather than put it to work and was punished as he deserved.

Consequently, that brilliant lamp which was lit for the sake of our salvation should always shine in us. For we have the lamp of the heavenly commandment and spiritual grace, to which David referred: *Your law is a lamp to my feet and a light to my path*[Ps 118:105]. Solomon also says this about it: *For the command of the law is a lamp*[Prov 6:23].

Therefore, we must not hide this lamp of law and faith. Rather, we must set it up in the Church, as on a lamp-stand, for the salvation of many, so that we may enjoy the light of truth itself and all believers may be enlightened.

June 13th

St. Anthony of Padua, Priest & Doctor

From a sermon by St. Anthony of Padua, Priest & Doctor

Actions speak louder than words

The man who is filled with the Holy Spirit speaks in different languages. These different languages are different ways of witnessing to Christ, such as humility, poverty, patience and obedience; we speak in those languages when we reveal in ourselves these virtues to others. Actions speak louder than words; let your words teach and your actions speak. We are full of words but empty of actions, and therefore are cursed by the Lord, since he himself cursed the fig tree when he found no fruit but only leaves. Gregory says: "A law is laid upon the preacher to practice what he preaches." It is useless for a man to flaunt his knowledge of the law if he undermines its teaching by his actions.

But the apostles *spoke as the Spirit gave them the gift of speech*. Happy the man whose words issue from the Holy Spirit and not from himself! For some men speak as their own character dictates, but steal the words of others and present them as their own and claim the credit for them. The Lord refers to such men and others like them in Jeremiah: *So, then, I have a quarrel with the prophets that steal my words from each other. I have a quarrel with the prophets, says the Lord, who have only to move their tongues to utter oracles. I have a quarrel with the prophets who make prophecies out of lying dreams, who recount them and lead my people astray with their lies and their pretensions. I certainly never sent them or commissioned them, and they serve no good purpose for this people, says the Lord*[Jer 23:30-40].

We should speak, then, as the Holy Spirit gives us the gift of speech. Our humble and sincere request to the Spirit for ourselves should be that we may bring the day of Pentecost to fulfillment, insofar as he infuses us with his grace, by using our bodily senses in a perfect manner and by keeping the commandments. Likewise we shall request that we may be filled with a keen sense of sorrow and with fiery tongues for confessing the faith, so that our deserved reward may be to stand in the blazing splendor of the saints and to look upon the triune God.

June 19th

St. Romuald, Abbot

From the life of St. Romuald by St. Peter Damian, Bishop & Doctor

Denying oneself and following Christ

Romuald lived in the vicinity of the city of Parenzo for three years. In the first year he built a monastery and appointed an abbot with monks. For the next two years he remained there in seclusion. In that setting, divine holiness transported him to such a summit of perfection that, breathed upon by the Holy Spirit, he foresaw many future events and comprehended with the rays of his intelligence hidden mysteries of the Old and New Testament.

Frequently he was seized by so great a contemplation of divinity that he would be reduced to tears with the boiling, indescribable heat of divine love. In this condition he would cry out: Beloved Jesus, beloved, sweet honey, indescribable longing, delight of the saints, sweetness of the angels, and other things of this kind. We are unable to express the ecstasy of these utterances, dictated by the Holy Spirit.

Wherever the holy man might arrange to live, he would follow the same pattern. First he would build an oratory with an altar in a cell; then he would shut himself in and forbid access.

Finally, after he had lived in many places, perceiving that his end was near, he returned to the monastery he had built in the valley of Castro. While he awaited with certainty his approaching death, he ordered a cell to be constructed there with an oratory in which he might isolate himself and preserve silence until death.

Accordingly the hermitage was built, since he had made up his mind that he would die there. His body began to grow more and more oppressed by afflictions and was already failing, not so much from weakness as from the exhaustion of great age. One day he began to feel the loss of his physical strength under all the harassment of increasingly violent afflictions. As the sun was beginning to set, he instructed two monks who were standing by to go out and close the door of the cell behind them; they were to come back to him at daybreak to celebrate matins. They were so concerned about his end that they went out reluctantly and did not rest immediately. On the contrary, since they were worried that their master might die, they lay hidden near the cell and watched this precious treasure. For some time they continued to listen attentively until they heard neither movement nor sound. Rightly guessing what had happened, they pushed open the door, rushed in quickly, lit a candle and found the holy man lying on his back, his blessed soul snatched up into heaven. As he lay there, he seemed like a neglected heavenly pearl that was soon to be given a place of honor in the treasury of the King of kings.

June 21st

St. Aloysius Gonzaga

From a letter to his mother by St. Aloysius Gonzaga, Religious

God's mercies shall be my song for ever

May the comfort and grace of the Holy Spirit be yours for ever, most honored lady. Your letter found me lingering still in this region of the dead, but now I must rouse myself to make my way on to heaven at last and to praise God for ever in the land of the living; indeed I had hoped that before this time my journey there would have been over. If charity, as Saint Paul says, means *to weep with those who weep and rejoice with those who are glad*[Rom 12:15], then, dearest mother, you shall rejoice exceedingly that God in his grace and his love for you is showing me the path to true happiness, and assuring me that I shall never lose him.

The divine goodness, most honored lady, is a fathomless and shoreless ocean, and I confess that when I plunge my mind into thought of this it is carried away by the immensity and feels quite lost and bewildered there. In return for my short and feeble labors, God is calling me to eternal rest; his voice from heaven invites me to the infinite bliss I have sought so languidly, and promises me this reward for the tears I have so seldom shed.

Take care above all things, most honored lady, not to insult God's boundless loving kindness; you would certainly do this if you mourned as dead one living face to face with God, one whose prayers can bring you in your troubles more powerful aid than they ever could on earth. And our parting will not be for long; we shall see each other again in heaven; we shall be united with our Savior; there we shall praise him with heart and soul, sing of his mercies for ever, and enjoy eternal happiness. When he takes away what he once lent us, his purpose is to store our treasure elsewhere more safely and bestow on us those very blessings that we ourselves would most choose to have.

I write all this with the one desire that you and all my family may consider my departure a joy and favor and that you especially may speed with a mother's blessing my passage across the waters till I reach the shore to which all hopes belong. I write the more willingly because I have no clearer way of expressing the love and respect I owe you as your son.

June 22nd

St. Paulinus of Nola, Bishop

From a letter by St. Paulinus of Nola, Bishop

God everywhere produces his love in his people through the Holy Spirit

You have shown, my lord, that you bear within you true charity and perfect love toward my humble person. Truly holy and deservedly blessed, you are a most desirable friend, for my cousin Julian on his return from Carthage delivered the letter which conveyed to us the shining light of your sanctity. As a result it seems to me that I am not just now coming to know your love for me but rather recognizing it as something I was already aware of. For clearly this love of yours came forth from the one *who predestined us for himself from the foundation of the world*[Eph 1:4]. In him, the maker of all that is to be, we were made before we were born, *because he made us and not we ourselves*[Ps 99:3]. Shaped by his work and his foreknowledge, then, we were already joined by charity into a likeness of wills and a union of faith, or a faith of unity, that anticipated our present acquaintance. So before we met in person, we became known to each other in the revelation of the Spirit.

Hence I give thanks and boast in the Lord, who, one and the same throughout the world, produces his love in his people through the Holy Spirit whom he pours out upon all flesh. With the flow of the river he gladdens his city among whose citizens he rightly established you to be the first *among the princes of his people*[Ps 112:8] in your apostolic see. Likewise, he wanted me, whom he raised up when I was downtrodden, and lifted up from the earth when I was destitute, to be numbered among your associates. But I am more grateful for that gift of the Lord by which he established a place for me in your heart and allowed me so to penetrate your affections that I might claim a personal trust in your love. Moved by such kindnesses and gifts, I could not love you in a merely casual or negligent way.

But you should know everything about me and you should be aware that I am a sinner of long standing; It is not so long ago that *I was led out of darkness and the shadow of death*[Ps 106:14]; only recently have I begun to breathe in the air of life; only recently have I put my hand to the plough and taken up the cross of Christ. I need to be helped by your prayers to persevere to the end. And if you should lighten my burden by your intercession, this is the reward that will be added on to your merits, for the holy man who helps a laborer (I dare not call myself a brother) *will be exalted like a great city*[Prov 11:11].

We have sent to you a loaf of bread in token of our unity; it symbolizes as well the substance of the Trinity. By accepting it you will make it a bread of blessing.

June 22nd

St. John Fisher, Bishop & Martyr & St. Thomas More, Martyr

From a letter written in prison to his daughter, Margaret, by St. Thomas More

With good hope I shall commit myself wholly to God

Although I know well, Margaret, that because of my past wickedness I deserve to be abandoned by God, I cannot but trust in his merciful goodness. His grace has strengthened me until now and made me content to lose goods, land, and life as well, rather than to swear against my conscience. God's grace has given the king a gracious frame of mind toward me, so that as yet he has taken from me nothing but my liberty. In doing this His Majesty has done me such great good with respect to spiritual profit that I trust that among all the great benefits he has heaped so abundantly upon me I count my imprisonment the very greatest. I cannot, therefore, mistrust the grace of God. Either he shall keep the king in that gracious frame of mind to continue to do me no harm, or else, if it be his pleasure that for my other sins I suffer in this case as I shall not deserve, then his grace shall give me the strength to bear it patiently, and perhaps even gladly.

By the merits of his bitter passion joined to mine and far surpassing in merit for me all that I can suffer myself, his bounteous goodness shall release me from the pains of purgatory and shall increase my reward in heaven besides.

I will not mistrust him, Meg, though I shall feel myself weakening and on the verge of being overcome with fear. I shall remember how Saint Peter at a blast of wind began to sink because of his lack of faith, and I shall do as he did: call upon Christ and pray to him for help. And then I trust he shall place his holy hand on me and in the stormy seas hold me up from drowning.

And if he permits me to play Saint Peter further and to fall to the ground and to swear and forswear, may God our Lord in his tender mercy keep me from this, and let me lose if it so happen, and never win thereby! Still, if this should happen, afterward I trust that in his goodness he will look on me with pity as he did upon Saint Peter, and make me stand up again and confess the truth of my conscience afresh and endure here the shame and harm of my own fault.

And finally, Margaret, I know this well: that without my fault he will not let me be lost. I shall, therefore, with good hope commit myself wholly to him. And if he permits me to perish for my faults, then I shall serve as praise for his justice. But in good faith, Meg, I trust that his tender pity shall keep my poor soul safe and make me commend his mercy.

And, therefore, my own good daughter, do not let your mind be troubled over anything that shall happen to me in this world. Nothing can come but what God wills. And I am very sure that whatever that be, however bad it may seem, it shall indeed be the best.

June 24th

Nativity of St. John the Baptist

From a sermon by St. Augustine, Bishop & Doctor

The voice of one crying in the wilderness

The Church observes the birth of John as a hallowed event. We have no such commemoration for any other fathers; but it is significant that we celebrate the birthdays of John and of Jesus. This day cannot be passed by. And even if my explanation does not match the dignity of the feast, you may still meditate on it with great depth and profit. John was born of a woman too old for childbirth; Christ was born of a youthful virgin. The news of John's birth was met with incredulity, and his father was struck dumb. Christ's birth was believed, and he was conceived through faith.

Such is the topic, as I have presented it, for our inquiry and discussion. But as I said before, if I lack either the time or the ability to study the implications of so profound a mystery, he who speaks within you even when I am not here will teach you better; it is he whom you contemplate with devotion, whom you have welcomed into your hearts, whose temples you have become.

John, then, appears as the boundary between the two testaments, the old and the new. That he is a sort of boundary the Lord himself bears witness, when he speaks of *the law and the prophets up until John the Baptist*[Lk 16:16]. Thus he represents times past and is the herald of the new era to come. As a representative of the past, he is born of aged parents; as a herald of the new era, he is declared to be a prophet while still in his mother's womb. For when yet unborn, he leapt in his mother's womb at the arrival of blessed Mary. In that womb he had already been designated a prophet, even before he was born; it was revealed that he was to be Christ's precursor, before they ever saw one another. These are divine happenings, going beyond the limits of our human frailty. Eventually he is born, he receives his name, his father's tongue is loosened. See how these events reflect reality.

Zechariah is silent and loses his voice until John, the precursor of the Lord, is born and restores his voice. The silence of Zechariah is nothing but the age of prophecy lying hidden, obscured, as it were, and concealed before the preaching of Christ. At John's arrival Zechariah's voice is released, and it becomes clear at the coming of the one who was foretold. The release of Zechariah's voice at the birth of John is a parallel to the rending of the veil at Christ's crucifixion. If John were announcing his own coming, Zechariah's lips would not have been opened. The tongue is loosened because a voice is born. For when John was preaching the Lord's coming he was asked, *Who are you*[Jn 1:22]*?* And he replied: *I am the voice of one crying in the wilderness*[Jn 1:22]. The voice is John, but the Lord *in the beginning was the Word*[Jn 1:1]. John was a voice that lasted only for a time; Christ, the Word in the beginning, is eternal.

June 27th

St. Cyril of Alexandria, Bishop & Doctor

From a letter by St. Cyril of Alexandria, Bishop & Doctor

Defender of the divine motherhood of the Virgin Mary

That anyone could doubt the right of the holy Virgin to be called the Mother of God fills me with astonishment. Surely she must be the Mother of God if our Lord Jesus Christ is God, and she gave birth to him! Our Lord's disciples may not have used those exact words, but they delivered to us the belief those words enshrine, and this has also been taught us by the holy fathers.

In the third book of his work on the holy and consubstantial Trinity, our father Athanasius, of glorious memory, several times refers to the holy Virgin as "Mother of God." I cannot resist quoting his own words: "As I have often told you, the distinctive mark of holy Scripture is that it was written to make a twofold declaration concerning our Savior; namely, that he is and has always been God, since he is the Word, Radiance and Wisdom of the Father; and that for our sake in these latter days he took flesh from the Virgin Mary, Mother of God, and became man."

Again further on he says: "There have been many holy men, free from all sin. Jeremiah was sanctified in his mother's womb, and John while still in the womb leaped for joy at the voice of Mary, the Mother of God." Athanasius is a man we can trust, one who deserves our complete confidence, for he taught nothing contrary to the sacred books.

The divinely inspired Scriptures affirm that the Word of God was made flesh, that is to say, he was united to a human body endowed with a rational soul. He undertook to help the descendants of Abraham, fashioning a body for himself from a woman and sharing our flesh and blood, to enable us to see in him not only God, but also, by reason of this union, a man like ourselves.

It is held, therefore, that there are in Emmanuel two entities, divinity and humanity. Yet our Lord Jesus Christ is nonetheless one, the one true Son, both God and man; not a deified man on the same footing as those who share the divine nature by grace, but true God who for our sake appeared in human form. We are assured of this by Saint Paul's declaration: *When the fullness of time came, God sent his Son, born of a woman, born under the law, to redeem those who were under the law and to enable us to be adopted as sons*[Gal 4:4-5].

June 28th

St. Irenaeus, Bishop, Doctor & Martyr

From the treatise Against Heresies by St. Irenaeus, Bishop, Doctor and Martyr

Life in man is the glory of God; the life of man is the vision of God

The glory of God gives life; those who see God receive life. For this reason God, who cannot be grasped, comprehended or seen, allows himself to be seen, comprehended and grasped by men, that he may give life to those who see and receive him. It is impossible to live without life, and the actualization of life comes from participation in God, while participation in God is to see God and enjoy his goodness.

Men will therefore see God if they are to live; through the vision of God they become immortal and attain to God himself. As I have said, this was shown in symbols by the prophets: God will be seen by men who bear his Spirit and are always waiting for his coming. As Moses said in the Book of Deuteronomy: *On that day we shall see, for God will speak to man, and man will live*[Deut 5:24].

God is the source of all activity throughout creation. He cannot be seen or described in his own nature and in all his greatness by any of his creatures. Yet he is certainly not unknown. Through his Word the whole creation learns that there is one God the Father, who holds all things together and gives them their being. As it is written in the Gospel: *No man has ever seen God, except the only-begotten Son, who is in the bosom of the Father; he has revealed him*[Jn 1:18].

From the beginning the Son is the one who teaches us about the Father; he is with the Father from the beginning. He was to reveal to the human race visions of prophecy, the diversity of spiritual gifts, his own ways of ministry, the glorification of the Father, all in due order and harmony, at the appointed time and for our instruction. Where there is order, there is also harmony; where there is harmony, there is also correct timing; where there is correct timing, there is also advantage.

The Word became the steward of the Father's grace for the advantage of men, for whose benefit he made such wonderful arrangements. He revealed God to men and presented men to God. He safeguarded the invisibility of the Father to prevent man from treating God with contempt and to set before him a constant goal toward which to make progress. On the other hand, he revealed God to men and made him visible in many ways to prevent man from being totally separated from God and so cease to be. Life in man is the glory of God; the life of man is the vision of God. If the revelation of God through creation gives life to all who live upon the earth, much more does the manifestation of the Father through the Word give life to those who see God.

June 29th

Saints Peter and Paul, Apostles

From a sermon by St. Augustine, Bishop & Doctor

The martyrs realized what they taught

This day has been made holy by the passion of the blessed apostles Peter and Paul. We are, therefore, not talking about some obscure martyrs. *For their voice has gone forth to all the world, and to the ends of the earth their message*[Ps 18:4-5]. These martyrs realized what they taught: they pursued justice, they confessed the truth, they died for it.

Saint Peter, the first of the apostles and a fervent lover of Christ, merited to hear these words: *I say to you that you are Peter*[Mt 16:18], for he had said: *You are the Christ, the Son of the living God*[Mt 16:16]. Then Christ said: *And I say to you that you are Peter, and on this rock I will build my Church*[Mt 16:18]. On this rock I will build the faith that you now confess, and on your words: *You are the Christ, the Son of the living God*[Mt 16:16], I will build my Church. For you are Peter, and the name Peter comes from *petra*, the word for "rock," and not vice versa. "Peter" comes, therefore, from *petra*, just as "Christian" comes from Christ.

As you are aware, Jesus chose his disciples before his passion and called them apostles; and among these almost everywhere Peter alone deserved to represent the entire Church. And because of that role which he alone had, he merited to hear the words: *To you I shall give the keys of the kingdom of heaven*[Mt 16:19]. For it was not one man who received the keys, but the entire Church considered as one. Now insofar as he represented the unity and universality of the Church, Peter's preeminence is clear from the words: *To you I give,* for what was given was given to all. For the fact that it was the Church that received the keys of the kingdom of God is clear from what the Lord says elsewhere to all the apostles: *Receive the Holy Spirit, adding immediately, whose sins you forgive, they are forgiven, and whose sins you retain, they are retained*[Jn 20:21-23].

Rightly then did the Lord after his resurrection entrust Peter with the feeding of his sheep. Yet he was not the only disciple to merit the feeding of the Lord's sheep; but Christ in speaking only to one suggests the unity of all; and so he speaks to Peter, because Peter is the first among the apostles. Therefore do not be disheartened, Peter; reply once, reply twice, reply a third time. The triple confession of your love is to regain what was lost three times by your fear. You must loose three times what you bound three times; untie by love that which your fear bound. Once, and again, and a third time did the Lord entrust his sheep to Peter.

Both apostles share the same feast day, for these two were one; and even though they suffered on different days, they were as one. Peter went first, and Paul followed. And so we celebrate this day made holy for us by the apostles' blood. Let us embrace what they believed, their life, their labors, their sufferings, their preaching and their confession of faith.

June 30th

First Martyrs of the Church of Rome

From a letter to the Corinthians by St. Clement I of Rome, Pope & Martyr

Though victims of jealousy, they gave the finest example

Let us leave behind the examples from times of old, and come to those who struggled closest to us; let us consider the noble models of our own generation. It was through jealousy and envy that the greatest and most upright pillars of the Church were persecuted and struggled unto death. Let us set before our eyes the good apostles. First of all, Peter, who because of unreasonable jealousy, suffered not merely once or twice but many times, and, having thus given his witness, went to the place of glory that he deserved. It was through jealousy and conflict that Paul showed the way to the prize for perseverance. He was put in chains seven times, sent into exile, and stoned; a herald both in the east and the west, he achieved a noble fame by his faith. He taught justice to all the world and, when he had reached the limits of the western world, he gave his witness before those in authority; then he left this world and was taken up into the holy place, a superb example of endurance.

Around these men with their holy lives there gathered a great throng of the elect, who, though victims of jealousy, gave us the finest example of endurance in the midst of many indignities and tortures. Through jealousy women were tormented like Dirce or the daughters of Danaus, suffering terrible and unholy acts of violence. But they courageously finished the course of faith and despite their bodily weakness won a noble prize. It was jealousy that separated wives from husbands, and violated the words of our father Adam: *This is now bone of my bones and flesh of my flesh*[Gen 2:23]. Jealousy and strife have overthrown great cities and uprooted mighty nations.

We are writing this, beloved, not only for your admonition but also as a reminder to ourselves; for we are placed in the same arena, and the same contest lies before us. Hence we ought to put aside vain and useless concerns and go straight to the glorious and venerable norm which is our tradition, and we should consider what is good, pleasing and acceptable in the sight of him who made us. Let us fix our gaze on the blood of Christ, realizing how precious it is to his Father, since it was shed for our salvation and brought the grace of repentance to all the world.

July 3rd

St. Thomas, Apostle

From a homily on the Gospels by St. Gregory the Great, Pope & Doctor

My Lord and my God

Thomas, one of the twelve, called the Twin, was not with them when Jesus cameJn 20:24. He was the only disciple absent; on his return he heard what had happened but refused to believe it. The Lord came a second time; he offered his side for the disbelieving disciple to touch, held out his hands, and showing the scars of his wounds, healed the wound of his disbelief.

Dearly beloved, what do you see in these events? Do you really believe that it was by chance that this chosen disciple was absent, then came and heard, heard and doubted, doubted and touched, touched and believed? It was not by chance but in God's providence. In a marvelous way God's mercy arranged that the disbelieving disciple, in touching the wounds of his master's body, should heal our wounds of disbelief. The disbelief of Thomas has done more for our faith than the faith of the other disciples. As he touches Christ and is won over to belief, every doubt is cast aside and our faith is strengthened. So the disciple who doubted, then felt Christ's wounds, becomes a witness to the reality of the resurrection.

Touching Christ, he cried out: *My Lord and my God*[Jn 20:28]*. Jesus said to him: Because you have seen me, Thomas, you have believed* [Jn 20:29]. Paul said: *Faith is the guarantee of things hoped for, the evidence of things unseen*. It is clear, then, that faith is the proof of what cannot be seen. What is seen gives knowledge, not faith. When Thomas saw and touched, why was he told: *You have believed because you have seen me* [Jn 20:29]? Because what he saw and what he believed were different things. God cannot be seen by mortal man. Thomas saw a human being, whom he acknowledged to be God, and said: *My Lord and my God* [Jn 20:28]. Seeing, he believed; looking at one who was true man, he cried out that this was God, the God he could not see.

What follows is reason for great joy: *Blessed are those who have not seen and have believed* [Jn 20:29]. There is here a particular reference to ourselves; we hold in our hearts one we have not seen in the flesh. We are included in these words, but only if we follow up our faith with good works. The true believer practices what he believes. But of those who pay only lip service to faith, Paul has this to say: *They profess to know God, but they deny him in their works*[Titus 1:16]. Therefore James says: *Faith without works is dead*[Jas 2:14-26].

July 4th

St. Elizabeth of Portugal

From a sermon attributed to St. Peter Chrysologus, Bishop & Doctor

Blessed are the peacemakers

Blessed are the peacemakers, the evangelist said, dearest brethren*, for they shall be called sons of God*[Mt 5:9]. Truly Christian virtues grow in a man who enjoys the unchangeable possession of Christian peace, nor does one come to the title of son of God except through that of peacemaker.

Peace, dearest brethren, rescues man from servitude, provides him with the name of a free man, changes his identity before God together with his condition, from a servant to a son, and from a slave to a free man. Peace among brethren is the will of God, the joy of Christ, the completion of holiness, the rule of justice, the teacher of truth, the guardian of morals and a praiseworthy discipline in every regard. Peace lends strength to our prayers; it is the way our petitions can reach God easily and be credited; it is the plenitude which fulfills our desires. Peace is the mother of love, the bond of concord and the manifest sign of a pure soul, one which seeks to please God, which seeks to be fulfilled and has its desire rewarded. Peace must be preserved according to the Lord's precepts, as Christ said: *I leave you peace, my peace I give you*[Jn 14:27], that is, as I left you in peace, in peace shall I find you. As Christ left the world, he wished to leave the gift he wanted to find when he returned.

We have a commandment from heaven to retain his gift; his one word is: "I shall find what I left." God's is the planting of peace in the root, but the uprooting is from the enemy; for, just as brotherly love comes from God, so hatred comes from the devil; therefore, we must condemn our hatred of men, for it is written: *He who hates his brother is a murderer*[1 Jn 3:15].

Now you see, dearest brethren, why we should love peace and cultivate harmony: because they beget and nurture love. But you know also from the apostle John that, *Love comes from God*[1 Jn 4:7], and that whoever is not with God does not possess love.

Let us therefore, my brethren, keep the commandments, which are life for us; let us carry on together the obligations of our brotherhood in profound peace; let us bind one another with the ties of salvific charity in this mutual love which *covers a multitude of sins*[1 Pet 4:8]. Love ought to be embraced with the grasp of all our desires, since the goods it provides amount to as many rewards. We must keep peace before all other virtues, since God is always in peace.

Love peace, and all the world will be tranquil and quiet. By doing so you store up rewards for me, and joy for yourselves, that the Church of God may be founded on the bond of peace and may cling to perfect observance in Christ

July 5th

St. Anthony Zaccaria, Priest

From a sermon to fellow members of his society by St. Anthony Zaccaria, Priest

The follower of the apostle Paul

We are fools for Christ's sake[1 Cor 4:10]: our holy guide and most revered patron was speaking about himself and the rest of the apostles, and about the other people who profess the Christian and apostolic way of life. But there is no reason, dear brothers, that we should be surprised or afraid; *for the disciple is not superior to his teacher, nor the slave to his master*[Mt 10:24-26]. We should love and feel compassion for those who oppose us, rather than abhor and despise them, since they harm themselves and do us good, and adorn us with crowns of everlasting glory while they incite God's anger against themselves. And even more than this, we should pray for them and not be overcome by evil, but overcome evil by goodness. We should heap good works *like red-hot coals* of burning love *upon their heads*[Prov 25:21-22], as our Apostle urges us to do, so that when they become aware of our tolerance and gentleness they may undergo a change of heart and be prompted to turn in love to God.

In his mercy God has chosen us, unworthy as we are, out of the world, to serve him and thus to advance in goodness and to bear the greatest possible fruit of love in patience. We should take encouragement not only from the hope of sharing in the glory of God's children, but also from the hardships we undergo.

Consider your calling[1 Cor 1:26-29], dearest brothers; if we wish to think carefully about it we shall see readily enough that its basis demands that we who have set out to follow, admittedly from afar, the footsteps of the holy apostles and the other soldiers of Christ, should not be unwilling to share in their sufferings as well. *We should keep running steadily in the race we have started, not losing sight of Jesus, who leads us in our faith and brings it to perfection*[Heb 12:1-2]. And so since we have chosen such a great Apostle as our guide and father and claim to follow him, we should try to put his teaching and example into practice in our lives. Such a leader should not be served by faint-hearted troops, nor should such a parent find his sons unworthy of him.

July 6th

St. Maria Goretti, Virgin & Martyr

From a homily at the canonization of St. Maria Goretti by Pope Pius XII

I have no fear, for you are with me

It is well known how this young girl had to face a bitter struggle with no way to defend herself. Without warning a vicious stranger burst upon her, bent on raping her and destroying her childlike purity. In that moment of crisis she could have spoken to her Redeemer in the words of that classic, *The Imitation of Christ:* "Though tested and plagued by a host of misfortunes, I have no fear so long as your grace is with me. It is my strength, stronger than any adversary; it helps me and gives me guidance." With splendid courage she surrendered herself to God and his grace and so gave her life to protect her virginity.

The life of this simple girl – I shall concern myself only with highlights – we can see as worthy of heaven. Even today people can look upon it with admiration and respect. Parents can learn from her story how to raise their God-given children in virtue, courage and holiness; they can learn to train them in the Catholic faith so that, when put to the test, God's grace will support them and they will come through undefeated, unscathed and untarnished.

From Maria's story carefree children and young people with their zest for life can learn not to be led astray by attractive pleasures which are not only ephemeral and empty but also sinful. Instead they can fix their sights on achieving Christian moral perfection, however difficult and hazardous that course may prove. With determination and God's help all of us can attain that goal by persistent effort and prayer.

Not all of us are expected to die a martyr's death, but we are all called to the pursuit of Christian virtue. This demands strength of character though it may not match that of this innocent girl. Still, a constant, persistent and relentless effort is asked of us right up to the moment of our death. This may be conceived as a slow steady martyrdom which Christ urged upon us when he said: *The kingdom of heaven is set upon and laid waste by violent forces*[Mt 11:12].

So let us all, with God's grace, strive to reach the goal that the example of the virgin martyr, Saint Maria Goretti, sets before us. Through her prayers to the Redeemer may all of us, each in his own way, joyfully try to follow the inspiring example of Maria Goretti who now enjoys eternal happiness in heaven.

July 11th

St. Benedict, Abbot

From the Rule of Benedict, Abbot

Put Christ before everything

Whenever you begin any good work you should first of all make a most pressing appeal to Christ our Lord to bring it to perfection; that he, who has honored us by counting us among his children, may never be grieved by our evil deeds. For we must always serve him with the good things he has given us in such a way that he may never – as an angry father disinherits his sons or even like a master who inspires fear – grow impatient with our sins and consign us to everlasting punishment, like wicked servants who would not follow him to glory.

So we should at long last rouse ourselves, prompted by the words of Scripture: *Now is the time for us to rise from sleep*[Rom 13:11-13]. Our eyes should be open to the God-given light, and we should listen in wonderment to the message of the divine voice as it daily cries out: *Today, if you shall hear his voice, harden not your hearts*[Heb 3:15]; and again: *If anyone has ears to hear, let him listen to what the Spirit is saying to the churches*[Rev 3:22]. And what does the Spirit say? *Come my sons, listen to me; I will teach you the fear of the Lord*[Ps 33:12]. *Hurry, while you have the light of life, so that death's darkness may not overtake youJn 12:35*.

And the Lord as he seeks the one who will do his work among the throng of people to whom he makes that appeal, says again: *Which of you wants to live to the full; who loves long life and the enjoyment of prosperity*[Ps 33:13-15]*?* And, if when you hear this you say, I do, God says to you: If you desire true and everlasting life, *keep your tongue from evil and your lips from deceit; turn away from evil and do good; seek peace and pursue it*[Ps 33:13-15]. And when you have done these things my eyes will be upon you and my ears will be attentive to your prayers; and before you call upon my name I shall say to you: Behold, *I am here*. What could be more delightful, dearest brothers, than the voice of our Lord's invitation to us? In his loving kindness he reveals to us the way of life.

And so, girded with faith and the performance of good works, let us follow in his paths by the guidance of the Gospel; then we shall deserve to see him *who has called us into his kingdom*[1 Thes 2:12]. If we wish to attain a dwelling-place in his kingdom we shall not reach it unless we hasten there by our good deeds.

Just as there exists an evil fervor, a bitter spirit, which divides us from God and leads us to hell, so there is a good fervor which sets us apart from evil inclinations and leads us toward God and eternal life. Monks should put this fervor into practice with an overflowing love: that is, they should *surpass each other in mutual esteem*[Phil 2:3], accept their weaknesses, either of body or of behavior, with the utmost patience; and vie with each other in acceding to requests. No one should follow what he considers to be good for himself, but rather what seems good for another. They should display brotherly love in a chaste manner; fear God in a spirit of love; revere their abbot with a genuine and submissive affection. Let them put Christ before all else; and may he lead us all to everlasting life.

July 13th

St. Henry

From the ancient Life of St. Henry

He provided the Church with the benefits of peace and tranquility

After the most blessed servant of God had been anointed king, he was not satisfied with the anxieties of his realm; so, in order to attain the crown of immortality, he determined to campaign for the King of all, for to serve him is to rule. Accordingly, he applied the utmost energy to the extension of religious worship and began to enrich the churches with property and to furnish them with extensive adornment. He reestablished the see of Bamberg in his own domain, dedicating it to Peter and Paul, the princes of the apostles, and to the most revered Saint George, the martyr; by a special law he submitted it to the holy Church of Rome, to pay the honor due by divine right to the first see and also to secure his foundation under Rome's patronage. But to show more clearly how carefully this holy man provided his church with the benefits of peace and tranquillity even after his death, we here include his letter of establishment.

"Henry, king by the preordained mercy of God, to all the sons of the Church, both future and present. By the most salutary instructions of sacred eloquence we are taught and advised to abandon temporal riches, to lay aside earthly goods, and to strive to reach the eternal and everlasting dwelling-places in heaven. For present glory is fleeting and meaningless, while it is possessed, unless in it we can glimpse something of heaven's eternity. But God's mercy toward the human race provided a useful remedy when he made the reward for earthly existence a share in our heavenly country.

"Therefore, not unmindful of this clemency and aware that by the gratuitous consideration of divine mercy we were raised up to a position of regal dignity, we think it fitting not only to enlarge the churches constructed by our ancestors, but for the greater glory of God to build new ones and to raise them up as the most grateful gifts of our devotion. Furthermore, not turning a deaf ear to the Lord's commandments and obediently following divine urgings, we desire to take the treasures of divine generosity bestowed on us by his bounty and store them in heaven, where thieves cannot dig them up or steal them and rust or moth may not destroy them. Moreover, when we reflect upon all that we have now stored up, our heart will be often drawn with longing and love.

"Accordingly we wish to make known to all the faithful that we have designated a portion of our paternal heritage called Babenberch to be raised to the dignity of an episcopal see so that there we ourselves and our parents may be held in glorious memory, and that the sacrifice of salvation may be offered constantly for all the faithful."

July 14th

St. Camillus de Lellis, Priest

From the life of St. Camillus, by his companion

Serving the Lord in the brethren

Let me begin with holy charity. It is the root of all the virtues and Camillus' most characteristic trait. I can attest that he was on fire with this holy virtue – not only toward God, but also toward his fellowmen, and especially toward the sick. The mere sight of the sick was enough to soften and melt his heart and make him utterly forget all the pleasures, enticements and interests of this world. When he was taking care of his patients, he seemed to spend and exhaust himself completely, so great was his devotion and compassion. He would have loved to take upon himself all their illness, their every affliction, could he but ease their pain and relieve their weakness.

In the sick he saw the person of Christ. His imagination was so vivid that, while feeding them, he perceived his patients as other Christ's. He would even beg of them the gift of forgiveness for his sins. His reverence in their presence was as great as if he were really and truly in the presence of his Lord. In his conversations he talked of nothing more often or with greater feeling than of holy charity. He would have liked to plant this virtue in every human heart.

To enkindle the enthusiasm of his religious brothers for this all-important virtue, he used to impress upon them the consoling words of Jesus Christ: *I was sick and you visited me*[Mt 25:36-40]. He seemed to have these words truly graven on his heart, so often did he say them over and over again.

Great and all-embracing was Camillus' charity. Not only the sick and dying, but every other needy or suffering human being found shelter in his deep and kind concern. Indeed, his heartfelt concern for the poor led him to say often: "If there were no poor people in the world, we should have to go below the earth to look for them and rescue them, to show them compassion and do them good!"

July 15th

St. Bonaventure, Bishop & Doctor

From the Journey of the Mind to God by St. Bonaventure, Bishop & Doctor

Mystical wisdom is revealed by the Holy Spirit

Christ is both the way and the door. Christ is the staircase and the vehicle, like the *throne of mercy over the Ark of the Covenant*[Ex 25:17; Heb 9:5], and *the mystery hidden from the ages*[Cor 1:26]. A man should turn his full attention to this throne of mercy, and should gaze at him hanging on the cross, full of faith, hope and charity, devoted, full of wonder and joy, marked by gratitude, and open to praise and jubilation. Then such a man will make with Christ a *pasch,* that is, a passing-over. Through the branches of the cross he will pass over the Red Sea, leaving Egypt and entering the desert. There he will taste the hidden manna, and rest with Christ in the sepulcher, as if he were dead to things outside. He will experience, as much as is possible for one who is still living, what was promised to the thief who hung beside Christ: *Today you will be with me in paradise*[Lk 23:43].

For this passover to be perfect, we must suspend all the operations of the mind and we must transform the peak of our affections, directing them to God alone. This is a sacred mystical experience. It cannot be comprehended by anyone unless he surrenders himself to it; nor can he surrender himself to it unless he longs for it; nor can he long for it unless the Holy Spirit, whom Christ sent into the world, should come and inflame his innermost soul. Hence the Apostle says that this mystical wisdom is revealed by the Holy Spirit.

If you ask how such things can occur, seek the answer in God's grace, not in doctrine; in the longing of t will, not in the understanding; in the sighs of prayer, not in research; seek the bridegroom not the teacher; God and not man; darkness not daylight; and look not to the light but rather to the raging fire that carries the soul to God with intense fervor and glowing love. The fire is God, and the furnace is in Jerusalem, fired by Christ in the ardor of his loving passion. Only he understood this who said: *My soul chose hanging and my bones death*[Job 7:15]. Anyone who cherishes this kind of death can see God, for it is certainly true that: *No man can look upon me and live*[Ex 33:20].

Let us die, then, and enter into the darkness, silencing our anxieties, our passions and all the fantasies of our imagination. Let us pass over with the crucified Christ *from this world to the Father*[Jn 16:28], so that, when the Father has shown himself to us, we can say with Philip: *It is enough*[Jn 14:8]. We may hear with Paul: *My grace is sufficient for you;* and we can rejoice with David, saying: *My flesh and my heart fail me, but God is the strength of my heart and my heritage for ever*[Ps 72:26]. *Blessed be the Lord for ever, and let all the people say: Amen. Amen*[Ps 105:47-48]*!*

July 16th

Our Lady of Mount Carmel

From a sermon by St. Leo the Great, Pope & Doctor

Mary conceived in her soul before she conceived in her body

A royal virgin of the house of David is chosen. She is to bear a holy child, one who is both God and man. She is to conceive him in her soul before she conceives him in her body. In the face of so unheard of an event she is to know no fear through ignorance of the divine plan; the angel tells her what is to be accomplished in her by the Holy Spirit. She believes that there will be no loss of virginity, she who is soon to be the mother of God. Why should she lose heart at this new form of conceiving when she has been promised that it will be effected through the power of the Most High? She believes, and her faith is confirmed by the witness of a previous wonder: against all expectation Elizabeth is made fruitful. God has enabled a barren woman to be with child; he must be believed when he makes the same promise to a virgin.

The son of God who was *in the beginning with God, through whom all things were made, without whom nothing was made*[Jn 1:1-3], became man to free him from eternal death. He stooped down to take up our lowliness without loss to his own glory. He remained what he was; he took up what he was not. He wanted to join the very nature of a servant to that nature in which he is equal to God the Father. He wanted to unite both natures in an alliance so wonderful that the glory of the greater would not annihilate the lesser, nor the taking up of the lower diminish the greatness of the higher.

What belongs to each nature is preserved intact and meets the other in one person: lowliness is taken up by greatness, weakness by power, mortality by eternity. To pay the debt of our human condition, a nature incapable of suffering is united to a nature capable of suffering, and true God and true man are forged into the unity that is the Lord. This was done to make possible the kind of remedy that fitted our human need: *one* and the same *mediator between God and men*[1 Tim 2:5] able to die because of one nature, able to rise again because of the other. It was fitting, therefore, that the birth which brings salvation brought no corruption to virginal integrity; the bringing forth of Truth was at the same time the safeguarding of virginity.

Dearly beloved, this kind of birth was fitting for Christ, the power and the wisdom of God: a birth in which he was one with us in our human nature but far above us in his divinity. If he were not true God, he would not be able to bring us healing; if he were not true man, he would not be able to give us an example.

And so at the birth of our Lord, the angels sing in joy: *Glory to God in the highest*, and they proclaim *peace to his people on earth*[Lk 2:14] as they see the heavenly Jerusalem being built from all the nations of the world. If the angels on high are so exultant at this marvelous work of God's goodness, what joy should it not bring to the lowly hearts of men?

July 21st

St Lawrence of Brindisi, Priest & Doctor

From a sermon by Saint Lawrence of Brindisi, Priest & Doctor

Preaching is an apostolic duty

There is a spiritual life that we share with the angels of heaven and with the divine spirits, for like them we have been formed in the image and likeness of God. The bread that is necessary for living this life is the grace of the Holy Spirit and the love of God. But grace and love are nothing without faith, since without faith it is impossible to please God. And faith is not conceived unless the word of God is preached. *Faith comes through hearing, and what is heard is the word of Christ*[Rom 10:17]. The preaching of the word of God, then, is necessary for the spiritual life, just as the planting of seed is necessary for bodily life.

Christ says: *The sower went out to sow his seed*[Lk 8:5-15]. The sower goes out as a herald of justice. On some occasions we read that the herald was God, for example, when with a living voice from heaven he gave the law of justice to a whole people in the desert.

On other occasions, the herald was an angel of the Lord, as when he accused the people of transgressing the divine law at Bochim, in the place of weeping. At this all the sons of Israel, when they heard the angel's address, became sorrowful in their hearts, lifted up their voices, and wept bitterly. Then again, Moses preached the law of the Lord to the whole people on the plains of Moab, as we read in Deuteronomy. Finally, Christ came as God and man to preach the word of the Lord, and for the same purpose he sent the apostles, just as he had sent the prophets before them.

Preaching, therefore, is a duty that is apostolic, angelic, Christian, divine. The word of God is replete with manifold blessings, since it is, so to speak, a treasure of all goods. It is the source of faith, hope, charity, all virtues, all the gifts of the Holy Spirit, all the beatitudes of the Gospel, all good works, all the rewards of life, all the glory of paradise: *Welcome the word that has taken root in you, with its power to save you*[Jas 1:21].

For the word of God is a light to the mind and a fire to the will. It enables man to know God and to love him. And for the interior man who lives by the Spirit of God through grace, it is bread and water, but a bread sweeter than honey and the honeycomb, a water better than wine and milk. For the soul it is a spiritual treasure of merits yielding an abundance of gold and precious stones. Against the hardness of a heart that persists in wrongdoing, it acts as a hammer. Against the world, the flesh and the devil it serves as a sword that destroys all sin.

July 22nd

St. Mary Magdalene

From a homily on the Gospels by St. Gregory the Great, Pope & Doctor

She longed for Christ, though she thought he had been taken away

When Mary Magdalene came to the tomb and did not find the Lord's body, she thought it had been taken away and so informed the disciples. After they came and saw the tomb, they too believed what Mary had told them. The text then says: *The disciples went back home*[Jn 20:10-11], and it adds: *but Mary wept and remained standing outside the tomb* [Jn 20:10-11].

We should reflect on Mary's attitude and the great love she felt for Christ; for though the disciples had left the tomb, she remained. She was still seeking the one she had not found, and while she sought she wept; burning with the fire of love, she longed for him who she thought had been taken away. And so it happened that the woman who stayed behind to seek Christ was the only one to see him. For perseverance is essential to any good deed, as the voice of truth tells us: *Whoever perseveres to the end will be saved*[Mt 24:13].

At first she sought but did not find, but when she persevered it happened that she found what she was looking for. When our desires are not satisfied, they grow stronger, and becoming stronger they take hold of their object. Holy desires likewise grow with anticipation, and if they do not grow they are not really desires. Anyone who succeeds in attaining the truth has burned with such a love. As David says: *My soul has thirsted for the living God; when shall I come and appear before the face of God*[Ps 41:2-4]? And so also in the Song of Songs the Church says: *I was wounded by love;* and again: *My soul is melted with love.*

Woman, why are you weeping? Whom do you seek [Jn 20:15]? She is asked why she is sorrowing so that her desire might be strengthened; for when she mentions whom she is seeking, her love is kindled all the more ardently.

Jesus says to her: Mary [Jn 20:16]. Jesus is not recognized when he calls her "woman"; so he calls her by name, as though he were saying: Recognize me as I recognize you; for I do not know you as I know others; I know you as yourself. And so Mary, once addressed by name, recognizes who is speaking. She immediately calls him *rabboni,* that is to say, *teacher,* because the one whom she sought outwardly was the one who inwardly taught her to keep on searching.

July 23rd

St. Bridget

From the prayers attributed to St. Bridget

A prayer to Christ our Savior

Blessed are you, my Lord Jesus Christ. You foretold your death and at the Last Supper you marvelously consecrated bread which became your precious body. And then you gave it to your apostles out of love as a memorial of your most holy passion. By washing their feet with your holy hands, you gave them a supreme example of your deep humility.

Honor be to you, my Lord Jesus Christ. Fearing your passion and death, you poured forth blood from your innocent body like sweat, and still you accomplished our redemption as you desired and gave us the clearest proof of your love for all men. Blessed may you be, my Lord Jesus Christ. After you had been led to Caiaphas, you, the judge of all men, humbly allowed yourself to be handed over to the judgment of Pilate. Glory be to you, my Lord Jesus Christ, for the mockery you endured when you stood clothed in purple and wearing a crown of sharp thorns. With utmost endurance you allowed vicious men to spit upon your glorious face, blindfold you and beat your cheek and neck with cruelest blows. Praise be to you, my Lord Jesus Christ. For with the greatest patience you allowed yourself like an innocent lamb to be bound to a pillar and mercilessly scourged, and then to be brought, covered with blood, before the judgment seat of Pilate to be gazed upon by all. Honor be to you, my Lord Jesus Christ. For after your glorious body was covered with blood, you were condemned to death on the cross, you endured the pain of carrying the cross on your sacred shoulders, and you were led with curses to the place where you were to suffer. Then stripped of your garments, you allowed yourself to be nailed to the wood of the cross. Everlasting honor be to you, Lord Jesus Christ. You allowed your most holy mother to suffer so much, even though she had never sinned nor ever even consented to the smallest sin. Humbly you looked down upon her with your gentle loving eyes, and to comfort her you entrusted her to the faithful care of your disciple. Eternal blessing be yours, my Lord Jesus Christ, because in your last agony you held out to all sinners the hope of pardon, when in your mercy you promised the glory of paradise to the penitent thief.

Eternal praise be to you, my Lord Jesus Christ, for the time you endured on the cross the greatest torments and sufferings for us sinners. The sharp pain of your wounds fiercely penetrated even to your blessed soul and cruelly pierced your most sacred heart till finally you sent forth your spirit in peace, bowed your head, and humbly commended yourself into the hands of God your Father, and your whole body remained cold in death.

Blessed may you be, my Lord Jesus Christ. You redeemed our souls with your precious blood and most holy death, and in your mercy you led them from exile back to eternal life.

Blessed may you be, my Lord Jesus Christ. For our salvation you allowed your side and heart to be pierced with a lance; and from that side water and your precious blood flowed out abundantly for our redemption.

Glory be to you, my Lord Jesus Christ. You allowed your blessed body to be taken down from the cross by your friends and laid in the arms of your most sorrowing mother, and you let her wrap your body in a shroud and bury it in a tomb to be guarded by soldiers.

Unending honor be to you, my Lord Jesus Christ. On the third day you rose from the dead and appeared to those you had chosen. And after forty days you ascended into heaven before the eyes of many witnesses, and there in heaven you gathered together in glory those you love, whom you had freed from hell.

Rejoicing and eternal praise be to you, my Lord Jesus Christ, who sent the Holy Spirit into the hearts of your disciples and increased the boundless love of God in their spirits.

Blessed are you and praiseworthy and glorious for ever, my Lord Jesus. You sit upon your throne in your kingdom of heaven, in the glory of your divinity, living in the most holy body you took from a virgin's flesh. So will you appear on that last day to judge the souls of all the living and the dead; you who live and reign with the Father and the Holy Spirit for ever and ever. Amen.

July 25th

St. James, Apostle

From a homily on Matthew by St. John Chrysostom, Bishop & Doctor

Sharers in the suffering of Christ

The sons of Zebedee press Christ: *Promise that one may sit at your right side and the other at your left*[Mt 20:21-24]. What does he do? He wants to show them that it is not a spiritual gift for which they are asking, and that if they knew what their request involved, they would never dare make it. So he says: *You do not know what you are asking* [Mt 20:21-24], that is, what a great and splendid thing it is and how much beyond the reach even of the heavenly powers. Then he continues: *Can you drink the cup which I must drink and be baptized with the baptism which I must undergo* [Mt 20:21-24]? He is saying: "You talk of sharing honors and rewards with me, but I must talk of struggle and toil. Now is not the time for rewards or the time for my glory to be revealed. Earthly life is the time for bloodshed, war and danger."

Consider how by his manner of questioning he exhorts and draws them. He does not say: "Can you face being slaughtered? Can you shed your blood?" How does he put his question? *Can you drink the cup?* Then he makes it attractive by adding: *which I must drink*, so that the prospect of sharing it with him may make them more eager. He also calls his suffering a baptism, to show that it will effect a great cleansing of the entire world. The disciples answer him: *We can!* Fervor makes them answer promptly, though they really do not know what they are saying but still think they will receive what they ask for.

How does Christ reply? *You will indeed drink my cup and be baptized with my baptism* [Mt 20:21-24]. He is really prophesying a great blessing for them, since he is telling them: "You will be found worthy of martyrdom; you will suffer what I suffer and end your life with a violent death, thus sharing all with me. *But seats at my right and left side are not mine to give; they belong to those for whom the Father has prepared them* [Mt 20:21-24]." Thus, after lifting their minds to higher goals and preparing them to meet and overcome all that will make them desolate, he sets them straight on their request.

Then the other ten became angry at the two brothers [Mt 20:21-24]. See how imperfect they all are: the two who tried to get ahead of the other ten, and the ten who were jealous of the two! But, as I said before, show them to me at a later date in their lives, and you will see that all these impulses and feelings have disappeared. Read how John, the very man who here asks for the first place, will always yield to Peter when it comes to preaching and performing miracles in the Acts of the Apostles. James, for his part, was not to live very much longer; for from the beginning he was inspired by great fervor and, setting aside all purely human goals, rose to such splendid heights that he straightway suffered martyrdom.

July 26th

Saints Joachim and Ann, Parents of Mary

From a sermon by St. John Damascene, Bishop & Doctor

By their fruits you will know them

Ann was to be the mother of the Virgin Mother of God, and hence nature did not dare to anticipate the flowering of grace. Thus nature remained sterile, until grace produced its fruit. For she who was to be born had to be a first-born daughter, since she would be the mother of the first-born of all creation, *in whom all things are held together*[Col 1:17].

Joachim and Ann, how blessed a couple! All creation is indebted to you. For at your hands the Creator was offered a gift excelling all other gifts: a chaste mother, who alone was worthy of him.

And so rejoice, Ann, that *you were sterile and have not borne children; break forth into shouts, you who have not given birth*[Isa 54:1]. Rejoice, Joachim, because from your daughter *a child is born for us, a son is given us, whose name is Messenger of great counsel and universal salvation, mighty God*[Isa 9:6; Mt 1:18-25]. For this child is God.

Joachim and Ann, how blessed and spotless a couple! You will be known by the fruit you have borne, as the Lord says: *By their fruits you will know them*[Mt 7:15-20]. The conduct of your life pleased God and was worthy of your daughter. For by the chaste and holy life you led together, you have fashioned a jewel of virginity: she who remained a virgin before, during and after giving birth. She alone for all time would maintain her virginity in mind and soul as well as in body.

Joachim and Ann, how chaste a couple! While safeguarding the chastity prescribed by the law of nature, you achieved with God's help something which transcends nature in giving the world the Virgin Mother of God as your daughter. While leading a devout and holy life in your human nature, you gave birth to a daughter nobler than the angels, whose queen she now is. Girl of utter beauty and delight, daughter of Adam and mother of God, blessed the loins and blessed the womb from which you come! Blessed the arms that carried you, and blessed your parents' lips, which you were allowed to cover with chaste kisses, ever maintaining your virginity. *Rejoice in God, all the earth. Sing, exult and sing hymns*[Ps 95:11]. Raise your voice, raise it and be not afraid.

July 29th

St. Martha

From a sermon by St. Augustine, Bishop & Doctor

Blessed are they who deserved to receive Christ in their homes

Our Lord's words teach us that though we labor among the many distractions of this world, we should have but one goal. For we are but travelers on a journey without as yet a fixed abode; we are on our way, not yet in our native land; we are in a state of longing, not yet of enjoyment. But let us continue on our way, and continue without sloth or respite, so that we may ultimately arrive at our destination.

Martha and Mary were sisters, related not only by blood but also by religious aspirations. They stayed close to our Lord and both served him harmoniously when he was among them. Martha welcomed him as travelers are welcomed. But in her case, the maidservant received her Lord, the invalid her Savior, the creature her Creator, to serve him bodily food while she was to be fed by the Spirit. For the Lord willed to put on the form of a slave, and under this form to be fed by his own servants, out of condescension and not out of need. For this was indeed condescension, to present himself to be fed; since he was in the flesh he would in fact be hungry and thirsty.

Thus was the Lord received as a guest who *came unto his own and his own received him not; but as many as received him, he gave them the power to become sons of God*[Jn 1:11-13], adopting those who were servants and making them his brothers, ransoming the captives and making them his coheirs. No one of you should say: "Blessed are they who have deserved to receive Christ into their homes!" Do not grieve or complain that you were born in a time when you can no longer see God in the flesh. He did not in fact take this privilege from you. As he says: *Whatever you have done to the least of my brothers, you did to me*[Mt 25:40-45].

But you, Martha, if I may say so, are blessed for your good service, and for your labors you seek the reward of peace. Now you are much occupied in nourishing the body, admittedly a holy one. But when you come to the heavenly homeland will you find a traveler to welcome, someone hungry to feed, or thirsty to whom you may give drink, someone ill whom you could visit, or quarrelling whom you could reconcile, or dead whom you could bury?

No, there will be none of these tasks there. What you will find there is what Mary chose. There we shall not feed others, we ourselves shall be fed. Thus what Mary chose in this life will be realized there in all its fullness; she was gathering fragments from that rich banquet, the Word of God. Do you wish to know what we will have there? The Lord himself tells us when he says of his servants, *Amen, I say to you, he will make them recline and passing he will serve them*[Lk 12:37].

July 30th

St. Peter Chrysologus, Bishop & Doctor

From a sermon by St. Peter Chrysologus, Bishop & Doctor

The sacrament of Christ's incarnation

A virgin conceived, bore a son, and yet remained a virgin. This is no common occurrence, but a sign; no reason here, but God's power, for he is the cause, and not nature. It is a special event, not shared by others; it is divine, not human. Christ's birth was not necessity, but an expression of omnipotence, a sacrament of piety for the redemption of men. He who made man without generation from pure clay made man again and was born from a pure body. The hand that assumed clay to make our flesh deigned to assume a body for our salvation. That the Creator is in his creature and God is in the flesh brings dignity to man without dishonor to him who made him.

Why then, man, are you so worthless in your own eyes and yet so precious to God? Why render yourself such dishonor when you are honored by him? Why do you ask how you were created and do not seek to know why you were made?

Was not this entire visible universe made for your dwelling? It was for you that the light dispelled the overshadowing gloom; for your sake was the night regulated and the day measured, and for you were the heavens embellished with varying brilliance of the sun, the moon and the stars. The earth was adorned with flowers, groves and fruit; and the constant marvelous variety of lovely living things was created in the air, the fields, and the seas for you, lest sad solitude destroy the joy of God's new creation. And the Creator still works to devise things that can add to your glory. He has made you in his image that you might in your person make the invisible Creator present on earth; he has made you his legate, so that the vast empire of the world might have the Lord's representative. Then in his mercy God assumed what he made in you; he wanted now to be truly manifest in man, just as he had wished to be revealed in man as in an image. Now he would be in reality what he had submitted to be in symbol.

And so Christ is born that by his birth he might restore our nature. He became a child, was fed, and grew that he might inaugurate the one perfect age to remain for ever as he created it. He supports man that man might no longer fall. And the creature he had formed of earth he now makes heavenly; and what he had endowed with a human soul he now vivifies to become a heavenly spirit. In this way he fully raised man to God, and left in him neither sin, nor death, nor travail, nor pain, nor anything earthly, with the grace of our Lord Christ Jesus, who lives and reigns with the Father in the unity of the Holy Spirit, now and for ever, for all the ages of eternity. Amen.

July 31st

St. Ignatius of Loyola, Priest

From the life of St. Ignatius from his own words by Luis Gonzalez

Put inward experiences to the test to see if they come from God

Ignatius was passionately fond of worldly books of fiction and tales of knight-errantry. When he felt he was getting better, he asked for some of these books to pass the time. But no book of that sort could be found in the house; instead they gave him a life of Christ and a collection of the lives of saints written in Spanish.

By constantly these books he began to be attracted to what he found narrated there. Sometimes in the midst of his he would reflect on what he had read. Yet at other times he would dwell on many of the things which he had been accustomed to dwell on previously. But at this point our Lord came to his assistance, insuring that these thoughts were followed by others which arose from his current .

While the life of Christ our Lord or the lives of the saints, he would reflect and reason with himself: "What if I should do what Saint Francis or Saint Dominic did?" In this way he let his mind dwell on many thoughts; they lasted a while until other things took their place. Then those vain and worldly images would come into his mind and remain a long time. This sequence of thoughts persisted with him for a long time.

But there was a difference. When Ignatius reflected on worldly thoughts, he felt intense pleasure; but when he gave them up out of weariness, he felt dry and depressed. Yet when he thought of living the rigorous sort of life he knew the saints had lived, he not only experienced pleasure when he actually thought about it, but even after he dismissed these thoughts, he still experienced great joy. Yet he did not pay attention to this, nor did he appreciate it until one day, in a moment of insight, he began to marvel at the difference. Then he understood his experience: thoughts of one kind left him sad, the others full of joy. And this was the first time he applied a process of reasoning to his religious experience. Later on, when he began to formulate his spiritual exercises, he used this experience as an illustration to explain the doctrine he taught his disciples on the discernment of spirits.

August 1st

St. Alphonsus Liguori, Bishop & Doctor

From a sermon by St. Alphonsus Liguori, Bishop & Doctor

On the love of Christ

All holiness and perfection of soul lies in our love for Jesus Christ our God, who is our Redeemer and our supreme good. It is part of the love of God to acquire and to nurture all the virtues which make a man perfect.

Has not God in fact won for himself a claim on all our love? From all eternity he has loved us. And it is in this vein that he speaks to us: "O man, consider carefully that I first loved you. You had not yet appeared in the light of day, nor did the world yet exist, but already I loved you. From all eternity I have loved you."

Since God knew that man is enticed by favors, he wished to bind him to his love by means of his gifts: "I want to catch men with the snares, those chains of love in which they allow themselves to be entrapped, so that they will love me." And all the gifts which he bestowed on man were given to this end. He gave him a soul, made in his likeness, and endowed with memory, intellect and will; he gave him a body equipped with the senses; it was for him that he created heaven and earth and such an abundance of things. He made all these things out of love for man, so that all creation might serve man, and man in turn might love God out of gratitude for so many gifts.

But he did not wish to give us only beautiful creatures; the truth is that to win for himself our love, he went so far as to bestow upon us the fullness of himself. The eternal Father went so far as to give us his only Son. When he saw that we were all dead through sin and deprived of his grace, what did he do? Compelled, as the Apostle says, by the superabundance of his love for us, he sent his beloved Son to make reparation for us and to call us back to a sinless life.

By giving us his Son, whom he did not spare precisely so that he might spare us, he bestowed on us at once every good: grace, love and heaven; for all these goods are certainly inferior to the Son: *He who did not spare his own Son, but handed him over for all of us; how could he fail to give us along with his Son all good things*[Rom 8:32]*?*

August 2nd

St. Eusebius of Vercelli, Bishop

From a letter by St. Eusebius of Vercelli, Bishop

I have run the race; I have kept the faith

Dearly beloved, I know now that you are safe, as I was hoping, and I felt that I had paid you a visit, by being suddenly transported over the face of the earth like Habakkuk, when the angel brought him to Daniel. When I receive a letter from one of you and see in your writings your goodness and love, joy mingles with tears, and my desire to continue is checked by my weeping. Both emotions are inescapable, as they vie with each other in discharging their duty of affection, when such a letter satisfies my longing for you.

Days pass in this way as I imagine myself in conversation with you, and so I forget my past sufferings. Consolations surround me on all sides: your firm faith, your love, your good works. In the midst of so many great blessings I soon imagine myself in your company, in exile no longer.

Dearly beloved, I rejoice in your faith, in the salvation that comes from faith, in your good works, which are not confined to your own surroundings but spread far and wide. Like a farmer tending a sound tree, untouched by ax or fire because of its fruit, I want not only to serve you in the body, good people that you are, but also to give my life for your well-being.

Somehow or other I have managed with difficulty to complete this letter. I asked God constantly to keep the guards away hour by hour, and to allow the deacon to bring you some kind of greeting in writing, not simply news of my suffering. So I beg you to keep the faith with all vigilance, to preserve harmony, to be earnest in prayer, to remember me always, so that the Lord may grant freedom to his Church which is suffering throughout the world, and that I may be set free from the sufferings that weigh upon me, and so be able to rejoice with you.

I also ask and beseech you in God's mercy, that each one of you should add his own name to the greeting in this letter. Of necessity I cannot write to each of you as was my custom. So in this letter I ask you all – brothers and holy sisters, sons and daughters, men and women, old and young – to be content with this greeting and to be good enough to give my respectful good wishes to those who are outside the community and are kind enough to be my friends.

August 4th

St. John Mary Vianney, Priest

From the catechetical instructions by St. John Mary Vianney, Priest

The glorious duty of man: to pray and to love

My little children, reflect on these words: the Christian's treasure is not on earth but in heaven. Our thoughts, then, ought to be directed to where our treasure is. This is the glorious duty of man: to pray and to love. If you pray and love, that is where a man's happiness lies.

Prayer is nothing else but union with God. When one has a heart that is pure and united with God, he is given a kind of serenity and sweetness that makes him ecstatic, a light that surrounds him with marvelous brightness. In this intimate union, God and the soul are fused together like two bits of wax that no one can ever pull apart. This union of God with a tiny creature is a lovely thing. It is a happiness beyond understanding.

We had become unworthy to pray, but God in his goodness allowed us to speak with him. Our prayer is incense that gives him the greatest pleasure.

My little children, your hearts are small, but prayer stretches them and makes them capable of loving God. Through prayer we receive a foretaste of heaven and something of paradise comes down upon us. Prayer never leaves us without sweetness. It is honey that flows into the soul and makes all things sweet. When we pray properly, sorrows disappear like snow before the sun.

Prayer also makes time pass very quickly and with such great delight that one does not notice its length. Listen: Once when I was a purveyor in Bresse and most of my companions were ill, I had to make a long journey. I prayed to the good God, and, believe me, the time did not seem long.

Some men immerse themselves as deeply in prayer as fish in water, because they give themselves totally to God. There is no division in their hearts. O, how I love these noble souls! Saint Francis of Assisi and Saint Colette used to see our Lord and talk to him just as we talk to one another.

How unlike them we are! How often we come to church with no idea of what to do or what to ask for. And yet, whenever we go to any human being, we know well enough why we go. And still worse, there are some who seem to speak to the good God like this: "I will only say a couple of things to you, and then I will be rid of you." I often think that when we come to adore the Lord, we would receive everything we ask for, if we would ask with living faith and with a pure heart.

August 5th

Dedication of St. Mary Major

From a homily delivered at the Council of Ephesus by St. Cyril of Alexandria, Bishop & Doctor

In praise of Mary, Mother of God

I see here a joyful company of Christian men met together in ready response to the call of Mary, the holy and ever-virgin Mother of God. The great grief that weighed upon me is changed into joy by your presence, venerable Fathers. Now the beautiful saying of David the psalmist: *How good and pleasant it is for brothers to live together in unity*[Ps 132:1], has come true for us.

Therefore, holy and incomprehensible Trinity, we salute you at whose summons we have come together to this church of Mary, the Mother of God.

Mary, Mother of God, we salute you. Precious vessel, worthy of the whole world's reverence, you are an ever-shining light, the crown of virginity, the symbol of orthodoxy, an indestructible temple, the place that held him whom no place can contain, mother and virgin. Because of you the holy gospels could say: *Blessed is he who comes in the name of the Lord*[Ps 117:26;Lk 13:35].

We salute you, for in your holy womb he, who is beyond all limitation, was confined. Because of you the holy Trinity is glorified and adored; the cross is called precious and is venerated throughout the world; the heavens exult; the angels and archangels make merry; demons are put to flight; the devil, that tempter, is thrust down from heaven; the fallen race of man is taken up on high; all creatures possessed by the madness of idolatry have attained knowledge of the truth; believers receive holy baptism; the oil of gladness is poured out; the Church is established throughout the world; pagans are brought to repentance.

What more is there to say? Because of you the light of the only-begotten Son of God has shone upon those who sat in darkness and in the shadow of death; prophets pronounced the word of God; the apostles preached salvation to the Gentiles; the dead are raised to life, and kings rule by the power of the holy Trinity.

Who can put Mary's high honor into words? She is both mother and virgin. I am overwhelmed by the wonder of this miracle. Of course no one could be prevented from living in the house he had built for himself, yet who would invite mockery by asking his own servant to become his mother?

Behold then the joy of the whole universe. Let the union of God and man in the Son of the Virgin Mary fill us with awe and adoration. Let us fear and worship the undivided Trinity as we sing the praise of the ever-virgin Mary, the holy temple of God, and of God himself, her Son and spotless Bridegroom. To him be glory for ever and ever. Amen.

August 6th

The Transfiguration of the Lord

From a sermon on the transfiguration of the Lord by Anastasius of Sinai, Bishop

It is good for us to be here

Upon Mount Tabor, Jesus revealed to his disciples a heavenly mystery. While living among them he had spoken of the kingdom and of his second coming in glory, but to banish from their hearts any possible doubt concerning the kingdom and to confirm their faith in what lay in the future by its prefiguration in the present, he gave them on Mount Tabor a wonderful vision of his glory, a foreshadowing of the kingdom of heaven. It was as if he said to them: "As time goes by you may be in danger of losing your faith. To save you from this I tell you now that *some standing here* listening to me *will not taste death until they have seen the Son of Man coming*[Mt 16:28] in the glory of his Father." Moreover, in order to assure us that Christ could command such power when he wished, the evangelist continues: *Six days later, Jesus took with him Peter, James and John, and led them up a high mountain where they were alone. There, before their eyes, he was transfigured. His face shone like the sun, and his clothes became as white as light. Then the disciples saw Moses and Elijah appear, and they were talking to Jesus*[Mt 17:1-6].

These are the divine wonders we celebrate today; this is the saving revelation given us upon the mountain; this is the festival of Christ that has drawn us here. Let us listen, then, to the sacred voice of God so compellingly calling us from on high, from the summit of the mountain, so that with the Lord's chosen disciples we may penetrate the deep meaning of these holy mysteries, so far beyond our capacity to express. Jesus goes before us to show us the way, both up the mountain and into heaven, and – I speak boldly – it is for us now to follow him with all speed, yearning for the heavenly vision that will give us a share in his radiance, renew our spiritual nature and transform us into his own likeness, making us for ever sharers in his Godhead and raising us to heights as yet undreamed of.

Let us run with confidence and joy to enter into the cloud like Moses and Elijah, or like James and John. Let us be caught up like Peter to behold the divine vision and to be transfigured by that glorious transfiguration. Let us retire from the world, stand aloof from the earth, rise above the body, detach ourselves from creatures and turn to the Creator, to whom Peter in ecstasy exclaimed: *Lord, it is good for us to be here*[Mt 17:4].

It is indeed good to be here, as you have said, Peter. It is good to be with Jesus and to remain here for ever. What greater happiness or higher honor could we have than to be with God, to be made like him and to live in his light?

Therefore, since each of us possesses God in his heart and is being transformed into his divine image, we also should cry out with joy: *It is good for us to be here*[Mt 17:4] – here where all things shine with divine radiance, where there is joy and gladness and exultation; where there is nothing in our hearts but peace, serenity and stillness; where God is seen. For here, in our hearts, Christ takes up his abode together with the Father, saying as he enters: *Today salvation has come to this house*[Lk 19:1-9]. With Christ, our hearts receive all the wealth of his eternal blessings, and there where they are stored up for us in him, we see reflected as in a mirror both the firstfruits and the whole of the world to come.

August 7th

St. Sixtus II, Pope & Martyr, and Companions, Martyrs

From a letter by St. Cyprian, Bishop & Martyr

We know that the soldiers of Christ are not slain but crowned

I did not write to your community at once, dearest brother, because all the clergy, exposed as they are to the imminent danger of being put to the test and prepared in a spirit of dedication for the divine glory of heaven, were quite unable to leave here. But you must know that the messengers whom I dispatched to Rome have now returned. I sent them to find out the truth and report back whatever may have been decreed in our regard, for many conflicting and unreliable rumors are current.

The true state of affairs is this. Valerian has issued an edict to the Senate to the effect that bishops, presbyters and deacons shall suffer the death penalty without delay. Senators, distinguished men and members of the equestrian class, are to be deprived of their rank and property, and if, after forfeiting their wealth and privileges, they still persist in professing Christianity, they too are to be sentenced to death. Ladies of the upper classes are to be deprived of their property and exiled. In the case of members of the imperial staff, any who have either previously confessed or do now confess to being Christians shall have their property confiscated and shall be assigned as prisoners to the imperial estates.

To this decree the Emperor Valerian attached a copy of the letter he had sent to the provincial governors concerning us. Every day we are hoping that this letter will arrive, for we are standing firm in faith and ready to endure suffering, in expectation of winning the crown of eternal life through the help and mercy of the Lord. I must also inform you that Sixtus was put to death in a catacomb on the sixth of August, and four deacons with him. Moreover, the prefects in Rome are pressing this persecution zealously and without intermission, to such a point that anyone brought before them is punished and his property is claimed by the treasury.

I ask you to make these facts known to the rest of our fellow bishops, in order that by the exhortation of their pastors the brethren everywhere may be strengthened and prepared for the spiritual combat. Let all our people fix their minds not on death but rather on immortality; let them commit themselves to the Lord in complete faith and unflinching courage and make their confession with joy rather than in fear, knowing that in this contest the soldiers of God and Christ are not slain but rather win their crowns.

Farewell in the Lord, dearest brother.

August 7th

St. Cajetan, Priest

From a letter by St. Cajetan, priest

Christ dwells in our hearts by faith

I am a sinner and do not think much of myself; I have recourse to the greatest servants of the Lord, that they may pray for you to the blessed Christ and his Mother. But do not forget that all the saints can not endear you to Christ as much as you can yourself. It is entirely up to you. If you want Christ to love you and help you, you must love him and always make an effort to please him. Do not waver in your purpose, because even if all the saints and every single creature should abandon you, he will always be near you, whatever your needs.

You know, of course, that we are pilgrims in this world, on a journey to our true home in heaven. The man who becomes proud loses his way and rushes to death. While living here we should strive to gain eternal life. Yet of ourselves we cannot achieve this since we have lost it through sin; but Jesus Christ has recovered it for us. For this reason we must always be grateful to him and love him. We must always obey him, and as far as possible remain united with him.

He has offered himself to be our food. How wretched is the man who knows nothing of such a gift! To us has been given the opportunity to receive Christ, son of the Virgin Mary, and we refuse him. Woe to the man who does not care enough to receive him. My daughter, I want what is good for myself; I beg the same for you. Now there is no other way to bring this about than to ask the Virgin Mary constantly to come to you with her glorious Son. Be bold! Ask her to give you her Son, who in the blessed sacrament of the altar is truly the food of your soul. Readily will she give him to you, still more readily will he come to you, giving you the strength to make your way fearlessly through this dark wood. In it large numbers of our enemies lie in wait, but they cannot reach us if they see us relying on such powerful help.

Nor, my child, must you receive Jesus Christ simply as a means to further your own plans; I want you to surrender to him, that he may welcome you and, as your divine Savior, do to you and in you whatever he wills. This is what I want, this is what I beg of you, this, as far as I can, is what I compel you to do.

August 8th

St. Dominic, Priest

From various writings on the history of the Order of Preachers

He spoke with God or about God

Dominic possessed such great integrity and was so strongly motivated by divine love, that without a doubt he proved to be a bearer of honor and grace. He was a man of great equanimity, except when moved to compassion and mercy. And since a joyful heart animates the face, he displayed the peaceful composure of a spiritual man in the kindness he manifested outwardly and by the cheerfulness of his countenance.

Wherever he went he showed himself in word and deed to be a man of the Gospel. During the day no one was more community-minded or pleasant toward his brothers and associates. During the night hours no one was more persistent in every kind of vigil and supplication. He seldom spoke unless it was with God, that is, in prayer, or about God; and in this matter he instructed his brothers.

Frequently he made a special personal petition that God would deign to grant him a genuine charity, effective in caring for and obtaining the salvation of men. For he believed that only then would he be truly a member of Christ, when he had given himself totally for the salvation of men, just as the Lord Jesus, the Savior of all, had offered himself completely for our salvation. So, for this work, after a lengthy period of careful and provident planning, he founded the Order of Friars Preachers.

In his conversations and letters he often urged the brothers of the Order to study constantly the Old and New Testaments. He always carried with him the gospel according to Matthew and the epistles of Paul, and so well did he study them that he almost knew them from memory.

Two or three times he was chosen bishop, but he always refused, preferring to live with his brothers in poverty. Throughout his life, he preserved the honor of his virginity. He desired to be scourged and cut to pieces, and so die for the faith of Christ. Of him Pope Gregory IX declared: "I knew him as a steadfast follower of the apostolic way of life. There is no doubt that he is in heaven, sharing in the glory of the apostles themselves."

August 10th

St. Lawrence, Deacon & Martyr

From a sermon by St. Augustine, Bishop & Doctor

He ministered the sacred blood of Christ

The Roman Church commends to us today the anniversary of the triumph of Saint Lawrence. For on this day he trod the furious pagan world underfoot and flung aside its allurements, and so gained victory over Satan's attack on his faith.

As you have often heard, Lawrence was a deacon of the Church at Rome. There he ministered the sacred blood of Christ; there for the sake of Christ's name he poured out his own blood. Saint John the apostle was evidently teaching us about the mystery of the Lord's supper when he wrote: *Just as Christ laid down his life for us, so we ought to lay down our lives for the brethren*[1 Jn 3:16]. My brethren, Lawrence understood this and, understanding, he acted on it. Just as he had partaken of a gift of self at the table of the Lord, so he prepared to offer such a gift. In his life he loved Christ; in his death he followed in his footsteps.

Brethren, we too must imitate Christ if we truly love him. We shall not be able to render better return on that love than by modeling our lives on his. *Christ suffered for us, leaving us an example, that we should follow in his steps*[1 Pet 2:21]. In saying this, the apostle Peter seems to have understood that Christ suffered only for those who follow in his steps, in the sense that Christ's passion is of no avail to those who do not. The holy martyrs followed Christ even to shedding their life's blood, even to reproducing the very likeness of his passion. They followed him, but not they alone. It is not true that the bridge was broken after the martyrs crossed; nor is it true that after they had drunk from it, the fountain of eternal life dried up.

I tell you again and again, my brethren, that in the Lord's garden are to be found not only the roses of his martyrs. In it there are also the lilies of the virgins, the ivy of wedded couples, and the violets of widows. On no account may any class of people despair, thinking that God has not called them. Christ suffered for all. What the Scriptures say of him is true: *He desires all men to be saved and to come to knowledge of the truth*[1 Tim 2:4].

Let us understand, then, how a Christian must follow Christ even though he does not shed his blood for him, and his faith is not called upon to undergo the great test of the martyr's sufferings. The apostle Paul says of Christ our Lord: *Though he was in the form of God he did not consider equality with God a prize to be clung to*[Phil 2:5-11]. How unrivaled his majesty! *But he emptied himself, taking on the form of a slave, made in the likeness of men, and presenting himself in human form*[Phil 2:5-11]. How deep his humility!

Christ humbled himself. Christian, that is what you must make your own. *Christ became obedient.* How is it that you are proud? When this humbling experience was completed and death itself lay conquered, Christ ascended into heaven. Let us follow him there, for we hear Paul saying: *If you have been raised with Christ, you must lift your thoughts on high, where Christ now sits at the right hand of God*[Col 3:1].

August 11th

St. Clare, Virgin

From a letter to Blessed Agnes of Prague by St. Clare, Virgin

Behold the poverty, humility and love of Christ

Happy indeed is she who is granted a place at the divine banquet, for she may cling with her inmost heart to him whose beauty eternally awes the blessed hosts of heaven; to him whose love inspires love, whose contemplation refreshes, whose generosity satisfies, whose gentleness delights, whose memory shines sweetly as the dawn; to him whose fragrance revives the dead, and whose glorious vision will bless all the citizens of that heavenly Jerusalem. For he is the splendor of eternal glory, *the brightness of eternal light, and the mirror without cloud*[St. Clare].

Queen and bride of Jesus Christ, look into that mirror daily and study well your reflection, that you may adorn yourself, mind and body, with an enveloping garment of every virtue, and thus find yourself attired in flowers and gowns befitting the daughter and most chaste bride of the king on high. In this mirror blessed poverty, holy humility and ineffable love are also reflected. With the grace of God the whole mirror will be your source of contemplation.

Behold, I say, the birth of this mirror. Behold his poverty even as he was laid in the manger and wrapped in swaddling clothes. What wondrous humility, what marvelous poverty! The King of angels, the Lord of heaven and earth resting in a manger! Look more deeply into the mirror and meditate on his humility, or simply on his poverty. Behold the many labors and sufferings he endured to redeem the human race. Then, in the depths of this very mirror, ponder his unspeakable love which caused him to suffer on the wood of the cross and to endure the most shameful kind of death. The mirror himself, from his position on the cross, warned passersby to weigh carefully this act, as he said: *All of you who pass by this way, behold and see if there is any sorrow like mine*[Lam 1:12]. Let us answer his cries and lamentations with one voice and one spirit: *I will be mindful and remember, and my soul will be consumed within me*[Lam 3:20]. In this way, queen of the king of heaven, your love will burn with an ever brighter flame.

Consider also his indescribable delights, his unending riches and honors, and sigh for what is beyond your love and heart's content as you cry out: *Draw me on! We will run after you in the perfume of your ointment*[Song 1:3-4], heavenly spouse. Let me run and not faint until you lead me into your wine cellar; your left hand rests under my head, your right arm joyfully embraces me, and you kiss me with the sweet kiss of your lips. As you rest in this state of contemplation, remember your poor mother and know that I have indelibly written your happy memory into my heart, for you are dearer to me than all the others.

August 13th

St. Pontian, Pope & Martyr, and St. Hippolytus, Priest & Martyr

From a letter by St. Cyprian, Bishop and Martyr

Invincible faith

With what praises can I extol you, most valiant brothers? What words can I find to proclaim and celebrate your brave hearts and your persevering faith? Examined under the fiercest torture, you held out until your ordeal was consummated in glory; it was not you who yielded to the torments but rather the torments that yielded to you. No respite from pain was allowed by the instruments of your torture, but your very crowning signaled the end of pain. The cruel butchery was permitted to last the longer, not so that it might overthrow the faith that stood so firm, but rather that it might dispatch you, men of God, more speedily to the Lord.

The crowd in wonder watched God's heavenly contest, this spiritual battle that was Christ's. They saw his servants standing firm, free in speech, undefiled in heart, endowed with supernatural courage, naked and bereft of the weapons of this world, but as believers equipped with the arms of faith. Tortured men stood there stronger than their torturers; battered and lacerated limbs triumphed over clubs and claws that tore them.

Savage and prolonged beating could not overcome such invincible faith, even when the bodies of God's servants were so mangled that no whole members were left to suffer punishment, but only wounds remained. Enough blood flowed to quench the fire of persecution, a glorious river to cool even the burning heat of hell. What a divine display it was, how sublime and magnificent! How pleasing did the sworn allegiance and loyalty of his soldiers render the dead in God's sight! In the psalms, where the Holy Spirit speaks to us and counsels us, it is written: *Precious in the sight of God is the death of his holy ones*[Ps 115:15]. Rightly is that death called "precious," for at the price of blood it purchased immortality and won God's crown through the ultimate act of courage.

How happy Christ was to be there, how gladly he fought and conquered in such servants! He protects their faith and gives strength to believers in proportion to the trust that each man who receives that strength is willing to place in him. Christ was there to wage his own battle; he aroused the soldiers who fought for his name; he made them spirited and strong. And he who once for all has conquered death for us, now continually conquers in us.

How blessed is this Church of ours, so honored and illuminated by God and ennobled in these our days by the glorious blood of martyrs! In earlier times it shone white with the good deeds of our brethren, and now it is adorned with the red blood of martyrs. It counts both lilies and roses among its garlands. Let each of us, then, strive for the highest degree of glory, whichever be the honor for which he is destined; may all Christians be found worthy of either the pure white crown of a holy life or the royal red crown of martyrdom.

August 14th

St. Maximilian Mary Kolbe, Priest & Martyr

From the letters of St. Maximilian Mary Kolbe, Priest & Martyr

Apostolic zeal for the salvation and sanctification of souls

The burning zeal for God's glory that motivates you fills my heart with joy. It is sad for us to see in our own time that indifferentism in its many forms is sp like an epidemic not only among the laity but also among religious. But God is worthy of glory beyond measure, and therefore it is of absolute and supreme importance to seek that glory with all the power of our feeble resources. Since we are mere creatures we can never return to him all that is his due.

The most resplendent manifestation of God's glory is the salvation of souls, whom Christ redeemed by shedding his blood. To work for the salvation and sanctification of as many souls as possible, therefore, is the preeminent purpose of the apostolic life. Let me, then, say a few words that may show the way toward achieving God's glory and the sanctification of many souls.

God, who is all-knowing and all-wise, knows best what we should do to increase his glory. Through his representatives on earth he continually reveals his will to us; thus it is obedience and obedience alone that is the sure sign to us of the divine will. A superior may, it is true, make a mistake; but it is impossible for us to be mistaken in obeying a superior's command. The only exception to this rule is the case of a superior commanding something that in even the slightest way would contravene God's law. Such a superior would not be conveying God's will.

God alone is infinitely wise, holy, merciful, our Lord, Creator, and Father; he is beginning and end, wisdom and power and love; he is all. Everything other than God has value to the degree that it is referred to him, the maker of all and our own redeemer, the final end of all things. It is he who, declaring his adorable will to us through his representatives on earth, draws us to himself and whose plan is to draw others to himself through us and to join us all to himself in an ever deepening love.

Look, then, at the high dignity that by God's mercy belongs to our state in life. Obedience raises us beyond the limits of our littleness and puts us in harmony with God's will. In boundless wisdom and care, his will guides us to act rightly. Holding fast to that will, which no creature can thwart, we are filled with unsurpassable strength.

Obedience is the one and the only way of wisdom and prudence for us to offer glory to God. If there were another, Christ would certainly have shown it to us by word and example. Scripture, however, summed up his entire life at Nazareth in the words: *He was subject to them*[Lk 2:51 ~ the Finding in the Temple]; Scripture set obedience as the theme of the rest of his life, repeatedly declaring that he came into the world to do his Father's will.

Let us love our loving Father with all our hearts. Let our obedience increase that love, above all when it requires us to surrender our own will. Jesus Christ crucified is our sublime guide toward growth in God's love.

We will learn this lesson more quickly through the Immaculate Virgin, whom God has made the dispenser of his mercy. It is beyond all doubt that Mary's will represents to us the will of God himself.

By dedicating ourselves to her we become in her hands instruments of God's mercy even as she was such an instrument in God's hands. We should let ourselves be guided and led by Mary and rest quiet and secure in her hands. She will watch out for us, provide for us, answer our needs of body and spirit; she will dissolve all our difficulties and worries.

August 15th

Assumption of the Blessed Virgin Mary

From the apostolic constitution *Munificentissimus Deus* by Pope Pius XII

Your body is holy and excelling in splendor

In their homilies and sermons on this feast the holy fathers and great doctors spoke of the assumption of the Mother of God as something already familiar and accepted by the faithful. They gave it greater clarity in their preaching and used more profound arguments in setting out its nature and meaning. Above all, they brought out more clearly the fact that what is commemorated in this feast is not simply the total absence of corruption from the dead body of the Blessed Virgin Mary but also her triumph over death and her glorification in heaven, after the pattern set by her only Son, Jesus Christ.

Thus Saint John Damascene, preeminent as the great preacher of this truth of tradition, speaks with powerful eloquence when he relates the bodily assumption of the loving Mother of God to her other gifts and privileges: "It was necessary that she who had preserved her virginity inviolate in childbirth should also have her body kept free from all corruption after death. It was necessary that she who had carried the Creator as a child on her breast should dwell in the tabernacles of God. It was necessary that the bride espoused by the Father should make her home in the bridal chambers of heaven. It was necessary that she, who had gazed on her crucified Son and been pierced in the heart by the sword of sorrow which she had escaped in giving him birth, should contemplate him seated with the Father. It was necessary that the Mother of God should share the possessions of her Son, and be venerated by every creature as the Mother and handmaid of God."

Saint Germanus of Constantinople considered that it was in keeping not only with her divine motherhood but also with the unique sanctity of her virginal body that it was incorrupt and carried up to heaven: "In the words of Scripture, you appear *in beauty*. Your virginal body is entirely holy, entirely chaste, entirely the house of God, so that for this reason also it is henceforth a stranger to decay: a body changed, because a human body, to a preeminent life of incorruptibility, but still a living body, excelling in splendor, a body inviolate and sharing in the perfection of life."

Another early author declares: "Therefore, as the most glorious Mother of Christ, our God and Savior, giver of life and immortality, she is enlivened by him to share an eternal incorruptibility of body with him who raised her from the tomb and took her up to himself in a way he alone can tell."

All these reasonings and considerations of the holy Fathers rest on Scripture as their ultimate foundation. Scripture portrays the loving Mother of God, almost before our very eyes, as most intimately united with her divine Son and always sharing in his destiny.

Above all, it must be noted that from the second century the holy Fathers present the Virgin Mary as the new Eve, most closely associated with the new Adam, though subject to him in the struggle against the enemy from the nether world. This struggle, as the first promise of a redeemer implies, was to end in perfect victory over sin and death, always linked together in the writings of the Apostle of the Gentiles.

Therefore, just as the glorious resurrection of Christ was an essential part of this victory and its final trophy, so the struggle shared by the Blessed Virgin and her Son was to end in the glorification of her virginal body. As the same Apostle says: *When this mortal body has clothed itself in immortality, then will be fulfilled the word of Scripture: Death is swallowed up in victory*[1 Cor 15:54].

Hence, the august Mother of God, mysteriously united from all eternity with Jesus Christ in one and the same decree of predestination, immaculate in her conception, a virgin inviolate in her divine motherhood, the whole-hearted companion of the divine Redeemer who won complete victory over sin and its consequences, gained at last the supreme crown of her privileges – to be preserved immune from the corruption of the tomb, and, like her Son, when death had been conquered, to be carried up body and soul to the exalted glory of heaven, there to sit in splendor at the right hand of her Son, the immortal King of the ages.

August 16th

St. Stephen of Hungary

From admonitions to his son by St. Stephen

Son, listen to your father's instruction

My dearest son, if you desire to honor the royal crown, I advise, I counsel, I urge you above all things to maintain the Catholic and apostolic faith with such diligence and care that you may be an example for all those placed under you by God and that all the clergy may rightly call you a man of true Christian profession. Failing to do this, you may be sure that you will not be called a Christian or a son of the Church. Indeed, in the royal palace after the faith itself, the Church holds second place, first propagated as she was by our head, Christ; then transplanted, firmly constituted and spread through the whole world by his members, the apostles and holy fathers. And though she always produced fresh offspring, nevertheless in certain places she is regarded as ancient.

However, dearest son, even now in our kingdom the Church is proclaimed as young and newly planted; and for that reason she needs more prudent and trustworthy guardians lest a benefit which the divine mercy bestowed on us undeservedly should be destroyed and annihilated through your idleness, indolence or neglect.

My beloved son, delight of my heart, hope of your posterity, I pray, I command, that at every time and in everything, strengthened by your devotion to me, you may show favor not only to relations and kin, or to the most eminent, be they leaders or rich men or neighbors or fellow-countrymen, but also to foreigners and to all who come to you. By fulfilling your duty in this way you will reach the highest state of happiness. Be merciful to all who are suffering violence, keeping always in your heart the example of the Lord who said: *I desire mercy and not sacrifice*[Hos 6:6; Mt 9:13]. Be patient with everyone, not only with the powerful, but also with the weak.

Finally be strong lest prosperity lift you up too much or adversity cast you down. Be humble in this life, that God may raise you up in the next. Be truly moderate and do not punish or condemn anyone immoderately. Be gentle so that you may never oppose justice. Be honorable so that you may never voluntarily bring disgrace upon anyone. Be chaste so that you may avoid all the foulness of lust like the pangs of death.

All these virtues I have noted above make up the royal crown and without them no one is fit to rule here on earth or attain the heavenly kingdom.

August 19th

St. John Eudes, Priest

From a treatise on the admirable Heart of Jesus by St. John Eudes, Priest

The source of salvation and true life

I ask you to consider that our Lord Jesus Christ is your true head and that you are a member of his body. He belongs to you as the head belongs to the body. All that is his is yours: breath, heart, body, soul and all his faculties. All of these you must use as if they belonged to you, so that in serving him you may give him praise, love and glory. You belong to him as a member belongs to the head. This is why he earnestly desires you to serve and glorify the Father by using all your faculties as if they were his.

He belongs to you, but more than that, he longs to be in you, living and ruling in you, as the head lives and rules in the body. He desires that whatever is in him may live and rule in you: his breath in your breath, his heart in your heart, all the faculties of his soul in the faculties of your soul, so that these words may be fulfilled in you: *Glorify God and bear him in your body, that the life of Jesus may be made manifest in you*[1 Cor 6:20].

You belong to the Son of God, but more than that, you ought to be in him as the members are in the head. All that is in you must be incorporated into him. You must receive life from him and be ruled by him. There will be no true life for you except in him, for he is the one source of true life. Apart from him you will find only death and destruction. Let him be the only source of your movements, of the actions and the strength of your life. He must be both the source and the purpose of your life, so that you may fulfill these words: *None of us lives as his own master and none of us dies as his own master. While we live, we are responsible to the Lord, and when we die, we die as his servants. Both in life and death we are the Lord's. That is why Christ died and came to life again, that he might be Lord of both the dead and the living*[Rom 14:7-9].

Finally, you are one with Jesus as the body is one with the head. You must, then, have one breath with him, one soul, one life, one will, one mind, one heart. And he must be your breath, heart, love, life, your all. These great gifts in the follower of Christ originate from baptism. They are increased and strengthened through confirmation and by making good use of other graces that are given by God. Through the holy eucharist they are brought to perfection.

August 20th

St. Bernard, Abbot & Doctor

From a sermon by St. Bernard, Abbot & Doctor

I love because I love, I love that I may love

Love is sufficient of itself, it gives pleasure by itself and because of itself. It is its own merit, its own reward. Love looks for no cause outside itself, no effect beyond itself. Its profit lies in its practice. I love because I love, I love that I may love. Love is a great thing so long as it continually returns to its fountainhead, flows back to its source, always drawing from there the water which constantly replenishes it. Of all the movements, sensations and feelings of the soul, love is the only one in which the creature can respond to the Creator and make some sort of similar return however unequal though it be. For when God loves, all he desires is to be loved in return; the sole purpose of his love is to be loved, in the knowledge that those who love him are made happy by their love of him.

The Bridegroom's love, or rather the love which is the Bridegroom, asks in return nothing but faithful love. Let the beloved, then, love in return. Should not a bride love, and above all, Love's bride? Could it be that Love not be loved?

Rightly then does she give up all other feelings and give herself wholly to love alone; in giving love back, all she can do is to respond to love. And when she has poured out her whole being in love, what is that in comparison with the unceasing torrent of that original source? Clearly, lover and Love, soul and Word, bride and Bridegroom, creature and Creator do not flow with the same volume; one might as well equate a thirsty man with the fountain.

What then of the bride's hope, her aching desire, her passionate love, her confident assurance? Is all this to wilt just because she cannot match stride for stride with her giant, any more than she can vie with honey for sweetness, rival the lamb for gentleness, show herself as white as the lily, burn as bright as the sun, be equal in love with him who is Love? No. It is true that the creature loves less because she is less. But if she loves with her whole being, nothing is lacking where everything is given. To love so ardently then is to share the marriage bond; she cannot love so much and not be totally loved, and it is in the perfect union of two hearts that complete and total marriage consists. Or are we to doubt that the soul is loved by the Word first and with a greater love?

August 21st

St. Pius X, Pope

From the apostolic constitution *Divino afflatu* of Pope St. Pius X

The song of the Church

The collection of psalms found in Scripture, composed as it was under divine inspiration, has, from the very beginnings of the Church, shown a wonderful power of fostering devotion among Christians as they offer to God *a continuous sacrifice of praise, the harvest of lips blessing his name*[Heb 13:15]. Following a custom already established in the Old Law, the psalms have played a conspicuous part in the sacred liturgy itself, and in the divine office. Thus was born what Basil calls *the voice of the Church*[St. Basil: Every Psalm is the Voice of the Church], that singing of psalms, which is *the daughter of that hymn of praise* (to use the words of our predecessor, Urban VIII) *which goes up unceasingly before the throne of God and of the Lamb*[Rev 5:8; 8:3-4], and which teaches those especially charged with the duty of divine worship, as Athanasius says, *the way to praise God, and the fitting words in which to bless him*. Augustine expresses this well when he says: *God praised himself so that man might give him fitting praise; because God chose to praise himself man found the way in which to bless God*.

The psalms have also a wonderful power to awaken in our hearts the desire for every virtue. Athanasius says: *Though all Scripture, both old and new, is divinely inspired and has its use in teaching, as we read in Scripture itself, yet the Book of Psalms, like a garden enclosing the fruits of all the other books, produces its fruits in song, and in the process of singing brings forth its own special fruits to take their place beside them*. In the same place Athanasius rightly adds: *The psalms seem to me to be like a mirror, in which the person using them can see himself, and the stirrings of his own heart; he can recite them against the background of his own emotions*. Augustine says in his Confessions: *How I wept when I heard your hymns and canticles, being deeply moved by the sweet singing of your Church. Those voices flowed into my ears, truth filtered into my heart, and from my heart surged waves of devotion. Tears ran down, and I was happy in my tears*.

Indeed, who could fail to be moved by those many passages in the psalms which set forth so profoundly the infinite majesty of God, his omnipotence, his justice and goodness and clemency, too deep for words, and all the other infinite qualities of his that deserve our praise? Who could fail to be roused to the same emotions by the prayers of thanksgiving to God for blessings received, by the petitions, so humble and confident, for blessings still awaited, by the cries of a soul in sorrow for sin committed? Who would not be fired with love as he looks on the likeness of Christ, the redeemer, here so lovingly foretold? His was *the voice* Augustine *heard in every psalm, the voice of praise, of suffering, of joyful expectation, of present distress*.

August 22nd

Queenship of Mary

From a homily by St. Amadeus of Lausanne, Bishop

Queen of the world and of peace

Observe how fitting it was that even before her assumption the name of Mary shone forth wondrously throughout the world. Her fame spread everywhere even before she was raised above the heavens in her magnificence. Because of the honor due her Son, it was indeed fitting for the Virgin Mother to have first ruled upon earth and then be raised up to heaven in glory. It was fitting that her fame be spread in this world below, so that she might enter the heights of heaven on overwhelming blessedness. Just as she was borne from virtue to virtue by the Spirit of the Lord, she was transported from earthly renown to heavenly brightness.

So it was that she began to taste the fruits of her future reign while still in the flesh. At one moment she withdrew to God in ecstasy; at the next she would bend down to her neighbors with indescribable love. In heaven angels served her, while here on earth she was venerated by the service of men. Gabriel and the angels waited upon her in heaven. The virgin John, rejoicing that the Virgin Mother was entrusted to him at the cross, cared for her with the other apostles here below. The angels rejoiced to see their queen; the apostles rejoiced to see their lady, and both obeyed her with loving devotion.

Dwelling in the loftiest citadel of virtue, like a sea of divine grace or an unfathomable source of love that has everywhere overflowed its banks, she poured forth her bountiful waters on trusting and thirsting souls. Able to preserve both flesh and spirit from death she bestowed health-giving salve on bodies and souls. Has anyone ever come away from her troubled or saddened or ignorant of the heavenly mysteries? Who has not returned to everyday life gladdened and joyful because his request had been granted by the Mother of God?

She is a bride, so gentle and affectionate, and the mother of the only true bridegroom. In her abundant goodness she has channeled the spring of reason's garden, the well of living and life-giving waters that pour forth in a rushing stream from divine Lebanon and flow down from Mount Zion until they surround the shores of every far-flung nation. With divine assistance she has redirected these waters and made them into streams of peace and pools of grace. Therefore, when the Virgin of virgins was led forth by God and her Son, the King of kings, amid the company of exulting angels and rejoicing archangels, with the heavens ringing with praise, the prophecy of the psalmist was fulfilled, in which he said to the Lord: *At your right hand stands the queen, clothed in gold of Ophir*[Ps 44:10].

August 23rd

St. Rose of Lima, Virgin

From the writings of St. Rose of Lima, Virgin

Let us know the love of Christ which surpasses all knowledge

Our Lord and Savior lifted up his voice and said with incomparable majesty: "Let all men know that grace comes after tribulation. Let them know that without the burden of afflictions it is impossible to reach the height of grace. Let them know that the gifts of grace increase as the struggles increase. Let men take care not to stray and be deceived. This is the only true stairway to paradise, and without the cross they can find no road to climb to heaven."

When I heard these words, a strong force came upon me and seemed to place me in the middle of a street, so that I might say in a loud voice to people of every age, sex and status: "Hear, O people; hear, O nations. I am warning you about the commandment of Christ by using words that came from his own lips: We cannot obtain grace unless we suffer afflictions. We must heap trouble upon trouble to attain a deep participation in the divine nature, the glory of the sons of God and perfect happiness of soul."

That same force strongly urged me to proclaim the beauty of divine grace. It pressed me so that my breath came slow and forced me to sweat and pant. I felt as if my soul could no longer be kept in the prison of the body, but that it had burst its chains and was free and alone and was going very swiftly through the whole world saying:

"If only mortals would learn how great it is to possess divine grace, how beautiful, how noble, how precious. How many riches it hides within itself, how many joys and delights! Without doubt they would devote all their care and concern to winning for themselves pains and afflictions. All men throughout the world would seek trouble, infirmities and torments, instead of good fortune, in order to attain the unfathomable treasure of grace. This is the reward and the final gain of patience. No one would complain about his cross or about troubles that may happen to him, if he would come to know the scales on which they are weighed when they are distributed to men."

August 24th

St. Bartholomew, Apostle

From a homily on the first letter to the Corinthians by St. John Chrysostom, Bishop & Doctor

The weakness of God is stronger than men

It was clear through unlearned men that the cross was persuasive, in fact, it persuaded the whole world. Their discourse was not of unimportant matters but of God and true religion, of the Gospel way of life and future judgment, yet it turned plain, uneducated men into philosophers. How the foolishness of God is wiser than men, and his weakness stronger than men!

In what way is it stronger? It made its way throughout the world and overcame all men; countless men sought to eradicate the very name of the Crucified, but that name flourished and grew ever mightier. Its enemies lost out and perished; the living who waged war on a dead man proved helpless. Therefore, when a Greek tells me I am dead, he shows only that he is foolish indeed, for I, whom he thinks a fool, turn out to be wiser than those reputed wise. So too, in calling me weak, he but shows that he is weaker still. For the good deeds which tax-collectors and fishermen were able to accomplish by God's grace, the philosophers, the rulers, the countless multitudes cannot even imagine.

Paul had this in mind when he said: *The weakness of God is stronger than men*[1 Cor 1:25.] That the preaching of these men was indeed divine is brought home to us in the same way. For how otherwise could twelve uneducated men, who lived on lakes and rivers and wastelands, get the idea for such an immense enterprise? How could men who perhaps had never been in a city or a public square think of setting out to do battle with the whole world? That they were fearful, timid men, the evangelist makes clear; he did not reject the fact or try to hide their weaknesses. Indeed he turned these into a proof of the truth. What did he say of them? That when Christ was arrested, the others fled, despite all the miracles they had seen, while he who was leader of the others denied him!

How then account for the fact that these men, who in Christ's lifetime did not stand up to the attacks by the Jews, set forth to do battle with the whole world once Christ was dead – if, as you claim, Christ did not rise and speak to them and rouse their courage? Did they perhaps say to themselves: "What is this? He could not save himself but he will protect us? He did not help himself when he was alive, but now that he is dead he will extend a helping hand to us? In his lifetime he brought no nation under his banner, but by uttering his name we will win over the whole world?" Would it not be wholly irrational even to think such thoughts, much less to act upon them?

It is evident, then, that if they had not seen him risen and had proof of his power, they would not have risked so much.

August 25th

St. Louis of France

From a spiritual testament to his son by St. Louis

A just king rules the earth

My dearest son, my first instruction is that you should love the Lord your God with all your heart and all your strength. Without this there is no salvation. Keep yourself, my son, from everything that you know displeases God, that is to say, from every mortal sin. You should permit yourself to be tormented by every kind of martyrdom before you would allow yourself to commit a mortal sin.

If the Lord has permitted you to have some trial, bear it willingly and with gratitude, considering that it has happened for your good and that perhaps you well deserved it. If the Lord bestows upon you any kind of prosperity, thank him humbly and see that you become no worse for it, either through vain pride or anything else, because you ought not to oppose God or offend him in the matter of his gifts.

Listen to the divine office with pleasure and devotion. As long as you are in church, be careful not to let your eyes wander and not to speak empty words, but pray to the Lord devoutly, either aloud or with the interior prayer of the heart.

Be kindhearted to the poor, the unfortunate and the afflicted. Give them as much help and consolation as you can. Thank God for all the benefits he has bestowed upon you, that you may be worthy to receive greater. Be just to your subjects, swaying neither to right nor left, but holding the line of justice. Always side with the poor rather than with the rich, until you are certain of the truth. See that all your subjects live in justice and peace, but especially those who have ecclesiastical rank and who belong to religious orders.

Be devout and obedient to our mother the Church of Rome and the Supreme Pontiff as your spiritual father. Work to remove all sin from your land, particularly blasphemies and heresies.

In conclusion, dearest son, I give you every blessing that a loving father can give a son. May the three Persons of the Holy Trinity and all the saints protect you from every evil. And may the Lord give you the grace to do his will so that he may be served and honored through you, that in the next life we may together come to see him, love him and praise him unceasingly. Amen.

August 25th

St. Joseph Calasanz, Priest

From the writings of St. Joseph Calasanz, Priest

Let us try to cling to Christ and please him alone

Everyone knows the great merit and dignity attached to that holy ministry in which young boys, especially the poor, receive instruction for the purpose of attaining eternal life. This ministry is directed to the well-being of body and soul; at the same time that it shapes behavior it also fosters devotion and Christian doctrine. In doing this it performs for the young boys the very same service as their guardian angels.

Moreover the strongest support is provided not only to protect the young from evil, but also to rouse them and attract them more easily and gently to the performance of good works. Whatever the type of condition, it is well known that when the young are given this help the change for the better is so great that it becomes impossible to distinguish those who are educated from those who are not. Like the twigs of plants the young are easily influenced, as long as someone works to change their souls. But if they are allowed to grow hard, we know well that the possibility of one day bending them diminishes a great deal and is sometimes utterly lost.

All who belong to the society of men, and especially all Christians, praise those who increase the human dignity of young boys, especially poor boys by giving them a proper education. Above all, parents are happy that their children are led through straight paths. Civil leaders rejoice to gain upright subjects and good citizens. The Church is especially joyful that others who love Christ and proclaim the Gospel are added to its following.

All who undertake to teach must be endowed with deep love, the greatest patience, and, most of all, profound humility. They must perform their work with earnest zeal. Then, through their humble prayers, the Lord will find them worthy to become fellow workers with him in the cause of truth. He will console them in the fulfillment of this most noble duty, and, finally, will enrich them with the gift of heaven.

As Scripture says: *Those who instruct many in justice will shine as stars for all eternity*[Dn 12:3]. They will attain this more easily if they make a covenant of perpetual obedience and strive to cling to Christ and please him alone, because, in his words: *What you did to one of the least of my brethren, you did to me*[Mt 25:40].

August 27th

St. Monica

From the Confessions of St. Augustine, Bishop & Doctor

Let us gain eternal wisdom

The day was now approaching when my mother Monica would depart from this life; you knew that day, Lord, though we did not. She and I happened to be standing by ourselves at a window that overlooked the garden in the courtyard of the house. At the time we were in Ostia on the Tiber. We had gone there after a long and wearisome journey to get away from the noisy crowd, and to rest and prepare for our sea voyage. I believe that you, Lord, caused all this to happen in your own mysterious ways. And so the two of us, all alone, were enjoying a very pleasant conversation, *forgetting the past and pushing on to what is ahead*[Phil 3:13]. We were asking one another in the presence of the Truth - for you are the Truth - what it would be like to share the eternal life enjoyed by the saints, which *eye has not seen, nor ear heard, which has not even entered into the heart of man*[1 Cor 2:9]. We desired with all our hearts to drink from the streams of your heavenly fountain, the fountain of life.

That was the substance of our talk, though not the exact words. But you know, O Lord, that in the course of our conversation that day, the world and its pleasures lost all their attraction for us. My mother said: "Son, as far as I am concerned, nothing in this life now gives me any pleasure. I do not know why I am still here, since I have no further hopes in this world. I did have one reason for wanting to live a little longer: to see you become a Catholic Christian before I died. God has lavished his gifts on me in that respect, for I know that you have even renounced earthly happiness to be his servant. So what am I doing here?"

I do not really remember how I answered her. Shortly, within five days or thereabouts, she fell sick with a fever. Then one day during the course of her illness she became unconscious and for a while she was unaware of her surroundings. My brother and I rushed to her side but she regained consciousness quickly. She looked at us as we stood there and asked in a puzzled voice: "Where was I?"

We were overwhelmed with grief, but she held her gaze steadily upon us, and spoke further: "Here you shall bury your mother." I remained silent as I held back my tears. However, my brother haltingly expressed his hope that she might not die in a strange country but in her own land, since her end would be happier there. When she heard this, her face was filled with anxiety, and she reproached him with a glance because he had entertained such earthly thoughts. Then she looked at me and spoke: "Look what he is saying." Thereupon she said to both of us, "Bury my body wherever you will; let not care of it cause you any concern. One thing only I ask you, that you remember me at the altar of the Lord wherever you may be." Once our mother had expressed this desire as best she could, she fell silent as the pain of her illness increased.

August 28th

St. Augustine, Bishop & Doctor

From the Confessions of St. Augustine, Bishop & Doctor

O eternal truth, true love and beloved eternity

Urged to reflect upon myself, I entered under your guidance into the inmost depth of my soul. I was able to do so because *you were my helper.* On entering into myself I saw, as it were with the eye of the soul, what was beyond the eye of the soul, beyond my spirit: your immutable light. It was not the ordinary light perceptible to all flesh, nor was it merely something of greater magnitude but still essentially akin, shining more clearly and diffusing itself everywhere by its intensity. No, it was something entirely distinct, something altogether different from all these things; and it did not rest above my mind as oil on the surface of water, nor was it above me as heaven is above earth. This light was above me because it had made me; I was below it because I was created by it. He who has come to know the truth knows this light.

O eternal truth, true love and beloved eternity. You are my God. To you do I sigh day and night. When I first came to know you, you drew me to yourself so that I might see that there were things for me to see, but that I myself was not yet ready to see them. Meanwhile you overcame the weakness of my vision, sending forth most strongly the beams of your light, and I trembled at once with love and dread. I learned that I was in a region unlike yours and far distant from you, and I thought I heard your voice from on high: "I am the food of grown men; grow then, and you will feed on me. Nor will you change me into yourself like bodily food, but you will be changed into me."

I sought a way to gain the strength which I needed to enjoy you. But I did not find it until I embraced *the mediator between God and men, the man Christ Jesus, who is above all, God blessed for ever*[1 Tim 2:5]. He was calling me and saying: *I am the way of truth, I am the life*[Jn 14:6]. He was offering the food which I lacked the strength to take, the food he had mingled with our flesh. For *the Word became flesh*[Jn 1:14], that your wisdom, by which you created all things, might provide milk for us children.

Late have I loved you, O Beauty ever ancient, ever new, late have I loved you! You were within me, but I was outside, and it was there that I searched for you. In my unloveliness I plunged into the lovely things which you created. You were with me, but I was not with you. Created things kept me from you; yet if they had not been in you they would not have been at all. You called, you shouted, and you broke through my deafness. You flashed, you shone, and you dispelled my blindness. You breathed your fragrance on me; I drew in breath and now I pant for you. I have tasted you, now I hunger and thirst for more. You touched me, and I burned for your peace.

August 29th

Beheading of St. John the Baptist, Martyr

From a homily by St. Bede the Venerable, Priest & Doctor

Precursor of Christ in birth and death

As forerunner of our Lord's birth, preaching and death, the blessed John showed in his struggle a goodness worthy of the sight of heaven. In the words of Scripture: *Though in the sight of men he suffered torments, his hope is full of immortality*[Wis 3:1-4]. We justly commemorate the day of his birth with a joyful celebration, a day which he himself made festive for us through his suffering and which he adorned with the crimson splendor of his own blood. We do rightly revere his memory with joyful hearts, for he stamped with the seal of martyrdom the testimony which he delivered on behalf of our Lord.

There is no doubt that blessed John suffered imprisonment and chains as a witness to our Redeemer, whose forerunner he was, and gave his life for him. His persecutor had demanded not that he should deny Christ, but only that he should keep silent about the truth. Nevertheless, he died for Christ. Does Christ not say: *I am the truth*[Jn 14:6]? Therefore, because John shed his blood for the truth, he surely died for Christ.

Through his birth, preaching and baptizing, he bore witness to the coming birth, preaching and baptism of Christ, and by his own suffering he showed that Christ also would suffer.

Such was the quality and strength of the man who accepted the end of this present life by shedding his blood after the long imprisonment. He preached the freedom of heavenly peace, yet was thrown into irons by ungodly men; he was locked away in the darkness of prison, though he came bearing witness to the Light of life and deserved to be called a bright and shining lamp by that Light itself, which is Christ. John was baptized in his own blood, though he had been privileged to baptize the Redeemer of the world, to hear the voice of the Father above him, and to see the grace of the Holy Spirit descending upon him. But to endure temporal agonies for the sake of the truth was not a heavy burden for such men as John; rather it was easily borne and even desirable, for he knew eternal joy would be his reward.

Since death was ever near at hand through the inescapable necessity of nature, such men considered it a blessing to embrace it and thus gain the reward of eternal life by acknowledging Christ's name. Hence the apostle Paul rightly says: *You have been granted the privilege not only to believe in Christ but also to suffer for his sake*[Phil 1:29]. He tells us why it is Christ's gift that his chosen ones should suffer for him: *The sufferings of this present time are not worthy to be compared with the glory that is to be revealed in us*[Rom 8:18].

September 3rd

St. Gregory the Great, Pope & Doctor

From a homily on Ezekiel by St. Gregory the Great, Pope & Doctor

For Christ's love I do not spare myself in speaking of him

Son of man, I have made you a watchman for the house of Israel[Ezek 3:17]. Note that a man whom the Lord sends forth as a preacher is called a watchman. A watchman always stands on a height so that he can see from afar what is coming. Anyone appointed to be a watchman for the people must stand on a height for all his life to help them by his foresight.

How hard it is for me to say this, for by these very words I denounce myself. I cannot preach with any competence, and yet insofar as I do succeed, still I myself do not live my life according to my own preaching.

I do not deny my responsibility; I recognize that I am slothful and negligent, but perhaps the acknowledgment of my fault will win me pardon from my just judge. Indeed when I was in the monastery I could curb my idle talk and usually be absorbed in my prayers. Since I assumed the burden of pastoral care, my mind can no longer be collected; it is concerned with so many matters.

I am forced to consider the affairs of the Church and of the monasteries. I must weigh the lives and acts of individuals. I am responsible for the concerns of our citizens. I must worry about the invasions of roving bands of barbarians, and beware of the wolves who lie in wait for my flock. I must become an administrator lest the religious go in want. I must put up with certain robbers without losing patience and at times I must deal with them in all charity.

With my mind divided and torn to pieces by so many problems, how can I meditate or preach wholeheartedly without neglecting the ministry of proclaiming the Gospel? Moreover, in my position I must often communicate with worldly men. At times I let my tongue run, for if I am always severe in my judgments, the worldly will avoid me, and I can never attack them as I would. As a result I often listen patiently to chatter. And because I too am weak, I find myself drawn little by little into idle conversation, and I begin to talk freely about matters which once I would have avoided. What once I found tedious I now enjoy.

So who am I to be a watchman, for I do not stand on the mountain of action but lie down in the valley of weakness? Truly the all-powerful Creator and Redeemer of mankind can give me in spite of my weaknesses a higher life and effective speech; because I love him, I do not spare myself in speaking of him.

September 8th

Nativity of the Blessed Virgin Mary

From a discourse by St. Andrew of Crete, Bishop

The old has passed away, all things are made new

The fulfillment of the law is Christ himself[Mt 5:17-20], who does not so much lead us away from the letter as lift us up to its spirit. For the law's consummation was this, that the very lawgiver accomplished his work and changed letter into spirit, summing everything up in himself and, though subject to the law, living by grace. He subordinated the law, yet harmoniously united grace with it, not confusing the distinctive characteristics of the one with the other, but effecting the transition in a way most fitting for God. He changed whatever was burdensome, servile and oppressive into what is light and liberating, so that we should be enslaved no longer *under the elemental spirits of the world*[Gal 4:3], as the Apostle says, nor held fast as bondservants under the letter of the law.

This is the highest, all-embracing benefit that Christ has bestowed on us. This is the revelation of the mystery, this is the emptying out of the divine nature, the union of God and man, and the deification of the manhood that was assumed. This radiant and manifest coming of God to men most certainly needed a joyful prelude to introduce the great gift of salvation to us. The present festival, the birth of the Mother of God, is the prelude, while the final act is the foreordained union of the Word with flesh. Today the Virgin is born, tended and formed, and prepared for her role as Mother of God, who is the universal King of the ages.

Justly then do we celebrate this mystery since it signifies for us a double grace. We are led toward the truth, and we are led away from our condition of slavery to the letter of the law. How can this be? Darkness yields before the coming of light, and grace exchanges legalism for freedom. But midway between the two stands today's mystery, at the frontier where types and symbols give way to reality, and the old is replaced by the new.

Therefore, let all creation sing and dance and unite to make worthy contribution to the celebration of this day. Let there be one common festival for saints in heaven and men on earth. Let everything, mundane things and those above, join in festive celebration. Today this created world is raised to the dignity of a holy place for him who made all things. The creature is newly prepared to be a divine dwelling place for the Creator.

September 9th

St. Peter Claver, Priest

From a letter by St. Peter Claver, Priest

To preach the Gospel to the poor, to heal the broken hearted, to proclaim pardon to captives

Yesterday, May 30, 1627, on the feast of the Most Holy Trinity, numerous blacks, brought from the rivers of Africa, disembarked from a large ship. Carrying two baskets of oranges, lemons, sweet biscuits, and I know not what else, we hurried toward them. When we approached their quarters, we thought we were entering another Guinea. We had to force our way through the crowd until we reached the sick. Large numbers of the sick were lying on the wet ground or rather in puddles of mud. To prevent excessive dampness, someone had thought of building up a mound with a mixture of tiles and broken pieces of bricks. This, then, was their couch, a very uncomfortable one not only for that reason, but especially because they were naked, without any clothing to protect them.

We laid aside our cloaks, therefore, and brought from a warehouse whatever was handy to build a platform. In that way we covered a space to which we at last transferred the sick, by forcing a passage through bands of slaves. Then we divided the sick into two groups: one group my companion approached with an interpreter, while I addressed the other group. There were two blacks, nearer death than life, already cold, whose pulse could scarcely be detected. With the help of a tile we pulled some live coals together and placed them in the middle near the dying men. Into this fire we tossed aromatics. Of these we had two wallets full, and we used them all up on this occasion. Then, using our own cloaks, for they had nothing of this sort, and to ask the owners for others would have been a waste of words, we provided for them a smoke treatment, by which they seemed to recover their warmth and the breath of life. The joy in their eyes as they looked at us was something to see.

This was how we spoke to them, not with words but with our hands and our actions. And in fact, convinced as they were that they had been brought here to be eaten, any other language would have proved utterly useless. Then we sat, or rather knelt, beside them and bathed their faces and bodies with wine. We made every effort to encourage them with friendly gestures and displayed in their presence the emotions which somehow naturally tend to hearten the sick.

After this we began an elementary instruction about baptism, that is, the wonderful effects of the sacrament on body and soul. When by their answers to our questions they showed they had sufficiently understood this, we went on to a more extensive instruction, namely, about the one God, who rewards and punishes each one according to his merit, and the rest. We asked them to make an act of contrition and to manifest their detestation of their sins. Finally, when they appeared sufficiently prepared, we declared to them the mysteries of the Trinity, the Incarnation and the Passion. Showing them Christ fastened to the cross, as he is depicted on the baptismal font on which streams of blood flow down from his wounds, we led them in reciting an act of contrition in their own language.

September 13th

St. John Chrysostom, Bishop & Doctor

From a homily by St. John Chrysostom, Bishop & Doctor

Life to me means Christ, and death is gain

The waters have risen and severe storms are upon us, but we do not fear drowning, for we stand firmly upon a rock. Let the sea rage, it cannot break the rock. Let the waves rise, they cannot sink the boat of Jesus. What are we to fear? Death? *Life to me means Christ, and death is gain*[Phil 1:21]. Exile? *The earth and its fullness belong to the Lord*[Ps 23:1]. The confiscation of our goods? *We brought nothing into this world, and we shall surely take nothing from it*[Job 1:21; 1 Tim 6:7]. I have only contempt for the world's threats, I find its blessings laughable. I have no fear of poverty, no desire for wealth. I am not afraid of death nor do I long to live, except for your good. I concentrate therefore on the present situation, and I urge you, my friends, to have confidence.

Do you not hear the Lord saying: *Where two or three are gathered in my name, there am I in their midst*[Mt 18:20]? Will he be absent, then, when so many people united in love are gathered together? I have his promise; I am surely not going to rely on my own strength! I have what he has written; that is my staff, my security, my peaceful harbor. Let the world be in upheaval. I hold to his promise and read his message; that is my protecting wall and garrison. What message? *Know that I am with you always, until the end of the world*[Mt 28:20]!

If Christ is with me, whom shall I fear? Though the waves and the sea and the anger of princes are roused against me, they are less to me than a spider's web. Indeed, unless you, my brothers, had detained me, I would have left this very day. For I always say: *Lord, your will be done*[Mt 6:9-13]; not what this fellow or that would have me do, but what you want me to do. That is my strong tower, my immovable rock, my staff that never gives way. If God wants something, let it be done! If he wants me to stay here, I am grateful. But wherever he wants me to be, I am no less grateful.

Yet where I am, there you are too, and where you are, I am. For we are a single body, and the body cannot be separated from the head nor the head from the body. Distance separates us, but love unites us, and death itself cannot divide us. For though my body die, my soul will live and be mindful of my people.

You are my fellow citizens, my fathers, my brothers, my sons, my limbs, my body. You are my light, sweeter to me than the visible light. For what can the rays of the sun bestow on me that is comparable to your love? The sun's light is useful in my earthly life, but your love is fashioning a crown for me in the life to come.

September 14th

The Exaltation of the Holy Cross

From a discourse by St. Andrew of Crete, Bishop

The cross is Christ's glory and triumph

We are celebrating the feast of the cross which drove away darkness and brought in the light. As we keep this feast, we are lifted up with the crucified Christ, leaving behind us earth and sin so that we may gain the things above. So great and outstanding a possession is the cross that he who wins it has won a treasure. Rightly could I call this treasure the fairest of all fair things and the costliest, in fact as well as in name, for on it and through it and for its sake the riches of salvation that had been lost were restored to us.

Had there been no cross, Christ could not have been crucified. Had there been no cross, life itself could not have been nailed to the tree. And if life had not been nailed to it, there would be no streams of immortality pouring from Christ's side, blood and water for the world's cleansing. The legal bond of our sin would not be canceled, we should not have obtained our freedom, we should not have enjoyed the fruit of the tree of life and the gates of paradise would not stand open. Had there been no cross, death would not have been trodden underfoot, nor hell despoiled.

Therefore, the cross is something wonderfully great and honorable. It is great because through the cross the many noble acts of Christ found their consummation – very many indeed, for both his miracles and his sufferings were fully rewarded with victory. The cross is honorable because it is both the sign of God's suffering and the trophy of his victory. It stands for his suffering because on it he freely suffered unto death. But it is also his trophy because it was the means by which the devil was wounded and death conquered; the barred gates of hell were smashed, and the cross became the one common salvation of the whole world.

The cross is called Christ's glory; it is saluted as his triumph. We recognize it as the cup he longed to drink and the climax of the sufferings he endured for our sake. As to the cross being Christ's glory, listen to his words: *Now is the Son of Man glorified, and in him God is glorified, and God will glorify him at once*[Jn 13:31]. And again: *Father, glorify me with the glory I had with you before the world came to be*[Jn 17:5]. And once more: *Father, glorify your name. Then a voice came from heaven: I have glorified it and will glorify it again*[Jn 12:28]. Here he speaks of the glory that would accrue to him through the cross. And if you would understand that the cross is Christ's triumph, hear what he himself also said: *When I am lifted up, then I will draw all men to myself*[Jn 12:32]. Now you can see that the cross is Christ's glory and triumph.

September 15th

Our Lady of Sorrows

From a sermon by St. Bernard, Abbot & Doctor

His mother stood by the cross

The martyrdom of the Virgin is set forth both in the prophecy of Simeon and in the actual story of our Lord's passion. The holy old man said of the infant Jesus: *He has been established as a sign which will be contradicted*[Lk 2:34]. He went on to say to Mary: *And your own heart will be pierced by a sword*[Lk 2:35].

Truly, O blessed Mother, a sword has pierced your heart. For only by passing through your heart could the sword enter the flesh of your Son. Indeed, after your Jesus – who belongs to everyone, but is especially yours – gave up his life, the cruel spear, which was not withheld from his lifeless body, tore open his side. Clearly it did not touch his soul and could not harm him, but it did pierce your heart. For surely his soul was no longer there, but yours could not be torn away. Thus the violence of sorrow has cut through your heart, and we rightly call you more than martyr, since the effect of compassion in you has gone beyond the endurance of physical suffering.

Or were those words: *Woman, behold your Son*[Jn 19:25-29], not more than a sword to you, truly piercing your heart, cutting through to the division between soul and spirit? What an exchange! John is given to you in place of Jesus, the servant in place of the Lord, the disciple in place of the master; the son of Zebedee replaces the Son of God, a mere man replaces God himself. How could these words not pierce your most loving heart, when the mere remembrance of them breaks ours, hearts of stone and iron though they are!

Do not be surprised, brothers, that Mary is said to be a martyr in spirit. Let him be surprised who does not remember the words of Paul, that one of the greatest crimes of the Gentiles was that they were without love. That was far from the heart of Mary; let it be far from her servants.

Perhaps someone will say: "Had she not known before that he would die?" Undoubtedly. "Did she not expect him to rise again at once?" Surely. "And still she grieved over her crucified Son?" Intensely. Who are you and what is the source of your wisdom that you are more surprised at the compassion of Mary than at the passion of Mary's Son? For if he could die in body, could she not die with him in spirit? He died in body through a love greater than anyone had known. She died in spirit through a love unlike any other since his.

September 16th

St. Cornelius, Pope & Martyr, and St. Cyprian, Bishop & Martyr

From a letter by St. Cyprian, Bishop & Martyr

A faith that is ready and unshaken

Cyprian sends greetings to his brother Cornelius. My very dear brother, we have heard of the glorious witness given by your courageous faith. On learning of the honor you had won by your witness, we were filled with such joy that we felt ourselves sharers and companions in your praiseworthy achievements. After all, we have the same Church, the same mind, the same unbroken harmony. Why then should a priest not take pride in the praise given to a fellow priest as though it were given to him? What brotherhood fails to rejoice in the happiness of its brothers wherever they are?

Words cannot express how great was the exultation and delight here when we heard of your good fortune and brave deeds: how you stood out as leader of your brothers in their declaration of their faith, while the leader's confession was enhanced as they declared their faith. You led the way to glory, but you gained many companions in that glory; being foremost in your readiness to bear witness on behalf of all, you prevailed on your people to become a single witness. We cannot decide which we ought to praise, your own ready and unshaken faith or the love of your brothers who would not leave you. While the courage of the bishop who thus led the way has been demonstrated, at the same time the unity of the brotherhood who followed has been manifested. Since you have one heart and one voice, it is the Roman Church as a whole that has thus borne witness.

Dearest brother, bright and shining is the faith which the blessed Apostle praised in your community. He foresaw in the spirit the praise your courage deserves and the strength that could not be broken; he was heralding the future when he testified to your achievements; his praise of the fathers was a challenge to the sons. You unity, your strength have become shining examples of these virtues to the rest of the brethren.

Divine providence has now prepared us. God's merciful design has warned us that the day of our own struggle, our own contest, is at hand. By that shared love which binds us closely together, we are doing all we can to exhort our congregation, to give ourselves unceasingly to fasting, vigils and prayers in common. These are the heavenly weapons which give us the strength to stand firm and endure; they are the spiritual defenses, the God-given armaments that protect us.

Let us then remember one another, united in mind and heart. Let us pray without ceasing, you for us, we for you; by the love we share we shall thus relieve the strain of these great trials.

September 16th ~ Alternative

From the proconsular Acts of the martyrdom of St. Cyprian, Bishop & Martyr

In such a just cause there is no need for deliberation

On the morning of the fourteenth of September a great crowd gathered at the Villa Sexti, in accordance with the order of the governor Galerius Maximus. That same day the governor commanded Bishop Cyprian to be brought before him for trial in the court of Sauciolum. After Cyprian was brought in, the governor asked him: "Are you Thascius Cyprian?" And the bishop replied: "Yes, I am." The governor Galerius Maximus said: "Have you posed as the pontiff of a sacrilegious group?" The bishop answered: "I have." Then the governor said: "Our most venerable emperors have commanded you to perform the religious rites." Bishop Cyprian replied: "I will not do so." Galerius Maximus said: "Consider your position." Cyprian replied: "Follow your orders. In such a just cause there is no need for deliberation."

Then Galerius Maximus, after consulting with his council, reluctantly issued the following judgment: "You have long lived with your sacrilegious convictions, and you have gathered about yourself many others in a vicious conspiracy. You have set yourself up as an enemy of the gods of Rome and our religious practices. The pious and venerable emperors, the Augusti, Valerian and Gallienus, and Valerian the most noble of Caesars, have been unable to draw you back to the observance of their holy ceremonies. You have been discovered as the author and leader of these heinous crimes, and will consequently be held forth as an example for all those who have followed you in your crime. By your blood the law shall be confirmed." Next he read the sentence from a tablet: "It is decided that Thascius Cyprian should die by the sword." Cyprian responded: "Thanks be to God!"

After the sentence was passed, a crowd of his fellow Christians said: "We should also be killed with him!" There arose an uproar among the Christians, and a great mob followed after him. Cyprian was then brought out to the grounds of the Villa Sexti, where, taking off his outer cloak and kneeling on the ground, he fell before the Lord in prayer. He removed his dalmatic and gave it to the deacons, and then stood erect while waiting for the executioner. When the executioner arrived, Cyprian told his friends to give the man twenty-five gold pieces. Cloths and napkins were being spread out in front of him by the brethren. Then the blessed Cyprian covered his eyes with his own hands, but when he was unable to tie the ends of the linen himself, the priest Julian and the sub-deacon Julian fastened them for him.

In this way the blessed Cyprian suffered, and his body was laid out at a nearby place to satisfy the curiosity of the pagans. During the night Cyprian's body was triumphantly borne away in a procession of Christians who, praying and bearing tapers and torches, carried the body to the cemetery of the governor Macrobius Candidianus which lies on the Mappalian Way near the fish ponds. Not many days later the governor Galerius Maximus died.

The most blessed martyr Cyprian suffered on the fourteenth of September under the emperors Valerian and Gallienus, in the reign of our true Lord Jesus Christ, to whom belong honor and glory for ever. Amen.

Septembee 17th

St. Robert Bellarmine, Bishop & Doctor

From a treatise On the Ascent of the Mind to God
by St. Robert Bellarmine, Bishop and Doctor

Incline my heart to your decrees

Sweet Lord, you are meek and merciful[Ps 85:15]. Who would not give himself wholeheartedly to your service, if he began to taste even a little of your fatherly rule? What command, Lord, do you give your servants? *Take my yoke upon you* [Mt 11:28-30.], you say. And what is this yoke of yours like? *My yoke,* you say, *is easy and my burden light*[Mt 11:28-30.] Who would not be glad to bear a yoke that does not press hard but caresses? Who would not be glad for a burden that does not weigh heavy but refreshes? And so you were right to add: *And you will find rest for your souls.* And what is this yoke of yours that does not weary, but gives rest? It is, of course, that first and greatest commandment: *You shall love the Lord your God with all your heart*[Deut 6:4-5; Mt 22:37-40]. What is easier, sweeter, more pleasant, than to love goodness, beauty and love, the fullness of which you are, O Lord, my God?

Is it not true that you promise those who keep your commandments a reward more desirable than great wealth and sweeter than honey? You promise a most abundant reward, for as your apostle James says: *The Lord has prepared a crown of life for those who love him*[Jas 1:12]. What is this crown of life? It is surely a greater good than we can conceive of or desire, as Saint Paul says, quoting Isaiah: *Eye has not seen, ear has not heard, nor has it so much as dawned on man what God has prepared for those who love him*[1 Cor 2:9.]

Truly then the recompense is great for those who keep your commandments. That first and greatest commandment helps the man who obeys, not the God who commands. In addition, the other commandments of God perfect the man who obeys them. They provide him with what he needs. They instruct and enlighten him and make him good and blessed. If you are wise, then, know that you have been created for the glory of God and your own eternal salvation. This is your goal; this is the center of your life; this is the treasure of your heart. If you reach this goal, you will find happiness. If you fail to reach it, you will find misery.

May you consider truly good whatever leads to your goal and truly evil whatever makes you fall away from it. Prosperity and adversity, wealth and poverty, health and sickness, honors and humiliations, life and death, in the mind of the wise man, are not to be sought for their own sake, nor avoided for their own sake. But if they contribute to the glory of God and your eternal happiness, then they are good and should be sought. If they detract from this, they are evil and must be avoided.

September 19th

St. Januarius, Bishop & Martyr

From a sermon by St. Augustine, Bishop & Doctor

For you I am a bishop; with you I am a Christian

The day I became a bishop, a burden was laid on my shoulders for which it will be no easy task to render an account. The honors I receive are for me an ever present cause of uneasiness. Indeed, it terrifies me to think that I could take more pleasure in the honor attached to my office, which is where its danger lies, than in your salvation, which ought to be its fruit. This is why being set above you fills me with alarm, whereas being with you gives me comfort. Danger lies in the first; salvation in the second.

To be honest with you, my obligations involve me in so much turmoil that I feel as though I were tossed by storms on a great ocean. When I remember by whose blood I have been redeemed, this thought brings me peace, as though I were entering the safety of a harbor; and I am consoled, as I carry out the arduous duties of my own particular office, by the blessings which we all have in common. By finding my chief joy therefore in the redemption, which I share with you, and not in my office, which has placed me over you, I shall the more truly be your servant; and so not only fulfill the Lord's command, but also show myself not ungrateful to him for making me your fellow servant. For my Redeemer has a claim upon my love, and I do not forget how he questioned Peter, and asked: *Do you love me, Peter? Then feed my sheep*[Jn 21:15-17]. He asked this once, then again and then a third time. He inquired about his love, and then he gave him work to do; for the greater one's love is, the easier is the work.

How shall I repay the Lord for all the blessings he has given me[Ps 115:12-13]*?* I could say perhaps that I repay him by feeding his sheep, but even though I do this, *it is not really I who do it, but the grace of God within me*[1 Cor 15:10]. So when all that I do is the gift of God's grace, how can I possibly repay him? As a matter of fact, I hope to be repaid myself, and this for the very reason that I love him freely and feed his sheep. But, you may ask, if I feed his sheep because I love him freely, how can I demand payment for feeding them? It is indeed unthinkable to ask for a recompense for love freely given unless that recompense is the loved one himself.

But even if feeding his sheep could repay him for redeeming me, what could repay him for having made me his shepherd? To be a good shepherd I depend entirely on his grace, for without his help I should be a very bad one, there is so much evil in me. Pray, then, that I may not be a bad shepherd, but a good one.

And for you, my brothers, *I also pray and warn you against failing to cooperate with the grace you receive from God*[2 Cor 6:1]. Make my ministry a fruitful one. You are God's garden, and you should therefore welcome the laborer who does the visible work of planting and watering the seed, even though the growth comes from one who works invisibly within you. Help me both by your prayers and by your obedience, for then it will be a pleasure for me, not to preside over you, but to serve you.

September 20th

Andrew Kim Taegŏn, Priest & Martyr, St. Paul Chŏng Hasang, and Companions, Martyrs

From the final exhortation of Andrew Kim Taegŏn, Priest & Martyr

Love and perseverance are the crown of faith

My brothers and sisters, my dearest friends, think again and again on this: God has ruled over all things in heaven and on earth from the beginning of time; then reflect on why and for what purpose he chose each one of us to be created in his own image and likeness.

In this world of perils and hardship if we did not recognize the Lord as our Creator, there would be no benefit either in being born or in our continued existence. We have come into the world by God's grace; by that same grace we have received baptism, entrance into the Church, and the honor of being called Christians. Yet what good will this do us if we are Christians in name alone and not in fact? We would have come into the world for nothing, we would have entered the Church for nothing, and we would have betrayed even God and his grace. It would be better never to have been born than to receive the grace of God and then to sin against him. Look at the farmer who cultivates his rice fields. In season he plows, then fertilizes the earth; never counting the cost, he labors under the sun to nurture the seed he has planted. When harvest time comes and the rice crop is abundant, forgetting his labor and sweat, he rejoices with an exultant heart. But if the crop is sparse and there is nothing but straw and husks, the farmer broods over his toil and sweat and turns his back on that field with a disgust that is all the greater the harder he has toiled.

The Lord is like a farmer and we are the field of rice that he fertilizes with his grace and by the mystery of the incarnation and the redemption irrigates with his blood, in order that we will grow and reach maturity. When harvest time comes, the day of judgment, those who have grown to maturity in the grace of God will find the joy of adopted children in the kingdom of heaven; those who have not grown to maturity will become God's enemies and, even though they were once his children, they will be punished according to their deeds for all eternity.

Dearest brothers and sisters: when he was in the world, the Lord Jesus bore countless sorrows and by his own passion and death founded his Church; now he gives it increase through the sufferings of his faithful. No matter how fiercely the powers of this world oppress and oppose the Church, they will never bring it down. Ever since his ascension and from the time of the apostles to the present, the Lord Jesus has made his Church grow even in the midst of tribulations.

For the last fifty or sixty years, ever since the coming of the Church to our own land of Korea, the faithful have suffered persecution over and over again. Persecution still rages and as a result many who are friends in the household of the faith, myself among them, have been thrown into prison and like you are experiencing severe distress. Because we have become the one Body, should not our hearts be grieved for the members who are suffering? Because of the human ties that bind us, should we not feel deeply the pain of our separation?

But, as the Scriptures say, God numbers the very hairs of our head and in his all-embracing providence he has care over us all. Persecution, therefore, can only be regarded as the command of the Lord or as a prize he gives or as a punishment he permits. Hold fast, then, to the will of God and with all your heart fight the good fight under the leadership of Jesus; conquer again the diabolical power of this world that Christ has already vanquished. I beg you not to fail in your love for one another, but to support one another and to stand fast until the Lord mercifully delivers us from our trials.

There are twenty of us in this place and by God's grace we are so far all well. If any of us is executed, I ask you not to forget our families. I have many things to say, yet how can pen and paper capture what I feel? I end this letter. As we are all near the final ordeal, I urge you to remain steadfast in faith, so that at last we will all reach heaven and there rejoice together. I embrace you all in love.

September 21st

St. Matthew, Apostle & Evangelist

From a homily by St. Bede the Venerable, Priest & Doctor

Jesus saw him through the eyes of mercy and chose him

Jesus saw a man called Matthew sitting at the tax office, and he said to him: Follow me[Mt 9:9]. Jesus saw Matthew, not merely in the usual sense, but more significantly with his merciful understanding of men.

He saw the tax collector and, because he saw him through the eyes of mercy and chose him, he said to him: *Follow me*. This following meant imitating the pattern of his life – not just walking after him. St. John tells us: *Whoever says he abides in Christ ought to walk in the same way in which he walked*[1 Jn 2:6].

And he rose and followed him[Mt 9:9]. There is no reason for surprise that the tax collector abandoned earthly wealth as soon as the Lord commanded him. Nor should one be amazed that neglecting his wealth, he joined a band of men whose leader had, on Matthew's assessment, no riches at all. Our Lord summoned Matthew by speaking to him in words. By an invisible, interior impulse flooding his mind with the light of grace, he instructed him to walk in his footsteps. In this way Matthew could understand that Christ, who was summoning him away from earthly possessions, had incorruptible treasures of heaven in his gift.

As he sat at table in the house, behold many tax collectors and sinners came and sat down with Jesus and his disciples[Mt 9:10]. This conversion of one tax collector gave many men, those from his own profession and other sinners, an example of repentance and pardon. Notice also the happy and true anticipation of his future status as apostle and teacher of the nations. No sooner was he converted than Matthew drew after him a whole crowd of sinners along the same road to salvation. He took up his appointed duties while still taking his first steps in the faith, and from that hour he fulfilled his obligation and thus grew in merit.

To see a deeper understanding of the great celebration Matthew held at his house, we must realize that he not only gave a banquet for the Lord at his earthly residence, but far more pleasing was the banquet set in his own heart which he provided through faith and love. Our Savior attests to this: *Behold I stand at the door and knock; if anyone hears my voice and opens the door, I will come in to him and eat with him, and he with me*[Rev 3:20].

On hearing Christ's voice, we open the door to receive him, as it were, when we freely assent to his promptings and when we give ourselves over to doing what must be done. Christ, since he dwells in the hearts of his chosen ones through the grace of his love, enters so that he might eat with us and we with him. He ever refreshes us by the light of his presence insofar as we progress in our devotion to and longing for the things of heaven. He himself is delighted by such a pleasing banquet.

September 26th

Saints Cosmas and Damian, Martyrs

From a sermon by St. Augustine, Bishop & Doctor

The martyrs' death was bought by the death of Christ and it is precious in his sight

In the glorious deeds of the holy martyrs who everywhere adorn the Church, we verify the truth of what we have been singing: *Precious in the sight of the Lord is the death of his saints*[Ps 115:15]. They are precious in our sight and in the sight of him in whose name it was done. The price paid for these deaths was the death of one man. How many deaths indeed this one man bought by dying, for if he had not died, the grain of wheat would not have been multiplied! You have heard what he said as he drew near to his passion, our redemption: *If the grain of wheat does not fall to the ground and die, it remains barren, but if it dies, it is very fruitful*[Jn 12:24].

On the cross Christ effected a great exchange. There the purse containing the price to be paid for us was opened. When the soldier's lance cut its way into his side, the price paid for the whole world flowed forth. The martyrs and all the faithful were bought with it, but the faith of the martyrs was also tested: their blood bore witness to their faith. They gave back what had been paid for them and lived up to what Saint John says: *As Christ laid down his life for us, so we should lay down our lives for our brothers*[1 Jn 3:16]. Elsewhere we read: *You have taken your seat at the great table; consider carefully what is set before you, for you must prepare the same in return*[Prov 23:1]. The great table is the one at which the Lord of the banquet is himself the food. No one feeds the guests with his very self, yet that is what Christ the Lord does. He invites and he is the food and drink. The martyrs took careful note of what they ate and drank, so that they might return the same.

But how could they return the same unless the one who had first given it, gave them also the means of making a return? *What shall I give back to the Lord for all that he has given me? I shall take the cup of salvation*[Ps 115:12-13]. What cup is that? The bitter and saving cup of suffering, the cup the sick man would be afraid to put to his lips unless the doctor had drunk of it first. That is the cup meant here, and we find Christ himself speaking of it: *Father, if possible, let this cup pass away from me*[Mt 26:39]. Of it the martyrs said: *I shall take the cup of salvation and call upon the name of the Lord*[Ps 115:12-13].

Are you not afraid that you may fail the test? But why should you be? *I shall call upon the name of the Lord*[Ps 115:12-13]. How else did the martyrs overcome, except that in them he overcame who said: *Rejoice, for I have overcome the world*[Jn 16:33]? The Lord of heaven directed their minds and tongues; through them he overcame the devil on earth and crowned them as martyrs in heaven. Happy are they who have thus drunk of this cup, for their suffering is over, and they have received their honors.

September 27th

St. Vincent de Paul, Priest

From a writing of St. Vincent de Paul, Priest

Serving the poor is to be our first preference

Even though the poor are often rough and unrefined, we must not judge them from external appearances nor from the mental gifts they seem to have received. On the contrary, if you consider the poor in the light of faith, then you will observe that they are taking the place of the Son of God who chose to be poor. Although in his passion he almost lost the appearance of a man and was considered a fool by the Gentiles and a stumbling block by the Jews, he showed them that his mission was to preach to the poor: *He sent me to preach the good news to the poor*[Isa 61:1-3; Lk 4:18]. We also ought to have this same spirit and imitate Christ's actions, that is, we must take care of the poor, console them, help them, support their cause.

Since Christ willed to be born poor, he chose for himself disciples who were poor. He made himself the servant of the poor and shared their poverty. He went so far as to say that he would consider every deed which either helps or harms the poor as done for or against himself. Since God surely loves the poor, he also loves those who love the poor. For when one person holds another dear, he also includes in his affection anyone who loves or serves the one he loves. That is why we hope that God will love us for the sake of the poor. So when we visit the poor and needy, we try to be understanding where they are concerned. We sympathize with them so fully that we can echo Paul's words: *I have become all things to all men*[1 Cor 9:22]. Therefore, we must try to be stirred by our neighbors' worries and distress. We must beg God to pour into our hearts sentiments of pity and compassion and to fill them again and again with these dispositions.

It is our duty to prefer the service of the poor to everything else and to offer such service as quickly as possible. If a needy person requires medicine or other help during prayer time, do whatever has to be done with peace of mind. Offer the deed to God as your prayer. Do not become upset or feel guilty because you interrupted your prayer to serve the poor. God is not neglected if you leave him for such service. One of God's works is merely interrupted so that another can be carried out. So when you leave prayer to serve some poor person, remember that this very service is performed for God. Charity is certainly greater than any rule. Moreover, all rules must lead to charity. Since she is a noble mistress, we must do whatever she commands. With renewed devotion, then, we must serve the poor, especially outcasts and beggars. They have been given to us as our masters and patrons.

September 28th

St. Wenceslaus, Martyr

From the first old Slavic legend

The throne of the king who judges the poor in honesty shall be strengthened for ever

At the death of Vratislaus the people of Bohemia made his son Wenceslaus their king. He was by God's grace a man of utmost faith. He was charitable to the poor, and he would clothe the naked, feed the hungry and offer hospitality to travelers according to the summons of the Gospel. He would not allow widows to be treated unjustly; he loved all his people, both rich and poor; he also provided for the servants of God, and he adorned many churches.

The men of Bohemia, however, became arrogant and prevailed upon Boleslaus, his younger brother. They told him, "Your brother Wenceslaus is conspiring with his mother and his men to kill you."

On the feasts of the dedication of the churches in various cities, Wenceslaus was in the habit of paying them a visit. One Sunday he entered the city of Boleslaus on the feast of Saints Cosmas and Damian, and after hearing Mass, he planned to return to Prague. But Boleslaus, with his wicked plan in mind, detained him with the words: "Why are you leaving, brother?" The next morning when they rang the bell for matins, Wenceslaus, on hearing the sound, said: "Praise to you, Lord; you have allowed me to live to this morning." And so he rose and went to matins.

Immediately Boleslaus followed him to the church door. Wenceslaus looked back at him and said: "Brother, you were a good subject to me yesterday." But the devil had already blocked the ears of Boleslaus and perverted his heart. Drawing his sword Boleslaus replied: "And now I intend to be a better one!" With these words he struck his brother's head with his sword. But Wenceslaus turned and said: "Brother, what are you trying to do?" And with that he seized Boleslaus and threw him to the ground. But one of Boleslaus' counselors ran up and stabbed Wenceslaus in the hand. With his hand wounded, he let go of his brother and took refuge in the church. But two evil men struck him down at the church door; and then another rushed up and ran him through with a sword. Thereupon Wenceslaus died with the words: *Into your hands, O Lord, I commend my spirit*[Ps 30:6; Lk 23:46]!

September 29th

Saints Michael, Gabriel and Raphael, Archangels

From a homily on the Gospels by St. Gregory the Great, Pope & Doctor

The word "angel" denotes a function rather than a nature

You should be aware that the word "angel" denotes a function rather than a nature. Those holy spirits of heaven have indeed always been spirits. They can only be called angels when they deliver some message. Moreover, those who deliver messages of lesser importance are called angels; and those who proclaim messages of supreme importance are called archangels.

And so it was that not merely an angel but the archangel Gabriel was sent to the Virgin Mary. It was only fitting that the highest angel should come to announce the greatest of all messages.

Some angels are given proper names to denote the service they are empowered to perform. In that holy city, where perfect knowledge flows from the vision of almighty God, those who have no names may easily be known. But personal names are assigned to some, not because they could not be known without them, but rather to denote their ministry when they came among us. Thus, Michael means "Who is like God?"; Gabriel is "The Strength of God"; and Raphael is "God's Remedy."

Whenever some act of wondrous power must be performed, Michael is sent, so that his action and his name may make it clear that no one can do what God does by his superior power. So also our ancient foe desired in his pride to be like God, saying: *I will ascend into heaven; I will exalt my throne above the stars of heaven; I will be like the Most High*[Isa 14:13]. He will be allowed to remain in power until the end of the world when he will be destroyed in the final punishment. Then, he will fight with the archangel Michael, as we are told by John: *A battle was fought with Michael the archangel*[Rev 12:7-17].

So too Gabriel, who is called God's strength, was sent to Mary. He came to announce the One who appeared as a humble man to quell the cosmic powers. Thus God's strength announced the coming of the Lord of the heavenly powers, mighty in battle.

Raphael means, as I have said, God's remedy, for when he touched Tobit's eyes in order to cure him, he banished the darkness of his blindness. Thus, since he is to heal, he is rightly called God's remedy.

September 30th

St. Jerome, Priest & Doctor

From the prologue of the commentary on Isaiah by St. Jerome, Priest & Doctor

Ignorance of Scripture is ignorance of Christ

I interpret as I should, following the command of Christ: *Search the Scriptures,* and *Seek and you shall find*[Mt 7:7-8]. Christ will not say to me what he said to the Jews: *You erred, not knowing the Scriptures and not knowing the power of God*[Mt 22:29]. For if, as Paul says, Christ is the power of God and the wisdom of God, and if the man who does not know Scripture does not know the power and wisdom of God, then ignorance of Scripture is ignorance of Christ.

Therefore, I will imitate the head of a household who brings out of his storehouse things both new and old, and says to his spouse in the Song of Songs: *I have kept for you things new and old, my beloved*[Song 7:13]. In this way permit me to explain Isaiah, showing that he was not only a prophet, but an evangelist and an apostle as well. For he says about himself and the other evangelists: *How beautiful are the feet of those who preach good news, of those who announce peace*[Isa 52:7; Rom 10:14-15]. And God speaks to him as if he were an apostle: *Whom shall I send, who will go to my people*[Isa 6:8]? And he answers: *Here I am; send me* [Isa 6:8].

No one should think that I mean to explain the entire subject matter of this great book of Scripture in one brief sermon, since it contains all the mysteries of the Lord. It prophesies that Emmanuel is to be born of a virgin and accomplish marvelous works and signs. It predicts his death, burial and resurrection from the dead as the Savior of all men. I need say nothing about the natural sciences, ethics and logic. Whatever is proper to holy Scripture, whatever can be expressed in human language and understood by the human mind, is contained in the book of Isaiah. Of these mysteries the author himself testifies when he writes: *You will be given a vision of all things, like words in a sealed scroll. When they give the writings to a wise man, they will say: Read this. And he will reply: I cannot, for it is sealed. And when the scroll is given to an uneducated man and he is told: Read this, he will reply: I do not know how to read*[Isa 29:11-12].

Should this argument appear weak to anyone, let him listen to the Apostle: *Let two or three prophets speak, and let others interpret; if, however, a revelation should come to one of those who are seated there, let the first one be quiet*[1 Cor 14:29]. How can they be silent, since it depends on the Spirit who speaks through his prophets whether they remain silent or speak? If they understood what they were saying, all things would be full of wisdom and knowledge. But it was not the air vibrating with the human voice that reached their ears, but rather it was God speaking within the soul of the prophets, just as another prophet says: *It is an angel who spoke in me*[Zech 4:4]; and again, *Crying out in our hearts, Abba, Father,* and *I shall listen to what the Lord God says within me*[Gal 4:6].

October 1st

St. Thérèse of the Child Jesus, Virgin & Doctor

From the autobiography of St. Theres of the Child Jesus, Virgin & Doctor

In the heart of the church I will be love

Since my longing for martyrdom was powerful and unsettling, I turned to the epistles of Saint Paul in the hope of finally finding an answer. By chance the twelfth and thirteenth chapters of the first epistle to the Corinthians caught my attention, and in the first section I read that not everyone can be an apostle, prophet or teacher, that the Church is composed of a variety of members, and that the eye cannot be the hand. Even with such an answer revealed before me, I was not satisfied and did not find peace.

I persevered in the and did not let my mind wander until I found this encouraging theme: *Set your desires on the greater gifts. And I will show you the way which surpasses all others*[1 Cor 12:31]. For the Apostle insists that the greater gifts are nothing at all without love and that this same love is surely the best path leading directly to God. At length I had found peace of mind.

When I had looked upon the mystical body of the Church, I recognized myself in none of the members which Saint Paul described, and what is more, I desired to distinguish myself more favorably within the whole body. Love appeared to me to be the hinge for my vocation. Indeed I knew that the Church had a body composed of various members, but in this body the necessary and more noble member was not lacking; I knew that the Church had a heart and that such a heart appeared to be aflame with love. I knew that one love drove the members of the Church to action, that if this love were extinguished, the apostles would have proclaimed the Gospel no longer, the martyrs would have shed their blood no more. I saw and realized that love sets off the bounds of all vocations, that love is everything, that this same love embraces every time and every place. In one word, that love is everlasting.

Then, nearly ecstatic with the supreme joy in my soul, I proclaimed: O Jesus, my love, at last I have found my calling: my call is love. Certainly I have found my proper place in the Church, and you gave me that very place, my God. In the heart of the Church, my mother, I will be love, and thus I will be all things, as my desire finds its direction.

October 2nd

The Holy Guardian Angels

From a sermon by St. Bernard, Abbot & Doctor

That they might guard you in all your ways

He has given his angels charge over you to guard you in all your ways[Ps 90:11]. *Let them thank the Lord for his mercy; his wonderful works are for the children of men*[Ps 106:8]. Let them give thanks and say among the nations, the Lord has done great things for them. O Lord, what is man that you have made yourself known to him, or why do you incline your heart to him? And you do incline your heart to him; you show him your care and your concern. Finally, you send your only Son and the grace of your Spirit, and promise him a vision of your countenance. And so, that nothing in heaven should be wanting in your concern for us, you send those blessed spirits to serve us, assigning them as our guardians and our teachers.

He has given his angels charge over you to guard you in all your ways[Ps 90:11]. These words should fill you with respect, inspire devotion and instill confidence; respect for the presence of angels, devotion because of their loving service, and confidence because of their protection. And so the angels are here; they are at your side, they are with you, present on your behalf. They are here to protect you and to serve you. But even if it is God who has given them this charge, we must nonetheless be grateful to them for the great love with which they obey and come to help us in our great need.

So let us be devoted and grateful to such great protectors; let us return their love and honor them as much as we can and should. Yet all our love and honor must go to him, for it is from him that they receive all that makes them worthy of our love and respect.

We should then, my brothers, show our affection for the angels, for one day they will be our coheirs just as here below they are our guardians and trustees appointed and set over us by the Father. We are God's children although it does not seem so, because we are still but small children under guardians and trustees, and for the present little better than slaves.

Even though we are children and have a long, a very long and dangerous way to go, with such protectors what have we to fear? They who keep us in all our ways cannot be overpowered or led astray, much less lead us astray. They are loyal, prudent, powerful. Why then are we afraid? We have only to follow them, stay close to them, and we shall dwell under the protection of God's heaven.

October 4th

St. Francis of Assisi

From a letter written to all the faithful by St. Francis of Assisi

We must be simple, humble and pure

It was through his archangel, Saint Gabriel, that the Father above made known to the holy and glorious Virgin Mary that the worthy, holy and glorious Word of the Father would come from heaven and take from her womb the real flesh of our human frailty. Though he was wealthy beyond reckoning, he still willingly chose to be poor with his blessed mother. And shortly before his passion he celebrated the Passover with his disciples. Then he prayed to his Father saying: *Father, if it be possible, let this cup be taken from me*[Mt 26:39].

Nevertheless, he reposed his will in the will of his Father. The Father willed that his blessed and glorious Son, whom he gave to us and who was born for us, should through his own blood offer himself as a sacrificial victim on the altar of the cross. This was to be done not for himself through whom all things were made, but for our sins. It was intended to leave us an example of how to follow in his footsteps. And he desires all of us to be saved through him, and to receive him with pure heart and chaste body.

O how happy and blessed are those who love the Lord and do as the Lord himself said in the gospel: *You shall love the Lord your God with your whole heart and your whole soul, and your neighbor as yourself*[Deut 6:4-5; Mt 22:37-40]. Therefore, let us love God and adore him with pure heart and mind. This is his particular desire when he says: *True worshipers adore the Father in spirit and truth*[Jn 4:23]. For all who adore him must do so in the spirit of truth. Let us also direct to him our praises and prayers saying: *Our Father, who art in heaven,* since *we must always pray and never grow slack*.

Furthermore, let us produce worthy fruits of penance. Let us also love our neighbors as ourselves. Let us have charity and humility. Let us give alms because these cleanse our souls from the stains of sin. Men lose all the material things they leave behind them in this world, but they carry with them the reward of their charity and the alms they give. For these they will receive from the Lord the reward and recompense they deserve. We must not be wise and prudent according to the flesh. Rather we must be simple, humble and pure. We should never desire to be over others. Instead, we ought to be servants who are submissive to every human being for God's sake. The Spirit of the Lord will rest on all who live in this way and persevere in it to the end. He will permanently dwell in them. They will be the Father's children who do his work. They are the spouses, brothers and mothers of our Lord Jesus Christ.

October 6th

St. Bruno, Priest

From a letter to his Carthusian sons by St. Bruno, Priest

My spirit rejoices in the Lord

From the frequent and pleasant reports of our most blessed brother, I know of your reasoned and truly praise worthy discipline, carried out with unwavering rigor. Since I have heard of your holy love and constant pursuit of honesty and virtue, my spirit rejoices in the Lord. I rejoice and am drawn to praise and give thanks to God, and still I long to love him. I rejoice, as I should, in the growing fruits of your strength, and yet I grieve and grow ashamed that I lie idle and senseless in the mire of my sins.

Therefore rejoice, my dearest brothers, because you are so blessed and because of the bountiful hand of God's grace upon you. Rejoice, because you have escaped the various dangers and shipwrecks of the stormy world. Rejoice, because you have reached the quiet and safe anchorage of a secret harbor Many wish to come into this port, and many make great efforts to do so, yet do not achieve it. Indeed many, after reaching it, have been thrust out, since it was not granted them from above.

Therefore, my brothers, you should consider it certain and well-established that whoever partakes of this desirable good, should he in any way lose it, will grieve to his death, if he has any regard or concern for the salvation of his soul.

My dearest lay brothers, of you I say: *My soul magnifies the Lord*[Lk 1:46-55]. For I have learned of the generosity of his mercy toward you from the report of your prior and dearest father; he rejoices and takes great pride in you. And let us rejoice that since you are unacquainted with the knowledge of letters, almighty God will inscribe in your hearts with his finger not only his love but also the knowledge of his holy law. By your work you show what you love and what you know. When you observe true obedience with prudence and enthusiasm, it is clear that you wisely pick the most delightful and nourishing fruit of divine Scripture.

October 7th

Our Lady of the Rosary

From a sermon by St. Bernard, Abbot & Doctor

We should meditate on the mysteries of salvation

The child to be born of you will be called holy, the Son of God, the fountain of wisdom, the Word of the Father on high. Through you, blessed Virgin, this Word will become flesh, so that even though, as he says: *I am in the Father and the Father is in me*[Jn 14:11], it is still true for him to say: "I came forth from God and am here."

In the beginning was the Word[Jn 1:1]. The spring was gushing forth, yet still within himself. Indeed, *the Word was with God*[Jn 1:1], truly dwelling in inaccessible light. And the Lord said from the beginning: *I think thoughts of peace and not of affliction*[Jer 29:11]. Yet your thought was locked within you, and whatever you thought, we did not know; for who knew the mind of the Lord, or who was his counselor?

And so the idea of peace came down to do the work of peace: *The Word was made flesh and* even now *dwells among us*[Jn 1:14]. It is by faith that he dwells in our hearts, in our memory, our intellect and penetrates even into our imagination. What concept could man have of God if he did not first fashion an image of him in his heart? By nature incomprehensible and inaccessible, he was invisible and unthinkable, but now he wished to be understood, to be seen and thought of.

But how, you ask, was this done? He lay in a manger and rested on a virgin's breast, preached on a mountain, and spent the night in prayer. He hung on a cross, grew pale in death, and roamed free among the dead and ruled over those in hell. He rose again on the third day, and showed the apostles the wounds of the nails, the signs of victory; and finally in their presence he ascended to the sanctuary of heaven.

How can we not contemplate this story in truth, piety and holiness? Whatever of all this I consider, it is God I am considering; in all this he is my God. I have said it is wise to meditate on these truths, and I have thought it right to recall the abundant sweetness, given by the fruits of this priestly root; and Mary, drawing abundantly from heaven, has caused this sweetness to overflow for us.

October 9th

Saints Denis, Bishop, and his Companions, Martyrs

From a commentary on psalm 118 by St. Ambrose, Bishop & Doctor

Be a faithful and courageous witness

As there are many kinds of persecution, so there are many kinds of martyrdom. Every day you are a witness to Christ. You were tempted by the spirit of fornication, but feared the coming judgment of Christ and did not want your purity of mind and body to be defiled: you are a martyr for Christ. You were tempted by the spirit of avarice to seize the property of a child and violate the rights of a defenseless widow, but remembered God's law and saw your duty to give help, not act unjustly: you are a witness to Christ. Christ wants witnesses like this to stand ready, as Scripture says: *Do justice for the orphan and defend the widow*[Isa 1:17]. You were tempted by the spirit of pride but saw the poor and the needy and looked with loving compassion on them, and loved humility rather than arrogance: you are a witness to Christ. What is more, your witness was not in word only but also in deed.

Who can give greater witness than one *who acknowledges that the Lord Jesus has come in the flesh*[1 Jn 4:2] and keeps the commandments of the Gospel? One who hears but does not act, denies Christ. Even if he acknowledges him by his words, he denies him by his deeds. How many will say to Christ: *Lord, Lord, did we not prophesy and cast out devils and work many miracles, all in your name*[Mt 7:22]*?* On that day he will say to them: *Depart from me, all you evildoers*[Mt 7:23]. The true witness is one who bears witness to the commandments of the Lord Jesus and supports that witness by deeds.

How many hidden martyrs there are, bearing witness to Christ each day and acknowledging Jesus as the Lord! The Apostle knew this kind of martyrdom, this faithful witness to Christ. *This is our boast,* he said, *the witness of our conscience*[2 Cor 1:12]. How many have borne witness in public but denied it in private! *Do not believe every spirit,* he said, but know *from their fruits*[1 Jn 4:1] whom you should believe. Be faithful and courageous when you are persecuted within, so that you may win approval when you are persecuted in public. Even in those unseen persecutions there are kings and governors, judges with terrible power. You have an example in the temptation endured by the Lord.

In another place we read: *Do not let sin be king in your mortal body*[Rom 6:12]. You see the kings before whom you are made to stand, those who sit in judgment over sinners, where sin is in control. There are as many kings as there are sins and vices; it is before these kings that we are led and before these we stand. These kings have their thrones in many hearts. But if anyone acknowledges Christ, he immediately makes a prisoner of this kind of king and casts him down from the throne of his own heart. How shall the devil maintain his throne in one who builds a throne for Christ in his heart?

October 9th

St. John Leonardi, Priest

From a letter to Pope Paul V by St. John Leonardi, Priest

I will tell you what the Lord requires of you

Those who want to work for moral reform in the world must seek the glory of God before all else. Because he is the source of all good, they must wait for his help, and pray for it in this difficult and necessary undertaking. They must then present themselves to those they seek to reform, as mirrors of every virtue and as lamps on a lamp-stand. Their upright lives and noble conduct must shine before all who are in the house of God. In this way they will gently entice the members of the Church to reform instead of forcing them, lest, in the words of the Council of Trent, they demand of the body what is not found in the head, and thus upset the whole order of the Lord's household.

They will be like skilled physicians taking great pains to dispose of all the diseases that afflict the Church and require a cure. They will ready themselves to provide suitable remedies for each illness.

As far as remedies applicable to the whole Church are concerned, reform must begin with high and low alike, with superiors and inferiors. Yet the reformers must look first to those who are set over the rest, so that reform can begin at the point from which it may spread to others.

Be especially concerned with cardinals, patriarchs, archbishops, bishops and priests, whose particular duty is the care of souls, and make them men to whom guidance of the Lord's flock can be safely entrusted. So let us work down from the highest to the lowest, from superiors to inferiors. Those men who must initiate ecclesiastical reform must not be looked down upon.

Nothing should be left untried that can train children from early childhood in good morals and in the earnest practice of Christianity. To this end nothing is more effective than pious instructions in Christian doctrine. Children should be entrusted only to good and God-fearing teachers.

These are the thoughts, most holy Father, that the Lord has chosen to inspire in me for the present on this most important matter. If at first glance they appear difficult, compare them with the magnitude of the situation. Then they will seem very easy indeed. Great works are accomplished only by great men, and great men should be involved in great works.

October 14th

St. Callistus I, Pope & Martyr

From a treatise to Fortunatus by St. Cyprian, Bishop and Martyr

In times of peace the testimony of a good conscience wins the crown

The sufferings of this present time are not to be compared with the glory that is to be revealed in us[Rom 8:18]. Who would not strive wholeheartedly to attain to such glory, to become a friend of God and straightway rejoice with Christ, receiving heavenly rewards after earth's torment and suffering? Soldiers of this world take pride in returning to their home country in triumph after they have defeated the enemy. How much greater is the glory in returning triumphantly to heaven after conquering the devil. The bold deceiver is laid low, the trophies of victory are restored to the place from which Adam was cast out for his sin. We offer to the Lord a most acceptable gift, our incorrupt faith, the unshaken courage of our spirit and the glorious pride of our dedication. We accompany him when he comes to take vengeance on his enemies; sitting at his side at the judgment seat, sharing in Christ's inheritance, we are on an equal footing with the angels and enjoy the possession of a heavenly kingdom together with the patriarchs, apostles and prophets. What persecution can defeat such thoughts, what torture overwhelm them?

The spirit of a strong and stable character strengthened by meditation endures; this unshaken spirit, which is strengthened by a certain and solid faith in the future will be enlivened against all the terrors of the devil and threats of this world. During persecution the earth is closed off from us, but heaven lies open; the Antichrist threatens, but Christ protects us; death is brought on, but eternal life follows. What an honor, what happiness to depart joyfully from this world, to go forth in glory from the anguish and pain, in one moment to close the eyes that looked on the world of men and in the next to open them at once to look on God and Christ! The speed of this joyous departure! You are suddenly withdrawn from earth to find yourself in the kingdom of heaven.

These are the thoughts you must grasp with your heart and mind and reflect on day and night. If persecution should overtake such a soldier of God, it will not overcome one so virtuously prepared for battle. Even if our summons should come sooner, our faith which was prepared for the witness of martyrdom will not go unrewarded. For we would immediately receive our reward by God's judgment. In time of persecution the battle wins the crown, but in peace it is the testimony of a good conscience.

October 15th

St. Teresa of Avila, Virgin & Doctor

From a work by St. Teresa of Avila, Virgin & Doctor

Let us always be mindful of Christ's love

If Christ Jesus dwells in a man as his friend and noble leader, that man can endure all things, for Christ helps and strengthens us and never abandons us. He is a true friend. And I clearly see that if we expect to please him and receive an abundance of his graces, God desires that these graces must come to us from the hands of Christ, through his most sacred humanity, in which God takes delight.

Many, many times I have perceived this through experience. The Lord has told it to me. I have definitely seen that we must enter by this gate if we wish his Sovereign Majesty to reveal to us great and hidden mysteries. A person should desire no other path, even if he is at the summit of contemplation; on this road he walks safely. All blessings come to us through our Lord. He will teach us, for in beholding his life we find that he is the best example.

What more do we desire from such a good friend at our side? Unlike our friends in the world, he will never abandon us when we are troubled or distressed. Blessed is the one who truly loves him and always keeps him near. Let us consider the glorious Saint Paul: it seems that no other name fell from his lips than that of Jesus, because the name of Jesus was fixed and embedded in his heart. Once I had come to understand this truth, I carefully considered the lives of some of the saints, the great contemplatives, and found that they took no other path: Francis, Anthony of Padua, Bernard, Catherine of Siena. A person must walk along this path in freedom, placing himself in God's hands. If God should desire to raise us to the position of one who is an intimate and shares his secrets, we ought to accept this gladly.

Whenever we think of Christ we should recall the love that led him to bestow on us so many graces and favors, and also the great love God showed in giving us in Christ a pledge of his love; for love calls for love in return. Let us strive to keep this always before our eyes and to rouse ourselves to love him. For if at some time the Lord should grant us the grace of impressing his love on our hearts, all will become easy for us and we shall accomplish great things quickly and without effort.

October 16th

St. Hedwig, Religious

From the life of St. Hedwig, Religious by a contemporary author

She was always directed toward God

Hedwig knew that those living stones that were to be placed in the building of the heavenly Jerusalem had to be smoothed out by buffetings and pressures in this world, and that many tribulations would be needed before she could cross over into the glory of her heavenly homeland. And so she exposed herself completely to the waters of suffering and continually exhausted her body with rigorous chastisement. Because of such great daily fasts and abstinences she grew so thin that many wondered how such a feeble and delicate woman could endure these torments.

She afflicted herself with continual mortification of the flesh, but she did so with prudent discretion. The more attentively she kept watch, the more she grew in the strength of the spirit and in grace, and the more the fire of devotion and divine love blazed within her. She was often borne aloft with such ardent desire and impelled toward God that she would no longer be aware of the things that were around her.

Just as her devotion made her always seek after God, so her generous piety turned her toward her neighbor, and she bountifully bestowed alms on the needy. She gave aid to colleges and to religious persons dwelling within or outside monasteries, to widows and orphans, to the weak and the feeble, to lepers and those bound in chains or imprisoned, to travelers and needy women nursing infants. She allowed no one who came to her for help to go away uncomforted.

And because this servant of God never neglected the practice of all good works, God also conferred on her such grace that when she lacked human means to do good, and her own powers failed, the divine power of the sufferings of Christ strengthened her to respond to the needs of her neighbors. And so through divine favor she had the power to relieve the bodily and spiritual troubles of all who sought her help.

October 16th

St. Margaret Mary Alacoque, Virgin

From a letter by St. Margaret Mary Alacoque, virgin

We must know the love of Christ which surpasses all knowledge

It seems to me that our Lord's earnest desire to have his sacred heart honored in a special way is directed toward renewing the effects of redemption in our souls. For the Sacred Heart is an inexhaustible fountain and its sole desire is to pour itself out into the hearts of the humble so as to free them and prepare them to lead lives according to his good pleasure.

From this divine heart three streams flow endlessly. The first is the stream of mercy for sinners; it pours into their hearts sentiments of contrition and repentance. The second is the stream of charity which helps all in need and especially aids those seeking perfection to find the means of surmounting their difficulties. From the third stream flow love and light for the benefit of his friends who have attained perfection; these he wishes to unite to himself so that they may share his knowledge and commandments and, in their individual ways, devote themselves wholly to advancing his glory.

This divine heart is an abyss of all blessings, and into it the poor should submerge all their needs. It is an abyss of joy in which all of us can immerse our sorrows. It is an abyss of lowliness to counteract our foolishness, an abyss of mercy for the wretched, an abyss of love to meet our every need.

Therefore, you must unite yourselves to the heart of our Lord Jesus Christ, both at the beginning of your conversion in order to obtain proper dispositions, and at its end in order to make reparation. Are you making no progress in prayer? Then you need only offer God the prayers which the Savior has poured out for us in the sacrament of the altar. Offer God his fervent love in reparation for your sluggishness. In the course of every activity pray as follows: "My God, I do this or I endure that in the heart of your Son and according to his holy counsels. I offer it to you in reparation for anything blameworthy or imperfect in my actions." Continue to do this in every circumstance of life. And every time that some punishment, affliction or injustice comes your way, say to yourself: "Accept this as sent to you by the Sacred Heart of Jesus Christ in order to unite yourself to him."

But above all preserve peace of heart. This is more valuable than any treasure. In order to preserve it there is nothing more useful than renouncing your own will and substituting for it the will of the divine heart. In this way his will can carry out for us whatever contributes to his glory, and we will be happy to be his subjects and to trust entirely in him.

October 17th

St. Ignatius of Antioch, Bishop & Martyr

From a letter to the Romans by St. Ignatius of Antioch, Bishop & Martyr

I am God's wheat and shall be ground by the teeth of wild animals

I am writing to all the churches to let it be known that I will gladly die for God if only you do not stand in my way. I plead with you: show me no untimely kindness. Let me be food for the wild beasts, for they are my way to God. I am God's wheat and shall be ground by their teeth so that I may become Christ's pure bread. Pray to Christ for me that the animals will be the means of making me a sacrificial victim for God.

No earthly pleasures, no kingdoms of this world can benefit me in any way. I prefer death in Christ Jesus to power over the farthest limits of the earth. He who died in place of us is the one object of my quest. He who rose for our sakes is my one desire. The time for my birth is close at hand. Forgive me, my brothers. Do not stand in the way of my birth to real life; do not wish me stillborn. My desire is to belong to God. Do not, then, hand me back to the world. Do not try to tempt me with material things. Let me attain pure light. Only on my arrival there can I be fully a human being. Give me the privilege of imitating the passion of my God. If you have him in your heart, you will understand what I wish. You will sympathize with me because you will know what urges me on.

The prince of this world is determined to lay hold of me and to undermine my will which is intent on God. Let none of you here help him; instead show yourselves on my side, which is also God's side. Do not talk about Jesus Christ as long as you love this world. Do not harbor envious thoughts. And supposing I should see you, if then I should beg you to intervene on my behalf, do not believe what I say. Believe instead what I am now writing to you. For though I am alive as I write to you, still my real desire is to die. My love of this life has been crucified, and there is no yearning in me for any earthly thing. Rather within me is the living water which says deep inside me: "Come to the Father." I no longer take pleasure in perishable food or in the delights of this world. I want only God's bread, which is the flesh of Jesus Christ, formed of the seed of David, and for drink I crave his blood, which is love that cannot perish.

I am no longer willing to live a merely human life, and you can bring about my wish if you will. Please, then, do me this favor, so that you in turn may meet with equal kindness. Put briefly, this is my request: believe what I am saying to you. Jesus Christ himself will make it clear to you that I am saying the truth. Only truth can come from that mouth by which the Father has truly spoken. Pray for me that I may obtain my desire. I have not written to you as a mere man would, but as one who knows the mind of God. If I am condemned to suffer, I will take it that you wish me well. If my case is postponed, I can only think that you wish me harm.

October 18th

St. Luke, Evangelist

From a homily on the gospels by St. Gregory the Great, Pope & Doctor

The Lord follows his preachers

Beloved brothers, our Lord and Savior sometimes gives us instruction by words and sometimes by actions. His very deeds are our commands; and whenever he acts silently he is teaching us what we should do. For example, he sends his disciples out to preach two by two, because the precept of charity is twofold-love of God and of one's neighbor.

The Lord sends his disciples out to preach in twos in order to teach us silently that whoever fails in charity toward his neighbor should by no means take upon himself the office of preaching.

Rightly is it said that he sent them ahead of him into every city and place where he himself was to go. For the Lord follows after the preachers, because preaching goes ahead to prepare the way, and then when the words of exhortation have gone ahead and established truth in our minds, the Lord comes to live within us. To those who preach Isaiah says: *Prepare the way of the Lord, make straight the paths of our God*[Isa 40:3-8; Lk 3:3-6]. And the psalmist tells them: *Make a way for him who rises above the sunset.* The Lord rises above the sunset because from that very place where he slept in death, he rose again and manifested a greater glory. He rises above the sunset because in his resurrection he trampled underfoot the death which he endured. Therefore, we make a *way for him who rises above the sunset*[Ps 67:2-5] when we preach his glory to you, so that when he himself follows after us, he may illumine you with his love.

Let us listen now to his words as he sends his preachers forth: *The harvest is great but the laborers are few. Pray therefore the Lord of the harvest to send laborers into his harvest*[Lk 10:2]. That the harvest is good but the laborers are few cannot be said without a heavy heart, for although there are many to hear the good news there are only a few to preach it. Indeed, see how full the world is of priests, but yet in God's harvest a true laborer is rarely to be found; although we have accepted the priestly office we do not fulfill its demands.

Think over, my beloved brothers, think over his words: *Pray the Lord of the harvest to send laborers into his harvest*[Mt 9:38]. Pray for us so that we may be able to labor worthily on your behalf, that our tongue may not grow weary of exhortation, that after we have taken up the office of preaching our silence may not bring us condemnation from the just judge.

October 19th

Saints Isaac Jogues and John de Brebeuf, priests and martyrs, and their Companions, martyrs

From the spiritual diaries by St. John de Brébeuf, Priest & Martyr

May I die only for you, Jesus, who willingly died for me

For two days now I have experienced a great desire to be a martyr and to endure all the torments the martyrs suffered.

Jesus, my Lord and Savior, what can I give you in return for all the favors you have first conferred on me? I *will take* from your hand *the cup* of your sufferings and *call on your name*[Ps 115:12-13]. I vow before your eternal Father and the Holy Spirit, before your most holy Mother and her most chaste spouse, before the angels, apostles and martyrs, before my blessed fathers Saint Ignatius and Saint Francis Xavier-in truth I vow to you, Jesus my Savior, that as far as I have the strength I will never fail to accept the grace of martyrdom, if some day you in your infinite mercy should offer it to me, your most unworthy servant.

I bind myself in this way so that for the rest of my life I will have neither permission nor freedom to refuse opportunities of dying and shedding my blood for you, unless at a particular juncture I should consider it more suitable for your glory to act otherwise at that time. Further, I bind myself to this so that, on receiving the blow of death, I shall accept it from your hands with the fullest delight and joy of spirit. For this reason, my beloved Jesus, and because of the surging joy which moves me, here and now I offer my blood and body and life. May I die only for you, if you will grant me this grace, since you willingly died for me. Let me so live that you may grant me the gift of such a happy death. In this way, my God and Savior, *I will take* from your hand *the cup* of your sufferings and *call on your name*: Jesus, Jesus, Jesus!

My God, it grieves me greatly that you are not known, that in this savage wilderness all have not been converted to you, that sin has not been driven from it. My God, even if all the brutal tortures which prisoners in this region must endure should fall on me, I offer myself most willingly to them and I alone shall suffer them all.

October 19th

St. Paul of the Cross, Priest

From a letter by St. Paul of the Cross, Priest

We preach Christ crucified

It is very good and holy to consider the passion of our Lord and to meditate on it, for by this sacred path we reach union with God. In this most holy school we learn true wisdom, for it was there that all the saints learned it. Indeed when the cross of our dear Jesus has planted its roots more deeply in your hearts, then will you rejoice: "To suffer and not to die," or, "Either to suffer or to die," or better: "Neither to suffer, nor to die, but only to turn perfectly to the will of God."

Love is a unifying virtue which takes upon itself the torments of its beloved Lord. It is a fire reaching through to the inmost soul. It transforms the lover into the one loved. More deeply, love intermingles with grief, and grief with love, and a certain blending of love and grief occurs. They become so united that we can no longer distinguish love from grief nor grief from love. Thus the loving heart rejoices in its sorrow and exults in its grieving love.

Therefore, be constant in practicing every virtue, and especially in imitating the patience of our dear Jesus, for this is the summit of pure love. Live in such a way that all may know that you bear outwardly as well as inwardly the image of Christ crucified, the model of all gentleness and mercy. For if a man is united inwardly with the Son of the living God, he also bears his likeness outwardly by his continual practice of heroic goodness, and especially through a patience reinforced by courage, which does not complain either secretly or in public. Conceal yourselves in Jesus, crucified and hope for nothing except that all men be thoroughly converted to his will.

When you become true lovers of the Crucified, you will always celebrate the feast of the cross in the inner temple of the soul, bearing all in silence and not relying on any creature. Since festivals ought to be celebrated joyfully, those who love the Crucified should honor the feast of the cross by enduring in silence with a serene and joyful countenance, so that their suffering remains hidden from men and is observed by God alone. For in this feast there is always a solemn banquet, and the food presented is the will of God, exemplified by the love of our crucified Christ.

October 23rd

St. John of Capistrano, Priest

From the treatise Mirror of the Clergy by St. John of Capistrano, Priest

The lives of good clerics bring light and serenity

Those who are called to the table of the Lord must glow with the brightness that comes from the good example of a praiseworthy and blameless life. They must completely remove from their lives the filth and uncleanness of vice. Their upright lives must make them like the salt of the earth for themselves and for the rest of mankind. The brightness of their wisdom must make them like the light of the world that brings light to others. They must learn from their eminent teacher, Jesus Christ, what he declared not only to his apostles and disciples, but also to all the priests and clerics who were to succeed them, when he said: *You are the salt of the earth. But what if salt goes flat? How can you restore its flavor? Then it is good for nothing but to be thrown out and trampled underfoot*[Mt 5:13].

Truly the unclean, immoral cleric is trampled underfoot like worthless manure. He is saturated with the filth of vice and entangled in the chains of sin. In this condition he must be considered worthless both to himself and to others. As Gregory says: "When a man's life is frowned upon, it follows that his preaching will be despised."

Presbyters who are born leaders deserve to be doubly honored, especially those who labor in preaching and teaching[1 Tim 5:17]. It is indeed a double task that worthy priests perform, that is to say, it is both exterior and interior, both temporal and spiritual, and, finally, both a passing task and an eternal one.

Even though they dwell on earth and are bound by the same necessities of nature along with all mortal creatures, at the same time they are engaged in earnest communication with the angels in heaven, so that they may be pleasing to their king and learn how to serve him. Therefore, just as the sun rises over the world in God's heaven, so clerics *must let their light shine before men so that they may see their good deeds and give praise to their heavenly Father*[Mt 5:16].

You are the light of the world[Mt 5:14]. Now a light does not illumine itself, but instead it diffuses its rays and shines all around upon everything that comes into its view. So it must be with the glowing lives of upright and holy clerics. By the brightness of their holiness they must bring light and serenity to all who gaze upon them. They have been placed here to care for others. Their own lives should be an example to others, showing how they must live in the house of the Lord.

October 24th

St. Anthony Claret, Bishop

From a work by St. Anthony Mary Claret, Bishop

The love of Christ drives us on

Driven by the fire of the Holy Spirit, the holy apostles traveled throughout the earth. Inflamed with the same fire, apostolic missionaries have reached, are now reaching and will continue to reach the ends of the earth, from one pole to the other, in order to proclaim the word of God. They are deservedly able to apply to themselves those words of the apostle Paul: *The love of Christ drives us on*[2 Cor 5:14-17].

The love of Christ arouses us, urges us to run, and to fly, lifted on the wings of holy zeal. The man who truly loves God also loves his neighbor. The truly zealous man is also onc who loves, but he stands on a higher plane of love so that the more he is inflamed by love, the more urgently zeal drives him on. But if anyone lacks this zeal, then it is evident that love and charity have been extinguished in his heart. The zealous man desires and achieves all great things and he labors strenuously so that God may always be better known, loved and served in this world and in the life to come, for this holy love is without end.

Because he is concerned also for his neighbor, the man of zeal works to fulfill his desire that all men be content on this earth and happy and blessed in their heavenly homeland, that all may be saved, and that no one may perish for ever, or offend God, or remain even for a moment in sin. Such are the concerns we observe in the holy apostles and in all who are driven by the apostolic spirit.

For myself, I say this to you: The man who burns with the fire of divine love is a son of the Immaculate Heart of Mary, and wherever he goes, he enkindles that flame; he desires and works with all his strength to inflame all men with the fire of God's love. Nothing deters him: he rejoices in poverty; he labors strenuously; he welcomes hardships; he laughs off false accusations; he rejoices in anguish. He thinks only of how he might follow Jesus Christ and imitate him by his prayers, his labors, his sufferings, and by caring always and only for the glory of God and the salvation of souls.

October 28th

Saints Simon and Jude, Apostles

From a commentary on the gospel of John
by St. Cyril of Alexandria, Bishop & Doctor

As the Father sent me, so I am sending you

Our Lord Jesus Christ has appointed certain men to be guides and teachers of the world and stewards of his divine mysteries. Now he bids them to shine out like lamps and to cast out their light not only over the land of the Jews but over every country under the sun and over people scattered in all directions and settled in distant lands.

That man has spoken truly who said: *No one takes honor upon himself, except the one who is called by God*[Heb 5:4], for it was our Lord Jesus Christ who called his own disciples before all others to a most glorious apostolate. These holy men became the *pillar and mainstay*[1 Tim 3:15] of the truth, and Jesus said that he was sending them just as the Father had sent him.

By these words he is making clear the dignity of the apostolate and the incomparable glory of the power given to them, but he is also, it would seem, giving them a hint about the methods they are to adopt in their apostolic mission. For if Christ thought it necessary to send out his intimate disciples in this fashion, just as the Father had sent him, then surely it was necessary that they whose mission was to be patterned on that of Jesus should see exactly why the Father had sent the Son. And so Christ interpreted the character of his mission to us in a variety of ways. Once he said: *I have come to call not the righteous but sinners to repentance*[Lk 5:32]. And then at another time he said: *I have come down from heaven, not to do my own will, but the will of him who sent me. For God sent his Son into the world, not to condemn the world, but that the world might be saved through him*[Jn 6:38-46].

Accordingly, in affirming that they are sent by him just as he was sent by the Father, Christ sums up in a few words the approach they themselves should take to their ministry. From what he said they would gather that it was their vocation to call sinners to repentance, to heal those who were sick whether in body or spirit, to seek in all their dealings never to do their own will but the will of him who sent them, and as far as possible to save the world by their teaching.

Surely it is in all these respects that we find his holy disciples striving to excel. To ascertain this is no great labor; a single of the Acts of the Apostles or of Saint Paul's writings is enough.

November 1st

All Saints

From a sermon by St. Bernard, Abbot & Doctor

Let us make haste to our brethren who are awaiting us

Why should our praise and glorification, or even the celebration of this feastday mean anything to the saints? What do they care about earthly honors when their heavenly Father honors them by fulfilling the faithful promise of the Son? What does our commendation mean to them? The saints have no need of honor from us; neither does our devotion add the slightest thing to what is theirs. Clearly, if we venerate their memory, it serves us, not them. But I tell you, when I think of them, I feel myself inflamed by a tremendous yearning.

Calling the saints to mind inspires, or rather arouses in us, above all else, a longing to enjoy their company, so desirable in itself. We long to share in the citizenship of heaven, to dwell with the spirits of the blessed, to join the assembly of patriarchs, the ranks of the prophets, the council of apostles, the great host of martyrs, the noble company of confessors and the choir of virgins. In short, we long to be united in happiness with all the saints. But our dispositions change. The Church of all the first followers of Christ awaits us, but we do nothing about it. The saints want us to be with them, and we are indifferent. The souls of the just await us, and we ignore them.

Come, brothers, let us at length spur ourselves on. We must rise again with Christ, we must seek the world which is above and set our mind on the things of heaven. Let us long for those who are longing for us, hasten to those who are waiting for us, and ask those who look for our coming to intercede for us. We should not only want to be with the saints, we should also hope to possess their happiness. While we desire to be in their company, we must also earnestly seek to share in their glory. Do not imagine that there is anything harmful in such an ambition as this; there is no danger in setting our hearts on such glory.

When we commemorate the saints we are inflamed with another yearning: that Christ our life may also appear to us as he appeared to them and that we may one day share in his glory. Until then we see him, not as he is, but as he became for our sake. He is our head, crowned, not with glory, but with the thorns of our sins. As members of that head, crowned with thorns, we should be ashamed to live in luxury; his purple robes are a mockery rather than an honor. When Christ comes again, his death shall no longer be proclaimed, and we shall know that we also have died, and that our life is hidden with him. The glorious head of the Church will appear and his glorified members will shine in splendor with him, when he forms this lowly body anew into such glory as belongs to himself, its head.

Therefore, we should aim at attaining this glory with a wholehearted and prudent desire. That we may rightly hope and strive for such blessedness, we must above all seek the prayers of the saints. Thus, what is beyond our own powers to obtain will be granted through their intercession.

November 2nd

All Souls

From a book on the death of his brother Satyrus by St. Ambrose, Bishop & Doctor

Let us die with Christ, to live with Christ

We see that death is gain, life is loss. Paul says: *For me life is Christ, and death a gain*[Phil 1:21]. What does "Christ" mean but to die in the body, and receive the breath of life? Let us then die with Christ, to live with Christ. We should have a daily familiarity with death, a daily desire for death. By this kind of detachment our soul must learn to free itself from the desires of the body. It must soar above earthly lusts to a place where they cannot come near, to hold it fast. It must take on the likeness of death, to avoid the punishment of death. The law of our fallen nature is at war with the law of our reason and subjects the law of reason to the law of error. What is the remedy? *Who will set me free from this dead body? The grace of God, through Jesus Christ, our Lord*[Rom 7:24-25].

We have a doctor to heal us; let us use the remedy he prescribes. The remedy is the grace of Christ, the dead body our own. Let us then be exiles from our body, so as not to be exiles from Christ. Though we are still in the body, let us not give ourselves to the things of the body. We must not reject the natural rights of the body, but we must desire before all else the gifts of grace.

What more need be said? It was by the death of one man that the world was redeemed. Christ did not need to die if he did not want to, but he did not look on death as something to be despised, something to be avoided, and he could have found no better means to save us than by dying. Thus his death is life for all. We are sealed with the sign of his death; when we pray we preach his death; when we offer sacrifice we proclaim his death. His death is victory; his death is a sacred sign; each year his death is celebrated with solemnity by the whole world.

What more should we say about his death since we use this divine example to prove that it was death alone that won freedom from death, and death itself was its own redeemer? Death is then no cause for mourning, for it is the cause of mankind's salvation. Death is not something to be avoided, for the Son of God did not think it beneath his dignity, nor did he seek to escape it.

Death was not part of nature; it became part of nature. God did not decree death from the beginning; he prescribed it as a remedy. Human life was condemned because of sin to unremitting labor and unbearable sorrow and so began to experience the burden of wretchedness. There had to be a limit to its evils; death had to restore what life had forfeited. Without the assistance of grace, immortality is more of a burden than a blessing.

The soul has to turn away from the aimless paths of this life, from the defilement of an earthly body; it must reach out to those assemblies in heaven (though it is given only to the saints to be admitted to them) to sing the praises of God. We learn from Scripture how God's praise is sung to the music of the harp: *Great and wonderful are your deeds, Lord God Almighty; just and true are your ways, King of the nations. Who will not revere and glorify your nature? You alone are holy; all nations will come and worship before you*[Rev 15:3-4].

The soul must also desire to witness your nuptials, Jesus, and to see your bride escorted from earthly to heavenly realities, as all rejoice and sing: *All flesh will come before you*. No longer will the bride be held in subjection to this passing world but will be made one with the spirit.

Above all else, holy David prayed that he might see and gaze on this: *One thing I have asked of the Lord, this I shall pray for: to dwell in the house of the Lord all the days of my life, and to see how gracious is the Lord*[Ps 26:4].

November 3rd

St. Martin de Porres, Religious

From a homily at the Canonization of St. Martin De Porres by Pope John XXIII

"Martin the charitable"

The example of Martin's life is ample evidence that we can strive for holiness and salvation as Christ Jesus has shown us: first by loving God *with all your heart, with all your soul, and with all your mind; and second, by loving your neighbor as yourself*[Mk 12:30-31].

When Martin had come to realize that Christ Jesus *suffered for us and that he carried our sins on his body to the cross, he would meditate with remarkable ardor and affection about Christ on the cross*[1 Pet 2:24]. Whenever he would contemplate Christ's terrible torture he would be reduced to tears. He had an exceptional love for the great sacrament of the eucharist and often spent long hours in prayer before the blessed sacrament. His desire was to receive the sacrament in communion as often as he could.

Saint Martin, always obedient and inspired by his divine teacher, dealt with his brothers with that profound love which comes from pure faith and humility of spirit. He loved men because he honestly looked on them as God's children and as his own brothers and sisters. Such was his humility that he loved them even more than himself and considered them to be better and more righteous than he was.

He did not blame others for their shortcomings. Certain that he deserved more severe punishment for his sins than others did, he would overlook their worst offenses. He was tireless in his efforts to reform the criminal, and he would sit up with the sick to bring them comfort. For the poor he would provide food, clothing and medicine. He did all he could to care for poor farmhands, blacks and mulattoes who were looked down upon as slaves, the dregs of society in their time. Common people responded by calling him "Martin the charitable."

The virtuous example and even the conversation of this saintly man exerted a powerful influence in drawing men to religion. It is remarkable how even today his influence can still move us toward the things of heaven. Sad to say, not all of us understand these spiritual values as well as we should, nor do we give them a proper place in our lives. Many of us, in fact, strongly attracted by sin, may look upon these values as of little moment, even something of a nuisance, or we ignore them altogether. It is deeply rewarding for men striving for salvation to follow in Christ's footsteps and to obey God's commandments. If only everyone could learn this lesson from the example that Martin gave us.

November 4th

St. Charles Borromeo, Bishop

From a sermon given during the last synod he attended

Practice what you preach

I admit that we are all weak, but if we want help, the Lord God has given us the means to find it easily. One priest may wish to lead a good, holy life, as he knows he should. He may wish to be chaste and to reflect heavenly virtues in the way he lives. Yet he does not resolve to use suitable means, such as penance, prayer, the avoidance of evil discussions and harmful and dangerous friendships. Another priest complains that as soon as he comes into church to pray the office or to celebrate Mass, a thousand thoughts fill his mind and distract him from God. But what was he doing in the sacristy before he came out for the office or for Mass? How did he prepare? What means did he use to collect his thoughts and to remain recollected?

Would you like me to teach you how to grow from virtue to virtue and how, if you are already recollected at prayer, you can be even more attentive next time, and so give God more pleasing worship? Listen, and I will tell you. If a tiny spark of God's love already burns within you, do not expose it to the wind, for it may get blown out. Keep the stove tightly shut so that it will not lose its heat and grow cold. In other words, avoid distractions as well as you can. Stay quiet with God. Do not spend your time in useless chatter.

If teaching and preaching is your job, then study diligently and apply yourself to whatever is necessary for doing the job well. Be sure that you first preach by the way you live. If you do not, people will notice that you say one thing, but live otherwise, and your words will bring only cynical laughter and a derisive shake of the head.

Are you in charge of a parish? If so, do not neglect the parish of your own soul, do not give yourself to others so completely that you have nothing left for yourself. You have to be mindful of your people without becoming forgetful of yourself.

My brothers, you must realize that for us churchmen nothing is more necessary than meditation. We must meditate before, during and after everything we do. The prophet says: *I will pray, and then I will understand*[1 Cor 14:14-19]. When you administer the sacraments, meditate on what you are doing. When you celebrate Mass, reflect on the sacrifice you are offering. When you pray the office, think about the words you are saying and the Lord to whom you are speaking. When you take care of your people, meditate on the Lord's blood that has washed them clean. In this way, *all that you do becomes a work of love*[1 Cor 16:14].

This is the way we can easily overcome the countless difficulties we have to face day after day, which, after all, are part of our work: in meditation we find the strength to bring Christ to birth in ourselves and in other men.

November 9th

Dedication of Saint John Lateran

From a sermon by St. Caesarius of Arles

We have all been made temples of God through baptism

My fellow Christians, today is the birthday of this church, an occasion for celebration and rejoicing. We, however, ought to be the true and living temple of God. Nevertheless, Christians rightly commemorate this feast of the church, their mother, for they know that through her they were reborn in the spirit. At our first birth, we were vessels of God's wrath; reborn, we became vessels of his mercy. Our first birth brought death to us, but our second restored us to life.

Indeed, before our baptism we were sanctuaries of the devil; but after our baptism we merited the privilege of being temples of Christ. And if we think more carefully about the meaning of our salvation, we shall realize that we are indeed living and true temples of God. *God does not dwell only in structures fashioned by human hands*[Acts 7:48], in homes of wood and stone, but rather he dwells principally in the soul made according to his own image and fashioned by his own hand. Therefore, the apostle Paul says: *The temple of God is holy, and you are that temple*[1 Cor 3:16].

When Christ came, he banished the devil from our hearts, in order to build in them a temple for himself. Let us therefore do what we can with his help, so that our evil deeds will not deface that temple. For whoever does evil, does injury to Christ. As I said earlier, before Christ redeemed us, we were the house of the devil, but afterward, we merited the privilege of being the house of God. God himself in his loving mercy saw fit to make of us his own home.

My fellow Christians, do we wish to celebrate joyfully the birth of this temple? Then let us not destroy the living temples of God in ourselves by works of evil. I shall speak clearly, so that all can understand. Whenever we come to church, we must prepare our hearts to be as beautiful as we expect this church to be. Do you wish to find this basilica immaculately clean? Then do not soil your soul with the filth of sins. Do you wish this basilica to be full of light? God too wishes that your soul be not in darkness, but that the light of good works shine in us, so that he who dwells in the heavens will be glorified. Just as you enter this church building, so God wishes to enter into your soul, for he promised: *I shall live in them, and I shall walk the corridors of their hearts*[2 Cor 6:16].

November 10th

St. Leo the Great, Pope & Doctor

From a sermon by St. Leo the Great, Pope & Doctor

The minister of a special calling

Although the universal Church of God is constituted of distinct orders of members, still, in spite of the many parts of its holy body, the Church subsists as an integral whole, just as the Apostle says: *We are all one in Christ*[Gal 3:28], nor is anyone separated from the office of another in such a way that a lower group has no connection with the head. In the unity of unity of faith and baptism, our community is then undivided. There is a common dignity, as the apostle Peter says in these words: *And you are built up as living stones into spiritual houses, a holy priesthood, offering spiritual sacrifices which are acceptable to God through Jesus Christ*[1 Pet 2:5]. And again: *But you are a chosen people, a royal priesthood, a holy nation, a people of election*[1 Pet 2:9].

For all, regenerated in Christ, are made kings by the sign of the cross; they are consecrated priests by the oil of the Holy Spirit, so that beyond the special service of our ministry as priests, all spiritual and mature Christians know that they are a royal race and are sharers in the office of the priesthood. For what is more king-like than to find yourself ruler over your body after having surrendered your soul to God? And what is more priestly than to promise the Lord a pure conscience and to offer him in love unblemished victims on the altar of one's heart?

Because, through the grace of God, it is a deed accomplished universally on behalf of all, it is altogether praiseworthy and in keeping with a religious attitude for you to rejoice in this our day of consecration, to consider it a day when we are especially honored. For indeed one sacramental priesthood is celebrated throughout the entire body of the Church. The oil which consecrates us has richer effects in the higher grades, yet it is not sparingly given in the lower.

Sharing in this office, my dear brethren, we have solid ground for a common rejoicing; yet there will be more genuine and excellent reason for joy if you do not dwell on the thought of our unworthiness. It is more helpful and more suitable to turn your thoughts to study the glory of the blessed apostle Peter. We should celebrate this day above all in honor of him. He overflowed with abundant riches from the very source of all graces, yet though he alone received much, nothing was given over to him without his sharing it. The Word made flesh lived among us, and in redeeming the whole human race, Christ gave himself entirely.

November 11th

St. Martin of Tours, Bishop

From a letter by Sulpicius Severus

Martin the poor and humble man

Martin knew long in advance the time of his death and he told his brethren that it was near. Meanwhile, he found himself obliged to make a visitation of the parish of Candes. The clergy of that church were quarreling, and he wished to reconcile them. Although he knew that his days on earth were few, he did not refuse to undertake the journey for such a purpose, for he believed that he would bring his virtuous life to a good end if by his efforts peace was restored in the church.

He spent some time in Candes, or rather in its church, where he stayed. Peace was restored, and he was planning to return to his monastery when suddenly he began to lose his strength. He summoned his brethren and told them he was dying. All who heard this were overcome with grief. In their sorrow they cried to him with one voice: "Father, why are you deserting us? Who will care for us when you are gone? Savage wolves will attack your flock, and who will save us from their bite when our shepherd is struck down? We know you long to be with Christ, but your reward is certain and will not be any less for being delayed. You will do better to show pity for us, rather than forsake us."

Thereupon he broke into tears, for he was a man in whom the compassion of our Lord was continually revealed. Turning to our Lord, he made this reply to their pleading: "Lord, if your people still need me, I am ready for the task; your will be done."

Here was a man words cannot describe. Death could not defeat him nor toil dismay him. He was quite without a preference of his own; he neither feared to die nor refused to live. With eyes and hands always raised to heaven he never withdrew his unconquered spirit from prayer. It happened that some priests who had gathered at his bedside suggested that he should give his poor body some relief by lying on his other side. He answered: "Allow me, brothers, to look toward heaven rather than at the earth, so that my spirit may set on the right course when the time comes for me to go on my journey to the Lord." As he spoke these words, he saw the devil standing near. "Why do you stand there, you bloodthirsty brute?" he cried. "Murderer, you will not have me for your prey. Abraham is welcoming me into his embrace."

With these words, he gave up his spirit to heaven. Filled with joy, Martin was welcomed by Abraham. Thus he left this life a poor and lowly man and entered heaven rich in God's favor.

November 12th

St. Josaphat, Bishop & Martyr

From the Encyclical Letter *Ecclesiam Dei* by Pope Pius XI

He gave his life for the unity of the Church

In designing his Church God worked with such skill that in the fullness of time it would resemble a single great family embracing all men. It can be identified, as we know, by certain distinctive characteristics, notably its universality and unity.

Christ the Lord passed on to his apostles the task he had received from the Father: *I have been given all authority in heaven and on earth. Go, therefore, and make disciples of all nations*[Mt 28:18-20]. He wanted the apostles as a body to be intimately bound together, first by the inner tie of the same faith and love *which flows into our hearts through the Holy Spirit*[Rom 5:5], and, second, by the external tie of authority exercised by one apostle over the others. For this he assigned the primacy to Peter, the source and visible basis of their unity for all time. So that the unity and agreement among them would endure, God wisely stamped them, one might say, with the mark of holiness and martyrdom.

Both these distinctions fell to Josaphat, archbishop of Polock of the Slavonic rite of the Eastern Church. He is rightly looked upon as the great glory and strength of the Eastern Rite Slavs. Few have brought them greater honor or contributed more to their spiritual welfare than Josaphat, their pastor and apostle, especially when he gave his life as a martyr for the unity of the Church. He felt, in fact, that God had inspired him to restore worldwide unity to the Church and he realized that his greatest chance of success lay in preserving the Slavonic rite and Saint Basil's rule of monastic life within the one universal Church.

Concerned mainly with seeing his own people reunited to the See of Peter, he sought out every available argument which would foster and maintain Church unity. His best arguments were drawn from liturgical books, sanctioned by the Fathers of the Church, which were in common use among Eastern Christians, including the dissidents. Thus thoroughly prepared, he set out to restore the unity of the Church. A forceful man of fine sensibilities, he met with such success that his opponents dubbed him "the thief of souls."

November 13th

St. Frances Xavier Cabrini

From a homily at the Canonization of St. Frances Xavier Cabrini by Pope Pius XII

A humble woman who lived a virtuous life

Inspired by the grace of God, we join the saints in honoring the holy virgin Frances Xavier Cabrini. She was a humble woman who became outstanding not because she was famous, or rich or powerful, but because she lived a virtuous life. From the tender years of her youth, she kept her innocence as white as a lily and preserved it carefully with the thorns of penitence; as the years progressed, she was moved by a certain instinct and a supernatural zeal to dedicate her whole life to the service and greater glory of God.

She welcomed delinquent youths into safe homes and taught them to live upright and holy lives. She consoled those who were in prison and recalled to them the hope of eternal life. She encouraged prisoners to reform themselves and to live honest lives.

She comforted the sick and the infirm in the hospitals and diligently cared for them. She extended a friendly and helping hand especially to immigrants and offered them necessary shelter and relief, for having left their homeland behind, they were wandering about in a foreign land with no place to turn for help. Because of their condition she saw that they were in danger of deserting the practice of Christian virtues and their Catholic faith.

Where did she acquire all that strength and the inexhaustible energy by which she was able to perform so many good works and to surmount so many difficulties involving material things, travel and men?

Undoubtedly she accomplished all this through the faith which was always so vibrant and alive in her heart; through the divine love which burned within her; and, finally, through constant prayer by which she was so closely united with God from whom she humbly asked and obtained whatever her human weakness could not obtain.

In the face of the endless cares and anxieties of life, she never let anything turn her aside from striving and aiming to please God and to work for his glory for which nothing, aided by God's grace, seemed too laborious, or difficult, or beyond human strength.

November 15th

St. Albert the Great, Bishop & Doctor

From a commentary on the gospel of Luke by St. Albert the Great, Bishop & Doctor

He was a shepherd and doctor who built up the body of Christ

Do this in remembrance of me[Lk 22:14-20; 1 Cor 11:23-26]; . Two things should be noted here. The first is the command that we should use this sacrament, which is indicated when he says: *Do this*. The second is that this sacrament commemorates the Lord's going to death for our sake.

Do this. Certainly he would demand nothing more profitable, nothing more pleasant, nothing more beneficial, nothing more desirable, nothing more similar to eternal life. We will look at each of these qualities separately.

This sacrament is profitable because it grants remission of sins; it is most useful because it bestows the fullness of grace on us in this life. *The Father of spirits instructs us in what is useful for our sanctification*[St. Albert]. And his sanctification is in Christ's sacrifice, that is, when he offers himself in this sacrament to the Father for our redemption, to us for our use. *I consecrate myself for their sakes. Christ, who through the Holy Spirit offered himself up without blemish to God, will cleanse our consciences from dead works to worship the living God*[Heb 9:14].

Nor can we do anything more pleasant. For what is better than God manifesting his whole sweetness to us. *You gave them bread from heaven, not the fruit of human labor, but a bread endowed with all delight and pleasant to every sense of taste. For this substance of yours revealed your kindness toward your children, and serving the desire of each recipient, it changed to suit each one's taste*[St. Albert].

He could not have commanded anything more beneficial, for this sacrament is the fruit of the tree of life. Anyone who receives this sacrament with the devotion of sincere faith will never taste death. *It is a tree of life for those who grasp it, and blessed is he who holds it fast*[Prov 3:18]. *The man who feeds on me shall live on account of me*[Jn 6:57].

Nor could he have commanded anything more lovable, for this sacrament produces love and union. It is characteristic of the greatest love to give itself as food. *Had not the men of my tent exclaimed: Who will feed us with his flesh to satisfy our hunger*[Job 31:31]*?* as if to say: I have loved them and they have loved me so much that I desire to be within them, and they wish to receive me so that they may become my members. There is no more intimate or more natural means for them to be united to me, and I to them.

Nor could he have commanded anything which is more like eternal life. Eternal life flows from this sacrament because God with all sweetness pours himself out upon the blessed.

November 16th

St. Margaret of Scotland

From the pastoral constitution on the Church in the Modern World of the Second Vatican Council

The sanctity of marriage and the family

Husband and wife, by the covenant of marriage, are no longer two, but one flesh. By their intimate union of persons and of actions they give mutual help and service to each other, experience the meaning of their unity, and gain an ever deeper understanding of it day by day.

This intimate union in the mutual self-giving of two persons, as well as the good of the children, demands full fidelity from both, and an indissoluble unity between them.

Christ the Lord has abundantly blessed this richly complex love, which springs from the divine source of love and is founded on the model of his union with the Church.

In earlier times God met his people in a covenant of love and fidelity. So now the Savior of mankind, the Bridegroom of the Church, meets Christian husbands and wives in the sacrament of matrimony. Further, he remains with them in order that, as he loved the Church and gave himself up for her, so husband and wife may, in mutual self-giving, love each other with perpetual fidelity.

True married love is caught up into God's love; it is guided and enriched by the redeeming power of Christ and the saving action of the Church, in order that the partners may be effectively led to God and receive help and strength in the sublime responsibility of parenthood.

Christian partners are therefore strengthened, and as it were consecrated, by a special sacrament for the duties and the dignity of their state. By the power of this sacrament they fulfill their obligations to each other and to their family and are filled with the spirit of Christ. This spirit pervades their whole lives with faith, hope and love. Thus they promote their own perfection and each other's sanctification, and so contribute together to the greater glory of God.

Hence, with parents leading the way by example and family prayer, their children – indeed, all within the family circle – will find it easier to make progress in natural virtues, in salvation and in holiness. Husband and wife, raised to the dignity and the responsibility of parenthood, will be zealous in fulfilling their task as educators, especially in the sphere of religious education, a task that is primarily their own.

Children, as active members of the family, contribute in their own way to the holiness of their parents. With the love of grateful hearts, with loving respect and trust, they will return the generosity of their parents and will stand by them as true sons and daughters when they meet with hardship and the loneliness of old age.

November 16th

St. Gertrude, Virgin

From the Revelations by St. Gertrude, Virgin

Your thoughts of me are thoughts of peace

May my soul bless you, O Lord God my Creator, may my soul bless you. From the very core of my being may all your merciful gifts sing your praise. Your generous care for your daughter has been rich in mercy; indeed it has been immeasurable, and as far as I am able I give you thanks. I praise and glorify your great patience which bore with me even though, from my infancy and childhood, adolescence and early womanhood, until I was nearly twenty-six, I was always so blindly irresponsible. Looking back I see that but for your protecting hand I would have been quite without conscience in thought, word or deed. But you came to my aid by giving me a natural dislike of evil and a natural delight in what is good, and provided me with necessary correction from those among whom I lived. Otherwise I should now have to admit to doing my own will whenever the opportunity offered itself, living like some pagan in a pagan society, and never understanding that you, my God, reward good deeds while punishing evil. Yet you had chosen me to be specially trained to serve you. I was a child of five when I began to live in a convent surrounded by your most devoted friends.

To make amends for the way I previously lived, I offer you, most loving Father, all the sufferings of your beloved Son, from that first infant cry as he lay on the hay in the manger, until that final moment when, bowing his head, with a mighty voice, Christ gave up his spirit. I think, as I make this offering, of all that he underwent, his needs as a baby, his dependence as a young child, the hardships of youth and the trials of early manhood.

To atone for all my neglect I offer, most loving Father, all that your only-begotten Son did during his life, whether in thought, word or deed. That sacred life was, I know, utterly perfect in all respects, from the moment he descended from your heavenly throne and came into this world, until finally he presented the glory of his victorious human nature to you, his Father.

And now, as an act of thanksgiving, I praise and worship you, Father, in deepest humility for your most loving kindness and mercy. Though I was hurrying to my eternal loss, your thoughts of me were thoughts of peace and not of affliction, and you lifted me up with so many great favors. To these you added the inestimable gift of your intimate friendship, and in various ways allowed me to possess your Son’s own heart, that most noble ark of God united with the Godhead. You refused me no delight that could be mine.

Finally, you drew me to yourself by your faithful promises of the good things you would give me from the hour of my death. So great are these promises that for their sake alone, even if you had given me nothing besides, my heart would sigh for you always and be filled with a lively hope.

November 17th

St. Elizabeth of Hungary, Religious

From a letter of Conrad of Marburg, spiritual director of St. Elizabeth

Elizabeth recognized and loved Christ in the poor

From this time onward Elizabeth's goodness greatly increased. She was a lifelong friend of the poor and gave herself entirely to relieving the hungry. She ordered that one of her castles should be converted into a hospital in which she gathered many of the weak and feeble. She generously gave alms to all who were in need, not only in that place but in all the territories of her husband's empire. She spent all her own revenue from her husband's four principalities, and finally she sold her luxurious possessions and rich clothes for the sake of the poor.

Twice a day, in the morning and in the evening, Elizabeth went to visit the sick. She personally cared for those who were particularly repulsive; to some she gave food, to others clothing; some she carried on her own shoulders, and performed many other kindly services. Her husband, of happy memory, gladly approved of these charitable works. Finally, when her husband died, she sought the highest perfection; filled with tears, she implored me to let her beg for alms from door to door.

On Good Friday of that year, when the altars had been stripped, she laid her hands on the altar in a chapel in her own town, where she had established the Friars Minor, and before witnesses she voluntarily renounced all worldly display and everything that our Savior in the gospel advises us to abandon. Even then she saw that she could still be distracted by the cares and worldly glory which had surrounded her while her husband was alive. Against my will she followed me to Marburg. Here in the town she built a hospice where she gathered together the weak and the feeble. There she attended the most wretched and contemptible at her own table.

Apart from those active good works, I declare before God that I have seldom seen a more contemplative woman. When she was coming from private prayer, some religious men and women often saw her face shining marvelously and light coming from her eyes like the rays of the sun.

Before her death I heard her confession. When I asked what should be done about her goods and possessions, she replied that anything which seemed to be hers belonged to the poor. She asked me to distribute everything except one worn out dress in which she wished to be buried. When all this had been decided, she received the body of our Lord. Afterward, until vespers, she spoke often of the holiest things she had heard in sermons. Then, she devoutly commended to God all who were sitting near her, and as if falling into a gentle sleep, she died.

November 18th

Dedication of the Basilicas of Saints Peter and Paul, Apostles

From a sermon by St. Leo the Great, Pope & Doctor

Peter and Paul, offspring of the divine seed

Precious in the eyes of the Lord is the death of his holy ones[Ps 115:15]. No type of cruelty can tear down the religion established by the mystery of Christ's cross. The Church is not diminished by persecutions, but rather increased. The field of the Lord is always being enriched with a more abundant harvest, while the seeds which are sown one by one yield a manifold return.

From this field those two famous shoots of the divine seed burst forth into a great progeny, witnessed by thousands of blessed martyrs. To emulate the apostles' triumph, these martyrs have adorned our city far and wide with people clothed in purple and shining brilliantly, and they have crowned it with a diadem fashioned by the glory of many precious stones.

On the commemoration of all the saints it is right for us to rejoice in this heavenly band, fashioned by God as models of patience and support for our faith; but we must glory and exult even more in the eminence of these two forebears, whom the grace of God raised to so high a summit among all the members of the Church, and established like two eyes that bring light to the body whose head is Christ.

As to their merits and virtues, which no words can describe, we should not think of any difference or distinction between them; their calling was the same, their labors were similar, theirs was a common death.

Our experience has shown, as our predecessors have proved, that we may believe and hope that in all the labors of the present life, by the mercy of God, we shall always be helped by the prayers of our special patrons. Just as we are humbled by our own sins, so we shall be raised up by the merits of these apostles.

November 21st

Presentation of Mary

From a sermon by St. Augustine, Bishop & Doctor

She who believed by faith, conceived by faith

Stretching out his hand over his disciples, the Lord Christ declared: *Here are my mother and my brothers; anyone who does the will of my Father who sent me is my brother and sister and my mother*[Mt 12:48-50]. I would urge you to ponder these words. Did the Virgin Mary, who believed by faith and conceived by faith, who was the chosen one from whom our Savior was born among men, who was created by Christ before Christ was created in her – did she not do the will of the Father? Indeed the blessed Mary certainly did the Father's will, and so it was for her a greater thing to have been Christ's disciple than to have been his mother, and she was more blessed in her discipleship than in her motherhood. Hers was the happiness of first bearing in her womb him whom she would obey as her master.

Now listen and see if the words of Scripture do not agree with what I have said. The Lord was passing by and crowds were following him. His miracles gave proof of divine power, and a woman cried out: *Happy is the womb that bore you, blessed is that womb*[Lk 11:27]*!* But the Lord, not wishing people to seek happiness in a purely physical relationship, replied: *More blessed are those who hear the word of God and keep it*[Lk 11:28] Mary heard God's word and kept it, and so she is blessed. She kept God's truth in her mind, a nobler thing than carrying his body in her womb. The truth and the body were both Christ: he was kept in Mary's mind insofar as he is truth, he was carried in her womb insofar as he is man; but what is kept in the mind is of a higher order than what is carried in the womb.

The Virgin Mary is both holy and blessed, and yet the Church is greater than she. Mary is a part of the Church, a member of the Church, a holy, an eminent – the most eminent – member, but still only a member of the entire body. The body undoubtedly is greater than she, one of its members. This body has the Lord for its head, and head and body together make up the whole Christ. In other words, our head is divine – our head is God.

Now, beloved, give me your whole attention, for you also are members of Christ; you also are the body of Christ. Consider how you yourselves can be among those of whom the Lord said: *Here are my mother and my brothers*[Mt 12:48-50]. Do you wonder how you can be the mother of Christ? He himself said: *Whoever hears and fulfils the will of my Father in heaven is my brother and my sister and my mother*[Mt 12:48-50]. As for our being the brothers and sisters of Christ, we can understand this because although there is only one inheritance and Christ is the only Son, his mercy would not allow him to remain alone. It was his wish that we too should be heirs of the Father, and co-heirs with himself.

Now having said that all of you are brothers of Christ, shall I not dare to call you his mother? Much less would I dare to deny his own words. Tell me how Mary became the mother of Christ, if it was not by giving birth to the members of Christ? You, to whom I am speaking, are the members of Christ. Of whom were you born? "Of Mother Church," I hear the reply of your hearts. You became sons of this mother at your baptism, you came to birth then as members of Christ.

Now you in your turn must draw to the font of baptism as many as you possibly can. You became sons when you were born there yourselves, and now by bringing others to birth in the same way, you have it in your power to become the mothers of Christ.

November 22nd

St. Cecilia, Virgin, Martyr

From a discourse on the psalms by St. Augustine, Bishop & Doctor

Sing to God with songs of joy

Praise the Lord with the lyre, make melody to him with the harp of ten strings! Sing to him a new song[Ps 32:2]. Rid yourself of what is old and worn out, for you know a new song. A new man, a new covenant- a new song. This new song does not belong to the old man. Only the new man learns it: the man restored from his fallen condition through the grace of God, and now sharing in the new covenant, that is, the kingdom of heaven. To it all our love now aspires and sings a new song. Let us sing a new song not with our lips but with our lives.

Sing to him a new song, sing to him with joyful melody [Ps 32:3]. Every one of us tries to discover how to sing to God. You must sing to him, but you must sing well. He does not want your voice to come harshly to his ears, so sing well, brothers!

If you were asked, "Sing to please this musician," you would not like to do so without having taken some instruction in music, because you would not like to offend an expert in the art. An untrained listener does not notice the faults a musician would point out to you. Who, then, will offer to sing well for God, the great artist whose discrimination is faultless, whose attention is on the minutest detail, whose ear nothing escapes? When will you be able to offer him a perfect performance that you will in no way displease such a supremely discerning listener?

See how he himself provides you with a way of singing. Do not search for words, as if you could find a lyric which would give God pleasure. Sing to him "with songs of joy." This is singing well to God, just singing with songs of joy.

But how is this done? You must first understand that words cannot express the things that are sung by the heart. Take the case of people singing while harvesting in the fields or in the vineyards or when any other strenuous work is in progress. Although they begin by giving expression to their happiness in sung words, yet shortly there is a change. As if so happy that words can no longer express what they feel, they discard the restricting syllables. They burst out into a simple sound of joy, of jubilation. Such a cry of joy is a sound signifying that the heart is bringing to birth what it cannot utter in words.

Now, who is more worthy of such a cry of jubilation than God himself, whom all words fail to describe? If words will not serve, and yet you must not remain silent, what else can you do but cry out for joy? Your heart must rejoice beyond words, soaring into an immensity of gladness, unrestrained by syllabic bonds. *Sing to him with songs of joy.*

November 23rd

St. Clement I, Pope & Martyr

From a letter to the Corinthians by St. Clement, Pope & Martyr

Wonderful are God's gifts

Beloved, how blessed and wonderful are God's gifts! There is life everlasting, joy in righteousness, truth in freedom, faith, confidence, and self-control in holiness. And these are the gifts that we can comprehend; what of all the others that are being prepared for those who look to him. Only the Creator, the Father of the ages, the all-holy, knows their grandeur and their loveliness. And so we should strive to be found among those who wait for him so that we may share in these promised gifts. And how is this to be, beloved brothers? It will come about if by our faith our minds remain fixed on God; if we aim at what is pleasing and acceptable to him, if we accomplish what is in harmony with his faultless will and follow the path of truth, rejecting all injustice, viciousness, covetousness, quarrels, malice and deceit.

This is the path, beloved, by which we find our salvation, Jesus Christ, the high priest of our sacrifices, the defender and ally in our helplessness. It is through him that we gaze on the highest heaven, through him we can see the reflection of God's pure and sublime countenance, through him the eyes of our hearts have been opened, through him our foolish and darkened understanding opens toward the light, and through him the Lord has willed that we should taste everlasting knowledge. *He reflects God's majesty* and *is as much superior to angels as the name he has obtained is more excellent than theirs* .

Let us then serve in his army, brothers, following his blameless commands with all our might. The great cannot exist without the small, nor the small without the great; they blend together to their mutual advantage. Take the body, for example. The head is nothing without the feet, just as the feet are nothing without the head. The smallest parts of our body are necessary and valuable to the whole. All work together and are mutually subject for the preservation of the whole body.

Our entire body, then, will be preserved in Christ Jesus, and each of us should be subject to his neighbor in accordance with the grace given to each. The stronger should care for the weak, and the weak should respect the stronger. The wealthy should give to the poor, and the poor man should thank God that he has sent him someone to supply his needs. The wise should manifest their wisdom not in words but in good deeds, and the humble should not talk about their own humility but allow others to bear witness to it. Since, therefore, we have all this from him, we ought to thank him for it all. Glory to him for ever. Amen.

November 23rd

St. Columban, Abbot

From an instruction by St. Columban, abbot

Man's likeness to God, if preserved, imparts high dignity

Moses wrote in the law: *God made man in his image and likeness*[Gen 1:27]. Consider, I ask you, the dignity of these words. God is all-powerful. We cannot see or understand him, describe or assess him. Yet he fashioned man from clay and endowed him with the nobility of his own image. What has man in common with God? Or earth with spirit? – for *God is a spirit.* It is a glorious privilege that God should grant man his eternal image and the likeness of his character. Man's likeness to God, if he preserves it, imparts high dignity.

If man applies the virtues planted in his soul to the right purpose, he will be like God. God's commands have taught us to give him back the virtues he sowed in us in our first innocence. The first command is *to love our Lord with our whole heart because he loved us first*[1 Jn 4:19] from the beginning, before our existence. Loving God renews his image in us. Anyone who loves God keeps his commandments, for he said: *If you love me, keep my commandments*[Jn 14:15]. His command is that we love each other. In his own words: *This is my command, that you love each other as I also have loved you*[Jn 15:12].

True love is shown not merely *in word, but in deed and in truth*[1 Jn 3:18]. So we must turn back our image undefiled and holy to our God and Father, for his is holy; in the words of Scripture: *Be holy, for I am holy*[Lev 19:2; 1 Pet 1:16]. We must restore his image with love, for he is love; in John's words: *God is love*[1 Jn 4:8] . We must restore it with loyalty and truth, for he is loyal and truthful. The image we depict must not be that of one who is unlike God; for one who is harsh and irascible and proud would display the image of a despot.

Let us not imprint on ourselves the image of a despot, but let Christ paint his image in us with his words: *My peace I give you, my peace I leave with you*[Jn 14:27]. But the knowledge that peace is good is of no benefit to us if we do not practice it. The most valuable objects are usually the most fragile; costly things require the most careful handling. Particularly fragile is that which is lost by wanton talk and destroyed with the slightest injury of a brother. Men like nothing better than discussing and minding the business of others, passing superfluous comments at random and criticizing people behind their backs. So those who cannot say: *The Lord has given me a discerning tongue, that I may with a word support him who is weary*[Isa 50:4] should keep silent, or if they do say anything it should promote peace.

November 24th

Saints Andrew Dung-Lac, Priest, and his Companions, Martyrs

From a letter of St. Paul Le-Bao-Tinh sent to students of the Seminary of Ke-Vinh in 1843

The martyrs' share in Christ's victory

I, Paul, in chains for the name of Christ, wish to relate to you the trials besetting me daily, in order that you may be inflamed with love for God and join with me in his praises, *for his mercy is for ever*[Ps 135:1-27]. The prison here is a true image of everlasting hell: to cruel tortures of every kind—shackles, iron chains, manacles—are added hatred, vengeance, calumnies, obscene speech, quarrels, evil acts, swearing, curses, as well as anguish and grief. But the God who once freed the three children from the fiery furnace is with me always; he has delivered me from these tribulations and made them sweet, *for his mercy is for ever*[Ps 135:1-27].

In the midst of these torments, which usually terrify others, I am, by the grace of God, full of joy and gladness, because I am not alone—Christ is with me.

Our master bears the whole weight of the cross, leaving me only the tiniest, last bit. He is not a mere onlooker in my struggle, but a contestant and the victor and champion in the whole battle. Therefore upon his head is placed the crown of victory, and his members also share in his glory.

How am I to bear with the spectacle, as each day I see emperors, mandarins, and their retinue blaspheming your holy name, O Lord, *who are enthroned above the Cherubim and Seraphim?* Behold, the pagans have trodden your cross underfoot! Where is your glory? As I see all this, I would, in the ardent love I have for you, prefer to be torn limb from limb and to die as a witness to your love.

O Lord, show your power, save me, sustain me, that in my infirmity your power may be shown and may be glorified before the nations; grant that I may not grow weak along the way, and so allow your enemies to hold their heads up in pride.

Beloved brothers, as you hear all these things may you give endless thanks in joy to God, from whom every good proceeds; bless the Lord with me, *for his mercy is for ever*[Ps 135:1-27]. *My soul proclaims the greatness of the Lord, my spirit rejoices in God my Savior, for he has looked with favor on his lowly servant and from this day all generations will call me blessed*[Lk 1:46-55], *for his mercy is for ever*[Ps 135:1-27].

O praise the Lord, all you nations, acclaim him all you peoples, for God chose what is weak in the world to confound the strong, God chose what is low and despised to confound the noble[Ps 117:1-29]. Through my mouth he has confused the philosophers who are disciples of the wise of this world, *for his mercy is for ever*[Ps 135:1-27].

I write these things to you in order that your faith and mine may be united. In the midst of this storm I cast my anchor toward the throne of God, the anchor that is the lively hope in my heart.

Beloved brothers, for your part *so run that you may attain the crown, put on the breastplate of faith*[1 Cor 9:24] and take up *the weapons* of Christ *for the right hand and for the left*[2 Cor 6:7], as my patron Saint Paul has taught us. *It is better for you to enter life with one eye or crippled than, with all your members intact, to be cast away*[Mt 18:7-9].

Come to my aid with your prayers, that I may have the strength to fight according to the law, and indeed *to fight the good fight*[2 Tim 4:5] and to fight until the end and so finish the race. We may not again see each other in this life, but we will have the happiness of seeing each other again in the world to come, when, standing at the throne of the spotless Lamb, we will together join in singing his praises and exult for ever in the joy of our triumph. Amen.

November 30th

St. Andrew, Apostle

From a homily on the Gospel of John by St. John Chrysostom, Bishop & Doctor

We have found the Messiah

After Andrew had stayed with Jesus and had learned much from him, he did not keep this treasure to himself, but hastened to share it with his brother. Notice what Andrew said to him: *We have found the Messiah, that is to say, the Christ*[Jn 1:41]. Notice how his words reveal what he has learned in so short a time. They show the power of the master who has convinced them of this truth. They reveal the zeal and concern of men preoccupied with this question from the very beginning. Andrew's words reveal a soul waiting with the utmost longing for the coming of the Messiah, looking forward to his appearing from heaven, rejoicing when he does appear, and hastening to announce so great an event to others. To support one another in the things of the spirit is the true sign of good will between brothers, of loving kinship and sincere affection.

Notice, too, how, even from the beginning, Peter is docile and receptive in spirit. He hastens to Jesus without delay. *He brought him to Jesus*[Jn 1:42], says the evangelist. But Peter must not be condemned for his readiness to accept Andrew's word without much weighing of it. It is probable that his brother had given him, and many others, a careful account of the event; the evangelists, in the interest of brevity, regularly summarize a lengthy narrative. Saint John does not say that Peter believed immediately, but that *he brought him to Jesus*[Jn 1:42]. Andrew was to hand him over to Jesus, to learn everything for himself. There was also another disciple present, and he hastened with them for the same purpose.

When John the Baptist said: *This is the Lamb,* and *he baptizes in the Spirit*[Jn 1:33], he left the deeper understanding of these things to be received from Christ. All the more so would Andrew act in the same way, since he did not think himself able to give a complete explanation. He brought his brother to the very source of light, and Peter was so joyful and eager that he would not delay even for a moment.

December 3rd

St. Francis Xavier, Priest

From the letters to St. Ignatius by St. Francis Xavier, Priest

Woe to me if I do not preach the Gospel

We have visited the villages of the new converts who accepted the Christian religion a few years ago. No Portuguese live here-the country is so utterly barren and poor. The native Christians have no priests. They know only that they *are* Christians. There is nobody to say Mass for them; nobody to teach them the Creed, the Our Father, the Hail Mary and the Commandments of God's Law.

I have not stopped since the day I arrived. I conscientiously made the rounds of the villages. I bathed in the sacred waters all the children who had not yet been baptized. This means that I have purified a very large number of children so young that, as the saying goes, they could not tell their right hand from their left. The older children would not let me say my Office or eat or sleep until I taught them one prayer or another. Then I began to understand: "The kingdom of heaven belongs to such as these."

I could not refuse so devout a request without failing in devotion myself. I taught them, first the confession of faith in the Father, the Son and the Holy Spirit, then the Apostles' Creed, the Our Father and Hail Mary. I noticed among them persons of great intelligence. If only someone could educate them in the Christian way of life, I have no doubt that they would make excellent Christians.

Many, many people hereabouts are not becoming Christians for one reason only: there is nobody to make them Christians. Again and again I have thought of going round the universities of Europe, especially Paris, and everywhere crying out like a madman, riveting the attention of those with more learning than charity: "What a tragedy: how many souls are being shut out of heaven and falling into hell, thanks to you!"

I wish they would work as hard at this as they do at their books, and so settle their account with God for their learning and the talents entrusted to them.

This thought would certainly stir most of them to meditate on spiritual realities, to listen actively to what God is saying to them. They would forget their own desires, their human affairs, and give themselves over entirely to God's will and his choice. They would cry out with all their heart: *Lord, I am here! What do you want me to do?* Send me anywhere you like – even to India.

December 4th

St. John Damascene, Priest & Doctor

From The Statement of Faith by St. John Damascene, Priest & Doctor

You have called me, Lord, to minister to your people

O Lord, you led me from my father's loins and formed me in my mother's womb. You brought me, a naked babe, into the light of day, for nature's laws always obey your commands.

By the blessing of the Holy Spirit, you prepared my creation and my existence, not because man willed it or flesh desired it, but by your ineffable grace. The birth you prepared for me was such that it surpassed the laws of our nature. You sent me forth into the light by adopting me as your son and you enrolled me among the children of your holy and spotless Church.

You nursed me with the spiritual milk of your divine utterances. You kept me alive with the solid food of the body of Jesus Christ, your only-begotten Son and our God, and you let me drink from the chalice of his life-giving blood, poured out to save the whole world.

You loved us, O Lord, and gave up your only-begotten Son for our redemption. And he undertook the task willingly and did not shrink from it. Indeed, he applied himself to it as though destined for sacrifice, like an innocent lamb. Although he was God, he became man, and in his human will, became obedient to you, God his Father, *unto death, even death on a cross*[Phil 2:5-11].

In this way you have humbled yourself, Christ my God, so that you might carry me, your stray sheep, on your shoulders. You let me graze in green pastures, refreshing me with the waters of orthodox teaching at the hands of your shepherds. You pastured these shepherds, and now they in turn tend your chosen and special flock. Now you have called me, Lord, by the hand of your bishop to minister to your people. I do not know why you have done so, for you alone know that. Lord, lighten the heavy burden of the sins through which I have seriously transgressed. Purify my mind and heart. Like a shining lamp, lead me along the straight path. When I open my mouth, tell me what I should say. By the fiery tongue of your Spirit make my own tongue ready. Stay with me always and keep me in your sight.

Lead me to pastures, Lord, and graze there with me. Do not let my heart lean either to the right or to the left, but let your good Spirit guide me along the straight path. Whatever I do, let it be in accordance with your will, now until the end.

And you, O Church, are a most excellent assembly, the noble summit of perfect purity, whose assistance comes from God. You in whom God lives, receive from us an exposition of the faith that is free from error, to strengthen the Church, just as our Fathers handed it down to us.

December 6th

St. Nicholas, Bishop

From a treatise on John by St. Augustine, Bishop & Doctor

The strength of love ought to overcome the fear of death

When the Lord asks Peter if he loves him, he is asking something he already knows. Yet he does not ask only once, but a second and third time. Each time Peter's answer is the same: *You know I love you*[Jn 21:15-17]. Each time the Lord gives him the same command: *Tend my sheep*[Jn 21:15-17].

Peter had denied Christ three times, and to counter this he must profess his faith three times. Otherwise his tongue would seem quicker to serve fear than love, and the threat of death would seem to have made him more eloquent than did the presence of life. If denying the shepherd was proof of fear, then the task of love is to tend his flock.

When those who are tending Christ's flock wish that the sheep were theirs rather than his, they stand convicted of loving themselves, not Christ. And the Lord's words are a repeated admonition to them and to all who, as Paul writes sadly, are seeking their own ends, not Christ's.

Do you love me? Tend my sheep[Jn 21:15-17]. Surely this means: "If you love me, your thoughts must focus on taking care of my sheep, not taking care of yourself. You must tend them as mine, not as yours; seek in them my glory, not yours; my sovereign rights, not yours; my gain, not yours. Otherwise you will find yourself among those who belong to the 'times of peril,' those who are guilty of self-love and the other sins that go with that beginning of evils."

So the shepherds of Christ's flock must never indulge in self-love; if they do they will be tending the sheep not as Christ's but as their own. And of all vices this is the one that the shepherds must guard against most earnestly: seeking their own purposes instead of Christ's, furthering their own desires by means of those persons for whom Christ shed his blood.

The love of Christ ought to reach such a spiritual pitch in his shepherds that it overcomes the natural fear of death which makes us shrink from the thought of dying even though we desire to live with Christ. However distressful death may be, the strength of love ought to master the distress. I mean the love we have for Christ who, although he is our life, consented to suffer death for our sake.

Consider this: if death held little or no distress for us, the glory of martyrdom would be less. But if the Good Shepherd, who laid down his life for his sheep, has made so many of those same sheep martyrs and witnesses for him, then how much more ought Christ's shepherds to fight for the truth even to death and to shed their blood in opposing sin? After all, the Lord has entrusted them with tending his flock and with teaching and guiding his lambs.

With his passion for their example, Christ's shepherds are most certainly bound to cling to the pattern of his suffering, since even the lambs have so often followed that pattern of the chief shepherd in whose one flock the shepherds themselves are lambs. For the Good Shepherd who suffered for all mankind has made all mankind his lambs, since in order to suffer for them all he made himself a lamb.

December 7th

St. Ambrose, Bishop & Doctor

From a letter by St. Ambrose, Bishop & Doctor

By the grace of your words win over your people

You have entered upon the office of bishop. Sitting at the helm of the Church, you pilot the ship against the waves. Take firm hold of the rudder of faith so that the severe storms of this world cannot disturb you. The sea is mighty and vast, but do not be afraid, for as Scripture says: *he has founded it upon the seas, and established it upon the waters*[Psalm 24:2].

The Church of the Lord is built upon the rock of the apostles among so many dangers in the world; it therefore remains unmoved. The Church's foundation is unshakable and firm against the assaults of the raging sea. Waves lash at the Church but do not shatter it. Although the elements of this world constantly beat upon the Church with crashing sounds, the Church possesses the safest harbor of salvation for all in distress. Although the Church is tossed about on the sea, it rides easily on rivers, especially those rivers that Scripture speaks of: *The rivers have lifted up their voice*[Ps 92:2-4]. These are the rivers flowing from the heart of the man who is given drink by Christ and who receives from the Spirit of God. When these rivers overflow with the grace of the Spirit, they lift up their voice.

There is also a stream which flows down on God's saints like a torrent. There is also a rushing river giving joy to the heart that is at peace and makes for peace. Whoever has received from the fullness of this river, like John the Evangelist, like Peter and Paul, lifts up his voice. Just as the apostles lifted up their voices and preached the Gospel throughout the world, so those who drink these waters begin to preach the good news of the Lord Jesus.

Drink, then, from Christ, so that your voice may also be heard. Store up in your mind the water that is Christ, the water that praises the Lord. Store up water from many sources, the water that rains down from the clouds of prophecy.

Whoever gathers water from the mountains and leads it to himself or draws it from springs, is himself a source of dew like the clouds. Fill your soul, then, with this water, so that your land may not be dry, but watered by your own springs.

He who reads much and understands much, receives his fill. He who is full, refreshes others. So Scripture says: *If the clouds are full, they will pour rain upon the earth*[Eccl 11:3].

Therefore, let your words be rivers, clean and limpid, so that in your exhortations you may charm the ears of your people. And by the grace of your words win them over to follow your leadership. Let your sermons be full of understanding. Solomon says: *The weapons of the understanding are the lips of the wise*[Prov 16:21-23]; and in another place he says: *Let your lips be bound with wisdom*[St. Ambrose]. That is, let the meaning of your words shine forth, let understanding blaze out. See that your addresses and expositions do not need to invoke the authority of others, but let your words be their own defense. Let no word escape your lips in vain or be uttered without depth of meaning.

December 8th

The Immaculate Conception of the Blessed Virgin Mary

From a sermon by St. Anselm, Bishop & Doctor

Virgin Mary, all nature is blessed in you.

Blessed Lady, sky and stars, earth and rivers, day and night – everything that is subject to the power or use of man – rejoice that through you they are in some sense restored to their lost beauty and are endowed with inexpressible new grace. All creatures were dead, as it were, useless for men or for the praise of God, who made them. The world, contrary to its true destiny, was corrupted and tainted by the acts of men who served idols. Now all creation has been restored to life and rejoices that it is controlled and given splendor by men who believe in God.

The universe rejoices with new and indefinable loveliness. Not only does it feel the unseen presence of God himself, its Creator, it sees him openly, working and making it holy. These great blessings spring from the blessed fruit of Mary's womb.

Through the fullness of the grace that was given you, dead things rejoice in their freedom, and those in heaven are glad to be made new. Through the Son who was the glorious fruit of your virgin womb, just souls who died before his life-giving death rejoice as they are freed from captivity, and the angels are glad at the restoration of their shattered domain.

Lady, full and overflowing with grace, all creation receives new life from your abundance. Virgin, blessed above all creatures, through your blessing all creation is blessed, not only creation from its Creator, but the Creator himself has been blessed by creation.

To Mary God gave his only-begotten Son, whom he loved as himself. Through Mary God made himself a Son, not different but the same, by nature Son of God and Son of Mary. The whole universe was created by God, and God was born of Mary. God created all things, and Mary gave birth to God. The God who made all things gave himself form through Mary, and thus he made his own creation. He who could create all things from nothing would not remake his ruined creation without Mary.

God, then, is the Father of the created world and Mary the mother of the re-created world. God is the Father by whom all things were given life, and Mary the mother through whom all things were given new life. For God begot the Son, through whom all things were made, and Mary gave birth to him as the Savior of the world. Without God's Son, nothing could exist; without Mary's Son, nothing could be redeemed.

Truly the Lord is with you, to whom the Lord granted that all nature should owe as much to you as to himself.

December 9th

St. Juan Diego

From a homily on the Canonization of Juan Diego by John Paul II, Pope

The Virgin Mary brought comfort to Juan Diego

He has lifted up the humble[Lk 1:52]. God the Father looked down onto Juan Diego, a simple Mexican Indian and enriched him not just with the gift of rebirth in Christ but also with the sight of the face of the Blessed Virgin Mary and a role in the task of evangelizing the entire continent of America. From this we can see the truth of the words of St Paul: *those whom the world thinks common and contemptible are the ones that God has chosen – those who are nothing at all to show up those who are everything*[1 Cor 1:27-31].

This fortunate man, whose name, Cuauhtlatoatzin, means "the eagle that speaks," was born around 1474 in Cuauhtitlan, part of the kingdom of Texcoco. When he was an adult and already married, he embraced the Gospel and was purified by the waters of baptism along with his wife, setting out to live in the light of faith and in accordance with the promises he had made before God and the Church.

In December 1531, as he was travelling to the place called Tlaltelolco, he saw a vision of the Mother of God herself, who commanded him to ask the Bishop of Mexico to build a church on the site of the vision. The bishop asked him for some proof of this amazing event. On 12 December the Blessed Virgin Mary appeared to Juan Diego once more and told him to climb to the top of the hill called Tepeyac and pick flowers there and take them away with him. It was impossible that any flowers should grow there, because of the winter frosts and because the place was dry and rocky. Nevertheless Juan Diego found flowers of great beauty, which he picked, collected together in his cape, and carried to the Virgin. She told him to bring the flowers to the bishop as a proof of the truth of his vision. In the bishop's presence Juan Diego unfolded his cape and poured out the flowers; and there appeared, miraculously imprinted on the fabric, the image of the Virgin of Guadalupe, which from that moment onwards became the spiritual centre of the nation.

The church was built in honor of the Queen of Heaven. Juan Diego, moved by piety, left everything and dedicated his life to looking after this tiny hermitage and to welcoming pilgrims. He trod the way to sanctity through love and prayer, drawing strength from the eucharistic banquet of our Redeemer, from devotion to his most holy Mother, from communion with the holy Church and obedience to her pastors. Everyone who met him was overwhelmed by his virtues, especially his faith, love, humility, and other-worldliness.

Juan Diego followed the Gospel faithfully in the simplicity of his daily life, always aware that God makes no distinction of race or culture but invites all to become his children. Thus it was that he enabled all the indigenous peoples of Mexico and the New World to become part of Christ and the Church.

Juan Diego walked with God until his last day, in 1548, when God called him to himself. Through the centuries his memory has been associated with the apparition of Our Lady of Guadalupe and has reached the furthest regions of the Earth.

December 11th

St. Damasus I, Pope

From a treatise against Faustus by St. Augustine, Bishop & Doctor

We celebrate the martyrs with the veneration of love and fellowship

We, the Christian community, assemble to celebrate the memory of the martyrs with ritual solemnity because we want to be inspired to follow their example, share in their merits, and be helped by their prayers. Yet we erect no altars to any of the martyrs, even in the martyrs' burial chapels themselves.

No bishop, when celebrating at an altar where these holy bodies rest, has ever said, "Peter, we make this offering to you," or "Paul, to you," or "Cyprian, to you." No, what is offered is offered always to God, who crowned the martyrs. We offer in the chapels where the bodies of those he crowned rest, so the memories that cling to those places will stir our emotions and encourage us to greater love both for the martyrs whom we can imitate and for God whose grace enables us to do so.

So we venerate the martyrs with the same veneration of love and fellowship that we give to the holy men of God still with us. We sense that the hearts of these latter are just as ready to suffer death for the sake of the Gospel, and yet we feel more devotion toward those who have already emerged victorious from the struggle. We honor those who are fighting on the battlefield of this life here below, but we honor more confidently those who have already achieved the victor's crown and live in heaven.

But the veneration strictly called "worship," or latria, that is, the special homage belonging only to the divinity, is something we give and teach others to give to God alone. The offering of a sacrifice belongs to worship in this sense (that is why those who sacrifice to idols are called idol-worshipers), and we neither make nor tell others to make any such offering to any martyr, and holy soul, or any angel. If anyone among us falls into this error, he is corrected with words of sound doctrine and must then either mend his ways or else be shunned.

The saints themselves forbid anyone to offer them the worship they know is reserved for God, as is clear from the case of Paul and Barnabas. When the Lycaonians were so amazed by their miracles that they wanted to sacrifice to them as gods, the apostles tore their garments, declared that they were not gods, urged the people to believe them, and forbade them to worship them.

Yet the truths we teach are one thing, the abuses thrust upon us are another. There are commandments that we are bound to give; there are breaches of them that we are commanded to correct, but until we correct them we must of necessity put up with them.

December 12th

Our Lady of Guadalupe

From a report by Don Antonio Valeriano, a Native American author of the sixteenth century

The Voice of the Turtledove has been heard in our land

At daybreak one Saturday morning in 1531, on the very first days of the month of December, an Indian named Juan Diego was going from the village where he lived to Tlatelolco in order to take part in divine worship and listen to God's commandments. When he came near the hill called Tepeyac, dawn had already come, and Juan Diego heard someone calling him from the very top of the hill: "Juanito, Juan Dieguito."

He went up the hill and caught sight of a lady of unearthly grandeur whose clothing was as radiant as the sun. She said to him in words both gentle and courteous: "Juanito, the humblest of my children, know and understand that I am the ever virgin Mary, Mother of the true God through whom all things live. It is my ardent desire that a church be erected here so that in it I can show and bestow my love, compassion, help, and protection to all who inhabit this land and to those others who love me, that they might call upon and confide in me. Go to the Bishop of Mexico to make known to him what I greatly desire. Go and put all your efforts into this."

When Juan Diego arrived in the presence of the Bishop, Fray Juan de Zumarraga, a Franciscan, the latter did not seem to believe Juan Diego and answered: "Come another time, and I will listen at leisure."

Juan Diego returned to the hilltop where the Heavenly Lady was waiting, and he said to her: "My Lady, my maiden, I presented your message to the Bishop, but it seemed that he did not think it was the truth. For this reason I beg you to entrust your message to someone more illustrious who might convey it in order that they may believe it, for I am only an insignificant man."

She answered him: "Humblest of my sons, I ask that tomorrow you again go to see the Bishop and tell him that I, the ever virgin holy Mary, Mother of God, am the one who personally sent you."

But on the following day, Sunday, the Bishop again did not believe Juan Diego and told him that some sign was necessary so that he could believe that it was the Heavenly Lady herself who sent him. And then he dismissed Juan Diego.

On Monday Juan Diego did not return. His uncle, Juan Bernardino, became very ill, and at night asked Juan to go to Tlatelolco at daybreak to call a priest to hear his confession.

Juan Diego set out on Tuesday, but he went around the hill and passed on the other side, toward the east, so as to arrive quickly in Mexico City and to avoid being detained by the Heavenly Lady. But she came out to meet him on that side of the hill and said to him: "Listen and understand, my humblest son. There is nothing to frighten and distress you. Do not let your heart be troubled, and let nothing upset you. Is it not I, your Mother, who is here? Are you not under my protection? Are you not, fortunately, in my care? Do not let your uncle's illness distress you. It is certain that he has already been cured. Go up to the hilltop, my son, where you will find flowers of various kinds. Cut them, and bring them into my presence."

When Juan Diego reached the peak, he was astonished that so many Castilian roses had burst forth at a time when the frost was severe. He carried the roses in the folds of his *tilma* (mantle) to the Heavenly Lady. She said to him: "My son, this is the proof and the sign which you will bring to the Bishop so that he will see my will in it. You are my ambassador, very worthy of trust."

Juan Diego set out on his way, now content and sure of succeeding. On arriving in the Bishop's presence, he told him: "My lord, I did what you asked. The Heavenly Lady complied with your request and fulfilled it. She sent me to the hilltop to cut some Castilian roses and told me to bring them to you in person. And this I am doing, so that you can see in them the sign you seek in order to carry out her will. Here they are; receive them."

He immediately opened up his white mantle, and as all the different Castilian roses scattered to the ground, there was drawn on the cloak and suddenly appeared the precious image of the ever virgin Mary, Mother of God, in the same manner as it is today and is kept in her shrine of Tepeyac.

The whole city was stirred and came to see and admire her venerable image and to offer prayers to her; and following the command which the same Heavenly Lady gave to Juan Bernardino when she restored him to health, they called her by the name that she herself had used: "the ever virgin holy Mary of Guadalupe."

December 12th Alternative

From the message of Pope Paul VI to the Mexican people

The best homage to Mary: loving God and neighbor

Beloved sons and daughters, we wish to unite our voice to that filial hymn which the Mexican people raise up today to the Mother of God. Devotion to the most holy Virgin of Guadalupe must be for all of you a constant and specific demand for authentic Christian renewal. The crown which she expects from all of you is not so much a material one as a precious spiritual crown, shaped by a profound love of Christ and a sincere love of all: the two commandments which sum up the gospel message. The same most holy Virgin, with her example, guides us on these two paths.

In the first place, she exhorts us to make Christ the center and summit of our whole Christian life. She remains hidden, with supreme humility, so that the image of her Son might appear to humanity with all its incomparable brightness. For this reason, true Marian devotion reaches its fullness and its most rightful expression when it is a path to the Lord and directs all its love toward him, just as Mary knew how to do, so as to intertwine in one and the same impulse the tenderness of a mother and the piety of a creature.

But in addition, and precisely because she loved Christ so dearly, our Mother fulfilled perfectly that second commandment which must be the norm of all human relations: the love of neighbor. How beautiful and delicate was the intervention of Mary at the wedding feast of Cana, when she moved her Son to accomplish the first miracle of turning the water into wine solely to help those young spouses! It is a complete sign of the constant love of the Virgin for humanity in need, and ought to be an example for all those who seek to be considered truly her sons and daughters.

Christians can do no less than to show solidarity in seeking a solution to the situation of those to whom the bread of culture has not yet come nor the opportunity of honorable and justly remunerated work. They cannot remain indifferent while new generations find no path for the realization of their legitimate aspirations, and while part of humanity continues to be placed at the margins of the advantages of civilization and progress. For this reason, on this celebrated feast, we urge you from our heart to give your Christian life a clear social sense--as the Council has asked--that you may always be in the front line in all efforts to attain progress, and in all the initiatives for improving the situation of those who suffer want. See in each person a brother or a sister--a brother or sister in Christ--in such a way that the love of God and the love of the neighbor become united in the same love, alive and operative, which is the only thing that can redeem the miseries of the world, renewing it in its most profound root, the human heart.

The person who has much should be conscious of his or her obligation to serve and contribute with generosity to the good of all. The person who has little or who has nothing should, with the help of a just society, make every effort at self-improvement and of going beyond self, and even in cooperating in the progress of those who suffer the same situation. And, all of you, feel the obligation to unite fraternally so as to help forge this new world for which the human race longs.

This is what the Virgin of Guadalupe asks of you today, this fidelity to the Gospel, of which she knew how to be the most eminent example.

Upon you, dearly beloved sons and daughters, we implore with confidence the maternal benevolence of the Mother of God and Mother of the Church, in order that she may continue to protect your nation and to direct and impel it more and more along the paths of progress, communal love, and a peaceful life together.

December 12th Optional Memorial

St. Jane Frances de Chantel, Religious

From The Memoirs by the secretary of St. Jane Frances de Chantal, Religious

Love is as strong as death

One day Saint Jane spoke the following eloquent words, which listeners took down exactly as spoken:

"My dear daughters, many of our holy fathers in the faith, men who were pillars of the Church, did not die martyrs. Why do you think this was?" Each one present offered an answer; then their mother continued. "Well, I myself think it was because there is another martyrdom: the martyrdom of love. Here God keeps his servants and handmaids in this present life so that they may labor for him, and he makes of them both martyrs and confessors. I know," she added, "that the Daughters of the Visitation are meant to be martyrs of this kind and that, by the favor of God, some of them, more fortunate than others in that their desire has been granted, will actually suffer such a martyrdom."

One sister asked what form this martyrdom took. The saint answered: "Yield yourself fully to God, and you will find out! Divine love takes its sword to the hidden recesses of our inmost soul and divides us from ourselves. I know one person whom love cut off from all that was dearest to her, just as completely and effectively as if a tyrant's blade had severed spirit from body."

We realized that she was speaking of herself. When another sister asked how long the martyrdom would continue, the Saint replied: "From the moment when we commit ourselves unreservedly to God, until our last breath. I am speaking, of course, of great-souled individuals who keep nothing back for themselves, but instead are faithful in love. Our Lord does not intend this martyrdom for those who are weak in love and perseverance. Such people he lets continue on their mediocre way, so that they will not be lost to him; he never does violence to our free will."

Finally, the saint was asked whether this martyrdom of love could be put on the same level as martyrdom of the body. She answered: "We should not worry about equality. I do think, however, that the martyrdom of love cannot be relegated to a second place, for *love is as strong as death*[Song 8:6]. For the martyrs of love suffer infinitely more in remaining in this life so as to serve God, than if they died a thousand times over in testimony to their faith and love and fidelity."

December 13th

St. Lucy, Virgin & Martyr

From the book On Virginity by St. Ambrose, Bishop & Doctor

You light up your grace of body with your splendor of soul

You are one of God's people, of God's family, a virgin among virgins; you light up your grace of body with your splendor of soul. More than others you can be compared to the Church. When you are in your room, then, at night, think always on Christ, and wait for his coming at every moment.

This is the person Christ has loved in loving you, the person he has chosen in choosing you. He enters by the open door; he has promised to come in, and he cannot deceive. Embrace him, the one you have sought; turn to him, and be enlightened; hold him fast, ask him not to go in haste, beg him not to leave you. The Word of God moves swiftly; he is not won by the lukewarm, nor held fast by the negligent. Let your soul be attentive to his word; follow carefully the path God tells you to take, for he is swift in his passing.

What does his bride say? *I sought him, and did not find him; I called him, and he did not hear me*[Song 5:6]. Do not imagine that you are displeasing to him although you have called him, asked him in, opened the door to him,and that this is the reason why he has gone so quickly; no, for he allows us to be constantly tested. When the crowds press him to stay, what does he say in the Gospel? *I must preach the word of God to other cities, because I have been sent for that*[Lk 4:43]. But even if it seems to you that he has left you, go out and seek him once more.

Who but holy Church is to teach you how to hold Christ fast? Indeed, she has already taught you, if you only understood her words in Scripture: *How short a time it was when I left them before I found him whom my soul has loved. I held him fast, and I will not let him go*[Song 3:1-5].

How do we hold him fast? Not by restraining chains or knotted ropes but by bonds of love, by spiritual reins, by the longing of the soul.

If you also, like the bride, wish to hold him fast, seek him and be fearless of suffering. It is often easier to find him in the midst of bodily torments, in the very hands of persecutors.

His bride says: *How short a time it was after I left them* [Song 3:1-5]. In a little space, after a brief moment, when you have escaped from the hands of your persecutors without yielding to the powers of this world, Christ will come to you, and he will not allow you to be tested for long.

Whoever seeks Christ in this way, and finds him, can say: *I held him fast, and I will not let him go before I bring him into my mother's house, into the room of her who conceived me*[Song 3:4]. What is this "house," this "room," but the deep and secret places of your heart?

Maintain this house, sweep out its secret recesses until it becomes immaculate and rises as a spiritual temple for a holy priesthood, firmly secured by Christ, the cornerstone, so that the Holy Spirit may dwell in it.

Whoever seeks Christ in this way, whoever prays to Christ in this way, is not abandoned by him; on the contrary, Christ comes again and again to visit such a person, for he is with us until the end of the world.

December 14th

St. John of the Cross, Priest & Doctor

From a Spiritual Canticle by St. John of the Cross, Priest & Doctor

The knowledge of the mystery hidden in Christ Jesus

Though holy doctors have uncovered many mysteries and wonders, and devout souls have understood them in this earthly condition of ours, yet the greater part still remains to be unfolded by them, and even to be understood by them.

We must then dig deeply in Christ. He is like a rich mine with many pockets containing treasures: however deep we dig we will never find their end or their limit. Indeed, in every pocket new seams of fresh riches are discovered on all sides.

For this reason the apostle Paul said of Christ: *In him are hidden all the treasures of the wisdom and knowledge of God*[Col 2:3]. The soul cannot enter into these treasures, nor attain them, unless it first crosses into and enters the thicket of suffering, enduring interior and exterior labors, and unless it first receives from God very many blessings in the intellect and in the senses, and has undergone long spiritual training.

All these are lesser things, disposing the soul for the lofty sanctuary of the knowledge of the mysteries of Christ: this is the highest wisdom attainable in this life.

Would that men might come at last to see that it is quite impossible to reach the thicket of the riches and wisdom of God except by first entering the thicket of much suffering, in such a way that the soul finds there its consolation and desire. The soul that longs for divine wisdom chooses first, and in truth, to enter the thicket of the cross.

Saint Paul therefore urges the Ephesians *not to grow weary in the midst of tribulations*[Eph 3:13], but to be *rooted and grounded in love, so that they may know with all the saints the breadth, the length, the height and the depth – to know what is beyond knowledge, the love of Christ, so as to be filled with all the fullness of God*[Eph 3:17-19].

The gate that gives entry into these riches of his wisdom is the cross; because it is a narrow gate, while many seek the joys that can be gained through it, it is given to few to desire to pass through it.

December 21st

St. Peter Canisius, Priest & Doctor

From the writings by St. Peter Canisius, Priest & Doctor

A spiritual experience

Before he set out for Germany – he is rightly called the second apostle of that country – Saint Peter Canisius received the apostolic blessing, and underwent a profound spiritual experience. He describes it in these words.

"Eternal High Priest, you allowed me in your boundless goodness to commend the fruit and confirmation of that blessing to your apostles, to whom men go on pilgrimage to the Vatican and who there work wonders under your guidance. It was there that I experienced great consolation and the presence of your grace, offered to me through these great intercessors. They too gave their blessings, and confirmed the mission to Germany; they seemed to promise their good will to me as an apostle of that country. You know, Lord, how strongly and how often you committed Germany to my care on that very day: I was to continue to be solicitous for it thereafter, I was to desire to live and die for it.

"At length, it was as if you opened to me the heart in your most sacred body: I seemed to see it directly before my eyes. You told me to drink from this fountain, inviting me, that is, to draw the waters of my salvation from your wellsprings, my Savior. I was most eager that streams of faith, hope and love should flow into me from that source. I was thirsting for poverty, chastity, obedience. I asked to be made wholly clean by you, to be clothed by you, to be made resplendent by you.

"So, after daring to approach your most loving heart and to plunge my thirst in it, I received a promise from you of a garment made of three parts: these were to cover my soul in its nakedness, and to belong especially to my religious profession. They were peace, love and perseverance. Protected by this garment of salvation, I was confident that I would lack nothing but all would succeed and give you glory."

December 23rd

St. John of Kanty, Priest

From a letter by Pope Clement XIII

In heart and speech he was attuned to God

Saint John of Kanty deserves a high place among the great saints and scholars who practice what they preach and defend the true faith against those who attack it. When heresy and schism were gaining ground in neighboring territories, his teaching at the University of Krakow was untainted by any error. At the pulpit he fought to raise the standard of holiness among the faithful, and his preaching was reinforced by his humility, his chastity, his compassion, his bodily penance and other qualities of a dedicated priest and apostle.

He was a unique contribution to the reputation and credit of the professors of the university; he also bequeathed a wonderful example to those of his profession, an inspiration of complete dedication to duty and to their teaching – in theology and other sciences – for the honor and glory of the one God.

With the sense of worship that he brought to his teaching of the sacred sciences he combined humility. He never put himself above another, but treated himself as of no account, even though he was acknowledged by all as their master. So far was he from pretenses that he even wished to be an object of contempt in the eyes of all who underestimated his worth. He could take their insults and cutting remarks in stride.

With his humility went a rare and childlike simplicity: the thoughts of his heart were revealed in his words and actions. If he suspected that someone had taken offense at speaking the truth, before going to the altar he would ask forgiveness for what was not so much his own sin as the other person's misunderstanding. Every day after his round of duties he would go straight from the lecture room to church. There he would spend long hours in contemplation and prayer before the hidden Christ of the Eucharist. The God in his heart and the God on his lips were one and the same God.

December 26th

St. Stephen, First Martyr

From a sermon of St. Fulgentius of Ruspe, Bishop

The armament of love

Yesterday we celebrated the birth in time of our eternal King. Today we celebrate the triumphant suffering of his soldier. Yesterday our king, clothed in his robe of flesh, left his place in the virgin's womb and graciously visited the world. Today his soldier leaves the tabernacle of his body and goes triumphantly to heaven.

Our king, despite his exalted majesty, came in humility for our sake; yet he did not come empty-handed. He brought his soldiers a great gift that not only enriched them but also made them unconquerable in battle, for it was the gift of love, which was to bring men to share in his divinity. He gave of his bounty, yet without any loss to himself. In a marvelous way he changed into wealth the poverty of his faithful followers while remaining in full possession of his own inexhaustible riches.

And so the love that brought Christ from heaven to earth raised Stephen from earth to heaven; shown first in the king, it later shone forth in his soldier. Love was Stephen's weapon by which he gained every battle, and so won the crown signified by his name. His love of God kept him from yielding to the ferocious mob; his love for his neighbor made him pray for those who were stoning him. Love inspired him to reprove those who erred, to make them amend; love led him to pray for those who stoned him, to save them from punishment. Strengthened by the power of his love, he overcame the raging cruelty of Saul and won his persecutor on earth as his companion in heaven. In his holy and tireless love he longed to gain by prayer those whom he could not convert by admonition.

Now at last, Paul rejoices with Stephen, with Stephen he delights in the glory of Christ, with Stephen he exalts, with Stephen he reigns. Stephen went first, slain by the stones thrown by Paul, but Paul followed after, helped by the prayer of Stephen. This, surely, is the true life, my brothers, a life in which Paul feels no shame because of Stephen's death, and Stephen delights in Paul's companionship, for love fills them both with joy. It was Stephen's love that prevailed over the cruelty of the mob, and it was Paul's love that covered the multitude of his sins; it was love that won for both of them the kingdom of heaven.

Love, indeed, is the source of all good things; it is an impregnable defense, and the way that leads to heaven. He who walks in love can neither go astray nor be afraid: love guides him, protects him, and brings him to his journey's end.

My brothers, Christ made love the stairway that would enable all Christians to climb to heaven. Hold fast to it, therefore, in all sincerity, give one another practical proof of it, and by your progress in it, make your ascent together.

December 27th

St. John, Apostle & Evangelist

From tractates on the first letter of St. John by St. Augustine, Bishop & Doctor

Life itself was revealed in the flesh

Our message is the Word of life. We announce what existed from the beginning, what we have heard, what we have seen with our own eyes, what we have touched with our own hands[1 Jn 1:1]. Who could touch the Word with his hands unless *the Word was made flesh and lived among us*[Jn 1:14]?

Now this Word, whose flesh was so real that he could be touched by human hands, began to be flesh in the Virgin Mary's womb; but he did not begin to exist at that moment. We know this from what John says: *What existed from the beginning*[1 Jn 1:1.] Notice how John's letter bears witness to his Gospel, which you just heard a moment ago: *In the beginning was the Word, and the Word was with God*[Jn 1:1.].

Someone might interpret the phrase *the Word of life* to mean a word about Christ, rather than Christ's body itself which was touched by human hands. But consider what comes next: *and life itself was revealed*[1 Jn 1:2]. Christ therefore is himself the Word of life.

And how was this life revealed? It existed from the beginning, but was not revealed to men, only to angels, who looked upon it and feasted upon it as their own spiritual bread. But what does Scripture say? *Mankind ate the bread of angels*[Ps 77:25].

Life itself was therefore revealed in the flesh. In this way what was visible to the heart alone could become visible also to the eye, and so heal men's hearts. For the Word is visible to the heart alone, while flesh is visible to bodily eyes as well. We already possessed the means to see the flesh, but we had no means of seeing the Word. The Word was made flesh so that we could see it, to heal the part of us by which we could see the Word.

John continues: *And we are witnesses and we proclaim to you that eternal life which was with the Father and has been revealed among us*[1 Jn 1:2] – one might say more simply, "revealed to us."

We proclaim to you what we have heard and seen[1 Jn 1:1.]. Make sure that you grasp the meaning of these words. The disciples saw our Lord in the flesh, face to face; they heard the words he spoke, and in turn they proclaimed the message to us. So we also have heard, although we have not seen.

Are we then less favored than those who both saw and heard? If that were so, why should John add: *so that you too may have fellowship with us*[1 Jn 1:3]? They saw, and we have not seen; yet we have fellowship with them, because we and they share the same faith.

And our fellowship is with God the Father and Jesus Christ his Son. And we write this to you to make your joy complete[1 Jn 1:2-3] – complete in that fellowship, in that love and in that unity.

December 28th

The Holy Innocents, Martyrs

From a sermon of St. Quodvultdeus, Bishop

They cannot speak, yet they bear witness to Christ

A tiny child is born, who is a great king. Wise men are led to him from afar. They come to adore one who lies in a manger and yet reigns in heaven and on earth. When they tell of one who is born a king, Herod is disturbed. To save his kingdom he resolves to kill him, though if he would have faith in the child, he himself would reign in peace in this life and for ever in the life to come.

Why are you afraid, Herod, when you hear of the birth of a king? He does not come to drive you out, but to conquer the devil. But because you do not understand this you are disturbed and in a rage, and to destroy one child whom you seek, you show your cruelty in the death of so many children.

You are not restrained by the love of weeping mothers or fathers mourning the deaths of their sons, nor by the cries and sobs of the children. You destroy those who are tiny in body because fear is destroying your heart. You imagine that if you accomplish your desire you can prolong your own life, though you are seeking to kill Life himself.

Yet your throne is threatened by the source of grace-so small, yet so great-who is lying in the manger. He is using you, all unaware of it, to work out his own purposes freeing souls from captivity to the devil. He has taken up the sons of the enemy into the ranks of God's adopted children.

The children die for Christ, though they do not know it. The parents mourn for the death of martyrs. The child makes of those as yet unable to speak fit witnesses to himself. See the kind of kingdom that is his, coming as he did in order to be this kind of king. See how the deliverer is already working deliverance, the Savior already working salvation.

But you, Herod, do not know this and are disturbed and furious. While you vent your fury against the child, you are already paying him homage, and do not know it.

How great a gift of grace is here! To what merits of their own do the children owe this kind of victory? They cannot speak, yet they bear witness to Christ. They cannot use their limbs to engage in battle, yet already they bear off the palm of victory.

December 29th

St. Thomas Becket, Bishop & Martyr

From a letter by St. Thomas Becket, Bishop

Without real effort, no one wins the crown

If we who are called bishops desire to understand the meaning of our calling and to be worthy of it, we must strive to keep our eyes on him whom God appointed high priest for ever, and to follow in his footsteps. For our sake he offered himself to the Father upon the altar of the cross. He now looks down from heaven on our actions and secret thoughts, and one day he will give each of us the reward his deeds deserve.

As successors of the apostles, we hold the highest rank in our churches; we have accepted the responsibility of acting as Christ's representatives on earth; we receive the honor belonging to that office, and enjoy the temporal benefits of our spiritual labors. It must therefore be our endeavor to destroy the reign of sin and death, and by nurturing faith and uprightness of life, to build up the Church of Christ into a holy temple in the Lord.

There are a great many bishops in the Church, but would to God we were the zealous teachers and pastors that we promised to be at our consecration, and still make profession of being. The harvest is good and one reaper or even several would not suffice to gather all of it into the granary of the Lord. Yet the Roman Church remains the head of all the churches and the source of Catholic teaching. Of this there can be no doubt. Everyone knows that the keys of the kingdom of heaven were given to Peter. Upon his faith and teaching the whole fabric of the Church will continue to be built until we all reach full maturity in Christ and attain to unity in faith and knowledge of the Son of God.

Of course many are needed to plant and many to water now that the faith has spread so far and the population become so great. Even in ancient times when the people of God had only onc altar, many teachers were needed; how much more now for an assembly of nations which Lebanon itself could not provide with fuel for sacrifice, and which neither Lebanon nor the whole of Judea could supply with beasts for burnt offerings! Nevertheless, no matter who plants or waters, God gives no harvest unless what he plants is the faith of Peter, and unless he himself assents to Peter's teaching. All important questions that arise among God's people are referred to the judgment of Peter in the person of the Roman Pontiff. Under him the ministers of Mother Church exercise the powers committed to them, each in his own sphere of responsibility.

Remember then how our fathers worked out their salvation; remember the sufferings through which the Church has grown, and the storms the ship of Peter has weathered because it has Christ on board. Remember how the crown was attained by those whose sufferings gave new radiance to their faith. The whole company of saints bears witness to the unfailing truth that without real effort no one wins the crown.

December 31st

St. Sylvester I, Pope

From the Ecclesiastical History by St. Eusebius of Caesarea, Bishop

The Peace of Constantine

Glory to God the almighty, the King of the universe, for all his gifts, and gratitude to Jesus Christ, the Savior and Redeemer of our souls, through whom we pray that this peace may be preserved for us stable and unshaken for ever: a peace that will keep us safe from troubles outside as well as from all anxieties and disturbances of soul. When this bright and radiant day, darkened by no cloud, shone with heavenly light on the churches of Christ throughout the world, even those outside our community, though they had not the same cause for rejoicing, shared at least some of the blessings that God had bestowed on us. For us above all, who had placed our hopes in Christ, there was inexpressible joy and a heavenly happiness shone on every face. Every place that a short time before had been laid waste by the tyrants' wickedness we now saw restored to life, recovering, as it seemed, from a long and deadly disease. Churches were once again rising from the ground high into the air, far surpassing in splendor and magnificence the ones that had previously been stormed and destroyed.

Then came the spectacle that we had prayed and hoped for: dedication festivals throughout the cities, and the consecration of the newly erected houses of worship. For this there were convocations of bishops, gatherings of pilgrims from far distant lands, warm and loving contact between the different communities, as the members of Christ's body united in complete harmony. The mysterious prophecy: *There came together bone to bone and joint to joint*[Ezek 37:5-10] was thus fulfilled, as were all the other prophecies which had been unerringly proclaimed by type and symbol. All the members were filled with the grace of the one divine Spirit, all were of one mind, with the same enthusiasm for the faith, and on the lips of all there was one hymn of praise.

Yes, and our bishops performed religious rites with full ceremonial, priests officiated at the liturgy, the solemn ritual of the Church, chanting psalms, proclaiming the other parts of our God-given Scriptures, and celebrating the divine mysteries. Baptism was also administered, the sacred symbol of our Savior's passion.

Without the slightest distraction, men and women of all ages united in prayer and thanksgiving, their minds and hearts full of joy as they gave glory to God the giver of all good gifts.

FEASTS